Baby
Names
Day by Day

Baby Names

* Day by Day *

Stephanie Zia

hamlyn

First published in Great Britain in 2005 by Hamlyn,
a division of Octopus Publishing Group Ltd
2–4 Heron Quays, London E14 4JP

Distributed in the United States and Canada by
Sterling Publishing Co., Inc.
387 Park Avenue South, New York,
NY 10016-8810

ISBN 0 600 61249 X
EAN 9780600612490

A CIP catalogue record for this book is available
from the British Library.

Printed and bound in China

10 9 8 7 6 5 4 3 2 1

Contents

Introduction

Naming a baby is one of the most important and exciting things a new parent will do, and there is now a wider range of names to choose from than ever before. The choice of names includes those inherited from English-speaking cultures, those from Continental Europe, Africa, Asia and beyond, and those from classical literature and mythology, religious texts and ancient folklore.

It is important to think about your child's name in combination with his or her surname as well as with the names of other family members. Having a Mona and a Lisa in the same household is certain to prompt some smiles, as will a combination of William and Harry. Be careful that you do not inadvertently create 'amusing' initials, such as Thomas Witt (T Witt) or Barbara Ursula Matthews (BUM) – your child will not thank you for your choice! You also need to think about how your child will feel about his or her name at school, college and work. You may want to give your baby the name of a famous sportsperson or singer – but how long will these names have any relevance, even to you?

This book will help you to choose names that you and your partner like and that also have a special significance for your child. Four boys' and four girls' names are included for every day of the year, including 29 February, and if you don't want to choose one of the names associated with your baby's birthday, why not look for one that is connected with another important date, such as your wedding anniversary? The meanings of names are also included to help you finalize your decision, so sit back, take your time and enjoy this very special task.

January

January

1

Jerome, Gerome, Jerry

The reclusive author *J.D. Salinger* was born *Jerome David Salinger* on this day in 1919. After writing short stories for the *New Yorker* and *Esquire* magazines, he published *The Catcher in the Rye*, his first and only novel, in 1951. It was an immediate success and sells to this day.

Meaning holy name

Julius, Julian, Julyan, Julien, Jolyon, Jolly

The Julian calendar was introduced by *Julius Caesar* in 45BC. Although the Greek astronomer and mathematician Sosigenes of Alexandria persuaded Caesar to do this, it was Caesar himself who worked out the number of days in each month. The year 46BC had to have an extra 90 days so that it could catch up with the seasons.

Meaning youthful

Milt, Milton

The legendary jazz vibraphone player *Milt Jackson* was born on this day in 1923. He was a founder member of the Modern Jazz Quartet, one of the most influential jazz ensembles of all time. His best-known composition, 'Bags Groove', takes its title from his own nickname, Bags.

Meaning town with a mill

Bartolomé, Bartholomew, Bartholomeus, Barthelmey, Barthel, Bart, Bartel, Barth

Today is the birthday of the Spanish painter *Bartolomé Esteban Murillo*. Born in Seville in 1617, he specialized in the joyous, harmonious side of the religious life. He influenced the English painters John Constable and Sir Joshua Reynolds.

Meaning son of a ploughman

Aurora, Aurelia, Aurelie, Aurie, Auristela

In Roman myth *Aurora* is the Roman goddess of the dawn, making her name an appropriate one for the first day of the year. The sun is her brother, the moon her sister. She flies across the sky, bringing the light of dawn and crying tears of dew.

Meaning dawn

Whitney

On this day in 1993 *Whitney Houston*'s platinum single 'I Will Always Love You' was number one in the United States and Britain. It stayed at the top of the US charts for 11 weeks. She has won a total of six Grammy awards, and her biggest-selling album was *The Bodyguard* (1992).

Meaning white island

Kala

Kala is the name that was given to the first baby to be born in the millennium year 2000. The full name of the girl, who comes from Tonga in the South Pacific, is Kala Sosefina Milleniume Kauvaka. Tonga was the first country in the world to see the dawn of the new millennium.

Meaning time

Roxane, Roxine, Roxana, Roxy, Roxanna, Roxanne

Roxane means dawn in Persian, an appropriate name for the beginning of the year. It is said to have been the name of the wife of Alexander the Great, king of Macedonia in Greece and conqueror of a vast empire. Roxane, the daughter of a Bactrian prince, was responsible for the death of Alexander's second wife, but was herself murdered in 310BC.

Meaning dawn

Gregory, Greg

Today is the feast day of *St Gregory of Nazianus*, who became bishop of Constantinople (now Istanbul) in 379. His spiritual writings, among them an apologetic oration, have been hugely influential. Gregory has been a consistently popular name over the centuries and was adopted by 16 popes and two antipopes.

Meaning watchful, vigilant

Isaac, Ike, Kizaak, Ikie, Ikey

Isaac Asimov, the Russian-born biochemist and writer, was born on this day in 1920. A prolific writer, he became one of the most influential science-fiction authors of the 20th century, adding the word 'robotics' to the English language.

Meaning he will laugh

Chick, Chuck, Chic

Chick Churchill, keyboard player with 1970s rock band Ten Years After, was born on this day in 1949. The band, formed in 1967, had two hit albums in Britain, *Undead* (1968) and *Stonedhenge* (1970), and played at the Woodstock Festival in 1969.

From Charles, meaning free man

Pernell

The US boxer *Pernell Whitaker* was born on this day in 1964. After winning a gold medal at the 1984 Olympic Games in the lightweight division, he became world champion at lightweight, light-welter weight and light-middle weight. His nickname was Sweet Pea.

From Peter, meaning rock, stone

Christie

Christie Turlington, the US supermodel, was born this day in 1969. After a decade at the peak of her modelling career, representing Calvin Klein and Armani among others, she wrote two books on yoga and appeared on the cover of *Time* magazine illustrating the science of yoga.

From Christine, meaning follower of Christ

Elara

Elara, the 12th satellite of the planet Jupiter, was discovered on this day in 1905. According to some versions of the legend, the giant Tityus was the son of Elara and Zeus. Tityus was so large that when he lay down he covered 3.6 hectares (9 acres) of ground.

From Ellar, meaning storeroom, cellar

Therese, Theresa, Teresa, Terese, Teresita

St Therese of Lisieux, a French Carmelite nun, was born on this day in 1873. Also known as Little Flower, she was canonized in 1925. Her autobiography, *The Story of a Soul*, tells of her visions of Jesus. She said: 'What matters in life is not great deeds but great love.'

Meaning harvest, reap

Rachel, Rachael, Rachelle, Rachele, Raquel, Rahel, Ray, Rae, Raoghnailt

Dame Rachel Waterhouse was born on this day. For more than 30 years she was a member of the council of the UK Consumers' Association, and for eight years she was chairman of the Association. She later became president of the Birmingham Consumer Group.

Meaning innocent as a lamb

Mel, Melville, Melvil

Mel Gibson, Australian actor, film director and philanthropist, was born on this day in 1956. His film *The Passion of the Christ* (2003) was phenomenally successful. In 2004 he donated $10 million (about £5.6 million) to children's hospitals around the world to help children with serious medical conditions.

Meaning bad settlement

Ronald, Ronnie, Ron

J.R.R. Tolkien, author of *The Hobbit* and the trilogy *The Lord of the Rings*, was born *John Ronald Reuel Tolkien* in Bloemfontein, South Africa, on this day in 1892. *The Lord of the Rings*, which has not been out of print since it was published in 1954–5, spawned the most successful feature film trilogy of all time.

From Reginald, meaning strong ruler

Stephen, Steve, Steven, Stevenson

Stephen Stills, the US singer and songwriter, was born on this day in 1945. In the 1960s and 1970s he played with Buffalo Springfield and Crosby, Stills, Nash and Young before going solo. One of Crosby, Stills, Nash and Young's biggest hits was 'Love the One You're With' (1971).

Meaning garland, crown

Sergio, Serge, Sargent, Sarge

Sergio Leone, the Italian film director born on this day in 1929, is best known for devising the spaghetti western genre, the first of which, *A Fistful of Dollars* (1964), starred the then-unknown Clint Eastwood. Leone went on to make *The Good, the Bad and the Ugly* (1966) and *Once upon a Time in the West* (1969), among others.

Meaning military attendant

Aretha, Areta, Aretta, Retha

On 3 January 1987 *Aretha Franklin*, one of the greatest US soul singers of all time, became the first woman to be inducted into the Rock-and-Roll Hall of Fame. The uncontested queen of soul has had many hits, including 'Respect' and 'I Say a Little Prayer'.

Meaning virtuous

Genevieve, Geneva, Genovefa, Guinevere, Genovera

Today is the feast day of *St Genevieve*, the patron saint of Paris. Her prayers are said to have stopped the Huns, led by Attila, from invading Paris in 451. *Genevieve* is also the title of the 1953 film about the London-to-Brighton car rally.

Meaning kinswoman

Marion, Marian, Marianna, Marianne, Maryanne

Marion Davies, US actress and comedienne of the 1920s and 1930s and better known as the companion of newspaper publisher William Randolph Hearst, was born on this day in 1897. A star of more than 45 films, she was also a hugely popular socialite and philanthropist.

Meaning graceful

Danica, Danika

The US actress *Danica McKellar* was born on 3 January 1975 in La Jolla, California. She played Winnie Cooper in TV's *The Wonder Years* (1988–93) and Debbie Dobs in *The Twilight Zone* (1985–6), and she also appeared in the series *The West Wing* (2002).

Meaning morning star

Fabian, Fabe, Faber, Fabio, Fabiano, Fabien

The *Fabian Society*, the socialist intellectual movement, was founded in London on this day in 1884. Committed to gradual not revolutionary social reform, its early members included George Bernard Shaw and Sidney and Beatrice Webb.

Meaning bean

Floyd, Lloyd

The US boxer *Floyd Patterson* was born in Waco, Texas, on 4 January 1935. The winner of a gold medal at the 1952 Olympic Games, he had a unique style of boxing, holding his gloves high and springing forwards unexpectedly. In 1956, at 21, he became the youngest heavyweight champion ever.

Meaning grey-haired

Jakob, Jake, Jacob, Jacobus

One half of the Brothers Grimm, *Jakob Grimm* was born on this day in 1785. Fearing that old folktales would be lost forever, he and his brother Wilhelm began collecting and preserving them while they were still at university. First published in 1812, the famous stories have been translated into more than 160 languages.

Meaning supplanter

Louis, Lewis, Luis, Lewes, Luthais, Lugaidh, Luigi, Lou

Louis Braille, the French inventor of Braille, was born on this day in 1809. He became blind at the age of three after an accident with one of his father's leather-working tools, and he later used this tool to invent the code that enables blind people to read and write. All the letters are made up of patterns of six dots.

Meaning famous warrior

Anastasia, Anstice, Ana

In Russia 4 January is the name day of *St Anastasia*, a Dalmatian saint, martyred in about 304 at Srem Mitrovica (now in Serbia). The name is often associated with Russia because of Grand Duchess Anastasia, daughter of Tsar Nicholas II, who was assassinated with other members of the royal family at Yekaterinburg in 1918. Many women later claimed to be she.

Meaning awakening, resurrection

Dyan, Dyana

Dyan Cannon, the US actress known for her role as Judge Jennifer 'Whipper' Cone in the TV series *Ally McBeal* (1997), was born on this day in 1937 in Tacoma, Washington. She was married for a time to the actor Cary Grant, and they had one daughter, Jennifer.

From Diana, meaning goddess of the moon and hunting

Fiona, Fionn

On this day in 2000 *Fiona Thornewil* and Catherine Hartley became the first British women ever to reach the South Pole. It took them two months to walk across the continent of Antarctica. Fiona and her husband, Mike, also became the first married couple to reach the South Pole.

Meaning white, fair

Phyllis, Phyllida, Phillida, Phylis

The much-quoted US journalist *Phyllis Battelle* was born on this day in 1922. From 1955 right the way through until 1988 she wrote a weekly column, syndicated all over America, called 'Assignment America'.

Meaning leafy, foliage

Juan

King *Juan Carlos* of Spain was born in Rome on this day in 1938, while his parents were living in exile. When he became king in 1975 he relinquished all dictatorial rights set in place by Francisco Franco and became a constitutional monarch. So popular, many Spaniards call themselves Juancarlists rather than monarchists,

From John, meaning God has shown me favour

Umberto, Humbert

Umberto Eco, the Italian philosopher and writer, was born on this day in 1932. He became world famous after the publication of *The Name of the Rose* (1980), one of the first novels written in the postmodern style. It sold over 10 million copies and has been translated into 30 languages.

Meaning bright warrior

Paramhansa

Paramhansa Yogananda, founder of the Self-Realization Fellowship, was one of the 20th-century's greatest emissaries of Indian thought and philosophy to the West. He was born on this day in 1893, and his book *Autobiography of a Yogi* (1946) is still in print.

Meaning supreme soul

Zebulon, Zebulun, Zabulon, Zeb, Lonny

The US explorer and soldier *Zebulon Montgomery Pike* was born on 5 January 1779. He led the expedition (named after him) that mapped the territory to the headwaters of the River Mississippi and of the Red and Arkansas Rivers. The book of the expedition was a bestseller. Pike County, Ohio, and Pikes Peak in Colorado are named after him.

Meaning dwelling

Diane, Dian, Dianne, Dyanne

US actress *Diane Keaton* was born on this day in 1946. She won an Oscar for her affectionate performance in the title role in Woody Allen's film *Annie Hall* (1977). Later on in her career she won a Golden Globe and was also nominated for an Oscar for her performance in the film *Something's Gotta Give* (2003), in which she starred opposite Jack Nicholson.

From Diana, meaning goddess of the moon and hunting

Janica, Janika

The Croatian skier *Janica Kostelic* was born on 5 January 1982 in Zagreb. The champion slalom skier won the Alpine Skiing World Cup in 2001 and 2003, and won a silver and three gold medals at the 2002 Winter Olympics.

From John, meaning God has shown me favour

Raisa

Raisa Gorbachev, the former first lady of the Soviet Union, was born on 5 January 1932. Raisa Maksimovna Titorenko met Mikhail Gorbachev at Moscow State University, where she was studying sociology. She was the first Russian leader's wife to have a highly visible public profile.

Meaning adaptable, easy-going

Pamela, Pam, Pammy, Pamella, Pammie

Pamela Sue Martin, the US actress known for her role as Fallon Carrington in the TV soap opera *Dynasty*, was born on this day in 1953. She played the part from 1981 to 1984. She is a director as well as an actress, running her own theatre company in Idaho.

Meaning all sweet

Earl, Earle, Earlyl, Erle, Erl

Earl Scruggs, the US banjo player who developed the bluegrass style of playing, was born on this day in 1924. He was only ten years old when he invented his unique three-finger pick, which has since become known throughout the world as Scruggs Style Picking.

Meaning nobleman

Kasper, Kaspar, Casper, Caspar, Gaspar, Gaspard, Gasper, Jasper

In Poland 6 January is the name day for *Kasper*, the German form of Jasper, which is a Persian name. Kasper (Caspar), Melchior and Balthasar are the names traditionally ascribed to the Magi or three wise men, who travelled to Bethlehem to visit the newborn Jesus.

From Jasper, meaning treasurer

Khalil

Khalil Gibran, the philosophical essayist, artist, novelist and mystical poet, was born in Lebanon on this day in 1883. A major influence on US pop culture, he spent two years in Paris studying art under Auguste Rodin. His best-known work is his collection of 26 poetic essays, *The Prophet* (1923).

Meaning friend

Rowan, Roan, Rowen, Rowe

Rowan Atkinson, the British comedy actor famous for his roles in the TV series *Blackadder* and *Mr Bean*, was born on this day in 1955. *Mr Bean* has been televised in more than 200 countries, and the movie, *Bean* (1997), was one of the highest-earning British films ever, taking a massive $240 million worldwide.

Meaning little red one

Maria, Marya

The Italian physician and educator *Maria Montessori* opened her first school and day-care centre for working-class children in Rome on this day in 1907. The Montessori Method is based on her particular philosophy that education should be based on the laws of nature, not the prejudices of adult society.

From Mary, meaning bitter

Nigella

Nigella Lawson, British cookery writer and TV celebrity chef, was born on this day in 1960. Her first cookery book, *How Not To Eat*, was an immediate success. *How to be a Domestic Goddess* earned her the Author of the Year award at the British Book Awards in 2001. She has two children, Cosima and Bruno.

Meaning black

Tiffany, Tiphani

The name *Tiffany* is traditionally bestowed on girls born on the Feast of the Epiphany (6 January), which is the 12th day of Christmas. The 1961 movie *Breakfast at Tiffany's*, based on the novel by Truman Capote and starring Audrey Hepburn, is one of the most popular films of all time.

Meaning appearing to God

Viola, Violanto

Viola is the heroine of William Shakespeare's play *Twelfth Night*. Rescued from a storm at sea, she shows a strong, independent spirit and determination to survive by dressing as a boy so that she can work as a page to Duke Orsino.

From Violet, meaning shy flower

Jann, Jan

Jann Wenner, founder of *Rolling Stone* magazine, was born on this day in 1946. The magazine, known for its high journalistic content, was first published in the Haight-Ashbury area of San Francisco in 1967, the same place and time as the flower-power 'Summer of Love'.

From John, meaning God has shown me favour

Gerald, Ger, Gereld, Garold, Gerry

British naturalist, author and zookeeper *Gerald Durrell* was born on this day in 1925. He is best known for his autobiographical book *My Family and Other Animals* (1956). He was the younger brother of the novelist Lawrence Durrell.

Meaning ruling spear

Nicholas, Nicolas, Niccolo, Nichol, Nicol, Nicolai, Nick, Nik, Nikki, Nickie, Nikos

Nicholas Cage, US actor, producer and director, and nephew of the film director Francis Ford Coppola, was born on this day in 1964. He won the best actor Oscar for his performance in *Leaving Las Vegas* (1995). He has been married (not at the same time) to Patricia Arquette and Lisa Marie Presley.

Meaning victorious, conqueror

Millard

Millard Fillmore, the 13th president of the United States, was born on this day in 1800. Raised in poverty in a log cabin in Finger Lakes, New York County, his first job was as an apprentice to a cloth dresser. His path to the presidency began when he studied law after serving in the army.

Meaning triumphant, strong

Bernadette, Bernadine, Bernadina, Berneta, Bernita, Bernie

Bernadette Soubirous, the French saint, was born on this day in 1844. She is best known for the visions she experienced at Lourdes and her declaration that the spring waters there had been given healing powers by the Virgin Mary.

From Bernard, meaning brave as a bear

Septima

Septima is the female version of the Latin name Septimus, meaning seventh. In the 19th century the male form was often used for the seventh-born child in a family, but the name could be given to a child born on the seventh day of a month.

Meaning seventh born

Trudie, Trudy, Trude, Truda

Trudie Styler was born on this day in 1956. The wife of rock star Sting, she is an actress and author. She also runs a successful film company, Xingu Films, which produces environmental documentaries and feature films, including *Lock, Stock and Two Smoking Barrels* (1998).

From Gertrude, meaning strong spear

Zora, Zorana, Zorah, Zorina

The African-American novelist *Zora Neale Hurston* was born on this day in 1891. She studied as an anthropologist and brought folktales, voodoo and magic to her novels, of which *Their Eyes Were Watching God* (1937) is her best known. She has been a major influence on many black women writers.

Meaning dawn

Bobby, Bob, Bobbie

On this day in 1958 the 14-year-old chess player *Bobby Fischer* won the US chess championship. Considered to be one of the greatest chess players of all time, he went on to win the world championship in 1972, when he defeated the Russian master Boris Spassky.

From Robert, meaning bright, famous

David, Dave, Dav, Davey, Davie, Davy, Davon, Davis, Dewi, Dafydd, Dai, Davidson

David Bowie, one of the most influential rock stars from the early 1970s to the present time, was born David Jones on this day in 1947. His appeal and originality lay in his invention of the concept album, most notably *The Rise and Fall of Ziggy Stardust and the Spiders from Mars* (1972).

Meaning beloved

Elvis

The king of rock and roll was born on this day in 1935. With a string of hit records and films made during the 1950s and early 1960s and a distinctive style of dress and performance, *Elvis Presley* became a role model for many young people.

Meaning not known

Lucian, Lucien

In France 8 January is the feast day of St Lucian, who was martyred at Beauvais early in the Christian era. The British artist *Lucian Freud* is one of the most enigmatic and highly regarded artists of the 20th century. His highly sensual portraits are mainly of his family, friends and lovers.

From Lucius, meaning light

Ami, Amie

The US actress *Ami Dolenz* was born on this day in 1969. She is the daughter of Samantha Juste and the actor and musician, Mickey Dolenz, who used to be in the group The Monkees. She has three sisters: Charlotte, Emily and Georgia.

From Amy, meaning beloved

Emily

Emily Greene Balch, the US academic, writer and pacifist, was born on this day in 1867. She received the Nobel Prize for peace in 1946, mainly for her work with the Women's International League for Peace and Freedom, which she helped found during the First World War.

Meaning rival

Shirley, Shirlie, Shirleen, Shirlene, Shirlee

The Welsh singer *Shirley Bassey* was born on this day in 1937. Although her musical output over the past 40 years has been prolific, she is probably best known for her recording of the theme tune to the James Bond film *Goldfinger* (1964).

Meaning bright clearing

Yvette, Yvetta

The US actress *Yvette Mimieux* was born to her French father and Spanish mother on this day in 1942. She made her film debut as a girl from the far, far future in the 1960 screen version of H.G. Wells's *The Time Machine*. The year she travelled from was 802701.

From Yvonne, meaning yew

Adrian, Adrien, Adriano, Ade, Addie, Adie, Hadrian

This is the feast day of *St Adrian of Canterbury*, who was born in Africa. He was twice offered the post of archbishop of Canterbury, but preferred to become abbot at St Augustine's in Canterbury. His tomb has been associated with various miracles.

Meaning from the coast

Charles, Charlie, Charley, Chas, Chaz, Chay, Carolos, Karl, Carlo, Carlos, Karol, Karel

On this day in 1834 *Charles Darwin* arrived in Port San Julian, Patagonia, on board HMS *Beagle*. During this trip the British naturalist carried out much of the research that was subsequently published in his revolutionary book *On the Origin of Species by Means of Natural Selection* (1859).

Meaning free man

Ralph, Ralf, Rauf, Rafe, Ralphie

The British architect *Ralph Tubbs* was born on this day in 1912. He is best known for his design for the Dome of Discovery, which featured in the Festival of Britain in 1951. This was the largest dome in existence at the time and considered a remarkable technological achievement.

Meaning wise, strong

Tiberius

It is the birthday today of *Tiberius Hemsterhuis*, who was born in Groningen, the Netherlands, on 9 January 1685. A mathematical genius, at the age of 20 he became the professor of mathematics and philosophy at Amsterdam University, but he was more interested in ancient languages, for which he eventually became famous.

Meaning of the River Tiber

Gracie, Grace, Gracia, Gratia, Grazia

The British comedy actress and singer *Gracie Fields* was born on this day in Rochdale, Lancashire, in 1898. She was a huge success both in the theatre and as a film actress. Two of her best-known films were *Sally in Our Alley* (1931) and *Looking on the Bright Side* (1931).

Meaning grace

Dixie

Joan Baez, the US folk singer, was born on this day in 1941. *The Night They Drove Old Dixie Down* is one of her best-known songs. She supported various civil rights and pacifist causes, which went hand in hand with her singing career. In the 1960s and 1970s she toured and recorded with singer and songwriter Bob Dylan.

Meaning gracious gift of God

Nona, Nonie

Literally meaning 'nine' or 'ninth', the name *Nona* was often reserved for the ninth-born child in a 19th-century family. As families are not as large these days, this name could equally well be used for a girl born on the ninth day of the month (or even in the ninth month of the year).

Meaning ninth

Simone, Simonne, Simona, Simonette, Simonetta

The French intellectual, philosopher, feminist and novelist *Simone de Beauvoir* was born on this day in 1908. She was as famous for her own work as for being the lifelong companion of the existentialist philosopher, Jean-Paul Sartre. Her best-known work is her study of female oppression, *The Second Sex* (1953).

From Simon, meaning to hear, to be heard

Robinson

On this day in 1887 the poet *Robinson Jeffers* was born in Pittsburgh, Pennsylvania. His poetry celebrates the beauty of the landscape around Carmel and Big Sur in California, where he built and lived in a stone cottage. He also built a 12-metre (40-foot) stone tower nearby, which features in many of his poems.

Meaning son of Robert

Ruben, Reuben

Ruben Dario is the penname of the revolutionary Spanish poet, journalist and diplomat, who was born on 10 January 1867 in Metapa, Nicaragua. The town was later renamed Ciudad Dario (City of Dario) in his honour. His real name was Felix Rubén García Sarmiento.

Meaning behold a son

Paul, Paolo, Pablo, Pavel, Pasha

On this day in 1908 the actor *Paul Henreid* was born in Austria. His real name was Paul George Julius von Hernreid, but he changed it when he went to Hollywood in the 1930s. His films included *Goodbye Mr Chips* (1939), *Casablanca* (1942) and *Now Voyager* (1942).

Meaning small

Rod, Roddy, Rodrick, Roderic, Roderigo, Rodrigo

The British rock singer *Rod Stewart* was born on this day in 1945. Although he started his singing career on the folk circuit, he is best known for his work during the 1970s both as a solo artist and with his band the Faces.

From Roderick, meaning famous, powerful

Barbara, Barbra, Barbie, Barby, Babb, Babette, Babita, Bab, Babs, Babby, Bar, Barb, Bairbre, Barbro, Varvara

Barbara Hepworth, the British sculptor, was born on this day in 1903. Considered one of the most important 20th-century sculptors, many of her large, abstract pieces are on permanent display in the gardens of the studio in St Ives, Cornwall, where she worked until her death.

Meaning stranger

Emma, Ema, Emmi, Emmie, Emmy, Emmye, Em

Emma Bunton, formerly a member of the Spice Girls, was born on this day in 1976. Having shed her 'Baby Spice' image, she has since carved a successful solo career for herself.

Meaning entire, whole

Krista, Kristabel, Christabel

The US actress *Krista Tesreau* celebrates her birthday on this day. Born in 1964, she is best known for playing the role of Mindy Lewis for six years in the US daytime TV drama *Guiding Light*, for which she succeeded in winning the 1987 daytime Emmy nomination for outstanding ingénue in a drama series.

Meaning beautiful follower of Christ

Fawn

Fawn McKay Brodie was born in the US on this day in 1915. She was a teacher and a biographer, best known for *No Man Knows My History*, her biography of Joseph Smith, the founder of the Church of the Latter-day Saints. She was excommunicated from the Church for apostasy.

Meaning young deer

Rahul

It is the birthday today of the Indian cricketer *Rahul Sharad Dravid*, who was born in Indore, Madhya Pradesh, on this day in 1973. He has been nicknamed 'the Wall' because of his solid batting. He was named Player of the Year and Test Player of the Year in 2004 and is vice-captain of the national team.

Meaning son of Lord Buddha

Jason, Jasun

The British actor *Jason Connery* was born on this day in 1963. Coming from outstanding acting stock – his father is Sean Connery and his mother is Diane Cilento – his choice of career was hardly a surprising one.

Meaning healer

Ranulph, Ranulf, Randy

On 11 January 1981 the British explorer *Ranulph Fiennes* and his intrepid team achieved the longest and fastest crossing of Antarctica. They travelled 4,025 kilometres (2,500 miles) to reach Scott's base in a record 75 days. His Jack Russell, Bothie, who accompanied him also set a record of being the first dog to travel to both the North and South Poles.

From Randolf, meaning shield, wolf

Shomari

The US footballer *Shomari Buchanan* was born on this day in 1977. He has played in both the Arena Football League and AF2, and is the wide receiver of the Corpus Christi Hammerheads from the IFL (Intense Football League).

Meaning forceful

Amelia, Amalia, Amealia, Amelea

On this day in 1935 *Amelia Earhart* became the first person to fly solo across the Pacific Ocean, from Honolulu to California. Just three years earlier she had gained international fame by becoming the first woman to fly solo across the Atlantic, and she received numerous awards for her flying feats.

Meaning hard-working

Kathleen, Cathleen, Caitlin

On this day in 1922 the British film and stage actress *Kathleen Byron* was born. She was a leading actress in the 1940s, and her film credits included *A Matter of Life and Death* (1946) and *Black Narcissus* (1946). *One of Our Dinosaurs is Missing* (1976) was among her later films.

Meaning pure maiden

Juanita

Juanita Kreps was born on this day in 1921. As well as being appointed the first woman director of the New York Stock Exchange, she was also the first woman to become secretary of commerce, a post she held from 1977 to 1979 in President Jimmy Carter's administration.

From Jane, meaning God's gift of grace

Anna, Ana, Annika, Anula, Anusia, Anuska

On this day in 1949 the British leading actress *Anna Calder-Marshall* was born. Among her many films have been *Pussycat, Pussycat, I Love You* (1970), *Wuthering Heights* (1970) and *Anna Karenina* (1997).

From Anne, meaning God has favoured me

Anthony, Antony, Antoin, Antonio, Antonino, Antoine, Anton, Ant, Tony

Anthony Andrews, the British actor with boyish good looks, was born on this day in 1948. Although he has appeared in many films, his performance as *Sebastian Flyte* in the 1981 TV adaptation of Evelyn Waugh's *Brideshead Revisited* is undoubtedly his most memorable role.

Meaning not known

Benedict, Benedic, Bendick, Benedetto, Benedicto, Benedix, Benet

Today is the feast day for *St Benedict Biscop*, who was born in the north of England in about 628. He founded monasteries at Wearmouth and Jarrow in the north-eastern region, Northumbria.

Meaning blessed

Haruki

Haruki Murakami, the iconic Japanese author, was born on this day in 1949. He ran a jazz club in Tokyo before taking up writing. When his novel *Norwegian Wood* sold 4 million copies on publication, sales were referred to as the 'Murakami boom'.

Meaning spring tree

Arcadius

Today is the feast day of the little known *St Arcadius*, who lived in the early 4th century. Because he refused to offer sacrifices to idols, he was executed in a particularly gruesome way, but continued to testify to his faith until the very last moment of his life.

Meaning not known

Hattie, Hatty, Hettie, Hetty

Hattie Ophelia Caraway was the first woman senator in the United States. She was appointed to complete her husband's term as senator on his death in 1931, but was elected in her own right to represent the state of Arkansas on 12 January 1932, a position she held until 1945.

From Henrietta, meaning ruler of the home

Jetta

The girl's name *Jetta* is derived from the precious stone jet. The black semi-precious gemstone is considered a lucky connection for people born under the star sign Capricorn (between 22 December and 20 January).

Meaning black

Luise, Lousitte, Loyce, Liusade

Luise Rainer, the German-born actress, was born on this day in 1910. She moved to Hollywood in 1935, where her birthplace was amended to Austria, and before the end of the decade had won two Academy Awards for best actress. Unwilling to toe the studio line, she stopped making films in the mid-1940s.

From Louis, meaning famous warrior

Maggie, Maigrghread, Magaidh, Margalo

The Scottish blues and soul singer *Maggie Bell* was born on this day in 1945. She first appeared in the limelight with her group Stone the Crows, but when it broke up in 1973 she became a successful artist in her own right.

From Margaret, meaning pearl

13 JANUARY

Olin, Olen

Olin Chaddock Wilson was born on 13 January 1909. He was the recipient of the first ever PhD in astronomy given by the California Institute of Technology. His speciality was a study of the phases of spectroscopy, and he was elected to the National Academy of Sciences in 1960.

From Olaf, meaning descendant

Jay

The US author *Jay McInerney* was born on this day in 1955. He has written a handful of novels and many short stories and articles since he rose to fame with the publication in 1983 of his first novel *Bright Lights, Big City*.

Meaning crow, jay

Orlando

British actor *Orlando Bloom* was born on this day in 1977. Named after the character in Virginia Woolf's 1928 novel of the same name, he is best known for the role of Legolas in the film trilogy *The Lord of the Rings* (2001–03).

From Roland, meaning famous land

Patrick, Pat, Padraic, Padruig, Peyton, Patrizio, Patrice

The US actor *Patrick Dempsey* was born on this day in 1966. One of the top leading men in the 1980s and 1990s, he avoided being typecast and played a wide variety of roles in such films as *In a Shallow Grave* (1988) and *Happy Together* (1990).

Meaning well-born

Ernestine, Ernesta

Ernestine Rose, who is regarded as America's first Jewish feminist, was born in Poland on this day in 1810. She left home when she was 17, travelled around Europe and in 1836 moved to New York. Her rebellious tendencies were apparent early on and equipped her in her fight for women's rights and the abolition of slavery in the 1840s and 1850s.

Meaning purposeful, serious

Gwen, Gwennie, Gwendoline, Gwendolyn, Gwyn

Gwen Verdon, US dancer and actress, was born on this day in 1925. She had distinctive red hair and a temperament to match, but she was considered to be Broadway's best dancer throughout the 1950s and 1960s.

From Gwendolen, meaning fair, blessed

Hilary, Hillary, Hillery, Hilaria, Hilaire

Today is the feast day of the 4th-century bishop *St Hilary of Poitiers*. He wrote extensively, notably his work *On the Trinity* and commentaries on the Psalms and the Gospel of St Matthew. Although the name Hilary was originally borne by men, it is now more often given to girls.

Meaning cheerful

Ivetta, Ivette

Today is the feast day of *St Ivetta of Huy*. This 12th-century saint, who was born in the Netherlands, is the patron saint of brides and of large families.

From Yvette, meaning yew

Bart

The cartoon show *The Simpsons* received its first TV airing on this day in 1990. The cartoon, created by Matt Groening, is centred around the lives in small-town Springfield of Homer, Marge, *Bart*, Lisa and baby Maggie. It is now an institution, and Bart is a hero for many a young boy.

Meaning son of the ploughman

Hugh, Hughy, Hughie, Hewe

The British writer *Hugh Lofting* was born on this day in 1886. From 1912 he lived in the USA, where he wrote and illustrated the Dr Dolittle books, the first of which, *The Story of Dr Dolittle*, appeared in 1920. His other books include *Gub Gub's Book* (1932) and *Tommy, Tilly and Mrs Tubbs* (1934).

Meaning mind, spirit

Trevor, Trefor

British theatre director Sir *Trevor Nunn* was born on 14 January 1940. When he was 28 he became the youngest ever artistic director of the Royal Shakespeare Company. As well as directing all the classics, he has also produced a string of London's most successful stage musicals, including *Cats* and *Les Misérables*.

Meaning large homestead

Rolla, Rollo

The scientist and inventor *Rolla Harger* was born in the US on this day in 1890. He is famous for inventing a device that could detect the presence of alcohol in humans, which he named a Drunkometer. He put a chemical into a balloon which had been blown into: if the person had been drinking, the chemical would change colour.

From Rolf, meaning renowned wolf

Berthe, Bertha, Bertina, Berty, Berta

The French impressionist artist *Berthe Morisot* was born on this day in 1841. Regarded by many as a 'feminine' artist because of the domestic subject matter she chose to paint, she did, in fact, open up many opportunities for female artists in the latter part of the 19th century.

Meaning shining

Faye, Fay, Fae

Faye Dunaway, the US actress, was born on this day in 1941. She is best known for her first film, *Bonnie and Clyde* (1967), in which she played the outlaw Bonnie Parker. During the 1970s and 1980s she played many difficult roles, including Evelyn Mulwray in *Chinatown* (1974). She received an Oscar for her performance in *Network* (1976).

From Faith, meaning loyal

Martina, Marta, Martine, Martyna

Today's date marks the day in 1985 when Czech-born tennis player *Martina Navratilova* won her 100th tennis tournament. Seven times the number one player in the world, she was Wimbledon singles champion an astonishing nine times. She also won the US Open four times, the French Open twice and the Australian Open three times.

Meaning war-like

Maud, Maude, Maudle

On 14 January 1939 Norway laid claim to the part of Antarctica that lies between 20°W and 45°E. This piece of land is called *Queen Maud Land*, and it was named in honour of Maud, queen of Norway, the wife of Haakon VII.

Meaning strong in battle

15 JANUARY

Ivor, Ifor, Ivar, Iver

Ivor Novello, the Welsh singer and entertainer, was born on this day in 1893. He wrote and performed in many light operatic musicals, including *Careless Rapture* (1936) and *Perchance to Dream* (1945), but is perhaps best known as the composer of the favourite First World War song 'Keep the Home Fires Burning'.

Meaning warrior with bow

Lloyd, Floyd

The US film star *Lloyd Bridges* was born on this day in 1913. Father of actors Jeff and Beau Bridges, Lloyd was best known for his role as deepsea diver Mike Nelson in the children's underwater adventure series *Sea Hunt* (1958–60).

Meaning grey-haired

Martin, Martie, Marty, Marino, Marton, Martainn, Martino

The African-American civil rights leader *Martin Luther King Jr* was born on this day in 1929. One of the best-loved leaders in US history, in 1964 he became the youngest-ever winner of the Nobel Prize for peace. He will forever be remembered for his rousing 1963 speech, 'I have a dream'.

Meaning war-like

Gene

The US jazz drummer *Gene Krupa* was born in Chicago on this day in 1909. He made his first recording in 1927 and toured as a soloist before joining Benny Goodman's orchestra in 1933. A film based on his life, *Drum Crazy* (1960), had Krupa playing on the soundtrack, although he was played by the actor Sal Mineo.

From Eugene, meaning noble, well-born

Elizabeth, Elisabeth, Elisabet, Elisabetta, Lizabeta, Lizbeth, Lizzy, Lizzie, Lize, Liza, Liz, Betty, Bettie, Bet, Eliza, Elisa, Elissa, Elzieta, Elspeth

Queen *Elizabeth I* of England was crowned at Westminster Abbey on this day in 1559. The last of the Tudors, she reigned for 45 years, a period that has since become known as the Elizabethan era.

Meaning consecrated to God

Ita, Ide

Today is the feast day of *St Ita*, who was born in Ireland in about 570. She led a convent of dedicated women in County Limerick, where she is greatly revered to this day. Ita is said to have performed many extraordinary miracles, and one report claims that she lived entirely on food sent down from heaven.

From Ide, meaning thirst

Odette

The premiere of Pyotr Tchaikovsky's ballet *Swan Lake* took place in St Petersburg on 15 January 1895. It tells the story of a princess, *Odette*, who is turned into the queen of the swans by an evil sorcerer. She can be returned to human form only by a suitor who swears his eternal love for her.

Meaning home-lover

Charo

The singer, dancer, comedian, actress and classical guitar virtuoso *Charo* celebrates a birthday today. The Hollywood star was voted the best guitarist in the world by *Guitar* magazine. She went to court to prove she was born in 1951, not 1941 as officially stated, and won her case.

From Rosario, meaning rosary

Brian, Bryan, Briant, Brien, Bryant

The British composer *Brian Ferneyhough* was born in Coventry in the English Midlands on this day in 1943. His orchestral piano, vocal, chamber and choral pieces have been performed around the world. He has held numerous academic posts, and in 1999 he was appointed professor of music at the University of California.

Meaning high, noble

Lucius, Luc, Lucais, Lucas, Luce, Lucio

On this day in 1967 *Lucius Amerson* became the first black sheriff in a Southern state of the USA. His election as sheriff of Alabama was a milestone in US history. He was so popular that he was re-elected four times, with a total of 20 years in office.

Meaning light

Philip, Phil, Phill, Phelps, Philly, Phillie, Phillopa, Philips, Pilib, Filip, Filli, Filib

On 16 January 1556 *Philip II* became king of Spain. He reigned through Spain's 'golden age' when the Spanish Empire extended to large parts of South and Central America as well as the Low Countries. Although he conquered Portugal, he lost his navy in the Armada against England in 1588.

Meaning lover of horses

Francisco, Francesco, Frantioek

Francisco Scavullo, one of America's leading photographers, was born on this day in 1921. His photographs have appeared on the covers of virtually every top fashion magazine, and he took the cover shots for *Cosmopolitan* magazine for 30 years. He also worked on film posters, including Barbra Streisand's remake of *A Star is Born* (1976).

Meaning Frenchman

Dolly

On this day in 1964 the musical version of *Hello, Dolly!* received its premiere at St James Theatre, New York. At the first performance Carol Channing took the leading part of Dolly, the widowed matchmaker on the look-out for a good catch for herself.

From Dorothea, meaning gift of God

Ethel, Ethyl, Ethylyn, Ethelda

Ethel Merman, the US star of stage musicals, was born in Astoria, New York, on this day in 1908. She enjoyed enormous success in a host of Broadway musicals, and she also appeared in films, including *Follow the Leader* (1930) and *Alexander's Ragtime Band* (1938).

Meaning noble

Kate, Katie

Kate Moss, the willowy supermodel, was born on this day in 1974. Her waif-like appearance heralded a new direction for female models. In addition to her highly successful modelling career, Kate has appeared in films and music videos.

From Katherine, meaning pure maiden

Penelope, Penny, Pen

The composer Niccolò Piccinni was born on this day in 1728. Although he was Italian, he is remembered for the operas he wrote for the French court, including *Penelope*, which received its first performance at the Palace of Fontainebleau in 1785. It tells the story of the wife of Odysseus, who waits faithfully for his return from the Trojan War.

Meaning not known

Benjamin, Beniamino, Benjie, Ben, Benny, Bennie, Benyamin

Benjamin Franklin, the US statesman, scientist and philosopher, was born on this day in 1706. One of the leaders of the American Revolution, he took part drafting both the Declaration of Independence and the Constitution. He was America's first postmaster general.

Meaning son of the south

Nevil, Neville, Nev

Nevil Shute, the British engineer and author, was born on this day in Ealing, London, in 1899. He wrote many novels, mostly adventure stories, of which *A Town Like Alice* (1949) is probably his best known. It is less well known that he was involved in the development of retractable undercarriages in aeroplanes.

Meaning new settlement

Gaspard, Gaspar, Gasper

The Swiss botanist and anatomist *Gaspard Bauhin* was born in Basel on this day in 1560. He published several important works on botany and anatomy, including *Theatrum anatomicum* (1605) and *Pinax theatri bontanica* (1623).

From Jasper, meaning treasurer

Vido

Vido Musso, the tenor saxophonist notable for his big band solos, was born on 17 January 1913. In the 1930s he began making his name playing around the Los Angeles area with Stan Kenton. He reached the peak of his career in the 1940s, playing with Benny Goodman's orchestra.

Meaning not known

Alva, Almha

Alva Vanderbilt-Belmont, manager and financier of the American Woman's Suffrage Movement, was born on this day in 1853. She was one of the richest and most powerful women in the USA and was considered a leader of the women's movement at least half a century before it became a fashionable cause.

Meaning white lady

Antonia, Anthonia, Atoni, Antonina, Toinette

In Bulgaria, Greece and Hungary 17 January is the name day for *Antonia*, the female form of Antony. Antonius was a Roman family name, the most famous holder in history being Mark Antony. The 'h' crept into Anthony and Anthonia in the 16th century, so that the name would be associated with *anthos*, the Greek word for flower.

Meaning not known

Moira, Moyra

Moira Shearer, the Scottish dancer and actress, was born on this day in 1926. Her first love was ballet, and it was as a dancer that she became famous in her role in the highly successful film *The Red Shoes* (1948). Her other film credits include *Peeping Tom* (1959).

From Mary, meaning bitter

Gay, Gaye, Gai

On 17 January 1969 *Marvin Gaye* was at the top of the charts with his classic recording 'I Heard it Through the Grapevine'. He was born Marvin Pentz Gay Junior in Washington D.C. He added the 'e' to his surname when he was an adult, emulating one of his heroes, Sam Cooke.

Meaning lively

Cary, Carey

The charismatic film star *Cary Grant* was born on this day in 1904 to a working-class family in Horfield, Bristol, in England. His real name was Archibald Alexander Leach. He was equally at home playing comedy, serious drama and thrillers, and he excelled in Alfred Hitchcock's *North by Northwest* (1959).

From Charles, meaning free man

Kevin, Kev, Kevan, Keven, Kevon

US actor *Kevin Costner* was born on 18 January 1955. He has appeared in many popular films, including *The Untouchables* (1987), as well as blockbusters, such as *Dances with Wolves* (1990), which he also directed.

Meaning handsome, beloved

Sachio

Sachio Kinugasa, the Japanese baseball star, was born on this day in 1947. He shot to fame on 13 June 1987 when he played his 2,131st consecutive game, smashing the astonishing achievement of New York Yankees legend Lou Gehrig, whose record had stood for 48 years.

Meaning fortunately born

Kirk, Kirkley, Kirkwood

Kirk Varnedoe was born on this day in 1946. One of America's most distinguished art curators, he was director of painting and sculpture at New York's Museum of Modern Art for 12 years. He went on to become the art historian at the Institute for Advanced Study at Princeton, New Jersey.

Meaning church

Constance, Connie

The US actress and singer *Constance Moore* was born on this day in 1919. In the early 1960s she appeared in the TV series *Window on Main Street*, but she is better known for her films, which included *Show Business* (1943) and *Hats off to Rhythm* (1947).

Meaning constancy

Margaret, Margaretta, Margarita, Margaret, Margriet

Today is the feast day of *St Margaret of Hungary*, the daughter of King Bela IV, who built a convent for Dominican nuns in the capital city of Budapest, which Margaret entered and where she remained for the rest of her life, undertaking many penances to keep herself humble.

Meaning pearl

Mable, Mabel, Mabe, Amabel, Maible, Maybele, Moibeal

The US Olympic runner *Mable Ferguson* was born on this day in 1955. With her team mates she won a silver medal for the 400 metre relay at the Olympic Games held in Munich in 1972.

Meaning lovely, good-humoured

Sylvia, Syl, Sylva, Zilva, Zilvia, Silva, Sil, Silvana, Silvia, Silvie

British suffragette *Estelle Sylvia Pankhurst* was born on this day in 1882. She devoted her life to various socialist, pacifist and women's causes, and was instrumental in the campaign for women's suffrage and other social changes in the years before the First World War.

Meaning from the forest

19 JANUARY

Edgar, Edgard, Ned, Neddie

The US writer *Edgar Allan Poe* was born on this day in 1809. He is best known for his short stories, such as 'The Fall of the House of Usher', but is also considered to be the inventor of the detective story with 'The Murders in the Rue Morgue' and 'The Mystery of Marie Rogét'.

Meaning prosperous guardian

Marius, Mario

Today is the feast day of *St Marius*. A rich Perisan, Marius, together with his wife Martha, gave away all his wealth to the poor. For their piety in burying the ashes of executed Christians, Marius and Martha were themselves martyred, and their remains were buried in Rome on the Via Cornelia.

Meaning war-like

Javier, Xavier

Javier Pérez de Cuéllar, the Peruvian diplomat who was secretary general of the United Nations from 1982 until 1991, was born on this day in 1920. He became prime minister of Peru in November 2000 after the incumbent, Alberto Fujimori, resigned over corruption charges.

Meaning new house

Stefan, Steffen, Stephanus

The Swedish tennis star *Stefan Edberg* was born on this day in 1966. Among his many tennis accolades are twice winning Wimbledon (in 1988 and 1990) and being ranked number one in the world in 1990 and 1991.

From Stephen, meaning garland, crown

Indira

On 19 January 1966 *Indira Ghandi* was elected the first woman prime minister of India. She held this office until 1977, and again between 1980 and 1984. She was a highly skilled politician and gained a reputation throughout the world as a formidable stateswoman.

Meaning beauty

Janis, Janice, Janetta, Janette, Janna, Jana, Jan

The US blues and psychedelic rock singer *Janis Joplin* was born on this day in 1943. Her remarkable singing talents catapulted her into stardom in the late 1960s and 1970s, when she had a string of gold and platinum albums.

From Jane, meaning God's gift of grace

Nina, Nena, Nineta, Ninetta

The British writer *Nina Bawden* was born in London on this day in 1925. She has written books for children, including *Carrie's War* (1973), about a child evacuated to Wales during the Second World War, and *The Peppermint Pig* (1975). Among her books for adults are *Tortoise by Candlelight* (1963) and *The Ruffian on the Stair* (2001).

From Antonina, meaning not known

Patricia, Pat, Patrice, Patriza, Patsy, Patti, Patty

The US author of psychological mystery novels *Patricia Highsmith* was born on this day in 1921. Her first book, *Strangers on a Train* (1950), was made into a classic film by Alfred Hitchcock in 1951. Her most famous character, Tom Ripley, appeared in a number of her novels, including *The Talented Mr Ripley* (1955), also filmed in 1999.

Meaning well-born

Buzz

US astronaut *Buzz Aldrin* was born on this day in 1930. Edwin Eugene Aldrin was a member of the NASA team on *Apollo 11* that made the momentous first landing on the moon in July 1969. With Neil Armstrong, he spent over two hours walking on the moon's surface.

Meaning not known

Fabian, Fabe, Faber, Fabio, Fabiano, Fabien

Today is the feast day of *St Fabian*, who became pope in 236. It is said that when it was time to elect a new pope, a dove descended on to Fabian's head, and he was chosen by popular acclaim. He was martyred during the persecution of Christians organized by the Roman emperor, Decius.

Meaning bean

Federico, Frederico, Fredericus

The Italian film director *Federico Fellini* was born on this day in 1920. Many of his films, such as *La Strada* (1954), *La Dolce Vita* (1960), *Roma* (1972) and *Amarcord* (1973), are characterized by bizarre and fantastic events and people, and by their almost circus-like qualities.

Meaning peaceful ruler

Gordian, Gordianus

The Roman emperor *Gordian III* was born Marcus Antonius Gordianus on 20 January 225. His mother was Antonia Gordiana. Good-looking and youthful as well as kind, he was a much-loved and highly esteemed emperor, and was known as Gordianus Pius.

Meaning lion-like

Agnes, Agna, Aigneis, Agneta, Agnola, Annis, Ina, Ines, Inessa, Inez, Nessa, Nesta, Nessi, Neysa

Today is the eve of the feast of *St Agnes*. She is the patron saint of engaged couples, and legend has it that if a young girl fasts on this day, she will dream of her future husband during the night. Her emblem is a lamb.

Meaning pure, chaste

Carol, Carole, Carola

The US figure skater *Carol Heiss Jenkins* was born on this day in 1940. She won a gold medal in the 1960 Winter Olympic Games at Squaw Valley, California. She made history by being awarded first-place votes by all nine judges.

Meaning melody

Joy, Joyce, Joice, Joicelin, Joicelyn, Joycelin, Joycelyn, Joya

The Austrian-born naturalist and conservationist *Joy Adamson* was born on this day in 1910. She will forever be associated with the lioness, Elsa, whose life she saved. Her account of these events in Kenya was published in her bestselling book, *Born Free* (1960), which was subsequently made into a successful film in 1966.

Meaning joyful

Ruth, Ruthie

The so-called first lady or queen of American dance, *Ruth St Denis* was born on this day in 1878. Although often compared with her European contemporary Isadora Duncan, they had different approaches to solo dance. Ruth's dancing had a strong spiritual element, and she was passionate about Eastern culture and mythology.

Meaning compassionate friend

21 JANUARY

Abel

On this day in 1643 the Dutch explorer *Abel Tasman* discovered the archipelago of Tonga in the South Pacific Ocean. In the earlier part of the same expedition, which was financed by the Dutch East India Company, he was the European who 'discovered' New Zealand and Tasmania.

Meaning breath

Billy, Bill

The singer and musician *Billy Ocean* was born in Trinidad on this day in 1950. He moved to Britain when he was eight, and by his early 20s was recording hit records. In 1984 he became an international star when his song 'Caribbean Queen' reached number one.

From William, meaning desiring to defend

Ethan, Etan

Ethan Allen, the American revolutionary, was born on this day in 1738. A staunch patriot, he was in command of a force called the Green Mountain Boys, which fought for the independence of the area that is now Vermont.

Meaning firm, long-lived

Russell, Russel, Rust, Russet, Rusty

On this day in 1853 a US physician called Dr *Russell Hawes* patented the envelope-folding machine. His knowledge of anatomy enabled him to design a machine that complemented the movements of the worker thereby enabling production of 2,500 envelopes an hour.

Meaning little red one

Geena

The US film and TV actress *Geena Davis* was born on this day in 1956. Of the scores of films she has made, she is perhaps best known for her portrayal of Thelma in the Ridley Scott road movie *Thelma and Louise* (1991), which was nominated for several awards.

Meaning silvery

Ingrid, Ingaberg, Inga, Ingeborg, Ingebiorg, Inger, Ingibiorg, Ingunna

Princess *Ingrid Alexandra* of Norway was born on this day in 2004. She is the first child of this Scandinavian country's Crown Prince Haakon and Crown Princess Mette-Marit. Princess Ingrid is second in line to the Norwegian throne.

Meaning beautiful child

Sophia, Sophie, Sophy, Sofia, Sofie, Sadhbha, Sadhbh

The first British woman to qualify as a doctor, *Sophia Louisa Jex-Blake* was born on this day in 1840. In the mid-1800s women were not permitted to train as doctors, nor were they accepted by the British Medical Association. Through her determination, Sophia Jex-Blake was able to change the law and open the gates for women doctors.

Meaning wisdom

Jenufa

On this day in 1904 in Brno, Czechoslovakia, Leos Janácek's opera *Jenufa* was first performed. It is based on a play entitled *Her Stepdaughter* by Gabriela Preissova, about Jenufa, who is loved by two men and finds happiness only after suffering from the jealousy of one of her suitors.

From Genevieve, meaning kinswoman

Manfred, Manfried

The romantic poet known as Lord Byron was born George Gordon Byron, 6th baron Byron, on this day in 1788. His dramatic poem *Manfred* (1817) is his most Gothic work, telling of a man who loved his sister, Astarte, and can find no peace.

Meaning peaceful hero

Satyen, Satyendra

Satyen Bose, the eminent Indian physicist, was born on this day in 1894. His paper on quantum theory was only four pages long, but Alfred Einstein saw its importance immediately. He translated the work into German, and the radiation formula became known as the Einstein-Bose statistic.

Meaning similar

Ramsay, Ramsey

On this day in 1924 *Ramsay MacDonald* became the first Labour prime minister of Britain. He came from a humble Scottish background and had had little formal education, but he developed a reputation for rousing speeches and served two terms in office.

Meaning island of wild garlic

Sam, Sammy, Sammie

The legendary US soul singer *Sam Cooke* was born on this day in 1931. He made the transition from his gospel roots to the emerging sound of the late 1950s and early 1960s, developing a distinctive crooning style. *Chain Gang* (1960) and *Twistin' the Night Away* (1962) are probably his best-known songs.

From Samuel, meaning asked of God

Beatrice, Bea, Beitris

The influential socialist and co-founder of the Fabian Society *Beatrice Potter Webb* was born on this day in 1858. Together with her husband, Sidney Webb, she was responsible for an enormous amount of writing on social issues, which helped shaped the Labour movement in Britain. They also founded the London School of Economics and Political Science in 1895.

Meaning bringer of happiness

Cleopatra

On 22 January 1881 a red granite obelisk called *Cleopatra's Needle* was erected in New York's Central Park. The obelisk, which is over 20 metres (65 feet) high, is one of a pair of pre-Christian edifices that formerly stood outside the Caesarium Temple in Alexandria, Egypt. The second obelisk is on the Embankment in London.

Meaning father's glory

Blaesilla, Blessilla

This is the feast day of *St Blaesilla*. The daughter of St Paula, she lived in the 4th century. She studied Hebrew and was a student of St Jerome. She married Furius, the son of Titiana. St Jerome wrote about her virtuous, saintly life.

Meaning not known

Roberta, Robertha, Roberthe, Robinette, Robnia, Robinia, Ruberta, Ruperta, Bertie, Bobbie, Bobby, Bobette, Bobina

Dr *Roberta Bonder*, a neurologist, was selected as one of the first six Canadians to travel into space. On 22 January 1992 she became the first Canadian woman in space, on board *Discovery*.

From Robert, meaning bright, famous

23 JANUARY

Derek, Derrick, Derk, Darrick, Derry

The West Indian poet and playwright *Derek Walcott* was born on this day in 1930. He has lived most of his life in Trinidad, and he writes about the clashes between European and West Indian cultures. In 1992 he was awarded the Nobel Prize for literature.

Meaning ruler of the people

Django, Djan, Djanden, Djani, Djaren, Djarimin

The Belgian gypsy guitarist *Django Reinhardt* was born on this day in 1910 in Liverchies, near Charleroi. In partnership with the violinist Stéphane Grappelli, he changed the sound of US jazz in the 1930s and beyond. He had a unique way of playing the guitar that many have tried and failed to emulate since.

Meaning lord of the hallowed land

Rutgar, Rutger

Today is the birthday of the Dutch actor *Rutgar Hauer*. Born in 1944, his international career took off in 1981 when he starred opposite Sylvester Stallone in *Nighthawk*. He is best remembered, however, for his role as the android in Ridley Scott's *Blade Runner* (1982).

Meaning famous spear

Fletcher

On this day in 1790 *Fletcher Christian* landed on Pitcairn Island together with his fellow mutineers from HMS *Bounty*. Christian had been the leader of the mutiny against Captain William Bligh, who was cast adrift with 18 other men in an open boat, eventually reaching the safety of Timor.

Meaning maker of arrows

Caroline, Carolina, Caryn, Carey, Charleen, Charlene, Charline, Sharleen, Sharlene, Sharline

Princess *Caroline of Monaco* was born on this day in 1957. The eldest daughter of Prince Rainier and Princess Grace (formerly the actress Grace Kelly), Caroline has two siblings, Albert and Stephanie. She is second in line to the throne after Albert.

Meaning free woman

Chita, Conchita, Concha, Conception, Concepcion, Conceptia

Actress *Chita Rivera* was born on this day in 1933 in Washington D.C. She made her name as Anita in the Broadway premiere of *West Side Story* (1957) and went on to win many awards, including two Tony Awards for best leading actress in a musical.

Meaning beginning

Jeanne, Jenete, Jeniece

The French film actress *Jeanne Moreau* was born on this day in 1928. Among her huge list of credits, she has starred in over 100 films, appeared in TV productions and has written and directed a number of films. One of her most famous starring roles from her early career was as Catherine in François Truffaut's *Jules et Jim* (1961).

From Jane, meaning God's gift of grace

Nancy, Nan, Nana

On 23 January 1993 US skater *Nancy Kerrigan* won first place in the US Female Figure Skating Championships. She started skating when she was six years old and won her first competition when she was just 15. She was the first woman to perfect the triple-triple combination, which had previously been attempted only by men.

From Anne, meaning God has favoured me

Jef, Jeff, Jeffers

On this day in 1984 the revolutionary Apple Macintosh personal computer was unveiled to the world. One of its inventors, *Jef Raskin*, had the idea for a user-friendly computer that would operate in the way humans think rather than as machines work. It was named after his favourite fruit.

From Geoffrey, meaning peaceful ruler

Albin, Albinus

The Swiss novelist poet *Albin Zollinger* was born on this day in 1895. The son of a mechanic, he grew up in Zurich and Argentina. He trained as a teacher and remained in the job all his life. His poetry began appearing in the 1930s in the Swiss intellectual magazine *The Time*.

Meaning white, bright

Warren, Waring, Werner

The US singer and songwriter *Warren Zevon* was born on this day in 1947. He received a classical piano training, but then moved into folk circles, spending time with the Everly Brothers. He is best known for his often strange lyrics and for his many high-profile musical collaborations.

Meaning warrior, game-keeper

Hadrian, Adrian, Adriano, Adrien, Ado

The Roman emperor *Hadrian* was born Publius Aelius Hadrianus on this day in AD76. Born in Italica, Spain, he managed to rule without getting into much serious conflict, largely thanks to the walls he had built, the most famous being Hadrian's Wall, parts of which can still be seen running across northern England.

From Adrian, meaning from the coast

Tatyana, Tatiana, Tanya

The US actress and singer *Tatyana Ali* was born Tatyana Marisol Ali on this day in 1979. Her first big role was as Ashley Banks in the nineties TV show *The Fresh Prince of Bel-Air*. She began singing on the show, and her first album, *Daydreaming*, rose to number six in the US charts.

Meaning not known

Edith, Edie, Editha, Edithe, Ediva, Edythe, Eadie, Eadith, Eaidie, Eady, Eda

The US novelist *Edith Wharton* was born on this day in 1862. She wrote more than 40 books, of which *The House of Mirth* (1905) and the Pulitzer Prize-winning *The Age of Innocence* (1920) are among the best loved. Her novels treat the American upper classes with subtle satire and irony, which gained her a wide readership.

Meaning successful in battle

Felicia, Felice, Felicidad, Felicie, Felis, Felise, Feliza, Felicity

In Poland and Lithuania 24 January is the name day for *Felicia*. Everyone with this name will receive small gifts and bunches of flowers from their friends and family. It is the female form of Felix, a Roman name meaning successful and lucky.

Meaning good fortune

Nastassja, Natasha

The German-born actress *Nastassja Kinski* was born on this day in 1961. The daughter of actor Klaus Kinski, she came to fame in her award-winning performance of the lead role in Roman Polanski's film *Tess* (1979). She is multilingual and has appeared in over 60 films and TV shows.

Meaning Christmas

Robert, Bob, Rob, Bobby, Robbie, Rip, Rabby, Rabbie, Rab, Roban

The Scottish poet *Robert Burns*, widely known as Rabbie Burns, was born on this day in 1759. Every year Burns's Night is celebrated in Scottish communities worldwide with a symbolic supper of haggis, neeps (turnips or swede) and tatties (potatoes), a plentiful supply of alcohol and readings of Burns's poems and songs.

Meaning bright, famous

Edmund, Edmond, Edmondo, Edmundo, Odon

On this day in 1540 *St Edmund Campion* was born in London. Having escaped religious persecution in England, he became a member of the Society of Jesus in France, returning to England for a Jesuit mission. Hanged in 1581, he was canonized in 1886.

Meaning rich protector

Yousseff, Yusuf

Today is the birthday of *Yousseff Chahaine*, the Egyptian film director, who was born in Alexandria, Egypt, in 1926. He studied film in California before returning to the Middle East. Famous throughout the Arab world, he won the 50th anniversary Palme d'Or at Cannes for his 1997 film *Massir*.

Meaning God increases

William, Will, Willie, Willy, Bill

The British author *William Somerset Maugham* was born in Paris on this day in 1874. He qualified as a surgeon and turned to writing on a full-time basis only in 1897. Among his best known works are the autobiographical *Of Human Bondage* (1915), and *The Moon and Sixpence (1919)*, *East of Suez* (1922) and *Cakes and Ale* (1930).

Meaning desiring to defend

Clementine, Clementina, Clemency, Clementia, Clemencia

On this day in 1994 the US space probe *Clementine* was launched with the important but unglamorous task of tracking meteoroids and man-made debris orbiting the earth.

Meaning merciful

Victoria, Victorine, Victoire, Vitoria, Vittoria, Tory

On this day in 1858 Princess *Victoria*, the eldest daughter of Queen Victoria, was married to Friedrich, crown prince of Prussia. Specially commissioned music by Felix Mendelssohn was played on the occasion; the 'Wedding March' from *A Midsummer Night's Dream* has become one of the most popular wedding compositions.

Meaning victorious one

Corazón

Cory Aquino, president of the Philippines 1986 –92, was born *Corazón Cojuangco Aquino* on this day in 1933. After her husband Benigno Aquino was assassinated in 1983 she became the focus of the opposition to the autocrat Ferdinand Marços.

Meaning heart

Virginia, Ginny, Ginnie, Jinny, Virgi, Virgie, Virg, Vergy

The British novelist *Adeline Virginia Woolf* was born on this day in 1882. A central figure in the Bloomsbury Group in London and co-founder with her husband of the Hogarth Press, she developed a modern style of writing using stream of consciousness. Among her most memorable novels are *Mrs Dalloway* (1925), *To the Lighthouse* (1927), *Orlando* (1928) and *The Waves* (1931).

Meaning virgin

Grantly, Grantley, Grant, Grenville

The pioneering British obstetrician *Grantly Dick-Read* was born on this day in 1890. In his book *Natural Childbirth* (1933) he showed how the fear of childbirth contributed to muscle tension. He promoted the provision of more information for women about childbirth and worked for the National Childbirth Trust.

Meaning great one

Ancel, Ancell

US scientist *Ancel Benjamin Keys* was born on this day in 1904. He was a pioneering nutritionist, who studied the influence of diet on health. He also established the modern epidemiology of cardiovascular disease (CVD). He lived to be two weeks short of 101 years old.

Meaning God-like

Sydney, Sidney, Sid, Syd

This day in 1788 marked the day on which a group of British explorers landed at Botany Bay near *Sydney*, Australia, and Arthur Philip, the commander of the group, established the first European settlement there. To commemorate the event, 26 January is celebrated as Australia Day.

Meaning wide land by a marsh

Timothy, Timotheus, Timoid, Tymon, Tim, Timmie, Timmy, Timotoo

Today is the feast day for *St Timothy*. He lived in Lystra in Asia Minor and is regarded as the first bishop of Ephesus. He was one of St Paul's disciples, as well as a close friend and confidant of his mentor. Like Paul, he devoted his life to spreading the Gospel.

Meaning honouring God

Jacqueline, Jackeline, Jackelyn, Jacketta, Jaclyn, Jacklyn, Jacky, Jackie, Jacobina, Jacqueleine, Jacquelyn, Jacquetta, Jacqui, Jamesina, Jaquith

The British cellist *Jacqueline du Pré* was born on this day in 1945. She was only 20 when she made a recording of Elgar's *Cello Concerto*. Her expressive interpretation of the work made her a star.

From Jacob, meaning supplanter

Julia, Juline, Julina, Sile, Sileas

The US architect *Julia Morgan* was born on this day in 1872. One of the first women to graduate with a degree in civil engineering and the first woman architect to graduate in Paris, she designed over 700 buildings, ranging from public and educational buildings to private houses.

Meaning youthful

Cecilia, Cecelia, Cecile, Cecille, Cecily, Cele, Cicely, Ciel, Cissie, Sissie, Sisle, Sisile, Sileas, Sisley

Paul Simon and Art Garfunkel's album *Bridge over Troubled Water* was released on this day in 1970. It was at the top of the album charts for ten weeks and spawned several singles. *Cecilia*, which has Paul Simon's first use of South African rhythms, peaked at number four in the US singles charts.

Meaning patron saint of music

Paula, Paola, Paule, Paulena, Paulita, Pauli, Paulie, Pavla

Today is the feast day of *St Paula*, who was born in Rome in 347. She and her husband, Toxotius, had five children, and they were held up as an example of the ideal married couple.

From Paul, meaning little

27 JANUARY

Lewis, Louis, Luis, Lewes, Luthais, Lugaidh, Luigi, Lou

Lewis Carroll, the British mathematician and author, was born Charles Lutwidge Dodgson on this day in 1832. His classic works are *Alice's Adventures in Wonderland* (1865) and *Through The Looking Glass and What Alice Found There* (1872). He created his penname by anglicizing the Latin forms of his first two names, Carolus Lodovicus.

Meaning famous warrior

Seth

The US rock musician *Seth Justman* was born on this day in 1951. As the keyboard player for the J. Geils Band and its main songwriter, Seth's talents and production skills had much to do with the group's mega success.

Meaning appointed by God

Vivian, Vivien, Vyvyan, Viv, Ninian

On 27 January 1976 the Antiguan cricketer *Vivian Richards*, known as Viv, scored his first test century playing for the West Indies against Australia. He was the successful captain of the West Indian team from 1985 to 1991, was Wisden cricketer of the year in 1977 and Wisden cricketer of the century in 2000.

Meaning lively

Wolfgang, Wolfe, Wolfram

The Austrian composer *Wolfgang Amadeus Mozart* was born on this day in 1756. Considered to be one of the greatest composers ever, Mozart's prodigious gifts were evident from the age of five. He produced a huge number of major compositions, and his wide variety of musical works are as popular today as they ever were.

Meaning approaching wolf

Angela, Angel, Angeline, Angelina, Angelita

Today is the feast day of *St Angela Merici*, who was born in 1474. At a time when education for woman was reserved for nuns and the rich, she founded the Company of St Ursula, the first order of nuns to be devoted to the education of poor girls.

Meaning heavenly messenger

Donna, Dona

The US actress *Donna Reed* was born on this day in 1921. Brought up on a farm, her great beauty meant she was destined for a more glamorous life. She had many starring film roles in the 1940s and 1950s, most notably in *It's a Wonderful Life* (1946) and *From Here to Eternity* (1953).

Meaning noble lady

Georgia, George, Georgana, Georganne, Georgene, Georgina, Georgette, Georgiana, Georgianna, Georgie, Georgine, Georgy, Giorgia

On this day in 1785 the *University of Georgia* was founded. It was the first state-supported university in the USA, and about 61,200 hectares (151,225 acres) were set aside to build a seminary of learning. Today, there are 14 colleges and schools on the original site.

Meaning farm girl

Mairead

The Northern Irish peace activist *Mairead Corrigan* was born on this day in 1944. She was co-founder of the Community of Peace People, which has been at the forefront of encouraging a peaceful resolution to the troubles. She was awarded the Nobel Prize for peace in 1976.

From Margaret, meaning pearl

Claes, Claus, Claud, Colley, Klaus, Neacail

The Swedish sculptor *Claes Oldenberg* was born on this day in 1929. Although he was born in Sweden, he moved to the USA and studied art at Yale University. He played an important role in New York's emerging Pop Art scene of the late 1950s. His best-known works are enormous depictions of everyday objects, such as ironing boards, scissors and plugs.

From Nicholas, meaning victorious, conqueror

Parry

Parry O'Brien, the US track and field athlete, was born on this day in 1932. In four consecutive Olympic Games, between 1952 and 1964, he won two gold medals, one silver and came fourth in the shot put.

Meaning protector

Jackson

The US artist *Jackson Pollock* was born on this day in 1912. The pioneer of abstract expressionism, he challenged traditional methods of painting by fixing his huge canvases to the floor or wall and pouring or dripping paint, sand and other material on them. Instead of brushes, he moved the paint around with sticks, knives or a trowel.

Meaning son of Jack

Ronnie, Ron, Ronny, Reynold, Rene, Renault, Renaud

The jazz musician and club owner *Ronnie Scott* was born on this day in 1927. The jazz club in London's Soho that bears his name opened in 1959. Ronnie Scott would often make a stage appearance himself, playing tenor saxophone.

From Reginald, meaning strong ruler

Colette, Collete, Collette, Nicolette

The French novelist *Colette* was born on this day in 1873. Her full name was Sidonie-Gabrielle Colette, but she became known by her surname. She wrote over 50 novels and many short stories, all of which had an autobiographical element and were often about the joys and pain of love.

Meaning victorious

Kathleen, Kathlene, Kathryn, Kathy, Kathie

On 28 January 1903 the English physicist and mathematician *Kathleen Lonsdale* was born. She devoted much of her working life to the study of crystals and has a rare diamond, Lonsdaleite, named after her. She was the first woman to be elected a fellow of the Royal Society and the first woman professor at University College, London.

Meaning pure maiden

Susan, Sue, Susy, Suzie, Suzy, Susi, Susie, Sukey, Suki, Suky

The US writer and critic *Susan Sontag* was born on this day in 1933. She wrote novels, short stories, plays and several works of non-fiction and essays, and she also wrote and directed four films and several plays. She was a human rights activist for over 20 years and received many prizes and accolades for both this and her literary work.

Meaning lily, rose

Zerlina

On this day in 1840 the opera *Fra Diavolo* by the French composer Daniel Auber premiered in Paris. The complicated plot involves the loyal *Zerlina*, daughter of an innkeeper, a bandit, some stolen jewels, betrayal and the triumph of true love.

Meaning not known

29 JANUARY

Anton, Antonino, Antonio, Antons, Antin

The writer *Anton Chekhov* was born on this day in 1860. Considered the greatest Russian storyteller and dramatist, Chekhov's acute observations of both the comic and tragic in life found expression in his short stories and plays, the best known of which are *Uncle Vanya* (1900), *The Three Sisters* (1901) and *The Cherry Orchard* (1904).

From Anthony, meaning not known

Frederick

The composer *Frederick Delius* was born on this day in 1862. Although he was born in Bradford in the north of England, both his parents were German. He is best known for his songs and small orchestral pieces, often pastoral in theme, especially *On Hearing the First Cuckoo in Spring*.

Meaning peaceful ruler

Morris, Morrie, Morry, Morice, Moritz, Morel

On this day in 1929 the US guide dog organization, the Seeing Eye, was founded by Swiss dog breeder Dorothy Eustis, who was persuaded by a blind American, *Morris Frank*, to train one of her dogs to be his eyes. Morris and guide dog Buddy travelled the USA promoting the scheme to make the world accessible to the blind.

From Maurice, meaning dark, swarthy

Romain, Romanus

The French writer *Romain Rolland* was born in Clamecy, Nievre, on 29 January 1866. He won the Nobel Prize for literature in 1915 for his ten-volume cycle *Jean-Christophe*. A pacifist, he looked to Eastern philosophy for inspiration.

From Roman, meaning from Rome

Eugénie, Eugenia

On this day in 1856 the marriage took place in the Tuileries Palace in Paris between Napoleon III and *Eugénie de Montijo*, a Spanish noblewoman renowned for her beauty. She and her husband were forced to flee France in 1870. Settling in Britain, she became a friend of Queen Victoria's.

Meaning noble, well-born

Germaine, Germain

The Australian feminist writer and academic *Germaine Greer* was born on this day in 1939. Considered one of the most significant feminists of the 20th century, she is probably best known for her first book, *The Female Eunuch*, published in 1970. She is also a university lecturer and a media commentator on artistic and social issues.

Meaning from Germany

Oprah, Ophrah, Ophra, Ofra

The US TV talk-show hostess and actress *Oprah Winfrey* was born on this day in 1954. Although her first claim to fame was as an actress in the film *The Color Purple* (1985), it is the *Oprah Winfrey Show* that has led to her being named as one of the 100 most influential people of the 20th century. The show has been broadcast for nearly 20 years and has won numerous awards.

Meaning fawn

Charity, Caridad, Karita

On 29 January 1966 the musical comedy *Sweet Charity* premiered at the Palace Theatre, New York. With a score by Cy Coleman and lyrics by Dorothy Fields to a story by Neil Simon, it was an instant success. Its songs included 'Big Spender' and 'If My Friends Could See Me Now'.

Meaning love

Franklin, Frank

On this day in 1882 the 32nd president of the USA, *Franklin Delano Roosevelt*, was born in Hyde Park, New York. Although he was partially paralysed by poliomyelitis, he was an active campaigner and politician. During his presidency the New Deal was put in place, and he promoted a system of social security. His 'fireside chats' were a well-loved and familiar part of his style.

Meaning free man

Slatan

Slatan Dudow, the Bulgarian theatre and film director, was born on this day in 1903. He studied theatre in Berlin in the 1920s, moving on to film-making after meeting Sergei Eisenstein, his greatest influence. His best-known film is *To Whom Does the World Belong?* (1932).

From Sultan, meaning king

Nikolaus, Nikos, Niles

The architectural historian *Nikolaus Pevsner* was born on this day in 1902. Although he was born and educated in Germany, Pevsner became a British citizen and dedicated over 20 years to editing the 46-volume series, *The Buildings of England*. He also wrote the influential *An Outline of European Architecture* (1942).

From Nicholas, meaning victorious, conqueror

Mungo

The Scottish surgeon and explorer *Mungo Park* set off on an expedition on 30 January 1804 to discover the source of the River Niger. This was part of a larger British plan to find out more about Africa's interior. Having had some success on his travels, he returned to England a celebrity.

Meaning dear friend

Eleanor, Elonore, Eleonora, Elonore Eleanora, Eleanore, Elinor, Elinora, Eleanor, Elinore

The US women's rights campaigner *Eleanor Smeal* was born on this day in 1939. President of the Feminist Majority Foundation, for 30 years she worked for justice in many cases affecting the rights of women in the USA. Her later campaigns focused on women's rights in Afghanistan.

From Helen, meaning light

Jemima, Jemmie, Jemie

Jemima Khan was born on 30 January 1974. The beautiful heiress, daughter of Sir James and Annabel Goldsmith, gave up her university studies and a promising horse-riding career to be a politician's wife in Lahore, Pakistan. She is active in several high-profile, international charities.

Meaning dove

Elise, Elysia, Elysium, Elicia

Elise Cavanna, the multitalented artist, actress, singer, chef and dancer, was born on 30 January 1902. One of the pioneers of abstraction and modernism in art, she also studied dance under Isadora Duncan. An independent spirit, she was extremely tall and, for a while, had purple hair.

Meaning blissful sweetness

Vanessa, Van, Vania, Vanna, Vannie, Vanni, Vanny, Vanya

The British actress *Vanessa Redgrave*, star of film, stage and TV, was born on this day in 1937. All the members of her immediate family are or were actors – her parents Rachel Kempson and Sir Michael Redgrave, brother Corin, sister Lynn and daughters Natasha and Joely Richardson.

Meaning not known

31 JANUARY

Asa, Ase

On 31 January 1893 the Coca-Cola trademark was registered. The seven-year-old company was owned by *Asa Candler*, and he was determined to make the 'tonic beverage made from a secret formula' more popular. Rather than selling the drink exclusively at soda fountains in pharmacies, he had the bright idea of bottling it to make it more widely accessible – and the rest is history.

Meaning doctor, healer

Justin, Just, Justino, Justus, Justinian

The US pop star *Justin Timberlake* was born on 31 January 1981. He started singing in a band, NSYNC, when he was only 14. The sales of his first solo album, *Justified*, reached triple platinum.

Meaning fair, just

Neil, Neal, Niles, Nils, Niels, Niall, Nels, Neill, Neel, Neall

The Canadian rock star *Neil Young* made his first public appearance at the age of 17 on 31 January 1963. He has been in and out of the limelight ever since with his band Crazy Horse, with Crosby, Stills, Nash and Young and on his own. Several hits in the early 1970s, most notably 'Heart of Gold' (1972), made him into a superstar.

Meaning champion

Norman, Normand, Normie, Norris, Norm

US writer *Normal Mailer* was born on this day in 1923. He became famous in his mid-20s with the publication of his first novel, *The Naked and the Dead* (1948). He is considered to be one of the world's major writers but is often controversial.

Meaning man from the north

Anna, Ana, Annika, Anula, Anuska

The legendary ballerina *Anna Pavlova* was born in Russia on 31 January 1881. Her fragility and daintiness set her apart from other ballet dancers of the period. Her powerful performances of *La Cygne* (The Dying Swan) sealed her destiny as one of the greatest dancers ever.

From Anne, meaning God has favoured me

Beatrix, Trix, Trixie, Trixy

Queen *Beatrix of the Netherlands* was born on this day in 1938. She was crowned in 1980, after her mother, Queen Juliana, abdicated. She is renowned for carrying out her duties with formality and professionalism, and for creating a modern, efficient and people-friendly monarchy. Her eldest son will take over the throne when she decides to vacate the position.

Meaning bringer of happiness

Minnie, Minny, Helma, Mina, Guilla, Wilhelmina, Welma, Velma, Willa

British actress and singer *Minnie Driver* was born on 31 January 1971. The name Minnie stuck after her sister had trouble pronouncing her real name, Amelia. She has made about 15 films, and received an Academy Award for her role in *Good Will Hunting* (1997).

Meaning protector

Tallulah, Tallu, Tallula, Tally, Tallie

Tallulah Bankhead, the iconic US actress, was born on this day in 1903. Named after the town Tallulah Falls, Georgia, she loved being the centre of attention, even as a child. She became known for her wild personality and wit as well as her acting ability in every medium.

Meaning princess, abundance

February

February

Clark, Clarke, Clerk

The US actor *Clark Gable* was born on 1 February 1901. His first major acting roles were for MGM, and he swiftly became the studio's most important star. He won an Oscar for *It Happened One Night* (1934) and five years later played Rhett Butler in *Gone with the Wind*. He was the epitome of manliness for a whole generation of women.

Meaning cleric, scholar

Boris

Boris Yeltsin was born on this day in 1931. In 1991 he won 57 per cent of the popular vote to become the first ever democratically elected leader of Russia. He fired his entire cabinet four times.

Meaning fighter

Harvey, Harve, Herv, Herve, Hervey

On 1 February 1887 a 48.5-hectare (120-acre) citrus farm outside Los Angeles, owned by property developer *Harvey Wilcox*, was renamed Hollywood by his wife. He had intended to sell off the plot of land to like-minded conservative prohibitionists, but this was not to be. The official founder of Hollywood would not believe his eyes if he saw how his plot looks today.

Meaning worthy in battle

Stanley, Stanly, Stan, Stanleigh

Stanley Matthews, the legendary British soccer player who was nicknamed the wizard of dribble, was born on this day in 1915 in Hanley, Staffordshire. He started playing for Stoke City when he was 14 years old, and after the war he joined Blackpool FC, where he stayed for 14 years. He also played for England and was the first professional footballer to be knighted (in 1964).

Meaning from the stony meadow

Evonne, Ivonne, Evette

The Australian Aboriginal tennis star *Evonne Goolagong* won her first senior tennis tournament in Australia on this day in 1971. She went on to win the French, Italian, Australian and Wimbledon titles, and clocked up a staggering 88 tournament wins by the time she retired in 1982.

From Yvonne, meaning yew

Josceline, Joscelin, Jocelyn, Joscelyn, Joscelyne, Joselen, Joselin, Joseline, Joselyn, Joselyne, Joslin, Josilen, Josilene

The British cookery writer *Josceline Dimbleby* was born on 1 February 1943. She has written many bestselling cookery books and has won two prestigious awards for writing about food; she also had a food column in the *Daily Telegraph*.

Meaning fair, just

Sherilyn, Cherilyn

Sherilyn Fenn is the enigmatically beautiful US actress who played Audrey Horne in David Lynch's cult TV hit *Twin Peaks* (1990). She went on to work in many feature films, including Lynch's feature *Wild at Heart* (1990). She was born on this day in 1965 in Detroit, Michgan.

From Cherie, meaning beloved

Muriel, Meriel, Muire, Murielle

The Scottish author *Muriel Spark* was born on this day in 1918. She has had almost 50 books published since she started writing in 1945, including novels, poems, short stories and literary criticism. Despite this prolific output, she will forever be associated with her bestseller, *The Prime of Miss Jean Brodie* (1961).

Meaning sea bright

Finnegan, Finn, Finlay, Fingal, Findley, Findlay

The Irish modernist writer James Joyce was born on 2 February 1882. He developed a unique experimental style of writing that involved using invented words, puns and allusions. His best-known works are *Dubliners* (1914), *Portrait of the Artist as a Young Man* (1916), *Ulysses* (1922) and *Finnegans Wake* (1939).

Meaning fair, white

Mark, Marc, Marco, Marcus

On this day in 1863 an unknown author, Samuel Langhorne Clemens, decided to adopt the pseudonym *Mark Twain*. He went on to shape US literature and is the author of the evocative *The Adventures of Tom Sawyer* (1876) and *The Adventures of Huckleberry Finn* (1884).

Meaning follower of Mars

Solomon, Salomon, Solamon, Solly, Soloman, Sol, Sollie, Zollie, Zolly

US philanthropist *Solomon Robert Guggenheim* was born on this day in 1861. His father made a fortune in the copper industry. Solomon started collecting modern art when he retired from the firm. A permanent home for his collection was designed by Frank Lloyd Wright, and the Gugenheim Museum opened in New York in 1959.

Meaning peaceful, wise

Rebop, Rabab

On this day in 1992 a son, *Rebop*, was born to musician and record producer Todd Rundgren and Michelle Gray. Todd Rundgren has produced countless albums for a wide range of musicians, from Shaun Cassidy to the Psychedelic Furs.

Meaning musical instrument

Elaine, Laney

The US actress *Elaine Stritch* was born on this day in 1926. Known for her brash character and deep, strident voice, she has had a 60-year plus career singing and acting on stage and in film and on TV. One of the strongest characters in show business, her indomitable spirit has carried her through the bad times as well as the good.

From Helen, meaning light

Eva, Eve, Evelina, Eveline, Evelyn, Evie, Evita, Evonne

This day in 1963 was the birth date of a singer with one of the greatest voices of all time: *Eva Cassidy*. Because it was impossible to categorize her musical style, she failed to receive the recognition she deserved during her lifetime. She was also a talented painter and a great lover of nature.

Meaning giver of life

Louise, Louisitte, Louisette, Loyce, Luise, Labhaoise, Liusade

The opera *Louise* by Gustave Charpentier received its first performance on 2 February 1900 in Paris. An instant success, it chronicles the love affair of Louise, a working-class girl, and her poet suitor, Julien. It is a universal and moralistic tale about duty to family (the father was unhappy about their relationship) and the power of love.

From Louis, meaning famous warrior

Farrah

The US actress *Farrah Fawcett* was born on this day in 1947. She came to fame when she starred, as Farrah Fawcett-Majors, in the original TV series of *Charlie's Angels* (1977–82) with Kate Jackson and Jaclyn Smith. She later made films, including *Logan's Run* (1976) and *Strictly Business* (1979).

Meaning not known

Felix, Felicio, Felizio, Felice

The German composer *Felix Mendelssohn* was born on 3 February 1809. Often thought of as one of music's underrated geniuses, he wrote in just about every musical form, but his most famous compositions are possibly the incidental music (including the 'Wedding March') to *A Midsummer Night's Dream* and *Fingal's Cave* overture.

Meaning good fortune

Alvar, Alva, Alvah

Alvar Aalto, the innovative Finnish designer and architect, was born on 3 February 1898. His designs include the distinctive laminated birchwood furniture, and his buildings include the Finlandia concert hall in Helsinki and the campus for the Helsinki University of Technology.

Meaning exalted one

Frankie, Frank, Franz, Franchot, Fran

The British singer *Frankie Vaughan* was born in Liverpool on this day in 1928. He started singing in the late 1940s in variety theatres and became known for his dapper appearance in top hat and tails. He made forays into film, even starring with Marilyn Monroe on one occasion.

From Francis, meaning free man

Noël, Nowell, Newell, Newel, Natale, Natal

The English actor and writer *Noël Coward* was knighted on 3 February 1970. He epitomized 'Englishness' and despite his camp appearance became an idol for many men. His songs ranged from sentimental to satirical, such as 'Mad Dogs and Englishmen' and 'Some Day I'll Find You'.

Meaning Christmas

Gertrude, Gartred, Gert, Gertie, Gertrud, Gerda, Gerty, Gertudis, Gertruda

The US writer *Gertrude Stein* was born on 3 February 1874. Truly eccentric, she spent most of her life in Paris, where her home was a magnet for many artists and writers in the period between the two world wars. Her most famous and accessible book is *The Autobiography of Alice B. Toklas* (1933), which is, in fact, her own autobiography.

Meaning strong spear

Blythe, Blyth, Blith, Blithe

Today is the birthday of the actress *Blythe Danner*, who was born on this day in 1944 in Zaire, where her parents were missionaries. As well as being a successful actress, speaking seven languages and once swimming the English Channel, she is the mother of Gwyneth and Jake Paltrow.

Meaning happy, joyful

Mabel, Mable, Mabe, Amabel, Maible, Maybele, Moibeal

On this day in 1900 the British cabaret star *Mabel Mercer* was born in Burton-upon-Trent, Staffordshire. She lived in Paris for some years, honing her singing skills, and spent the rest of her life in New York. Her forte was live performance, where her human warmth was much in evidence.

Meaning lovely, good-humoured

Maura

US actress *Maura Tierney* was born on 3 February 1965. Having progressed from small roles in TV series and films to more high-profile ones, she is best known for playing Abby Lockhart in the long-running and ever-popular TV series *ER*.

Meaning dark, swarthy

Fernand, Fernando, Hernando, Ferd, Ferdie, Ferdy

The French cubist painter *Fernand Léger* was born on this day in Argentan, Normandy, in 1881. He was the first artist to take cubism into the realm of non-figurative abstraction. He also designed for the theatre and ballet, and made experimental-style films.

From Ferdinand, meaning daring adventurer

Gua

Gua Yuehua, the Chinese table tennis champion, celebrates his birthday today. In China table tennis is a major sport, and Gua is a national hero. Among world players he is ranked as one of the best competitors ever.

Meaning dark

Conwell, Connell, Conall

The US writer *Russell Conwell Hoban* was born in Lansdale, Pennsylvania, on 4 February 1925, but lived in London from 1969. His books include works for adults and children, his most famous being *The Mouse and his Child* (1967), *Turtle Diary* (1975) and *Riddley Walker* (1980).

Meaning strong wolf

Harrison

On this day in 1805 British novelist and editor *William Harrison Ainsworth* was born in Manchester. Among his 39 historical romances were *Rookwood* (1834), which romanticized the career of the highwayman Dick Turpin, and he wrote about Herne the Hunter in *Windsor Castle* (1843). Some of his books were illustrated by George Cruikshank.

Meaning son of Harry

Isablita, Isabel, Ishbel, Isobel, Ysabeu, Ysabel, Ysabella, Ysabelle, Ysobel, Ysobella, Ysobelle Bel, Bella, Belle

On this day in 1931 *Isabelita Perón* was born in La Rioja, Argentina. A nightclub dancer, she became the third wife of Argentine president Juan Perón in July 1974. After Perón's death in 1974 she became president, but was overthrown in a military coup.

Meaning consecrated to God

Natalie, Natalia, Natale, Natala, Nathalie, Natica, Natika, Natividad, Nattie, Netta, Nettie, Netty, Noel, Noelle, Novella

The Australian singer *Natalie Imbruglia* was born on 4 February 1975. Like Kylie Minogue, her career began on the set of the TV soap opera *Neighbours*.

Meaning Christmas

Rosa, Rosalia, Rosaleen, Rosalie, Rosel, Rosella, Roselle, Rosena, Rosene, Rosetta, Rosette, Rosia, Rosie, Rosy

The civil rights activist *Rosa Lee Parks* was born on 4 February 1913. In 1955 she sparked a year-long boycott of the bus system in Montgomery, Alabama, by refusing to give up her seat for a white passenger. This led to the end of segregation.

Meaning rose

Joan, Jeanne

Today is the feast day of *St Joan of France*, the daughter of Louis XI and Charlotte of Savoy. The king married her off to the duke of Orléans, but when he became king, the marriage was annulled. Joan then founded an order of nuns, the Annonciades, to pray and work for peace.

From Jane, meaning God's gift of grace

Duff

It is the birthday today of Guns N' Roses bass player *Duff McKagan*, who was born in Seattle, Washington, on 5 February 1964. He played in 31 bands in the Los Angeles area, including Ten Minute Warning and the Fartz, before joining Guns N' Roses.

Meaning dark

Boyd

The Scottish inventor of the rubber tyre, *John Boyd Dunlop* was born on this day in 1840. A vet by profession, he moved from Edinburgh to Belfast, where he built up a large practice. He had to travel to see his animal patients, and the solid wheels of the day combined with the rough roads of Ireland spurred him on to invent a wheel for a more comfortable ride.

Meaning light-haired

Adlai, Adley, Adli, Adly

Adlai Ewing Stevenson, US politician and diplomat, was born in Los Angeles on this day in 1900. From 1961 to 1965 he was US ambassador to the United Nations and generally had greater appeal in Europe than in the USA. His speeches were published as *Call to Greatness* (1954) and *What I Think* (1956).

Meaning God is just

Willard

The US actor *Willard Parker* was born Worster van Eps on 5 February 1912. Most of his roles were in action adventure movies, such as *A Slight Case of Murder* (1938) and *The Great Jesse James Raid* (1953), and he was also in the TV series *Tales of the Texan Rangers* (1955–7).

Meaning brave, resolute

Agatha, Agathe, Agata, Agace, Agathy, Aggy, Aggie, Agueda

Today is the feast day of *St Agatha*. She is believed to have been born in Sicily in the 3rd century, and legend recounts that when she rejected her suitor, Quintian, he denounced her for being a Christian. She is the patron saint of bell-founders.

Meaning of impeccable virtue

Esme, Esmée

It is the birthday today of *Esme Creed-Miles*, the daughter of actress Samantha Morton and Charlie Creed-Miles. She was born in London on 5 February 2000. Samantha was nominated for a best supporting actress Oscar for her part in Woody Allen's *Sweet and Lowdown* (1999) and for best actress for *In America* (2004).

Meaning esteemed

Jessica, Jessalyn

On 5 February 1928 the US soprano *Jessica Dragonette* was the first entertainer ever to appear on TV. Known as the queen of the radio and princess of song, she was one of the most popular entertainers in the 1920s and 1930s.

Meaning rich one

Melina

The Greek actress *Melina Mercouri* was born on 5 February 1923. After gaining international fame as a film star, notably in *Never on Sunday* (1960), she returned to her homeland and went into politics. In the early 1990s she became minister for culture and was subsequently a candidate for the office of mayor of Athens.

Meaning yellow canary

Marley, Marly

Bob Marley, the king of reggae, was born on this day in 1945 near Kingston, Jamaica. Every year this day is celebrated throughout Jamaica as Bob Marley Day. With his band the Wailers, Bob Marley was responsible for bringing his particular brand of music to all corners of the globe, and his music is inextricably linked to his Rastafarian religion.

Meaning from the lake in the meadow

Christopher, Christophe, Christoph, Christoforo, Chrostophorus, Cristobal

The English playwright *Christopher Marlowe* was born on 6 February 1564. He is probably the most important and best known of William Shakespeare's contemporaries, and his plays include *Edward II* (1590) and *The Tragical History of Dr Faustus* (1604).

Meaning carrier of Christ

Axl, Axel, Absalom

Axl Rose was born on this day in 1962 in Lafayette, Indiana. His original name was William Bruce Rose, but he chose Axl because, with Rose, it forms an interesting unprintable anagram. In 1985 he formed the band Guns N' Roses, a unique mould of heavy rock and punk.

Meaning my father is peace

Masha, Mashiro

Masha Masaharu celebrates his birthday today. The Japanese actor and pop star was born in Nagasaki in 1969. He is known throughout Japan by his nickname, Masha, the legend being that his father had such poor teeth that when he tried to say Masaharu it came out Mashaharu.

Meaning broad-minded

Mamie, Manette, Manon, Mara, Maretta, Marette

The beautiful Hollywood screen sex siren *Mamie van Doren*, who was born Lucille Olander in South Dakota on this day in 1931, was known as one of the three Ms, along with Marilyn Monroe and Jane Mansfield. Universal Pictures named her after President Eisenhower's wife.

From Mary, meaning bitter

ZsaZsa, Zsa-Zsa, Zsa

Another screen sex symbol born today, in 1917, is *ZsaZsa Gabor*. Like Mamie van Duren, she was better known for being herself than for any of her roles. From being chosen as Miss Hungary in 1936, she was married no fewer than nine times.

From Susan, meaning lily, rose

Anne, Ann, Annie

On this day *Anne*, queen of Britain and Ireland, was born in London in 1665. She was the daughter of the duke of York (later James II) and Anne Hyde, and the younger sister of Mary, who married William of Orange. Anne married George, prince of Denmark, and they had 17 children, of whom only one survived infancy – and he died aged 12.

Meaning God has favoured me

Dorothy, Dorothea, Dorothoe, Dorete, Dorota, Drottya, Dosia, Thea, Dot, Dottie, Dotty, Dora, Dory, Dorothi, Dorothoe, Theodora

Today is the feast day of *St Dorothy of Cappadocia*, who was imprisoned for her beliefs in the late 3rd century, but managed to convert two women warders to Christianity. She was, however, martyred in 303. Her symbol is a basket laden with fruit.

Meaning gift of God

Charles, Charlie, Charley, Chas, Chaz, Chay, Carolos, Karl, Carlo, Carlos, Karol, Karel

The British author *Charles John Huffam Dickens* was born near Portsmouth on 7 February 1812. Famous for his novels of social commentary in the Victorian era, many of which were satirical, he is one of the few authors whose books have never been out of print.

Meaning free man

An

An Wang, the American-Chinese computer genius and philanthropist, was born on 7 February 1920 in Shanghai, China. Founder of Wang Laboratories, he invented the pulse transfer controller, a crucial part of the computer's memory device.

Meaning peace

Eddie, Ed, Eddy

The British comedian *Eddie Izzard* was born on this day in 1962 in Aden, Yemen, and was raised in Northern Ireland, Wales and on the south coast of England. His unique style of comic delivery together with his penchant for cross-dressing have proved enormously successful around the globe, and he has a large and loyal following.

From Edward, meaning prosperous guardian

Garth

US country singer *Garth Brooks* was born in Yukon, Oklahoma, on 7 February 1962. He has been awarded many accolades for his contributions to country music and is the bestselling country music singer and songwriter of all time.

Meaning not known

Petula, Petronella, Petronelle, Petronia, Petronilla, Petronille, Pierette, Petra, Petrina, Perrine

On 7 February 1966 the number one record in the US singles charts was 'My Love' by *Petula Clark*. A wartime child star, Petula has been famous all her life. She has been making records for over 50 years and has recorded over 1,000 songs.

Meaning steady

Hattie, Hatty, Hettie, Hetty

The British comic actress *Hattie Jacques* was born on this day in 1924. She began her career as a radio actress before moving to films and TV. She is best known for her performances on TV with Eric Sykes and in the *Carry On* films, of which she made 14. She was married to the actor John Le Mesurier.

From Henrietta, meaning ruler of the home

Dora, Dory

On this day in 1924 British actress *Dora Bryan* was born Dora Broadbent in Southport, Lancashire. She has appeared in films, the theatre and in many TV series. Her first film was *Odd Man Out* (1946), and she took the lead in the London run of *Hello, Dolly!* in 1966. On TV she was in the long-running *Mother's Ruin* (1994).

From Dorothy, meaning gift of God

Laura, Laure, Laurel, Laurie, Lora, Loralie, Loree, Lorelie

The US author *Laura Ingalls Wilder* was born on 7 February 1867 in Pepin, Wisconsin. She is best known for her novel *Little House on the Prairie* (1935). With her family she lived a tough frontier life in Kansas, Minnesota, Iowa and South Dakota.

Meaning laurel wreath

Dean, Deane, Dene, Dino

US actor *James Dean* was born on 8 February 1931. Although his acting career was tragically cut short, his performance in *Rebel without a Cause* (1955) led to his becoming a role model for teenagers of his generation and many since.

Meaning from the valley

Myron, Merrill

It is US actor *Myron McCormick*'s birthday today. Born in 1908, he was one of the founding members of Princeton's University Players, whose later alumni included James Stewart and Henry Fonda. Myron played Luther Billis in the 1949 stage premiere of *South Pacific*. He was also in the film *The Hustler* (1961).

Meaning fragrant oil

Nick, Nicky, Nichol, Nicol, Nicolai, Nik, Nikki, Nickie, Nikos

The US actor *Nick Nolte* was born Nicholas King Nolte on this day in 1940. He has featured in over 50 films, including *The Prince of Tides* (1991), *Lorenzo's Oil* (1992) and *Affliction* (1997). He has received several Oscar nominations and won the New York Critics award for best actor for his role in *Cape Fear* (1991).

From Nicholas, meaning victorious, conqueror

Phileas

The author and science-fiction pioneer *Jules Verne*, who was born on this day in 1828, was the creator of *Phileas Fogg*, the hero of his novel *Around the World in Eighty Days* (1873). Verne had already enjoyed success with *Twenty Thousand Leagues Under the Sea* (1869).

From Phyllis, meaning leafy, foliage

Evangeline, Evangelina, Vancy, Vangie

Evangeline Adams, the first famous American astrologer, was born on this day in 1868 at 8.30 am in New Jersey, which makes her an Aquarian with Pisces rising. Among her predictions were the Second World War, the 1929 stock market crash and the deaths of Enrico Caruso and Edward VII.

Meaning bearer of glad tidings

Catherine, Catharine, Katherine, Katharine, Kathryn, Cathryn, Cathy, Kathy, Catharina, Cathelle, Cathie, Cathleen, Catriona

On this day in 1725 *Catherine I*, empress of Russia, succeeded to the throne. Although she came from a humble background and was uneducated, her common sense and steely determination enabled her to perform her duties with great success.

Meaning pure maiden

Elly, Ellie

The Dutch soprano *Elly Ameling* was born in Rotterdam on this day in 1933. She has spent over 40 years recording and touring the world, performing in all the major opera houses. Her range is broad, her repertoire extending from Bach and Mozart to Britten and Gershwin.

From Eleanor, meaning light

Lana, Alana, Alanah, Alanna, Alina, Allene, Allyn, Lanetta, Lanette

The actress *Lana Turner* was born on 8 February 1921. Variously nicknamed the Sweater Girl and the Nightclub Queen, her glamour-girl image and lifestyle were sometimes counterproductive to her acting career.

Meaning bright, fair

Brendan, Brendon, Brendis, Brenna, Bryn, Bren

Brendan Behan, the powerfully political Irish playwright and author, was born on this day in 1923. His first international success was in 1954 with his play *The Quare Fellow*, which transferred from Dublin to the Theatre Royal, London, where it was produced by Joan Littlewood.

Meaning prince

Nelson, Nels, Nils, Nilson

On 9 February 1994 *Nelson Mandela* became the first black president of South Africa. One of the greatest moral and political leaders of our time, he was responsible for creating a new multiracial South Africa free from the oppression of apartheid. After a lifetime of struggle, setbacks and 25 years' imprisonment, Nelson Mandela has emerged as a 20th-century hero.

Meaning son of Neal

Travis, Travers, Travus

US country rocker *Travis Tritt* was born on 9 February 1963. He is something of a rebel and has remained on the sidelines of the country music boom. His later career has been marked by a return to his bluegrass roots.

Meaning from the crossroads

Ansbert, Ansbald, Ansas, Ansard

Today is the feast day of *St Ansbert of Fontenelle*, abbot of Fontenelle, Rouen, France. He lived in the 7th century and was the confessor to the king of the Ostrogoths. For a short while he was bishop of Rouen.

Meaning not known

Alice, Alyce, Ali, Allie, Ally, Allys, Allyce, Alys, Alis, Allis, Ailish, Alla, Aleece, Alecia

African-American author *Alice Walker* was born on 9 February 1944. Her best-known book, *The Color Purple* (1982), won a Pulitzer prize and was made into a successful film. Her other novels include *The Temple of My Familiar* (1989) and *By the Light of My Father's Smile* (2001).

Meaning truth

Carmen, Carmina, Carmia, Carmine, Carma, Carmacita, Carmelita, Carmencita, Carmita, Charmaine

The Portuguese-Brazilian singer, dancer and actress *Carmen Miranda* was born near Lisbon, Portugal, on this day in 1909. She became known as 'the lady in the tutti-frutti hat' because of the fruit-adorned headdresses she favoured, but this image belied her talents as a samba superstar.

Meaning singer with a beautiful voice

Kenya

Today is the birthday of *Kenya Julia Miabi Sarah Jones*, the daughter of Natassja Kinski and Quincy Jones, who was born on 9 February 1993. Natassja Kinski's most famous film appearances include the title role of *Tess* (1979) and *Paris, Texas* (1984).

Meaning African country

Mia, Meah, Mea

US actress *Mia Farrow* was born on 9 February 1945. Her partners have included Frank Sinatra, André Previn and Woody Allen. She is mother to 14 children, nine of them adopted. Her most famous films are *Rosemary's Baby* (1968), *The Great Gatsby* (1974) and several of Woody Allen's.

From Mary, meaning bitter

Clifford

Clifford T. Ward, the popular but underrated British singer and songwriter of the 1970s, was born on 10 February 1946. The ex-teacher had only one hit single, 'Gaye', but many of his songs were recorded by other artists, and he had a loyal following of fans.

Meaning ford by the cliff

Bertolt, Berthold, Berthoud, Bertold

Bertolt Brecht, the German poet and dramatist, was born on this day in 1898. His revolutionary way of staging plays, designed to shock the audience, became known as epic theatre. His methods of alienating his audiences were so successful that there were riots at his early plays.

Meaning brilliant ruler

Samuel, Sammy, Sam

On this day in 1824 *Samuel Plimsoll*, British social reformer and member of Parliament, was born in Bristol. He is known as the sailors' friend because of his campaign to pass the 1876 Merchant Shipping Act, which required shipowners to mark all their ships with a line indicating the level to which they could be loaded.

Meaning asked of God

Tom, Tommy, Tomlin, Tomkin, Tomaso, Thom

The cartoon cat and mouse *Tom and Jerry* made their screen debut on this day in 1940. Tom, the devilish cat, is always trying to outwit Jerry in their riotous chases around the kitchen, but Tom is continually thwarted by the impish mouse. The two have delighted generations of children and adults for over 60 years.

From Thomas, meaning twin

Sharon, Sharron, Sharri, Sharry, Shari

On this day in 1958 US actress *Sharon Stone* was born in Meadville, Pennsylvania. Stardom came at the age of 32 through her performance in the film *Basic Instinct* (1992), and in 1995 she received a Golden Globe and an Oscar nomination for her role in *Casino* (1995).

Meaning beautiful and exotic princess

Leontyne, Leontine, Leontina

The US soprano *Leontyne Price* was born in Laurel, Mississippi, on this day in 1927. After studying at the Juilliard School of Music, her powerful and extraordinarily far-ranging voice landed her the role of Bess in the Broadway opening of *Porgy and Bess* (1935) and set her on the road to stardom.

Meaning lion-like

Neva, Nevada

Neva Patterson was born on this day in 1925 in Nevada. A TV star of the 1950s, she has appeared in more than 400 TV dramas, as well as working in the theatre and movies. Her most famous roles are in *The Solid Gold Cadillac* (1956) and *An Affair to Remember* (1957).

Meaning white as the moon

Stella, Stelle, Estelle, Estrelita, Estella, Estrella

Stella Adler, Marlon Brando's acting teacher, was born on 10 February 1902. For many years she was the most famous drama coach in the USA. She studied with Constantin Stanislavsky, and together they founded the style of teaching known as 'method acting', where the actor totally inhabits his character on and off set.

Meaning star

Drake

On this day in 1573 the English explorer Sir *Francis Drake* first set eyes on the Pacific Ocean. Of the five ships with which he left England, only the *Golden Hind* survived the perilous journey. This expedition lasted for three years and covered some 58,000 kilometres (36,000 miles).

Meaning dragon

Gerry, Ger, Gery

Gerry Goffin, one half of the prolific songwriting duo Goffin and King, was born on 11 February 1939. The 'King' is Carole King, his wife from 1959 until 1968. Among their many successful songs is 'Take Good Care of My Baby', a hit for Bobby Vee in 1961.

From Gerald, meaning ruling spear

Gaetano, Gaétan, Cayetano

On this day in 1840 *Gaetano Donizetti*'s opera *La Fille du régiment* (The Daughter of the Regiment) was performed in Paris for the first time. Donizetti is known as a composer of Italian operas, but he also wrote string quartets, orchestral works and some church music.

Meaning person from Caieta

Honoré, Honor

On 11 February 1568 the French writer *Honoré d'Urfé* was born in Marseilles. His main work was the five-volume *Astrée* (1610–27), which is about 5th-century shepherds and shepherdesses. It is regarded as the most important French pastoral novel and influenced the philosopher Rousseau.

Meaning honour

Jennifer, Jenny, Jen

The US actress *Jennifer Aniston* was born on this day in 1969. Famous for her role as Rachel in the long-running TV soap *Friends*, she has also enjoyed leading roles in a number of films, including *The Object of My Affection* (1998) and *Office Space* (1999).

From Genevieve, meaning kinswoman

Lydia, Lidia, Lidie, Lydie, Lida

The American anti-slavery activist *Lydia Marie Child* was born on 11 February 1902 in Medford, Massachusetts. A novelist and journalist, she was on the executive committee of the American Anti-Slavery Society and edited the *National Anti-Slavery Standard* in 1841–3.

Meaning cultured one

Brandy, Brandais, Brandea, Brandice

The US pop singer and actress *Brandy* was born Brandy Rayana Norwood on this day in 1979 in McComb, Mississippi. She has had several chart hits, including the platinum-selling 'Baby' (1995), and stars in the title role of the TV sitcom *Moesha* (1996). She has a daughter called Sy'rai.

Meaning brandy

Sheryl, Sherrie, Sherry

Today is the birthday of US rock singer and songwriter *Sheryl Crow*, who was born on 11 February 1964 in Kennett, Missouri. Her first album, *Tuesday Night Music Club* (1994), was an immediate hit, and the single 'All I Wanna Do' (1994) was a favourite in the 1990s.

From Cherie, meaning beloved

Abraham, Abe, Abram, Abran, Avram, Bram, Ibrahim, Abie

US president *Abraham Lincoln* was born on 12 February 1809. The day was declared a national holiday in 1892 and is celebrated to this day. Lincoln was the 16th president, but only the first Republican to hold this office.

Meaning father of the multitudes

Julian, Julyan, Julien, Jolyon, Jolly

Today is the feast day of *St Julian the Hospitaller*. Legend recounts how Julian, a nobleman, mistakenly killed his father and mother. In penance, he and his loyal wife built a hospital for the poor near a swiftly flowing river, and he helped travellers ford the river. One day, he helped a leper, who turned out to be a messenger from God.

Meaning youthful

Franco, Francesco

Franco Zeffirelli, the multitalented opera, theatre and film producer and designer, was born Gianfranco Corsi in Florence, Italy, on this day in 1923. Over five decades he has produced and directed a huge body of acclaimed work, from Oscar-nominated feature films to opera.

Meaning free man

Lorne, Lorrie, Lorry

The Canadian actor *Lorne Green* was born today in Ottawa in 1915. He is best known for his portrayal of Ben Cartwright, the burly ranch owner in the long-running TV series *Bonanza*. One of the best known of all TV westerns, it ran for 430 episodes in the late 1950s and 1960s.

From Lawrence, meaning crowned with laurels

Chynna, Cyna, China

It is the birthday today of *Chynna Phillips*, daughter of John and Michelle Phillips, of the 1960s group the Mamas and the Papas. She had her own band, Wilson Phillips, formed with Wendy and Carnie Wilson, children of former Beach Boy, Brian Wilson. In 2004 they released their fourth album, *California*.

Meaning nation of China

Jayne, Jaynell

This day in 1984 marked British Jayne Torvill and Christopher Dean's Olympic gold medal win for ice dancing at the Winter Olympics in Sarajevo, in the former Yugoslavia. The memorable event gave a new lease of life to Ravel's *Bolero*.

Meaning God's victorious smile

Judy, Judie

The US children's author *Judy Blume* was born on 12 February 1938. She was one of the first writers of teenage fiction to tackle taboo subjects, such as divorce, and has been applauded for her use of real-life settings and realistic endings. Her works include *Deenie* (1973) and *Superfudge* (1980).

From Judith, meaning admired, praised one

Louisa

American first lady *Louisa Adams* was born on this day in 1775. Her husband, John Quincy Adams, served one term as president in 1825–9. Louisa Adams was notable as being the only first lady in history not to have been born in America: she was born in England of an English mother, although her father was American.

From Louis, meaning famous warrior

Oliver, Olivero, Olivan, Ollie, Oliveiro, Nolly, Nollie, Noll

The British actor *Oliver Reed* was born on 13 February 1938. Famous for his macho image, both on and off the screen, his best-known films include *Women in Love* (1969) and *The Devils* (1970). He died during the making of his last film, *Gladiator* (2000).

Meaning symbol of peace

Jerry, Jerold, Jerrold, Jere

Jerry Springer, the talk-show host, was born in London on this day in 1944, in London. At the age of 33 he was voted mayor of Cincinatti – one of the youngest people ever to hold that office in the USA. His massively successful talk show was turned into a hit musical, *Jerry Springer, The Opera*, in 2003.

From Jeremy, meaning exalted by the Lord

Blair

Blair Moody, US senator and journalist, was born Arthur Edson Blair on this day in 1902. As well as being a delegate to the Democratic National Convention, he was a prolific journalist, covering the Second World War in Britain, Africa and Italy.

Meaning from the plain

Thelston

The cricketer *Thelston Payne* celebrates his birthday today. The West Indian wicket-keeper and left-handed batsman was born Thelston Rodney O'Neale Payne on 13 February 1957 in Foul Bay, St Philip, Barbados. He is a coach for the National Sports Council.

Meaning not known

Barbie, Barb, Barbetta, Barb, Bas

On this day in 1959 the Barbie doll was first available for sale to the public. Still manufactured by the US company Mattel (earning them millions of dollars a year), one Barbie doll is bought somewhere in the world every half a second.

Meaning stranger

Esther, Eister, Etty, Eister, Hester, Hessy, Hesther, Hetty

On 13 February 1870 *Esther Morris* was the first woman to be appointed a justice of the peace in the USA. She became a symbol of the women's rights movement, and her independent attitudes and indefatigable support of women's issues were widely praised.

Meaning star

Kim

The US actress *Kim Novak* was born Marilyn Novak on 13 February 1933. The pinnacle of her career was her appearance as two characters in Alfred Hitchcock's *Vertigo* (1958). She continued to make films and appear on TV, but never achieved the same success.

From Kimberley, meaning clearing, wood

Stockard

Today is the birthday of *Stockard Channing*. The Harvard-educated US actress was born on 13 February 1944. She first came to public notice in the movie *Grease* (1978), and has since won an Emmy for her role as Abby Bartlett in the highly popular TV series *The West Wing* (1999), as well as a Tony for her stage performance in *A Day in the Death of Joe Egg* (1985).

Meaning from the yard of tree stumps

Valentine

Today is, of course, the feast day of *St Valentine*. Little is known about the original Valentine, although a church built in Rome in the mid-4th century was dedicated to St Valentine, who may have been a martyred bishop of Terni. The first recorded Valentine card was sent in 1477.

Meaning healthy, strong

Carl, Karl, Carlo, Carlos, Karol, Karel

The US journalist *Carl Bernstein*, who broke the Watergate scandal, was born on 14 February 1944. He and his fellow journalist, Bob Woodward, were reporters on the *Washington Post* and their investigation into the Watergate scandal led to the resignation of President Richard Nixon in 1974.

From Charles, meaning free man

Cyril, Cyrille, Caireall

As well as being the feast day of St Valentine, today is the feast day of *St Cyril*, who, with his brother Methodius, was a missionary in eastern Europe. They were known as the apostles of the Slavs and are especially revered in the Czech Republic, Slovakia and Croatia. St Cyril is credited with inventing the Cyrillic alphabet.

Meaning lord

Robert, Bob, Rob, Bobby, Robbie, Rip, Rabby, Rabbie, Rab, Roban

The British economist *Thomas Robert Malthus* was born on this day in 1766 in Dorking, Surrey. He published his controversial *An Essay on the Principle of Population* in 1798, arguing that population tends to increase more quickly than the means of subsistence.

Meaning bright, famous

Fatima

It is the birthday today of soccer player *Fatima Leyva*, who was born in 1980. She has played for the Mexican national team in many international events, including the World Cup (1999) and the PanAmerican Games (1999, 2003). She also broadcasts as a commentator for Telemundo.

Meaning from Our Lady of Fatima

Calisto, Callisto

The Italian composer Pietro Francesco Cavalli was born on this day in 1602 in Crema. He wrote church music and many operas, of which *La Calisto* (1651) is still performed. It tells of the nymph Calisto, who is pursued by Jove but is turned into a bear by Juno. She eventually becomes the constellation of Ursa Minor.

Meaning fair, good

Meg, Meta, Meggie

US actress *Meg Tilly* was born on Valentine's Day in 1960. Originally a dancer, Meg made her debut in Alan Parker's film *Fame* (1980), but back problems forced her to pursue an acting career, and she has appeared in *The Big Chill* (1983), *Psycho II* (1983) and *The Two Jakes* (1990).

From Margaret, meaning pearl

Lois

The Canadian actress *Lois Maxwell* was born on this day in 1927. She worked in Hollywood in the 1940s but then moved to Britain, and she will be best remembered for her performance as *Miss Moneypenny* in many of the James Bond films, beginning with *Dr No* in 1962 and continuing until *A View to Kill* in 1985.

Meaning not known

Galileo, Galil

Galileo Galilei, the inventor of the telescope, was born on 15 February 1564 in Pisa, Italy. The founder of modern science dropped out of medical college with no qualifications and became a teacher. He reported his first sightings through his telescope in a book called *Sidereus Nuncius* (Starry Messenger), which was published in 1610.

Meaning neighbour

Demetrius, Demeitiri, Dimitri, Dimitry, Dimity, Dmitry, Dmitri, Demeter

The first president of the International Olympic Committee (IOC) was born on this day in 1835. *Demetrius Vikelas* was born in Ermoupolis on the island of Syros. The first Olympics of the modern era were held in 1900 in Athens.

Meaning earth lover

Cyrus, Cy

The US inventor *Cyrus Hall McCormick* was born on this day in 1809 in Rockbridge County, Virginia. His modifications to the mechanical grain reaper combined with his marketing and business skills to bring him huge commercial success.

Meaning sun

Matt, Mattison, Mathe, Matty, Mattie, Mat, Mats, Mate, Mata, Matyas, Massey

Matt Groening, the creator of *The Simpsons*, was born on 15 February 1954. What began as a comic strip in a newspaper is now one of the most popular TV series ever. In real life, Matt's parents are called Homer and Marge, and his sisters are Lisa and Maggie.

Meaning gift of God

Claire, Clare, Clareta, Clarette, Clarine, Clarabelle, Clarabella

The British actress *Claire Bloom* was born on this day in 1931. She has appeared in many Shakespearean plays as well as scores of other classic roles, both on the stage and in film. Many consider her to be one of the most talented and beautiful actresses of the era.

Meaning bright, shining

Georgina, Georgiana, Georgette, Georgie, Georgia, Giorgia, Georgy, Georgine, Georgene

In France, Hungary and Poland 15 February is the name day for *Georgina*, the female form of George, which is derived from the Greek for farmer, *ge* being Greek for earth. The name became popular in the 18th century, when George was the name of four successive monarchs.

Meaning girl from the farm

Hilda, Hilde, Hildie, Hildy, Hild

Che Guevara's daughter *Hilda* was born on 15 February 1956. She was the daughter of his first wife, also called Hilda, who, like Che Guevara, was a revolutionary involved in the Cuban cause.

Meaning battle maid

Brownell

The political activist and outspoken campaigner for the US suffrage movement *Susan Brownell Anthony* was born on this day in 1820. She devoted 50 years of her life to this cause, and her dying words, 'failure is impossible', became the rallying cry of the suffragettes.

Meaning dweller on the brown hill

Machito

Cuban band leader *Machito* was born Francisco Raúl Gutiérrez Grillo on this day in 1908 in Havana, Cuba. The son of a cigar manufacturer, he became one of the leading figures of the 1940s Afro-Cuban jazz scene in New York. His story was told in the 1987 film *Machito: A Latin Jazz Legacy*.

Meaning not known

John, Johnnie, Johnny, Jon

The tennis player *John McEnroe* was born on this day in 1959. Famous for his volatile temper as much as for his superb tennis, he was at the top of the men's tennis circuit in the early 1980s, winning Wimbledon three times and the US Open four times. He also excelled in doubles tennis, winning many top competitions.

Meaning God has shown me favour

LeVar, Levardis

The US actor *LeVar Burton* was born on 16 February 1957. Best known for his performances as Geordi LaForge in *Star Trek: The Next Generation* (1987), he has also produced many episodes of the series. He produced and hosted Emmy award-winning *Reading Rainbow* (1983) and played Kunta Kinte in *Roots* (1977).

Meaning not known

Iain, Ian

The Scottish writer *Iain Banks* was born on 16 February 1954. He gained national recognition with his first novel, *The Wasp Factory*, in 1984. This compulsively readable Gothic horror story was later televised. He has written a further ten literary novels, and nine science-fiction novels, penned under the name Iain M. Banks.

Meaning God's gift

Juliana, Juliana, Juliane, Julianna, Julianne

Today is the feast day of *St Juliana of Cumae*, who is especially venerated in the Netherlands. In art she is often depicted battling against a winged devil or leading the captured devil by a chain. Spurned by both her father and her suitor, Juliana died a martyr.

Meaning youthful

Gretchen, Grethe

Gretchen Wyler, the actress and animal rights campaigner, was born on 16 February 1932. The vice-president of the Humane Society of the USA since 2002, she has received many awards and accolades for her work in animal welfare.

From Margaret, meaning pearl

Katharine, Katherine, Catherine, Catharine, Kathryn, Cathryn, Cathy, Kathy, Catharina, Cathelle, Cathie, Cathleen, Catriona

US actress *Katharine Cornell* was born on this day in 1893. She was born in Berlin, but her parents were American and she made her stage debut in New York with the Washington Square Players in 1917. She was noted for her performances in *Saint Joan* and *Romeo and Juliet*.

Meaning pure maiden

Charlotte, Carlotta, Karlotte, Lottie, Charlie

On 16 February 1892 Jules Massenet's opera *Werther* received its first performance in Vienna. It tells how *Charlotte*, who is loved by Werther but is engaged to be married to Albert, chooses duty before love. It all ends in tears.

Meaning free woman

17 FEBRUARY

Alan, Alain, Alair, Aland, Alano, Allan, Allen, Allyn, Allie, Ailean

The British actor *Alan Bates* was born on this day in 1934. He preferred performing the works of the great modern playwrights, and he chose his film roles with care, taking the parts of Gabriel Oak in *Far from the Madding Crowd* (1967) and Rupert Birkin in *Women in Love* (1969).

Meaning handsome

Myles, Miles

On this day in 1621 *Myles Standish* became the first commander of the Plymouth Colony, the settlement of Puritan pilgrims from Britain who arrived in North America on the *Mayflower*. Standish was born in Lancashire and had been a soldier of fortune in the Netherlands.

Meaning soldier

René, Rene, Rennie, Renny, Renato

The French physician *René Laënnec* was born on this day in 1781 in Brittany. He became known as the father of knowledge of pulmonary disease. He also invented the stethoscope in order to avoid embarrassment when he wanted to listen to young women's chests.

Meaning reborn

Arcangelo

Arcangelo Corelli was born on this day in 1653 in Fusignano, Italy. Equally famed as a composer and a violinist, he also taught and did much to make sure that the new instrument became one of the most important in classical music. Vivaldi, Handel and Bach were all influenced by him.

Meaning chief of the angels

Edna, Edny, Ed, Eddie

Australian Barry Humphries, the alter ego and creator of the larger-than-life Melbourne housewife *Dame Edna Everage* and of Sir Les Patterson, the Australian cultural attaché, was born on this day in 1934 in Melbourne. In 1982 he received the Order of Australia.

Meaning delight, pleasure

Brenda, Bren

The Irish actress *Brenda Fricker* was born on this day in 1945. She made her name in Britain through her performances (1986–90) in the long-running TV series *Casualty*, but this slightly rebellious yet rock solid actress won international acclaim and an Academy Award for her part in the film *My Left Foot* (1989).

Meaning fiery

Stacey, Stacia, Stacie, Stacy

Stacey McClean of the British child pop group S Club Juniors was born on this day in 1989. She beat off fierce competition to win a coveted place in the group, which was mentored by pop superstars S Club 7. Stacey lives in Blackpool, in the north of England, and her favourite singer is Whitney Houston

From Anastasia, meaning awakening, resurrection

Dodie

The US singer *Dodie Stevens* was born Geraldine Ann Pasquale on this day in 1947. She rose to number three in the US charts in 1959 with the song 'Pink Shoelaces'. She later toured with Sergio Mendes's band before becoming a highly prolific session singer.

Meaning beloved

Andrés, Andreas, Andrej

Andrés Segovia, the Spanish classical guitar master, was born on this day in 1894 in Linares, Spain. Known as the father of the modern classical guitar movement, his great achievement was to make the guitar as respected in the classical world as the violin and piano.

From Andrew, meaning warrior

Pluto

On this day in 1930 the planet *Pluto* was discovered. The ninth planet from the Sun is named after the Roman god of the Underworld. The Walt Disney cartoon character Pluto was named after the planet. It is also the name of the oldest Linux User Group, based in Italy.

Meaning wealth, riches

Len, Lennie, Lenny, Leoner, Lennard

The British writer *Len Deighton* was born in London on 18 February 1929. He has written over 25 thrillers, including *The Ipcress File* (1962), which was filmed in 1965, with Michael Caine creating the unforgettable role of Harry Palmer (unnamed in the book).

From Leonard, meaning brave as a lion

Enzo

The Italian car manufacturer *Enzo Anselmo Ferrari* was born on 18 February 1898 in Modena. He became a racing driver with Alfa Romeo in 1920, but in 1927 he founded the company that bears his name to supply parts for other racing teams. In 1940 he began designing his own cars, and his marque went on to become the most successful in the world of Formula One.

From Lorenzo, meaning laurel crown

Toni, Tonia, Tonya, Toinette, Tony

The African-American author *Toni Morrison* was born Chloe Anthony Morrison on 18 February 1931 in Lorain, Ohio. She has won many awards, including the Pulitzer prize for *Beloved* (1987). In 1993 she became the first African-American woman to win the Nobel Prize for literature.

From Antonia, meaning not known

Cybill, Cybil

The US actress and model *Cybill Shepherd* was born on this day in 1950. Her film career took off after she appeared on the front cover of a magazine and was spotted by director Peter Bogdanovich, for whom she made *The Last Picture Show* (1971). She also appeared in the TV series *Moonlighting* (1985–9).

From Sybil, meaning prophetess

Sinead, Sine, Seon, Sean, Seonaid

The Irish actress *Sinead Cusack* was born on 18 February 1948. Her father, three sisters (Sorcha, Niamh and Catherine) and husband (Jeremy Irons) are all in the acting profession too. Her first film was *David Copperfield* (1969), and she has also appeared in the TV programme *Have Your Cake and Eat It* (1997).

From Jane, meaning God's gift of grace

Yoko

Today is the birthday of Japanese artist *Yoko Ono*, who was born in Tokyo in 1933. She is best known for her marriage to Beatle member John Lennon. Their wedding took place on the Rock of Gibraltar on 20 March 1969. They have one son, Sean Tara Ono Lennon, who was born on the same day of the year as his father.

Meaning positive

Sven, Swen, Svend, Svenson, Svensen, Swensen, Swenson

Sven Anders Hedin, the Swedish explorer, was born on this day in 1865. He travelled throughout Persia and Mesopotamia, charting large areas of remote lands, such as Tibet, Khurasan and Turkistan. He wrote popular accounts of his travels, the most famous being *Through Asia* (1898) and *Across the Gobi Desert* (1931).

Meaning youth

Smokey

US singer *Smokey Robinson*, the Tamla Motown star, was born in Detroit on 19 February 1940. He not only wrote and sang with his band, the Miracles, but was also Motown's second in command, writing, producing and auditioning, and helping to shape the Motown sound.

Meaning smoky

Conrad, Connie, Kon, Rad, Con, Conroyo

Today is the feast day of *St Conrad of Piacenza*. Born in 1290, he lived as a hermit in Noto, Sicily, for 36 years. His reputation for performing miracles was already widespread when he was visited by the bishop of Syracuse, to whom he gave some newly baked cakes from his bare cell.

Meaning brave counsel

Lee, Leroy, Leight, Leigh

US actor *Lee Marvin* was born on 19 February 1924. A direct descendant of Thomas Jefferson, one of his most memorable performances was his gravelly rendition of 'Wandering Star' in the film *Paint Your Wagon* (1969), in which he starred with Clint Eastwood.

Meaning clearing, wood

Amy, Amee, Ami, Amie, Aimee

The Chinese-American writer *Amy Tan* was born on 19 February 1952. Her bestselling first novel, *The Joy Luck Club* (1988), examines the relationship between Chinese mothers and their Chinese-American daughters. Her subsequent novels include *The Year of No Flood* (1995) and *The Hundred Secret Senses* (1995).

Meaning beloved

Merle, Merl, Myrle, Meryl, Merlina, Myrlene, Merola, Merrill, Merla

Hollywood actress *Merle Oberon* was born Estelle Merle O'Brien Thompson on 19 February 1911 in Bombay, India. Her father was Anglo-Irish, her mother Anglo-Sinhalese. The first of her four husbands was the film director Alexander Korda, with whom she worked on the unfinished *I Claudius* (1937).

Meaning blackbird

Hana

The Czech tennis star *Hana Mandlikova* was born on 19 February 1962. In her 12-year career, between 1978 and 1990, she won four major singles titles, including the US Open twice, but the Wimbledon title eluded her.

From Joanna, meaning God is gracious

Phoenix

Spice Girl Melanie Brown (formerly known as Scary Spice) gave birth to a daughter, *Phoenix Chi*, on 19 February 1999. According to legend, the phoenix is a bird of which only one exists, a new bird rising from the ashes of the old one. Chi is a Nigerian protective spirit.

Meaning legendary bird

French

US actor *French Stewart*, who is best known for playing Harry Solomon in the hit TV sitcom *Third Rock from the Sun* (1996), was born on 20 February 1964. French is his real name, and he is the fourth member of his family to be so named. His movies include *Home Alone: Taking Back the House* (2002) and *Inspector Gadget* (1999).

Meaning from France

Ansel, Ancell, Ansell, Anslem

One of the world's masters of photography, *Ansel Easton Adams* was born on this day in 1902 in San Francisco. A childhood trip to Yosemite in the Sierre Nevada, California, was the inspiration for his celebrated series of western landscapes. He was also a passionate conservationist.

Meaning follow of the nobleman

Joshua, Josh

The seaman and adventurer *Joshua Slocum* was born in Wilmot, Nova Scotia, on 20 February 1844. In 1898 he became the first person to sail single-handed around the world, in a fishing boat called *Spray*. He consequently wrote *Sailing Alone Around the World* (1899).

Meaning God's salvation

Kelsey

US actor *Kelsey Grammer* was born in the Caribbean Virgin Islands on this day in 1955. Famous for his roles in the TV comedy shows *Cheers* (1982) and *Frasier* (1993), he was named the highest paid actor in the USA in 2001.

Meaning island dweller

Cindy, Cindie, Cinderella

US model *Cindy Crawford* was born on 20 February 1966. She sacrificed a career in chemical engineering to become the first, and possibly the highest paid, of a new breed of supermodel.

Meaning girl from the ashes

Imogen, Imogene

The British actress *Imogen Stubbs* was born on this day in 1961. She achieved notable success on stage with the Royal Shakespeare Company, the director of which, Trevor Nunn, subsequently became her husband. She has also appeared in several movies, including *Sense and Sensibility* (1995) and *Twelfth Night* (1996).

Meaning girl, maiden

Kylie, Kyla, Kylah, Kilah, Kylynn

Australian singer *Kylie Minogue* had her first British number one on 20 February 1988 with 'I Should Be So Lucky'. The actress and singer has since gone on to become an iconic figure of the early 21st century all over the world.

Meaning pretty one

Tara, Tarah, Terra

On 20 February 1998 *Tara Lipinski* became the youngest ever woman to win an Olympic figure-skating title. A year earlier, in March 1997, the skater, from Pennsylvania, was the youngest world champion. She has since moved on to acting roles on TV and in film.

Meaning hill

Tadd, Tadley, Thad, Taddy, Tadda, Tad, Thada, Thaddeus, Thaddaus, Thaddea, Thada, Taddeo, Tadeo

The African-American bandleader, pianist and composer *Tadd Dameron* was born Tadley Ewing Peake on 21 February 1917 in Cleveland. He wrote and arranged for many bands, including Dizzy Gillespie. In 1948 his orchestral piece, *Soulphony*, was premiered at Carnegie Hall.

Meaning courageous

Damien, Daimen

Today is the feast day of *St Peter Damian*, who was born in Ravenna in 1007. He joined a community of hermits and later became bishop of Ostia. He was critical of clerical laxity and wrote widely on theological and canonical subjects.

Meaning tamer

Hubert, Hobart, Hobbard, Hoyt, Hube

The French fashion designer *Hubert de Givenchy* was born Hubert James Marcel Taffin de Givenchy on 21 February 1927. He opened the fashion house that bears his name in 1952, and the outfits he created for Audrey Hepburn and Jackie Kennedy epitomized his style.

Meaning bright spirit

Wystan

W.H. Auden, regarded as one of the greatest poets in the English language, was born on 21 February 1907 in York, England, but moved to the USA in 1939. His full name was *Wystan Hugh Auden*. His poem 'Funeral Blues' achieved new heights of popularity after it was featured in the film *Four Weddings and a Funeral* (1994).

Meaning battle stone

Charlotte, Charlotta, Charo

The Welsh singer *Charlotte Church* was born on 21 February 1986. She became an international success when she was 13 years old with the release of her first album of classical recordings. She subsequently developed a diverse repertoire, which increased her appeal and made her into one of the bestselling crossover female artists.

Meaning free woman

Anaïs, Ana

The US writer *Anaïs Nin* was born in Paris on this day in 1903. From 1914 she lived mostly in New York, and her books were influenced by surrealism and psychoanalysis. Among her works are *A Spy in the House of Love* (1954) and *Collages* (1964). Her short stories were collected in *Under a Glass Bell* (1944).

Meaning God has favoured me

Jilly, Jill, Jillie

British writer *Jilly Cooper* was born in Hornchurch, London, on this day in 1942. She was a journalist with the *Sunday Times* and with the *Mail on Sunday*, but is better known for her novels, including *Riders* (1978), *Polo* (1991) and *Appassionata* (1996).

From Gillian, meaning nestling

Nina, Nena, Nineta, Ninetta

The US jazz and soul singer *Nina Simone* was born on 21 February 1933. A child prodigy and a classically trained pianist, she turned to singing and became known as the 'high priestess of soul'. She gained an enormous international following and an unrivalled legendary status.

From Antonina, meaning not known

Frank, Franklin, Francklin, Frankie, Franklyn

On this day in 1879 *Frank Winfield Woolworth* opened his first 'five and dime' store in New York. His idea was to sell products at discounted prices to undercut the local merchants, and this continued successfully for 100 years. The British subsidiary, which opened in 1909, continues to trade in the UK.

Meaning free man

George, Georg, Georgie, Georgy, Giorgio, Gordie, Gordy

The first president of the USA, *George Washington* was born in Bridges Creek, Virginia, on 22 February 1732. He was a general during the War of Independence before being elected president from 1789 to 1797. He is often known as the father of his country.

Meaning farmer

Bruce

Popular British entertainer *Bruce Forsyth* was born in Edmonton, London, on this day in 1928. He is best known for his appearances on TV shows, beginning his career with *Sunday Night at the London Palladium* (1958–60). He hosted *The Generation Game* (1971–8, 1990–95) and compered the popular *Play Your Cards Right* (1980–87).

Sparky, Spark

US baseball manager *Sparky Anderson* was born on this day in 1934. He was the only manager to win the World Series in both leagues, Detroit in AL in 1984, and Cincinatti in NL in 1975. In 2000 he was admitted to the Baseball Hall of Fame.

Meaning man about town

Drew

US film star *Drew Barrymore* was born on 22 February 1975. Her grandfather was the actor John Barrymore, and Drew was the maiden name of her great-grandmother, Georgiana. She started making films when she was five years old, appearing in *E.T. The Extra-Terrestrial* (1982). Later, she starred in *Never Been Kissed* (1998) and the film versions of the TV show *Charlie's Angels* (2000, 2003).

Meaning courageous

Julie

British actress *Julie Walters* was born on this day in 1950. She will probably always be associated with her marvellous portrayal of Rita in the film *Educating Rita* (1983) and as Ron Weasly's mum in the *Harry Potter* movies (2001, 2002, 2004).

Meaning youthful

Sylvette, Syl, Sil, Silva, Silvana, Silvia, Silvie, Slyvana, Sylva, Zilivia, Zilvia

Today is the birthday of French actress *Sylvette Miou-Miou*, who was born Sylvette Hzry on 22 February 1950. In her first major role she starred with Gérard Depardieu in *Les Valseuses* (1974). She was in *Coup de foudre* (1983) with Isabelle Huppert and *Dog Day* (1984) with Lee Marvin.

From Sylvia, meaning from the forest

Edna

US poet *Edna St Vincent Millay* was born in Rockland, Maine, on this day in 1892. She won a Pulitzer Prize for *The Harp Weaver and Other Poems* (1923), and she also wrote the libretto for the opera *The King's Henchman* (1927).

Meaning delight, pleasure

Meyer, Meir, Meier, Mayr, Myer, Mayor, Myerson

The founder of the Rothschild banking dynasty, *Meyer Rothschild* was born on this day in 1744. The son of a poor moneylender, he was apprenticed to a bank when he was 13 years old. He began trading in rare coins and antiques and went on to become one of Germany's wealthiest men.

Meaning bringer of light

Elston

The baseball player *Elston Howard* was born on 23 February 1929. The first African-American to play for the Yankees, he introduced the hinged catcher's mitt, the precursor of the modern one-handed catch. After a short spell at Boston he returned to the Yankees team to coach for the next nine years.

Meaning estate of the noble one

Snooky, Snooks, Snookie, Snooker

On this day in 1950 a song called 'The Old Master Painter' sung by *Snooky Lanson* entered the US charts. In the 1950s it was recorded by six different artists: Peggy Lee, Mel Tormé, Phil Harris, Dick Haymes and Frank Sinatra.

Meaning not known

Lazarus, Lazar, Elizer, Eleazar

Today is the feast day of *St Lazarus Zographos*, often known as St Lazarus the Painter. A monk, he lived in Constantinople (now Istanbul) in the 9th century. As a punishment for having painted holy images, his hand was burned, but it healed and he was able to re-paint what had been destroyed.

Meaning helped by God

Helena, Helene, Ilcane, Ilena, Illonna, Illone, Ilona, Isleen

Czech tennis player *Helena Sukova* was born on 23 February 1965. The highest world ranking that she managed to achieve was fifth in 1986, but she remained in the top ten women seeds until 1989.

From Helen, meaning light

Majel

Today is the birthday of the TV and film actress *Majel Barrett*, best known for her role as Nurse Christine Chapel in *Star Trek* (1969–71). She also played Lwaxana Troi, Deanna's mother, in *Star Trek: The Next Generation* (1990–96). She was married to Gene Roddenberry, and they had a son called Rod.

From Mabel, meaning amiable, loving

Régine, Regina, Ragan, Raina, Raine, Rayna, Regan, Regine, Reina, Reine, Rina

Régine Crespin, the celebrated French mezzo-soprano, was born in Marseilles on this day in 1927. Her 1962 US debut at the Metropolitan Opera House, New York, as the Marschallin in *Der Rosenkavalier* is one of the legendary performances in opera. She wrote about it in her memoirs, *On Stage, Off Stage* (1997).

Meaning queen born to rule

Dakota

Today is the birthday of US child star *Dakota Fanning*, who was born on this day in 1994. She could read aged two and won the Broadcast Film Critics award for best young actor/actress when she was seven. She starred in *The Cat in the Hat* (2003) and *Hide and Seek* (2005).

Meaning friend, partner

Wilhem, Vilhem, Vilem, Viliam, Vasili, Vasily, Guillaume, Guillermo

Wilhem Grimm was born on this day in 1786. With his brother Jakob he gathered some of the world's most enduring fairy stories from the Bremen and Hanau area in Germany. The first volume was published in 1812, and two further volumes appeared in 1815 and 1822.

Meaning valiant protector

Winslow, Windsor, Winchell, Winfred, Wingate, Winthrop, Winward, Winfrey

Winslow Homer, the US landscape artist, was born on this day in 1836. He is best known for his seascapes, which he painted around Maine. After 20 years, he switched from oil to watercolour.

Meaning from the friend's hill

Mac

The founder of *Apple Mac* computers, Steven Jobs was born on this day in 1955. He succeeded in revolutionizing the personal computer and became a multimillionaire before the age of 30. In 1986 he co-founded the animation studio Pixar, producing the highly successful *A Bug's Life* (1998), *Toy Story* (1995) and *Toy Story 2* (1999).

Meaning son of

Honus

Today is the birthday of *Honus Wagner*, born in Mansfield (now Carnegie), Pennsylvania, on February 24 1874. He is the greatest shortstop baseball player in history, and the Honus baseball trading card is the most valuable ever. Known as the Mona Lisa of baseball cards, it is worth $1.5 million (about £833,000).

Meaning not known

Kristin, Cristen, Kristen, Krystina, Kristine, Kirsten, Kristina

US actress *Kristin Davis* was born in Boulder, Colorado, on 24 February 1965. Her most notable role was as Charlotte York in the hugely popular TV series *Sex and the City* (1998). She also hosts MTV's *200 Greatest Pop Icons*.

Meaning follower of Christ

Renata, Renate, Renée, Renette

One of the leading Italian sopranos of her generation, *Renata Scotto* was born in Savona on this day in 1936. She stepped into Maria Callas's shoes at La Scala, Milan, and subsequently sang with the Metropolitan Opera House in New York for 20 years.

Meaning reborn

Adela, Della, Dell, Adella, Adela

Today is the feast day of *St Adela*. Princess Adela was the youngest daughter of King William I of England, known as William the Conqueror, and was born in around 1062. She lived in England, where she endowed churches and monasteries.

Meaning noble

Lulu

On this day in 1979 Alban Berg's opera *Lulu* received its first complete performance in Paris. Lulu, who embodies female sensuality, has a string of lovers, and she rises – and falls – through society. Berg died before he could complete the work, which was finished by the Austrian composer Friedrich Cerha.

Meaning pearl

Samson, Sampson, Sansone, Sanson

The Kenyan athlete *Samson Kitur* was born on 25 February 1966. Many Kenyans have succeeded at 800 metres and above, but he was unique at the time for competing in the 400 metres. He won the bronze medal in the 1992 Olympic Games and at the 1993 World Championships.

Meaning sun

Zeppo

Zeppo Marx was born Herbert Marx in New York on this day in 1901. The 'sensible' Marx brother, Zeppo acted as understudy to his brothers and was, less famously, an inventor, his innovations including a watch for monitoring the pulse rates of patients.

Meaning not known

Anthony, Antony, Antoin, Antonio, Antonino, Antoine, Anton, Ant, Tony

On this day in 1917 British writer and critic *Anthony Burgess* was born John Anthony Burgess Wilson in Manchester. As well as novels, including *A Clockwork Orange* (1962), *Heavenly Powers* (1980) and *Any Old Iron* (1989), he wrote film scripts and critical studies

Meaning not known

Meher, Merwan, Mihir

Meher Baba, the Indian mystic, was born on this day in 1894. He was born Merwan Shehariarji Irani in Poona, India. Central to his teachings was the belief that universal love and devotion could heal the ills of the modern world.

Meaning sun

Elkie, Elke, Elisa, Elissa

British singer *Elkie Brooks* was born Elaine Bookbonder on 25 February 1945. She first achieved success with the band Vinegar Joe in the early 1970s and then launched into an extremely fruitful solo career in which she dominated the album charts for many years.

From Alice, meaning truth

Ida

The first ever US female coastguard *Ida Lewis* was born on this day in 1842. She was a lighthouse keeper for the whole of her life, against much opposition, and became known as the bravest woman in America, having saved 18 lives during her service.

Meaning prosperous

Teá, Teara, Tiara

Teá Leoni was born Elizabeth Teá Pantaleoni in New York on this day in 1966. The producer and actress is best known for her role as Nora Wilde in TV's *The Naked Truth* (1995). She has a son, Kid Duchovny, and a daughter, Madelaine West Duchovny.

Meaning turban, flower

Walburga

Today is the feast day of the English *St Walburga*, who joined a mission to Germany, where she became abbess of a large monastery at Heidenheim. The German Walpurgisnachts is named after her, and she was associated with witchcraft and other legends.

Meaning strange fortress

Johnny, Johnnie, Jonny

US country legend *Johnny Cash* was born on 26 February 1932. A musical giant, his career spanned four decades, during which he recorded 1,500 songs. His influence on countless musicians from all fields is immeasurable.

Meaning God has shown me favour

Kuwata

It is the birthday today of *Kuwata Keisuke*, one of Japan's best-known singers, who was born on 26 February 1956. His first success was as lead singer and songwriter for the 1970s group the Southern All Stars. The band has had many hits, including 'Mampy-no-G-spot' (1995). He has also directed a number of films.

Meaning not known

Levi, Levin

Levi Strauss was born in Bavaria on this day in 1829. After emigrating to the USA he opened a clothes manufacturing business, and in 1873 the world's first jeans were made. Levi Strauss is now a multinational company with global recognition.

Meaning united

Victor, Vic, Vick, Victoire, Vittorio

French writer *Victor Hugo* was born on this day in 1802. Today his best-known work is the novel *Les Misérables* (1862), but he also wrote plays and poetry. Exiled from Paris in 1851, he lived in the Channel Islands, where he wrote many of his major novels.

Meaning conqueror

Margaret, Maggie, Magaidh, Maigrghread, Margalo, Margao, Margarieta, Margaretha, Margarethe, Margaretta, Margarita, Marge, Margery, Marge, Marget, Margetta, Margharita

On 26 February 1960 *Princess Margaret*, sister to Queen Elizabeth II, married Anthony Armstrong-Jones. It was the first 'modern' royal ceremony, thanks to the wider availability of TV. Anthony Armstrong-Jones became a famous photographer.

Meaning pearl

Sissieretta, Sissierette, Sissie, Sis

The African-American soprano *Sissieretta Jones* was born on this day in 1869. Nicknamed the Black Patti after the opera star Adelina Patti, she never recorded, but in 1927 a record label called Black Patti was launched, named after Sissieretta.

Meaning not known

Sandie, Sandy, Sashenka, Zandra

British singer *Sandie Shaw* was born on 26 February 1947. Her first number one single was 'There's Always Something There to Remind Me' (1964), and this was followed by two more chart toppers, including the Eurovision Song Contest winner 'Puppet on a String' (1967).

From Sandra, meaning helper of mankind

Betty, Bettie, Bet

US actress *Betty Hutton* was born on this day in 1921. She made her name singing and dancing her way through many movies in the 1940s. She was in *The Fleet's In* (1942), *Star Spangled Rhythm* (1942) and *Annie Get Your Gun* (1950), in which she starred with Howard Keel.

From Elizabeth, meaning consecrated to God

Gavin, Gaven, Gawain, Gavan, Gawen

BBC news reporter *Gavin Esler* was born on this day in 1953. He started his career as a reporter in Northern Ireland, was the BBC US correspondent for several years in the late 1980s and has since become a familiar face as a BBC news presenter.

Meaning battle hawk

Dexter, Dex, Deck, Decca

Dexter Gordon, the jazz tenor saxophonist, was born in Los Angeles on this day in 1923. He first played with the Lionel Hampton Band at the beginning of the 1940s. He reached his peak during that decade, playing with all the greats of the New York jazz scene, from Charlie Parker to Miles Davis.

Meaning right-handed

Paddy, Padraic, Padraig, Padruig

The British politician *Paddy Ashdown* was born on 27 February 1941. After a career in the Royal Marines, he entered Parliament and was leader of the Liberal Democrats from 1988 to 1999. He is now the international community's high representative in Bosnia and Herzegovina.

From Patrick, meaning well-born

Navarro

It is the birthday today of N. Scott Momaday. The Kiowa Indian poet, printmaker and author was born *Navarro Scott Momaday* on this day in Oklahoma in 1934. His first novel, *The House Made of Dawn*, won the 1969 Pulitzer Prize.

Meaning plains

Joanne, Jo Anne, Joan, Jo

US actress *Joanne Woodward* was born on this day in 1930 in Thomasville, Georgia, and became a star after her appearance in *The Three Faces of Eve* (1957). She has been married to Paul Newman since 1958, and they have appeared together in many films.

From Jane, meaning God's gift of grace

Ellen, Ellyn, Elin, Elena, Ellin, Elyn, Elen

British actress *Ellen Alicia Terry* was born on 27 February 1847. Called the greatest English actress of the 19th century, her serious acting career did not start until she was 31, but over the next 20 years she played most of Shakespeare's leading ladies.

Meaning light mercy

Elizabeth, Elisabeth, Elisabet, Elisabetta, Lizabeta, Lizbeth, Lizzy, Lizzie, Lize, Liza, Liz, Betty, Bettie, Bet, Eliza, Elisa, Elissa, Elzieta, Elspeth

Actress *Elizabeth Taylor* was born on this day in 1932. She made her name in *National Velvet* (1944), but is as well known for her husbands: Nick Hilton, Michael Wilding, Mike Todd, Eddie Fisher and Richard Burton, whom she married twice and with whom she made several films.

Meaning consecrated to God

Gaby, Gabbie, Gabby

The asteroid *Gaby* was discovered on 27 February 1930. Gaby is short for Gabriel. The first Gabriel was the Archangel Gabriel, God's messenger, who brought Mary the news that she was pregnant with a special child. It is still used as a male name, but is more popular as a girl's name.

From Gabrielle, meaning woman of God

Linus

The US scientist *Linus Pauling* was born on this day in 1901. He was as famous for his scientific achievements as he was for his role as humanitarian and social activist. He received the Nobel Prize twice – for chemistry and for peace – the only person ever to have achieved this.

Meaning flax-coloured hair

Wallace, Wallache, Wallis, Wallie, Wally, Walsh, Welch, Welsh

On 28 February 1935 US chemist *Wallace Carothers* made a discovery that changed the course of history. He and his colleagues discovered a remarkable fibre that came to be known as nylon.

Meaning Welshman, stranger

Zero

The legendary Broadway actor *Zero Mostel* was born on 28 February 1915. He won three Tony awards: for his performances in Ionescu's play *Rhinoceros* in 1961, in Sondheim's *A Funny Thing Happened on the Way to the Forum* in 1962 and, most memorable of all, for his performance as Tevye in *Fiddler on the Roof* in 1964.

Meaning seeds

Jojst

On this day Swiss mathematician *Jojst Burgi* was born in 1552 in Liechtenstein, Switzerland. He is best known for inventing the logarithm system at the same time as, but independently of, the Scottish mathematician John Napier.

Meaning not known

Loretta, Lauriette, Lorette, Lorita, Lorenza, Lor, Lori, Lorie

On this day in 1983 the final episode of the American TV series *M*A*S*H* was aired. More than 250 episodes were spawned from the film of the same name about a team of medical workers at a field hospital in the Korean War. It cleverly combined humour with an anti-war message. *Loretta Swit* memorably played Major Margaret 'Hot Lips' Houlihan, the main female character.

From Laura, meaning laurel wreath

Mercedes, Mercy, Mercia, Merci

The American-Cuban actress *Mercedes Ruehl* was born on 28 February 1954. She won an Oscar and accompanying stardom for her role as Jeff Bridges's girlfriend in *The Fisher King* (1991). She went on to appear in *Gia* (1998) and *Out of the Cold* (1999).

Meaning compassionate, merciful

Stephanie, Stephania, Stephena, Stephenia, Stephenie, Steff, Stefany, Stafa, Steffie, Stevie, Stevenia

The English actress *Stephanie Beacham* was born on 28 February 1949. She is best known for her role as Sable Colby in the US TV soap opera *The Colbys* (1985).

Meaning garland, crown

Billie-Jean

On this day in 1984 Michael Jackson won seven Grammy awards for the biggest-selling album of all time, *Thriller*. *Billie-Jean* was just one of its tracks that became a massive hit single.

From William, meaning resolute ruler, and Jean, meaning God's gift of grace

29 FEBRUARY

Note: 29 February occurs only every fourth year on a leap year. Most people born on this day choose to celebrate three out of every four birthdays on February 28, and therefore names significant for that day could also be considered for a child born on a leap day.

Blaine, Blain, Blane

On this day in 1904 a man was born in Germany and was christened with 26 names, one for each letter of the alphabet. His second name, naturally beginning with a B, was *Blaine*.

Meaning thin, source of river

Jeff, Jeffers, Jeffery, Jeffrey, Jeffry

The New York rapper *Jeff 'Ja Rule' Atkins* was born on 29 February 1976. In addition to his own solo work, he has rapped on some of Jennifer Lopez's hits and has undertaken some acting roles.

Meaning peaceful ruler

Gioacchino

Gioacchino Rossini, the Italian composer, was born in Pesaro on this day in 1792. His most famous operas are *The Barber of Seville* and *La Cenerentola*. The overture to his opera *William Tell* became widely known when it was used as the theme tune for the 1950s and 1960s TV show *The Lone Ranger*.

From John, meaning God has shown me favour

Joss, Josh, Josh

The British actor *Joss Ackland* was born on 29 February 1928. He started acting in the early 1950s and has over 150 screen performances to his credit. He has a reputation for playing smug, vaguely villainous characters.

Meaning God's salvation

Ann, Anne, Annie

The founder of the Shaker Movement, *Ann Lee*, known as Mother Ann, was born on 29 February 1736. An offshoot religious sect, the Shakers originated in England and then emigrated to the USA, where their numbers peaked at about 6,000 in the mid-19th century. They led a pacifist, co-operative, ritualized existence within strict rules.

Meaning God has favoured me

Tempest, Tempestta

On this day one of the most colourful and original stars of the burlesque stage, *Tempest Storm*, was born in 1928. She went from chorus girl to striptease star of stage and screen. It was rumoured that her lovers included Elvis Presley, President Kennedy and Sammy Davis Jr.

Meaning storm

Michèle, Michelle

The French actress *Michèle Morgan* was born on this day in 1920. She was a leading lady in many French films from the mid-1930s, also making films in the USA and Britain. She made *Passage to Marseilles* (1944) with Humphrey Bogart and *The Fallen Idol* (1948) with Ralph Richardson.

Meaning like the Lord

Jocelyn, Joscelyn, Joscelyne, Joselen, Joselin, Joseline, Joselyn, Joselyne, Joslin, Josilen, Josilene

On this day in 1968 British radio astronomer Dr *Jocelyn Bell Burnell* announced the discovery of the first 'pulsar' (pulsating radio source). She joined the staff of the Royal Observatory in Edinburgh and later became manager of the James Clerk Maxwell Telescope on Hawaii.

Meaning fair, just

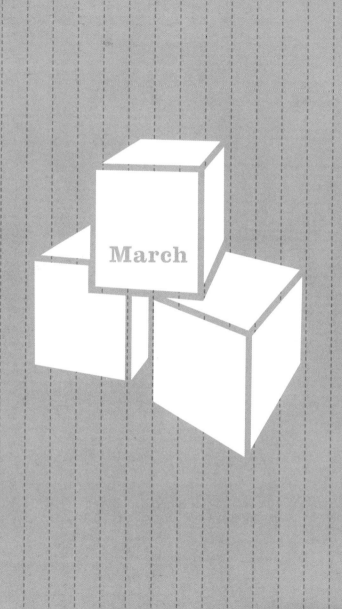

March

March

Lytton, Litton

The writer *Lytton Strachey* was born Giles Lytton Strachey on this day in 1880 in London, England. At Cambridge University he was a member of the group called the Apostles along with Leonard Woolf and E.M. Forster. This later grew into the famous Bloomsbury Group, of which he was a leading member.

Meaning farm on the side of a hill

Glenn, Glen, Glyn, Glynn

Glenn Miller, the US musician and bandleader, was born in Clarinda, Iowa, on this day in 1904. His big band was hugely popular in the late 1930s and 1940s. His first Hollywood film recording produced his first smash hit number entitled 'Chattanooga Choo-choo'.

Meaning valley

Oskar, Oscar

Oskar Kokoschka, the expressionist artist, was born in Pöchlarn, Austria, on 1 March 1886. He was one of the three greats in Viennese art, the other two being Klimt and Schiele. He had a passionate affair with Alma Mahler, the widow of the composer Gustav Mahler.

Meaning gentle friend, divine spear

Sandro

Sandro Botticelli, the Italian Renaissance artist, was born Allesandro di Marino Filipepi on this day in 1445. He took his second name from his brother's nickname, Il Botticello (the little barrel). Discovered by the Pre-Raphaelites, it was to be over five centuries before he made his name.

From Alessandro, meaning protector

Dinah, Dina, Dine

The US singer and actress *Dinah Shore* was born in Winchester, Tennessee, on this day in 1917. She studied sociology, but was determined to be a singer, performing on Nashville radio and then travelling to New York to sing with various bands. Her recording 'Yes, My Darling Daughter' was a hit, and she also appeared in various films, including *Follow the Boys* (1944) and *Till the Clouds Roll By* (1946).

Meaning judgement

Lillian, Lil, Lilia, Lilian, Liliana, Liliane, Lilias, Lili, Lilly, Lily, Lilyan

Lillian M.N. Stevens, who was born on this day in 1844, was a noted campaigner for the temperance movement in the USA. She also did a lot of work on securing penal reform for women and took up the cause for neglected and delinquent children.

Meaning lily

Sable

Today is the birthday of *Sable Alexandra Worthy*, who was born on 1 March 1990, the daughter of the Los Angeles Lakers basketball player James 'Big Game James' Worthy. James was voted the most outstanding player of 1982.

Meaning black

Alberta, Albertina, Albertine, Alverta, Auberta

Alberta Hunter, the African-American blues singer, was born on this day in 1895. She wrote many of her own songs and worked with many of the jazz greats, including Louis Armstrong and Sidney Bechet. She became a star of New York musical reviews.

Meaning intelligent, noble

Theodore, Dore, Feodor, Feodore

Dr *Theodore Seuss*, the author of *The Cat in the Hat* books for children, was born on 2 March 1904. When he was commissioned to write his first book, his brief was to overcome the 'boringness' of children's books and use only 250 words. His books were an instant hit.

Meaning gift of God

Lou, Louie, Lewie, Lew

Lou Reed, one of the foremost rock musicians of the late 20th century, was born on this day in 1943. His poetic songs get to the core of the seedier side of life, but his best-known song is probably 'Perfect Day'.

From Lewis, meaning famous warrior

Rory, Rorry, Rorie, Roderick, Ruaidhri

Irish blues and rock guitarist *Rory Gallagher* was born on 2 March 1948. During his 30-year career he gained a worldwide following and sold over 30 million records. He eschewed most of the trappings of stardom and lived simply, devoting himself to his music.

Meaning red king

Orrin, Oran, Orren, Oren

Orrin Keepnews, a major figure in the jazz world and regarded as one of the greatest jazz record producers of all time, was born on this day in 1923. He started several classic jazz record labels, producing, among others, Duke Ellington, Thelonius Monk, Sonny Rollins, Bill Evans and John Coltrane.

Meaning fair-skinned

Laraine, Larraine, Larayne, Larine, Larina, Lorraine

US actress *Laraine Newman* was born on 2 March 1952. She was in the original cast of *Saturday Night Live* (1980) and has been in many movies and TV shows since, including *Third Rock from the Sun* (1996), *The Flintstones* (1996) and *Monsters Inc.* (2001).

Meaning famous in battle

Scarlett, Scarlet, Scarletta

Mick Jagger and Jerry Hall's eldest daughter, *Elizabeth Scarlett*, was born on 2 March 1984. Following in her mother's modelling footsteps, she is the 'face' of the cosmetics company Lancôme. When she was just 17 she was photographed for the cover of US *Vogue*.

Meaning the colour scarlet

Slava

Today is the birthday of *Slava Zaitsev*, one of the leading Russian fashion designers. Since the fall of communism there has been an explosion of fashion and design in Russia. Zaitsev also makes enticing perfumes, including Maroussia, which captures snowy Russian winters, vodka and roaring fires in a bottle.

Meaning glory

Heather

The US actress *Heather McComb* was born on this day in 1977 in Barnegat, New Jersey. She began acting at the age of two when she appeared in an advertisement for the publisher's clearing house. Her first big lead was as Jubilee in the TV film *Generation X* (1996).

Meaning heather

3 MARCH

Ronan

Singer with the Irish boy band Boyzone, *Ronan Keating* was born on this day in 1977. He joined the band when he was only 16 and within a couple of years had sold 12 million albums. After his solo success with the theme tune from the film *Notting Hill* (1999), he left Boyzone and became a superstar in his own right.

Meaning little seal

Sholem, Sholom

One of Yiddish literature's most popular and best-loved authors, *Sholem Aleichem* was born on this day in 1859 as Sholem Rabinovitch. He pioneered the Jewish 'laughter through tears' style of humour. The musical *Fiddler on the Roof* is based on his work.

Meaning peace

Bertrand, Bertram, Bartram, Beltram, Beltran, Beltrando, Berty, Bert

On this day in 1999 *Bertrand Piccard* and Brian Jones set off from Château d'Oex, Switzerland, to circumnavigate the world nonstop in a hot-air balloon. They succeeded, landing in Egypt 19 days, 21 hours and 47 minutes later.

Meaning bright raven

Jance, Jancsi, Janos

Jance Garfat, the bass player for Dr Hook and the Medicine Show, was born on this day in 1944. A pop country rock band, Dr Hook had a succession of hits in the 1970s, including the enduring 'Sylvia's Mother' (1972) and 'The Cover of Rolling Stone' (1973).

Meaning God's gracious gift

Lys, Lysandra

Today is the birthday today of the first ever winner of the Eurovision Song Contest. *Lys Assia*, who was born on 3 March 1926 in Argau, Switzerland, sang 'Refrain'. She also competed in 1957 and 1958.

Meaning liberator

Miranda, Randa, Myranda, Merande, Mandy, Mira

British actress *Miranda Richardson* was born on this day in 1958. Her first success was as Ruth Ellis in *Dance with a Stranger* (1984), and she tends to take on challenging roles. On TV she was known as Queenie in the hugely popular comedy series *Blackadder* (1983).

Meaning admired

Florida, Florie, Florrie, Florenz, Florentea, Floryn, Flo

On this day in 1845 *Florida* became the 27th state of the USA. Known the world over as the Sunshine State, Florida is the home of Disneyland, orange juice and Cape Canaveral (Cape Kennedy), from where rockets are launched into space.

Meaning blooming flower

Cunegund, Kunigund, Gundel, Kunza, Konne, Kuni, Konne

Today is the feast day of the German *St Cunegund*. She was the wife of Holy Roman Emperor Henry II, who was also canonized. After her husband's death in 1024, Cunegund entered the nunnery she had founded at Kaufungen. She and her husband had been great supporters of Benedictine monasticism.

Meaning fighting family

Brooklyn, Brook

The eldest son of English megastar soccer player David Beckham and his ex-Spice Girl (Posh Spice) wife Victoria, *Brooklyn Beckham* was born on 4 March 1999. He is named after the famous bridge in New York. He and his younger brother have Sir Elton John and Liz Hurley for godparents, along with Victoria's brother and sister.

Meaning brook

Knute, Knut, Canute

The Norwegian *Knute Rockne* was born on this day in 1888. One of the most charismatic and greatest US college football coaches of all time – the great George 'Gupper' Gupp was one of his players – he took Notre Dame through five seasons without a single loss or a draw.

Meaning knot

Landon, Langdon, Langston

The US footballer *Landon Donovan* was born on this day in 1982. When he was 17 he began playing for Bayern Leverkusen in Germany. The San Jose Earthquakes player led the US team to the quarter finals of the 2002 World Cup.

Meaning from the long hill

Vermont

On this day in 1791 Vermont became the 14th state of the USA. The Lake Champlain region had been claimed by the French in 1609 and the name of the state comes from their description of the beautiful scenery, Les Verts Monts (the green mountains).

Meaning green mountains

Patsy, Pat, Patti, Patty

The British actress *Patsy Kensit* was born on this day in 1968. She began acting at the age of four, and one of her early roles was as Mia Farrow's daughter. She appeared in *Lethal Weapon II* (1989) opposite Mel Gibson and married two rock stars, Jim Kerr and Liam Gallagher.

From Patricia, meaning well-born

Chastity

Chastity Bono, the daughter of Sonny and Cher, was born on this day in 1969. Sonny and Cher's biggest hit, 'I Got You Babe', was at the top of the charts for three weeks in August 1965, and their loving duet became one of pop TV's earliest classic moments.

Meaning pure

Jeanette, Jenette, Jenete, Jeniece

On this day in 1917 *Jeanette Rankin* of Montana became the first woman member of the US House of Representatives. A dedicated pacifist, she was one of the leaders of the resistance movement to the Vietnam War that eventually succeeded in bringing US troops back home.

Meaning God's gift of grace

Miriam, Mimi, Mitzi, Mearr

The South African singer and actress *Miriam Makeba* was born on 4 March 1932. In 1966 she won a Grammy for the best folk recording for her collaboration with Harry Belafonte, *An Evening With Belafonte/Makeba* (1966).

From Mary, meaning bitter

Paolo, Paley, Pablo

The Italian film director *Pier Paolo Pasolini* was born in Bologna on this day in 1922. As well as directing movies, such as *The Gospel According to St Matthew* (1964) and *The Decameron* (1970), he wrote novels, newspaper articles and published several volumes of poetry.

From Paul, meaning little

Rex, Rey

The British actor *Rex Harrison* was born on this day in 1908 in Cheshire. Sexy Rexy, as he was known, starred in countless films, but is best remembered for his portrayal of Professor Higgins in *My Fair Lady*, which he played on stage and on film (1964), winning an Oscar for the latter.

Meaning king

Richard, Rich, Richerd, Ritch, Ritchie, Ricard, Diccon, Dickon, Dick, Dickie

On this day in 1750 *Richard III* became the first of Shakespeare's plays ever to be performed in the USA when it was staged at the Nassau Street Theatre, New York. It was the fourth play in the historical cycle that began with *Henry VI, Parts 1, 2* and 3, written early in his career.

Meaning power, wealth

Heitor

The Brazilian composer *Heitor Villa-Lobos* was born on this day in 1887. Among the greatest of all South American composers, his work covered a broad spectrum, from choral music for schoolchildren to full symphonic works. He composed some of the best classical guitar pieces ever written.

From Hector, meaning steady, unswerving

Samantha, Sam

British actress *Samantha Eggar* was born on this day in 1939. She was nominated for an Oscar for her performance in *The Collector* (1965), which was based on the novel by John Fowles and which also starred Terence Stamp. She has made numerous films since then, including *The Astronaut's Wife* (1999).

Meaning guarded by God, listener

Ruby, Rubette, Rubia, Rubina, Rubie

On this day in 1955 *Ruby Murray* had a number one UK hit with a song called 'Softly, Softly'. The singer, who came from Belfast, Northern Ireland, dominated the charts in the 1950s. In 1955 she had five singles in the UK Top 40 at the same time, still an unbeaten record.

Meaning precious jewel

Rosa, Rosalee, Rosaleen, Roselle, Rosel, Rosella, Rosena, Rosene, Rosette

The Polish-German Jewish Marxist politician *Rosa Luxemburg* was born on this day in 1871. She founded the *Red Flag* newspaper and was the co-founder of Spartakusbund (Spartacus League), which later became the German Communist Party.

Meaning rose ·

Clodagh

The British singer and actress *Clodagh Rogers* was born on 5 March 1947 in Ballymena, Northern Ireland. She shot to fame in Britain with her Eurovision Song Contest entry 'Jack in the Box' (1971). She didn't win, but the song was a hit. She was immortalized in the Monty Python sketch 'The Cycle Tour'.

Meaning Irish river

Ettore

The Italian mathematician *Ettore Bortolotti* was born on this day in 1866 in Bologna. He wrote and edited numerous manuscripts and held several professorships. He was professor of infinitesimal calculus at Modena University, which must rank as one of the best-named academic postings.

Meaning hold, check

Gabriel, Gabriello, Gabe, Gabie, Gabby

The Nobel Prize-winning author *Gabriel García Marquez* was born on this day in 1928 in Colombia. The seamless merging of realism and fantasy in his stories is a peerless example of the Latin American genre known as magic realism. *100 Years of Solitude* (1967) is one of his best-known works.

Meaning God's messenger

Michelangelo

Michelangelo Buonarroti, the towering genius of Renaissance art, was born on this day in 1495. His first love was sculpture. His best-known works are the frescoes on the ceiling of the Sistine Chapel in Rome and his colossal statue of David.

From Michael, meaning like the Lord, and Angelo, meaning angel

Cyrano, Cyrenaica

The French soldier, novelist and dramatist *Savinien Cyrano de Bergerac* was born on this day in 1619. He is remembered today for the play written about him by Edmond Rostand (1987). The character, with a huge wit and nose to match, played by Gérard Depardieu in the film version of 1990, bore little resemblance to the real-life Cyrano.

Meaning from Cyrene

Kiki, Kiku

The British singer *Kiki Dee* was born on this day in 1947. The first European to sign with Tamla Motown, her biggest hits came later, both duets with Elton John: 'Don't Go Breaking My Heart' (1976) and 'True Love' (1993).

Meaning chrysanthemum

Valentina, Valentine, Valida, Valeda, Valencia, Val

Valentina Tereshkova, the first woman in space, was born on 16 June 1963, the daughter of a tractor driver. Her hobby was parachute jumping, and this led her to train as a cosmonaut. She was launched from the Soviet space station on 16 June 1963 and orbited the Earth 48 times.

Meaning healthy, strong

Kiri

Dame *Kiri te Kanawa* was born in Gisborne, New Zealand, on this day in 1944, adopted by her Irish mother and Maori father. Though already well known in opera, she became internationally famous when she sang at the wedding of Prince Charles and Lady Diana Spencer in 1981.

Meaning mountain

Elizabeth, Elisabeth, Elisabet, Elisabetta, Lizabeta, Lizbeth, Lizzy, Lizzie, Lize, Liza, Liz, Betty, Bettie, Bet, Eliza, Elisa, Elissa, Elzleta, Elspeth

On this day in 1805 the English poet *Elizabeth Barrett Browning* was born in Coxhoe, Durham. She eloped with the poet Robert Browning in 1846, and they lived in Florence.

Meaning consecrated to God

Edwin, Edlin, Eduino

Sir *Edwin Henry Landseer*, the British painter, was born on this day in 1802. Particularly noted for his paintings of animals, he also sculpted the lions in London's Trafalgar Square. He was just 13 years old when he first exhibited at the Royal Academy.

Meaning prosperous friend

Willard

Willard Scott was born on this day in 1934. The weatherman, famous for his appearances on the US TV show *Today* (1980), started his career on radio. He used to supplement his income playing Bozo the Clown on local TV. This led to his becoming the first ever Ronald McDonald clown.

Meaning brave, resolute

Piet, Pietro

The artist *Piet Cornelis Mondrian* was born at Amersfoot, the Netherlands, on this day in 1872. The painter, who became famous for his deceptively simple abstract coloured square paintings, was a primary school teacher before he turned to art.

From Peter, meaning rock, stone

Maurice, Morris

On this day in 1875 the French composer *Maurice Ravel* was born in Ciboure near the Pyrenees. Although he wrote two operas, *L'Heure espagnole* and *L'Engant et les sortilèges*, he is probably best known for *Boléro* (1928), which will be forever associated with British ice dance stars Jayne Torvill and Christopher Dean.

Meaning dark, swarthy

Felicity, Felicitas

Today is the feast day of *St Felicity*, who was martyred with her companion, St Perpetua. They, and four men, Secundulus, Saturninus, Saturus and Revocatus, were arrested in Carthage and imprisoned for their faith. They were condemned to death by wild beasts.

Meaning good fortune

Louisa, Louise, Lou

On this day in 1832 US author *Louisa May Alcott* was born in Germantown, Philadelphia. She was a nurse during the Civil War, and achieved fame with her novel *Little Women* (1868), which she followed up with *Little Men* (1871) and *Jo's Boys* (1886). She became involved in women's suffrage and other reform movements.

From Louis, meaning famous warrior

Janet, Janetta, Janette, Jana, Jan

Janet Guthrie, the pioneering US racing driver, was born on this day in 1938. An aerospace engineer, flying instructor and pilot by profession, in March 1977 she became the first woman to compete in the Indianapolis 500. Her driving suit and crash helmet are displayed at the Smithsonian Institution in Washington D.C.

From Jane, meaning God's gift of grace

Lorena, Laurene, Lauretta, Laurette, Laurie

The US journalist *Lorena A. Hickok* was born on 7 March 1893. After interviewing Eleanor Roosevelt, she became a great friend and confidante of the first lady. She wrote a biography of Eleanor and together they wrote *Women of Courage*, a book about women in politics.

From Laura, meaning laurel wreath

Kenneth, Ken, Keneth, Kent, Kenny, Kennith

Kenneth Grahame, the Scottish author of *The Wind in the Willows* (1908), was born on this day in 1859 in Edinburgh. He wrote the story for his son, and the crazy character of Toad was based on him. Grahame worked in the Bank of England for most of his life.

Meaning handsome

Aidan, Aiden, Eden

Aidan Quinn, the US actor, was born on 8 March 1959. He played Dez, Madonna's love interest, in *Desperately Seeking Susan* (1985). In 1986 he was nominated for an Emmy for his performance in *An Early Frost* (1986).

Meaning fiery little one

Anslem, Ansel, Anselme, Anshelm, Anse, Elmo

The German artist *Anslem Kiefer* was born in Donaueschingen on 8 March 1945. Kiefer studied under Joseph Beuys and is one of Germany's major contemporary painters. After travelling the world, he settled in France, where he has a 14-hectare (35-acre) studio compound.

Meaning follower of a nobleman

Ruggiero

The Italian composer *Ruggiero Leoncavallo* was born on this day in Naples in 1857. His first opera, *Pagliacci*, was performed in Milan in 1892. He went on to write a version of *La Bohème* (1897), *Zaza* (1900) and *Der Roland* (1904).

Meaning pirate

Cyd

The Hollywood dancer and actress *Cyd Charisse* was born Tula Ellice Finkelea in Amarillo, Texas, on this day in 1921. She had several movie roles as a ballerina, including *Mission to Moscow* (1943) and *Something to Shout About* (1943). She danced with Fred Astaire in the *Zeigfeld Follies* (1946).

Meaning public hill

Lynn, Lynne, Lynette, Linnet, Lyn

The English actress *Lynn Redgrave* was born Lyn Rachel Redgrave on 8 March 1943. Her family is a famous acting dynasty: her parents were Michael Redgrave and Rachel Kempson, her sister is Vanessa Redgrave and her nieces are Natasha and Joely Richardson and Jemma Redgrave.

Meaning waterfall, idol

Pudentiana

Today is the feast day of *St Pudentiana*. She was the daughter of a Roman senator, and legend has it that she is the girl mentioned in a letter of St Paul to Timothy. She is said to have helped Christians with their burials and to have given all her money to the poor.

Meaning she who should be ashamed

Mariska, Markiska, Maris, Marissa, Marisa

It is the birthday today of the Dutch TV hostess, actress and model *Mariska Hulscher*, who was born on 8 March 1964 in Delft, Holland.

Meaning of the sea

9

Dominic, Dom, Domingo, Dominik, Dominy

Today is the feast day of the Italian *St Domininc Savio*. He was a devout Christian, who was praying by himself when he was four, was an altar boy at five and began studying for the priesthood at twelve. He is the patron saint of altar boys and the falsely accused.

Meaning born on the day of the Lord

Mickey, Mick, Mickie

Mickey Spillane, the US author and occasional actor, was born Frank Morrison Spillane in New York on this day in 1918. His novel *I the Jury* (1947) introduced the famous private eye Mike Hammer. Spillane played Hammer in the film *The Girl Hunters* (1963).

Diminutive of Michael, meaning like the Lord

Yuri, Uri, Uriah, Urias, Uriel

Yuri Gagarin, the first man in space, was born Yuri Alekeyevich Gagarin on this day in 1934. He made his historic flight on 12 April 1961 aboard *Vostok* 1. While in flight he was swiftly promoted from lowly Second Lieutenant to Major, a promotion that was announced by Tass, the official news agency of the former Soviet Union.

Meaning the Lord's light

Amerigo, Emmerich, Emmery, Emery, Emory, Merrick

Amerigo Vespucci was born on this day in 1512. The Italian navigator was the first person in the world to write about the Americas. The mapper who named America is said to have taken the name for the country from the feminine form of Vespucci's penname, Americus Vespucius.

Meaning industrious ruler

Frances, Francesca, Francisca, Franciska, Françoise

Today is the feast day of *St Frances of Rome*. She was born in Rome in 1354, the daughter of a nobleman, and was married when she was only 13. She spent her life serving the poor, guided by an archangel, who was visible only to her. She is the patron saint of cars and their drivers, and so this is the day on which cars are blessed.

From Frances, meaning free

Juliette, Juliet, Julietta, Julina, Juline

The French actress *Juliette Binoche* was born on this day in 1964. She is the highest-paid actress in the history of France. Her first big role was in *The Unbearable Lightness of Being* (1984). She won an Oscar for best supporting actress for *The English Patient* (1996).

From Julia, meaning youthful

Keely

US jazz singer *Keely Smith* was born in Norfolk, Virginia, on 9 March 1932. With her band leader husband, Louis Prima, she had her first hit in 1958 with 'That Ol' Black Magic'. She made a comeback in 2000 with what many consider to be the best album she has produced.

Meaning beautiful one

Daja, Danya, Danyelle, Danice

The Czech tennis star *Daja Betanova* was born on this day in 1983. She played for her country in the 2000 Olympic Games when she was just 17 years old, and she has beaten several top names in grand slam tournaments.

From Danielle, meaning God is my judge

Bix

Bix Beiderbecke was born on this day in 1903. A jazz cornet and pianist, he took his inspiration from the French impressionist composers, especially Ravel, Satie and Debussy. Each summer the Bix Beiderbecke Memorial Jazz Festival draws thousands to his birthplace in Davenport, Iowa.

Meaning not known

Warner, Verner, Werner

On this day in 1918 *Warner Brothers* released its first film. It was called *Four Years in Germany*. It was, however, to be nearly ten years before the brothers – Jack, Sam, Albert and Harry – had their first success, with the first talkie, *The Jazz Singer* (1927), starring Al Jolson.

Meaning protecting army

Cristus

Cristus James, the son of Crystal Gayle and Bill Gatizmo, was born on this day in 1986. Crystal Gayle is a country singer who crossed into the mainstream with her international hit 'Don't it Make My Brown Eyes Blue' (1977).

Meaning carrier of Christ

Mykola

The Ukrainian composer, conductor, pianist and folksong collector *Mykola Vytaliyevich Lysenkno* was born on this day in 1842. He founded the Ukrainian School of Music and was revered in his country. His son, Ostap, became a music teacher, and his daughter, Maryana, a pianist.

Meaning victorious people's army

Eva, Eve, Evita, Ewa

The British soprano *Eva Turner* was born on this day in 1892 in Oldham, Lancashire. She was among the first to sing *Turandot*, and her performance of the aria 'In questa reggia' was recorded in 1930. She was professor of music at Oklahoma University in 1950–59 before returning to London to teach at the Royal Academy of Music.

Meaning life

Neneh

The singer *Neneh Cherry* was born in Stockholm on this day in 1964. She moved to London and played in several bands, including the Cherries, the Slits and Rip Rig and Panic. Her first solo album, *Raw Like Sushi* (1990), spawned the worldwide hit single 'Buffalo Stance' (1990).

Meaning not known

Jezebel, Jezebella, Jezebelle

On 10 March 1938 the play *Jezebel* opened on Broadway. It wasn't hugely successful, but was turned into a movie and made a star of a young actress called Bette Davis. She got the part only as compensation for missing out on the role of Scarlett O'Hara in the film *Gone With the Wind*.

Meaning follower of idols

Elena, Eleanor, Elinor, Elinore, Elinora, Ellie, Eleonore

The Russian tennis player *Elena Dovina* was born on this day in 1983. Elena, who is 1.88 metres (6 feet 2 inches) tall, reached her first final at Estoil in 2001. In 2002 she got to the US Open quarter finals, beating Jelena Dokic in a major upset.

From Helen, meaning light

Douglas, Doug, Douggie, Douggy, Dug, Duglass

On this day in 1952 the British writer *Douglas Adams* was born in Cambridge. His cult science-fiction comedy *The Hitchhiker's Guide to the Galaxy* began its life as a BBC radio series (1982) before becoming a classic series of bestselling books, and a feature film.

Meaning from the dark stream

Troy

The US racing driver *Troy Ruttman* was born on this day in 1930. When he was just 22 years old he became the youngest person ever to win the Indianapolis 500. He went on to become the first ever Indy 500 winner to race in Formula One at Reims, France.

Meaning curly-haired

Paul, Pavel, Pauley, Pablo, Paolo

On this day in 1997 *Paul McCartney* went to Buckingham Palace to receive a knighthood from the queen. In 2003, at the age of 61, he became a father again when his second wife, Heather, gave birth to a girl, Beatrice Milly.

Meaning little

Shane

The actor *Shane Ritchie* was born Shane Patrick Roche in London on this day in 1964 to Irish parents. He is best known in Britain for his role as Alfie Moon in the TV soap opera *Eastenders*. Shane started his career as a Pontins holiday camp bluecoat called Shane Skywalker.

From John, meaning God has shown me favour

Chelsea, Chelsy, Chelsie, Chelsey, Kelsie

The *Royal Hospital, Chelsea*, in London was founded on this day in 1682 by King Charles II as a home for unfit soldiers. Today it is still the home for war veterans. Known as Chelsea Pensioners, they can be seen in their smart red uniforms around the King's Road area of Chelsea.

Meaning port of ships

Thora, Thorberta, Thorberte, Throbertha, Thordia, Thorberthe, Thordis

The US actress *Thora Birch* was born on this day in 1982. One of her early successes was beating 4,000 others to land a role in the film *Paradise* (1991), starring Don Johnson and Melanie Griffiths. She played Jane Burnham in *American Beauty* (1999) and received her first Golden Globe nomination for *Ghost World* (2000).

Meaning thunder

LeToya, Letoya, Letizia, Letka, Letofumaua, Letrice

The US singer *LeToya Luckett* was born in Houston, Texas, on this day in 1981. One of the original members of the hugely successful band Destiny's Child, she released her debut solo album in the summer of 2004.

Meaning not known

Anissa, Anise, Anish

The US actress *Anissa Jones* was born on 11 March 1958. She became famous while still a child, appearing without a break in the TV sitcom *Family Affair* for six years (1966). She sang and danced with Elvis Presley in *The Trouble with Girls* (1969).

Meaning charming, friendly

Jack

The US author *Jack Kerouac* was born on this day in 1922. He wrote his best-known novel, *On the Road* (1957), on one continuous piece of paper roll. The book, charting his adventures travelling across America with Dean Moriarty, heralded the emergence of the 1950s beat generation.

From John, meaning God has shown me favour

Vaslav, Vassily, Vassi, Vasya, Vas, Vasili

On this day in 1888 *Vaslav Nijinsky*, the outstanding Russian ballet dancer, was born in Kiev, Ukraine. Principal dancer of Diaghilev's Ballet Russes until 1914, he danced the leading roles in *Le Pavilion d'Armida* and *Les Sylphides* with the equally legendary Pavlova.

Meaning royal

Kemal, Cemal

Kemal Attatürk, the founder of modern Turkey, was born on this day in 1881. He introduced many reforms to unite the people, including equal rights for women, and he also encouraged his people to wear Western-style dress.

Meaning beauty

Roy, Conroy, Leroy

On this day in 1962 *Roy Orbison*'s 'Dream Baby (How Long Must I Dream)' entered the US Top 10. Born Roy Kelton Orbison, he never appeared without his trademark dark sunglasses. He influenced many artists of the 1970s, including Van Halen, Mick Jagger and John Lennon.

Meaning red-haired

Googie, Georgette

British actress *Googie Withers* was born Georgette Lizette Withers on this day in 1917 in Karachi, Pakistan. Appearing in many movies in the 1930s and 1940s, including *One of Our Aircraft is Missing* (1942), one of her most memorable later performances was in the movie *Shine* (1996). Her daughter is the actress Joanna McCallum.

Meaning little pigeon

Liza, Eliza, Elisa, Lize

US singer and actress *Liza Minnelli* was born Liza May to Judy Garland and Vincent Minnelli in Los Angeles on this day in 1946. She was named after the Gershwin song 'Liza' and her grandmother, May. In 1972 she won an Oscar for her performance as Sally Bowles in the film *Cabaret*.

From Elizabeth, meaning consecrated to God

Corrina, Corinne, Corinna, Correna, Cora, Corissa, Corella, Corett, Coretta, Corette

It is the birthday today of *Corrina Grant Gill*, the daughter of country music superstars Vince Gill and Amy Grant. She was born on 12 March 2001. Her father has won 15 Grammys, has been voted entertainer of the year twice and has sold over 22 million albums.

Meaning maiden

Juliette, Juliet, Juliotta

On this day in 1912 the US Girl Scouts organization was founded by *Juliette Gordon Low*. At first, they were called Girl Guides, like their British counterparts. Juliette was born Juliette Magill Kinzie Gordon in Savannah, Georgia, where everyone knew her as Daisy.

Meaning youthful

Roderic, Roderick, Rod, Roddy, Rurik, Rodrigo, Roddie, Rodd, Rodrick, Rodric

Today is the feast day of *St Roderic*. During the time of the Moorish occupation of Spain, Roderic was a priest. His family used force to try to make him give up his Christian beliefs, but he held steadfastly on to them.

Meaning rich, renowned ruler

Hugo, Huey, Hughes

Hugo Wolf, the Austrian composer, was born in Windischgraz on this day in 1860. He is best known for his song settings, and unusually for the time, he emphasized the importance of the lyrics, insisting that the inspiration for his music came from the words and not the other way round.

From Hugh, meaning mind, spirit

Dennis, Dennison, Denny, Deny, Denzil, Dionisio, Dion

Dennis the Menace first appeared on this day in 1951. One of the most enduring cartoon characters ever, Dennis, with his sidekick Gnasher the dog, came into the world with the comic *The Beano*. There is a park in Monterey named after him – the Dennis the Menace Park.

From Dionysus, meaning lover of wine

Herbie, Heriberto, Herb, Harbert, Harbin

On this day in 1969 the Walt Disney film *The Love Bug* was released. *Herbie*, the star of the film, was a white VW Beetle with a mind of its own. The last Herbie Beetle was made on 30 July 2003 in Puebla, Mexico, but an updated version of the Beetle has since been produced.

From Herbert, meaning brilliant warrior

Abigail, Abigael, Abbe, Abbey, Abbie, Abby

Abigail Fillmore, first lady of the USA from 1850 to 1853, was born on this day in 1798 in Saratoga County, New York. She married Millard Fillmore in 1825, and the couple had one son, Millard Powers Fillmore, and one daughter, Mary Abigail, known as Abby.

Meaning father's joy

Ina, Ines, Inessa, Inez

Ina Ray Hutton, the US tap dancer and singer, was born on 13 March 1916. At the height of the big band era of 1940s New York, Ina formed her own all-girl big band, Ina Ray Hutton and her Melodears. Full of energy, she would dance the jitterbug while she conducted.

From Agnes, meaning pure, chaste

Annabeth, Anabeth

The US actress *Annabeth Gish* was born on 13 March 1971 in Alberquerque, New Mexico. The star of TV's *The X-Files* (1998) and *The West Wing* (1999) also appeared in the feature film *The Celestine Prophecy* (2005), based on the bestselling book by James Redfield.

Meaning full of grace, house of God

Glenne, Glenna, Glenn, Glenine, Glennis

The US actress *Glenne Headly* was born on this day in 1955. She starred in many movies, including *Steppenwolf* (1974) with John MalKovich, to whom she was married from 1982 to 1990. Glenne is in fact one of the oldest names ever recorded.

Meaning valley

Albert, Ailbert, Aldabert, Aubert, Adelbert, Bert, Delbert, Elbert

The theoretical physicist *Albert Einstein* was born on 14 March 1879. Most famed for his theory of relativity, his surname has become synonymous with the word genius the world over. Albert became a popular name in Britain after Queen Victoria's marriage to Prince Albert.

Meaning noble

Michael, Mike, Mick, Micky, Mickey, Michel, Micah, Mischa, Mitch, Mitchell

The British actor Sir *Michael Caine* was born Maurice Joseph Micklewhite in Rotherhithe, London, on this day in 1933. Famous for his cockney accent, the Oscar-winning (for *Hannah and Her Sisters*, 1986) star of many memorable movies also runs several restaurants.

Meaning like the Lord

Quincy, Quintus, Quinlan

Quincy Jones was born in Chicago on this day in 1933. He started in the 1950s as a trumpet player, but diversified as a highly successful singer, composer, arranger, conductor, record producer, film and TV director, record company executive and magazine publisher.

Meaning from the estate of the fifth son

Perry

The first gold record was awarded on this day in 1958. It was presented to the US singer *Perry Como* by the Recording Industry Association of America for his hit song 'Catch a Falling Star'.

Meaning from the pear tree

Megan, Meghann, Meaghan, Meghan, Meagan

The Canadian actress *Megan Follow* was born on this day in 1968. She has starred in many stage plays and films. She won two Gemini Awards for her performance in *Anne of Green Gables* (1999), including for best performance by a lead actress. She has two children, Lyla Anne and Russell.

Meaning strong

Matilda, Mathilda, Matilde, Matelda, Mattie

Today is the feast day of *St Matilda*, who was born at Engern in Westphalia in about 895. She was the wife of the German king, Henry I (known as the Fowler), and was renowned for her great generosity to the poor and the church. She also founded many monasteries, including those at Quedlinburg and Nordhausen.

Meaning strong in battle

Teresa, Teressa, Therese, Toireasa

On this day in 1953 *Teresa Brewer* hit the top of the US charts with 'Till I Waltz Again with You'. She stayed at number one for seven weeks. The song was then recorded by Dick Todd, Russ Morgan, the Harmonicats, Ruby Wright, Tommy Sosebee and the Five Balls – all in 1953.

Meaning harvest, reap

Meredith, Meridith, Meri, Merry

It is the birthday today of *Meredith Salenger*, the US TV and movie actress. She began her movie career in *Annie* (1982) and has appeared in many other features and TV dramas since. In 1999 she starred in *Lake Placid* (1999).

Meaning protector of the sea

Gordon, Gordan, Gorden, Gordie, Gordy

On this day in 1909 *Harry Gordon Selfridge* opened his famous department store, Selfridges. The American was visiting London with his wife, Rosalie, and they weren't impressed by the shops, so he opened his own store at the unfashionable end of Oxford Street with £400,000.

Meaning from the cornered hill

Shunzhi

Today is the birthday of *Shunzhi*, the second emperor of the Chinese Manchu Qing dynasty. Born in 1638, he was the first Quin emperor to rule over the whole of China. He became emperor at the age of five years old.

Meaning sage progenitor

Ry, Rye

Ry Cooder was born in Los Angeles, California, on this day in 1947. Best known for his slide guitar work, especially in the memorable score for the film *Paris, Texas* (1984), he produced *Buena Vista Social Club* (1997).

Meaning from the riverbank

Sly, Si, Silas, Silvan, Silvano, Sylvan

Sly Stone celebrates his birthday today. He was born Sylvester Stewart in Dallas, Texas, on 15 March 1944. His band Sly and the Family Stone was pivotal in the development of soul, funk and psychedelia in the 1960s and 1970s.

From Sylvester, meaning from the forest

Verree

The US film actress *Verree Teasdale* was born on this day in 1906. She was one of the actresses to make the transition from silent films to the talkies and had a leading role in the classic *A Star is Born* (1937). She was married to another silent movie star, Adolphe Menjou.

Meaning not known

Isabella, Isabedau, Isabelle, Isbel, Issy, Izzie

The Irish playwright Lady *Isabella Augusta Gregory* was born near Coole, County Galway, on 15 March 1852. A founding member of the Abbey Theatre in Dublin, she collaborated there with the poet and playwright W.B. Yeats. She wrote many of her plays in the dialect of western Ireland.

Meaning consecrated to God

Sedna

On this day in 2004 the discovery of *90377 Sedna* was announced. The trans-Neptunian planetoid Sedna is the furthest distance at which any natural object in the solar system has ever been observed. The discovery was a collaboration between Caltech, Yale and Gemini.

Meaning not known

Persia, Persis

Persia Crawford Campbell was born on this day in 1898. She was perhaps the world's first consumer rights expert. With her academic background in consumer economics, she advised government departments and organized consumers and educated them to understand their rights.

Meaning from Persia

Arthur, Artur, Artie, Arturo, Aurthur, Artus, Art

On this day in 1900 the British archaeologist Sir *Arthur Evans* uncovered Knossos on Crete. The Minoan city was thought to be nothing more than a Greek myth, but the excavations revealed a fantastically intact city, with images of bulls and other artefacts that make it one of the most exciting archaeological finds ever.

Meaning strong as a rock

Gerbrand. Gerbrant, Gerbants, Brand

The Dutch poet and playwright *Gerbrand Adrianensz Bredero* was born on 16 March 1585 in Amsterdam. The house where he was born, 41 Nes Canal, still stands, as does 244 Oude Zidjs Voorburgwal, where he lived for most of his life.

Meaning brand

Leo

The Australian actor *Leo McKern* was born on this day in 1920. The star of British TV stage and screen was Horace Rumpole in TV's *Rumpole of the Bailey* (1978), one of the 'Number Two' characters in the cult TV series *The Prisoner* (1967) as well as the holy man in the Beatles' film *Help* (1965).

Meaning lion

Sully, Sullivan

On this day in 1839 the French poet and essayist René-François-Armand Prudhomme, known by his penname *Sully-Prudhomme*, was born. In 1901 he was the first ever winner of the Nobel Prize for literature for his writings on solitude and war.

Meaning hawk-eyed

Henrietta, Henriette, Hendrika, Hettie, Henrika, Hetty

In Hungary today is the name day for *Henrietta*. Henrietta is the female form of Henry, and the name became popular in England in the 17th century after Charles I married the French princess Henrietta Maria, sister of Louis XIII.

Meaning ruler of the home

Sybille, Sybil, Sybyl, Sybella, Sibylle, Sib, Sibby, Sibell, Sibella, Sibie, Sibil, Sibilla

Sybille Bedford, the German-born author and biographer, was born on this day in 1911. Her autobiographical novel *Jigsaw* (1989) was nominated for the Booker Prize, and she is considered by many to be one of the finest women writers of the 20th century.

Meaning prophetess

Christa, Crista

On this day in 1928 *Christa Ludwig*, the German mezzo-soprano, was born in Berlin. She made her debut as Orlovsky in *Die Fledermaus* in 1946, and her repertoire ranged from Mozart to Richard Strauss. She is especially admired for her interpretation of Mahler.

From Christine, meaning follower of Christ

Gloria, Cloriana, Gloire, Glori, Glory, Gloriano, Glorianna, Glorianne

On this day in 1979 *Gloria Gaynor* topped the charts with her single 'I Will Survive', which was a hit all over the world. The song was also recorded by Diana Ross, and the Hermes House Band reached number one in the Dutch charts with the same song in 1994.

Meaning glorious one

17 MARCH

Nat, Nate, Nathan, Nattie

The legendary US singer *Nat 'King' Cole* was born Nathaniel Adams Coles in Montgomery, Alabama, on March 17 1915 (or possibly a few years later – no one is certain). Among his best-known songs were 'Mona Lisa' (1950) and 'Unforgettable' (1951). His daughter, Natalie, is also a singer.

Meaning gift of God

Rudolf, Rodolph, Dolph, Rollo

The great ballet dancer *Rudolf Kkhametovich Nureyev* was born on this day in 1938. In 1961 he defected to the West from Russia and later joined the Royal Ballet. His performances with his close friend Margot Fonteyn became legendary.

Meaning famous wolf

Gene

US singer *Gene Pitney* was born on 17 March 1941 in Rockville, New England. He had many hits in the 1960s, including 'Town without Pity' (1961) and '24 Hours from Tulsa' (1966). In 1990 his duet with Marc Almond, 'Something's Gotten Hold of My Heart', reached number one in Britain.

From Eugene, meaning noble, well-born

Cito

The baseball manager *Cito Caston* was born on 17 March 1944. As the manager of Toronto, he was the first African-American to manage a winning World Series team. He shared the 1991 *Sporting News* award for man of the year with Pat Gillick.

Meaning quickly

Gertrude, Gertie, Gert

Today is the feast day of *St Gertrude of Nivelles*, whose mother founded a monastery at Nivelles and made her daughter, Gertrude, its abbess, even though she was still in her teens. She is said to have carried out her responsibilities well, until she resigned, still only 30 years old.

Meaning strong spear

Penelope, Penny, Pen

The British writer *Penelope Lively* was born in Egypt on this day in 1933. She lived in England from the age of 12. She has written many novels and books for children, and is considered a master of the short story. Her works include *The Ghost of Thomas Kempe* (1973) and *Moon Tiger* (1987).

Meaning not known

Renee, Rene, Rennie

US actress, screenplay writer and author *Renee Taylor* was born on 17 March 1935. She has won many awards, including an Emmy nomination for her performance as the mother in the TV show *The Nanny* (1993), and an Oscar nomination for her screenplay. She has also written bestselling healthy diet books.

From Renata, meaning born again

Brittany

Brittany Daniel, the US model and actress, and her twin sister Cyntha, were born on this day in 1976 in Florida. After modelling for many teen magazines, playing the Doublemint Twin and taking TV roles, Brittany appeared in her first feature film, *The Basketball Diaries*, in 1995, with Leonardo de Caprio.

Meaning Britain

Cyril, Cyrillus, Cyrille, Cirilo, Cyrill, Cy

Today is the feast day of *St Cyril of Jerusalem*. He was bishop of Jerusalem, but spent many years in exile because of his opposition to the emperor. His lectures, *Catecheses*, with detailed instructions, survive and are one of the most precious of all Christian antiquities.

Meaning lord

Courtney, Courtenay, Corty, Court, Cortie, Cort, Curt

The British jazz saxophonist *Courtney Pine* was born in London of Jamaican parents on 18 March 1964. He is one of the most popular jazz musicians in Britain, and as well as playing and recording, he presents a radio show *The Jazz Crusades* on BBC Radio Two.

Meaning place

Grover

Grover Cleveland, who became the 22nd and 24th presidents of the USA, was born in New Jersey on this day in 1837. The first Democrat to be elected after the Civil War, he is the only president to leave the White House and return for a second term four years later.

Meaning from the grove

Wilson, Wills

US soul singer *Wilson Pickett* was born on this day in 1941 in Prattville, Alabama. He was one of the most popular soul singers of the 1960s. His many hits included 'In the Midnight Hour', 'Mustang Sally' and 'Funky Broadway'.

Meaning son of William

Serafina, Seraphina, Serafine, Seraphine, Sera

Today is the birthday of *Serafina Watts*, the daughter of Rolling Stones drummer Charlie Watts and his wife, Shirley. She was born on 18 March 1968. Charlie Watts is passionate about jazz and has formed several big bands with some of the top names in jazz.

Meaning ardent believer

Judith, Juditha, Judy, Judie

On this day in 1922 *Judith Kaplan Eisenstein* became the first girl in the USA to celebrate a Bat Mitzvah. A child prodigy, she studied sacred music and wrote and published a book of songs for Jewish children, the first of its kind. She also taught at the Jewish Theological Seminary.

Meaning admired, praised

Marilla

The US lawyer and pioneering campaigner for women's rights *Marilla Ricker* was born on this day in 1840. She was the first woman to be admitted to the New Hampshire Bar, the first woman to stand for election as governor of New Hampshire and also the first woman to vote in a state election.

Meaning flower

Latifah

One of the best-known female rappers in music, *Queen Latifah* was born Dana Owens on 18 March 1970 in Newark, New Jersey. She released her first album, *All Hail the Queen*, in 1989, and sang with David Bowie on his *Fame 90* (1990) remix.

Meaning delicate, sensitive

19

Tobias, Tioboid, Tobe, Tobiah, Tobit, Toby

The Scottish author *Tobias George Smollett* was born on 19 March 1721 in Dalquhurn, West Dunbartonshire. The son of a judge and a qualified surgeon, his best-known novels are *The Adventures of Roderick Random* (1748) and *The Adventures of Peregrine Pickle* (1751).

Meaning God is good

Jennings

On this day in 1860 *William Jennings Bryan*, known as the Commoner, was born in Salem, Illinois. He was candidate for the US presidency three times and represented Nebraska in Congress. He was known for his faith, fairness and his commitment to the ordinary American.

Meaning descendant of John

Wyatt, Wiatt

Wyatt Earp was born Wyatt Berry Stapp Earp in Monmouth, Illinois, on 19 March 1848. He became an assistant marshal in Dodge City, Kansas, and deputy marshal in Tombstone, Arizona, where he was involved in the gunfight at the OK Corral in 1881.

From Guy, meaning guide

Said, Sajid

Said Wilbert Musa, prime minister of Belize, was born on this day in 1944 in San Ignacio Cayo. He studied law in Britain and went on to become a magistrate in Belize. He wore jeans and a T-shirt at his inauguration.

Meaning one who worships God

Moms

Moms Mabley, the US stand-up comedienne, was born Loretta Mary Aiken in North Carolina on this day in 1899. At the peak of her career in the 1960s she was a major influence on Bill Cosby, Whoopi Goldberg and many others.

Meaning mum

Ursula, Ursola, Urule, Ursulette, Ursa, Ursuline, Ursy, Ursule

The Swiss-born actress *Ursula Andress* was born on this day in 1936. Her most memorable scene was in the Bond movie *Dr No* (1962), emerging from the sea in her bikini. She was in many other films, including *The Clash of the Titans* (1981).

Meaning little bear

Glenn, Glenna, Glenine, Glennis, Glynis

US actress *Glenn Close* was born in Greenwich, Connecticut, on 19 March 1947. She will always be remembered for her chilling performance in *Fatal Attraction* (1987), but she has also won Tonys for her performances in Broadway's *The Real Thing* (1984) and *Sunset Boulevard* (1995).

Meaning valley

Elizabeth, Elisabeth, Elisabet, Elisabetta, Lizabeta, Lizbeth, Lizzy, Lizzie, Lize, Liza, Liz, Betty, Bettie, Bet, Eliza, Elisa, Elissa, Elzieta, Elspeth

The British composer *Elizabeth Maconchy* was born in Hertfordshire on this day in 1907. She studied with Ralph Vaughan Williams and has written many chamber pieces and an opera for children, *The King of the Golden River* (1975). Her daughter is the composer Nicola Frances LeFanu.

Meaning consecrated to God

Henrik, Heinrick, Heinrich, Hendrock, Henrik

The Norwegian playwright *Henrik Johan Ibsen* was born on this day in 1828. He played a major part in the development of modern, realistic theatre, for before him, plays were written as moral dramas with firm conclusions and predictable endings.

From Henry, meaning home ruler

Napoleon, Apoleo, Appolon

Napoleon II, known as the Eaglet, was born François-Charles-Joseph Bonaparte on this day in 1811 in Paris. He was the son of Napoleon Bonaparte and his second wife, the Austrian princess, Marie-Louise, and he was emperor for just 16 days before Louis XVIII was restored to the French throne in 1815.

Meaning destroyer

Alfonso, Alphonso, Alfons, Alfonse, Alford, Alonso, Alonzo, Alphonsus, Fonz

The Mexican diplomat *Alfonso García Robles* was born on 20 March 1911. In 1982 he was awarded the Nobel Prize for peace for his invaluable work in setting up a nuclear-free zone in Latin America and the Caribbean. The Treaty of Ttlateloco was signed in 1967.

Meaning noble, ready

Caleb, Cal, Cale

The American realist painter *Caleb Bingham* was born on this day in 1811 in Augusta County, Virginia. He managed successfully to combine arts and politics. After painting frontier life in Missouri, he was elected state legislator and became a full-time politician.

Meaning bold

Harriet, Harriot, Harriotte, Hattie, Hatty, Hettie, Hetty, Harriette

On this day in 1852 *Harriet Beecher Stowe*'s famous anti-slavery novel *Uncle Tom's Cabin or Life Among the Lowly* was published. The writer was raised in Cincinnati, becoming an abolitionist, encouraged by her husband and brother.

From Henrietta, meaning ruler of the home

Vera, Verena, Verine, Verene, Veria, Verina

The British singer Dame *Vera Lynn* was born in London on 20 March 1917. She was famous during the Second World War for her rousing, anthem-like song 'We'll Meet Again' and for her radio show, *Sincerely Yours*, which sent messages to the troops abroad. Her nickname was the Forces' Sweetheart.

Meaning faith

Winta

The Norwegian pop star known simply as *Winta* was born Winta Efrem Negassi on this day in 1984. She was born in Oslo to Eritrean parents, who had fled to Norway to escape the civil war in their own country. In 2004 she released her first album, *daWorks*, to great acclaim.

Meaning desire

Patty, Patti, Pat

On this day in 1976 *Patty Hearst* was found guilty of bank robbery. The heiress, daughter of publisher Randolph Hearts, had been kidnapped in February 1974 by the radical group the Symbionese Liberation Army, which had, she claimed, brainwashed her into agreeing to join them in the robbery.

From Patricia, meaning well-born

Johann, Johan

The great composer *Johann Sebastian Bach* was born on this day in 1685 in Eisenach, Germany. The son of an organist, Johann was always repairing the instrument in his village church. He became as familiar with its working as with the sounds it could produce.

From John, meaning God has shown me favour

Viv

Viv Stanshall was born in London on this day in 1943. With Neil Innes he formed the Bonzo Dog Doo-Dah Band, which had a hit with 'I'm the Urban Spaceman' in 1968. Viv's unique style of humour predated the Monty Python comic phenomenon, and his most admired work is called 'Men Opening Umbrellas Ahead'.

Meaning lively

Ayrton

Ayrton Senna, the Formula One racing driver, was born on this day in 1960 in São Paulo, Brazil. He was one of the most popular Brazilians ever and was the indisputable star of motor racing throughout the 1980s, achieving 65 pole positions and winning 41 races.

Meaning not known

Modest, Modeste

The Russian composer *Modest Petrovich Musorgsky* was born on this day in 1839. He wrote *Night on the Bare Mountain*, popularized in the Disney film *Fantasia* (1940), as well as *Pictures at an Exhibition* (1874), which was later arranged by Maurice Ravel.

Meaning humble

Millie, Milli, Milicent, Mellicent, Melisendra, Melsende, Melisandra

This day in 1967 saw the release of the film *Thoroughly Modern Millie*, a homage to the New York jazz era. The film, which starred Julie Andrews as Millie Dillmount, won an Oscar for the best original musical score for the composer Elmer Bernstein.

Meaning industrious, strong

Selma, Anselma, Anselme, Zelma

The civil rights march that took place on this day in 1965 in *Selma*, Alabama, led by Martin Luther King Jr, resulted in the passing of the Voting Rights Act, 1965. The town of Selma was placed in the top five in a competition to find the prettiest painted places in the southeast USA.

Meaning divinely protected

Rochelle, Rochalla, Rochalle, Rochella, Rochette

The British S Club Junior member *Rochelle Wiseman* was born on this day in 1989. Nicknamed the Athletic Junior, she beat off fierce competition to win a coveted place in the child group, mentored by pop superstars S Club 7. She has three sisters: Jenny, Lauren and Emily.

Meaning small rock, stone

Santuccia, Santucci, Sante, Santo, Santi, Santarelli, Santilli, Santella, Santini, Santone

Today is the feast day of the Blessed *Santuccia Terrebotti*. The Italian nun, who lived in the latter part of the 12th century, became a Benedictine abbess and founded the Servants of Mary order.

Meaning sacristan

Orrin, Orin, Oran, Orren, Oren

The Republican US senator *Orrin Grant Hatch* was born on this day in 1934. As well as being a long-serving member of the Senate, Orrin Hatch is a noted composer, singer and songwriter, who wrote the song 'The Difference Makes the Difference' for his friend Muhammad Ali, the former boxer.

Meaning pale-skinned man

Artis, Artorious

The Latvian minister of foreign affairs *Artis Pabriks* was born on 22 March 1966. He is also a college rector and author of two books, *Latvia: Challenge of Change* (2001) and *The Baltic States: Estonia, Latvia and Lithuania* (2002).

Meaning courageous, noble

Glen, Glenn, Glynn

The Rhinestone Cowboy, *Glen Campbell*, was born in 1936 in Billstown, Arkansas. His father was a sharecropper, and Glen was one of 12 children. Among his best-known songs are 'Galveston' (1969) and 'Wichita Lineman' (1968).

Meaning from the valley

Zacharius, Zachary, Zachari, Zachee, Zack

On this day in 741 the Greek deacon *Zacharius* was elected pope. Because his correspondence with St Boniface survives, we know that he was a skilled and wise diplomat who wielded great influence in France and Germany.

Meaning God

Reese

Reese Witherspoon, the US actress, was born on 22 March 1976. In 2001 she starred in the film *Legally Blonde*, which was followed by *Legally Blonde II* (2003), movies that gained her the status of one of the highest paid Hollywood actresses. She has a daughter, Ava Elizabeth, and a son, Deacon Phillippe.

From Rhys, meaning ardour

Keira

British actress *Keira Knightley* was born on this day in 1985. Her appearance in the low-budget film *Bend It Like Beckham* (2002), which went on to be a major hit, led to roles in *Pirates of the Caribbean* (2003) and *Love Actually* (2003).

Meaning not known

Zaha

On 22 March 2004 the British-Iraqi architect *Zaha Hadid* was awarded the Pritzker prize for architecture, one of the most prestigious prizes in the field. She was the first woman to win this award and remains one of the most important female architects in the world.

Meaning not known

May, Maybritt, Maia

The actress *May Britt* was born Maybritt Wilkens in Lidingö, Sweden, on this day in 1933. She appeared in several Italian films in the 1950s, and married Sammy Davis Jr in 1960 at a time when interracial marriage was still forbidden in 31 of the US states.

Meaning May

23 MARCH

Damon, Damian, Damiano

Damon Albern, lead singer of the pop group Blur, was born on 23 March 1968. The album and single *Parklife* made Blur a central part of the Britpop explosion in the 1990s. They won awards for best band, best album, best single and best video at the 1995 Brit Awards.

Meaning tamer

Jurij, Jurgen, Jorin, Joris, Jorgen

Baron *Jurij Bartolomej Vega*, the Slovene mathematician, physicist and artillery officer, was born on this day in 1754. He is famous for his series of books of logarithm tables, but his major work, *The Treasury of All Logarithms*, was not published until 1974.

Meaning the farmer

Donald, Don, Donn, Donalt, Donaugh, Donnell, Donnie, Donny

Donald Campbell, the racing car driver and speedboat racer, was born on this day in 1921. In 1964 he became the first and only person to hold the world land speed record – 648.72kph (403.1mph) – and the world water speed record –444.7kph (276.33mph) – at the same time.

Meaning ruler of the world

Akira

Akira Kurosawa, the Japanese film director, was born in Tokyo on 23 March 1910. One of the most respected names in international cinema, among his many masterpieces is *Ran* (1985), a transposition of Shakespeare's *King Lear* to medieval Japan. In 1989 he received an Academy Award for lifetime achievement.

Meaning intelligent

Chaka, Chakra, Chakara, Shakra

Chaka Khan was born on 23 March 1953. The lead singer with the 1970s funk outfit Rufus was born Yvette Marie Stevens and brought up in the city of Chicago. After going solo, she recorded a cover of Prince's 'I Feel For You' (1984), which became an instant classic.

Meaning circle of energy

Hazel

The US star of stage musicals *Hazel Dawn* was born on this day in 1891. Her performance as Claudine in *The Pink Lady* (1911) brought her much acclaim when she sang 'My Beautiful Lady', while accompanying herself on the violin. She appeared in one film, *Margie* (1946).

Meaning Hazel tree

Pietra, Petrina, Petronia, Petronilla, Petronille, Perrine

Today is the birthday of *Sophie Eva Pietra Meloni*, the daughter of art film director Sherman Williams and US actor Christopher Meloni, star of the US TV series *Law and Order* (1990). Sophie was born in 2001.

Meaning rock, stone

Nicholle

The US actress *Nicholle Tom* celebrates a birthday today. She was born in Hinsdale, Illinois, on 23 March 1978. She plays Maggie Sheffield in the TV show *The Nanny* (1993). Her twin brother, David, and her sister, Heather, are also actors.

Meaning the people's victory

24

Harry, Hal, Harailt

On this day in 1874 *Harry Houdini* was born in Hungary as Erik Weisz. His upside-down escapes from straightjackets and vanishing elephants ensured his notoriety, as did his performances in silent movies. He had his own film company, the Houdini Picture Corporation.

Meaning From Harold, meaning army commander

Byron, Byram, Byran

The pianist *Byron Janis* was born on this day in 1928. In 1960 he became the first US artist to perform in the USSR. He has received countless honours, including the French Legion d'Honneur. He is married to Maria Cooper Janis, the daughter of actor Gary Cooper.

Meaning from the cottage, the bear

Joseph, Josiah, Juzef, Seosaidh, Jodu

US animator *Joseph Barbara* was born on 24 March 1911. With writer William Hanna, he created many memorable cartoon characters, including Yogi Bear and Quick Draw McGraw. One of their earliest creations, *Huckleberry House*, was the first cartoon to win an Emmy award.

Meaning God will increase

Hamlet

At the Academy Awards ceremony on this day in 1949 Lawrence Olivier won the best actor award for his performance in *Hamlet*, the movie version of Shakespeare's play. The film also won best picture of 1948. The role of Hamlet has long been seen as a benchmark in an actor's career.

Meaning small village

Olive, Olva, Livia, Nollie, Olivette

The South African writer *Olive Schreiner* was born on 24 March 1855. Her *Story of an African Farm* (1883) became one of the earliest feminist novels. It featured a heroine, called Lyndall, who lived on a remote ostrich farm, but still succeeded in controlling her own destiny.

Meaning symbol of peace

Lucia, Luciana, Lucida, Lacinia, Lucette, Lu, Luz

Lucia Chase, founding director of New York's American Ballet Theatre, was born on this day in 1907. Mikhail Baryshnikov was the artistic director of the company throughout the 1980s, and principal dancers have included Anton Dolin and Natalia Makarova.

Meaning bringer of light

Nivea, Niv, Ivea

The US singer *Nivea Hamilton* was born on 24 March 1982 in Atlanta, Georgia. Before becoming a solo artist, she was a lead vocalist with Mystical, singing on their multi-platinum, award-winning song 'Danger'.

Meaning snowy white

Keisha, Keesha, Keziah, Keishia, Kezia

When she was nominated for a best actress Oscar for her role as Paikea in *Whale Rider*, *Keisha Castle-Hughes* became the youngest actress ever to achieve the honour. She was born on this day in 1990 in Donnybrook, Western Australia, her dad Australian, her mum Maori. She was brought up in New Zealand.

Meaning cinnamon

25 MARCH

Lawrence, Larrance, Lars, Laurence, Laurent, Lauric, Lauritz, Lawrance, Lawry

David Lean, the director of *Lawrence of Arabia* (1962), was born in Croydon, near London, on this day in 1908. He made many admired films, including *In Which We Serve* (1942), which he co-directed with Noël Coward, *Brief Encounter* (1945) and *The Bridge on the River Kwai* (1957).

Meaning laurel crown

Elton

Flamboyant British singer songwriter *Elton John* was born Reginald Dwight on this day in 1947. With lyricist Bernie Taupin he has produced a string of hits, including 'Daniel', 'Rocket Man' and 'Candle in the Wind', which he sang, in modified form, at Princess Diana's funeral.

Meaning from the old farm

Titan, Toto, Titus

On this day in 1656 the Dutch astronomer Christian Huygens discovered the largest of Saturn's seven moons, *Titan*, so named by John Herschel in *Results of Astronomical Observations Made at the Cape of Good Hope* (1847).

Meaning giant

Bela

The Hungarian composer *Béla Bartók* was born on 25 March 1881 in Nagyszentmiklós (now Sinnicolau Mare, Romania). One of the founders of ethnomusicology (the study of music from non-Western cultures), he wrote much chamber and vocal music, as well as an opera, *Bluebeard's Castle* (1911), and two ballets, including *The Miraculous Mandarin* (1914–17).

Meaning white

Lark

The actress *Lark Voorhies* was born in Nashville, Tennessee, on 25 March 1974. Lark, a Jehovah's Witness, played Lisa Turtle in the TV show *Saved by the Bell* (1989), and has also appeared in the US TV soaps *The Bold and the Beautiful* (1987) and *Days of Our Lives* (1992).

Meaning bird

Gloria, Gloire, Glori, Gloriana, Gloriane, Glorianna, Glorianne, Glory

The US feminist writer *Gloria Steinem* was born in Toledo, Ohio, on this day in 1934. She founded several feminist groups and the magazine *Ms*. She was responsible for popularizing Irina Dunn's quote: 'A woman without a man is like a fish without a bicycle.'

Meaning glorious one

Simone, Simonetta, Simonette, Simona

The French actress *Simone Signoret* was born on 25 March 1921 in Wiesebaden, Germany. She won a best actress Oscar in 1949 for her performance in *Room at the Top* (1958). The singer Nina Simone took her stage name from the actress.

From Simon, meaning to hear, to be heard

Dula

Today is the feast day of *St Dula*, also known as Theodular. She was a virgin slave, martyred at Nicomedia in Asia Minor. She is the patron saint of maidservants.

Meaning pear

Tennessee, Tenysoon, Tenison, Tennison

The playwright *Tennessee Williams* was born on 26 March 1911 as Thomas Lanier Williams in Columbus, Mississippi. He also wrote novels, short stories and poetry. Among his best-known plays are *The Glass Menagerie* (1944) and *Cat on a Hot Tin Roof* (1955).

Meaning son of Dennis

Leigh, Lee, Bradley, Leroy

On this day in 1961 *Leigh Bowery* was born in a place called Sunshine, near Melbourne, Australia. An extravagant performance artist, he opened the best-known nightclub of the 1980s called Taboo, on which the West End play *Taboo* was based.

Meaning clearing, wood

Tristram

Tristram was an early pseudonym of British poet A.E. Housman, who was born on this day in 1859 in Fockbury, Worcestershire. His first writing appeared under this name in an Oxford undergraduate magazine, *Ye Rounde Table*. Housman is best known for his poem *A Shropshire Lad* (1896).

Meaning sorrowful one

Leonard, Leonhard, Leonid, Leonidas, Lonnard, Lenard

The US actor, film director, poet and photographer *Leonard Nimoy* was born in Boston, Massachusetts, on this day in 1931. Best known for his role as the half-Vulcan, half-human Spock in *Star Trek* (1969–71), his two autobiographies are catchily entitled *I am not Spock* (1977) and *I am Spock* (1995).

Meaning brave as a lion

Erica, Erika, Arik, Eric

Erica Jong, the US author, was born on this day in 1942. Her novel *Fear of Flying* (1973) was a landmark publication in feminist history. In it, Jong wrote in a revolutionary way about how women deal with their sexuality. Her later books have included *Fear of Fifty* (1994) and *Inventing Memory* (1997).

Meaning powerful ruler

Diana, Di, Deanna, Dee, Ddyanna, Dyane, Dyana, Dianne, Dianna, Diane, Dian, Diahann

Diana Ross was born on 26 March 1944. She began her career in the Primettes, which evolved into one of the greatest of all girl groups, the Supremes. They had 12 number one hits, peaking in September 1964 with 'Baby Love'. Diana went on to become a hugely successful solo star.

Meaning goddess of the moon and hunting

Miyoshi, Miya

On this day in 1958 a 22-year-old actress called *Miyoshi Umeki* won an Oscar for the best supporting actress for her role in the film *Sayonara*. She went on to star in *Flower Drum Song* (1961) and *A Girl Named Tamiko* (1962).

Meaning sacred house

Leeza, Leeze, Lezé

The US TV personality *Leeza Gibbons* was born on this day in 1957. The hostess of the multi-Emmy-nominated TV talk show *Leeza* (1994–2000), she works tirelessly for various children's and AIDs charities. She has a daughter, Alexis, and two sons, Troy and Nathan.

From Elizabeth, meaning consecrated to God

27 MARCH

Wilhelm, Wilkes, Wiley, Uilleam, Uilliam

Wilhelm Konrad von Roentgen, the physicist who discovered x-rays, was born on this day in 1845. He photographed objects hidden behind shields and finally part of his own skeleton using this new form of radiation. He called it x-radiation because so little was known about it.

Meaning determined protector

Quentin, Quent, Quintin, Quinton, Quintus

Quentin Tarantino, the movie director, was born on this day in 1963. He began by working in a video store and achieved his ambition when he directed one of the best cult movies, the Academy Award-winning *Pulp Fiction* (1994).

Meaning fifth born

Golo, Goloin, Gollwyn, Golly, Golochol, Godelieve

Today is the birthday of *Golo Mann*, son of the novelist Thomas Mann. Golo was a popular historian who published books from the 1940s to the 1970s. Thomas Mann won the Nobel Prize for literature in 1929, mainly for his epic novel *Buddenbrooks* (1901).

Meaning God's love

Cale, Caleb, Cal

The racing driver *Cale Yarborough* was born on this day in 1940. With three NASCAR national championships and four Daytona 500 wins to his credit, he is the fifth-best NASCAR driver of all times, with a total of 83 wins.

Meaning bold one

Sarah, Sara, Sarene, Sarette, Sari, Sarine, Sarita

The great jazz singer *Sarah Vaughan* was born on 27 March 1924. She was the singer's singer, the influence and inspiration for many other musicians. She had her first hit in 1947 with 'Tenderly'. In 1982 she won a Grammy for best jazz vocalist for *Gershwin Live*.

Meaning princess

Cherry, Cerios

On this day in 1912 the first *cherry* trees to be grown in the USA were planted in Washington. They were a present from Japan. The name Cherry was originally a derivation of the name Charity. Cerios, a later Welsh name, comes from the plant.

Meaning fruit tree

Mariah, Maria, Marie, Mariel, Marietta, Mariette, Marilla

Mariah Carey was born on this day in 1970. She was the only female artist to have had a number one song in the US charts every year in the 1990s. She was named after 'They Call the Wind Mariah', a song from the film *Paint Your Wagon* (1969).

From Mary, meaning bitter

Xuxa

Xuxa, the Brazilian film and TV star, was born Maria da Graca Xuxa Meneghul on this day in 1963. She hosts a long-running children's variety show, singing and dancing with her teen team, known as the Paquitas. She was a former girlfriend of Pelé, the legendary soccer star.

From Xerxes, meaning warrior

Dirk

The British actor Sir *Dirk Bogarde* was born Derek Jules Gaspard Ulric Niven van den Bogaerde on this day in 1921. His first leading role was in *Doctor in the House* (1954), and he went on to star in many films in the 1960s and 1970s. He also wrote a series of bestselling autobiographies.

From Derek, meaning ruler of the people

Raphael, Raffaello, Rafael, Rafe, Raff, Rafi

The Italian Renaissance painter and architect *Raphael* was born Raffaello Sanzio on this day in 1483. He is best known for his Madonnas and for his large frescoes in the Vatican in Rome.

Meaning healed by God

Maxim, Maximilian, Mamximiliano, Maxfield, Max, Maxey, Maxie, Maximilien, Maxy, Maxa, Maks, Maksim, Massimiliano

Maxim Gorky, the Russian author, was born Aleksei Maksimovich Peshkov on this day in 1868. He was a political activist and founder of the socialist realist literary school. He has had streets, a park, an aeroplane and the town of his birth named after him.

Meaning greatest

Aristide, Aristides

The French statesman *Aristide Briand* was born on 28 March 1862 in Nantes, France. He was a leading member of the French socialist party in the early 20th century, and he became prime minister in 1909. He was awarded the Nobel Prize for peace in 1926.

Meaning best kind

Reba, Riba, Riva

Reba McEntire, the US country singer and actress, was born on this day in 1955 in McAlester, Oklahoma. She was voted female vocalist of the year four times by the Country Music Association. She has a son, Shelby.

From Rebecca, meaning gentle

Rhoda, Rodina, Rhodia

The British artist *Rhoda Holmes Nicholls* was born in Coventry on this day in 1854. She was already well established in Europe when she moved to the US, where her watercolours were well received. She also taught and edited a magazine called *Palette & Brush*.

Meaning from Rhodes, garland of roses

Bernice, Berenice, Berny, Bernie, Bunny

Bernice King, the daughter of Coretta Scott King and Dr Martin Luther King Jr, was born on this day. She is an author, speaker, orator and ordained preacher. Her first speech was at the United Nations when she was just 17 years old.

Meaning herald of victory

Debbie, Debor, Debra, Devora, Debora

On this day in 1981 the New York pop band Blondie received a gold record for 'Rapture'. Blondie was one of the most successful groups of the late 1970s and early 1980s, and their lead singer, *Debbie Harry*, from whom the band took its name, remains a cultural icon.

From Deborah, meaning bee

29 ^{MARCH}

Edwin, Edd, Edlin, Eduino

The British architect Sir *Edwin Landseer Lutyens* was born in London on 29 March 1869. His greatest achievement was the laying out and building of New Delhi in India, but he also built many English country houses in his uniquely sophisticated but simple style.

Meaning prosperous friend

Albert, Ailbert, Aubert, Bert, Bertie, Aldabert, Berty, Delbert, Elbert

On this day in 1871 the *Royal Albert Hall* was opened in London. The circular building, affectionately known as the nation's village hall, is the venue for all manner of concerts and shows. It is dedicated to Queen Victoria's much-loved husband, Prince Albert.

Meaning illustrious, noble

Niall, Niell, Nels, Niels, Niles, Nils

The Irish actor *Niall MacGinnis* was born in Dublin on 29 March 1913. He appeared in many films from the 1930s through to the 1970s, including *Martin Luther* (1953), in which he took the title role, and *Jason and the Argonauts* (1963), in which he was Zeus.

From Neal, meaning champion

Elihu, Elias, Elijah, Eliot, Eliott, Ellis

The British inventor and electrical engineer *Elihu Thomson* was born in Manchester on this day in 1853. The inventor of the alternating current motor, he was instrumental in the founding of the General Electric Company in the USA and other major electrical companies in Britain and France.

Meaning the Lord is God

Pearl

African-American singer *Pearl Bailey* was born in Newport News, Virginia, on this day in 1918. She began singing in nightclubs in Washington D.C., Baltimore and New York, and then joined Cab Calloway's band before launching a solo career. She starred in many Broadway shows, including *St Louis Blues* in 1958 and *Porgy and Bess* in 1959.

Meaning pearl

Elle

Elle Macpherson, the Australian supermodel and actress, was born Eleanor Gow on this day in 1963. She has appeared in films, on the TV hit show *Friends*, runs her own successful lingerie business and was the first living person from show business to appear on an Australian stamp.

From Helen, meaning light

Regina, Regan, Reyna, Reine, Rina, Reina, Rain, Rane, Reyna, Rani, Raina

The US country singer *Regina Lee* was born on 29 March 1968. She was in Dave and Sugar, a group that had a number of hits in the 1970s, including 'The Door is Always Open' (1976), which won the CMA award for single of the year. It was the CMA vocal group of the year from 1976 to 1979.

Meaning queenly

Montana

On this day in 1994 *Montana Eve Hirsch* was born, the daughter of actor Judd Hirsch and his wife Bonni. Judd Hirsch is famous for his role as Alex in *Taxi* (1978–83), and later in his career he appeared in the movie *A Beautiful Mind* (2001).

Meaning mountain

Vincent, Vince, Vinny

The Dutch artist *Vincent van Gogh* was born on this day in 1853. One of the best-known and greatest painters in the history of European art, he made no money from his art when alive. Ironically, his painting *Irises* sold for a record $53.9 million on 30 March 1987, the anniversary of his birth.

From Victor, meaning conqueror

Warren, Warin, Wareine, Warrener, Waring

The US actor *Warren Beatty* was born Henry Warren Beaty on 30 March 1937 in Richmond, Virginia. As well as having appeared in many films, he is a multi-award-winning producer, screenwriter and director. He and his wife Annette Bening have four children: Kathlyn, Benjamin, Isabel and Ella Corinne.

Meaning warrior, game-keeper

Jethro

The British agricultural pioneer *Jethro Tull* was born on this day in 1674 in Basildon, Berkshire. He invented many agricultural tools, the most important being the seed drill in 1708. He also invented the horse-drawn hoe and modernized the plough.

Meaning excellent, without equal

Eric, Erik, Erick

The British guitar legend *Eric Clapton* was born Eric Patrick Clapp in Ripley, Surrey, on this day in 1945. In the 1960s he played in the Yardbirds and then the supergroup Cream before going solo. He has two daughters, Julia Rose and Ella May.

Meaning kingly

Akarova, Akarau, Akaru, Akarsani, Akaralyn, Akarisa, Akarino, Akarija

The Belgian dancer *Akarova* was born Marguerite Acarin on this day in 1904. The best-known Belgian dancer of the inter-war years, she did her own choreography, costumes, sets, lighting and even programmes. A film about her, *Akarova*, was made in 1991.

Meaning not known

Lene, Lenis, Lenata, Leninta, Lenta, Lenos

The US singer and songwriter *Lene Lovich* was born on 30 March 1954. She was an original and stylish performer on the British post-punk scene in the late 1970s, influencing artists like Bjork and P.J. Harvey. Her single 'Lucky Number' reached number three in the UK charts.

Meaning white as a lily

Norah, Nora

The US singer and songwriter *Norah Jones* was born on this day in 1979 in New York City and raised in Grapevine, Texas. Her 2003 album *Come Away with Me* sold 8 million copies in the USA alone and won her five Grammys, including those for album of the year and best new artist.

From Helen, meaning light

Jodie, Jody

On this day in 1989 *Jodie Foster* won an Oscar for her performance in the film *The Accused* (1988), directed by Jonathan Kaplan. She repeated the achievement just three years later when she received a second best actress award for playing FBI agent Clarice Starling in *The Silence of the Lambs* (1991).

From Judith, meaning admired, praised

31 MARCH

René, Renault, Renauld

René Descartes was born in France on this day in 1596. The founder of modern philosophy and the father of modern mathematics, he coined the phrase 'I think therefore I am' and invented the Cartesian co-ordinate system, a major cog in the development of modern calculus.

From Reginald, meaning mighty and powerful ruler

Nagisa

The US-based Japanese film director and writer *Nagisa Oshima* was born on 31 March 1932. Beginning in the 1950s he made many radical, politically aware films, including *A Town of Love and Hope* (1959) and *Taboo* (1996).

Meaning beach, waterside

Ewan, Evan, Evyn, Ewen, Avan, Owen

The Scottish actor *Ewan McGregor* was born in Crieff on this day in 1971. He has appeared in many films, including *Trainspotting* (1996) and *Shallow Grave* (1994). He motorcycled around the world in 2004, which led to his involvement with the charity UNICEF.

Meaning well-born young warrior

Andrew, Andie, Andy, Andre, Aindreas, Anders, Anderson, Andonis, Andrien

The English poet *Andrew Marvell* was born on 31 March 1621. He was the member of Parliament for Hull for 19 years from 1659 as well as being an important member of the metaphysical poetry movement. His famous poems include 'To His Coy Mistress' and 'The Garden'.

Meaning warrior

Fausta, Faustine

On 31 March 307 *Fausta*, the daughter of the Roman emperor Maximian, married the emperor Constantine the Great, who is known as the first Christian emperor. His leniency towards the new religion allowed it to spread throughout the Roman Empire.

Meaning fortunate

Liz, Lizzy, Lizzie, Lizbeta, Lizbeth

Liz Claiborne, the US fashion designer and business executive, was born in Brussels, Belgium, on this day in 1929. She concentrates on designing fashionable clothes that can be worn for work or leisure, and in 1980 she was named Entrepreneurial Woman of the Year.

From Elizabeth, meaning consecrated to God

Rhea, Rea

The US actress *Rhea Perlman* was born on 31 March 1948. She is best known for her role as Carla Tortelli in the TV sitcom *Cheers*. She is married to the actor Danny DeVito, and they have three children: Lucy, Gracie and Jake.

Meaning mother, poppy

Balbina, Balbine, Balbinia

Today is the feast day of *St Balbina*. She was a nun who lived in Rome in the 2nd century. She was the daughter of St Quirinus and is believed to be buried close to him in the Roman catacombs. She was baptized by St Alexander.

Meaning she who hesitates

April

April

Milan, Milano, Mila

Milan Kundera, the Czech author, was born on this day in 1927. His novel *The Unbearable Lightness of Being* (1984) brought him international acclaim. It was turned into an Oscar-nominated film (1987), starring Daniel Day-Lewis and Juliette Binoche.

Meaning beloved

Kiyonori, Kiyoshi

Kiyonori Kikutake was born on this day in 1928 in Fukuoka, Japan. One of the leading international figures in Japanese architecture, he is famous for his floating city, the Marine City Project. Floating systems remain one of his specialities.

Meaning purity

Ferrucio, Ferruco, Ferro

Ferruccio Busoni, the German-Italian composer, teacher and philosopher, was born on 1 April 1866. A child prodigy pianist, he grew up to be known as the Prophet of Electronic Music after his championing of the Dynamophone, a precursor of the modern-day synthesizer.

Meaning iron

Petrus, Petrie, Petri, Peto, Petor, Pyotr

On this day in 527 *Petrus Sabbaticus* was proclaimed by his uncle, the Roman Emperor Justin I, as his co-ruler and successor. Petrus was born in Auresina in the Balkans to Justin's sister, Vigilanta. He became emperor as Justinian I and married an actress called Theodora.

From Peter, meaning rock, stone

Ali, Allie, Alleye

Ali MacGraw was born on this day in 1938. She was a major film star in the 1970s, starring in *Love Story* (1970), *Goodbye Columbus* (1969) and *The Getaway* (1972). On the set of The Getaway she met actor Steve McQueen – they fell in love and got married.

From Alison, meaning truth

Wangari

Today is the birthday of *Wangari Muta Maathai*, who was born in Nyeri, Kenya, on 1 April 1940. The first East African woman to earn a PhD and the first African woman to receive the Nobel Prize for peace, she founded the Green Belt Movement, which has planted 12 million trees across Africa.

Meaning not known (Kikyu tribal name)

Venus, Vinny, Vinita, Venita

Today marks the beginning of the Roman festival of *Venus Verticorda*, which celebrated Venus, the goddess of love and beauty. Roman women would bathe themselves in the public bath-houses, adorn themselves with headdresses of myrtle leaves, wash all the statues of Venus and decorate them with flowers.

Meaning goddess of love and beauty

Cicely, Cecily, Cecilia

On this day in 1893 the British actress and singer *Cicely Esmeralda Courtneidge* was born in Sydney, Australia. Her father was Scottish and her mother was English. In the course of her long career she appeared in numerous productions on the West End stage. Her husband, actor and producer, Jack Hulbert, wrote her biography, *The Little Woman's Always Right*, in 1975.

Meaning not known

Emile, Emil, Emilio, Emlen, Emelen

Emile Zola, the French writer, was born on this day in 1840. Inspired by Charles Darwin, he founded the social reformist naturalism movement. As well as his novels, he is remembered for his intervention, *J'Accuse*, in the Dreyfus affair.

Meaning industrious

Max, Maxey, Maxy, Maxie, Maxa, Maks

Max Ernst, the German expressionist and surrealist painter, was born on this day in 1891. Ernst was one of the founders of both the dada and surrealist art movements. He was also inspirational in promoting abstract expressionism in the USA in the 1940s.

Meaning the greatest, without equal

Giovanni, Geovanni, Giovanny, Geovanny

The Italian librarian and philanderer *Giovanni Giacomo Casanova* was born in Venice on this day in 1725. As well his many female conquests, he met many celebrities, including Mozart, who was still unknown at the time. He also found time to be secretary to a cardinal, an abbé, a gambler, an alchemist and a violinist.

From John, meaning God has shown me favour

Halle, Haileigh, Haille, Haili, Haleigh, Hailley

On this day in 1930 *Haile Selassie* became emperor of Ethiopia. He attempted to Westernize his country and took it into the League of Nations, but he was deposed in 1974. He is revered by many groups, including Rastafarians, who refer to him as the Black Messiah, the saviour of all Africans.

Meaning hero

Emmylou, Emylou

Country music star *Emmylou Harris* was born on this day in 1947 in Birmingham, Alabama. She recorded her first album, *Gliding Bird*, in 1969. In 1980 'That Lovin' You Feeling Again' won a best vocal duo Grammy for the Emmylou and Roy Orbison partnership.

From Emily, meaning rival

Camille, Cammelia, Camella, Camile, Cammi, Cam, Camala, Camelia

Camille Paglia, the US academic and author, was born on this day in 1947. For many years she wrote for the popular on-line magazine www.salon.com. Her 1992 book *Sex, Art and American Culture* challenged the conventional views of femininsm and caused much controversy and discussion.

From Camilla, meaning noble, righteous

Jahanara, Janna

Jahanara Begum was born on this day in 1614. She was the beloved daughter of Shah Jahan of India and his wife Mumtaz Mahal. After her mother's death she became the most important woman in India. Besides being beautiful, she was artistic and kind to the poor.

Meaning paradise

Debralee, Deborahlee, Debraleigh

The film and TV actress *Debralee Scott* was born on this day in 1953. She was the star of the 1970s TV soap and sitcom *Mary Hartman Mary Hartman* and was also in *Angie* (1979), *Get Rich Quick* (1977) and *Welcome Back Kotter* (1975).

From Deborah, meaning bee

3 APRIL

Marlon, Merlin, Marl, Merl, Marlen

The US actor *Marlon Brando* was born on this day in 1924. His smouldering good looks and revolutionary method acting style made him a star in the 1950s, when he made *On the Waterfront* (1954). His most memorable roles were in *The Godfather* (1972) and *Last Tango in Paris* (1972).

Meaning falcon

Washington

The US author *Washington Irving* was born on this day in 1783. He wrote biographies and the short story 'Rip Van Winkle'. His first book was *A History of New York from the Beginning of the World to the End of the Dutch Dynasty, by Dietrich Knickerbocker* (1809).

Meaning from the estate of the wise one

Lawton, Laughton, Lawry, Lawler, Lawley, Lawford, Loring

The US politician *Lawton Mainor Chiles* was born in Polk County, Florida, on this day in 1930, and from 1991 to 1998 he was the 41st governor of the state. In 1970 he undertook a 1,615-kilometre (1,003-mile) walk across Florida, earning him the nickname Walkin' Lawton.

Meaning laurel crown

Icon Eyes

Today is the birthday of *Icon Eyes Cody*. The Cherokee actor became famous as the Crying Indian after he appeared on an anti-pollution commercial with a tear in his eye. He was actually an Italian-Sicilian, born Espera DeCorti in Louisiana, so Espera (meaning hope) would be a more suitable name for a child born on this day.

Meaning not known

Doris, Dorris, Dorise, Dorita, Dorice, Dora

The US actress and singer *Doris Day* was born Doris Mary Anne von Kappelhoff on 3 April 1924. She had 11 Top 20 albums and more than 50 hit singles, the most enduring being 'Que Sera Sera'. She works tirelessly for animal welfare.

Meaning from the sea

Zelda, Selda, Griselda, Griselde, Grizelda, Grishelde, Grishilda

On this day in 1920 *Zelda Sayre* married US writer F. Scott Fitzgerald. She was a dancer, painter and writer, and a major influence on Fitzgerald's work. Her high spirits and carefree attitude epitomized the Jazz Age flapper. They had a son, Scottie.

Meaning grey heroine

Sandrine, Sandrina, Sandrene, Sandrena

The French tennis star *Sandrine Testud* was born in Lyons on this day in 1972. She was ranked 13 in the world in 1997, but in 2002 she caused a major upset when she defeated number one seed Venus Williams to reach the final of the Dubai Open Era.

From Alexandra, meaning helper of mankind

Agape, Irene, Chionia

Today is the feast day of the sisters *St Agape, St Irene* and *St Chionia*. During the persecution of Emperor Maximian, they hid in the mountains of Thessalonika, living a life of prayer. When they were brought before the magistrate, they refused to eat food that had been offered to idols. They were burned.

Meaning love, peace and white as snow

Heath

The actor *Heath Ledger* was born Heath Andrew Ledger on 4 April 1979 in Perth, Western Australia. He has starred in many movies, including *The Patriot* (2001) and *A Knight's Tale* (2001). In 2003 he was named one of Australian *GQ* magazine's men of the year.

Meaning heathland

Muddy

The father of Chicago blues, *Muddy Waters* was born McKinley Morganfield on this day in 1915 in Rolling Fork, Mississippi. His music was a huge influence on rock, folk, jazz and country music, and the Rolling Stones took their name from one of his songs.

Meaning muddy

Graham, Graeme

The Irish TV host *Graham Norton* was born on this day in 1963. His openly camp humour and off-beat celebrity interview style, often incorporating the internet, together with his involvement of audience members, have made his shows unique and successful on both sides of the Atlantic.

Meaning from the grey lands

Aki

Aki Kaurismuki, the Finnish writer and film director, was born in Orimattila, Finland, on this day in 1957. He won the Cannes Grand Prix in 2002 for *The Man without a Past* (2002). He also owns several restaurants and a hotel-restaurant in the Helsinki area.

Meaning autumn

Maya, Mea, Kam, Kammie, Kamaya, Kamea

Dr *Maya Angelou*, the bestselling US author, was born Marguerite Johnson in St Louis on this day in 1928. She is a poet, educator, historian, actress, playwright, civil rights activist, producer and director. Her autobiography has the unforgettable title, *I Know Why the Caged Bird Sings* (1970).

Meaning illusion

Theodora, Theadora, Teodora, Teodore, Thea, Theadosia, Theda

On this day in 527 *Theodora* became empress of Byzantium. The wife of Emperor Justinian, she was a powerful yet sensual woman, and a pioneer in the enforcement of rights for women.

Meaning gift of God

Marguerite, Margueritta, Margharita, Margette, Margetta, Margerita

The French writer *Marguerite Duras* was born on 4 April 1914 in Gia Dinh, Indochina. Her best-known work is the autobiographical *L'Amant* (The Lover) (1984), which won France's prestigious literary award, the Prix Goncourt. It has been translated into 40 languages and was made into a film in 1991.

From Margaret, meaning pearl

Dorothea, Dorele, Dorota, Drottya, Dosia

On this day in 1802 the US humanitarian and social reformer *Dorothea Lynde Dix* was born in Hampden, Maine. She was a tireless campaigner for prison reform, stressing the need for education and care of the mentally ill. In the Civil War she was a superintendent of women nurses in the army.

From Dorothy, meaning gift of God

Spencer, Spenser, Spence

The US film actor *Spencer Bonaventure Tracy* was born on 5 April 1900 in Milwaukee, Wisconsin. He had two children, John and Louise (Susie). In 1941 he began a relationship with Katharine Hepburn that he was to sustain for the rest of his life. They made nine films together.

Meaning provider

Booker

Booker Taliaferro Washington was born into slavery in Franklin County, Virginia, on this day in 1856. He rose from illiteracy to assume the position of president of Tuskegee College, which he turned into the best college for African-Americans in the USA. He was the first black person to appear on a US postage stamp.

Meaning beech tree

Herbert, Harbert, Hebert, Heriberto, Hoireabard

Herbert von Karajan, the great Austrian conductor, was born on 5 April 1908 in Salzburg to a Romanian family with Greek roots. He was chief conductor of the Berlin Philharmonic for many years and lent his name to the development of the compact disc.

Meaning brilliant fighter

Elihu, Elias, Elijah

Elihu Yale, the first benefactor of Yale University, was born in Boston, Massachusetts, on this day in 1649. He was taken to England in 1652 and never returned to America. His fortune came from the British East India Company, and his original donation to the university amounted to £560, a large sum in those days.

Meaning the Lord is God

Irene, Irena, Irinia, Irenna, Erena, Eirene

Today is the feast day of *St Irene*. She ruled the Byzantine Empire on the death of her husband, Leo IV, and summoned the Second Nicene Council, which defined the veneration that might be shown to images. She was eventually deposed and exiled to the island of Lesbos.

Meaning peace

Aliza, Aliezo, Alizah, Aleeza, Aliezah, Alitza

Aliza Kashi, the Israeli actress and singer, was born on this day in 1940. She had a hit with her record 'Born Free' (1967) and was a regular on the *Merve Griffiths* TV show.

Meaning joyful

Bette, Betta, Betty, Betina, Betsy, Bessie, Bessy, Bess

The US film star *Bette Davis* was born in Lowell, Massachusetts, on this day in 1908. She was nominated for an Oscar for her performance in *Now Voyager* (1942), and in 1977 she became the first woman to receive the American Film Institute's lifetime achievement award. She wrote her life story in *The Lonely Life* (1962) and *Mother Goddam* (1975).

From Elizabeth, meaning consecrated to God

Agnetha, Agneta

The Swedish singer *Agnetha Faltskog* was born in Jonkoping on this day in 1950. She was in Abba, one of the most commercially successful pop acts of all time, which won the Eurovision Song Contest in 1974 with 'Waterloo'. She has recorded several albums as a soloist.

From Agnes, meaning pure, chaste

André, Andreas, Andrej, Andras

The pianist, conductor and composer *André Previn* was born Andreas Ludwig Priwin on 6 April 1929 in Berlin. His family emigrated to the USA when he was nine. He was the conductor of the LA Philharmonic and the London Symphony Orchestra, among others, and has composed numerous film scores and musicals.

From Andrew, meaning warrior

James, Jamie, Jim, Jock

James Dewey Watson, the co-discoverer of DNA, was born on this day in 1928. He and Francis Crick made their discovery in 1952 at the Cavendish Laboratory in Cambridge. They were awarded the Nobel Prize for physiology or medicine in 1962.

From Jacob, meaning supplanter

Lowell, Lovel, Lowe, Lovell

Lowell Thomas, the pioneering film-maker and broadcaster, was born on this day in 1892 in Woodington, Ohio. In the 1920s he filmed Lawrence of Arabia, and he also filmed the battlefields of the First World War. In the 1930s his NBC radio daily newscasts from around the world were required listening.

Meaning beloved one

Butch

The US outlaw *Butch Cassidy* was born Robert Leroy Parker in Beaver, Utah, on this day in 1866. He was a rancher, who, as leader of the Wild Bunch, robbed banks and trains. Many historians believe his intentions were honourable, dubbing him the Robin Hood of the West.

From Berton, meaning brilliant one's estate

Isolde, Iseult, Isoda, Ysold, Ysolda, Yseult, Eysllt, Isold

In Poland it is the name day for *Isolde*. The name was common in Europe until the 16th century, and it was revived after Richard Wagner's opera *Tristan und Isolde* (1859) became popular at the end of the 19th century.

Meaning fair one

Candace, Candice, Candida, Candy, Candie

The US actress *Candace Cameron* was born in Panama City on 6 April 1976. Her first major role was in the TV series *St Elsewhere* in the 1980s, and she then went on to star as D.J. Tanner in *Full House* (1987). She is married to the hockey player Valeri Bure, and they have three children.

Meaning brilliant white

Marilu, Marylou

The US actress and author *Marilu Henner* was born on this day in 1952. She starred in many plays and TV shows, including playing the role of Roxie Hart in the Broadway run of *Chicago* (1997). She created the Total Health Makeover, and her many books include *Healthy Kids* (1993) and *I Refuse to Raise a Brat* (1994).

From Mary, meaning bitter, and Louis, meaning famous warrior

Felicity, Felicita, Flick

On this day in 1944 the British singer *Felicity Palmer* was born in Cheltenham, Gloucestershire. She made her opera debut as Dido in 1971 and subsequently sang all over the world. She specialized in French songs, especially those of Messiaen and Poulenc.

Meaning good fortune

Ford, Bradford, Crawford

Francis Ford Coppola was born on 7 April 1939. The US film director, screenwriter, vintner and hotelier is famous for *The Godfather* trilogy of films (1972, 1974, 1990) and for *Apocalypse Now* (1979). The multi-Oscar winner runs resorts in Guatemala and Belize.

Meaning river crossing

Ravi

Ravi Shankar, the Indian sitar master, was born on this day in 1920. He became famous in the West after his meeting with George Harrison of the Beatles in the 1960s. He has written concertos for sitar and orchestra, as well as pieces for ballets, films and artists, including Yehudi Menuhin and Hosan Yamomoto.

Meaning sun

Wordsworth

The British poet *William Wordsworth* was born in Cockermouth, Cumberland, on this day in 1770. His most famous poem, 'Daffodils', begins: 'I wandered lonely as a cloud, that floats on high o'er vales and hills, when all at once I saw a crowd, a host of golden daffodils.'

Meaning from the wolf's farm

Story

On this day in 1983 the US astronaut *Story Musgrave* performed the first space shuttle walk on the maiden voyage of the space shuttle *Challenger*. He is a veteran astronaut of six missions, spending a total of 1,281 hours, 59 minutes and 22 seconds in space.

From Storr, meaning great man

Billie, Billy, Willa, Willette, Wilmette, Wyla, Mina, Minnie, Minny

The great US jazz singer *Billie Holiday* was born Eleanora Fagan in Philadelphia on 7 April 1915. Her mother, Sadie, was only 13 years old when she gave birth to Billie, and her father, the jazz guitarist Clarence Holiday, was just 15. She was played by Diana Ross in the film of her life, *Lady Sings the Blues* (1972).

Meaning desiring to defend

Aisha, Ashia

On this day in 1975 *Aisha Wonder*, Stevie Wonder's daughter, was born. He wrote his moving song 'Isn't She Lovely' about Aisha. Her name and the meaning of her name are mentioned in the song, and she can be heard crying at the beginning.

Meaning life

Netta, Nettie

The date 7 April 1969 is widely regarded as the symbolic birthday of the *Internet*. It began as ARPANET, the US Department of Defense net for ARPA (Advanced Research Projects Agency), working on decentralized networks, queuing theory and packet switching.

From Henrietta, meaning ruler of the home

Gabriela, Gabrielle Gabriella, Gabrila, Gabriele

The Chilean poet, diplomat and teacher *Gabriela Mistral* was born Lucila Godoy de Alcayaga in Vicuña in 1889. In 1915 she published *Sonetos de la muerte* (Sonnets of Death), and she was awarded the Nobel Prize for literature in 1945.

Meaning woman of God

Hywel, Hywell, Howell

The Welsh actor *Hywel Bennett* was born in Garnant on this day in 1944. He was at the National Theatre for five years before moving into films. Two of his best-known film performances are in *The Family Way* (1968) and *The Virgin Soldiers* (1970).

Meaning little alert one

Clint, Clinton

On 8 April 1986 the film star *Clint Eastwood* was voted mayor of Carmel, California, and he served for two years. The Oscar-winning actor and film director has his own film production company. He has been married twice and has seven children by five different women.

Meaning from the farm on the headland

Siddhartha, Sidd

Today is said to be the birthday of the Buddha, who was born Prince *Siddhartha* in 563BC to Queen Mahamaya in a park in Lumbini, southern Nepal. A pillar placed in the park by an Indian emperor in 3BC still stands. There are over 350 million followers of his teachings throughout the world.

Meaning supremely enlightened teacher

Kofi

The seventh secretary general of the United Nations, *Kofi Atta Annan* was born on 8 April 1938 in Kumasi, Ghana. He was a twin, with a sister called Efua. In 1962 he worked for the World Health Organization, then director of tourism in Ghana from 1974 to 1976.

Meaning born on a Friday

Dorothy, Dorothea, Dorothoe, Dorete, Dorota, Drottya, Dosia, Thea, Dot, Dottie, Dotty, Dora, Dory, Dorothi, Dorothoe, Theodora

On this day in 1930 the British actress *Dorothy Tutin* was born in London. She has appeared in many classical and modern plays, playing Queen Victoria in *Portrait of a Queen* (1965). Among her many films are *The Importance of Being Earnest* (1952) and *An Awfully Big Adventure* (1995).

Meaning God is gift

Vivienne, Viv, Vivia, Vivi, Vivyan, Vyvyan, Viviana, Viviane, Vivie, Vivien, Vivienna

The British fashion designer *Vivienne Westwood* was born Vivienne Isabel Swire in Glossop, Derbyshire, on this day in 1941. In the mid-1970s she and Malcolm McLaren designed punk outfits, which they sold in their shop in the King's Road, London. She has two sons, Ben and Joseph.

Meaning lively

Rachel, Rachael, Rachelle, Rachele, Raquel, Rahel, Rae, Raoghnailt

The British singer *Rachel Stevens* was born Rachel Lauren Stevens on this day in 1978. Once part of the group S Club 7, later S Club, she has since become a solo artist and actress.

Meaning innocent as a lamb

Ilka, Ica, Ilona

The US actress and writer *Ilka Chase* was born in New Jersey on this day in about 1903. She appeared in 21 films and wrote novels and travel books. She also hosted a popular radio show for women called *Luncheon at the Waldorf.*

Meaning flattering, light

9 APRIL

Sibrand, Sbot, Siboto, Sibragtus, Sibrant, Sibratus, Siccard, Siboldus, Sibot

The Dutch physician and chemist *Sibrand Acker Stratingh* was born on this day in 1785. In 1835 he produced the world's first electrical car, which didn't run on rails.

Meaning not known

Eadweard, Eduard, Edouard

Eadweard Muybridge, the pioneering British photographer, was born in Kingston-on-Thames on this day in 1830. He used multiple cameras, up to as many as 50, to capture movement in photographs, the best known being a series of a galloping horse.

From Edward, meaning prosperous guardian

Seaborn, Seabert, Seabright, Sebert

The US composer *Seaborn McDaniel Denson* was born in Arbacoochee, Alabama, on this day in 1854. With his brother Thomas he changed the face of American traditional Sacred Harp singing, setting up the Sacred Harp Publishing Company in the 1930s.

Meaning sea glorious

Isambard, Isenham

Isambard Kingdom Brunel, the British engineer, was born in Portsmouth on 9 April 1806. He built the Great Western Railway and many famous steamships. On his birthday the sun is said to shine all the way through the Box Tunnel of the Great Western Railway.

Meaning glittering iron

Ednita, Edna, Edny

The Puerto Rican singer and actress *Ednita Nazario* was born on this day in 1957. A celebrated recording star in her own country since the 1970s, in 1999 she appeared in the USA, starring in Paul Simon's Broadway show *Capeman*.

Meaning delight, pleasure

Leigh, Leah

Gillian Leigh Anderson, the US actress best known for her role as the FBI agent Dana Scully in the hit TV science-fiction series *The X-Files* (1998) was born on this day in Chicago in 1968. Her later films include *The Life and Opinions of Tristram Shandy, Gentleman* (2005) and *The Mighty Celt* (2005).

Meaning from the meadow

Marian, Mariana, Mariom, Maryanne

On this day in 1939 the African-American opera singer *Marian Anderson* sang 'God Bless America' on the steps of the Washington Lincoln Memorial. The concert was arranged by the first lady, Eleanor Roosevelt, after Marian had been banned from singing in a concert by the Daughters of the American Revolution.

Meaning graceful

Caryn, Carine, Caitrin, Catalina, Caterina, Caireen, Caitlin

The US actress *Caryn Richman* was born on this day in 1959. She played Gidget, the wife of Moondoggie, in the 1960s cult TV show *Gidget*. She was also in the long-running US TV soap *The Young and the Restless* (1973).

From Catherine, meaning pure maiden

Omar

Omar Sharif, the Egyptian actor and bridge player, was born on this day in 1932. He rode a camel into international stardom and women's imaginations in *Lawrence of Arabia* (1962). His performance in *Dr Zhivago* (1965) won him a Golden Globe.

Meaning first son, follower of the prophet

Ricky, Rick, Rickie, Ritch, Ritchie, Riocard

On this day in 1940 the Welsh singer *Ricky Valance* was born in Ynysddu. He became the first Welsh artist to have a number one record when 'Tell Laura I Love Her' topped the charts in 1960 and sold over a million copies. He is not to be confused with La Bamba singer Ritchie Valens.

Meaning wealthy, powerful

Montague, Montagu, Monty, Monte

The British author *Montague Summers* was born on this day in 1880. He was a clergyman who wrote books about vampires and werewolves, including *The History of Witchcraft and Demonology* (1926), and, most famously, translated the witch-hunting manual *Malleus Maleficarum*.

Meaning from the jagged mountain

Cosimo, Cosmo, Cosme, Cosmé

The Italian financier and philanthropist *Cosimo di Giovanni de' Medici* was born on this day in 1389. He was the first of the Medici political dynasty, which ruled Florence throughout the Renaissance. He brought Florence, Venice and Milan together, creating peace in northern Italy.

Meaning perfect order of the universe

Clare, Claire, Clara

On this day in 1903 the US playwright *Clare Luce Boothe* was born in New York City. She was managing editor of the magazine *Vanity Fair* in 1933–4, and her plays included *The Women* (1916) and *Margin for Error* (1939). She became US ambassador to Italy from 1953 to 1957.

Meaning famous

Mandy, Mandie, Manda

The US pop singer and actress *Mandy Moore* was born in Nashu, New Hampshire, on this day in 1984. She released her first single, 'Candy' (1999), when she was 15 years old. She played Lana, the cheerleader, in the film *The Princess Diaries* (2001).

From Amanda, meaning worthy of being loved

Katrina, Katrin, Katrine, Katryn

Katrina Leskanich of Katrina and the Waves was born on this day in 1959. The group had a big hit in 1985 with 'Walking on Sunshine', later covered by Dolly Parton. In 1997 they won the Eurovision Song Contest with 'Love Shine a Light'. Her autobiography is *Don't it Feel Good* (2005).

From Katherine, meaning pure maiden

Michiko, Michi

On April 10 1959 *Michiko Shoda* married the future emperor of Japan, Akihito, and became the first commoner to marry into the Japanese imperial family. She raised her three children, the Princes Naruhito and Akishino and Princess Nori.

Meaning child of beauty, the righteous way

11

Joel

Broadway icon *Joel Grey* was born on this day in Ohio in 1932. He was the tuxedoed, white-faced MC of the Kit Kat Club in the film *Cabaret* (1972) and the cuckolded husband Amos Hart in *Chicago* (1996), in which he sang the show-stopping number 'Mr Cellophane'.

Meaning the Lord is God

Sony

Masaru Ibuka was born on 11 April 1908. He was the co-founder of a little post-war recording company, which grew into the electronics giant *Sony* Corporation. The name comes from the Latin word *sonus*, which means sound, and Sonny was a trendy name for boys in Japan in the 1940s.

Meaning son of sound

Gervase, Ger, Jervis, Jarvis, Jervoise, Jarv, Jarvey

Gervase de Peyer, the world's most recorded clarinettist, was born in London on this day in 1926. The principal clarinettist of the London Symphony Orchestra for 17 years, he did much to popularize the instrument. In 1992 he founded the Melos Symphonia of Washington.

Meaning spear vassal

Emmett, Emmit, Emmott, Emmot, Emmy

Emmett Ashford was born on 11 April 1914. He made baseball history in 1966 when he became the first African-American to umpire in the majors. Vice-president Hubert Humphrey was in the Washington crowd of 44,468 to see Cleveland win 5–2 against the Senators.

Meaning hard-working ant

Gemma

Today is the feast day of *St Gemma Galgani*, who was born in Tuscany in 1878. Gemma wanted to become a nun, but was too ill, eventually becoming paralysed. The Angel Gabriel cured her by a miracle. A very modern saint, Gemma has a website, www.stgemma.com.

Meaning gem

Cerys

Cerys Matthews, the lead singer of the Welsh band Catatonia, was born on this day in 1969. Over a period of ten years Catatonia produced four hit albums and several singles. Cerys's first solo album, *Cockahoop* (2004), was co-produced in Nashville by Bob Dylan.

Meaning love

Godeberta, Godeberthe, Godberta, Godbertha, Gode, Godecin

It is the feast day today of *St Godeberta of Noyon*, a French abbess who lived in the 7th century. She eschewed a life of luxury to take the veil. She performed a miracle when she extinguished a fire by making the sign of the Cross. She is the patron saint of drought relief, of epidemics and of the town of Noyon.

Meaning not known

Cleotha, Otha

Cleotha Staples, the daughter of Pops Staples, was born in Drew, Mississippi, on this day in 1935. The Staples Singers with Pops and his children, Pervis, Cleotha and Mavis, were a famous gospel group with many hits, including 'Respect Yourself' (1971) and 'I'll Take You There' (1972).

From Cleopatra, meaning glory of the father

Al, Alwin, Alvin, Alvan, Alwyn

The US singer *Al Jarreau* was born on 12 April 1940 in Milwaukee, Wisconsin. His beautiful voice was first heard in his local church, where he sang in the choir. He has won five Grammy awards, the only singer to receive awards in the rhythm and blues, pop and jazz categories.

Meaning friend of all

Scott, Scottie, Scotty, Scot

Scott Turow was born in Chicago on this day in 1949. The author of such blockbusters as *Presumed Innocent* (1987) and *The Burden of Proof* (1990), he taught creative writing at Stanford before training in law. He was Chicago's assistant attorney, presiding over several high-profile cases.

Meaning tattooed warrior, from Scotland

Cassidy, Cass, Cassy

David Cassidy was born on 12 April 1950. The 1970s TV show *The Partridge Family* made him a teen idol. He became a solo artist, attracting Beatlemania-type attention wherever he went. He remains an actor and a singer, recording and appearing in Las Vegas and on Broadway.

Meaning curly haired, ingenious

Vince, Vinnie, Vin

The country music singer *Vince Gill* was born on this day in 1957 in Norman, Oklahoma. He got his big break on the road to fame in 1989 with the hit single 'When I Call Your Name', and since then he has become one of the most popular artists in the genre. In 2004 he received a Grammy for the best male country vocal performance.

From Victor, meaning the conqueror

Mollie, Moya

Mollie Moore Davis, the US poet and editor, was born on this day in 1844 at Talladega, Alabama. She edited a literary magazine, *Picayune*, which made her a leading social and literary light in Houston and, later, in New Orleans.

From Mary, meaning bitter

Tama

The US author *Tama Janowitz* was born on 12 April 1957. Her collection of short stories, *Slaves of New York* (1986), made her one of the leading figures of the thriving 1980s New York arts scene. With Bret Easton Ellis and Jay McInerney, she was part of the literary brat pack.

Meaning jewel

Montserrat, Monserrat

Spain's greatest living soprano, *Montserrat Caballé* was born on 12 April 1933. In 1965 she became an overnight sensation in New York when she sang in Donizetti's *Lucrezia Borgia*. She was great friends with the band Queen's Freddie Mercury, and they recorded a hit album together.

Meaning jagged mountain, monastery

Cerealia, Ceres, Cerelia, Cerelie, Cerellia

Today was the first day of an ancient Roman holiday called *Cerealia*, the games of Ceres. It lasted for seven days and was in honour of Ceres, the goddess of motherly love and growing plants, especially grain.

Meaning spring-like

13 APRIL

Seamus

The Irish poet *Seamus Heaney* was born on this day in 1939. One of the most important literary figures of the 20th century, he won the Nobel Prize for literature in 1995. Such a frenzy for tickets breaks out when he is about to give a 'live' reading that his fans are nicknamed Heanyboppers.

Meaning supplanter

Gary, Garry, Gari, Garey, Gare

The chess grandmaster *Gary Kasparov* was born Garri Weinstein on this day in 1963 at Baku, Azerbaijan. Champion from 1985 to 2000, four years later he remained the strongest player in the world. Kasparov is the Slavicized version of his mother's maiden name, Kasparian.

Meaning spearman

Arron, Aeron

Today is the birthday of *Arron Asham*, the Canadian hockey player, who was born on 13 April 1978 in Portage la Prairie, Manitoba. He plays forward for the New York Islanders in the US National Hockey League.

Meaning mountain of strength

Guadalupe, Lupe

The Mexican boxer *Lupe Pintor* was born in Cuajimalpa on this day in 1955. He boxed from 1974 until 1995, losing only 14 times, drawing twice and winning 56 times. After he retired he opened a boxing school in Mexico City.

Meaning river of black stones

Romola, Roma, Romella, Romelle, Romula

The queen of France *Caterina Maria Romola de' Medici*, better known as Catherine de' Medici, wife of Henry II, was born in Italy on 13 April 1519. In the 1550s she changed the course of fashion when she banned thick waists at court, bringing in the cult of the corset.

Meaning lady of Rome

Eudora, Eudore

Eudora Welty, the author of the American South, was born on this day in 1909 in Jackson, Mississippi. The internet e-mail program, Eudora, is named after her. Its creator, Steve Dorner, was reading her short story 'Why I Live at the PO' when he was building the system.

Meaning good gift

Page

Page Hannah was born on April 13 1964. The film and TV actress appeared in the US TV drama *Fame* (1986–7) and in the daytime drama *Search for Tomorrow* (1975). Her older sister is famed actress Darryl Hannah and her uncle is the cinematographer Haskell Wexler.

Meaning page to a lord

Nella, Nela, Nila

Nella Larsen, the African-American writer, was born in Chicago on this day in 1893. The novelist and activist is associated with the explosion of African-American literature and art in the Harlem district of New York, which came to be known as the Harlem Renaissance era.

Meaning from the Nile

Noah, Noam, Noach, Noe, Noa

On this day in 1828 US lexicographer *Noah Webster* published his two-volume *An American Dictionary of the English Language*. Webster made it his life's work to standardize the spelling and grammar throughout the USA and to make American English distinct from the language spoken in Britain.

Meaning peaceful, restful, wanderer

Akbar

One of India's finest classical musicians, *Ali Akbar Khan* was born on this day in 1922. Known as the Indian Johann Sebastian Bach, he plays an instrument called a sarode, which has 25 strings. He is revered equally for his playing techniques and for his compositions.

Meaning powerful

Cadaroc, Caddock, Caddoc, Cadawg

Today is the feast day of *St Cadaroc of Llandaff*, who was born in Brycheiniog, Wales, in the late 11th century. He looked after Prince Rhys's greyhounds and was a court harpist before becoming a monk. He was wonderful with animals and had a healing touch.

Meaning battle-sharp

Morton, Morten

Morton Subotnick, the US composer, was born on this day in 1993 in Los Angeles, California. Since writing 'Silver Apples of the Moon' in 1967, he has been at the forefront of innovative composition, often incorporating interactive computer music systems into his work.

Meaning from the farm on the moor

Storm

Today is the birthday of *Storm Brieann Sixx*, the daughter of Nikki Sixx, bass player with the Mötley Crüe. Storm was born on April 14 1994. Mötley Crüe had many hit albums in the 1980s, peaking with *Dr Feelgood* (1989), which reached number one in the pop charts.

Meaning tempest

Aprile

US soprano *Aprile Millo* was born on this day in 1958. In 1986 she sang the title role in Verdi's *Aida* in the Emmy-winning New York production. She then toured with the opera in Europe and South America. She has made several CDs, including *Presenting Aprile Millo* (1986).

From April, meaning the beginning of spring

Sonja, Sonia, Sonya

Sonja Kristina, singer with 1970s UK rock band Curved Air, was born on this day in 1949. She was one of the few women to be seen on stage in the 1970s progressive rock era. Sonja has since become a solo artist. Her CD *Cri de Coeur* was released in 2003.

From Sophia, meaning wisdom

Buffy, Buffee, Buffey, Buffie, Buffye

It is the birthday today of the actress Sarah Michelle Gellar of TV series *Buffy the Vampire Slayer* (1997) fame, who was born in New York City on 14 April 1977. She has starred in many movies, including *Scooby Doo* (2000), and was voted woman of the year in 2002 by *Glamour* magazine.

Meaning buffalo, from the plains

15 APRIL

Leonardo, Leonhard, Leonid, Leonidas, Lonnard

Leonardo da Vinci, artist, sculptor, theorist, inventor, anatomist and natural historian – the ultimate Renaissance man – was born on this day in 1452. He didn't learn Latin until he was 40, and this freedom from medieval thought enabled him to see the world in a unique and original way.

Meaning brave as a lion

Matthew, Mathew, Mathias, Matthias, Mattias, Matt, Mattison, Mathe, Matty, Mattie, Matt, Mat, Mats, Mate, Mata, Matyas, Massey

On this day in 1729 J.S. Bach's *St Matthew Passion* received its first performance in Leipzig. It was one of the many cantatas that Bach composed for holy days, and his music so distils the beauty and mystery of Christianity that he is sometimes called the Fifth Evangelist in Germany.

Meaning gift of God

Émile, Emil, Emlyn, Emlen, Emilio, Emelen

On this day in 1858 *Émile Durkheim*, the founder of modern sociology, was born in Epinal, France. He believed that it was possible to explain social phenomena by applying a rigorous methodology rather than simply looking at society in terms of a collection of individuals.

Meaning industrious

Bliss

The Canadian poet *William Bliss Carman* was born on this day in 1861 in Fredericton, New Brunswick. He was the best-known poet in Canada in his lifetime, publishing many volumes of verse.

Meaning joyful one

Millicent, Milissent, Milisent, Mellicent, Melisenda, Melisandra, Melsandra

Millicent Washburn Shinn, the US child psychologist, was born on this day in 1858. She worked in journalism, becoming a magazine editor by the time she was 25, but then went on to further education. Her most popular book was *The Biography of a Baby* (1900).

Meaning strong, industrious

Uta

On this day in 1996 the 25th Boston marathon was won by *Uta Pippig* of Germany in 2 hours, 27 minutes and 12.6 seconds. She also won in 1994 and 1996. She won the New York City marathon in 1993, the only German to do so, and the Berlin races in 1990, 1992 and 1995.

Meaning rich

Bessie, Bess, Bessy

The US blues singer *Bessie Smith* was born in Chattanooga, Tennessee, on this day in 1894. She was the highest-paid black entertainer of her time, touring the country each summer in her own railway carriage. Among her many hits was 'Downhearted Blues' (1923).

From Elizabeth, meaning consecrated to God

Claudia

The Italian actress *Claudia Cardinale* was born on this day in 1939. She became widely known after her appearance in Luchino Visconti's *The Leopard* (1962) and subsequently appeared in *The Pink Panther* (1963) and *The Adventures of Brigadier Gerard* (1970).

Meaning lame

Kingsley, Kinsley

Kingsley Amis, the British novelist, was born on this day in 1922. His novel *Lucky Jim* (1954), which was set in a provincial university and is one of the funniest novels ever written, was turned into a hugely successful film in 1957.

Meaning from the king's meadow

Spike

Spike Milligan, the British comedian, was born in India on this day in 1918. His unique sense of humour found outlets in books and on TV and radio shows over decades. He was one of the founder members of the Goons, and *The Goon Show*, which ran on the radio from 1951 to 1960, was a major influence on Monty Python.

Meaning sharp point

Hans

Sir *Hans Sloane*, the British physician and naturalist, was born on 16 April 1660 in Killyleagh, Ireland. He founded the Chelsea Physic Garden in London and was first physician to King George II. His museum and library formed the core collection of the British Museum.

From John, meaning God has shown me favour

Merco, Mercer

The US dancer and choreographer *Merce Cunningham* was born in Centralia, Washington, on this day in 1919. He founded New York's celebrated Merce Cunningham Dance Company, and formed a close collaboration with the experimental composer John Cage. Merce continued to perform in his 80s, crippled with arthritis but still beautiful.

Meaning merchant

Gabriella, Gabrila, Gabriele, Gabriela

Gabriella Sabatini, the beautiful Argentine tennis player, was born on this day in 1970. The winner of the 1990 US Open, she was one of the most glamorous women on the court, and in 1989 she launched her own perfume, with the original name, Gabriella Sabatini.

Meaning woman of God

Melody, Melodia, Melodie, Lodie, Lody

US actress *Melody Patterson* was born on this day in 1949. She is best known for her role as Jane Angelica Thrift – or Wrangler Jane as she became known – the fast-shooting cowgirl in the 1960s TV series *F-Troop*.

Meaning like a song

Dusty, Dustina, Dustine

Dusty Springfield, the soulful British pop star, was born on this day in 1939. Her early TV appearances showed Dusty sporting the then fashionable beehive hairstyle, taken up decades later by Marge Simpson. She began recording in the group the Springfields before going solo, and her biggest hit was 'You Don't Have to Say You Love Me' (1966).

Meaning fighter

Fifi

The Canadian actress *Fifi D'Orsay* was born Marie-Rose Angeline Yvonne Lussier on this day in 1904. Her long career began in New York, where she was known as Mademoiselle Fifi. When she was 67 years old she appeared in the Tony-winning Broadway musical *Follies*.

From Joseph, meaning he will add

17 APRIL

Ernie, Erny, Ernst

On this day in 1956 a new savings scheme was launched in Britain. Each savings bond purchased has a unique number, which is entered into a monthly prize draw. The numbers are picked at random by *Ernie*, which stands for Electronic Random Number Indicator Equipment.

From Ernest, meaning purposeful, serious

Riccardo, Ricard

Riccardo Patrese, the Formula One racing driver, was born on this day in 1954 in Padua, Italy. He won six Grand Prix championships and holds the record for the most Grand Prix starts: 256.

Meaning wealthy and powerful one

Thornton, Thorn, Thornley, Thornly, Thorneley

US writer *Thornton Wilder* was born Thornton Niven Wilder in Madison, Wisconsin, on 17 April 1897. He won the Pulitzer prize twice: in 1928 for his novel *The Bridge of San Luis Rey* and a decade on in 1938 for his play *Our Town*, which was made into a film in 1940.

Meaning from the thorny place

Sean, Seann, Seain

British actor *Sean Bean* was born in Sheffield in 1959. He is a popular film actor – he was Boromir in *The Fellowship of the Ring* (2001) and Ulysses in *Troy* (2004) – and he is a successful classical stage actor. He was in the production of *Macbeth* that was the first Shakespearian play in the West End to have its run extended.

From John, meaning God has shown me favour

Karen, Karena, Karin, Karyn, Katryn

The Danish writer *Karen Blixen* was born on this day in 1885. Under the penname Isak Dinesen she wrote *Out of Africa* (1937), a fascinating account of her life in Kenya running a coffee plantation, and in 1985 it was turned into a successful film starring Meryl Streep and Robert Redford, directed by Sydney Pollack.

From Katherine, meaning pure maiden

Olivia, Olive, Ollie

The beautiful British actress *Olivia Hussey* was born Olivia Osuna on 17 April 1951. She became a star at the age of 18 when she played Juliet in Franco Zeffirelli's 1968 film *Romeo and Juliet*. She also played Mary in Zeffirelli's TV series *Jesus of Nazareth* (1977).

Meaning symbol of peace

Sirimavo

The world's first woman prime minister, *Sirimavo Bandaranaike* was born Sirimavo Ratwatte Dias Bandaranaike in Sri Lanka on this day in 1916. She was the prime minister of Sri Lanka three times, in 1960–65, 1970–77 and 1994–2000.

Meaning not known

Graziella, Grazina, Grazia

The Italian soprano and opera director *Graziella Sciutti* was born in Turin on this day in 1932. After a successful career as a singer, in 1977 she made her debut as a director at Glyndebourne with Francis Poulenc's *La Voix humaine*.

Meaning grace, charm

Skip, Skippy, Skipp, Skipper

The US comedian *Skip Stephenson* was born in Nebraska on this day in 1940. He was best known for hosting the US TV show *Real People* from 1979 to 1984. He recorded an album, *The Real Comedy of Skip Stephenson* in 1980.

Meaning owner of the ship

Ardito, Ardley

The Italian explorer, mountaineer, geologist and cartographer *Ardito Desio* was born in Palmanova on this day in 1897. On one of his geological surveys of Libya he became among the first people to find oil. In 1990 he established a scientific base on Mount Everest.

Meaning from the meadow

Reeve

The actor *Reeve Carney* was born on this day in 1983. He is best known for his starring role as the young Ishamel Chambers in the film *Snow Falling on Cedars* (1999), which starred Ethan Hawke.

Meaning steward

Francis, Frank, Fran

On this day in 1740 Sir *Francis Baring*, a British financier, was born in Devon. He and his brother, John, the sons of a German immigrant, established the commercial and financial house, Baring Brothers, using the money they earned as directors of the British East India Company. The bank survived until 1995.

Meaning free man

Hayley, Haley

British actress *Hayley Mills* was born Hayley Catherine Rose Vivian Mills on 18 April 1946. Her role in the film *Whistle Down the Wind* (1961) made her a child star. She won a special Oscar for her extraordinary performance in the dual role as the twins in *The Parent Trap* (1961).

Meaning clearing

Trine, Trinny, Trinna, Trin

The javelin thrower *Trine Hattestad* was born in Lorenskog, Norway, on 18 April 1966. She broke the world record three times, and her first World Championship win was in Stuttgart in 1993. She has two children: Joachim and Robin.

From Katrine, meaning pure maiden

Celine

On this day in 1996 the Canadian singer *Celine Dion* topped the US charts with her song 'Because You Loved Me'. She dedicated her album *The Colour of My Love* to her manager, René Angélil, and their marriage was televised on Canadian TV. They have a son, René-Charles.

Meaning heavenly

Ivana, Ivanna, Ivanne, Iverna, Ivina, Iva

Irvana Brlic-Mazuranic was born in Ogulin, Croatia, on this day in 1874. She is widely recognized as Croatia's finest writer of children's books. She had six children of her own and devoted all her work to her family and their education. She initially wrote in French.

Meaning yew tree

Alexis, Alick, Alex

The father of British blues, Alexis Korner was born in Paris on this day in 1928. He moved to Britain and became a significant influence on the 1960s pop scene. With the band CCS he recorded 'Whole Lotta Love', which was the theme tune to the TV chart show *Top of the Pops*.

From Alexander, meaning protector of mankind

Hayden, Hadon, Haydn

The Canadian actor *Hayden Christensen* was born in Vancouver on 19 April 1981. His best-known role is Anakin Skywalker in *Star Wars Episode 2: Attack of the Clones* (2002). The film took over $300 million in the USA alone.

Meaning from the hedged valley

Dudley, Dud, Duddy, Diddie, Dudly

Dudley Moore, the British actor, comedian and musician, was born on this day in 1935. In the 1960s he starred in the classic TV comedy *Not Only... But Also...*, which featured not only Dudley but also Peter Cook. Dudley later moved to Hollywood, where his films included *10* (1979) and *Arthur* (1980).

Meaning from the people's meadow

Simpson, Simson, Sim

On this day in 1987 the very first episode of *The Simpsons*, a short cartoon called 'Good Night', was broadcast in the US on *The Tracey Ullman Show*. It is said that Tracey later tried to claim for a share in the profits from *The Simpsons*.

From Sampson, meaning sun's man

Bekka, Beckie, Becky, Bekky, Beka

The US singer *Bekka Bramlett* was born on this day in 1968 to gospel singers Delaney and Bonnie Bramlett. In the early 1990s she joined the band Fleetwod Mac, and she sang with Joe Cocker on the soundtrack song 'Take Me Home' for the movie *Blown Away* (1994)

From Rebecca, meaning captivator

Ashley

Ashley Judd, the US actress, was born in Kentucky on 19 April 1968, the daughter of country singer Naomi Judd. Ashley has starred in many films, including *Heat* (1995) and *Eye of the Beholder* (1999). She is married to the Scottish racing driver Dario Franchitti.

Meaning from the meadow with the ash tree

Paloma, Palometa, Palommita

The designer and businesswoman *Paloma Picasso* was born on this day in 1949. The daughter of Pablo Picasso and Françoise Gilot, she set up the Paloma Picasso Foundation in Switzerland to promote the work of her parents, particularly her mother, who was also an artist.

Meaning dove

Sheena, Sheela, Sheelah, Sheilah, Sine

On this day in 1991 *Sheena Easton* topped the US charts with her song 'Morning Train (AKA 9 to 5)'. Having already established her success in Britain, she went on to win a Grammy for the best new artist of 1982. She was born Sheena Shirley Orr in Belshill, Scotland, in 1959.

From Jane, meaning God's gift of grace

Luther, Lothaire, Lothar, Lothario, Lute

Luther Vandross, the African-American soul singer, was born in New York City on this day in 1951. He recorded a string of successful albums in the 1980s, including *Forever, for Always, for Love*. In 1989 he had a hit single with 'Here and Now'.

Meaning famous warrior

Holland

On this day in 1882 US general *Holland McTyeire Smith* was born in Seale, Alabama. He served in the Pacific in the Second World War, leading the marines to victory across the islands of Micronesia and Iwo Jima. He was nicknamed Howlin' Mad.

Meaning woodland

Godvin, Godwin, Godvine, Godwine, Godwyne, Godvyne

The US jazz drummer Beaver Harris was born *William Godvin Harris* on this day in 1936 in Pittsburgh, Pennsylvania. He was part of New York's avant-garde jazz scene of the 1960s, playing with Sonny Rollins, Dexter Gordon and Thelonious Monk, among others.

Meaning God's friend

Odilon, Odil

The French painter and lithographer *Odilon Redon* was born in Bordeaux on 20 April 1840. He was one of the major figures in the symbolist movement, and began to achieve fame after illustrating the realist novel *A retours* by Joris-Karl Huysmans in 1884.

Meaning rich

Agnes

Today is the feast day of *St Agnes of Montepulciano*, who was born in Tuscany. When she was nine years old she persuaded her parents to let her join the convent of Montepulciano, and by the time she was 15 she was mother superior of a convent at Procena. She lived a life of great self-discipline, and several visions and miracles are ascribed to her.

Meaning pure, chaste

Gro

Gro Harlem Brundtland was Norway's first woman prime minister She was born on 20 April 1939 and trained to be a doctor before turning to politics. She served as prime minister for nine years over two terms between 1986 and 1996, and since leaving office she has maintained her interest in the environment and the Third World.

Meaning gardener

Carys, Caryl, Carryl

Today is the birthday of *Carys Zeta Douglas*, the daughter of Catherine Zeta Jones and Michael Douglas. She was born on 20 April 2003, a sister for Dylan Michael Douglas. Catherine's middle name, Zeta, comes from a ship on which her great-grandfather sailed.

Meaning beloved

Dana, Dayna

On this day in 1970 'All Kinds of Everything' by the Irish singer *Dana* was number one in the British charts. She won the Eurovision Song Contest for Ireland with the song when she was just 19 years old and had several other hit records before turning to politics.

Meaning from Denmark

Gideon

Gideon Sundback, the Canadian inventor, patented the zip fastener on this day in 1913. At first called a separable fastener – the name zip came later – it was used for tobacco pouches and boots. Nobody thought of using it on clothing and luggage for another 20 years.

Meaning tree cutter

Iggy

Iggy Pop was born on this day in 1947. The wild front man of the New York band the Stooges was born James Newell Osterbert in Muskegon, Michigan. He shared a flat with David Bowie in Berlin, and Bowie collaborated with him on several of his albums.

From Igor, meaning hero

Alf, Alfy, Al, Alfie

On this day in 1959 *Alf Dean* became the big game world record holder when he caught the largest fish ever hooked by a rod and reel at Denial Bay, South Australia. It was a great white shark, 5.13 metres (16 feet 10 inches) long and weighing in at 1,208 kilograms (2,663 pounds).

From Alfred, meaning good adviser

Beuno, Beuve, Beuvelin

Today is the feast day of *St Beuno*, a 7th-century abbot. The grandson of a Welsh prince, it is said that his great uncle was King Arthur. Legend has it that he brought St Winifred back to life. He is the patron saint of sick infants, and children are still taken to his tomb in Clynnog Fawr, Caernarvonshire, in the hope that they will be healed.

Meaning good

Andie

US actress *Andie McDowell* was born Rosalie Anderson McDowell on 21 April 1958. She was spotted in a magazine by Hugh Hudson. She made her name in *Sex, Lies and Videotape* (1989) and *Groundhog Day* (1993), but she is probably best remembered for her performance in *Four Weddings and a Funeral* (1994).

Meaning loveable

Silvana

Silvana Mangano is widely acknowledged to have been the sexiest actress of Italy's neo-realist period. Born in Rome on this day in 1930, she won the title Miss Rome when she was just 16 years old. Her movie career began when she started dating the actor Marcello Mastroianni, and she later married the producer Dino de Laurentis.

Meaning wood dweller

Farida

The Dutch model *Farida van der Stoom* was born on this day in 1974. Farida is an African, Arabian and Indian name. In Africa and Arabia it means unique. In Indian it means turquoise.

Meaning unique, turquoise

Villette

The English writer Charlotte Brontë was born on 21 April 1816 in Thornton, Yorkshire. She and her sisters lived at the now-famous rectory at Haworth. As well as *Jane Eyre* (1847), *Shirley* (1849) and *The Professor* (1857), she wrote *Villette* (1853), which tells of Lucy Snowe's experiences in the town of Villette, which mirrored the author's stay in Brussels.

Meaning from the village

Aaron, Aeron, Arron, Aron

Aaron Spelling, one of the most prolific TV producers ever, was born in Dallas, Texas, on 22 April 1923. Among his myriad shows are *Charlie's Angels* (2000), *Melrose Place* (1992) and *Beverly Hills 90210* (1990). His first wife was Carolyn Jones, who memorably starred as Morticia in *The Addams Family* (1992).

Meaning exalted

Bowdoin

Today is the birthday of *Bowdoin Harold Brazell*, the son of TV soap actress Tina Arning and Jason Brazell. Tina Arning is best known for her role in the daytime US soap *The Young and the Restless* (1973). Bowdoin is a town in Maine.

Meaning not known

Yehudi

Yehudi Menuhin, the US-British violinist, was born in New York on this day in 1916. One of the best-known violinists ever to live, he was a dedicated yoga aficionado and helped popularize the discipline in the West. Nigel Kennedy was one of the graduates of his renowned school for the musically gifted.

From Judah, meaning to praise

Craig, Craggie

Bros bassist *Craig Logan* was born on 22 April 1969 in Kirkcaldy, Scotland. The group's first single, 'When Will I be Famous', is one of the anthems of the 1980s, reaching number two in the charts in 1988. Craig left the band in 1988, leaving Bros as the blonde duo, Matt and Luke Goss.

Meaning from the stony hill

Sheryl, Sheri, Sherrie, Sherry, Cheryl

The actress *Sheryl Lee* was born on this day in 1967 in Bavaria, Germany. She will be remembered as Laura Palmer, the pivotal character in David Lynch's surreal TV series, *Twin Peaks* (1990–91). She is married to Neil Diamond's son, Jesse, and they have a son, Elijah.

Meaning beloved

Julitta

On 22 April 2004 the Oscar-winning star of *Pollock* (2000), Marcia Gay Harden and her husband, Thaddaeus Scheel, became parents of twins, a girl, *Julitta Dee Harden Scheel*, and a boy, Hudson Harden Scheel.

From Julia, meaning youthful

Opportuna

Today is the feast day of *St Opportuna*, a French Benedictine abbess, who lived in the 8th century. When a donkey was stolen from her, a farmer wouldn't confess. The next day his field was sown with salt. He returned the donkey and gave the land to the nuns.

Meaning opportune, favourable

Sabine, Sabina, Saidhbhain, Savina

Sabine Applemans, the beautiful Belgian tennis star, was born on 22 April 1972. Ranked 16th in the world in 1997, she was one of only 47 people to defeat Steffi Graf during her professional career. She went on to become a TV presenter.

Meaning woman of Sabine

23

Hamlet

William Shakespeare, the greatest writer in the English language, was born on this day in 1564 and died on the same day in 1616. *Hamlet*, which was first performed in 1602, is widely regarded as his greatest play. The Shakespeare Memorial Theatre, Stratford-upon-Avon, was opened on this day in 1932.

Meaning little village

Vladimir, Vadim

Vladimir Nabokov, the Russian-born US writer, was born in St Petersburg on this day in 1899. After the Russian Revolution he and his family fled to Berlin and later to Paris, and it was not until 1940 that he moved to the USA. He wrote many novels, some under the penname Vladimir Serin, but will be best remembered for *Lolita* (1955).

Meaning royally famous

Sergey, Sergent, Sergio, Serge, Sergeant, Sargie, Sarge, Sargent

The Russian composer *Sergey Sergeyevich Prokofiev* was born in Sontsovka, Ukraine, on this day in 1891. He is best known for *Peter and the Wolf* (1936), but also wrote operas and ballets as well as the music for the films *Alexander Nevsky* (1938) and *Ivan the Terrible* (1942).

Meaning military attendant

Mallord, Mallard

Joseph Mallord William Turner, one of England's greatest artists, was born in London on 23 April 1775. He spent a lot of time in Venice and became known as the painter of light and water. Among his best-known works are *The Fighting Téméraire* (1839) and *Rain, Steam and Speed* (1844).

Meaning strong adviser

Saskia

The singer *Saskia* of Saskia and Serge was born on this day in 1947. The two are best known for their song 'Spinning Wheel'. Saksia's real name is Trudy van den Berg. Saskia, a German name, was the name of Rembrandt's wife.

Meaning Saxon woman

Tessa, Tess, Tessy

The British actress *Tessa Wyatt* was born on this day in 1948. She became famous in Britain in the 1970s for her role as Richard O'Sullivan's girlfriend Vicky in the TV sitcom *Robin's Nest*, which was itself a spin-off from *Man About the House*, also starring O'Sullivan.

From Theresa, meaning harvest, reap

Ngaio

The New Zealand author and theatre director *Ngaio Marsh* was born in Christchurch on this day in 1895. She is internationally famous for her 32 detective novels, featuring the detective Roderick Alleyn, while in New Zealand she is remembered for her theatrical productions. She also wrote the libretto for an opera entitled *A Unicorn for Christmas* (1962).

Meaning tree, clever

Jaime, Jaimee, Jaimey, Jamey, Jamie, Jaymee

The US actress and model *Jaime King* was born on 23 April 1979 in Omaha, Nebraska. She is said to have been named after Jaime Sommers, *The Bionic Woman* in the 1970s TV series, who was played by Lindsay Wagner. She often takes the name James King, though Jaime is a legitimate name for a girl.

Meaning I love

Clement, Clemence, Clem, Clemens, Clementius, Clemmy, Clim

Sir *Clement Freud*, the British writer, broadcaster and politician, was born on this day in 1924. Known for his dour, ironic manner, he became famous in Britain for partnering a bloodhound in a dog food commercial. He is the grandson of Sigmund and brother of Lucien.

Meaning kind, merciful

Digby

Digby Fairweather, the British jazz trumpeter and composer, was born on this day in 1946. As well as playing in his band Digby Fairweather's Half Dozen, with George Melly, among others, Digby writes and hosts a weekly jazz radio show on the UK's Jazz FM station.

Meaning from the settlement by the dyke

Stafford, Staffard

British politician Sir *Stafford Cripps* was born in London on 24 April 1889. He was the ambassador to the Soviet Union in Winston Churchill's wartime coalition government and president of the Board of Trade in Clement Attlee's post-war government, but he refused to serve under Ramsay MacDonald.

Meaning from the ford by the landing place

Thorbjorn, Torbjorn, Torborg

Thorbjorn Falldin, prime minister of Sweden three times between 1976 and 1982, was born on this day in 1926. He was the leader of the Centerpartiet from 1971 to 1985.

Meaning thunder bear

Bridget, Brigid, Brigida, Brigette, Brigitte, Brita, Brydie, Brieta, Brietta

Bridget Riley, one of Britain's best-known artists, was born on this day in 1931. Her paintings are in the style known as Op Art (optical illusion art), and she was inspired by Seurat's pointillism. Her abstract patterns, painted on large canvases, seem to dance before the eyes.

Meaning mighty, strong

Jill, Jillian, Jillie

Jill Ireland, the British actress, producer and writer, was born on this day in 1936. Her first film appearance was as a dancer in *Oh Rosalinda* (1955). She married Charles Bronson in 1966, and they worked together on many films, including the *Death Wish* series.

Meaning nestling

Barbra, Bab, Babb, Barb

The US actress, film producer and director *Barbra Streisand* was born on 24 April 1942 in Brooklyn, New York. She has won five Emmys, eight Golden Globes and two Oscars. Her first Oscar, awarded in 1967 as best actress for her part in *Funny Face*, was shared with Katharine Hepburn for her role in *The Lion in Winter*.

Meaning beautiful stranger

Courtnee, Courtenay, Courtney

The US actress, singer and dancer *Courtnee Draper* was born in Florida on this day in 1985. She plays Morgan Hudson in the TV soap *The Jersey*. Her feature films include *The Room* (1998) and *Tom Sawyer* (1998).

Meaning from the court

25 APRIL

Aurelio, Aurelius, Oriel, Oriole

The composer *Aurelio Signoretti*, who is known for his sacred music, was born in Italy on this day in 1567. The name Aurelio is the Spanish, Italian and Portuguese form of the Roman family names of Aurelius (masculine) and Aurelia (feminine).

Meaning golden

Guglielmo, Guillermo, Guillym

The Italian electrical engineer *Guglielmo Marconi* was born on this day in 1874. He sent the world's first transatlantic radio message in 1901 from transmitters in Cornwall, England, to St John's, Newfoundland. In 1909 he won the Nobel Prize for physics for his groundbreaking work on the development of the radio.

Meaning determined protector

Andrey

The Russian mathematician *Andrei Nikolayevich Kolmogorov* was born on 25 April 1903. He was the founder of algorithmic complexity theory, and he made major advances in the fields of probability theory and topology.

Meaning strong and manly

Padgett, Paget, Paige, Page

The US writer *Padgett Powell* was born on this day in 1952. The professor of creative writing at the University of Florida, he has published four novels and two collections of short stories. His short stories have also appeared in anthologies of the best American short stories.

Meaning page boy

Tu

Tu Simone Ayer Morrow was born on this day in 2001. She is the daughter of Debbon Ayer and Rob Morrow. Rob Morrow is best known for his role as Joel Fleischman in the TV hit *Northern Exposure* (1990). Tu is a Chinese name.

Meaning earth, soil

Renée, Rene, Renee, Renata

The US actress *Renée Zellweger* was born in Katy, Houston, on this day in 1969. The star of the *Bridget Jones* movies (2001 and 2004) was advised to change her surname to a simpler one, but she refused because she and her brothers are the first Zellwegers to be born in the USA.

Meaning born again

Talia

The US actress *Talia Shire* was born on 25 April 1946. She was nominated for two Oscars, for her performances in *The Godfather Part 2* (1974) and *Rocky* (1976). Her brother is the producer Francis Ford Coppola, and her sons, Jason and Robert Schwartzman, are both actors.

Meaning blooming

Ella, Ellie

Ella Fitzgerald, the US jazz singer, was born in Newport News, Virginia, on this day in 1918. She made her first record in 1932 and had her first hit in 1938 with 'A-tisket, A-tasket'. Admired for her beautiful voice and effortless phrasing, she also appeared in films, including *St Louis Blues* (1958).

Meaning beautiful fairy woman

Artemis, Artemas

The US humorist *Artemis Ward* was born Charles Farrar Browne on this day in 1834. His columns as Artemis, a New England carnival manager, were deliberately misspelled, full of bad grammar and hugely popular. He helped Mark Twain get his first story published.

Meaning gift of Artemis

Duane, Dwayne, Dewain, Dwain

The US guitarist *Duane Eddy* was born in Corning, New York, on this day in 1938. Described by *Billboard* magazine as the number one rock-and-roll instrumentalist of all time, his biggest hit was 'Because They're Young' (1960). He won a Grammy for best rock instrumental in 1986 for 'Peter Gunn'.

Meaning singer

Bernard, Bernhard, Burnard, Bernie, Bernardo, Bern, Berndt, Berard

The US author *Bernard Malamud* was born on 26 April 1914 in Brooklyn, New York. He won a Pulitzer Prize and the National Book Award for his novel *The Fixer* (1966), which is set in tsarist Russia. He is best known for his short stories, collected in, among others, *The Magic Barrel* (1958) and *Rembrandt's Hat* (1973).

Meaning brave as a bear

Law

The US landscape architect *Frederick Law Olmsted*, born in Hartford, Connecticut, on this day in 1822, designed many of America's greatest parks, including Prospect Park, Brooklyn, and the College of California campus at Berkeley, but is best known for Central Park, New York (1858).

From Lawrence, meaning crowned with laurels

Ruth-Anne, Ruthanne

The British trip-hop/electronica duo Olive were number one in the UK charts on this day in 1997 with 'You're Not Alone' and then released the widely admired CD *Extra Virgin* (1999). In 2004 the vocalist *Ruth-Anne* began working on her first solo album in Ibiza.

From Ruth, meaning compassionate friend, and Anne, meaning God has favoured me

Tionne, Tio

The actress and TLC singer *Tionne Watkins* was born Tionne Tenise Watkins in Des Moines, Iowa, on this day in 1970. Better known as T-Boz, she has a daughter, Chase, with the rapper Mack 10.

Meaning not known

Erminnie, Ermina, Erminina, Erminie, Erma

Erminnie Adele Platt Smith, the US anthropologist and geologist, was born on this day in 1836. Her specialities were mineralogy, crystallography and the Iroquois Indians. She had four sons and was the first woman to be inducted into the American Academy of Science.

Meaning army maid

Marnette, Marne, Marny, Marnie, Marni

The US actress *Marnette Patterson* was born on this day in 1980. While still in her teens she starred in the TV series *Movie Stars* (1999) and had parts in the movies *A Nightmare on Elm Street: The Dream Child* (1989) and *Sliver* (1993).

Meaning rejoice

27 APRIL

August, Auguste, Augustin, Agosto, Aguistin, Augie

The Pulitzer Prize-winning US playwright *August Wilson* was born on this day in 1945. His plays focused on 20th-century African-American life, and two of the best known are *Fences* (1987) and *The Piano Lesson* (1990).

Meaning exalted one

Nicolas, Nic, Nicol

The Russian-American composer *Nicolas Slonimsky* was born on 27 April 1894. As well as being a great champion of contemporary music, conducting the premieres of works by Varese and Ives, he wrote *The Lexicon of Musical Invective* (1952), a compilation of terrible reviews. He lived to the age of 101.

Meaning victorious army leader

Ace, Acey

Ace Frehley, the lead guitarist for the rock band Kiss, was born in the Bronx, New York, on 27 April 1951. Kiss, with their highly theatrical stage show, was one of the most successful acts of the heady 1970s decade. They peaked with their live double album *Alive* (1976).

Meaning unity

Hauge, Haig

The US physical chemist, science writer and editor of scientific literature *Philip Hauge Abelson* was born in Tacoma, Washington, on this day in 1913. In 1940, in collaboration with his colleague Edwin Mattison McMillan, he co-discovered neptunium, the first actinide series trans-uranium element ever discovered.

Meaning enclosure dweller

Zita, Sitha, Citha, Zetta, Zitao

Today is the feast day of *St Zita of Lucca*. She was born in Mosagerati, near Lucca, Italy, in 1218. She was a servant who often gave her food and her masters' food to the poor. She is the patron saint of butlers, homemakers, domestic servants, waiters and waitresses, and her emblem is a bunch of household keys.

Meaning sixth born

Sheena, Sheela, Sheelah, Sheilah

The Scottish singer and actress *Sheena Easton* was born on this day in 1959. She sang the theme tune for the James Bond film *For Your Eyes Only* (1981). She has appeared on Broadway in *The Man of La Mancha* (1992) and *Grease* (1996). She has two children, Jake and Skylar.

Meaning dim-sighted

Geraldine, Geraldina, Geralda

On this day in 1938 *Geraldine Appoyni* married King Zog of Albania. Although she was born in Hungary, she was the daughter of the US heiress Gladys Steuart and thus became the only member of a European royal family with American blood. They had one son, Leka Zogu.

From Gerald, meaning ruling spear

Coretta

Coretta Scott King, the civil rights activist and wife of Martin Luther King Jr, was born on this day in 1927. She and the Rev King had four children: Yolanda Denise, Martin Luther III, Dexter Scott and Bernice Albertine.

Meaning maiden

Rowland, Rowe, Roland, Roly, Rollo

The US political reporter and commentator *Rowland Evans* was born on 28 April 1921. The co-host of the CNN TV show *Evans & Novak*, he believed that political reporting was the most artistic of all journalistic reporting.

Meaning famous land

Nate

The US actor *Nate Richert* was born in St Paul, Minnesota, on this day in 1978. He is best known for his role as Harvey Kinkel, Sabrina's boyfriend, in the TV series *Sabrina The Teenage Witch* (1996–2000).

From Nathan, meaning gift of God

Anton, Ant

On this day in 1950 *Anton Karas* topped the US charts with his theme tune from the film *The Third Man* (1949). The zither music that accompanies the film instantly evokes the atmosphere of post-war Vienna.

From Anthony, meaning not known

Conradus, Con, Conn, Konradus, Kon, Konn

Dutch archaeologist *Conradus Leemans* was born on this day in 1809. He was the director of the Leiden Museum from 1839 until 1891, and during this time he catalogued the museum's Egyptian artefacts and edited a unique lithographic account of the collection.

Meaning brave counsel

Odette

On this day in 1912 *Odette Hallowes* was born Odette Marie Celine Brailly in Amiens. She became one of the great heroines of the French Resistance during the Second World War and was awarded the George Cross in 1946. The film *Odette* (1950), starring Anna Neagle, portrayed her wartime deeds.

Meaning riches, prosperity

Harper

The US novelist *Harper Lee* was born in Monroeville, Alabama, on this day in 1926. She wrote only one published book, *To Kill a Mockingbird* (1960), but it became an enduring and much-loved classic, made into a successful film starring Gregory Peck in 1962. She has received several honorary doctorates.

Meaning harp player

Simbi, Simbe, Simba

Simbi Khali, the US actress, was born on this day in 1971. She is best known for her role as Nina Campbell in the TV series *Third Rock from the Sun* (1996). She also appeared in the feature film *We Were Soldiers* (2002).

Meaning lion

Marcia, Marcella, Marcela, Marcelle, Marcie, Marcile, Marcille, Marcy

US actress *Marcia Strassman* was born on this day in 1948. She played Rick Moran's wife in *Honey, I Shrunk the Kids* (1989) and *Honey, I Blew up the Kid* (1992), and was Julie Kotter in the TV comedy series *Welcome Back Kotter* (1975).

Meaning belonging to Mars

29

Lonnie, Lon

The king of skiffle, *Lonnie Donegan* was born on 29 April 1931 in Glasgow, Scotland. He was the inspiration for many musicians, including John Lennon and Pete Townsend. In 1969 he wrote 'I'll Never Fall In Love Again' for Tom Jones.

From Lawrence, meaning crowned with laurels

Daniel, Dane, Danny, Darnell, Dan

The British actor *Daniel Day-Lewis* was born Daniel Michael Blake Day-Lewis on 29 April 1957 in London. The award-winning actor has starred in many films, including *The Unbearable Lightness of Being* (1987) and *My Left Foot* (1989).

Meaning the lord is my judge

Seinfeld, Feld, Felder

Jerry Seinfeld, the US comedian, writer and actor, was born in Brooklyn, New York, on this day in 1954. The TV series *Seinfeld* ran from 1989 until 1998 and was one of the most successful US comedy shows of all time.

Meaning field

Zane, Sian

US actor *Zane Carney* was born on this day in 1985. He is best known for his starring role in *Dave's World* (1993), a film based on the syndicated columns of the Pulitzer Prize-winning humorist Dave Barry.

From John, meaning God has shown me favour

Uma, Umar

The US film actress *Uma Thurman* was born Uma Karuna Thurman on this day in 1970. Her father, a professor of Indo-Tibetan Buddhist studies at Columbia University, called her Uma after a Hindu goddess of light and beauty.

Meaning flourishing

Joan, Joana, Joanna, Joanne, Jeanne

The date 29 April saw the turning point in the Hundred Years War between England and France. *Joan of Arc* had predicted she would save Orleans and, on this day in 1429, she marched on the city with French troops. The English retreated and she was wounded, as she had foreseen.

From Jane, meaning God's gift of grace

Michelle, Michelline, Michella, Micheline, Michel, Michaela, Micaela, Michaelina, Michaeline

The US actress Michelle Pfeiffer was born on this day in 1958 in Santa Ana, Orange County, California. She became one of the biggest film stars after being in *The Fabulous Baker Boys* (1989).

Meaning who is like God

Catherine, Catharine, Katherine, Katharine, Kathryn, Cathryn, Cathy, Kathy, Catharina, Cathelle, Cathie, Cathleen, Catriona

Today is the feast day of the mystic *St Catherine of Siena*. She entered a Dominican order and spent much of her time working among the sick, including people with leprosy, at the time a feared disease. When the plague broke out in Siena, she led her followers into the poorest areas of the town, even digging graves herself.

Meaning pure maiden

Franz

Franz Lehár, the Austro-Hungarian composer, was born in Komárón on this day in 1870. Known chiefly for his operettas, he lived in Vienna for most of his life. His music epitomizes the place and the era, perhaps none more so than *The Merry Widow* (1909).

From Francis, meaning free man

Connecticut

The US journalist *Vermont Connecticut Royster* was born on this day in 1914. He was the editor of the *Wall Street Journal* and then became president of its publishing house. His name is an excellent example of the American habit of naming children after places.

Meaning beside the long tidal river

Isaiah

Isaiah Lord Thomas III, the US basketball player and coach, was born on 30 April 1961 in Chicago, Illinois. In 1980 he was selected to play for the US Olympic team, but America boycotted the games because they were being held in Moscow.

Meaning God is my helper

Barrington

Reggae legend *Barrington Levy* was born on 30 April 1964 in Clarendon, Jamaica. One of Jamaica's biggest stars, he has enjoyed many hits, including 'When You're Young and in Love'. His album *Living Dangerously* (1998) featured famed guests Snoop Doggy Dogg and Long Beach Dub All-Stars.

Meaning town of Barr

Cloris, Chloris, Chlora, Chlori

The US actress *Cloris Leachman* was born on this day in 1926 in Des Moines, Iowa. She won a best supporting actress Oscar for her performance in *The Last Picture Show* (1971) and has since appeared in many movies, including *High Anxiety* (1978) and *Walk Like a Man* (1987).

Meaning green, spring fresh

Kirsten, Kirstin, Kirstina, Kirstie, Kirstyn

Kirsten Dunst, the US actress, was born on this day in 1982 in Point Pleasant, New Jersey. She has been in both *Spiderman* films (2002, 2004), and she starred with Tom Cruise and Brad Pitt in *Interview with the Vampire* (1994).

Meaning anointed one

Babette, Babs, Babita, Babb, Bab

It is the birthday today of *Alice Babette Toklas*, the long-standing companion and friend of US writer Gertrude Stein. Alice was born on 30 April 1877 in San Francisco, California, but she and Stein moved to Paris in 1902, where they hosted salons attended by the influential avant-garde artists and writers of the day, including Picasso, Matisse, Braque and Hemingway.

From Barbara, meaning stranger

Melisande

On this day in 1902 Claude Debussy's opera *Pelléas et Mélisande* received its first performance in Paris. It is a reworking of the play by Maurice Maeterlinck, in which misunderstandings about who loves whom and the effects of jealousy have tragic consequences.

Meaning industrious

May

May

Glenn, Glen, Glyn, Glynn,

The actor *Glenn Ford* was born Gwyllyn Samuel Newton Ford on this day in 1916 in Quebec, Canada. He served in France in the Second World War and became a star after his unforgettable performance alongside Rita Hayworth in the classic film noir, *Gilda* (1946).

Meaning valley

Fidel, Fidele, Fidelio

On 1 May 1961 the then prime minister of Cuba, *Fidel Castro*, made the historic announcement that there would be no more elections held in the country. He came to power in January 1959, when he overthrew the dictator Fulgencio Batista y Zaldivar and established a communist regime.

Meaning faithful

Suresh, Suren, Surendra

The successful Indian politician *Suresh Kalmadi* was born on 1 May 1944. He is a member of the Indian National Congress as well as being president of the Indian Olympic Association and the Asian Athletics Association.

Meaning Lord Indra

Orson, Urson

On this day in 1941 *Orson Welles*'s film *Citizen Kane* premiered in New York. One of the most influential films ever made, it was based on the life of the newspaper proprietor William Randolph Hearst. Welles himself was born in 1915 in Kenosha, Wisconsin.

Meaning little bear

Joanna, Joanne, Jo

Today is the birthday of British actress *Joanna Lumley*, who was born in Srinagar, Kashmir, in 1946. She appeared on TV as Purdey in *The New Avengers* (1976–7) and as Sapphire in *Sapphire and Steel* (1979–82), but she is now forever known as Patsy Stone in the classic comedy series *Absolutely Fabulous*.

From Jane, meaning God's gift of grace

Bona, Bonita, Bonne, Bonnibelle, Bonnie, Nita

In ancient Rome the first day of May was the festival of *Bona Dea*, the Roman goddess of fertility and healing. It was the day on which the sick and ailing were taken to her temples for healing. It was strictly an all-girl affair. An image of her face can be seen on many old Roman coins.

Meaning good goddess

Priscilla, Prisca, Pris, Prisilla, Prissie

On this day *Priscilla Beaulieu* married Elvis Presley. Born Priscilla Ann Wagner in 1945 in Brooklyn, New York, she met Elvis when she was 14 years old. They dated for eight years before she said 'I do'. Beaulieu is the name of her mother's second husband.

Meaning descendant of princes

May, Mai, Mae, Maya, Maia

In England *May Day* springtime celebrations, dating back to ancient times, include dancing around the maypole, traditional morris dancing and the crowning of a May queen. It is also Labour Day in many countries, when rallies and gatherings are held to support working people.

Meaning born in May

Valery, Valeria, Valerian

The great Russian conductor *Valery Abissalovich Gergiev* was born in Moscow on this day in 1953. As the artistic and general director of Moscow's Kirov Opera and Ballet, he has expanded their repertoire and kept them at the peak of artistic excellence. In 2003 he was seen conducting in the innovative film *Russian Ark*.

Meaning powerful stranger

Satyajit

The Bengali film director *Satyajit Ray* was born on this day in 1921. One of the greatest film directors and producers, in 1992 he received an Oscar for lifetime achievement and the Bharat Ratna award. He also wrote Bengali detective stories.

Meaning wedded to truth

Beckham, Becks, Beck, Bec

It is the birthday today of British soccer superstar *David Robert Joseph Beckham*, who was born in Leytonstone, London, in 1975. The captain of the English team and Real Madrid player is equally famous for his marriage to ex-Spice Girl, Victoria.

Meaning brook

Lorenz, Lorenze, Lorenzo, Lorenz

Lorenz Hart, the lyricist half of the Broadway song-writing team Rodgers and Hart, was born on this day in 1895. Among the creative partnership's best-known and most often performed songs are 'The Most Beautiful Girl in the World', 'Bewitched, Bothered and Bewildered', 'Blue Moon' and 'My Funny Valentine'.

From Lawrence, meaning crowned with laurels

Lesley, Leslie, Lesli, Lesly, Les

Lesley Gore, the US singer, was born on 2 May 1946. Her first single, 'It's My Party' (1963), went straight to number one in the US charts. Produced by Quincy Jones, she also had 1960s hits with 'That's the Way Boys Are', 'Judy's Turn to Cry' and 'She's a Fool'.

Meaning keeper of the grey fort

Donatella, Donata, Dinate, Donatiane, Donatielle, Donella, Donelle

Donatella Versace was born in Italy on 2 May 1955. She started designing knitwear in the 1970s while still a student and was already involved in the fashion business before she took over the empire of her brother, Gianni Versace, after his death. She has two children, Daniel and Allegra.

Meaning given by God

Jenna

Jenna Von Oy, the US actress and country singer, was born on 2 May 1977 in Stratford, Connecticut. She is best known for her role as Six LeMeure, Blossom's best friend, in the American TV series *Blossom* (1991).

Meaning little bird

Peggy, Peg

The British character actress and comedienne Peggy Mount was born on this day in 1916. She had a long career in films, from *Sailor Beware* (1956) to *Oliver!* (1968), and she provided one of the voices in *The Princess and the Goblin* (1992).

From Margaret, meaning pearl

3 MAY

Bing

Bing Crosby was born in Taconia, Washington, on this day in 1903. The celebrated actor and singer had hits spanning decades from 'White Christmas' in 1954, one of the bestselling records of all time, to 1977, when he recorded 'Peace on Earth' with David Bowie.

Meaning kettle-shaped hollow

Walker

The US boxing champion Sugar Ray Robinson was born *Walker Smith Jr* in Detroit, Michigan, on this day in 1921. He was the world welterweight champion and holds the record for most times champion in a division, winning the world middleweight division five times.

Meaning the walker

Anders, Anderson, Andie, Andonis

Anders Graneheim, the Swedish bodybuilder, was born on 3 May 1962. A champion through the 1980s, a documentary called *The Last Pose* was made about him as he prepared to enter the Masters' Mr Olympia competition in 2002.

From Andrew, meaning warrior

Macon, Makon, Macomb

On this day in 1845 *Macon B. Allen* became the first African-American to be admitted to the US Bar and thus became the first African-American to practise law in the USA. He initially became a justice in Massachusetts and then, in 1873, a judge in South Carolina.

Meaning to make

Golda, Goldie, Goldina

Golda Meir, prime minister of Israel between 1969 and 1974, was born on this day in Kiev, Ukraine, in 1898. Her family moved to the USA in 1906, and in 1921 she went to Palestine to work on a kibbutz, where her leadership qualities were soon recognized. She was the first person to be issued with an Israeli passport.

Meaning pure gold

Beulah

The US actress *Beulah Bondi* was born on 3 May 1888. She has the distinction of playing Jimmy Stewart's mother in four different feature films in a career that spanned more than 40 years.

Meaning she who is to be married

Jamaica

On this day in 1494 Christopher Columbus discovered *Jamaica*. The name Jamaica comes from the Arawak people of South America, who first settled there around 1000. They called it Xamayca, which means land of wood and water.

Meaning land of wood and water

Lucile

The US actress Mary Astor was born *Lucile Vasconcellos Langhanke* in Quincy, Illinois, on this day in 1906. A star in silent and talking movies, she became famous after playing the female lead opposite John Barrymore in *Beau Brummell* (1924) and *Don Juan* (1926).

Meaning light, illuminating the ignorant

Amos

The Israeli novelist and journalist *Amos Oz* was born Amos Klausner on this day in 1939. He was brought up at 18 Amos Street in the Kerem Avraham district of Jerusalem. He is a professor of literature at Ben-Gurion University in the town of Beersheba in southern Israel.

Meaning burden bearer

Florian, Floryan, Floriann

Today is the feast day of *St Florian*, who was a Roman soldier. Rather than arresting Christians during the Diocletian persecution, Florian joined the Christians. He was tortured and drowned for his beliefs and has become, by association, the patron saint of fire brigades.

Meaning flowering, flourishing

Manuel, Mannie, Mano, Manolo, Manny

Manuel Benitez Perez, the famous Spanish matador of the 1960s, was born on this day in 1936 in Palma del Rio, near Cordoba. In the ring he was known as El Cordobes. He brought a unique theatrical, acrobatic style to the ring.

From Emmanuel, meaning God is with us

Hosni

Hosni Mubarak, president of Egypt from 1981, was born Muhammad Hosni Said Mubarak on 4 May 1928. He is one of the most powerful leaders in the Middle East and has been actively involved in trying to find a peaceful settlement to the conflict in Palestine.

Meaning beauty, excellence

Audrey, Audra, Audey, Audie, Audry, Audery

Audrey Hepburn was born on this day in 1929. Star of *Roman Holiday* (1953) and *Breakfast at Tiffany's* (1971), she was a movie icon, but in 1988 she became a special ambassador for UNICEF, dedicating her life to underprivileged children and helping the world's poorest nations.

Meaning noble strength

Um, Om, Umm

Today is the birthday of the celebrated singer *Um Kalthum*, who might be described as the Elvis Presley or Maria Callas of the Arab world. She is one of the most loved and popular singers who has ever existed. She was born in Egypt in 1908 and lived there all her life. Her records still sell in their millions.

Meaning mother

Panama

On this day in 1904 work began on building the *Panama Canal*, the 82-kilometre (51-mile) long canal that links the Atlantic and Pacific Oceans. The first chief engineer was called John Findlay Wallace. Panama is S-shaped, which means that the Atlantic Ocean is on the canal's west side and the Pacific Ocean is on the east.

Meaning place of abundant fish

Monica, Monique, Monca, Monika, Moyna

Today is the feast day of *St Monica*, who was born in Tagaste, Algeria, in 322. The mother of St Augustine of Hippo, she prayed, successfully, for the conversion to Christianity of her pagan husband, Patricius, and of her son.

Meaning advice giver

Sage

Sage Stallone, son of Sylvester and brother of Seargeoh, celebrates a birthday today. He was born in Los Angeles, California, in 1976. In 1990 Sage starred in *Rocky V*, the last of the Rocky sequels, along with his father, Talia Shire and real-life boxer Tommy Morrison.

Meaning wise

Karl, Karlens, Carlan, Karol, Karel

Karl Marx, the German political philosopher and social theorist, was born on this day in 1818. He lived in Paris and London. His three-volume work, *Das Kapital* (1867, 1884, 1894), helped to launch the communist and socialist movements. He is buried in Highgate Cemetery, London.

From Charles, meaning free man

Tyrone

Tyrone Power, the US actor, was born on this day in Cincinnati, Ohio, either in 1914 or 1913 – no one is sure. The film idol of the 1930s and 1940s contributed much to the success of the then fledgling company Twentieth Century Fox.

Meaning the sovereign

Soren, Tor, Thordis, Thorbert, Thor

Soren Aabye Kierkegaard, the Danish philosopher, was born on 5 May 1813. Known as the father of existentialism, his purpose – to restore the individual and the choices each person makes to the centre of philosophical debate – crossed boundaries of writing, philosophy, theology and literary criticism.

Meaning thunder

Gabrielle, Gabriella, Gabriel, Gabrila, Abriella, Avrielle

Gabrielle Coco Chanel's most lasting creation, the perfume Chanel No. 5, went on sale today for the first time in 1921. It was named after the fifth day of the fifth month. When asked what she wore in bed, Marilyn Monroe famously replied 'nothing but Chanel No. 5'.

Meaning woman of God

Tammy, Tamara, Tamar, Tammie

Tammy Wynette, the US country singer and songwriter, was born Virginia Wynette Pugh on this day in 1942. Best known for 'Stand by Your Man', she trained as a hairdresser and renewed her licence every year in case she had to return to the day job.

Meaning perfection, palm tree

Amy, Aimeé

On this day in 1930 the British aviator *Amy Johnson* set out on her solo flight to Australia. She was the first woman to do so and won £10,000 for her pains. She later flew across the Atlantic Ocean and to India. She also set a new record for the flight from London to Cape Town.

Meaning beloved

Taylor

Today is the birthday of *Taylor Ann Hasselhoff*, who was born in 1990. She is the daughter of actress Pamela Bach and *Baywatch* actor David Hasselhoff, and is a sister to Hayley Amber. The Hasselhoffs undertake a great deal of valuable work for children's charities.

Meaning tailor

Sigmund, Sigisimon, Sigmond, Sigisimund

Sigmund Freud was born Sigismund Schlomo Freud on this day in 1856. He is the founder of the psychoanalytical school of psychology. His central theory was that much of human behaviour is controlled by the unconscious. He studied hypnotism and the meaning of dreams.

Meaning victorious protector

Valentino, Valente, Valentin

Rodolfo Alfonzo Raffaele Pierre Philibert Guglielmi di Valentina d'Antonguolia was born on this day in 1895 in Castellaneta, Italy. Better known as *Rudolph Valentino*, he was the first movie actor to have a huge following of fans. Coincidentally, 1895 was also the year cinema was invented.

Meaning good health

Stewart, Stuart, Steweard, Stew, Stu

Stewart Granger, the British actor, was born James Lablanche Steward on this day in 1913. He changed his name to avoid any confusion with the US actor James Stewart. He married three times; his second wife was the actress Jean Simmons.

Meaning steward

Gaston, Gascon

Gaston Leroux, the French author of *Phantom of the Opera*, was born in Paris on this day in 1868. He worked as a journalist, sailing the world as a correspondent before publishing *The Mystery of the Yellow Room*, his first novel, in 1908. *Phantom* appeared two years later.

Meaning from Gascony

Heather

On this day in 1935 John Ford's movie *The Informer* was premiered. It starred Victor McLaglen and the British actress *Heather Angel*, who went on to star in *Pride and Prejudice* (1940), but became known to a much wider audience when she appeared in the long-running TV soap *Peyton Place* (1964–9).

Meaning heather (the plant)

Shannon, Shannah

Today is the birthday of Canadian swimmer *Shannon Shakespeare*, who was born on 6 May 1977. She represented her country at 100 metres freestyle in the both the 1996 and the 2000 Olympic Games.

Meaning small but wise

Destiny, Destinée

On this day in 2000 'Say My Name' by *Destiny's Child* reached number one in the US charts. Destiny's Child is one of the most successful girl groups and in seven years has sold 40 million records. Beyoncé's father manages the band.

Meaning fate

Ghena, Gheina, Ghena, Ghenelle

The Bulgarian soprano *Ghena Dimitrova* was born on this day in Beglej in 1941. She is one of the top dramatic singers in international opera and has sung all over the world, including the Metropolitan Opera House in New York and La Scala in Milan, where she has appeared for several seasons.

Meaning not known

Ilyich

On this day in 1840 the great Russian composer *Pyotr Ilyich Tchaikovsky* was born in Kamsko-Votkinsk. He wrote ten operas, six symphonies and the famous ballets, *Swan Lake*, *The Sleeping Beauty* and *The Nutcracker*.

Meaning Ilya's son

Volker

The German playwright *Volker Braun* was born in Dresden on this day in 1939. His first play, *Die Kipper* (The Dumpers) (1965), was produced and then banned. In 2000 he was awarded the Georg-Buchner Preis, one of Germany's most celebrated literary awards.

Meaning people's guard

Archibald, Archie, Archibaldo, Archy, Arkady, Arky, Arch, Archambault

US poet *Archibald MacLeish* was born on 7 May 1892 in Glencoe, Illinois. He believed that the poet was a natural outsider, but later he reversed his position and took up public life. The name Archibald sounds old fashioned, but Archie has enjoyed something of a revival.

Meaning bold prince

Breckin

Breckin Meyer, the US actor and producer, was born on this day in 1974. He went to the same school as Drew Barrymore, who says he gave her her first kiss. She was 10, he 11. He has appeared in many movies, including *Clueless* (1995) and *Garfield, The Movie* (2004).

Meaning freckled

Haley, Hayley, Hailey, Haylee

'Rock Around the Clock', the song credited with marking the beginning of rock and roll, was released on this day in 1955 by *Bill Haley and the Comets*. It wasn't a success until it was used on the soundtrack of the film *The Blackboard Jungle* (1955), after which all hell broke loose. Haley is often used as a girl's name.

Meaning clearing

Giselle, Gisela, Gisele, Gisella, Gizela

In France, Hungary and Poland 7 May is the name day for *Giselle*, which is also the title of a romantic ballet first performed in Paris in 1841. The ballet, based on a German poem by Heinrich Heine, has music by the French composer Adolphe Adam.

Meaning promise

Evita, Vitia

On this day in 1919 María Eva Duarte de Perón, known to everyone simply as *Evita*, was born in Buenos Aries. She became the second wife of Juan Perón, the Argentine politician. She was worshipped by the working class of her country, and her life was made the subject of the musical (1978) by Tim Rice and Andrew Lloyd-Webber.

Meaning life giver

Totie, Tootie, Toots

Totie Fields, the US comedian, was born in Hartford, Connecticut, on this day in 1930. In 1978 she was voted entertainer of the year and female comedy star of the year. She wrote a book entitled *I Think I'll Start on Monday: The Official Eight and a Half Ounce Mashed Potato Diet* (1972).

From Sophie, meaning wisdom

Crosby, Crosbey, Crosbie

Irving Berlin's song 'White Christmas', sung by *Bing Crosby* in *Holiday Inn* (1942), was copyrighted on this day in 1942. It has sold over 30 million copies, making it one of the bestselling records of all time. It is the most valuable music ever copyrighted.

Meaning dweller at the crossroads

Lex

Lex Barker, the Tarzan actor, was born Alexander Crichlow Barker Jr on this day in 1919 in New York. When he dropped out of Princeton to become an actor, his family virtually disowned him. He made five Tarzan movies in all, the first being *Tarzan's Magic Fountain* (1949). He also had five wives.

From Alexander, meaning protector of mankind

Mattie, Mattias, Mata, Matty

Mattie Jay of Busted was born on 8 May 1983. The British pop rock trio Busted have had a number one UK single, 'What I Go to School for' (2003), in addition to a double platinum album. The fun, energetic young band won best pop act at the 2004 Brit Awards.

Meaning gift of God

David, Dave, Dav, Davey, Davie, Davy, Davon, Davis, Dewi, Dafydd, Dai, Davidson

One of the most travelled people on earth, Sir *David Attenborough* was born on this day in 1926. The naturalist and presenter of many award-winning TV series, including *Life on Earth* (1979), *The Living Planet* (1983) and *The Private Life of Plants* (1995), was also a senior manager for the BBC.

Meaning beloved

Augusta, Augistina, Augustine, Auguste, Gusta, Guss, Gussie

The US author *Augusta Wilson* was born on this day in 1835 in Wynnton, Georgia. A great supporter of the Confederate cause, she worked as a nurse during the Civil War and wrote several novels. Her novel *St Elmo* (1866) was staged as a play and turned into a silent movie.

Meaning sacred, majestic

Keelin, Keely

Keelin Curnuck was born on this day in 1972. She was Miss Venus Swimwear in 1994 and Miss New York USA in 1996. Keelin or Keely, a Gaelic name, is an appropriate name for any beautiful girl.

Meaning slender and fair, beautiful one

Toni, Tonia

The singer *Toni Tennille* was born on 8 May 1941. She was in the 1970s duo Captain and Tennille, with Daryl Dragon, her husband. She has since become a solo artist, although the couple are still married. Their British number one hit, 'Love Will Keep Us Together' (1975), remained in the charts for six months.

From Antonia, meaning beyond price

Ana, Anna, Annika, Anneka, Anula, Anusia, Anuska

Ana Maria Lombo was born on this day in 1978 in Medellin, Colombia. She is best known as a member of the teen band Eden's Crush, which was formed after appearing on the US reality TV show *Popstars*. They had a US chart hit with 'Get Over Yourself' in 2001.

From Anne, meaning God has favoured me

Roland, Rowland, Roley, Rollin, Rollo, Rowe

In Slovakia 9 May is the name day for *Roland*. The best-known Roland in history was the Frankish hero and knight of Charlemagne, whose death at Roncesvalles in 778 is celebrated in the *Chanson de Roland* (Song of Roland). The name first arrived in Britain after the Norman Conquest in 1066.

Meaning famous land

Howard, Howie

The British archaeologist and Egyptologist *Howard Carter* was born on this day in 1874. He is famous as the discoverer of KV62, the tomb of Tutankhamen, at Luxor, Egypt. Although those associated with the find were said to be cursed, he lived to a ripe old age.

Meaning chief guardian

Pancho

The tennis player *Pancho Gonzales* was born Ricardo Alonso Gonzalez in Los Angeles on 9 May 1928. He dominated the male tennis game for 12 years and has been named as one of the five greatest tennis players that have ever lived.

Meaning tuft, plume

Vance

The US astronaut *Vance DeVoe Brand* was born at Longmont, Colorado, on 9 May 1931. He flew on four missions, including the historic *Apollo-Soyuz* test project in 1975. He is currently deputy director of aerospace projects at NASA.

Meaning from the grain barn

Glenda, Glenn, Glynis, Glennis, Glenys

Glenda Jackson, the British actress and member of Parliament, was born on this day in 1936 at Birkenhead near Liverpool. The girl who once worked in Boots the Chemist won two Oscars – for *Women in Love* (1969) and *A Touch of Class* (1973) – before giving it all up for politics.

Meaning valley

Mona, Moyna

The US poet *Mona van Duyn* was born Mona Jan Van Duyn on 9 May 1921 in Waterloo, Iowa. The co-founder of the literary magazine *Perspective*, she published the collections *A Time of Bees* (1964), *Near Changes* (1990) and *Firefall* (1993).

From Monica, meaning advice giver

Kathryn, Kath, Kathy

Kathryn Kuhlman, the US faith healer 'who believed in miracles', was born Kathryn Johanna Kuhlman on 9 May 1907. She began her ministry as a travelling evangelist with her sister and brother-in-law. The Kathryn Kuhlman Foundation continues to thrive.

From Katherine, meaning pure maiden

Candice, Candace, Candide, Candida, Candie, Candy

The US actress *Candice Bergen* was born in Beverly Hills, California, on 9 May 1946. She was nominated for a best supporting actress Oscar and a Golden Globe for her performance in *Starting Over* (1979). She married Louis Malle, and they have a daughter, Chloe.

Meaning brilliant white

Fred, Freddie, Freddy

The US actor and dancer *Fred Astaire* was born Frederick Austerlitz on 10 May 1899. He is best remembered for his roles with his dancing partner Ginger Rogers, with whom he made ten films. The name Astaire, which he and his sister Adele adopted, comes from his uncle L'Astaire.

From Frederick, meaning peaceful ruler

Hèlio

The Brazilian racing driver *Hèlio Castroneves* was born on this day in 1975. He is one of the top drivers in North American open-wheel racing. He won the Indianapolis 500 in 2001 and 2002. His nickname is Spiderman, because he climbs the fence to the crowd when he wins.

Meaning healer

Vladislav, Vlad, Vladislava, Vyacheslav

One of the most popular journalists in Russia, TV anchorman *Vladislav Listyev* was born on 10 May 1956. He was the head of the ORT TV Channel and was a key player in bringing democracy to Russian TV. He hosted *The View*, a successful talk show, in the 1980s.

Meaning glory

Bono

Bono, the lead singer with U2, was born Paul David Hewson in Dublin, Ireland, on this day in 1960. He campaigns vigorously for Third World debt relief. The name Bono comes from Bona Vox, a hearing aid device with a name that means 'good voice'; it is also Italian slang for sexy.

Meaning good voice, sexy

Tamiyo

The Japanese ballerina *Tamiyo Kusakari* was born on 10 May 1965. She joined the Maki Asami Ballet Company in 1984 and came first in the Japan Ballet Competition in 1987. In 1997 she starred in the movie *Shall We Dance* directed by Suo Masayuk. It was a huge hit in Japan and has since been remade with Richard Gere.

Meaning benefit

Ella, Ellie

Ella Grasso, governor of Connecticut and the first woman to be elected as a US state governor in her own right, was born Ella Tambussi Grasso on this day in 1919. She began her career as a speech writer for the League of Women Voters in 1943.

Meaning beautiful fairy woman

Maybelle, Maybelline, Maibelle, Mabella, Mabel

The US country singer *Maybelle Carter* was born on this day in 1909. She has become known as Mother Carter, the stage name she would use when touring with her daughters during the 1940s. Her granddaughter is the country singer Carlene Carter.

Meaning my fair maid

Ariel, Ariella, Arielle

US philosopher and writer *Ariel Durant* was born on this day in 1898. She and her husband, Will, were key figures in establishing the post-war US Declaration of Interdependence. They co-wrote *The Story of Civilization* (1935–75). She was the *Los Angeles Times* woman of the year in 1965.

Meaning God's lioness

Irving, Irvine, Irwin, Ervin, Erwin

Songwriter *Irving Berlin* was born Israel Isidore Baline in 1888 in Siberia, emigrating to the US in 1893. The composer of 'God Bless America' and 'White Christmas' sold his first lyrics, 'Marie from Sunny Italy', in 1903. He was paid 37 cents.

Meaning friend of the sea

Constantine, Constantino, Constant, Constantin, Connie, Conn, Konstantin, Konstantine

On this day in 330 Constantinople became the new capital of the Roman Empire. It was named after the emperor, *Constantine I*, who had originally wanted it to be known as New Rome, but the name never caught on. Before 330 it was called Byzantium; today it is called Istanbul.

Meaning firm, unwavering

Salvador, Salvadore, Salvatore, Salvator, Salvidor

The leading painter of the surrealist movement, *Salvador Dalì*, was born Salvador Domenec Felipe Jacinto Dalì Domenech in Figueras on this day in 1904. With his twirly moustache, eccentric clothes and unusual lifestyle, the Spanish artist is as unforgettable as his art.

Meaning saviour

Camilo

On this day *Camilo José Cela*, the Nobel Prize-winning Spanish novelist and travel writer, was born in Iria Flavia, La Coruña, in 1916. He founded a writing style known as tremendisimo. *La Familia de Pascual Duarte* (The Family of Pascual Duarte) was his first novel, published in 1942, but his best known is *La Colmena* (The Hive) (1951).

Meaning free-born

Martha, Marta, Martella, Marthe, Marti, Martita, Martynne, Mattie, Matty

One of the most important figures in contemporary dance, *Martha Graham* was born on 11 May 1894. Named *Time* magazine's dancer of the century in 1998, she was presented with the Presidential Medal of Freedom in 1976 by Gerald Ford, whose wife, Betty, was one of her pupils.

Meaning mistress

Holly, Hollie

Holly Valance, the actress and singer, was born Holly Vukadinovic on this day in 1983 in New Zealand. Brought up in Australia, her grandfather was the cousin of British comedian Benny Hill. She began her career as Flick Scully in the Australian soap *Neighbours*.

Meaning bearer of good fortune

Mari, Maribell, Marybelle, Maribel

Mari Sandoz, born on 11 May 1896, was a US novelist, historian, biographer and teacher. She was born on the Mirage Flats, Hay Springs, Nebraska, and her writing brings alive the distinctive frontier dialogue and harshness of her home region.

From Mary, meaning bitter

Minnesota, Minne

On this day in 1858 *Minnesota*, on the Canadian border, became the 32nd state of the Union. Its name is derived from the regional name for the Minnesota River, *mini sota*, which means sky-tinted water or smoky-white water.

Meaning sky-tinted water, smoky-white water

Edward, Edouard, Eduard, Ewart, Eddy, Eddie, Ed

The father of the limerick, *Edward Lear* was born on this day in 1812 in Highgate, London. The youngest of 20 children, he was brought up by Ann, his eldest sister by 21 years. Although he is best remembered for his limericks, he was also a highly talented artist and illustrator.

Meaning prosperous guardian

Dante, Durant

Dante Gabriel Rossetti, the British poet, painter and translator, was born on 12 May 1828. With John Everett Millais and William Holman Hunt, he founded the Pre-Raphaelite Brotherhood in 1848, which aimed to return to the vivid colours and naturalism that had characterized art before the Renaissance master Raphael.

Meaning enduring friendship

Yogi

New York Yankee baseball hero *Lawrence Peter 'Yogi' Berra* was born on this day in 1925 in St Louis, Missouri. Awarded the accolade of most valuable player of the American League three times, he was named after an Indian yogi, and the cartoon Yogi Bear was named after him.

Meaning guru

Sullivan, Sully, Sullie

The US child actor *Sullivan Sweeten* was born on this day in 1995 in Brownwood, Texas. He and his brother Sawyer play twins in the US TV hit show *Everybody Loves Raymond* (1996), starring Ray Romano and Emmy winner Patricia Heaton.

Meaning with black eyes

Ina

In Latvia today is the name day for *Ina*. The name, originally Greek, grew from the pet names of girls with -ina at the end of their names, such as Christina, Marina, Edwina and so on. There are two Irish saints called Ina.

Meaning pure

Florence, Florencia, Florenza, Florinda, Florine, Floris, Florrie, Florry

The lady with the lamp, *Florence Nightingale* was born to a wealthy family on this day in 1820 in Florence, Italy. Her sister was also, less fortunately, named after her birthplace, Parthenope. Florence trained as a nurse in Germany and France before volunteering to help in the Crimean War.

Meaning flower

Bianca

On this day in 1971 *Bianca Perez Morena de Macias* married Mick Jagger at St Tropez town hall in the south of France. They honeymooned on a yacht sailing around the Mediterranean islands of Corsica and Sardinia. Bianca has become an outspoken advocate of the world's dispossessed.

Meaning white

Indra

The Indian yoga teacher and actress *Indra Devi* was born in Riga, Russia, on this day in 1899. An early disciple of Sri Tirumalai Krishnamacharya, she was known in Hollywood in the 1940s as the first lady of yoga. She lived to be 102.

Meaning chief of the gods

13 ^{MAY}

Sgeir, Ansgar, Asgerd

The second president of Iceland, *Sgeir Sergison* was born on 13 May 1894. He was educated as a theologian, but was too young when he qualified to be ordained. He was elected president of his country in 1952 and was re-elected unopposed in 1956, 1960 and 1964.

Meaning son of Raud

Harvey, Harve, Harv, Herv, Herve, Hervey

The US actor *Harvey Keitel* was born on this day in 1939. His mother was Polish, his father was Romanian and he was brought up in New York City. He played the romantic lead opposite Holly Hunter in Jane Campion's multi-award-winning film *The Piano* (1993), but is better known for gangster roles, including those in *Reservoir Dogs* (1991) and *Pulp Fiction* (1994).

Meaning worthy in battle

Steveland, Stevie

One of the greatest singers and songwriters in the USA, Stevie Wonder was born *Steveland Judkins Hardaway* in Saginaw, Michigan, on this day in 1950. He has received 22 Grammys and in 2004 was given Billboard's Century Award.

Meaning crowned one

Roch

The French-Canadian novelist *Roch Carrier* was born on 13 May 1937. An officer of the Order of Canada and Canada's national librarian as well as a novelist, he is also known for his *contes*, which are short short stories.

Meaning glory

Alison, Alyson, Aliss, Allie, Allyson

On this day in 1995 the British mountaineer *Alison Hargreaves* became the first woman to climb Everest without the help of sherpas or oxygen. She was only the second person ever to do this.

Meaning noble, well-born

Zoe, Zoey, Zoie

Actress *Zoe Wanamaker* was born on this day in 1949. The daughter of the US film director Sam Wanamaker, Zoe lives in Britain. She played Madam Hooch in *Harry Potter and the Philosopher's Stone* (2001) and is also well known for her role in the TV series *My Family* (2000).

Meaning life

Bea, Beata

Bea Arthur, the US actress best known for her role as Dorothy in the long-running TV hit *The Golden Girls* (1985), was born on 13 May 1926. Since then she narrated PETA's Kentucky Fried Cruelty video, exposing the abuse inherent in the factory farming of chickens.

From Beatrice, meaning blessed, divine one

Daphne

Dame *Daphne du Maurier*, the British novelist, was born on 13 May 1907 in London. She lived in Cornwall for most of her life, and many of her stories are set there, including *Jamaica Inn* (1936) and the mesmerizing *Rebecca* (1938), which was turned into an Oscar-winning film in 1940.

Meaning bay tree

Sidney, Sid, Syd

Sidney Bechet, the great jazz saxophonist, clarinettist and composer, was born on 14 May 1897 in New Orleans, Louisiana. His autobiography is called *Treat it Gentle* (1960), and the character Pablo in Hermann Hesse's novel *Steppenwolf* (1927) is said to be based on him.

Meaning wide land by a marsh

Norodom

Norodom Sihamoni, the ruler of Cambodia, was born on this day in 1953. The son of King Norodom Sihanouk and Queen Monieath, he was his country's ambassador to UNESCO before he was enthroned in October 2004.

Meaning not known

Eoin

The Irish writer *Eoin Colfer* was born on 14 May 1965 in Wexford. He is the author of the *Artemis Fowl* series of children's books. He describes the stories as contemporary fairytales, on which Raymond Chandler and James Bond are as much an influence as Cinderella is.

Meaning God's gracious gift

Troy

The 1960s singer *Troy Shondell* was born on this day in 1940 in Fort Wayne, Indiana. He recorded in the 1950s as Gary Shelton, his real name. In 1961 he had a US hit with 'This Time', which reached number six in the US charts.

Meaning from the land of the curly-haired people

Sian

The acclaimed Welsh actress *Sian Phillips* was born Jane Elizabeth Ailwen Phillips in Bettws, Carmarthenshire, on 14 May 1934. She is primarily a stage actress, but has also appeared in many films, including *Dune* (1984). She was married to Peter O'Toole, and they have two children.

From Jane, meaning God's gift of grace

Tania, Tanya, Titania

The conductor, composer and music director *Tania Leon* was born on 14 May 1943 in Havana, Cuba. In the 1970s she was the music director of New York's Dance Theatre of Harlem as well as music director of several Broadway shows, including *The Wiz* (1978).

Meaning fairy queen

Apple

Apple Blythe Alison Martin was born in London on this day in 2004 to actress Gwyneth Paltrow and Chris Martin. The press wondered if she had been named after Chris's computer, or the Big Apple, Gwyneth's home city. It is just as likely that the name came from the fruit, the symbol of wisdom.

Meaning symbol of wisdom

Shanice, Shani

The US rhythm and blues singer *Shanice* was born on 14 May 1973 in Pittsburgh, Pennsylvania. The Grammy-winning vocalist signed her first record contract when she was just 11 years old. She had an international hit in 1992 with the song 'I Love Your Smile'.

Meaning marvellous

15 MAY

Jasper, Gaspar, Gaspard, Gasper, Kasper, Kaspar, Casper, Caspar

The US artist *Jasper Johns* was born on 15 May 1930 in Augusta, Georgia. He is one of the most important and influential US painters of the mid-20th century and one of the best printmakers ever. His best-known painting is *Flag* (1955).

Meaning treasurer

Amadeus, Amadeo, Amando, Amadour

British dramatist Peter Shaffer was born on 15 May 1926 in Liverpool. He has written numerous award-winning plays, including *Amadeus* (1979), about the life of Mozart. Turned into a film in 1984, it won eight Oscars, including best picture.

Meaning loveable

Eno, Enos

The British musician, producer and music theorist *Brian Eno*, known to everyone as Eno, was born Brian Peter George St Jean le Baptiste de la Salle Eno on 15 May 1948. He began his career in the band Roxy Music with Bryan Ferry.

Meaning mortal

Tenzing

The mountaineer *Tenzing Norgay* was born in Nepal on 15 May 1914. As a sherpa he accompanied many Everest expeditions, but in 1952 he and Edmund Hillary were the first men to reach the summit. He subsequently founded a trekking holiday company, run by his son, Jamling.

Meaning protector of dharma

Madeleine, Madelia, Madella, Madelle, Madlin, Maddalene

Madeleine Albright, who became the 64th US secretary of state, was born Marie Jana Korbel in Prague, Czechoslovakia, on this day in 1937. Nominated to the position by President Bill Clinton, she was the first ever woman to become secretary of state.

Meaning tower of strength

Dympna, Dymphna, Dymphia, Dimphia, Dympha

Today is the feast day of *St Dympna*. After her mother died her father became mentally ill and tried to make his daughter his second wife. Dympna fled. Some say she is buried in Gheel, near Antwerp, but a grave in Ireland has become her shrine, where miraculous cures for insanity and epilepsy are said to have occurred.

Meaning nurse

Zara

Zara Phillips, the daughter of Princess Anne and Captain Mark Phillips, was born *Zara Anne Elizabeth Phillips* in London on this day in 1981. Unusual for a member of the royal family, it is a biblical name, chosen by Prince Charles who thought it suited her sudden and quick birth.

Meaning bright as dawn

Arletty, Arletta, Arlette, Arlina, Arline, Arlyne

The French singer, model and actress *Arletty* was born Léonie Bathait on 15 May 1898 in Courbevoie. She appeared in many classic French films of the 1930s and 1940s, including *Hotel du Nord* (1938) and *Les Enfants du Paradis* (1945).

From Arlene, meaning pledge

Laffit, Laffie, Lafferty, Laffey

Laffit Pincay Jr, the US jockey, had his first win ever on this day in 1964. He went on to become the jockey with the most wins in history, entering the Guinness Book of Records with an overwhelming total of 9,311 wins.

Meaning not known

Studs

The US writer and broadcaster *Studs Terkel* was born Louis Terkel in New York City in 1912. He won the Pulitzer Prize in 1985 for his book about the Second World War, *The Good War*. He is named after Studs Lonigan, the hero of the novelist James T. Farrell's gritty trilogy set in Chicago's South Side.

Meaning house

Pierce, Pierro, Piero, Piers, Pierrot, Petro

The Irish actor *Pierce Brosnan* was born Pierce Brendan Brosnan on this day in 1953 in Navan, County Meath. He played the role of James Bond in four Bond films, but previously he was Remington Steele in the US TV detective series of the same name.

From Peter, meaning rock, stone

Natwar

Natwar Singh, the Indian politician, was born on 16 May 1931. In May 2004 he became the external affairs minister of India in Manmohan Singh's cabinet. He has also published several books, including a tribute to E.M. Forster.

Meaning Lord Krishna

Olga, Olenka, Olva, Ollie, Elga, Helga

The Russian gymnast *Olga Korbut* was born Olga Valentinovna Korbut on this day in 1955. She won a silver and three gold medals at the 1972 Munich Olympics. She invented two new gymnastic moves, the Korbut Salto and the Korbut Flip.

Meaning holy

Antoinette, Antoinetta, Antonina

On this day in 1770 *Marie Antoinette* married the dauphin of France, the future Louis XVI. She was the daughter of the Habsburg empress of Austria, Maria Theresa, and the marriage sealed the alliance between Austria and France.

From Antonia, meaning beyond price

Debra, Devora, Debor, Debora

The US actress *Debra Winger* was born on this day in 1955 in Cleveland Heights, Ohio. She was nominated for best actress Oscars for her roles in *An Officer and a Gentleman* (1982), opposite Richard Gere, and *Shadowlands* (1993), opposite Anthony Hopkins.

From Deborah, meaning bee

Junko

On this day in 1975 *Junko Tabei* became the first woman to set foot on the peak of Mount Everest. The Japanese mountaineer was born in 1939 in Fukushima Prefecture. The all-woman team with which she went to Everest was supported by *Yomiuri*, a newspaper, and Nihon TV.

Meaning not known

17 MAY

Erik, Eric, Erich, Erick

The French composer *Erik Satie* was born in Honfleur, France, on 17 May 1866. One of the original avant-garde composers, he was an influence on many. When he was broke and asked by a patron if he wanted a drink, he responded by asking: 'Could I have a pair of socks instead?'

Meaning peaceful ruler

Pervis

Pervis Jackson, a member of the US 1970s soul group the Spinners, was born in New Orleans on this day in 1938. The group had many classic hits, including 'Could It be I'm Falling in Love' (1972) and 'Then Came You' (1974).

Meaning passage

Trent

US musician, producer and composer *Trent Reznor* was born on this day in 1965 in Mercer, Pennsylvania. He was the creative force behind Nine Inch Nails and produced the soundtrack for the hit computer game Quake.

Meaning surging

Dennis, Denis, Den, Denny

British playwright *Dennis Potter* was born on this day in 1935. He wrote many of the most innovative and highly acclaimed dramas to have been shown on TV, including *Vote, Vote, Vote for Nigel Barton* (1965) and *Blue Remembered Hills* (1979). *Pennies from Heaven* (1978) and *The Singing Detective* (1986) combined drama with 1930s music.

Meaning wine-lover

Máxima, Maximilian, Maxie

Today is the birthday of *Máxima Zorreguieta Cerruti*, the Argentine-born wife of Prince Willem-Alexander of the Netherlands. She was an investment banker before joining the Dutch royal family in February 2002 and becoming a princess of Orange.

From Maxine, meaning greatest

Zinka

The Croatian soprano *Zinka Milanov* was born on 17 May 1906 in Zagreb. She changed her name from Zinka Kunc when she made her debut at the Metropolitan Opera House in New York in 1937. She sang the title role in *Tosca* at La Scala, Milan, in 1950. When she returned to the Met she was hailed as a *primadonna assoluta*.

Meaning zinc

Enya

The Grammy-winning Irish singer *Enya* was born Eithne Ni Bhráonain on this day in 1961. Enya is the phonetic approximation of Eithne in Irish Gaelic. Ireland's bestselling solo artist started in the group Clannad.

Meaning kernel

Sasha, Sacha

The US actress *Sasha Alexander* was born Suzna Alexander in Los Angeles on this day in 1975. She is best known for her role as Caitlin Todd in the US TV drama *Navy NCIS* (2003). She also played Gretchen Witter in *Dawson's Creek* (1998).

Meaning helpmate

Rudjer

The Jesuit physicist, astronomer, mathematician, philosopher, diplomat and poet *Rudjer Boscovich*, sometimes known as Ruggiero Giuseppe Boscovich, was born in Dubrovnik on 18 May 1711. Using Newtonian mechanics, he devised an atomic theory that inspired Faraday to develop field theory for electromagnetic interaction.

From Roger, meaning famous spearman

Perry, Pierino, Peregrino

The US singer *Perry Como* was born Pierino Ronald Como in Canonsburg, Pennsylvania, on 18 May 1912. He had many hits over the decades, his first being 'Till the End of Time' (1945). He also had a popular series of TV shows, which ran from 1948 to 1994.

Meaning pear tree

Kian, Cian, Kean

On Tuesday, 18 May 2004, Oscar-winning actress Geena Davis gave birth, at the age of 47, to twin boys, *Kian William* and Kaiis Steven, younger brothers to her two-year-old daughter Alizeh. Geena's husband, Reza Jarrahy, is a doctor.

Meaning ancient

Ezio, Enzio

The Italian bass *Ezio Pinza* was born in Rome on 18 May 1892. One of the opera greats of the first half of the 20th century, he appeared at the Metropolitan Opera House in New York for 22 seasons, delivering over 750 performances. Following his operatic career, he starred in a number of musicals on Broadway, including *South Pacific* in 1949.

Meaning aquiline nose

Margot, Margo, Margory, Margorie

Dame *Margot Fonteyn*, Britain's most famous ballerina, was born Margaret Hookham in Reigate, Surrey, on this day in 1919. When Rudolf Nureyev joined the Royal Ballet in the 1960s, they became one of the most electric stage partnerships ballet has ever known.

From Margaret, meaning pearl

Helen, Helena, Helene

On this day in 1991 *Helen Sharman* became the first British astronaut to fly in space. She became an astronaut after hearing an advertisement on the radio while she was driving home from her job as a research technician for Mars, the chocolate manufacturers. She beat 13,000 other applicants.

Meaning light

Martika, Martita, Marti, Martie, Marty

The Cuban-American singer and actress *Martika* was born Marta Marrero on this day in 1969. She starred as Gloria on the Disney Channel's *Kids Inc* (1984). Her album *Markita* (1989) spawned the number one US hit 'Toy Soldiers' (1992).

From Martha, meaning the mistress

Miriam

The British character actress *Miriam Margolyes* was born on this day in 1941. She has been in dozens of films since *A Nice Girl Like Me* (1969), including the *Harry Potter* films (2001, 2002, 2004) as well as *Ladies in Lavender* (2004) and *The Life and Death of Peter Sellers* (2004).

From Mary, meaning bitter

Yves, Ives, Ivo, Ivor, Ivar, Iven, Yven, Yvar

Today is the feast day of *St Yves*, who was born at Kermnartin, France, in 1303 and became a lawyer. He eventually entered the service of the bishops of Rennes and, later, of Treguier. After becoming a priest, he put his legal knowledge at the disposal of his parishioners.

Meaning warrior with bow

Edison

On this day in 1926 *Thomas Edison* spoke on the radio for the first time. He contributed to the inventions of the phonograph, kinetoscope, Dictaphone, radio, electric light bulb, autograph printer and tattoo gun.

Meaning son of Ed

Dusty

Dusty Hill, the guitarist and vocalist with the band ZZ Top, was born on 19 May 1949 in Dallas, Texas. ZZ Top are famous for their hard rocking sound, of which 'Gimme All Your Loving' (1983) is typical, and for their unique visual style.

From Dustin, meaning valiant fighter

Livio, Livingston

The Italian athlete *Livio Berruti* was born in Turin on 19 May 1939. He won a gold medal in the 200 metres in the 1960 Olympic Games when he was 21 years old. He always ran wearing white socks and black glasses.

Meaning from Leif's town

Marilyn, Marylyn, Maryse, Marya, Marla

On this day in 1962 probably the best-known rendition of the song 'Happy Birthday' was sung. *Marilyn Monroe* crooned to President John F. Kennedy at a fund-raising event at New York's Madison Square Garden, and the film of the event has become one of her most famous scenes.

From Mary, meaning bitter

Fidelia, Fidela, Fidele, Fidelity

The US artist *Fidelia Bridges* was born in Salem, Massachusetts, on this day in 1834. Her best-known works have been of plants, flowers and birds in their natural surroundings. She also illustrated books and greetings cards.

Meaning faithful

Lorraine, Loraine, Larraine, Larayne, Larina, Larine

Lorraine Hansberry, the US playwright and artist, was born on this day in 1930. She was the first African-American to have a play on Broadway. *A Raisin in the Sun* (1959) was a critical success, winning the New York Drama Critics' Circle best play of the year award.

Meaning famous in battle

Joaquina, Joachina, Joachima, Joakima

Today is the feast day of *St Joaquina Vedruna de Mas*, who was born in Barcelona in 1783 and was canonized in 1959. She was married to a nobleman and had nine children. When she became a widow she founded the Institute of the Carmelite Sisters of Charity in Catalonia.

Meaning the Lord's judge

Honorè, Honoratus, Honorius

The French novelist *Honorè de Balzac* was born on 20 May 1799 in Tours, Indre-et-Loire. One of the creators of literary realism, he famously worked very long hours, writing in 15-hour sittings and drinking lots of black coffee.

Meaning honour

Zbigniew

Poland's leading composer of film scores, *Zbigniew Preisner* was born on this day in 1955. He wrote the scores for the acclaimed films of Krzysztof Kieslowski, including the Three Colours series, *Blue* (1993), *White* (1993) and *Red* (1994). He has also written film scores for Francis Ford Coppola and many others.

Meaning dispeller of anger

Bronson, Bronnie

The US actor *Bronson Alcott Pinchot* was born on this day in 1959 in New York City. He is best known for his role as Balki Bartokomous in the TV sitcom *Perfect Strangers* (1986–93), for which he was nominated for an Emmy.

Meaning son of the brown-haired one

Israel, Izzie, Issie

One of Hawaii's best-loved singers, *Israel 'Brudda Iz' Kamakawiwo'ole* was born on the island of Oahu on 20 May 1959. His medley of 'Somewhere Over the Rainbow' and 'What a Wonderful World' (1993) was used on many films and made him an international star.

Meaning the Lord's soldier

Cher, Cherilyn, Cherie

The US singer and actress *Cher* was born Cherilyn Sarkisian LaPier on 20 May 1946. She and her first husband, Sonny, became famous in the 1960s with 'I Got You Babe' (1965). She has two children with her second husband Gregg Allman: Chastity Bono and Elijah Blue.

Meaning beloved

Trebisonda

Trebisonda Valla, who was born on this day in 1916, became the first Italian woman to win an Olympic gold medal when she won the 80 metre hurdles at the 1936 Berlin Olympics. Trebisonda is Italian for Trabzon, a beautiful Turkish town beloved by her father. She was known by her nickname Ondina.

Meaning little wave

Sigrid, Sigrior

The Norwegian novelist *Sigrid Undset* was born in Kalundborg, Denmark, on this day in 1882. She won the Nobel Prize for literature in 1928 for her three-volume work *Kristin Lavransdatter*. Set in medieval Norway, it told the story, in modernist style, of the entire life of a woman from her birth to her death.

Meaning beautiful victory

Margery, Marjorie

On this day in 1904 the British writer of detective stories *Margory Louisa Allingham* was born in London. Her best-known character was the detective Albert Campion, who appeared in several of her books, including *Police at the Funeral* (1931) and *The Tiger in the Smoke* (1952).

From Margaret, meaning pearl

21 MAY

Albrecht

The great German painter, wood-carver and engraver *Albrecht Dürer* was born in Nuremberg to Hungarian parents on 21 May 1471. His famous woodcuts include *Apocalypse* (1498), *Melancolia* (1514) and a series on the Crucifixion.

From Albert, meaning bright nobility

Donny, Domhnall

On this day in May 1989 *Donny Osmond* was at the top of the charts with 'Soldier of Love'. Before becoming a solo artist, Donny sang with his brothers – Alan, Jay, Jimmy, Merril, Wayne, Tom and Virl – and his sister, Marie, in the Osmonds.

From Donald, meaning ruler of the world

Armand, Armando, Armin, Armond

The US industrialist and art collector *Armand Hammer* was born on 21 May 1898. The chief executive of Occidental Petroleum was a generous philanthropist, supporting many charitable causes, including setting up the Armand Hammer United World College of the American West.

Meaning army man

Rollin, Rollo, Roley, Rowe, Rowland

On this day in 1922 a cartoon called 'On the Road to Moscow' won the Pulitzer Prize. The cartoonist was *Rollin Kirby*, who was born in Galva, Illinois, in 1875. This was the first time a cartoon had won the prize, and Kirby repeated the achievement with 'News from the Outside World' (1924) and 'Tammany' (1928).

From Roland, meaning famous land

Kay, Kaya, Kayia

The British actress *Kay Kendall* was born Kay Justine Kendall McCarthy on this day in 1927 in Withernsea, Yorkshire. She was dancing in the Palladium chorus when she was 12 and made her first film, *Fiddlers Three*, in 1944. She was married to the actor Rex Harrison.

Meaning resting place

Innocentia, Innocent, Inocenczo

On this day in 1909 Sister *Maria Innocentia Hummel* was born Berta Hummel. She changed her name when she entered the convent of Siessen. The kindergarten art teacher's drawings were turned into the famous M.I. Hummel figurines by Franz Boebel.

Meaning innocent

Maybellene, Maybelle, Moibeal, Maible, Mabel

On this day in 1955 US rock-and-roll star Chuck Berry recorded what was to become his first big hit, *Maybellene*, which was originally called 'Ida May'. Chuck Berry's real name was the stately Charles Edward Anderson Berry, and he went on to have dozens of hit records.

From Amabel, meaning loveable

Rhonda

On this day in 1965 the Beach Boys were number one in the US charts with 'Help me, Rhonda'. The song was taken from the album *Summer Days (and Summer Nights!!)* and reached number 27 in the British charts.

Meaning grand

Morrissey, Morris, Morrison

The charismatic lead singer of the top 1980s indie band the Smiths was born Stephen Patrick Morrissey on 22 May 1959 in Manchester, in the north of England. The Mozzer, as he is affectionately known, subsequently became a solo artist and moved to Los Angeles.

Meaning Maurice's son

Quinn

Quinn Martin was born on 22 May 1922. He was one of the most successful US TV producers of all time, and for a period of 21 years he had at least one prime-time show on air each year. Among his series were *The Fugitive, The Untouchables* and *Barnaby Jones.* (1973)

Meaning intelligent, wise

Sun, Sunny

The jazz composer, bandleader and piano and synthesizer player *Sun Ra* was born Herman Poole Blount on 22 May 1914 in Birmingham, Alabama. He was given the nickname Sonny when he was a child, and Ra is the name of the ancient Egyptian god of the sun.

Meaning sun, cheerful

Tintin

It is the birthday today of the creator of the famous *Tintin* cartoons, Hergé. He was born Georges Remi in Belgium on 22 May 1907. He took his penname Hergé from the French pronunciation of R G, the reverse of his initials.

Meaning sweet

Annika, Anika, Aneka, Anneka

On this day in 2003 *Annika Sorenstam* became the first woman golfer to play the PGA tour for 58 years. She was born in Stockholm, Sweden, in 1970, and with winnings of over $15 million, she is one of the most successful female golfers ever.

From Anne, meaning God has favoured me

Naomi, Nomi, Nomie

The British supermodel *Naomi Campbell* was born on 22 May 1970 in Streatham, London. Besides modelling, she has also performed as an actress and singer. Her album *Baby Woman* (1995) sold over a million copies, mostly in Japan.

Meaning pleasant one

Letizia, Letitia, Lettie, Lettice, Letisha, Leshia, Leda, Laetitia, Loutitia

On this day in 2004 *Letizia Ortiz Rocasolano* married Felipe, the prince of Asturias and heir to the Spanish throne. She was born in Oviedo, Asturias province, Spain. Before her marriage she was a journalist and TV presenter.

Meaning joy, happiness

Zahra, Zahrah

Zahra Savannah Rock was born on this day in 2004. She is the daughter of US actor comedian Chris Rock and his wife, Malaak Compton-Rock. In March 2004 Chris Rock was named the funniest man in America by the magazine *Entertainment Weekly*.

Meaning blooming flower

Rubens, Rube, Ruben, Rubey, Ruby, Reuben

The Formula One racing driver *Rubens Barrichello* was born Rubens Gonclaves Barrichello on 23 May 1972. His birthplace was São Paulo, Brazil, and his nickname is Rubinho. Among other wins, in 2004 he won the first Formula One race hosted in Shanghai, China.

Meaning behold a son

Carolus, Carrol, Carroll, Caryl, Carol

The Swedish botanist Carl von Linné is usually known by his Latin name, *Carolus Linnaeus*. He was born in Stenbrohult, Smalandia, on 23 May 1707. One of the fathers of modern science, his work on the classification of all living things laid the foundations for both ecology and taxonomy.

Meaning free man

Marvin, Marwen, Marwin, Mervin, Merwyn, Merwin

The US middleweight boxer *Marvin Hagler* was born on 23 May 1954 in Brockton, Massachusetts. Known as Marvellous Marvin, he looked tough and had a strong, steely character, but had an endearing soft spot for his fans.

Meaning famous friend

Anatoli, Anatole, Anatol, Anatolio

The Russian chess grandmaster *Anatoli Yevgenyevic Karpov* was born in Zlatoust on 23 May 1951. He is the most successful tournament player in history and one of the greatest players in the history of chess. He learned how to play when he was four years old.

Meaning from the East

Rosemary, Rosemarie, Romy, Rosie, Rosy

The US actress and singer *Rosemary Clooney* was born in Maysville, Kentucky, on this day in 1928. Her first hit was 'Come on-a My House' (1951), and in 1954 she starred in the movie classic *White Christmas* with Bing Crosby. She is the aunt of actor George Clooney.

Meaning dew of the sea

Jewel

US singer and songwriter *Jewel* was born on this day in 1974. Her then boyfriend, Sean Penn, directed the video for her second single, the hugely successful 'You Were Meant for Me'. She has also written a multimillion-selling book of poetry, *A Night without Armor*.

Meaning most precious one

Arabella, Arabelle, Aralia, Arbel, Arbele, Arbelle, Arbelia, Bel

Arabella Mansfield, the first woman to practise as a lawyer in the USA, was born Belle Aurelia Babb at Sperry Station, Des Moines, on this day in 1846. She took her law exams in Henry County, Iowa, and was admitted to the Bar in 1869.

Meaning beautiful altar

Misty

The country singer *Misty Morgan* was born on this day in 1945. She and her husband, Jack Blanchard, had 15 country hits between 1969 and 1975. The husband and wife duo were born three years apart in the same hospital in Buffalo, New York.

Meaning misty

Dylan, Dillan, Dilly, Dilan

Bob Dylan was born Robert Allen Zimmerman on 24 May 1941 in Duluth, Minnesota. One of his first stage names was Elston Gunn, and his first band was called the Golden Chords. Dylan himself says that his name comes not, as is often suggested, from Dylan Thomas, but from his Uncle Dillon.

Meaning great sea

Emanuel, Emmanuel, Immanuel, Manuel, Manolo, Mano

Emanuel Gottlieb Leutze was born on this day in 1816. The painter was born in Germany, but was raised in the USA. His best-known work is *Washington Crossing the Delaware* (1851), which is in the Metropolitan Museum of Art, New York.

Meaning God is with us

Philips, Pilib, Phillopa, Philly, Phil, Phill, Philly, Phillie, Filip, Filli, Filib

The Dutch painter *Philips Wouwerman* was born on this day in 1619. He was born into an artistic family – his father, Paulus, and his brothers, Pieter and Jan, were also artists – and he studied under Frans Hals. He is best known for his equestrian, battle and hunting scenes.

From Philip, meaning lover of horses

Daniel, Danielle, Daniell, Dane, Darnell

Daniel Gabriel Fahrenheit was born on this day in 1686 in Gdansk, which was then in Germany. He invented the alcohol thermometer (1709) and the mercury thermometer (1714), as well as the measuring scale for temperatures, which was named after him.

Meaning God is my judge

Siobhan

The actress *Siobhan McKenna* was born Siobhan Giollamhuire Mic Cionnaith in Belfast, Northern Ireland, on this day in 1922. Mainly a stage actress, she was a member of the Dublin Abbey Theatre and played Hamlet in 1959. She was in a number of films, including *King of Kings* (1961) and *Dr Zhivago* (1965).

From Jane, meaning gift of God

Elsa

Elsa Maxwell, the US columnist, songwriter and hostess, was born on this day in 1883. She wrote more than 80 songs, but was best known for her extraordinary parties. She invented games and novelties that made everyone who was anyone want to attend.

Meaning noble

Lillian, Lilian, Lilliana, Lilliane, Lillis, Lilly, Lillyan, Lily, Lilyan

One of the first working female engineers, *Lillian Moller Gilbreth* was born on 24 May 1878. She and her husband, Frank Bunker Gilbreth, were not only pioneers in the field of industrial engineering, but they also had 12 children. She appeared on a US stamp in 1984.

Meaning lily

Kristin

The British actress *Kristin Scott Thomas* was born on 24 May 1960 in Redruth, Cornwall. She has appeared in many films, including *The English Patient* (1996), for which she was nominated for an Academy Award as best actress.

From Christine, meaning follower of Christ

25

Miles, Myles

The jazz trumpeter *Miles Davis* was born at Alton, Illinois, on this day in 1926. One of the greatest trumpeters, famed for his unique emotional improvisational style, Davis studied formally at the Juilliard School of Music in New York before joining Charlie Parker's band.

Meaning soldier

Ian, Iaian, Iain

The British actor Sir *Ian Murray McKellan* was born in Burnley, Lancashire, on 25 May 1939. His first Broadway role was in *Bent* (1979). Equally at home on stage and in film, he was Oscar-nominated for his performance as Gandalf in *The Lord of the Rings* trilogy (2001, 2002, 2003) and won a Tony for *Amadeus* (1980).

Meaning God is gracious

Lucas, Luce, Lucio, Lucais

On this day in 1977 the first *Star Wars* film was shown in the USA. Directed by *George Lucas*, the series of films, which started 'a long time ago, in a galaxy far, far away', became one of the biggest movie phenomenons of all time.

From Luke, meaning light

Igor

Igor Ivanovich Sikorsky was born in Kiev, Ukraine, on this day in 1889. The aviation pioneer, who designed the modern helicopter and the first four-engine aircraft, emigrated to the USA in 1919 after the Russian Revolution.

Meaning hero

Ginny, Ginnie, Jinny

US singer and broadcaster *Ginny Simms* was born on this day in 1915 in San Antonio, Texas. After singing in big bands in the 1930s, she hosted a popular forces radio show during the Second World War. She was in several films in the 1940s, including *Broadway Rhythm* (1944).

From Virginia, meaning virgin

Leta, Letha, Lethia, Leithia, Lethitha

Leta Stetter Hollingworth was born in Nebraska on 25 May 1886. She was a pioneer in the study of the psychology of women and the differences between the sexes, and she carried out many sociological and biological experiments on the woman's role in society.

Meaning sweet oblivion

Patti

The US actress *Patti D'Arbanville-Quinn* was born on this day in 1951. When she was 17 years old she appeared in the Andy Warhol film *Flesh*. She dated Cat Stevens in the 1960s, and he wrote 'Lady D'Arbanville' in her honour. She has four children: Jesse, Emmelyn, Alexandra and Liam.

From Patricia, meaning well-born

Lauryn

Lauryn Hill, the US hip hop singer and actress, was born in South Orange, New Jersey, on this day in 1975. In 1988 she formed the Fugees with Pras Michel and Wyclef Jean, and in 1996 their second album, *The Score*, went multi-platinum.

From Lauren, meaning crowned with laurels

Wayne, Wain, Waine

The US actor *John Wayne* was born Marion Robert Morrison in Winterset, Iowa, on this day in 1907. His parents changed his middle name to Michael after calling their next son Robert. The actor-to-be didn't like being called Marion and changed his name before he appeared in his first film, *The Drop Kick* (1927). He got his nickname the Duke from his Airedale dog, Little Duke.

Meaning wagon maker

Hank

Hank Williams Jr, the US country singer, was born Randall Hank Williams on 26 May 1949 in Shreveport, Louisiana. The son of country music pioneer Hank Williams Sr and father of Hank III, his hits include 'Standing in the Shadows' and 'Born to Boogie'.

From Henry, meaning ruler of the estate

Nobuhiro, Nobuharu, Nobuhiko, Nobuhisa, Nobuhito

The Japanese *manga-ka* (comic artist) *Nobuhiro Watsuki* was born on 26 May 1970. He is famous for *Rurouni Kenshin*, a series of stories about samurai warriors.

Meaning not known

Mickey, Mick, Mickie

British guitarist, singer and producer *Mick Ronson* was born on 26 May 1946 in Hull. Nicknamed Rono, he played and sang with David Bowie in the 1970s. He released three solo albums, and also produced records for Ian Hunter and Lou Reed, among others.

From Michael, meaning like the Lord

Mariana, Marianna, Marianne, Marian, Marion

Today is the feast day of *St Mariana of Quito*, who lived in Peru in the 17th century. She worked for the poor and needy, and taught Indian children in her own home. She died during an epidemic in Quito, when she offered her own life in expiation of the sins of others.

From Mary, meaning bitter

Sally, Sallie, Sal, Salaaidh, Sadye, Sadella

The first US woman in space, *Sally Kristen Ride* was born on this day in 1951 in Los Angeles, California. She made her trip in 1983 on the space shuttle *Challenger*. She was the third woman in space after the Russians Valentina Tereshkova and Svetalna Savitskaya.

From Sarah, meaning princess

Dorothea, Dorete, Dorota, Drottya, Dosia

The US photographer *Dorothea Lange* was born on 26 May 1895 in Hoboken, New Jersey. She is best known for her social documentary work illustrating victims of the Great Depression, including 'Migrant Mother' (1936), publishing her photographs in *An American Exodus* (1939).

From Dorothy, meaning gift of God

Mamie, Manette, Manon, Mara, Maretta, Marette

Mamie Smith was born on 26 May 1883. In 1920 she became the first African-American to make a vocal blues recording. The three songs, including 'Crazy Blues', sold a million copies in one year. She was also a dancer, pianist and actress.

From Mary, meaning bitter

27 MAY

Declan

British singer Elvis Costello made his stage debut on this day in 1977. He was born *Declan Patrick Aloysius McManus* in London on 25 August 1954. His father, Ross McManus, sang with Joe Loss. Costello's best-known songs include 'Less Than Zero' (1977) and 'Watchin' the Detectives' (1977).

Meaning man of prayer

Owen, Owain, Owens

On this day in 1998, in the international soccer match between England and Chile, *Michael Owen* became the youngest player ever to score for England. He was 18. The Real Madrid player has averaged just under a goal in every two international games he has ever played.

Meaning warrior, well-born

Yasuhiro, Yasuo

Yasuhiro Nakasone was born on 27 May 1917. Prime minister of Japan from 1982 to 1987, he was the first Japanese politician to attend the annual summit of the seven leading Western nations and thus became Japan's first globally recognized political figure.

Meaning peaceful one

Dashiell

The US novelist and screenwriter *Dashiell Hammett* was born on this day in 1894 in St Mary's County, Maryland. In *The Maltese Falcon* (1930) he created the character Sam Spade, who was played by Humphrey Bogart in the 1941 movie of the book and was based on the time Hammett worked as an operative for the Pinkerton Detective Agency in Baltimore.

Meaning page boy

Peri

The US actress *Peri Gilpin* was born on 27 May 1961 in Waco, Texas, and was raised in Dallas, Texas. The accomplished stage actress is best known for her role as radio producer Roz Doyle in the TV comedy hit *Frasier* (1993).

Meaning purity

Siouxsie

Singer *Siouxsie Sioux* was born on this day in 1957. In the 1970s she formed Siouxsie and the Banshees, one of the most popular and enduring bands on London's punk scene. She has made 14 albums and has acted as a stand-in DJ for BBC's John Peel.

From Susan, meaning lily, rose

Alina

The Romanian ballerina *Alina Cojocaru* was born on this day in 1981. A rising star with London's Royal Ballet Company, her performances in leading roles have received much acclaim. Alina is a Polish name.

Meaning bright, beautiful

Cilla, Cill

It is the birthday today of the British singer and entertainer *Cilla Black*. She was born Priscilla Maria Veronica White in Liverpool on 27 May 1943. She was a hat-check girl at the Cavern Club where the Beatles first played and was signed there by their manager, Brian Epstein.

From Priscilla, meaning of ancient descent

Neville, Nevile, Nevil, Nev

On 28 May 1937 the British prime minister Stanley Baldwin resigned and announced that *Neville Chamberlain* would be his successor. The new leader of the Conservative Party is now largely remembered for his appeasement of Adolf Hitler and Benito Mussolini, although he took Britain into the Second World War in September 1939.

Meaning new settlement

Taffy

The American ice hockey player *Taffy Abel* was born on this day in 1900 in Sault Sainte Marie, Michigan. He was the first Native American to carry the US flag at an opening ceremony of the Olympic Games, which he did at the Winter Olympics in Chamonix in 1924. The Taffy Abel ice rink in Michigan is named after him.

From David, meaning beloved

Arto, Arthol, Artel, Artlett, Artley, Arton

The US guitarist and singer *Arto Lindsay* was born on this day in 1953. His childhood years, which were spent in Brazil, had a significant influence on his sound, and the vocals are sometimes in Portuguese. He appeared with Madonna in *Desperately Seeking Susan* (1985).

From Bartholomew, meaning son of a ploughman

Warwick, Warrick

The British novelist *Warwick Deeping* was born on 28 May 1877 in Southend, Essex. The author of 40 novels was a bestseller on both sides of the Atlantic in the 1920s and 1930s, and he was much admired by his contemporaries, including George Orwell and Graham Greene.

Meaning strong fortress

Maeve, Mave, Meave

The Irish author *Maeve Binchy* was born in Dalkey, Ireland, on this day in 1940. Her highly readable books, which include *The Glass Lake* (1994) and *Scarlet Feather* (2000), often examine the differences between life in England and Ireland, and how her country has changed since the Second World War.

Meaning goddess, purple flower

Kylie, Kayleigh, Kayle, Kay, Leigh

Kylie Minogue, the Australian actress and singer, was born on this day in 1968. She rose to fame in the TV soap *Neighbours* (1986), playing opposite Jason Donavan. Known the world over simply as Kylie, her single 'Can't Get You Out Of My Head' reached number one in over 40 countries.

Meaning boomerang

Sondra

The US actress *Sondra Locke* was born on 28 May 1947. She was the long-term girlfriend of Clint Eastwood through the 1970s and appeared in many of his films, including *The Outlaw Josey Wales* (1976) and *Any Which Way You Can* (1980).

From Sandrine, meaning helper and defender of mankind

Edouilda, Edouarda, Edouardiana, Edourardina, Edouina

The world's first surviving quintuplets, the Dionne quintuplets, were born in Canada on this day in 1934. Their names were *Yvonne Edouilda Marie*, Annette Lilianne Marie, Marie Reine Alma, Emile Marie Jeanne and Cecile Marie Emilda.

Meaning not known

29 MAY

Gilbert, Gilbeirt, Gilleabart, Gill, Gillie, Gil

The British writer *Gilbert Keith Chesterton*, known as G.K. Chesterton, was born in London on this day in 1874. The author of the *Father Brown* stories, he was also a journalist, poet, novelist and playwright. He was progressive in many ways, but at the same time defended traditional morality and Christian orthodoxy.

Meaning bright pledge

Edmund, Edmon, Edmond, Edmondo, Edmonn

On this day in 1953 Sir *Edmund Hillary* and his sherpa guide, Tenzing Norgay, became the first people to climb to the summit of Mount Everest. New Zealander Hillary was an explorer as well as a mountaineer, and on 4 January 1958 he reached the South Pole.

Meaning rich protector

Yann, Yan

On 29 May 2003 the Booker Prize-winning novel *The Life of Pi* by *Yann Martel* was published. The son of a Canadian diplomat, Yann was brought up in several countries and is well travelled, which explains the broad cultural diversity in his novels.

From John, meaning God has shown me favour

Lazaro, Lazarus, Lazar, Elizer, Eleazar

Lazaro Cardenas del Rio, who was president of Mexico from 1934 until 1940, was born on this day in 1895 at Michoacán, Mexico. He had little formal education and began his working life in a printing shop. He became interested in politics after the Mexican Revolution.

Meaning helped by God

Nanette, Nanetta, Nanice, Nanine, Nanon, Nanna

The British actress *Nanette Newman* was born in 1934. A film star of the 1960s and 1970s, her films included *The Wrong Box* (1966) and *The Raging Moon* (1970). She has also written cookery books and books for children, collaborating with illustrators such as Beryl Cook.

From Anne, meaning God has favoured me

Melissa, Lissa, Melisa

Melissa Etheridge, the US singer, was born on this day in 1961. A big star in the 1990s, her fourth album, *Yes I Am*, sold 6 million copies in its first year on sale in the US. She won a Grammy for best female rock vocalist in 1995.

Meaning honey bee, forest nymph

Toy

LaToya Jackson, a member of the Jackson musical family, was born on 29 May 1956. She was the first of the Jacksons to pursue a solo career After the release of her hit 'Just Wanna Dance' (2004), she announced that she was changing her name from LaToya to *Toy*.

Meaning plaything

Robyn, Robin, Robina, Robinette, Robinia

The US ice figure skater *Robyn Petroskey* was born on this day in 1974 in Minneapolis, Minnesota. She trained in Colorado Springs, Colorado, and was the Midwest champion in 1996. She started ice skating when she was just three years old.

Meaning shining with fame

Peter, Pete, Petrie, Perrin, Pernell, Peadar, Parnell

The tsar of Russia, *Peter I*, known as Peter the Great, was born on this day in 1672. He ruled Russia from 1682 until his death in 1725 and forced a policy of Westernization on his people, even banning beards. He founded a new capital, St Petersburg, in 1703.

Meaning rock, stone

Benny, Bendick, Bendix, Benedic, Benedicto, Bengt, Benoit, Benot, Benet

The jazz clarinettist *Benny Goodman* was born on 30 May 1909. Known as the king of swing, his fame and influence in the world of jazz and swing compares to Elvis's reign over rock and roll, both bringing black music to the urban whites.

From Benedict, meaning blessed

Stepin

The African actor *Stepin Fetchit* was born on this day in 1892. He was the first black movie star, but there were no leading roles for black actors at the time, so he took the parts of servants, slaves and farmhands. He was so convincing in these various roles that people believed he was like the characters he portrayed.

From Stephen, meaning garland, crown

Trey

Co-creator and executive producer of TV cartoon *South Park*, *Trey Parker* was born on this day in 1972 at Conifer, Colorado. He and college buddy Matt Stone got *South Park* off the ground when they were asked to make a Christmas videocard for the then FoxLab executive Brian Graden.

Meaning the third

Ruta

The actress *Ruta Lee* was born Ruta Mary Kilmonis on 30 May 1936 in Quebec, Canada. Star of radio, stage and TV from the 1950s onwards, she has appeared in many feature films, from *Seven Brides for Seven Brothers* (1954) to *A Christmas Too Many* (2004).

Meaning friend

Zilpah

Zilpah Polly Grant Bannister, the ID feminist and educator, was born on May 30 1794. Her letters about early feminism together with details on her activities can be seen in the Adams Female Academy, the Ipswich Female Seminary and the Mount Holyoke Female Seminary. The name is from the *Book of Genesis*.

Meaning mother of Gad and Asher

Daffy, Daffodil

Mel Blanc, the voice behind cartoon character *Daffy Duck*, was born on this day in 1908. Blanc was the voice of many of the great Warner Brothers cartoon characters, including Tweety Bird, Bugs Bunny and Penelope Pitstop.

Meaning spring flower

Cornelia

The US writer and actress *Cornelia Otis Skinner* was born on this day in 1901. The daughter of actor Otis Skinner, she wrote, produced and acted in 'monodramas', including *The Wives of Henry VIII* (1931). She also wrote the humorous travel book *Our Hearts were Young and Gay* (1942).

Meaning womanly virtue

31

Walt, Wally, Wat

The leading male US poet of the 19th century, *Walt Whitman* was born on this day in 1819 on Long Island, New York. He published his first collection of poems, *Leaves of Grass*, in 1855 at his own expense. It made little impact, but has become his most celebrated work.

From Walter, meaning mighty warrior

Denholm

British actor *Denholm Elliot* was born on this day in 1922 in London. He appeared in many of the biggest films of the 1980s, including *Trading Places* (1983), *A Room with a View* (1985), *Raiders of the Lost Ark* (1981) and *Indiana Jones and the Last Crusade* (1989).

Meaning island valley

Ellsworth

Ellsworth Kelly, the US minimalist painter and sculptor, was born on this day in 1923. His discovery of surrealism and neo-plasticism while travelling in France led to his experimentation with automatic writing, geometric abstraction and, later, the laws of chance.

Meaning farmer

Sigisimund, Sigisimond

On this day in 1433 *Sigismund* was crowned as emperor of Rome. Despite opposition among the nobility of the time, he had become king of Bohemia in 1386 after his marriage to Mary, queen of Hungary. They had one daughter, named Barbara Celjska.

From Sigmund, meaning victorious protector

Brooke, Brook

The US actress *Brooke Shields* was born Christa Brooke Camille Shields on this day in 1965. She studied at Princeton before becoming an actress and starring in such films as *Blue Lagoon* (1980) and *Endless Love* (1981). Her first husband was Andre Agassi, the tennis star.

Meaning dweller near the brook

Wendy, Wenda, Wendeline

Wendy Smith, vocalist with Prefab Sprout, one of the most popular British bands of the 1980s and 1890s, was born in Middlesborough in 1963. She was a fan of the original duo, which had formed in 1982, and she joined the band in 1982. The name Wendy was created by J.M. Barrie for his play *Peter Pan* (1904).

Meaning not known

Hilla

Baroness *Hilla Rebay von Ehrenweisen* was born on this day in 1890. She was an avant-garde artist, and also a friend of Solomon R. Guggenheim and one of the driving forces behind the establishment of the Guggenheim Museum. The collection was first opened to the public in 1939 under the title the Museum of Non-Objective Painting.

From Hilary, meaning cheerful

Petronilla, Petronella

Today is the feast day *St Petronilla*. A woman believed to be her is illustrated in a 4th-century fresco in Rome, which shows her about to be put to death for having refused to marry Flaccus, a nobleman. She preferred to devote her life to Christ. Some legends say that she was the daughter of St Peter, although this is unlikely.

From Peter, meaning rock, stone

June

1 JUNE

Szymon, Szy

Szymon Goldberg, the Polish-born US violinist and conductor, was born on this day in 1909. The conductor of the New Japan Philharmonic in Tokyo, he also taught at Yale and the Juilliard School of Music in New York. In the 1930s he was the concertmaster of the Berlin Philharmonic.

From Simon, meaning to hear, to be heard

Paul

On this day in 1927 the much-loved British actor *Paul Eddington* was born in London. He was admired for his many fine stage performances, but is affectionately remembered for his appearances as the hapless minister, later prime minister, Jim Hacker, in the TV series *Yes, Minister* (1980–82) and *Yes, Prime Minister* (1986–8).

Meaning small

Edo

Edo de Waart, the eminent Dutch conductor and oboist, was born in Amsterdam on this day in 1941. When he was 23 he spent a year as assistant conductor to Leonard Bernstein, and since then he has been chief conductor of the Netherlands Opera and artistic director of the Sydney Symphony Orchestra.

Meaning gateway to the bay

Brigham, Brigg

Brigham Young, the Mormon leader, was born in Whitingham, Vermont, on 1 June 1801. He is known among Mormons as the Mormon Moses because he led his people through the desert to found a promised land in Salt Lake City, which is the thriving centre and global headquarters of the Mormon Church.

Meaning dweller where the bridge is enclosed

Heidi, Heidy, Hidie, Hildie, Hilde, Hild

Heidi Klum, the US supermodel, was born on this day in 1973 in Bergisch Gladbach, Germany. Heidi had undertaken several acting roles, including an appearance in the TV series *Sex and the City*. With Flavio Briatore, she has a daughter, Leni, born in May 2004.

From Hilda, meaning battle maid

Alanis

The Canadian singer, songwriter and actress *Alanis Morissette* was born on this day in 1974. Her third album, *Jagged Little Pill*, was a phenomenal hit, selling 30 million copies worldwide and spawning six hit singles, including 'You Oughta Know' and 'Ironic'.

From Alana, meaning bright, fair

Justine, Justina

Justine Henin-Hardenne, the Belgian tennis player, was born on this day in 1982. After winning the US and the French Open titles in 2003, beating Kim Clijsters both times, she was ranked the number one player in the world and was women's singles world champion in 2003.

From Jocelyn, meaning fair, just

Norma Jean

The iconic actress Marilyn Monroe was born *Norma Jeane Mortenson* on this day in 1926. Her mother, Gladys Pearl Monroe, had her baptized Norma Jeane Baker, Baker being the name of Gladys's first husband. Norma Jean was working as a parachute inspector when she was spotted by a photographer.

From Norma, meaning pattern, rule, and Jean, meaning God's gift of grace

Hardy, Hardey, Hardie, Hardi

Thomas Hardy, the British poet and novelist, was born on this day in 1980 in Upper Bockhampton, near Dorchester, Dorset. He trained as an architect in London, but returned to Dorset, which, as Wessex, was the setting of many of his novels, including *The Mayor of Casterbridge* (1886) and *Tess of the D'Urbervilles* (1891).

Meaning bold, daring

Stacy, Stacey

Stacy Keach, the US actor and narrator, was born on this day in 1941 in Savannah, Georgia. A Fulbright scholar at London's Royal Academy of Dramatic Art, he made his debut on Broadway in *Indians* (1969). He has provided the narrations for many National Geographic and Nova films.

Meaning prosperous, stable

Elgar, Alger, Algar

The British composer *Edward Elgar* was born on 2 June 1857 in Broadheath, Worcestershire. His music epitomizes the English countryside, and he once wrote: 'There is music in the air, music all around us, the world is full of it and you simply take as much as you require.'

Meaning noble spearman

Lester, Leicester

The British jockey *Lester Piggott* won his seventh Epsom Derby on this day in 1976 riding Empery and at odds of 10–1. The jockey won the classic race nine times between 1954 and 1983, the first time on Never Say Die when he was just 18 years old, a record number of Epsom Derby wins.

Meaning from the army camp

Hedda, Heddy, Hedy, Heddi

Hedda Hopper, the US gossip columnist and actress, was born on 2 June 1885. Born Elda Furry, she took her name from her then husband, the Broadway star DeWolf Hopper. *The Hedda Hopper Show* launched her movie society gossip career, which ran from 1939 until 1951.

Meaning born fighter

Prima, Primalia, Primavera

Prima Selleca Tesh, the daughter of Connie Selleca and John Tesh, was born on 3 June 1994. John Tesh is the host of TV's *Entertainment Tonight*. He is also a musician, and three of his new age music albums have sold a million copies each.

Meaning first born, child of the spring

Sally

US actress *Sally Kellerman* was born on this day in 1938. She was nominated for an Oscar for best supporting actress for her performance in Robert Altman's *M*A*S*H* (1970) and also appeared in Altman's *Prêt-à-Porter* (Ready to Wear) (1994).

From Sarah, meaning princess

Vita

The British poet and novelist *Vita Sackville-West* was born Victoria Mary Sackville-West in Knole, Kent, on this day in 1892. A passionate gardener, her home at Sissinghurst, Kent, is world famous. She also wrote novels, including *All Passion Spent* (1931) and *No Signposts in the Sea* (1961). She was married to the diplomat Harold Nicolson and had an affair with Virginia Woolf.

From Victoria, meaning victory

3 JUNE

Raoul, Raul, Radulf

Raoul Dufy, the French fauvist painter, was born on this day in 1877 in Le Havre, Normandy. The fauvist style is a cheerful, highly colourful hybrid of impressionism. It makes much use of the 'fauve colours', pink, white and blue.

From Ralph, meaning wise, strong

Allen, Allyn, Allie, Alanson

Allen Ginsberg, the US poet, was born on 3 June 1926 in Paterson, New Jersey. With Jack Kerouac, Gregory Corso and William Burroughs, he was at the centre of the 1950s beat movement, whose spiritual home was the San Francisco City Lights Bookstore. He is perhaps best known for *Howl and Other Poems* (1956).

From Alan, meaning handsome

Curtis, Curt, Kurt, Curelo

US soul legend *Curtis Mayfield* was born on this day in 1942 in Chicago. He had his first hit, 'For Your Precious Love', when he was 16, and joined the group the Impressions, playing guitar for them for 12 years. As well as many songs, including 'Move On Up', he wrote the soundtrack for *Superfly* (1972).

Meaning courteous

Kevin, Kev

Today is the feast day of *St Kevin*, who founded a monastery at Glendalough in County Wicklow, which became as famous for the beauty of its surroundings as for the learning and piety of the monks. St Kevin died at Glendalough in 618.

Meaning comely, beloved

Bellona

In ancient Rome 3 June was the festival day for *Bellona*, the goddess of war. Her temple was close to that of Mars on the Capitoline Hill, emphasizing her links to the god of war, whose wife or daughter or sister she is variously said to be. She is always depicted carrying a sword.

Meaning warlike

Colleen, Coleen, Colene, Cailin, Coline, Colline

Colleen Dewhurst, the Canadian actress, was born on this day in 1924. The winner of two Tonys and four Emmys, the stage actress made her TV debut in 1958 in *The Count of Monte Cristo*. She married actor George C. Scott twice, and they had two sons, Alex and Campbell.

Meaning young girl

Reilly, Riley

Reilly Marie Anspaugh, the daughter of Roma Downey and David Anspaugh, was born on 3 June 1996. David Anspaugh was the producer of TV's long-running *Hill Street Blues* (1981) as well as director of the feature films *Hoosiers* (1986) and *Wisegirls* (2002).

Meaning valiant

Clotilda, Clotilde, Chlotilde, Chrodelchilde, Chrodigild, Chrotechildis

Today is the feast day of *St Clotilda*. She was born in about 470 and married Clovis I, king of the Franks, whom she converted to Christianity. This event had a profound effect on the religion and culture of northwest Europe.

Meaning heroine

Noah, Noam, Noach, Noe, Noa

US actor *Noah Wyle* was born Noah Strausser Speer Wyle on 4 June 1971. He is best known for his role as Dr John Carter in the TV series *ER* and has been nominated five times for an Emmy and three times for a Golden Globe for best supporting actor in a TV series. He was in the cult film *Donnie Darko* (2001).

Meaning peaceful, restful, wanderer

Bruce, Brewster

On this day in 1984 'Born in the USA' by *Bruce Springsteen* was released. The single, from the album *Born to Run*, became an 1980s anthem. It was used by Ronald Reagan in his presidential campaign, even though it was actually a protest song about the treatment of Vietnam veterans.

Meaning thicket, woodland

Henning

Henning Carlsen, the Danish film director, was born in Denmark on this day in 1927. His first film was *Dilemma* (1962), and went on to achieve international recognition with his later film *Hunger* (1966), which won Per Oscarsson a best actor award at Cannes.

Meaning ruler of the estate

Petroc, Petrock, Pedrog, Perreux, Petrocus

Today is the feast day of *St Petroc*, who is especially revered in Cornwall and Brittany. He is believed to have lived in the 6th century, travelling from Wales to Cornwall, where he founded monasteries at Wethnoc and Bothmena. Helped by St Wethnoc and St Samson, he is said to have defeated and then converted a serpent.

Meaning rock, stone

Morgana, Morgan, Morgen

Morgana King, the US actress and jazz singer, was born on this day in 1930. She played Mama Corleone in *The Godfather* (1972) and *The Godfather Part 2* (1974). She sang in New York clubs in the 1950s and 1960s, and recorded an album, *A Taste of Honey* (1964).

Meaning from the sea shore

Angelina, Angeline, Angelita, Angelique

The US actress *Angelina Jolie* was born on this day in 1975 to actor John Voigt and Marcheline Bertrand. She won an Academy Award for her performance in *Girl, Interrupted* (1999) and has won three Golden Globes. She has an adopted son from Cambodia, named Maddox Chivan Thornton Jolie.

From Angela, meaning heavenly messenger

Bettina, Betina

The US TV newsreader *Bettina Gregory* was born on this day in 1946. During her 27 years with ABC her reports have appeared on *Good Morning America*, *World News Tonight* and *Nightline*. She is the channel's chief anchor for special events, which have included the millennium celebrations.

From Elizabeth, meaning consecrated to God

Rosalind, Rosalinda, Rosaline, Rosalyn, Rosalynd, Roslyn, Rozalind

Four times Oscar-nominated actress *Rosalind Russell* was born on this day in 1907 in Waterbury, Connecticut. Her nominations were for *My Sister Eileen* (1942), *Sister Kenny* (1946), *Mourning Becomes Electra* (1948) and *Auntie Mame* (1959).

Meaning fair and beautiful rose

Lorca

Federico García Lorca was born on this day in 1898 in Fuentes Vaqueros, Granada, Spain. A friend of Dalí and Buñuel, the celebrated poet and dramatist was also an artist, pianist and composer. His best-known works are the plays *Blood Wedding* (1933), *Yerma* (1934) and *The House of Bernarda Alba* (1945).

Meaning not known

Spalding, Spaulding

Spalding Gray was born on 5 June 1941. He is best known for his autobiographical monologues. One of these, 'Swimming to Cambodia', about his experiences on the set of *The Killing Fields*, was made into a film of the same title.

Meaning from the split meadow

Bushrod

George Washington's favourite nephew, *Bushrod Washington*, was born in Virginia on this day in 1762. He studied law and practised as a Federalist lawyer for more than 30 years. He was appointed the executor of his uncle's will and inherited his home, Mount Vernon.

Meaning not known

Socrates, Socrate, Socratis

The Greek philosopher *Socrates* was born in Athens on this day in 469BC. He was not only wise but also brave. Before becoming a philosopher he fought at the siege of Potidaea as well as the battles of Potidaea and Delium. 'The only true wisdom is knowing you know nothing,' is one of his famous sayings.

Meaning wise

Laurie, Lauritz

Laurie Anderson was born on 5 June 1947 in Chicago, Illinois. In 1981 the multimedia artist, violinist, composer, singer, sculptor and poet had a hit single in the UK with 'O Superman', part of a larger work entitled *United States, I–IV* (1983). In 2003 NASA chose Anderson to be its first appointed artist in residence.

From Lawrence, meaning crowned with laurels

Toni, Tonia

The Australian actress, singer and TV host *Toni Pearen* was born on this day in 1972. She appeared in the hugely popular Australian soap *E Street* throughout its run (1989) and has recorded several hit singles, of which 'In Your Room' and 'I Want You' were the most successful.

From Antonia, meaning beyond price

Precious

On this day in 2003 Alexander McCall Smith's novel *The No. 1 Ladies Detective Agency* was published in Britain to great acclaim. Its heroine is Botswanan *Precious Ramotswe*, who sells her late father's cattle and sets up a detective agency.

Meaning precious, dear

Ivy

British novelist Dame *Ivy Compton-Burnett* was born in London on this day in 1892. She published her first novel, *Dolores*, in 1911, and her later work includes *Mother and Son* (1955) and *A God and His Gifts* (1963). Many of her books are about large upper-class families in Edwardian society.

Meaning climbing plant

Nicko, Nico

Nicko McBrain, the drummer with Iron Maiden, was born on this day in 1954. Iron Maiden are one of the most important heavy metal bands, with album sales of over 100 million. Nicko's drumming style has been a major influence on many modern drummers.

Meaning victory

Bjorn

Tennis player *Björn Borg* was born on this day in 1956 in Södertälje, Sweden. He was ranked number one player in the world six times and won 11 grand slams, including five consecutive Wimbledon championships in 1976–80.

Meaning bear

Maximilian, Maxim, Maxime, Max

Maximilian, emperor of Mexico from 1864 to 1867, was born on 6 June 1832. He was the brother of the emperor of Austria, Franz Josef, and he was offered the throne of Mexico when the French army conquered that country. When, on US insistence, Napoleon III withdrew his troops from Mexico, Maximilian was captured and executed.

Meaning greatest

Aram

The Armenian composer *Aram Ilich Khachaturian* was born in Tbilisi, Georgia, on this day in 1903. Among his best-known pieces is his ballet *Spartacus*, which became familiar as the theme music for the popular 1970s British TV drama *The Onedin Line*. He also wrote film music, including for *Battle of Stalingrad* (1949) and *Othello* (1955).

Meaning from Armenia

Sydney, Sidney, Sid, Sidonia, Sidonie, Syd

The US actress *Sydney Walsh* was born in Bay Village on this day in 1961. She has appeared in the films *To Die For* (1989) and *Point Break* (1991), with Keanu Reeves, and she was also in the 1980s TV series *Hooperman*.

Meaning wide land by a marsh

Ninette, Nineta, Ninetta

The founder of the Royal Ballet, Dame *Ninette de Valois* was born Edris Stannus on 6 June 1898 in Baltibouys, Ireland. She changed her name by deed poll in 1921. She stopped dancing when she was 28 to promote ballet. Rudolph Nureyev was one of her students.

From Nina, meaning the daughter

Chelsea, Chelsy, Chelsie, Chelsey

The US comedienne *Chelsea Brown* was born in Illinois on this day in 1946. She is best known for her appearances on the fast-moving 1970s TV sketch show *Rowan and Martin's Laugh-In*. She was also in *Matt Lincoln* (1970).

Meaning landing place

Dee

The British singer *Dee C. Lee* was born Diane Sealey in London on this day in 1964. As well as pursuing her solo career, she has sung with Slam Slam, Nobukuzu Takemura, Feat and, most memorably, with Paul Weller's Style Council.

Meaning black, dark

Beau, Beauregard, Bo

Beau Brummell, the arbiter of fashion in Regency England, was born George Bryan Brummell on 7 June 1778. A friend of the Prince Regent (later George IV), he led the trend for stylish clothes with elaborate neckwear. One of his handy household tips was to polish boots with champagne.

Meaning beautiful

Knud, Knute, Cnut, Cnutte, Canute

The Danish explorer *Knud Johan Victor Rasmussen* was born in Jacobshavn, Greenland, on June 7 1879. He went on many expeditions between 1902 and 1924, the best known being his great sledge journey in 1921–4 from Greenland to the Bering Strait to collect Inuit songs and legends.

Meaning knot

Prince

The US singer *Prince* was born Prince Rogers Nelson on this day in 1958. He is also a highly rated guitarist, songwriter, pianist, record producer, film director and actor. The album *Purple Rain* (1984) sold over 13 million copies in the US alone and spent an impressive 24 weeks at the top of the charts.

Meaning chief

Rocky, Roc, Rockley, Rockly, Rockey

The popular US boxer and entertainer *Rocky Graziano* was born Thomas Rocco Barbella in New York City on this day in 1922. He became middleweight champion when he beat Tony Zale in the second of a series of three memorable fights, told in the movie *Raging Bull* (1980).

Meaning from the rock

Jessica, Jess

British-born US actress *Jessica Tandy* was born on this day in 1909. In the course of her long career she appeared in *Forever Amber* (1948) and *Rommel, Desert Fox* (1951), among many others, but became internationally famous with the Oscar-winning *Driving Miss Daisy* (1989) and the Oscar-nominated *Fried Green Tomatoes at the Whistle Stop Café* (1992).

Meaning not known

Delilah, Dalilia, Delila, Lila

Tom Jones, the singer of the famous song *Delilah* (1968), was born on this day in 1940. 'Delilah' shows off Tom Jones's rich voice at its most powerful and has become a great karaoke favourite. Before his shows Elvis Presley used to warm up his voice with a few verses of 'Delilah'.

Meaning gentle temptress

Cassidy

The US actress *Cassidy Rae* was born in Clermont, Florida, on 7 June 1976. Since the mid-1990s she has appeared in many TV shows and films, including *Melrose Place* (1992) and *Models Inc.* (1994) on TV and the feature *Extreme Days* (2001).

Meaning clever

Raven

India Raven Rich was born on 7 June 1991. She is the daughter of Catherine Oxenburg, who played Amanda Carrington in the eighties TV soap *Dynasty*. Catherine's mother is Princess Elizabeth of Yugoslavia and Serbia, which makes India Raven the great-great-great-great-great-great-great-granddaughter of Catherine the Great, ruler of Russia in 1762–96.

Meaning sleek black bird

Francis

Francis Crick, the co-discoverer of the structure of DNA, was born Francis Harry Compton Crick on this day in 1916 in Northampton. He and James Watson began working on Rosalind Franklin's x-ray research in Cambridge in 1951, and they won the Nobel Prize in physiology or medicine in 1962.

Meaning free man

Dilbert

The creator of the *Dilbert* comic strip, Scott Adams, was born on 8 June 1957 in Windham, New York. The characters in the cartoon were inspired by the telecommunications engineers at Crocker National Bank, San Francisco, with whom Adams had worked.

Meaning bright

Keenen, Keen, Keenan, Kienan

The US comedian, actor, director and writer *Keenen Ivory Wayans* was born on 8 June 1958 in New York City. His brothers, Damon, Marlon and Shawn, and his sister, Kim, are all Hollywood celebrities, as is his nephew, Damon Wayans Jr.

Meaning little ancient one

Boz

The US singer, guitarist and songwriter *Boz Scaggs* was born William Royce Scaggs on 8 June 1944 in Ohio. In 1976 he had three chart hits with the band Toto. In 2003 his album *But Beautiful* reached the top of the jazz charts. Boz was the penname used by Charles Dickens.

Meaning not known

Lexa, Lexie, Lexine

The Canadian actress *Lexa Doig* was born in Toronto on this day in 1973. Her mother is Filipino, and her father is Scottish. Best known for her role in *Andromeda*, the science fiction TV series (2000–4), she is married to actor Michael Shanks. They have a daughter, Mia Tabitha.

From Alexandra, meaning helper of mankind

Millicent, Melicent, Mellicent, Milicent, Milisent, Milissent, Melisande, Melisandra

The British actress, singer and comedienne *Millicent Martin* was born on 8 June 1934. Seen later in her career as Daphne's mother in TV's *Frasier* (1993), she became famous in Britain in the 1960s for her appearances on the TV satirical show *That Was The Week That Was*.

Meaning industrious, strong

Bonnie, Bonita, Bonnibelle, Bonne, Bona

Singer *Bonnie Tyler* was born Gaynor Hopkins on this day in 1953 in Skewen, South Wales. Her single 'Lost in France' (1975) was a big hit in Britain and Europe, and 'It's a Heartache' reached number five in the US charts. Her latest CD is called *Simply Believe*.

Meaning sweet, good

Syra

Today is the feast day of *St Syra of Troyes*. She was an Irish nun who lived in France in the 7th century. She was placed under the care of St Burgudofara, the abbess of Brie, and she proved to be a saintly nun of the utmost devotion and humility. Her feast day is celebrated in Troyes and in Ireland.

Meaning not known

9 JUNE

Jackie

The US comedian *Jackie Mason* was born in Sheboygan, Wisconsin, on this day in 1931. An ordained rabbi, his stand-up routines are often politically incorrect studies on Jewish and American life.

From John, meaning God has shown me favour

Cole, Coclbert, Colby, Coel, Coleman, Colman

The composer and lyricist *Cole Porter* was born in Peru, Indiana, on this day in 1891. His musicals include *Kiss Me Kate* (1948) and *Anything Goes* (1934), and among his numerous songs are 'Night and Day' and 'I Get A Kick Out of You'. He was in the French Foreign Legion during the First World War.

Meaning keeper of the doves

Albéric, Alberik, Aubrey, Aube, Auberon

The French composer *Albéric Magnard* was born in Paris on 9 June 1865. His father was the editor of *Le Figaro* and a bestselling author, and family connections made it possible for Albéric to study music. He wrote several symphonies and operas, and was even described as the French Bruckner.

Meaning elf ruler

Wayman, Waymon, Waymond

Wayman Tisdale, who was born in Tulsa on this day in 1964, has succeeded in two professions. He was an NBA basketball forward for the Phoenix Suns for 12 years and then became a musician. His CDs consistently reach the top of the contemporary jazz charts.

Meaning man by the road

Meta

The African-American sculptor *Meta Vaux Warwick* was born on this day in 1877. A student of Auguste Rodin's in Paris, she exhibited her sculptures all over the USA for more than 60 years.

From Margaret, meaning pearl

Letty, Lettie, Lettice, Leshia

Letty Cottin Pogrebin was born in New York on this day in 1939. A pioneering feminist, she has combined her campaigning for women's rights with Jewish values. As well as writing many books, she started *Ms.* magazine and the *National Women's Political Caucus*.

From Letitia, meaning joyous gladness

Felicie, Felicitas, Felicidad

On this day in 1843 *Bertha Félicie Sophie von Suttner* was born in Prague. She married an Austrian baron. She was a novelist, but was also a radical pacifist, founding the Austrian Society for Peace in 1891. She was awarded the Nobel Prize for peace in 1905, and her face appears on the Austrian euro.

Meaning good fortune

Aura, Auria, Aure

The Portuguese actress *Aura Abranches* was born in Lisbon on this day in 1896. She appeared on the stage and in films, including *O Primo Basilio* (1959) and *Rosa de Alfama* (1953). The name Aura is supposed to bestow gentility on its owner.

Meaning gentle breeze

Saul, Sauls, Solly, Sol, Zol, Zollie, Zolly

The US author *Saul Bellow* was born today in 1915 in Lachine, Quebec, to Russian parents. In 1976 he won the Nobel Prize for literature. He wrote his best-known novel, *The Adventures of Augie March* (1953), while he was on a Guggenheim fellowship in Paris.

Meaning asked for

Maxi, Maxie

Maxi Priest, the soulful British reggae artist, was born Max Elliot on 10 June 1962 in London. He changed his name when he became a Rastafarian. His single 'Close to You' was a hit on both sides of the Atlantic.

From Maxwell, meaning from the great well

Gardner, Gardiner, Gardener, Gardenor, Gardnard, Gar, Garden

Gardner McKay, the US actor, was born on this day in 1932. He starred as Captain Adam Troy in the 1960s classic series *Adventures in Paradise*. He also wrote, raised African lions and had a weekly radio show on Hawaiian public radio.

Meaning gardener

Sessue, Sesu

Sessue Hayakawa was born on this day in 1890 in Chiba, Japan. One of Hollywood's first superstars, he was earning over $5,000 a week in 1914. As well as acting, he produced, wrote, practised the martial arts, gave huge parties and was an ordained Zen monk.

Meaning not known

Leelee

The US actress *Leelee Sobieski* was born Liliane Rudabet Gloria Elsveta Sobieski in New York City in 1982. Her names reflect her rich Polish and French heritage – Elsveta is Polish for Elizabeth. She has appeared in many films, including *Eyes Wide Shut* (1999).

From Lilian, meaning pure in thought, word and deed

Judy, Judi, Judie

The US singer and actress *Judy Garland* was born Frances Ethel Gumm in Grand Rapids on this day in 1922. She made her first stage performance with her sisters before moving to Hollywood. She made a series of musicals with Mickey Rooney before appearing in *The Wizard of Oz* (1939). 'Over the Rainbow' made her an international star.

From Judith, meaning woman from Judaea

Rebecca, Rebekah, Rebekka, Rebeka, Rebeca, Reba, Becky, Beckie, Becka

Rebecca Latimer Felton, the first woman US senator, was born on this day in 1835 near Decatur, Georgia. The 87-year-old replaced Thomas E. Watson until a special election could be held. She held office for two days, the shortest time of any senator in office.

Meaning captivator

Lemisha, Lemuela, Lemuella, Lemma

Lemisha Grinstead, the singer with the US rhythm and blues band 702, was born on this day in 1978. While the Las Vegas-based band was riding high in the charts with 'Where My Girl's At', Lemisha gave birth to a baby boy, Tony Lyndon.

Meaning dedicated to God

11 JUNE

Jacques

The French underwater explorer *Jacques Cousteau* was born on 11 June 1910. His books and films of his numerous expeditions on his ship *Calypso* were immensely popular all over the world in the 1950s and 1960s. He won three Oscars, a Palme d'Or and many other awards.

From Jacob, meaning supplanter

Barnabas, Barney, Barny, Barnaby, Barnabus, Barnaba, Burnaby

Today is the feast day of *St Barnabas*. Originally from Cyprus, he was an important figure in the early years of the Christian Church in Antioch. He introduced St Paul to leading Christians in Jerusalem and travelled widely with him on his many missions.

Meaning son of consolation

Jamaaladeen, Jamal

Jamaaladeen Tacuma is one of the top electric jazz bassists in the bass-led world of free funk. He began his career in the mid-1970s with Ornette Coleman's Prime Time. He was born Rudy McDaniel on 11 June 1957 and changed his name when he converted to Islam.

Meaning beauty

Carlisle, Carlyle, Carlysle

The US composer *Carlisle Floyd* was born Carlisle Sessions Floyd Jr in Latta, California, on this day in 1926. His operas, for which he writes the libretto and the music, have won many awards. His opera *Susannah* (1955) was performed at the Metropolitan Opera House in New York in 1999.

Meaning tower of the castle

Galina

On this day in 1988 the athlete *Galina Chistyakova* set the world record in women's long jump in Leningrad (now St Petersburg), Russia. She jumped 7.52 metres (24 feet 8 inches). In 1989 she also set the world's triple jump record at 14.52 metres (47 feet 8 inches). She held five world indoor records for the triple jump and one for the long jump.

From Helen, meaning light'

Alaska

On this day in 1788 the Russian sea explorer *Gerasim Grigorevich Izmmaliov* reached Alaska and put it on the map. He mapped a large part of the Russian Far East and Alaska, known then as Russian America. Alyeska is the native Aleut word for great country.

Meaning great country

Jeannette, Janette, Janetta, Jenete

The first woman elected to the US House of Representatives, the social reformer *Jeannette Rankin* was born on this day in 1880. She voted against the US entry into both the First and Second World Wars, the only member of Congress to do so. She also opposed the Vietnam War.

From Jane, meaning God's gift of grace

Amalya, Amala, Amla

Michigan attorney *Amalya Lyle Kearse* was born on this day in 1937 in Vauxhall, New Jersey. She was the first African-American woman to be appointed to the US Court of Appeals for the Second Circuit. She is also a writer and a world-class bridge player.

Meaning pure, hope

Leo

Today is the feast day of *St Leo III*, who was elected pope on 26 December 795. In 800 he crowned Charlemagne emperor of the West at the Christmas Mass in St Peter's in Rome, setting a precedent that only the pope could confer the imperial crown.

Meaning lion

George

The 41st president of the USA, *George Herbert Walker Bush* was born on this day in 1924 in Milton, Massachusetts. After establishing an oil-drilling business he became director of the CIA. He was vice-president to Ronald Reagan, and during his own administration (1989–93) the US invaded Panama.

Meaning farmer

Chick, Chic, Chuck

The jazz pianist *Chick Corea* was born Armando Anthony Chick Corea on 12 June 1941 in Massachusetts. He began experimenting with electric sounds in the 1960s, playing in Miles Davis's band. In the early 1970s he headed the jazz funk rock band Return to Forever.

From Charles, meaning free man

Huey, Hubert, Hube, Hubbard, Hoyt, Hobart, Hobbard

On this day in 1935 US Senator *Huey Long*, known as the Kingfish, made the longest speech on Senate records. It lasted for 15 1/2 hours and contained 150,000 words. Long reformed and developed Louisiana's public services, but was notorious for his corruption and demagoguery.

Meaning bright spirit

Johanna, Joana, Joanna, Joanne, Johanne

On this day in 1827 the author *Johanna Spyri* was born Johanna Louise Heusser in Hirzel, Switzerland. Her much-loved children's book, *Heidi*, about an orphan who lives in the Alps with her grandfather, was published in 1881 and received instant acclaim.

From Jane, meaning God's gift of grace

Uta

Today is the birthday of the US stage actress and acting teacher *Uta Hagen*. Although she was raised in the US, she was born in Gottingen, Germany, and studied in London at the Royal Academy of Dramatic Arts (RADA). She did appear in films, but not until 1972.

Meaning rich

Djuna, Dijana

The US writer *Djuna Barnes* was born on this day in 1892. She wrote contemporary modern fiction, plays and newspaper columns, and became a key figure in Bohemian life in Paris in the 1920s and 1930s. She played a significant role in the development of modernist writing.

From Diana, meaning goddess of the moon and hunting

Jonilee

Jenilee Harrison, the US actress, was born on this day in 1959 in Northridge, California. She is best known for her roles as Jamie Ewing Barnes in the TV series *Dallas* (1978) and Cindy Snow in *Three's Company* (1977).

From Genevieve, meaning kinswoman

Malcolm

The British actor *Malcolm McDowell* was born on this day in 1943. His most memorable role was as Alex in Stanley Kubrick's controversial *A Clockwork Orange* (1971). He was nominated for a best actor award for his performance by the New York film critics circle.

Meaning dove

Butler

The Irish poet *William Butler Yeats* was born on 13 June l865. The winner of the 1923 Nobel Prize for literature wrote plays as well as poetry and was co-founder of the Abbey Theatre, Dublin. In addition, he served as a Senator in the Irish government.

Meaning butler

Christo, Christoforo, Christoph, Christophe

Christo Yavasheff, the Bulgarian installation artist, who is famous for wrapping up large buildings and bridges, was born on 13 June 1935. In the 1970s he hung a large curtain across a stretch of California, Chinese-wall style, and made a film about it called *Christo's Fence*.

From Christopher, meaning carrier of Christ

Whitley

Whitley Strieber, the US author, was born on 13 June 1945. A writer of horror novels, he co-wrote a book called *The Coming Global Superstorm*, which was the inspiration for the blockbuster movie *The Day After Tomorrow* (2004).

Meaning from the white meadow

Dorothy, Dorothea, Dorothoe, Dorete, Dorota, Drottya, Dosia, Thea, Dot, Dottie, Dotty, Dora, Dory, Dorothi, Dorothoe, Theodora

The British writer *Dorothy L. Sayers* was born on this day in 1893. The 'L' stands for Leigh, and she was insistent that it was never left out. She wrote religious essays, but is best remembered for her detective novels, which featured Lord Peter Wimsey and Harriet Vane.

Meaning gift of God

Fanny, Fan, Fanchon, Franny, Frannie

The English novelist and diarist *Fanny Burney* was born on 13 June 1752 in King's Lynn, Norfolk. Her first novel, *Evelina* (1778), made her famous. She went on to write *Cecilia* (1782) and *Camilla* (1796).

From Frances, meaning free

Lois, Loise, Eloise, Heloise, Eloisa

The first female film director, *Lois Weber* was born on 13 June 1881 at Allegheny, Pennsylvania. She wrote and directed for Universal Pictures and made films with a social conscience, including *Where Are My Children?* (1916). These caused outrage, but were hugely popular.

From Louis, meaning famous warrior

Mary-Kate and Ashley

Mary-Kate and *Ashley*, the twin actresses and businesswomen, were born on this day in 1986 at Sherman Oaks, California. They have their own production company and magazine as well as their own fashion and accessories line.

From Mary, meaning bitter, and Kate, meaning pure maiden

Ashley, meaning ash wood

14

Burl, Byrle

The US folk singer, author and actor Burl Charles Icle Ivanhoe, better known as *Burl Ives*, was born on 14 June 1909 in Hunt Township, Illinois. He was in the films *East of Eden* (1954), *Cat on a Hot Tin Roof* (1957) and *Our Man in Havana* (1959), and won an Oscar for his performance in *The Big Country* (1958).

Meaning cup-bearer

Cy, Cyrus, Ciro

The US composer, songwriter and jazz pianist *Cy Coleman* was born Seymour Kaufman on this day in 1929. He was a child prodigy, giving recitals at the Carnegie Hall before he was ten. With Carolyn Leigh he wrote Frank Sinatra's hits 'Witchcraft' and 'The Best is Yet to Come'. He won 14 Tonys, three Emmys and two Grammys.

Meaning sun god

Alonzo, Alonso, Alphonso, Alphonsus, Alfonso, Alfonse, Alfons, Alford

The US mathematician and logician *Alonzo Church* was born on 14 June 1903 in Washington D.C. He laid some of the foundations of theoretical computer science by developing lambda calculus, which showed the existence of an unsolvable problem.

Meaning noble and ready

Lash

The US cowboy actor *Lash LaRue* was born on this day in 1917. He became a star in the 1940s when he took the leading role in a series of Lash LaRue films. He was always dressed in black and carried a 4.6-metre (15-foot) bullwhip. He had a 1950s TV series called *Lash of the West*.

Meaning whip

Yasmine, Yasmin, Yasmina

The US TV and movie actress *Yasmine 'Yaz' Amanda Bleeth* was born on 14 June 1968 in New York City. The *Baywatch* (1989) actress is of French, German, Russian and Algerian descent, though her name, Yasmine, is Persian.

From Jasmin, meaning fragrant flower

Traylor

The US actress *Traylor Howard* was born on this day in 1966 in Orlando, Florida. She was Sharon Carter in *Two Guys, a Girl and a Pizza Place* (1998) and Joy Byrnes in the US TV series *Boston Common* (1997).

Meaning not known

Marla, Marya

Marla Gibbs, the US actress who plays Florence Johnston, the sarcastic maid, in *The Jeffersons* (1975), and Mary Jenkins in *227* (1978), celebrates a birthday today. She was born on 14 June 1931 in Chicago, Illinois.

From Mary, meaning bitter

Steffi, Steff, Steph, Stephanie, Stefanie, Stefany, Stevie

The German tennis superstar *Steffi Graf* was born Stefanie Maria Graf on 14 June 1969. The 1988 Olympic gold medal winner is the only one of the five grand slam (US, French, Australian and Wimbledon) winners to win it on four different surfaces: grass, hardcourt, clay and carpet.

Meaning crown, garland

15 JUNE

Waylon, Wayland, Way

Waylon Jennings, the country singing legend, was born on this day in 1937 in Littlefield, Texas. The first country artist to get a platinum disc, he did much to broaden the appeal of country music. He recorded over 60 albums and had 16 songs at the top of the country charts.

Meaning road land

Josiah

Josiah Henson, the first black person to appear on a Canadian stamp, was born into slavery on this day in 1789 in Maryland in the USA. In 1830 he escaped and founded a school in Canada for other escapees. His autobiography is said to be the inspiration for H.B. Stowe's *Uncle Tom's Cabin*.

Meaning fire of the Lord

Noddy, Noda

Noddy Holder, the lead singer with the 1970s British rock band Slade, was born on 15 June 1946 in Walsall in the Midlands of England. Slade's 1973 Christmas hit, 'Merry Xmas Everybody', is played in Britain almost as often as 'White Christmas' in the run-up to Christmas.

Meaning famous

Vitus

Today is the feast day of *St Vitus*, the patron saint of dancers, actors, comedians and epileptics. His emblem is a dog. He is the patron saint of Forio in Italy and of Bohemia, and there is a St Vitus Cathedral in Prague. Legend has it that he was martyred during the Diocletian persecution, but little is known about this saint.

Meaning lively

Malvina, Melvina, Melvine, Melva, Malvie, Malva, Melva

The US sculptor *Malvina Hoffman* was born on this day in 1887. She studied under Rodin and was one of the leading sculptors in the USA. She travelled widely for her series of 104 life-size bronzes called *Races of Mankind*, getting headhunters and warriors to pose for her.

Meaning smooth brow

Courtney, Courtenay

The US actress *Courtney Cox Arquette* was born on this day in 1964 in Birmingham, Alabama. As well as numerous movie roles, from 1994 to 2004 she played Monica Geller Bing in the TV series *Friends*. She is married to David Arquette and they have a daughter, Coco, born on 12 June 2004.

Meaning from the court

Elinore, Elinora

The US reformer *Elinore Morehouse Herrick* was born on 15 June 1895. She started in industry as a pieceworker in Buffalo, New York. She studied economics by running a boarding house and then became the executive secretary of the New York Consumer's League.

From Eleanor, meaning light

Germaine

Today is the feast day of *St Germaine of Pibrac*, who was born near Toulouse, France, in about 1579. She was badly treated by her step-mother, but one day, when her step-mother accused her of stealing a loaf to give to a beggar, she opened her apron to reveal spring flowers. She died soon after, and miracles were said to take place at her grave.

Meaning from Germany

Leopold, Leo, Lepp

James Joyce admirers everywhere know 16 June as Bloomsday. On this day his fictional creation, *Leopold Bloom*, travels around Dublin. Joyce's masterpiece *Ulysees* (1922) describes the various characters Leopold meets and the situations he gets into, all in one day.

Meaning brave for the people

Stan

On this day British-born comedian *Stan Laurel* was born Arthur Stanley Jefferson in Ulverston, Lancashire. He was the thin half of the Laurel and Hardy comic partnership, and the duo made numerous films between the late 1920s and the early 1950s, successfully making the transition from silent to talking pictures. *The Music Box* (1932) won an Oscar.

Meaning clearing, wood

Geronimo, Gerome

The Native American leader of the Apache, *Geronimo*, was born Goyathlay (One Who Yawns) on this day in 1829. He was born on Bedonkohe Apache land in what is now New Mexico. He got his name, which is the Spanish version of Jerome, from the Mexicans.

Meaning holy name

Tupac

The rap artist *Tupac Amaru Shakur* was born on 16 June 1971. He had quite a few nicknames, including Makaveli, Pac, 2Pacalypse and 2Pac. The meaning given is for the African name. The Inca meaning is shining serpent; the Arabic meaning is thankful to God.

Meaning warrior messenger

Joyce, Joice

On this day in 1938 the US novelist *Joyce Carol Oates* was born. She has written at least 45 novels, numerous essays and short stories. Her best known work is her short story 'Where are You Going, Where Have You Been?', which was made into a film called *Smooth Talk* (1985).

Meaning rejoice

Eileen, Eibhlin, Aveline, Avila, Avis

The British actress and screenwriter *Eileen Atkins* was born on this day in 1934. She has won many awards for her stage acting, including *Evening Standard* best actress for *The Killing of Sister George* (1965). She co-created the hit TV series *Upstairs Downstairs* (1971) and *The House of Elliot* (1993).

Meaning bird

Syrai

Today is the birthday of *Syrai Smith*, the daughter of the singer, actress and model, Brandy, and her husband, the music producer and songwriter, Robert Smith. Syrai was born on 17 June 2002. Syrai (or Sarai) is a biblical name, but according to the *Book of Genesis*, God changed it to Sarah.

From Sarah, meaning princess

Alma

The US religious leader and organizer *Alma Bridwell White* was born on 16 June 1862 in Kinniconick, Kentucky. At the beginning of the 20th century she led the Methodist Pentecostal Union Church in its divide from the mainstream Methodist Church.

Meaning nourishing, soul

17 JUNE

Tigran

Tigran Vartanovich Petrosian, the Armenian chess master, was born on 17 June 1929 in Tbilisi, Georgia. World chess champion in 1963 and 1966, beating Boris Spassky, in 1969 he beat Bobby Fischer, ending Fischer's winning streak of 20 consecutive wins. He then lost to Spassky in 1969.

Meaning shooting an arrow

Maurits, Maurizio, Maruicio, Maury, Maurey, Morel

On this day in 1898 the Dutch graphic artist who drew all those logic-defying mazes, with staircases that seem to go up as well as down at the same time, was born in Leeuwarden, the Netherlands. He was born *Maurits Cornelis Escher*, the son of a hydraulics engineer (which may explain a lot).

From Maurice, meaning dark, swarthy

Newton, Newt

Newton Leroy Gingrich, better known as Newt Gringrich, was the speaker of the US House of Representatives from 1995 to 1999. He was born Newton McPherson on this day in 1943 in Harrisburg, Pennsylvania. Gingrich is the name of his stepfather.

Meaning from the new estate

Ormond, Orman, Ormen, Ormin, Ormand

The US designer and architect *Charles Ormond Eames Jr* was born on 17 June 1907 in St Louis, Missouri. He married a woman called Ray and together they designed and built the famous Eames House in California, made out of industrial prefabricated steel.

Meaning spearman

Ebone, Ebony

US tennis champion *Venus Ebone Starr Williams* was born on 17 June 1980 in Lansing, Michigan. Among many other wins, she won the gold at the Sydney Olympics in 2000.

Meaning dark wood

Kami, Kamilah, Kamila

US actress *Kami Cotler* was born on 17 June 1965 in Long Beach, California. She played Elizabeth Walton in the US TV series *The Waltons* (1974–81). She also sang on the Waltons' album *A Waltons' Christmas, Together Again* (1999).

Meaning perfect one

Conchita, Concha, Conceptia, Conception, Concepcion

On this day in 1942, when they were at the height of their popularity, the Glenn Miller Orchestra recorded *Conchita, Marquita, Lolita, Pepita, Rosita, Juanita Lopez*. Glenn Miller's band was probably the most popular in the USA throughout the Second World War.

Meaning beginning

Amrita, Amritha

The Indian actress *Amrita Rao* was born on 17 June 1981. She studied psychology before becoming a model. She then took up acting, and her hit Bollywood films include *The Legend of Bhagat Singh* (2002), *Main Hoon Na* (2004) and *Deewar* (2004), with Akshaye Khanna.

Meaning nectar of immortality, elixir of youth

Keye, Key

Keye Luke was born on 18 June 1904 in Canton, China. He grew up in Seattle and became a film star in the 1930s when he played Charlie Chan's eldest son in *Charlie Chan in Paris* (1935). He has appeared in many films, including Woody Allen's *Alice* (1990).

Meaning son of the fiery one

Bud, Budd, Buddy

The original voice of Superman and Batman, *Bud Collyer* was born on 18 June 1908. He recorded *Superman* for radio in the 1940s and *Batman* for the 1960s TV cartoon. He hosted the 1960s US TV shows *Beat the Clock* and *To Tell the Truth*.

Meaning welcome messenger

Daron, Daren

Daron Malakian, the guitarist, producer and songwriter with the US band System of a Down, was born on this day in 1975. Along with Metallica and Slipnot, the band led the heavy-metal revolution of the late 1990s. He was voted fourth best guitarist of the year by *Metal Edge* magazine.

Meaning little great one

Vitali, Vito

Russian cosmonaut *Vitali Mikhailovich Zholobov* was born on this day in 1937 in Zburjevka, Ukraine. He was the flight engineer on the 1976 *Soyuz 21* mission and was in space for two months on the *Salyut 5* space station. In 1981 he became the director of a geological science research group.

Meaning vital

Marianna, Marianne

In Poland it is the name day for *Marianna*, and all the girls called Marianna will receive small gifts and bunches of flowers. The name comes from Marian, which was a pet name for Mary. Mary-Anne and Marianne are the French pet names.

From Marian, meaning graceful

Blanche, Blanch, Blanca

Blanche Sweet, the star of silent movies, was born in Chicago, Illinois, on 18 June 1895. She starred in many of D.W. Griffith's films, including *Home Sweet Home* (1914) and *Judith of Bethulia* (1913), which was the first full-length feature film to be made in the USA.

Meaning fair, white

Isabella, Isabel, Bella

The actress *Isabella Rossellini* was born on this day in 1952; she is the daughter of Ingrid Bergman and Roberto Rossellini. The beautiful actress starred in David Lynch's *Blue Velvet* (1986) and *Wild at Heart* (1990). Her autobiography, *Some of Me*, was published in 1997.

Meaning consecrated to God

Osanna

Today is the feast day of the Blessed *Osanna Andreasi of Mantua*. She was an Italian noblewoman and nun who lived in 15th-century Italy. She had her first mystical experience, a vision of paradise, at the age of five.

Meaning praise

19 JUNE

Blaise, Blayze, Blaze

The French mathematician, physicist and religious philosopher *Blaise Pascal* was born on 19 June 1623. His surname has been given to a programming language and a unit of pressure. He made many important discoveries, including the construction of mechanical calculators.

Meaning firebrand

Salman

The British author *Salman Rushdie* was born in Bombay, India, on 19 June 1947. His inventive book *Midnight's Children* (1980) won the 'Booker of Bookers', the best Booker Prize winner over 25 years. He is married to the actress and model Padma Lakshmi.

Meaning safe

Garfield

On this day in 1978 the worldwide celebrity cat *Garfield* made his first appearance. The comic strip was created by Jim Davis, who named the cat after his grandfather, James Garfield Davis. Jim was raised on a farm in Indiana with his brother and 25 cats.

Meaning battlefield

Tobias, Tobiah, Tioboid, Tobe, Toby, Tobit

The US author *Tobias Wolff* was born on this day in 1945. He is a professor at Stanford University, where he has taught creative writing since 1997. He has published several collections of short stories, and his novels include *The Barrack's Thief* (1990) and *Old School* (2003).

Meaning God is good

Aung San

Aung San Suu Kyi was born on this day in 1945. Aung San means father, Kyi means mother, and Suu is both grandmother and the day she was born. Her pro-democracy campaign against the repressive Burmese regime has made her an international heroine, and she was awarded the Nobel Prize for peace in 1991.

Meaning father

Phylicia, Phylis, Philis, Fylicia, Fillis, Filis, Fillida, Filida

The US actress *Phylicia Rashad* was the first African-American actress to win a Tony for best leading actress for her performance in *A Raisin in the Sun* (2004). She was born in Houston, Texas, on 19 June 1948 and is best known for her TV role as Claire Huxtable, Cosby's on-screen wife in *The Bill Cosby Show* (1996–2000).

From Phyllis, meaning leafy, foliage

Mulan

On this day in 1998 the Walt Disney Company released the animated feature *Mulan*. The story is based on the Chinese legend of Hua Mulan, from the Northern Wei dynasty. It tells of a woman who disguises herself as a man to take the place of her elderly father in the army.

Meaning magnolia blossom

Juliana, Giuliana

Today is the feast day of *St Juliana Falconieri*. She was born to a noble family in Florence, Italy, in 1270. When she was 14 she refused to enter into an arranged marriage and instead entered an order of nuns. She became the first superior of the order of Servite nuns, which she helped form.

Meaning youthful

Errol

Hollywood superstar of the 1930s, *Errol Flynn* was born Errol Leslie Thompson Flynn on 20 June 1909 in Tasmania, Australia. His swashbuckling leads included *Captain Blood* (1935), and he was a definitive Robin Hood in *The Adventures of Robin Hood* (1938).

From Earl, meaning nobleman

Lionel, Lion, Lionello

US singer *Lionel Richie* was born Lionel Brockman Richie Jr on this day in 1949. Before his successful solo career, with hits such as 'Three Times a Lady' and 'All Night Long', he was with the 1970s Motown group the Commodores.

Meaning young lion

Vikram

The novelist and poet *Vikram Seth* was born on this day in 1952 in Calcutta, India. His first novel, *The Humble Administrator's Garden* (1985), was followed by the highly acclaimed *A Suitable Boy* (1993) and *An Equal Music* (1999).

Meaning glorious king

Wolfe

Wolfe Tone was born Theobold Wolfe Tone in Ireland on this day in 1763. He was one of the founders of the United Irishmen movement, originally intended to be a political union between Catholics and Protestants.

Meaning man of courage

Olympia, Olympe, Olimpie, Olympie

Olympia Dukaki, the US-Greek actress, was born on 20 June 1931. She won an Academy Award for best supporting actress for her role in *Moonstruck* (1987). She also starred in the successful *Steel Magnolias* (1989) and has won an Obie and a Golden Globe.

Meaning heavenly one

Candy, Candace, Candice, Candie

The US actress *Candy Clark* was born on this day in 1947. She was nominated for a best supporting actress Oscar for her role in *American Graffiti* (1973). She also appeared in *The Man Who Fell to Earth* (1976) and *Buffy the Vampire Slayer* (1992).

Meaning pure, brilliant white

Tress, Trescha

Tress MacNellie was born on this day in 1951. The highly accomplished voice actor has provided voices for many cartoon characters, including Gadget from *Chip 'n' Dale Rescue Rangers*, Dot Warner from *Animaniacs* and several characters in *The Simpsons* and *Futurama*.

From Teresa, meaning harvester

Nicole, Nicholina, Nichola, Nickie, Nicol, Nicola, Nicolina, Nicoline, Nikki, Nikoletta

The actress *Nicole Kidman* was born on this day in 1967 in Honolulu, Hawaii. She was brought up in Australia from the age of four. Among the many highlights of her career are the movies *Moulin Rouge* (2001) and *The Hours* (2002), which won her a best actress Oscar.

Meaning people's victory

21 JUNE

Alexander, Alex, Al, Alejandro, Sandy, Aleksander, Aleesandro, Sandor

Alexander the Great was born on this day in 356BC. He succeeded his father, Philip, as king of Macedonia when he was only 20 and went on to conquer the majority of the known world. His subjects and troops believed him to be god-like and invincible.

Meaning defender of men

Jean-Paul, John-Paul, Jon-Paul, Giovanni-Paolo, Juan-Pablo

Jean-Paul Sartre, the French existentialist philosopher and novelist, was born on 21 June 1905. He dominated post-war intellectual life in France, and his philosophical theories reached a large audience through his award-winning novels.

From John, meaning God has shown me favour, and Paul, meaning small

Ray, Raymond, Redmond, Redmund, Raymonde, Raimondo, Ramón

Ray Davies, founder and leading member of the 1960s band the Kinks, was born on this day in 1944. One of the most respected British songwriters, he penned and played a string of hit songs and influenced a generation of musicians.

From Raymond, meaning protector

William, Will, Wills, Gwilim, Guillermo, Willem

Prince William, the first-born son of the heir to the British throne, Charles, Prince of Wales, and the late Diana, Princess of Wales, was born on this day in 1982. He is considered to be one of Britain's most eligible bachelors.

Meaning desiring to defend

Jane, Jayne, Jaynie, Juana, Giovanna, Jana

Jane Russell, the US actress, was born on this day in 1921. The brunette bombshell appeared in many films during the 1940s and 1950s, but the peak of her career was her role alongside Marilyn Monroe in *Gentlemen Prefer Blondes* (1953).

Meaning God's gift of grace

Litha

Litha is the Celtic word for midsummer, and the name is sometimes used for the celebration of the summer solstice, which falls on this day. J.R.R. Tolkien used the term for a midsummer festival in *The Lord of the Rings* (1954–5).

Meaning midsummer

Benazir

Benazir Bhutto was born on this day in 1953. She was prime minister of Pakistan in 1988–9 and 1993–6, the first woman to lead a Muslim country in modern times. She was also, while studying at Oxford, the first Asian woman to be president of the Oxford Union.

Meaning incomparable

Titania, Tatiana, Tania, Tanya

Titania is the name of the queen of the fairies in Shakespeare's play *A Midsummer Night's Dream*, and the name is often used to refer to fairy-like qualities. Titania is also the largest moon of the planet Uranus, which is considered to rule freedom and creativity in astrology.

Meaning giant

Thomas, Tomas, Tomaso

Today is the feast day of *St Thomas More*. Born in 1478, More was a devoted family man who bravely opposed Henry VIII on the matter of his divorce from his first wife, Catherine of Aragon, and his claim to be head of the Church of England. St Thomas More is the patron saint of lawyers.

Meaning twin

Champ

The US football player *Champ Bailey* was born Roland Champ Bailey on this day in 1978 in Folkston, Georgia. The Washington Redskins drafted him out of the University of Georgia, and he was subsequently traded to the Denver Broncos for the 2004 season. The Gaelic name Carlin means little champ.

Meaning champion

Alban, Albie, Alby, Albany, Albin, Alben, Albanus

Today is the feast day of *St Alban*. During the persecution of Christians in the 2nd century, Alban hid a priest in his house and saved his life at risk to his own. Alban had been a pagan, but he was so impressed by the priest that he converted to Christianity.

Meaning from Alba

Todd, Tod, Toddy, Toddie

Todd Rundgren, the US pop musician, was born on 22 June 1948. His eventful musical career, which spans four decades, has covered many different musical styles and concepts, including experimental music. He is renowned as a highly innovative musician.

Meaning fox

Meryl, Muriel, Mariel, Meriel, Merrill

Meryl Streep, the US actress, was born on this day in 1949. Considered to be one of the best film actresses of the 20th century, her performances have won her two Oscars and in 2004 she received a lifetime achievement award from the American Film Institute.

Meaning sea bright

Anne, Ann, Anna, Ana, Annie, Annika, Anneka, Anula, Anusia, Anuska

Anne Morrow Lindbergh, American author and pioneering aviator, was born on this day in 1906. She accompanied her husband, Charles, as co-pilot and navigator on groundbreaking explorations during the 1930s. She was the first US woman to obtain a glider pilot's licence.

Meaning God has favoured me

Cyndi, Cindie, Cindy, Cinderella

The US singer *Cyndi Lauper* was born on 22 June 1953 in Queen's, New York. Her debut album, *She's So Unusual* (1984), spawned the feminist 1980s anthem 'Girls Just Wanna Have Fun' and the classic 'Time After Time', which has been covered by no fewer than 70 artists, including Miles Davis.

Meaning girl of the ashes

Cicely

The British founder of the modern hospice movement, Dame *Cicely Saunders* was born in London on this day in 1918. Since she founded St Christopher's Hospice, Sydenham, in 1967, the movement has spread throughout Britain and she has received many honours for her work.

Meaning patron saint of music

23

Zizou, Zinédine, Zine

The French football player known as *Zizou* was born Zinédine Yazid Zidane on 23 June 1972. When France won the Football World Cup in 1998, he was voted the top player. He is considered to be one of the best footballers of all time .

Meaning (from Africa) not known

Oda

One of the great Japanese warlords, *Oda Nobunaga* was born on 23 June 1534. He not only conquered most of Japan on the battlefield, but he also established a business economy, introduced the tea ceremony and built the most beautiful castles Japan has ever seen. He still lives on as the star of video games.

Meaning small pointed spear

Filbert, Filberto, Philbert

Tanzanian sporting hero *Filbert Bayi* was born on this day in 1953. He set the world record for the 1,500 metres – 3 minutes, 32.16 seconds – at the 1974 Commonwealth Games in New Zealand. In 2003 he formed the Filbert Bayi Institution to promote young sporting talent in Tanzania.

Meaning brilliant one

Wiley

On this day in 1931 *Wiley Post* took off from Long Island to fly around the world, becoming the first pilot ever to do so in a single-engine plane. His first adventure in aviation was as a parachutist for a flying circus called Burell Tobbs and His Texas Topnotch Fliers.

From William, meaning desiring to defend

Etheldreda, Audrey

Today is the feast day of *St Etheldreda*, who was born in about 630. She was the daughter of King Anna and Queen Saewara of the East Angles, and in 660 she married Ecgfrith, king of Northumbria. She became abbess of Ely in 673 and is the patron saint of Cambridge.

Meaning noble maiden

Josephine, Josette

On this day in 1763 *Jospehine de Beauharnais* was born in Trois-Ilets, Martinique. She is remembered as the first wife of Napoleon Bonaparte, whom she married in 1796. She retained the title empress even after the marriage was dissolved in 1809.

Meaning she will add

Selma, Anselma, Anselme, Zelma

The US actress *Selma Blair* was born on 23 June 1972. Selma, whose Hebrew name is Batsheva, is married to Frank Zappa's son, Ahmet Emuukha Rodan Zappa. Her best-known films include *Cruel Intentions* (1999) and *Legally Blonde* (2001).

Meaning divinely protected

Rosetta, Rosette, Rosina, Rosena, Raisa, Rois, Rosita

Today is the birthday of *Rosetta Hightower*, singer with the 1960s group the Orlons. The group, formed when its members were at high school, had several hits in the early 1960s, including 'The Wah Watusi' (1962) and 'Don't Hang Up' (1962) and were one of the most popular bands to come out of Philadelphia.

Meaning flower

Beck, Bec

British guitarist *Jeff Beck* was born in Wallington, Surrey, on this day in 1944. In the 1960s he replaced Eric Clapton in the Yardbirds, and his blues-jazz-rock style took the group to new heights. He then formed the Jeff Beck Group with Ron Wood on bass and Rod Stewart on vocals.

Meaning brook, stream

Ambrose, Ambroise, Ambros, Ambrosi, Ambrosio, Ambrosius, Amby, Brose

The US satirist *Ambrose Bierce* was born Ambrose Gwinnett on this day in 1842. Nicknamed Bitter Bierce, he was a journalist, short story writer, critic and editor. His most lasting work, *The Devil's Dictionary*, was published in 1911.

Meaning belonging to the divine immortals

Riley, Reilly, Ryley

The earliest piece of minimalist music, *In C*, was written by the US composer *Terry Riley*, who was born on this day in 1935. His collaborative, improvisational writing style influenced many. The British group Curved Air took their name from his album *A Rainbow in Curved Air* (1971).

Meaning valiant, war-like

Horatio, Horatius

Horatio Kitchener was born in Ballylongford, County Kerry, on 24 June 1850. He was the moustachioed British field marshal who appeared on the First World War poster 'Your Country Needs You'. He fought in the Sudan and South Africa, and was secretary of state for war on the outbreak of war in 1914.

From Horace, meaning time-keeper, hours of the sun

Sherry, Sheryl, Sharleen

American actress *Sherry Stringfield* celebrates a birthday today. She was born on 24 June 1967. Sherry played the popular doctor Susan Lewis in the first series of the TV show *ER* (1994) and later (2001) returned to the show as head of emergency medicine.

From Caroline, meaning free woman

Fortuna, Fortune

On this day ancient Romans celebrated *Fortuna*, the goddess of fate. She had many manifestations: Fortuna Annonairia brought the luck of the harvest, and Fortuna Primigenia directed the fortune of a newborn child at the moment of birth.

Meaning woman of destiny

Anita

The Indian novelist *Anita Desai* was born in Mussorie, India, on this day in 1937. She has written for both adults and children. Among her best-known works are *Voices in the City* (1965), the collection of short stories *Games at Twilight* (1978) and *Fasting, Feasting* (1999).

From Anne, meaning God has favoured me

Sissel

The Norwegian singer *Sissel* was born Sissel Kyrkjebø in Bergen, Norway, on this day in 1969. She sang on the soundtrack for the film *Titanic* (1997) and sang the Winter Olympic Anthem at the opening ceremony of the 1994 Winter Olympics in Lillehammer, Norway.

Meaning without sight

25 JUNE

Orwell, Orell

The British author and essayist *George Orwell* was born Eric Arthur Blair on this day in 1903. His two best-known novels, *Animal Farm* (1945) and *Nineteen Eighty-Four* (1949), are political allegories. The latter has a character called Big Brother, who controlled the citizens, a name that was used decades later for a reality TV show.

Meaning golden, gilded

Kene, Keane, Kean, Keen, Keene

US actor *Kene Holliday* was born in Copaigue, Suffolk County, New York, on this day in 1949. He has been appearing regularly on TV since the early 1960s. He was Tyler Hudson, the private investigator, in *Matlock* (1986) and later appeared in *Hope and Faith* (2004).

Meaning sharp-witted

Mario, Marius, Marion

Today is the birthday of *Mario Calire*, the drummer with the Wallflowers, who was born on 25 June 1974. In 1998 the band's song 'One Headlight' won a Grammy for best rock song and best rock performance by a duo or group with vocal. The band's lead singer is Bob Dylan's son, Jakob.

Meaning war-like

Dikembe

The basketball player *Dikembe Mutombo* was born Dikembe Mutombo Mpolondo Mukamba Jean Jacques Wamutombo in Kinshasa, Zaire, on this day in 1966. Named 'overall good guy' by *US Sporting News* for his humanitarian work in the USA and Africa, he has personally donated the sum of $3.5 million towards the construction of a hospital in Kinshasa.

Meaning not known

Carly, Carleen, Karly, Karlie, Karleen, Karlene, Carlene

Carly Simon, the US singer and songwriter, was born in New York City on 25 June 1945, the daughter of Richard Simon, co-founder of the publisher Simon and Schuster. Among her best-known songs are 'You're So Vain' and the James Bond theme song, 'Nobody Does It Better'. She won an Oscar for 'Let the River Run', which was in the movie *Working Girl* (1988).

Meaning womanly

Birdsall, Bird

Birdsall Otis Edey was the president of the Girl Scouts of America and one of its earliest organizers. Bird, as she was always known, was born on this day in 1872. She was a published poet and edited the first and early editions of the Girl Scout *Leader* magazine.

Meaning bird nook

Karisma

The Indian film star *Karisma Kapoor* was born on 25 June 1974 into a family of Bollywood film stars. Also known by her nickname, Lolo, she won the best actress Filmfare Award for her first leading role in *Raja Hindustani* (1996). She is married to the industrialist Sanjay Kapoor.

Meaning favour, gift

Tansu

On this day in 1993 *Tansu Ciller* became Turkey's first woman prime minister. Born in Istanbul in 1946, she became the party leader of the True Path Party and went on to become the prime minister of a coalition government.

Meaning ornamented

Kelvin, Kelvan, Kelven, Kelwin

On this day in 1824 *William Thomson, 1st Baron Kelvin* was born in Belfast, Northern Ireland. He was a physicist who made great inroads into the field of thermodynamics. He was one of the first members of the Order of Merit, and he is buried in Westminster Abbey, London.

Meaning from the narrow stream

Parker, Parke, Park, Parkin

Colonel *Tom Parker*, Elvis Presley's formidable and ever-present manager, was born Andreas Cornelius van Kuijk in the Netherlands on 26 June 1909. He got the title Colonel as an honorary commission, bestowed on him by the governor of Louisiana, Jimmie Davis, in 1948.

Meaning park-keeper, little Peter

Laurie, Laurier, Laurits, Lauritz

The much-loved British writer *Laurie Lee* was born on this day in 1914. His autobiographical *Cider With Rosie* (1959), about his childhood in Stroud, and *As I Walked Out One Midsummer Morning* (1969), about his walk across Spain in the 1930s, remain popular.

Meaning crowned with a laurel

Anthelm, Anthaniel, Ante

Today is the feast day of St *Anthelm*. Born in 1107 in Savoy, France, Anthelm was a Carthusian monk and became prior of the Grande Chartreuse. He defended Pope Alexander II against the antipope, Victor IV. He became bishop of Belley, where his relics remain to this day.

Meaning judge, worthy of praise

Kaitlin, Kaitlyn, Kaitleen, Kaitlinlee, Kaitlynn, Kaitlynne

The US actress *Kaitlin Cullum* was born in Los Angeles on this day in 1986. Famous for her role as Libby, Grace's young daughter, in the 1990s hit TV series *Grace under Fire*, the grown-up Kaitlin is making her name in feature films.

Meaning pure beauty

Babe, Babb, Babby, Babette, Babs, Bab, Babita

On 26 June 1914 *Babe Didrikson Zaharias* was born in Texas. One of the greatest female athletes of all time, in the 1930s she held Olympic, American or world records in five different events. In the 1940s she became a champion golfer, winning an unequalled 17 straight tournaments.

From Barbara, meaning stranger

Gretchen, Grete, Grethe

It is the birthday today of US country music singer *Gretchen Wilson*. She was born in Pocahontas, Illinois, on 26 June 1973. Her single 'Redneck Woman' (2004) reached number one of the country singles charts, and her album *Here for the Party* (2004) entered the charts at number one.

From Margaret, meaning pearl

Terri, Terry, Terentia, Terencia, Terrie

Terri Nunn, the lead singer of Los Angeles band Berlin, was born on this day in 1961. In the 1980s Berlin had a hit with 'Take My Breath Away' from the soundtrack of *Top Gun* (1986), starring Tom Cruise and Kelly McGillis.

Meaning guardian

27 JUNE

Fingal, Finlay

In Sweden 27 June is the name day for *Fingal*. The name comes from Finn na Gael, meaning Finn the foreigner, the Scottish name for Finn mac Cool. In Celtic legend he was the giant who built the Giant's Causeway – hexagonal basalt stepping-stones on the north coast of Northern Ireland.

Meaning fair hero

Tobey, Tobe, Tioboid, Tobiah, Tobit, Toby

Tobey Maguire, the star of the two *Spiderman* films (2000, 2004), was born on this day in 1975. He also played Red Pollard, the underdog who becomes a champion, in the popular *Seabiscuit* (2003). In *Wonder Boys* (2000) he played opposite Michael Douglas and Frances McDormand.

Meaning God is good

Lafcadio

The author *Lafcadio Hearn*, who was born Patricio Lafcadio Tessima Carlos Hearn on 27 June 1850, was named after Lelukada in Greece, the place he was born. He moved from Dublin to the USA when he was 19 before settling in Japan. He is best known for his books on Japan, especially his collections of Japanese fairytales.

Meaning island of Greece

Raúl

The Spanish footballer *Raúl González Blanco*, known universally as Raúl, was born on this day in 1977. The Real Madrid striker is the all-time leading goal scorer for the national team. Every time he scores he kisses his wedding ring, acknowledging his wife, Mamen.

Meaning wise ruler, wolf

Aestas, Aesta

In ancient Rome today was the festival of *Aestas*, the goddess of summer, and marked the first day of summer in the Roman calendar. Images of Aestas always portray her as wearing nothing but a garland of corn. If it rains today, tradition says it will be a wet summer.

Meaning summer

Meera, Meira

The British comedian, writer, playwright, singer, journalist and actress *Meera Syal* was born on 27 June 1963 in Wolverhampton. In 2000 she received the media personality of the year award from the Commission for Racial Equality. She was made an MBE in 1997.

Meaning light

Efua

Efua Theodora Sutherland, the Ghanaian writer, theatre pioneer, children's author and dramatist, was born on this day in 1924. She founded several theatre companies and writing societies in Accra. Her plays include *Foriwa* (1962), *Edufa* (1967) and *The Marriage of Anansewa* (1975).

Meaning born on Friday

Rosalie, Rosalee, Rosaleigh

Rosalie Allen, the queen of the yodellers, was born on this day in 1924. She became a professional yodeller during the Second World War, singing on the New York *Swing Billies* radio show. She had several hit records, including 'I Wanna be a Cowboy's Sweetheart' and 'Guitar Polka'.

Meaning rosy meadow

Jean-Jacques

The Swiss-French philosopher and writer *Jean-Jacques Rousseau* was born on 28 June 1712. He coined the phrase 'noble savage', believing that man was corrupted by society, and he was one of the first to attack the institution of private property. His ideas and texts were influential on the French Revolution.

Meaning God is gracious

Mel, Melvin, Melvyn, Malvin, Mal, Melva

Mel Brooks, the US film producer, actor, writer and director, was born Melvin Kaminsky in Brooklyn, New York, on this day in 1926. He is one of the few people to have won one or more Oscars, Emmys, Tonys and Grammys. In 2004, he achieved renewed success with the stage version of his 1968 film *The Producers*.

Meaning bad settlement

Wesley, Wesleigh, Westleigh

The British evangelist and founder of Methodism, *John Wesley* was born at Epworth, Lincolnshire, on this day in 1703. He and his brother, Charles, formed the first 'Holy Club' at Oxford in 1729, and they were named Methodists because of their methodical habits.

Meaning from the west meadow

Giselher

The German composer *Giselher Wolfgang Klebe* was born in Mannheim on this day in 1925. His works include the operas *The Fatal Wishes* (1959) and *Jakobowsky and the Colonels* (1964), and the ballet symphony *The Will* (1972).

Meaning gentleman hostage

Aileen, Aleen, Alene, Ailey, Ailee, Aili, Aila

The US actress *Aileen Quinn* was born in Pennsylvania on this day in 1971. She was a child star of the 1970s and 1980s on both stage and screen. She is best known for playing the title role in the 1982 movie version of the play *Annie* (1982).

Meaning light

Carlotta, Carlota, Carllee, Carlitta, Carlita

The Italian ballerina *Carlotta Grisi* was born Caronne Adele Giuseppina Maria Grisi on this day in 1819. She was taken to the Paris Opera as Jules Perrot's protégée, and in 1841 she danced the leading part in the world premiere of *Giselle*.

Meaning manly

Tichina, Tiina

The US actress *Tichina Arnold* was born on this day in 1969. She is best known for her roles as Sharla Valentine in *All My Children* (1970) and Zena Brown in *Ryan's Hope* (1975).

Meaning anointed, follower of Christ

Lalla, Lala, Laleh

British actress *Lalla Ward* was born the Honourable Lady Sarah Ward on 28 June 1951. For two years (1963) she played the role of Romana in the cult TV series *Dr Who*. She is married to the author and scientist Richard Dawkins and has a step-daughter, Juliet.

Meaning tulip

29 JUNE

Leroy, Leroi

On this day in 1908 US composer and conductor *Leroy Anderson* was born in Cambridge, Massachusetts. He was the master of light orchestral music, and many of his works were introduced by the Boston Pops Orchestra. Still remembered are 'Sleigh Ride', 'Plink-plank-plunk' and 'The Typewriter', which was used in the 1959 film *But Not for Me*.

Meaning king

Kwam, Kwame

The US civil rights leader and black activist, famous for his black power speeches, *Kwam Touré* was born Stokley Carmichael on 29 June 1941. He was chairman of the Student Non-violent Co-ordinating Committee. He was married to the South African singer Miriam Makeba.

Meaning born on Saturday

Gilberto, Gilbert, Gilbeirt, Gilleabart, Gill, Gil

The Brazilian superstar singer *Gilberto Gil* was born in Salvador, Bahia, on this day in 1942. He is one of the most important artists in Brazil and enjoys a strong international following. When President Lula came to power he became the nation's minister for culture.

Meaning bright pledge

Shigechiyo, Shig, Shige

The world's oldest person whose age has been authentically recorded, *Shigechiyo Izumi* was born in Okinawa, Japan, on this day in 1865. He lived to be 120 years, 237 days. When examined at the age of 115 he was found to be in perfect health. He worked till he was 105.

Meaning not known

Petra, Perrine, Petula, Pierette, Perette

In Bulgaria, Finland, Lithuania, Slovakia and Sweden 29 June is the name day for people named Petra, which comes from Petrina, itself a form of Peter. Petra is also the name of a beautiful ancient city in Jordan.

From Peter, meaning rock, stone

Oriana, Oriane, Oria

The Italian-born US journalist *Oriana Fallaci* was born on this day in 1930. She has written novels and memoirs, and is a highly regarded political journalist. She has interviewed Indira Gandhi, the Ayatollah Khomeini and Henry Kissinger, among many others.

Meaning golden one

Frieda, Freidanna, Freda, Frida, Friedie, Freddie

The Scottish actress *Frieda Inescort* was born in Edinburgh on this day in 1901. She performed in 16 Broadway productions and appeared in many classic Hollywood films, including *The Dark Angel* (1935), *Pride and Prejudice* (1940) and *A Place in the Sun* (1951).

Meaning peace, joy

Kimberlin, Kimberlyn, Kimberley, Kimbra

The US actress *Kimberlin Brown* was born on 29 June 1961. She is best known for her role as Sheila Carter in the successful *The Bold and Beautiful*, which was first broadcast in March 1987 and went on to be shown in 98 countries with an audience of 450 million.

From Kimberley, meaning clearing, wood

Horace, Horatio, Horatius, Race

The French artist *Horace Vernet* was born on 30 June 1789. He was the son of the painter Carle Vernet. Horace was born in the Louvre, Paris, where his parents were staying during the French Revolution. He was especially famous for his military paintings of the Napoleonic era.

Meaning hour, time

Esa-Pekka

The Finnish conductor *Esa-Pekka Salonen* was born in Helsinki on 30 June 1958. His first important conducting role was with London's Philharmonia Orchestra in 1983. He went on to become the chief conductor and music director of the Los Angeles Philharmonic.

Meaning salvation by God, rock

Bryn

The drummer with the Fabulous Poodles, *Bryn B. Burrows* was born on this day in 1954. The Fabulous Poodles was a British 1970s band, which released several albums, including *Mirror Stars* (1978) and *Think Pink* (1979).

Meaning hill

Dominikus, Dominik

The German architect and master builder *Dominikus Zimmermann* was born on this day in 1685. His best-known building is the Wies Pilgrimage Church at Wieskirche, which he built with his brother, Johann Baptist, who was a master at frescoes.

Meaning born on the Lord's day

Phoebe, Phebe

On 30 June 1927 *Phoebe Fairgrave Omlie* became the first US woman to be issued with a pilot's licence. The pioneering aviatrix was born in 1902 in Des Moines. She developed a double parachute drop for the Glen Messer Flying Circus and won the Women's Air Derby in 1929.

Meaning bright sun

Vigdis

On this day in 1980 *Vigdis Finnbogadottir* was elected president of Iceland. She was re-elected in 1984 and 1988. She was born in Reykjavik in 1930 and worked as a French teacher and a tour guide before entering politics. In 1990 she was awarded the international leadership living legacy prize by the Women's International Centre.

Meaning wife of killer Hrapp

Lucile, Lucille

The Danish choreographer and dancer *Lucile Grahn* was born in Copenhagen on this day in 1819. She danced Astrid in the premiere of *Valdemar* and Quitteria in the premiere of *Don Quixote*, both by her tutor August Bournonville.

Meaning light

Fabiana, Fabianna, Fabia, Fabienne

The footballer *Fabiana Vallejos* was born on this day in 1985. She plays as number 14 in the Argentine national team. In the USA in 2003 she helped her team qualify for the FIFA Women's World Cup.

From Fabian, meaning bean

July

July

Gottfried, Gottfrid

On this day in 1646 German philosopher and mathematician *Gottfried Wilhelm Leibniz* was born in Leipzig. Leibniz was a great influence on the German Enlightenment, and although he invented calculus before Isaac Newton, Newton published his findings first.

Meaning peace of God

Myron, Myrlon

Myron Cohen was born on this day in 1902. Often called America's funniest storyteller, in the 1960s he made regular TV appearances on the *Ed Sullivan Show*. His style was to speak very slowly, keeping the audience gripped and hanging on for his next word.

Meaning myrrh

Farley, Farleigh, Fairley

The US actor *Farley Granger* was born on 1 July 1925. He started making movies in the early 1940s, and one of his first roles was in Hitchcock's film *Rope* (1948). He was also in the two long-running US TV soaps, *The Edge of Night* (1975–84) and *As the World Turns* (1956–95).

Meaning fern meadow

Dan, Danio, Danilo, Danillo, Danil, Daniil

US author *Dan Brown*'s internationally successful novel *The Da Vinci Code* was first published in Britain on this day in 2003. More than 2 million copies of this title have been sold around the world since it was first published.

Meaning God is my judge

Amandine, Amantee

The French novelist George Sand was born *Amandine Aurore Lucie Dupin* on this day in 1804. She took her penname from Jules Sandeau, who collaborated with her on her first novel and who was her first lover. She had two children, Maurice and Slange. She famously had a long affair with the composer Chopin.

Meaning worthy of love

Estée, Esteen, Estela, Estelee, Estelina

Estée Lauder, the US businesswoman and beautician, was born on 1 July 1906. She founded her company in New York in 1946 with just four products: a skin lotion, a cleansing oil, a crème pack and an all-purpose cream. The company, still controlled by the Lauder family, now employs over 20,000 people.

Meaning star

Liv

The US actress *Liv Tyler* was born on this day in 1977 to Aerosmith's lead singer, Steven Tyler, and model, Bebe Buell. She is best known for playing Arwen in the film version of *The Lord of the Rings* trilogy (2001, 2002, 2003).

Meaning protector

Missy, Melissa

The first female hip hop superstar, *Missy Elliott* was born Melissa Elliott on this day in 1971. Originally known as Missy 'Misdemeanour', she released her first album, *Supa Dupa Fly*, in 1977. The album and the single, 'The Rain (Supa Dupa Fly)', were huge hits.

Meaning honey bee

Hermann, Herman, Hermon, Harman

The German author *Hermann Hesse* was born in Württemberg on this day in 1877. His novels reflect his fascination with Eastern religions and Jungian psychoanalysis. His two best-known works are *Siddhartha* (1922) and *Steppenwolf* (1927). In 1946 he was awarded the Nobel Prize for literature.

Meaning army man

Tyrone

The British theatrical director, writer and producer *Tyrone Guthrie* was born on 2 July 1900 in Tunbridge Wells, Kent. He ran several British companies, including the Old Vic, and founded the Guthrie Theatre in Minnesota and the Shakespearean Festival in Ontario.

Meaning Owen's meadow

Vicente, Vico, Vicor, Victerrance

Vicente Fox Quesada, the president of Mexico since 2000, was born on this day in 1942. Mexico doesn't officially have first ladies, but since his marriage to Marta Sahagún in 2001, Fox sometimes refers to himself and his wife as the presidential couple.

Meaning victorious conqueror

Thurgood

The first African-American justice of the US Supreme Court, *Thurgood Marshall* was born on this day in 1908 in Baltimore, Maryland. He was named after his great-grandfather, Thoroughgood Marshall, a former slave who fought for the Union during the Civil War.

Meaning Thor (god of thunder)

Yancy, Yanci, Yancity

The US actress *Yancy Butler* was born on this day in 1970 in New York. Her father, Joe Butler, was the drummer with the 1960s group the Lovin' Spoonful. She works in features and on TV. In 2001 she had her own TV series, *Witchblade*.

Meaning windmill dweller

Rosa, Rosabel, Rosabella, Rosalee, Rosella, Roselle, Rosalia, Rosaleen, Roisin, Rosheen

Today is the name day for everyone called *Rosa* in Sweden. From Rose, an Old German name taken to England with the Norman Conquest, it originally meant fame or horse. It is now universally associated with the flower.

Meaning flower

Charlene, Charline, Char

Pluto's only known moon is Charon. It was named by its discoverer, James Christy, on 2 July 1978, after the figure from Greek mythology, but Christy changed the pronunciation from a hard 'ch' to a soft 'sh', after his wife *Charlene*, whose nickname is Char.

Meaning free woman

Lindsay, Lindsey, Lindsee, Lindslee, Lindoloy

The US actress *Lindsay Lohan* was born on this day in 1986. She is the acclaimed child star of the 1998 remake of the film *The Parent Trap*, in which she played both twins with amazing style. As a teenager she starred in *Freaky Friday* (2003) and *Mean Girls* (2004).

Meaning Lincoln's marsh

Franz, Frantz, Frantizec

The author *Franz Kafka* was born in Prague, then in Austrian Bohemia, on this day in 1883. He was one of the most important German-language writers of the 20th century, and the word Kafkaesque has entered the language. Many of his works have been adapted for stage and TV, including 'The Metamorphosis' (1916) *The Trial* (1925) and *The Castle* (1926).

Meaning of France

Sherlock

On this day in 1895 Sir Arthur Conan Doyle published a story called 'The Adventure of Black Peter', featuring the detective *Sherlock Holmes*. He was based on Conan Doyle's medical teacher, Joseph Bell, and the name Sherlock Holmes was made from the names of two cricketers.

Meaning shear lock, close-cut hair

Tom, Tomas

Two famous people named Tom were born on this day. The US actor *Tom Cruise* was born Thomas Cruise Mapother IV in Syracuse, New York, in 1962. Sir *Tom Stoppard*, the distinguished British playwright, was born Tomás Straussler in Ziln, Czechoslovakia, on July 3 1937.

Meaning twin

Stavros

The Greek shipping magnate *Stavros Nairchos* was born on this day in 1909. He built up a trade fleet with his uncle before the Second World War, pioneering the construction of supertankers in 1952. The increased demand for these enormous oil-carrying ships in the years following the war made him a billionaire. He married five times.

Meaning cross, crucifixion

Elizabeth, Elisabeth, Elisabet, Elisabetta, Lizabeta, Lizbeth, Lizzy, Lizzie, Lize, Liza, Liz, Betty, Bettie, Bet, Eliza, Elisa, Elissa, Elzieta, Elspeth

The British writer *Elizabeth Coles Taylor* was born on this day in 1912 in Reading, Berkshire. She worked as a governess and a librarian before writing the first of her 12 novels, *At Mrs Lippincote's* (1945). She described her own works as books in which 'practically nothing ever happens', but they accurately portray the lives of women in the 1950s and 1960s.

Meaning consecrated to God

Ludivine, Ludovica

The French actress *Ludivine Sagner* was born on this day in 1979 at La Celle-Saint-Cloud, Yvelines. In 2003 two of her films were shown at the Cannes festival, *The Swimming Pool* and *La Petite Lili*.

Meaning famous warrior

Asha

The Malaysian actress and TV presenter *Asha Gill* was born on this day in 1972. She is one of the leading stars in Malaysia's first British soap, *The City of the Rich*. She was nominated for best entertainment presenter in the Asian Television Awards in 2004.

Meaning hope

Yeardley, Yeardleigh

The US actress *Yeardley Smith* was born on this day in 1964. Rarely recognized, she is the voice of Lisa Simpson in *The Simpsons*. Her father is a journalist with the *Washington Post*.

Meaning of the yard

Nathaniel, Nathanial, Nataniel, Natanial, Nate, Nat, Nattie, Nathane'el

US writer *Nathaniel Hawthorne* was born on this day in 1804 in Salem, Massachusetts. Best remembered for his short stories and romance novels, he lived in Concord for a while, where his neighbours were Ralph Waldo Emerson and Henry David Thoreau.

Meaning gift of God

Collins

The US songwriter *Stephen Collins Foster* was born in Lawrenceville, Pennsylvania, on 4 July 1826. He could be regarded as the first writer of pop music, and he was responsible for many of the most popular songs of the mid-19th century, including 'Oh! Susanna' (1848), 'Jeannie with the Light Brown Hair' (1854) and 'Gentle Annie' (1856).

Meaning strong and virile

Mitch, Mitchel, Mitchell

The US bandleader *Mitch Miller* was born in Rochester, New York, on 4 July 1911. Hugely successful as a bandleader and producer, his 1960s TV programme *Sing Along with Mitch* took him to new heights of popularity. The sing-along songs on the show were subtitled and featured a little bouncing dot, which moved above the words

Meaning who is like God

Geraldo, Gerallt

TV anchorman *Geraldo Miguel Riviera* was born on this day in 1943. His colourful TV career has ranged from *Geraldo*, his 1980s pioneering 'trash TV' talk show, to war reporting. His biography, *Exposing Myself*, was published in 1991.

Meaning ruling spear

Ulrika, Ulrica, Ulrike, Elrica, Rica

In Sweden 4 July is the name day for *Ulrika*. In 1718 Ulrika Eleonora was elected queen of Sweden after the death of her brother. Ulrika Jonsson, the British-based TV personality, appeared regularly as team captain on the surreal TV show *Shooting Stars* (1993), with Vic Reeves and Bob Mortimer, where she was known as Ulrika-ka-ka-ka.

Meaning ruler over all

Gina, Luigina, Lugenia, Luevenia

The Italian actress and model *Gina Lollobrigida* was Born on 4 July 1927 in Subiaco near Rome. She was one of the curvaceous beauties of the 1950s, with only Marilyn Monroe and Sophia Loren to rival her. She has since become a businesswoman, sculptor and photographer.

Meaning famous warrior

Abigail

Abigail Van Buren, the US 'Dear Abby' advice columnist, was born on this day in 1918. Her real name was Pauline Esther Friedman Phillips. She and her twin, Esther Pauline Friedman, who wrote an advice column under the penname Ann Landers, were known as Eppie and Popo.

Meaning father's joy

Signy, Signe, Signi

The US actress *Signy Coleman* was born in Ross, California on 4 July 1960. Among her many TV appearances are as the character Celeste in *Santa Barbara* (1984), as Hope in *The Young and the Restless* (1973) and as Annie Dutton in *Guiding Light* (1952). She is married to Vincent Irizarry.

Meaning new victory

5 JULY

Cecil, Cecilio, Cecilius, Cece

The British diamond tycoon *Cecil Rhodes* was born on this day in 1853 at Bishop's Stortford, Hertfordshire. The African state of Rhodesia, now Zimbabwe, was named after him. He also founded the Rhodes Scholarships, which enable foreign nationals to study at Oxford University. Bill Clinton was one such beneficiary.

Meaning one who doesn't see

Dwight

On this day 1879 US public official *Dwight Filley Davis* was born in St Louis, Missouri. He was US secretary for war and governor general of the Philippines, but he is remembered because in 1900 he donated an international challenge cup for lawn tennis. This is known as the Davis Cup, which is competed for each year.

Meaning not known

Aneurin

History was made on this day in 1948 when *Aneurin 'Nye' Bevan* created the National Health Service in Britain. Since that day the people of Britain have paid National Insurance contributions on their salaries in return for unlimited free medical assistance.

Meaning truly golden

Etienne

Etienne de Silhouette was born on this day in 1709. He introduced stringent budget cuts to Louis XV's finances, after which his name became synonymous with cost-cutting. The shadow portraits of the time, created from sheets of paper and much cheaper than real ones, began to become known as silhouettes.

Meaning crowned

Adeline, Adelaide, Adelina, Adelind, Adelia, Adelaida, Addi, Adela

On 5 July 1916 two women set off from New York on a motorbike trip across the USA. When they arrived in San Diego, California, on 12 September 1916, Augusta and *Adeline Van Buren* became the first women ever to make a transcontinental motorcycle journey.

Meaning kind, well-born

Wanda

The Polish harpsichordist *Wanda Landowska* was born in Warsaw on this day in 1879. Although she made it her life's work to reintroduce the works of J.S. Bach on the harpsichord, she also inspired new works by Falla, Poulenc and other 20th-century composers. As the Second World War approached she fled to the USA, where she lived until her death.

Meaning wanderer

Presley, Presli, Preslie, Presly

Presley Tanita Tucker, the daughter of country music star Tanita Tucker, was born on 5 July 1989, a sister for Layla LaCosta and elder brother Beau Grayson. She was the Country Music Association's top female vocalist of the year in 1991.

Meaning priest's land

Edie, Edite, Edita, Edit

The US actress *Edie Falco* was born on this day in 1963 in Brooklyn, New York. She is best known for her role as Tony Soprano's wife, Carmela, in the TV hit *The Sopranos* and has received many awards for her performance, including the 1999 Golden Globe and 1999 Emmy for best actress.

Meaning blessed war

Sylvester, Sylvestre, Sylverstre, Sylvanus, Sylvan, Sylvian

Sylvester Stallone was born Michael Sylvester Enzio Stallone on 6 July 1946. A producer and director as well as an actor, he is best known for his film roles as Rambo and Rocky. He has five children: Sage Moonblood, Seargeoh, Sophia Rose, Sistine Rose and Scarlet Rose.

Meaning forest

Ned, Nedward

The US actor *Ned Beatty* was born in Louisville, Kentucky, in 1937. Originally a stage actor, he made his film debut in 1971 in John Boorman's *Deliverance*. The Oscar-nominated actor has since appeared in many successful features, and he is also Dan's father in *Roseanne*.

Meaning blessed guardian

Merv, Mervet

Merv Griffin, the US talk-show host, was born on 6 July 1925. As well as having his own enormously popular and successful chat show, Merv was responsible for the TV game shows *Jeopardy!* and *Wheel of Fortune*.

Meaning famous

Tenzin

Tenzin Gyatso, His Holiness the Dalai Lama, was born on this day in 1935. He was exiled from Tibet in 1959 after China invaded his country, but Tibetans still see regard him as their religious and political leader. Dalai means ocean, and Lama means spiritual teacher.

Meaning protector of dharma

Dolores, Deloris, Doloritas, Delorita, Delora, Delores

Dolores Claman, the Canadian musician and composer, was born on 6 July 1927. She is famous for composing many pieces, but especially for 'Hockey Night in Canada', which is known as Canada's second national anthem.

Meaning lady of sorrow

Frida, Frieda

The Mexican painter *Frida Kahlo* was born Magdalena Carmen Frieda Kahlo y Calderón on 6 July 1907. She was married to the artist Diego Rivera, whom she later divorced and then remarried. Her candid, shocking paintings of the female experience made her a feminist cult figure.

Meaning peace

Godelva, Goldelive, Godeleine, Godilva

Today is the feast day of *St Godelva*. When she was abandoned by her husband, Bertulf of Ghistelles, the young Godelva was badly treated by her cruel mother-in-law. Bertulf, meanwhile, arranged for her to be murdered. Bertulf was never charged, but soon after her death miracles were said to have occurred at her grave.

Meaning beloved of God

LaVerne, Laverne, Lavera

LaVerne Andrews of the US singing group the Andrews Sisters was born on this day in 1911 in Minneapolis, Minnesota. With her sisters Maxine and Patti, the Andrews Sisters sold over 60 million records. They entertained Allied troops worldwide in the Second World War with 'Boogie Woogie Bugle Boy' and 'Pennsylvania Polka'.

Meaning like the spring

Ringo

The drummer with the Beatles, *Ringo Starr*, was born Richard Starkey on this day in 1940. He wrote a few of the group's songs, including 'Octopus's Garden' and 'Don't Pass Me By'. He has three children: Zac, Jason and Lee.

Meaning peace be with you

Satchel

The legendary baseball player *Leroy Satchel Paige* was born on this day in 1906 in Mobile, Alabama. He was the hardest thrower in the African-American league, and this, together with his endearing colourful personality, made him a big crowd-puller.

Meaning sack, bag

Gustav, Gustave, Gustavo, Gustander, Gustaf

The Austrian composer and conductor *Gustav Mahler* was born on 7 July 1860. When he was alive he was acclaimed for his conducting, but it is for his symphonies and song cycles that he is admired today. His Eighth Symphony is known as the 'Symphony of a Thousand' from the huge forces of choir and orchestra that are required for its performance.

Meaning staff of the gods

Yul

Yul Brynner was born on 7 July 1915 in Sakhalin, Russia. He is best known for his role as King Mongkut of Siam in the stage and film versions of the musical *The King and I*. He won an Oscar for best actor and a Tony, one of only seven people to win both for the same role.

Meaning beyond the horizon

Cree, Creda

The US actress *Cree Summer* was born in California on 7 July 1970. Daughter of the actor Don Francks, she is the voice of Penny in *Inspector Gadget*. She also played Suzie in *The Rugrats* (1991) and *All Grown Up* (2003), and Belgamine in the computer game Final Fantasy X (2001).

Meaning creed

Xavier, Xaviera, Xavieralyn, Xaviere, Xavierlyn, Zavier

On this day in 1946 Mother *Francesca Xavier Cabrini* was canonized, the first American citizen to be made a saint. She founded more than 60 orphanages in New York, Chicago, Seattle, New Orleans and throughout South America and Europe. She is the patron saint of immigrants.

Meaning new house

Shelly, Shelley, Shelli, Shellia, Shellie

The US actress and producer *Shelly Duvall* was born in Houston, Texas, on this day in 1949. Her best-known role is *The Shining* (1980), in which she starred opposite Jack Nicholson. She also gave a memorable performance in Woody Allen's *Annie Hall* (1977).

Meaning meadow on a ledge

Lillien, Lilianna, Liliana, Lilien

Lillien Jane Martin, who was born on 7 July 1851, was a pioneer in the field of child psychology, and she also had a colourful old age. When she was 78 she travelled alone to Russia, when she was 81 she drove across the US and when she was 87 she did a six-month trek through South America.

Meaning gracious lilly

Roone, Rooney

The US TV sports pioneer *Roone Arlege* was born on 8 July 1931. Head of ABC News from 1977 to 1998 and Head of ABC from 1968 to 1986, he was the first person to bring live sporting events to the TV screen. He has four children: Elizabeth Ann, Susan Lee, Patricia Lu and Roone Pickney.

Meaning red-haired

Zeppelin, Zepp, Zeppo, Zep, Zeph, Zephan

The German inventor and army officer Count *Ferdinand von Zeppelin* was born on this day in 1838 in Constance, Baden. He invented the enormous rigid airship named after him, which first flew in 1900. There is a city near Frankfurt named Zeppelinheim in his honour.

Meaning God has protected

Raffi, Rafi

The Canadian-Egyptian author and entertainer *Raffi Cavoukian* was born on 8 July 1948 in Cairo, Egypt. His album *Singable Songs for the Very Young* has sold over 2 million copies. Two of his best-loved songs are 'Baby Beluga' and 'Bananaphone'. He has also written for adults.

Meaning exalted

Tavis

Tavis Werts, the trumpet and flugelhorn player for Reel Big Fish, was born on this day in 1977. Reel Big Fish was a southern Californian ska-punk band of the 1990s. In 1977 they had a big hit with the song 'Sell Out'.

Meaning twin

Anjelica

The US actress *Anjelica Houston* was born on 8 July 1951 in Los Angeles, but grew up in Ireland, Britain and Europe. Nominated for Golden Globes for her part as Morticia Addams in *The Addams Family* (1991) and *Addams Family Values* (1993), she won a best supporting actress Oscar for *Prizzi's Honor* (1985).

Meaning not known

Micheline, Michelina

The Swiss politician *Micheline Calmy-Rey* was born on this day in 1945. She is a member of the Social Democratic Party and was elected to the Swiss Federal Council in 2002. She is the head of the Federal Department of Foreign Affairs.

Meaning who is like God

Sunniva, Sunnifa, Synnove

Today is the feast day of *St Sunniva of Bergen*. She was an Irish princess who lived in the 10th century. She fled to Norway with several companions to escape from an arranged marriage to an invading pagan king, and she is the patron saint of Bergen and of Norway's west coast.

Meaning gift of the sun

Artemisia, Artemis

Artemisia Gentileschi, one of the most accomplished painters of the early baroque, was born in Rome on 8 July 1593. She was the first woman to portray historical and religious themes in paintings and the first to become a member of the Accademia dell'Arte del Disegno in Florence.

Meaning moon goddess

Elias, Elijah, Elihu, Eliot, Elliott, Ellis

The US inventor *Elias Howe* was born on 9 July 1819 in Spencer, Massachusetts. Charles Fredrick Weisenthal invented the sewing machine, but Elias refined the design and was awarded the first US patent for a sewing machine using lock stitch.

Meaning the Lord is God

Avitus, Avital

On 9 July 455 *Eparchius Avitus*, the Roman military commander in Gaul, became the emperor of the West. As master of the soldiers, he was away from Rome when it was invaded by the Vandals under Gaiseric, bringing the rule of Petronious Maximus to an end. He was later deposed and became bishop of Placentia.

Meaning father of dew

Shelton

US wrestler *Shelton Benjamin* was born on this day in 1975 in Minneapolis, Minnesota. A college athletics and wrestling champion, he trained with Brock Lesnar and formed a famous partnership with Redd Dogg Begnaud that was known as the Dogg Pound.

Meaning town in the valley

Hockney

British artist *David Hockney* was born in Bradford, Yorkshire, on this day in 1937. He lives in California, which has featured large in his paintings, especially the series of swimming pools. One of his best-known paintings is *Mr and Mrs Clark and Percy* (1970–71), and he has also designed sets for many major opera houses.

Meaning clearing where hocks grow

Courtney, Courtenay, Courtni, Courtny, Courtnie, Courtnei, Courtne, Courtnesia

Courtney Love was born on this day in 1964. The US singer and actress is best known for being the widow of Kurt Cobain, lead singer with the band Nirvana. Their daughter is Frances Bean Cobain.

Meaning territory of Curtis

Dorothy, Dorothea, Dorothoe, Dorete, Dorota, Drottya, Dosia, Thea, Dot, Dottie, Dotty, Dora, Dory, Dorothi, Dorothoe, Theodora

The US journalist *Dorothy Thompson* was born in Lancaster, New York, on this day in 1894. After the First World War she became a correspondent in Vienna and Berlin, her columns being syndicated through the *New York Herald Tribune*. She was one of the most widely read US commentators on European politics during this crucial period.

Meaning gift of God

Jaylen, Jaylene

Jaylen Dushone James, who was born on 9 July 2003, is the daughter of US actress Countess Vaughn and Joseph James. Countess Vaughn is best known for her role as Kim Parker in the US children's TV sitcom *Moesha* (1996–2000).

Meaning illustrious bird

Karin

The ballet dancer *Karin von Aroldingen* was born in Greiz, East Germany, on this day in 1941. She was a principal dancer with the New York City Ballet from 1972 to 1984. Her most memorable role was in Balanchine's choreography to Stravinsky's Violin Concerto.

Meaning blessed, pure, holy

Alvan

The US astronomer and telescope maker *Alvan Graham Clark* was born on 10 July 1832 in Fall River, Massachusetts. In 1862 he was testing a new 45-centimetre (18-inch) refracting telescope when he discovered Sirius B, the magnitude-8 companion of Sirius.

Meaning elf friend

Camille, Camile, Camilo

The French impressionist painter *Camille Pissaro* was born on this day in 1830 on St Thomas in the Virgin Islands. He moved to France in 1855 and helped to develop the pioneering impressionist style of painting, and exerted considerable influence over Paul Cézanne and Paul Gauguin.

Meaning free-born

Marcel, Marcellus, Marcello

The French author *Marcel Proust* was born Valentin-Louis-Georges-Eugène-Marcel Proust on on this day in 1871. His master work, *A la recherche du temps perdu* (Remembrance of Things Past), was set in Beauce where he spent his summers as a child. Fictionalized as Combray, it was renamed Illiers-Combray in honour of the novel.

Meaning little follower of Mars

Arlo, Arlow

The US folk musician *Arlo Guthrie* was born in New York on this day in 1947. He is the son of singer and composer Woody Guthrie. His story song 'Alice's Restaurant', a protest against the Vietnam War draft, lasts for 18 minutes, 20 seconds. It was turned into a movie of the same name in 1969.

Meaning hill

Hassiba

Hassiba Boulmerka, the Algerian athlete, was born on 10 July 1968. In 1991 she became the first African woman to win an athletics world title. She also became the first Algerian to win an Olympic title when she won the gold medal for the 1,500 metres at the 1992 Barcelona Olympics.

Meaning not known

Eunice

Eunice Mary Kenney Shriver was born on this day in 1921. Her father was Joseph P. Kennedy Sr, and her brother was President John F. Kennedy. She married the US ambassador to France, Robert Shriver Jr, and they had five children. She did much work for the Special Olympics.

Meaning happy, victorious

Yuka, Yuki

The Japanese author *Yuka Murayama* was born in Tokyo on 10 July 1964. In 1992 her novel *Egg of Angel* won the Shousetsu Subaru Shinjinshou Prize, and her popularity has been increasing ever since. She is fond of nature, and her publicity photograph is of a vase of flowers rather than her own face.

Meaning snow child

Ljuba, Ljubica

The soprano *Ljuba Welitsch* was born in Borissovo, Bulgaria, on this day in 1913. She became an Austrian citizen and sang all over the world, most notably at the Metropolitan Opera House in New York, where her performance in Richard Strauss's opera *Salome* in 1949 has never been forgotten.

Meaning love

Elwyn, Elwin, Elwood

The US essayist and author *Elwyn Brooks White* was born on 11 July 1899 in Mount Vernon, New York. He is best known for writing children's books and a writer's style guide, *The Elements of Style* (1935). In 1929 he and James Thurber wrote a spoof entitled *Is Sex Necessary?* He wrote for the *New Yorker* from the 1920s.

Meaning elf friend

Giorgio

The Italian fashion designer *Georgio Armani* was born in Piacenza, Italy, on this day in 1934. He trained in medicine in Milan and after military service worked in a department store. His first work as a designer was with Nino Cerruti, but he set up his own company in 1975, becoming especially famous for suits, blazers and jackets.

Meaning farmer

Tab, Tabib

Tab Hunter was born Andrew Arthur Kelm on 11 July 1931 in New York City. He was a 1950s teen idol actor, who had a hit record with 'Young Love' (1957). He appeared in more than 50 films, from *The Lawless* (1948) to an appearance with Divine in *Polyester* (1985).

Meaning physician

Esera, Eser

The US footballer *Esera Tavai Tuaolo* was born on 11 July 1968 in Honolulu, Hawaii, and played professional football for a period of nine years. After coming out amid a media frenzy, he has dedicated his life to helping the younger generation, both gay and straight.

Meaning achiever

Liona

Canada's first lady of the guitar, *Liona Maria Carolynne Boyd* was born in London on 11 July 1949. She has several honorary doctorates, and in 1986 she recorded the breakthrough rock-classical-new age album, *Persona*, with Yo-Yo Ma, David Gilmour and Eric Clapton.

Meaning lioness

Brett, Bretta, Brettalyn, Brettainee

The comedienne *Brett Somers* was born Audrey Somers on this day in New Brunswick in 1924. She appeared regularly on the 1960s TV show *Match Game*, playing foil to Charles Nelson Reilly. She was married to the actor Jack Klugman.

Meaning of Bretagne, France

Tanith, Tanitha

The Canadian-born US skater *Tanith Belbin* was born on 11 July 1984 in Kingston, Ontario. She began skating when she was two years old. She and her partner, Benjamin Agosto, have won many prizes and championships.

Meaning love goddess

Arnetia, Arneitha, Arnetria

Arnetia Walker was born on 11 July 1961. The US actress appeared on Broadway when she was just 16 in *Two Gentlemen of Verona*. Her TV credits include *The Fresh Prince of Bel Air* (1990), *NYPD Blue* (1993) and *The Cosby Mysteries* (1994).

Meaning not known

Josiah, Josicah

On this day in 1730 *Josiah Wedgwood*, the British pottery manufacturer, was born in Burslem, Staffordshire. The eldest member of the Wedgwood dynasty, he was the first to industrialize the manufacture of pottery. He was Charles Darwin's grandfather.

Meaning Yahweh supports

Henry, Henrik, Henri, Heinrick, Hendrick, Heinrich, Hanraoi, Hark

Henry David Thoreau was born David Henry Thoreau on this day in 1817. In 1845 the author and philosopher moved to a hut on the shores of Walden Pond, Concord, where he lived the simple life for two years. His classic spiritual memoir *Walden, of Life in the Woods* (1854) is based on his time there.

Meaning ruler of the home

Buckminster, Buck, Bucky

The US visionary, designer, architect, inventor and writer *Richard Buckminster Fuller* was born on 12 July 1895. He used the principles of structure in nature for a wide range of inventions, including the geodesic dome and the aerodynamic Dymaxion car.

Meaning place of the buck deer

Pablo

One of the most important literary figures of 20th-century South America, *Pablo Neruda* was born Ricardo Eliecer Neftali Reyes Basoalto on this day in 1904 in Paraal, Chile. His surrealistic poems made him famous, and he won many prizes, including the Nobel Prize for literature in 1971.

Meaning small, humble

Cheryl, Cheryle

Cheryl Ladd was born Cheryl Jean Stoppelmoor in Huron, South Dakota, on 12 July 1951. She was Kris Monroe on the TV series *Charlie's Angels* from 1977 to 1981. As well as many acting roles, she wrote a children's book series *The Adventures of Little Nettie Windship*.

Meaning beloved

Beah, Bea

The US actress, poet and activist *Beah Richards* was born on this day in 1926 in Vicksburg, Mississippi. In a career that lasted for more than 50 years, she appeared on TV, screen and stage, and she won an Oscar nomination for *Guess Who's Coming to Dinner* (1967). Later in her career she appeared as Mrs Benton in TV's *ER* (1994).

Meaning blessed traveller

Veronica, Veronique, Vonnie, Vonny

Today is the feast day of *St Veronica*, the woman who, according to tradition, dried the face of Jesus as he was on the way to Calvary. The cloth she used, it is said, was left with an impression of his features. A cloth known as the veil of Veronica is preserved in St Peter's, Rome.

Meaning true image

Rolonda, Rolynda, Rolanda, Ro, Rola, Rolande

The US TV talk-show hostess and actress *Rolonda Watts* was born in Winston-Salem, North Carolina, on this day in 1959. In 2001 she began playing the role of Cameron Reese in the Hollywood soap opera *Days of Our Lives*.

From Roland, meaning famous land

13 JULY

Harrison, Harris

Harrison Ford was born on 13 July 1942. The US actor's best-known roles are as Han Solo in the *Star Wars* series of films and as Indiana Jones in the *Raiders of the Lost Ark* series. In 2001 he was named by the *Guinness Book of Records* as the richest actor alive.

Meaning son of Harold

Julius, Jule, Jules, Jolyon, Joliet

Julius Caesar, the Roman military and political leader, was born in Rome on 13 July in 100BC. He extended the Roman Empire to the Atlantic Ocean and launched the first Roman invasion of Britain. He was married to Cornelia Cinnilla.

Meaning youthful

Wole, Oluwole

The first African to win the Nobel Prize for literature, *Wole Soyinka* was born Akinwande Oluwole Soyinka on 13 July 1934 in Nigeria. Imprisoned during the Nigerian Civil War, he wrote about his experiences in *The Man Died: Prison Notes* (1973). He is a goodwill ambassador for UNESCO.

Meaning not known

Cheech

Cheech Marin was born on this day in 1946. The Mexican-American comedian and actor and Tommy Chong formed Cheech and Chong, a 1970s hippie act, and recorded several feature films and albums together. As a solo actor Cheech co-starred with Don Johnson in the TV series *Nash Bridges* (1996–2001).

Meaning not known

Sezen, Sesen

The Turkish pop singer *Sezen Aksu* was born on this day in Izmir in 1954. A Eurovision Song Contest winner, she made the crossover from light pop to serious experimental musician on the world music scene and has gained a large international following.

Meaning to wish for more

Danitra, Danita

Danitra Vance was born on 13 July 1959 in Chicago, Illinois. In 1985 the US actress and comedienne became the first female African-American to appear regularly on *Saturday Night Live*. She won an Obie award in 1990 and has worked mainly on stage, but she was in the movie *Jumpin' at the Boneyard* (1991).

Meaning gracious

Mildred, Millie

Today is the feast day of *St Mildred*, who was born in about 700. After refusing an offer of marriage, she entered a convent at Minster, Thanet, Kent, which her mother had founded. She eventually became the abbess and acquired a reputation as a 'comforter to all in affliction'.

Meaning gentle, strong

Missy, Missi, Missie, Missa

The US child star actress *Missy Gold* was born in Greta Falls, Montana, on this day in 1970. Her best-known roles are in *Little Mo* (1978), two series of *Benson* and *Twirl* (1981).

Meaning honey bee

Northrop, Northrup

One of the most distinguished literary critics of the 20th century, the Canadian *Northrop Frye*, was born on this day in 1912 in Sherbrooke, Quebec. His work on the poetry of William Blake made his international reputation, but he also wrote widely on all literary subjects.

Meaning from the north farm

Woodrow, Woody

The folk singer Woody Guthrie was born *Woodrow Wilson Guthrie* on 14 July 1912 in Okemah, Oklahoma, in the year that Woodrow Wilson was elected president. He became famous in the 1930s for his radio performances of traditional folk music and protest songs.

Meaning path through the woods

Ingmar

The Swedish film and theatre director *Ingmar Bergman* was born on 14 July 1918 in Uppsala. His directing style favours intuition over intellect, and he is not over-assertive with his actors. Among his many films, *Persona* (1966) and *Cries and Whispers* (1973) are his own personal favourites.

Meaning famous son

Roosevelt

The US football star and singer *Roosevelt 'Rosey' Grier* was born on a peanut farm in Georgia on this day in 1932. The Los Angeles Rams star became a bodyguard to Robert F. Kennedy and then an actor and a Christian minister. He was in *Roots: The Next Generation* (1978).

Meaning rose field

Emmeline, Emmelina, Emeline, Emelina

British suffragette *Emmeline Pankhurst* was born in Manchester on 14 July 1858. Her three daughters, Christabel, Sylvia and Adela, were also involved in the early fight for votes for women. An early believer in direct action, Emmeline Pankhurst was jailed 15 times, but her goal was attained just weeks before she died.

Meaning whole, universal

Tonya, Tonia

The US singer and guitarist *Tonya Donnely* was born on this day in 1966. She was with the Throwing Muses and the Breeders, then she had her own band, Belly, before going solo. She has recorded several solo albums, which have been very well received.

Meaning worthy of praise

Kateri

Today is the feast day of the Native American saint, the Blessed *Kateri Tekakwitha*, the Lily of the Mohawks. She was born in 1656 in Ossernenon (Auriesville), New York, and lived a life of sanctity that made a great impression on all who knew her. She was the first Native American to be proposed for canonization.

Meaning blessed, pure, holy

Zita

The US actress *Zita Johann* was born on this day in 1904. She was in *The Mummy* (1932), in which she played opposite Boris Karloff, taking the dual roles of a princess from ancient Egypt and her modern reincarnation. She was also Nora Moran in *The Sin of Nora Moran* (1933).

Meaning young woman

Forest

Forest Whitaker, the US actor, was born on 15 July 1961. As well as appearing in more than 47 films, including *The Color of Money* (1986) and *Four Dogs Playing Poker* (2000), he has produced more than eight and directed five. He was the host of the TV series *The Twilight Zone* (2002).

Meaning forest, woods

Inigo

Inigo Jones, Britain's first major architect, was born in London on this day in 1573. One of the first Englishmen to study architecture in Italy, his two best-known buildings are in London: the Banqueting House, Whitehall (1619) and the Queen's House, Greenwich (1616).

Meaning fiery

Rembrandt, Brandt, Brand

One of the greatest painters who ever lived, *Rembrandt Harmensz van Rijn* was born in Leiden, in the Netherlands, on 15 July 1606. He settled in Amsterdam, soon achieving fame, and he completed around 600 paintings, 300 etchings and 2,000 drawings.

Meaning sword, blade

Kid

On this day in 1931 *Kid Chocolate* knocked out Benny Bass to become the world junior lightweight, Cuba's first world boxing champion. His nickname was the Cuban Bon-Bon. He won over a hundred fights as an amateur and had 21 knockouts in 21 professional fights.

Meaning child

Rosetta, Rosita, Rosa

On this day in 1799 the French captain, Pierre-François Bouchard, discovered the Rosetta Stone in the Egyptian port of *Rosetta*, today known as Rashid. Engraved with Greek text and Egyptian hieroglyphics, it was the key to unlocking the language of the ancient Egyptians.

Meaning beautiful rose

Lacey, Lacye, Lacy

Lacey Rose Gordon, the daughter of Glenn Gordon and Jackie Zeman, was born on 15 July 1992. Glenn Gordon is a director, screenwriter and producer. His films include *Picture Perfect* (1994) and *Love Affair* (1988).

Meaning of Lassy, Normandy

Iris, Irisa

Dame *Jean Iris Murdoch*, the Anglo-Irish philosopher and novelist, was born on this day in 1919. She wrote 26 novels in all, *The Sea, The Sea* winning the Booker Prize in 1978. Several were made into films, as was the biography of her own life, *Iris* (2002), which was written by her husband, John Bayley.

Meaning rainbow

Lolita, Lita, Lolyta

The Canadian actress *Lolita Davidovich* was born on this day in 1961 to Yugoslavian parents. Her first role was in *Blaze* (1989), in which she appeared opposite Paul Newman. She has been in many films, including *JFK* (1993) and TV's *Prison Stories: Women on the Inside* (1991).

Meaning sorrowful

Roald, Roal

The Norwegian explorer *Roald Engelbreth Gravning Amundsen* was born on 16 July 1872 into a family of shipowners and captains. He led the Antarctic expedition of 1910–12 and became the first man to reach the South Pole. He wrote several books, including *My Life as an Explorer* (1927).

Meaning famous ruler

Choi, Cho

The president of South Korea from 1979 to 1980, *Choi Kyu-ha* was born on this day in 1919. He began his career as a university professor and then became a manager in the ministry of agriculture. He was acting prime minister in 1975–6 and prime minister in 1976–9.

Meaning beautiful

Pinchas

The Israeli violinist, violist and conductor *Pinchas Zukerman* was born in Tel Aviv on 16 July 1948. He has recorded over a hundred works and has won two Grammys. He has two daughters, Arianna and Natalia, from his long marriage to flautist and novelist Eugenia Zukerman.

Meaning serpent's mouth

Helier

Today is the feast day of *St Helier*, who gave his name to the town on the Island of Jersey. It is believed that he was born in Belgium and was converted to Christianity by Cunibert. His father, a heathen, killed Cunibert, and Helier fled to the island of Jersey, where he lived as a hermit for 15 years before being killed by pirates.

Menaing not known

Ginger

Ginger Rogers, the US actress and dancer, was born Virginia Katherine McMath on 16 July 1911. During the 1940s she and Fred Astaire danced into legend through ten musicals, including *Top Hat* (1935) and *Follow the Fleet* (1936). Her autobiography, *Ginger: My Story*, was published in 1991.

Meaning spice of ginger

Bess, Bessy, Bessie

The US beauty queen and celebrity *Bess Myerson* was born on 16 July 1924. In 1945 she became the first Jewish woman to win the Miss America pageant and appeared on many TV shows in the 1950s and 1960s. She became a social activist for civil rights and a philanthropist.

Meaning consecrated to God

Marietta, Mariette

Marietta Holley, the US author and feminist, was born on this day in 1836 in Jefferson County, New York. She used the pseudonym Josiah Allen's Wife. Through her heroine, fictional Samantha Allen, she satirized the life of women in marriage and put forward her arguments for women's rights with wit and style. She was often compared to Mark Twain.

Meaning bitter

Rain

Rain Pryor, the daughter of Richard Pryor, was born on this day in 1969. She is an actress, singer, writer and producer on stage and screen. She has produced several successful stage shows and has appeared in many films, including *How the Grinch Stole Christmas* (2000).

Meaning rain

17

Shmuel

The Hebrew writer *Shmuel Yosef Agnon* was born Shmuel Yosef Czaczkes on 17 July 1888 in Buczacz in Austrian Galicia, now Ukraine. In 1966 he became the first Hebrew writer to win the Nobel Prize for literature, which he won jointly with the German poet and dramatist Nelly Sachs.

Meaning God has heard

Cory, Corie

The Canadian writer *Cory Doctorow* was born on 17 July 1971. An activist in the world of e-publishing, he actively campaigns for more freedom over works in copyright. His first novel, *Down and Out in the Magic Kingdom* (2003), was offered free online.

Meaning ravine

Perry, Perri

Erle Stanley Gardner, the creator of the fictional lawyer *Perry Mason*, was born on this day in 1889. He was a lawyer as well as an author and wrote under many pseudonyms, including Kyle Corning, Carleton Kendrake, Les Tillray and A.A. Fair.

Meaning pear tree

Donald, Donaldo, Donal, Donagh

The Canadian actor *Donald Sutherland* was born on 17 July 1935 in St John, New Brunswick. His early successes include *The Dirty Dozen* (1967) and *M*A*S*H* (1970), and his role in the latter as Captain Benjamin Franklin 'Hawkeye' Pierce made him a star.

Meaning world leader

Konnie, Konna, Kona

Konnie Huq, the British TV presenter, was born in Ealing, London, on this day in 1975. In 1997 she became the first Asian presenter of the long-running and popular BBC TV children's show *Blue Peter*. She has two sisters, Rupa and Nutun.

Meaning angular

Diahann, Dihann, Dihanna, Dijanna, Dijana

The US actress and singer *Diahann Carroll* was born on this day in 1935 in the Bronx, New York. She was the first African-American actress to star as a non-servant in her own TV series, *Julia* (1968). She was in the 1980s TV series *Dynasty* and *The Colbys*, and has been nominated for an Oscar and an Emmy.

Meaning divine

Phoebe, Phoebie

Phoebe Snow, the US singer and songwriter, was born on this day in 1952. She was part of the early 1970s New York Greenwich Village music scene and had a single, 'Poetry Man', in the US top five. *The Very Best of Phoebe Snow* features her 1977 show at the Carnegie Hall.

Meaning illuminated, pure

Berenice

The US photographer *Berenice Abbott* was born in Springfield, Ohio, on 17 July 1898. She was an artist and a technician, teaching photographic techniques, experimenting with various methods and writing books, including *The Guide to Better Photography* (1941).

Meaning victorious

Hunter, Hunt

The US journalist and author *Hunter S. Thompson* was born in Kentucky on this day in 1937. The 'S' stood for Stockton. He started his career as a sports journalist for *Rolling Stone* magazine. His best-known book is *Fear and Loathing in Las Vegas* (1971), which was filmed in 1998 with Johnny Depp and Benicio Del Toro.

Meaning hunter

Mandela, Mandel, Mandell

The former president of South Africa, *Nelson Rolihlahla Mandela* was born in Qunu in the Transkei on l8 July 1918. His father was the chief of the tiny village of Mvezo. He was awarded the Nobel Prize for peace jointly with F.W. de Klerk, who had been the president who released Mandela from prison.

Meaning almond

Dolph, Dolphus

Dolph Sweet was born on this day in 1920. The US TV actor and stage director is best remembered for his roles as policemen, first in the cult movie *You're a Big Boy Now* (1968), and later in his career as Chief Carl Kaninsky in the TV sitcom *Gimme a Break* (1981–5).

Meaning noble wolf

Hume

Hume Blake Cronyn, the Canadian stage and film actor and screenplay writer, was born in Ontario in 1911. He appeared in Alfred Hitchcock's *A Shadow of a Doubt* (1943), and was then nominated for a best supporting actor Oscar for his role in *The Seventh Cross* (1944).

Meaning supporter of peace

Darlene, Darleen, Darla, Darlin

Darlene Conley, who plays Sally Spectra in the TV soap *The Bold and the Beautiful* (1987), was born on this day in 1942. The US actress has been nominated for two Emmys and many other awards. She began her career as a Shakespearean actress on Broadway, and she was also in Hitchcock's *The Birds* (1963).

Meaning little darling

Nadia

On this day in 1976 the 14-year-old Romanian gymnast *Nadia Comaneci* took part in the uneven parallel bars event at the Olympic Games. She was so perfect that she was awarded the top score of ten by the judges, the first time such a score for this event had been recorded.

Meaning hope

Tenley, Taneli

The US Olympic figure skating champion *Tenley Albright* was born on this day in 1935. Shortly after winning her gold medal at the 1956 Olympic Games she went to Harvard Medical School and became a surgeon, pioneering new cancer treatment techniques. She is on the board of the Olympic executive committee and many other official bodies.

Meaning God is my judge

Pauline

The French mezzo-soprano *Michelle-Ferdinande-Pauline Viardot* was born in Paris on this day in 1821. She studied the piano with Franz Liszt and began her career in 1838 with an appearance in Rossini's opera *Othello*. She was a friend of Turgenev, Schumann and Brahms.

Meaning small

19 JULY

Ilie

The Romanian tennis player *Ilie Nastase* was born in Bucharest on 19 July 1946. He won 57 singles titles in his career, including the US Open in 1972 and 1975, the French Open in 1970 and 1973 and Wimbledon in 1973. He has also written two novels in French.

Meaning the Lord is my God

Topher

Topher Grace was born in Connecticut on this day in 1978. The US actor is best known for his role as Eric Forman in the sitcom *That 70s Show*. He's been in several features, including *Oceans 12* (2004). Topher is an unusual abbreviation for the name Christopher.

From Christopher, meaning carrier of Christ

Archibald, Arch, Archie, Archy, Archi, Archiambaud, Archibaldo, Archimbald

The Scottish novelist A.J. Cronin was born *Archibald Joseph Cronin* in Cardross on 19 July 1896. Two of his novels, *The Citadel* (1937) and *The Keys of the Kingdom* (1941), were turned into Oscar-nominated films. The character Dr Finlay, who came from his medical stories, became the basis of a long-running 1960s TV drama series.

Meaning truly bold

Campbell

The US actor, producer and director *Campbell Scott* was born on this day in 1961. He was the executive producer and acted in *The Daytrippers* (1997), was in David Mamet's *The Spanish Prisoner* (1997) and directed and produced *Off the Map* (2003).

Meaning crooked mouth

Natalya

The Russian ballerina *Natalya Bessmertnova* was born on this day in 1941. She is a member of the world-famous Bolshoi Ballet and one of Russia's leading ballet dancers. She is married to the choreographer Yuri Grigorovich.

Meaning Christmas day

Rosalyn, Rosalynd

Rosalyn Sussman Yalow was born on 19 July 1921. The US medical physicist was the co-winner of the 1977 Nobel Prize for physiology or medicine for her development of the radio-immuno-assay (RAI) technique. She began her career as a secretary to a leading biochemist.

Meaning beautiful rose

Clea

The US actress *Clea Lewis* was born in Cleveland Heights, Ohio, on this day in 1965. She was in Stephen Frears's movie *Hero* (1992), and she played Lisa in *Diabolique* (1996), with Sharon Stone and Isabelle Adjani. She also appeared in the TV series *Ellen* (1990).

Meaning praise, acclaim

Malinda

On this day in 1913 *Billboard* published its earliest known chart of popular music sales. Entitled 'Last Week's Ten Best Sellers among Popular Songs', it records that the number one top-selling music for that week was a song called 'Malinda's Wedding Day' – the first ever number one song.

Meaning dark beauty

Richard, Dick

The British zoologist and palaeontologist Sir *Richard Owen* was born on this day in Lancaster in 1804. He is remembered for having established the Natural History Museum, of which he was the first director. He named several fossils, including those of Iguanodon and Archaeopteryx, and coined the word dinosaur.

Meaning wealthy and powerful

Nam

The Korean-American artist *Nam June Paik* was born in Seoul on this day in 1932. A major international figure, he has achieved more than any other artist in the exploration of the use of TV and video in art. His installation for the 1988 Seoul Olympic Games consisted of a staggering 1,003 video monitors.

Meaning manly

Joseph, Jo, Joe

The French composer *Marie-Joseph-Alexandre Déodat de Sévérac* was born on this day in 1872 in St Félix-Lauragais, Haute-Garonne. He studied with d'Indy and Magnard, and while he was in Paris he was friends with Picasso, Roussel and Marie Laurencin. He wrote much piano music and many songs.

Meaning he will add

Destutt

French philosopher *Destutt de Tracy* was born Antoine-Louis-Claude Destutt, comte de Tracy, on 20 July 1754 in the Bourbonnais. His theories divided the conscious life into four faculties: perception, memory, judgement and will.

Meaning not known

Theda

The US silent film star *Theda Bara* was born Theodosia Burr Goodman in Avondale on this day in 1885. She was hugely popular and one of the first screen goddesses, nicknamed the Vamp. Only three of her 40 films survive. In 1921 she married the film director Charles Brabin.

Meaning gift of God

Hortense, Hortensia

The US lawyer and reformer *Hortense Sparks Ward* was born on this day in 1872. She worked hard lobbying for women's rights and succeeded in changing the law on the property rights of married women in Texas through a measure that came to be known as the Hortense Ward Law.

Meaning garden

Gisele, Gisella, Gizela

The German-Brazilian model *Gisele Bundchen*, said to have been the highest-earning model in the world in 2001, was born on this day in 1980. She was spotted by a model agency at São Paulo McDonalds when she was 14 years old. Her sisters, Raquel, Graziela, Gabriela, Rafaela and Patricia, are all aspiring models.

Meaning promise

Verna

The US actress *Verna Felton* was born in Salinas, California, on 20 July 1890. The voice of the Fairy Godmother in Disney's *Cinderella* (1950) and Hilda Crocker in TV's *December Bride* (1954–9), she is remembered as one of the greatest character actresses of her time.

Meaning alder tree

Marshall, Marshal

The Canadian writer *Herbert Marshall McLuhan* was born on 21 July 1911 in Edmonton. He specialized in writing philosophical books about human communications through the media, including *Understanding Media* (1964) and *The Medium is the Massage* (1967), and he coined the phrase global village.

Meaning steward

Ernest, Ernesto, Ernestus, Ernst

One of the giants of 20th-century American literature, *Ernest Miller Hemingway* was born on this day in 1921. A larger-than-life figure, his life has been as much debated as his books. As well as novels, he also wrote short stories, of which his spare style of writing made him a master.

Meaning purposeful, serious

Robin

The actor *Robin Williams* was born on this day in 1952. He started his career as the alien Mork in the 1970s TV series *Mork and Mindy*. A master of improvisation, his unique style has won him many awards, but he also works tirelessly for charity, working through the Windfall Foundation, which he established.

From Robert, meaning bright, famous

Cat

The singer *Cat Stevens* was born Stephen Demetre Georgiou on 21 July 1948. His 1970s albums spawned many classic songs, including 'Wild World' and 'Moonshadow'. Yusuf Islam, as he has been known since converting to Islam, founded the charities Muslim Aid and Small Kindness.

Meaning cat

Wastrada

Today is the feast day of *St Wastrada of Utrecht*. She lived in the Netherlands in the 7th century and was the mother of the missionary Gregory of Utrecht, the Benedictine monk who studied under St Boniface.

Meaning not known

Margene

The US actress *Margene Storey* was born on 21 July 1943 in Orange County, California. She was a member of the Mouseketeers, the Mickey Mouse Club, which was a long-running TV variety series in the 1950s.

Meaning pearl

Ali, Alia, Alea, Alya, Aliya, Aliyah

Ali Landry, the US actress, was born on this day in 1973 in Breaux Bridge, Louisiana. She was Miss Louisiana and Miss USA in 1996. The Arabic name Alia, from which Ali comes, was first used in the US by Muslims.

Meaning sublimity

Brandi, Brandy, Brandais, Brandea, Brandice

The woman's soccer star *Brandi Chastain* was born on 21 July 1968. The versatile two-footed player rose to international fame after scoring a penalty in the Women's World Cup Final in 1999, putting her in the limelight and on the covers of *Sportsweek*, *Time* and *Newsweek*.

Meaning brandy

Gregor, Gregorio, Gregorious, Gregiogair

The Austrian monk and geneticist *Gregor Johann Mendel* was born near Udrau today in 1822. He studied the inheritance traits of pea plants, growing and testing some 28,000 specimens in the garden of his monastery, and developed his law of inheritance, earning him the name the father of genetics.

Meaning watchful one

Terence, Terencio, Torrance, Terrene

The British actor *Terence Stamp* was born on this day in 1939. General Zod in *Superman 2* (1981) and Chancellor Valorum in *Star Wars Episode 1: The Phantom Menace* (1999), he has appeared in countless major features, including *Priscilla Queen of the Desert* (1994). The Kinks' song 'Waterloo Sunset' was inspired by his relationship with his then girlfriend, Julie Christie.

Meaning smooth, polished, tender

Rufus, Rufe, Ruff

The singer and songwriter *Rufus Wainwright*, son of singer and songwriter Loudon Wainwright III and Kate McGarrigle, was born on this day in 1973 in the USA, but brought up in Canada. A master of vocals and the piano, his unique musical style has been labelled baroque rock or popera.

Meaning red-haired

Selman, Selmer

The Nobel Prize-winning biochemist *Selman Abraham Waksman* was born in Russia on 22 July 1888. His studies of the decomposition of organic substances led to the discovery of many new antibiotics, such as streptomycin and neomycin.

Meaning divine protector

Magdalene, Magdalen, Magdallyn, Magdalane, Maighdlin, Mala, Malena

Today is the feast day of *St Mary Magdalene*. After Jesus cured her of 'seven devils', her tears washed his feet and her hair dried them. She found the empty tomb where Jesus appeared before her. She moved to France and spent 30 years alone in the desert, fed by angels.

From Madeleine, meaning tower of strength

Franka

The German film star *Franka Potente* was born on this day in 1974. The actress, who loves to play empowered women, had her first big Hollywood hit with *Run Lola Run* (1998). She then starred in *The Bourne Identity* (2002) and *The Bourne Supremacy* (2004).

Meaning free woman

Licia

The legendary US opera soprano *Licia Albanese* was born on this day in 1913. She was with the Metropolitan Opera in New York for 26 seasons, making a total of 427 performances, and joined the San Francisco Opera for 20 seasons. She was the Operetta Diva in Sondheim's *Follies* in 1985.

Meaning happy

Augusta, Augustina, Augustino, Gusta, Austine, Gussie

The psychologist *Augusta Fox Bronner* was born on 22 July 1881. With her husband, William Healy, she founded the first child guidance clinic, the Juvenile Psychopathic Institute, in 1909.

Meaning sacred, majestic

23 ^{JULY}

Emil, Emlen, Emelen, Emile, Emilio, Emlyn

The first person to receive an Oscar, *Emil Jannings* was born in Switzerland on this day in 1884. He won the Oscar for his roles in *The Way of All Flesh* (1928) and in Josef von Sternberg's *The Last Command* (1928). Originally a stage actor, he became an international star after appearing in *Quo Vadis* (1924).

Meaning industrious

Yuval

Hip hop drummer *Yuval Gabay* was born in Jerusalem on 23 July 1963. From 1993 to 2000 he played with the jazz/hip hop quartet Soul Coughing. He has since guested with many artists, including Suzanne Vega and Mono Puff, and played in two bands, Firewater and UV Ray.

Meaning stream

Austin, Austen

On this day in 1829 the first typewriter was patented by *William Austin Burt*, who, in 1836, also patented the solar compass. As well as being an inventor, he was a millwright, building over eight mills, Mount Vernon's first postmaster, a circuit judge and a state legislator and surveyor.

Meaning exalted one

Otto, Otho

Otto the Merry, duke of Austria, was born on this day in 1301. In 1327 he founded the Cistercian abbey of Neuberg an der Murz in Styria. The abbey retains much of its medieval character and can still be visited. Otto had a brother called Frederick the Handsome.

Meaning wealthy, prosperous

Charisma, Charis

US actress *Charisma Carpenter* was born on this day in 1970. Best known for playing Cordelia Chase in *Buffy the Vampire Slayer* (1989), her first TV appearance was in *Baywatch* (1997). With her husband, Damian Hardy, she has a son, Donovan Charles, born in 2003.

Meaning charisma, grace

Brigit, Brigitte, Birgitta

Today is the feast day of *St Brigit of Sweden*, who was born in 1303. When she was 13 she married the 18-year-old Ulf Gudmarsson. It was a happy marriage, and the couple were blessed with eight children. Together they made the pilgrimage to Santiago de Compostella.

Meaning strong, mighty

Coral, Corale, Coralie, Coraline

Actress *Coral Brown* was born in Melbourne, Australia, on 23 July 1913. She appeared in dozens of films from the 1940s to the 1980s, giving one of her most memorable performances as Alice Hargreaves, the original Alice in Lewis Carroll's books, in *Dreamchild* (1985).

Meaning sincere, from the sea

Hella, Helah

The US actress and singer *Hella Kurty* was born on 23 July 1900. She appeared in two films in the 1940s, *Hotel Reserve* (1946) and *Candlelight in Algeria* (1944).

Meaning rust

Gus, Gussy, Gustaf

Gus van Sant, the film producer, director and writer, was born on this day in 1952. His films include *Drugstore Cowboy* (1989), which launched Matt Dillon's career, *My Own Private Idaho* (1991), which made stars of River Phoenix and Keanu Reeves, and Oscar-winning *Good Will Hunting* (1997).

Meaning staff of the Goths

Simon, Simeon, Siomonn, Sim

The great South American revolutionary leader *Simón Bolívar*, known as the Liberator, was born Simon José Antonio de la Santaisima Trinidad Bolivar y Palacios on 24 July 1783. He fought the Spanish for the independence of Bolivia, Colombia, Ecuador, Panama, Peru and Venezuela.

Meaning to hear, to be heard

Alphonse, Alfons, Alfonso, Alonso

The Czech artist *Alphonse Mucha* was born in Ivancise on this day in 1860. The original art nouveau artist, his distinctive illustrations often depicted women in swirling costumes surrounded by more swirls, haloes and flowers. He also designed furniture, jewellery and wallpaper.

From Alphonso, Meaning noble, ready

Heinz

The white-haired British 1960s teen idol *Heinz* was born on 24 July 1942. Originally the bass player with the Tornados, which had a hit with 'Telstar' (1962), Heinz's hits, produced by Joe Meek, included 'Just Like Eddie', 'Country Boy' and 'Diggin' My Potatoes'. The then fledgling guitarist Jimmy Page contributed a session on one of his songs.

Meaning household ruler

Oriana, Oria, Oriane

Oriana Fallaci, the Italian journalist and author, was born in Florence on this day in 1929. She worked as a war correspondent in the Vietnam War and the Indo-Pakistan War, and also in South America and in the Middle East.

Meaning golden one

Mara, Damara, Damaris, Maris

Mara Wilson, the US child actress, was born on this day in 1987. She has been in several major features and gave remarkable performances in *Miracle on 34th Street* (1994) and *Matilda* (1996). She has since returned to her studies and hopes to become a writer.

Meaning gentle girl

Bella, Belle, Bell, Belva, Belvia

The US women's rights champion *Bella Abzug* was born on this day in 1920. She gained a seat in the House of Representatives in 1971 and campaigned fiercely against the Vietnam War and for gay and women's rights. She was chair of President Carter's National Advisory Commission on Women.

Meaning beautiful

Daveigh

It is *Daveigh Chase*'s birthday today. The US child actress was born on this day in 1990 in Las Vegas, Nevada. She has been in numerous films and TV shows since her debut at the age of eight, including *The Ring* (2002), *Donnie Darko* (2001) and TV's *Oliver Beene* (2003–4).

Meaning beloved

25 JULY

Maxwell, Maxi, Maxie

The US artist and illustrator *Maxwell Parish* was born on 25 July 1870. If you are ever in New York, you can see a sample of his work: a portrait of Nat King Cole in the King Cole Bar of the exclusive St Regis Hotel. This bar is the birthplace of the Bloody Mary.

Meaning spring of fresh water

Elias, Elihu, Elijah

The Nobel Prize-winning author *Elias Canetti* was born in Rustschuk, Bulgaria, on this day in 1905, but lived most of his life in London. His best-known work, *Masse und Macht* (Crowds and Power) (1960), incorporates the study of crowds and society with mythology and folklore.

Meaning the Lord is God

Katō

The Japanese samurai *Katō Kiyomasa* was born on 25 July 1562 in Owari Province. As well as being a fearsome warrior, who laid down strict rules for his men, he was a devoted member of Nichirin Shu Buddhism and is famed for the number of beautiful temples he built.

Meaning second of twins

Verdine, Verden, Verdon, Varden

Verdine White, of the 1970s group Earth, Wind and Fire, was born in Illinois on this day in 1951. The group's biggest success was the soundtrack to the film *That's the Way of the World* (1975). The single, 'Shining Star', a blend of funk, jazz, rock and African rhythms, became an instant classic.

Meaning from the green hill

Peggy

The US figure skater *Peggy Fleming* was born on this day in 1958. The only American to win a gold medal in the 1968 Olympic Games, in 1981 she became a sports broadcaster with ABC, where she has had a long and distinguished career. In 1980 she became the first ice skater ever to perform at the White House.

From Margaret, meaning pearl

Iman, Imani

The beautiful Somalian model and actress *Iman* was born Iman Abdulmajid in 1955. In 1992 she married David Bowie, and they have a daughter, Alexandria Zahra. Iman has her own range of cosmetics, Iman Beauty, which is suitable for all skin colours.

Meaning believer

Svetlana, Swetlana

On this day in 1984 *Svetlana Savitskaya* became the first woman to walk in space. The Russian cosmonaut was on her second space journey, aboard the *Salyut 7* space station. On her first journey in 1980 she became only the second woman ever to go into space.

Meaning star

Olympia, Olympie, Olympe, Olimpie

It is the birthday today of one of the youngest members of the Greek royal family, *Princess Maria-Olympia*. She was born in New York on 25 July 1996 to Crown Prince Paulos and the Anglo-American Crown Princess Marie Chantal Miller.

Meaning heavenly one

Aldous, Aldis, Aldo, Aldus

The British essayist and novelist *Aldous Leonard Huxley* was born on this day in 1894 in Godalming, Surrey. Huxley was the author of *Brave New World* (1932), one of the most important works of science fiction of the 20th century. The rock band the Doors took their name from his book entitled *The Doors of Perception* (1954).

Meaning from the old house

Blake

The US film producer and director *Blake Edwards* was born on 26 July 1922. Famous for the *Pink Panther* films starring Peter Sellers, he was awarded an honorary Oscar in 2004. He is married to Julie Andrews.

Meaning fair-skinned

Joachim, Joaquin, Akim

Today is the feast day of *St Joachim* and St Anne. Joachim is traditionally the father of the Virgin Mary and the husband of St Anne. An angel came and told him about Anne's pregnancy while he was away from home. The tomb of Joachim and Anne was found in Jerusalem in 1889.

Meaning Judgement of the Lord

Brenton

The US songwriter, rhythm and blues singer and pianist *Brenton Wood* was born on 26 July 1941 in Shreveport, Los Angeles. He had two big hits in the 1960s, 'The Oogum Boogum Song' (1967) and 'Gimme Little Sign' (1967).

Meaning prince

Vivian, Viv, Vivi, Vivia, Viviane

Vivian Vance, the actress who will always be remembered as Ethel, Lucy's friend and neighbour in the *I Love Lucy* shows, was born on this day in 1909. She had to be overweight and frumpy, even though she was actually younger than Lucy.

Meaning alive

Marjorie, Marjery, Marjory, Margery

The US actress *Marjorie Lord* was born on this day in 1918. Her first important role was in *Johnny Come Lately* (1943), in which she played opposite James Cagney. Her best-known role was as Danny Williams's wife in the TV show *Make Room for Daddy*, which ran in the 1950s and 1960s.

From Margaret, meaning pearl

Donaldina, Donalda

Donaldina Mackenzie Cameron, the social worker and missionary, was born on this day in 1869. She dedicated her life to tracking down Chinese pimps and rescuing Chinese girls and women brought illegally into San Francisco for prostitution or a harsh, short life of servitude.

Meaning ruler of the world

Nana, Nanna

The US actress *Nana Visitor* was born on 26 July 1957. She is best known for her role as Major Kira Nerys in TV's *Deep Space Nine*, a part she first undertook in 1993. She went on to play Roxie in the stage show *Chicago*.

Meaning courageous

27

Bugs, Burgess, Burg, Berg

On 27 July 1940 the world's best-known rabbit, the cartoon character *Bugs Bunny*, made his debut. Created by Chuck Jones as part of his Looney Tunes series, his instantly recognizable voice, with the catchphrase 'What's up Doc?', was created by Mel Blanc.

Meaning from the fortified town

Hilaire, Hillary, Hillery, Hilary, Hilaria

The poet and writer *Hilaire Belloc* was born on this day in 1870. 'The man who wrote a library' penned serious and comic verse, literary criticism, travel writing, religious and political commentary, biographies of Napoleon, Cromwell and James II and more. Between 1906 and 1910 he was a member of Parliament.

Meaning cheerful, merry

Giosué

Giosué Carducci, the Italian poet and teacher, was born in Val di Castello, near Pisa, on 27 July 1835. The greatest Italian literary figure of the latter half of the 19th century, he won the Nobel Prize for literature in 1906.

Meaning God saves

Pantaleon

Today is the feast day of the patron saint of physicians and midwives, *St Pantaleon*. During the Diocletian persecution he was arrested for being a Christian, but he wouldn't die: a stone was tied to his leg to drown him, but the stone floated; when he was thrown to wild animals, they fawned all over him. He was eventually beheaded.

Meaning lion of all

Bharati, Bharat

Bharati Mukherjee, the Indian-American novelist, was born on this day in 1940. The winner of the National Book Critics' Circle Award for her book *The Middleman and Other Stories* (1999), she teaches creative writing at the University of California, Berkeley.

Meaning goddess Saraswati

Juliana

US guitar player and singer and songwriter *Juliana Hatfield* was born on 27 July 1967. She studied at Berkley College of Music, Massachusetts, and was a member of the Boston band the Blake Babies before going solo.

From Julia, meaning youthful

Destiny, Destinée

On this day in 1999 the US girl band *Destiny's Child* released their second album, *Writing's on the Wall*. It spawned several dance hits, such as 'Say My Name', 'Bills, Bills, Bills' and 'Jumpin' Jumpin'', and secured their destiny.

Meaning fate

Grazia, Graziana, Graziella

Maria Grazia Cucinotta was born on 27 July 1969 in Messina, Sicily. The Italian actress was in the James Bond film *The World is Not Enough* (1999). She was also in *Il postino* (1994), the Italian film about the life of the Chilean poet Pablo Neruda.

Meaning grace

Samson, Sampson, Simson

Today is the feast day of *St Samson*, who is thought to have been born in South Wales in the late 5th century. His parents were Amon of Dyfed and Anna of Gwynned. Famed as a miracle worker, he travelled to Ireland and then France, where he settled. He became the bishop of Dol, where he built a monastery.

Meaning sun

Riccardo

The celebrated Italian conductor *Riccardo Muti* was born in Naples on this day in 1941. He won the Cantelli Prize for young conductors in 1967. Since 1986 he has been the musical director of the La Scala, Milan, and guests all over the world with the greatest orchestras.

Meaning wealthy, powerful

Ballington, Ballin, Balin

Ballington Booth was born on 28 July 1857 in Brighouse, Yorkshire, US. Son of William Booth, who founded the Salvation Army in Britain, Ballington and his wife, Maud, founded Volunteers of America in 1896 to help the poor, disabled, homeless and anyone in need.

Meaning mighty warrior

Coby, Cobi, Cobie

On this day in 1976 *Coby Dick*, the US vocalist and songwriter with the heavy metal band Papa Roach, was born. Papa Roach was formed in 1993 in Vacaville, northern California, and the group's first album was called *Potatoes for Christmas* (1994).

Meaning supplanter

Louisinne

Louisinne Havemeyer, who was born on 28 July 1855, was an art collector from the late 19th century until the 1920s, and she is particularly remembered for appreciating the worth of Corot portraits, rather than his landscapes, long before anyone else.

From Louis, meaning famous warrior

Jamison, Jamisa

Jamison Bess Belushi, the daughter of James and Jennifer Belushi, was born on this day in 1999. James, the brother of John Belushi, has appeared in many films, from *Trading Places* (1983) to *K.9: The Patrol Pack* (2004).

Meaning supplanter

Asia

The actress *Asia Fuqua* was born on 28 July 2002. She is the daughter of the US actress Lela Rochon Fuqua and the director Antoine Fuqua. Antoine directed *Training Day* (1997) and *King Arthur* (2004). Lela's hits include 'Any Given Sunday' (1999) and 'Waiting To Exhale' (1995).

Meaning east

Jacqueline, Jackeline, Jackelyn, Jacketta, Jaclyn, Jacklyn, Jacky, Jackie, Jacobina, Jacqueleine, Jacquelyn, Jacquetta, Jacqui, Jamesina, Jaquith

On this day in 1929 *Jacqueline Lee Bouvier* was born in Southampton, New York. She was a photographer with the *Washington Times Herald* and in 1953 married John F. Kennedy. In 1968 she married the shipping magnate Aristotle Onassis.

Meaning supplanter

29 JULY

Olaf, Olen, Olin, Olav

Today is the feast day of the patron saint of Norway, *St Olaf*, who was born in 995 and who became king of Norway in 1016. During the national struggle to make Norway an independent country, he was killed at Stiklestad. Although there is no record that he performed any miracles in his lifetime, they were reported at his shrine, around which Trondheim Cathedral was built.

Meaning descendant

Wanya, Wania

Wanya Morris, a member of the multi-Grammy award-winning quintet Boyz II Men, was born in Philadelphia, Pennsylvania, on 29 July 1973. Boyz II Men have had six number one singles, and their biggest hit was 'One Sweet Day' (1996).

Meaning worthy of praise

Booth, Both, Boothe, Boote, Boot

The US novelist and dramatist *Booth Tarkington* was born in Indianapolis on this day in 1869. His novels were the blockbusters of the day. *The Magnificent Ambersons* (1918) was filmed by Orson Welles in 1942 and won Booth the 1919 Pulitzer Prize.

Meaning from a market

Geddy

Geddy Lee, the influential bass player and vocalist with hard rock band Rush, celebrates a birthday today. He was born in 1953 in Toronto, Canada. Rush were huge in the 1980s, when the group's hits included 'A Farewell to Kings', 'Hemispheres' and 'Permanent Waves'.

Meaning not known

Thelma

The US actress *Thelma Todd* was born on this day in 1905 in Lawrence, Massachusetts. She appeared in many films throughout the late 1920s and early 1930s, but is best remembered for her performances in the Marx Brothers films *Monkey Business* (1931) and *Horse Feathers* (1932).

Meaning nurseling

Jeanetta

The US actress *Jeanetta Arnette* was born on 29 July 1967. She has appeared in many notable feature films since the 1970s, including *Teenage Graffiti* (1977), *Boys Don't Cry* (1999) and *The Shipping News* (2001).

Meaning God is gracious

Clara, Clarabella, Clareta, Clarette

The original 'It Girl', *Clara Bow* was born on this day in 1905. She wowed 1920s Hollywood in films like *The Plastic Age* (1925) and *Mantrap* (1926). She made 56 films in all, both silent and sound. Sixteen of them are available on video.

Meaning bright, shining girl

Salome

Today is the feast day of *St Salome* and St Judith of Niederaltaich. Salome was an English princess who lived in the 9th century. St Judith, the anchoress of Ober Altaich, Bavaria, was her niece. Salome is from the Hebrew greeting shalom.

Meaning peace

Arnold, Arnald, Arnaldo, Arnaud, Arne, Arnie, Arno, Arn

Arnold Schwarzenegger was born on this day in 1947. In 2003 the Hollywood star of *The Terminator* (1984) and *Total Recall* (1990) was elected as the 38th governor of the state of California. The Governor has become one of his many nicknames since taking office.

Meaning strong as an eagle

Thorstein, Thurston, Thurstan

The US economist and writer *Thorstein Bunde Veblen* was born on 30 July 1857 in Manitowoc County, Wisconsin. His best-known work is his satire *The Theory of the Leisure Class* (1899). He also wrote the influential essay 'Why Economics is Not an Evolutionary Science'.

Meaning Thor's jewel

Casey, Case

The baseball player and manager *Casey Stengel* was born Charles Dillon Stengel on this day in 1890. In his long career he managed the Brooklyn Dodgers, the Boston Braves, the New York Yankees and the New York Mets.

Meaning brave, watchful

Tatwin

Today is the feast day of St *Tatwin of Canterbury*. Born in Mercia (a former kingdom of central England), he took his vows at Briudun in Worcestershire. He was consecrated as archbishop of Canterbury on 10 June 731. He wrote poetry and riddles, some of which survive.

Meaning not known

Delta

The US actress *Delta Burke* was born on this day in 1956. A former beauty queen, Delta is best known for her role as Suzanne Sugarbaker in the US TV series *Designing Women* (1986). She is also an author, designer and spokesperson for real-size women everywhere.

Meaning fourth daughter

Emily

On this day in 1818 the British writer *Emily Brontë* was born in Thornton, Yorkshire. She wrote verse and one novel, *Wuthering Heights* (1847), which was filmed in 1939 with Laurence Olivier and Merle Oberon.

Meaning industrious, worker

Vivica, Viveca

The US actress *Vivica Fox* was born Vivica Anjanetta Fox on 30 July 1964. Her outstanding performance in the movie *Independence Day* (1996) led to starring roles in *Batman & Robin* (1987), *Soul Food* (1997) and *Kill Bill*, Vols. 1 and 2 (2004). Vivica's mother also has an unusual name, Everlyena.

Meaning living voice

Kate

British singer and songwriter *Kate Bush* was born in Bexleyheath, Kent, on 30 July 1958. Her first hit, 'Wuthering Heights' (1978), was the bestselling record in both Britain and the USA. Her successful single 'Running up That Hill' was taken from the album *Hounds of Love* (1985).

Meaning pure

31 JULY

Primo

The Italian author *Primo Levi* was born in Turin on 31 July 1919. A survivor of Auschwitz, he became internationally known after the publication of his novel *If Not Now, When?* (1982). His best-known work is a collection of short stories, *The Monkey's Wrench* (1978).

Meaning first-born son

Ahmet, Ahmed

Ahmet Ertegun, the co-founder of Atlantic records, was born on this day in 1923 in Istanbul, Turkey. The son of the Turkish ambassador to the USA, Ahmet was also a songwriter, penning 'Sweet Sixteen' and 'Chains of Love' as A. Nugetre (Ertegun spelled backwards).

Meaning highly praised

Lino

On this day in 1954 the Himalayan mountain K2 was climbed for the first time. The second highest mountain in the world after Everest, K2 is the harder climb of the two mountains. The two men who reached the summit were *Lino Lacadelli* and Achille Companogi. The Italian team was led by Ardito Desio.

Meaning praise

Morey

Morey Carr, the singer with the humorous pop trio the Playmates, was born on 31 July 1932 in Waterbury, Connecticut. The group's single 'Beep Beep' (1958) was in the charts for 12 weeks, peaking at number four.

Meaning dark-skinned

Cydonia

On 31 July 1976 NASA released an extraordinary photograph of the surface of Mars showing what looked like a human face. Photographed by the *Viking* 1 space probe, the strange land formation was in the *Cydonia* region of Mars.

Meaning not known

Joanne, Johanne

The children's author *Joanne K. Rowling*, better known as J.K. Rowling, was born on this day in 1965. The author of the *Harry Potter* books lives in Edinburgh with her doctor husband. She is the richest woman in Britain, wealthier even than the queen. 31 July is also Harry Potter's birthday.

From Jane, meaning God's gift of grace

Arnette, Arnetta

On 31 July 1981 *Arnette Hubbard* was installed as the first woman president of the National Bar Association. An attorney, public official and elected state court judge, Arnette was named as one of the 100 most influential African-Americans by *Ebony* magazine.

Meaning powerful eagle

Summer

On this day in 1992 *Summer Sanders* won the Olympic gold medal in the 200 metres butterfly. This made her the first US athlete at the Barcelona Olympics to win four medals. She became known as the first lady of American swimming.

Meaning season of summer

August

August

1 AUGUST

Melville, Melvil, Mel

The US author Herman Melville was born in New York City on this day in 1819. Best known as the author of *Moby Dick*, Melville wrote *Billy Budd*, left unfinished on his death, which was adapted into an opera by Benjamin Britten. He also wrote some short stories, including 'Bartleby the Scrivener', and the epic poem *Clarel* (1876).

Meaning bad settlement

Adam, Adamo, Adahamh, Adao, Adan

Adam Duritz, lead singer with the US group Counting Crows, was born on 1 August 1964 in Baltimore, Maryland. The group's albums include *August and Everything After* (1993), *Recovering the Satellites* (1996) and *This Desert Life* (1999).

Meaning of the red earth

Yves, Ives, Yvar

Yves Saint Laurent, the Algerian-born French fashion designer, was born on this day in 1936. The former assistant to Christian Dior is famous for empowering women with the trouser suit. He also gave them the see-through blouse, the trench coat and his perfume, Rive Gauche.

Meaning son of the archer

Dom

The US actor *Dom De Luise* was born on 1 August 1933 in Brooklyn, New York. He was a regular in Mel Brooks's movies, including *Blazing Saddles* (1973), *Silent Movie* (1976) and *Spaceballs* (1987), and many more, plus his own TV specials.

Meaning belonging to the Lord

Tempestt, Tempesta, Tempeste

The US actress *Tempestt Bledsoe* was born on 1 August 1973. She became a child star after playing Vanessa Huxtable, one of the daughters of the middle-class African-American family in the phenomenally successful *The Cosby Show*, which ran from 1984 to 1992.

Meaning stormy one

Landry

Landry Albright was born on this day in 1990. The child actress is best known for her role as Bridget Forrester in the US TV soap *The Bold and the Beautiful*. She was the third actress in the role, which she played from 1995 to 1998.

Meaning rough land

Faith

Today is the feast day of *St Faith* (Pistis), who, with her sisters St Hope (Elpis) and St Charity (Agape), are reputed to be the daughters of St Sophia, a name that itself means wisdom. The sisters are said to have been martyred during the persecution of Christians initiated under Hadrian, but there is no evidence that they existed.

Meaning faith

Augusta, Augustine, Austen

Augusta would be a suitable name for a girl born on the first day of August. It is the female form of Augustus, a Latin name that means majesty. In addition to being the name of two towns in the USA (in the states of Georgia and Maine), it was the name of the mother of George III, king of Britain and Hanover.

Meaning majestic, exalted

Carroll, Carrol, Caryl, Carol, Carolus

The US actor *Carroll O'Conner* has a birthday today. Better known as Archie Bunker from TV's *All in the Family* (1971), he has had eight Emmy nominations, winning five of them. He has also won a Golden Globe and a Peabody award.

Meaning free man

Hèlder, Hèldar

Hèlder Postiga, the Portuguese soccer player, was born in Vila do Conde on 2 August 1982. He is a striker for the Portuguese national team and for FC Porto. He played for the English premier team Tottenham Hotspur in 2004.

Meaning not known

James, Jimmy, Jimmie, Jim

US writer *James Baldwin* was born in Harlem, New York, on this day in 1924. His first novel, *Go Tell It on the Mountain* (1953), is an exploration of the discrimination that the author, an African-American, encountered in USA. He later became a spokesman for Martin Luther King Jr.

Meaning may God protect

Mojo

The satirical musician and songwriter *Mojo Nixon* was born on this day in 1957. His real name is Neill Kirby McMillan Jr, and he chose his stage name because he thought that they were two names that shouldn't even be near each other. His best-known song is 'Elvis is Everywhere'.

Meaning not known

Myrna, Merna, Mirna, Moina, Morna, Moyna

The US actress *Myrna Loy* was born Katerina Myrna Adele Williams on this day in 1905. Her first film was *Pretty Ladies* (1925), and by the 1930s she was the queen of Hollywood, with Clark Gable the king. Clark Gable, Leslie Howard and John Barrymore all fell for her, and Men-Must-Marry-Myrna clubs sprang up all over the US.

Meaning beloved

Ethel

On this day in 1881 the British novelist *Ethel Mary Dell* was born in Streatham, London. She wrote romantic stories, including *The Way of an Eagle* (1912), *The Lamp in the Desert* (1919), *The Black Knight* (1926) and *Sown among Thorns* (1939).

Meaning noble

Bernadine, Bernadina, Bernadene, Berna

Bernadine Healy, the first woman director of the US National Institution of Health, was born on this day in 1944. As president of the US Red Cross, she advises the White House on preparedness to respond to weapons of mass destruction.

Meaning brave as a bear

Ingeborg, Ingibiorg, Ingebiorg, Ingaberg, Inga

Princess Ingeborg of Sweden was born on this day in 1878. The Danish princess married Prince Charles of Sweden, and they had four children: Astrid Sophie Louise Thyra, later queen of the Belgians; Martha, later queen of Norway; Margaretha; and Carl.

Meaning hero's daughter

Elisha, Eliseo

On this day in 1811 the inventor of the elevator, or lift, *Elisha Graves Otis*, was born in Halifax, Vermont. He got the idea for a spring-operated device in 1852 when he found a way to stop hoisting machinery from falling down. His invention paved the way for skyscrapers and the modern city landscape the world over.

Meaning God is my helper

Brooke, Brook

The British poet *Rupert Chawner Brooke* was born on this day in 1887. After travelling in North America and New Zealand, he joined the Royal Navy and is now remembered as one of the poets of the First World War. Among his best-known poems are 'The Old Vicarage, Grantchester' and 'The Soldier'.

Meaning dweller by the brook

Shenouda, Shenute

On this day in 1923 *Shenouda III*, leader of the Coptic Orthodox Church, was born in Asyut, Egypt. A popular leader, committed to Christian unity, in 1973 he met the Catholic pontiff, Paul VI, in the first such meeting for over 1,500 years.

Meaning not known

Terry

The popular Irish broadcaster *Terry Wogan* was born Michael Terence Wogan on 3 August 1938 in Limerick, Ireland. The name Terry is often used as a shortened form of Terence, as here, but it is actually medieval and a name in its own right, with the same German source as Derek.

Meaning ruler of the people

Lydia, Lidie, Lidia

Today is the feast day of *St Lydia Purpurea*, St Paul's first known convert. She lived in Thyatira in Asia Minor and was a businesswoman, trading in purple cloth, the most expensive and sought-after of the time. She is the patron saint of dyers.

Meaning cultured

Juliana

The British writer of children's books *Juliana Horatia Ewing* was born on this day in 1841 in Ecclesfield, Yorkshire. Among her many titles are *Mrs Overtheway's Remembrances* (1869) and *Daddy Darwin's Dovecote* (1884). In addition, she wrote poetry for children, and her mother, Margaret Gatty, wrote books for children.

Meaning young in heart and mind

Miriam, Mimi, Mitzi

Mrs *Miriam Hargrave* of Yorkshire, in the north of England, became a British celebrity when she appeared on a reality TV show about learning to drive. Between 1962 and 1970 she failed her driving test an impressive 39 times. However, on 3 August 3 1970 she passed, making this a lucky day for Miriams everywhere.

From Mary, meaning bitter

JoMarie

The US actress *JoMarie Payton* was born on 3 August 1950. For nine seasons she played the bubbly Winslow mum on the TV show *Family Matters* (1989). She is also a singer and has released a jazz CD, which was produced by Billy Mitchek.

From Josephine, meaning she shall add, and Mary, meaning bitter

Domenico, Dominic, Dominik, Domingo, Dominy

The Italian painter *Domenico Morelli* was born on this day in 1826. He was a leader of the realist movement in Italy and is known for his large paintings on historical and biblical themes. He was professor of art at Naples Academy.

Meaning born on the Lord's day

Gaspar, Gasper, Gaspard, Caspar, Casper, Kaspar, Kasper, Jasper

Gaspar N´nez de Arce, who is known as the Spanish Tennyson, was born on 4 August 1834 in Valladolid, Spain. As well as writing poetry, he was the civil governor of Barcelona. He wrote about revolution, order, peace and freedom.

Meaning treasurer

Knut, Knute, Canute

The Nobel Prize-winning Norwegian novelist, dramatist and poet *Knut Hamsun* was born Knut Pedersen on this day in 1859. His first success was in 1890 with a novel called *Sult* (Hunger) about a starving writer; the modern edition has an introduction by Paul Auster.

Meaning knot

Osbert

The British writer and artist *Osbert Lancaster* was born in London on this day in 1908. After studying architecture he started to draw cartoons for the *Daily Express* newspaper and these often included Lady Maudie Littlehampton and her circle of friends. He also worked in the theatre, designing sets and costumes.

Meaning bright, famous

Timi, Timotea

The US singer *Timi Yuro* was born on 4 August 1941. She is best remembered for her top ten hit of the early 1960s, 'Hurt', which she recorded when she was just 18 years old. She had 11 songs in the top 100 between 1961 and 1965.

Meaning honouring God

Jody, Jodie

The British rock singer and guitarist *Jody Turner* was born on this day in 1963. When she was 13 she formed the all-female rock band Rock Goddess with her nine-year-old sister Julie. The group expanded and were together through the 1980s, recording two albums.

Meaning admired, praised

Marguerite, Marguerita

Queen Elizabeth, the Queen Mother, was born Lady *Elizabeth Angela Marguerite Bowes-Lyon* on this day in 1900. In 1920 she married the duke of York, who became king as George VI, and was the mother of Elizabeth II, queen of Great Britain and Northern Ireland, and of Princess Margaret. She lived to be 101 years old.

Meaning pearl

Perpetua, Perpetita

Today is the feast day of St *Perpetua*. She is believed to be one of the earliest saints, living in Rome in the 3rd century. She was married into a noble family, which also converted to Christianity with her friend and maid, who became St Felicitas. She is the patron saint of cattle and martyrs.

Meaning continuous

Armstrong, Armie, Arm

The first man to walk on the moon, *Neil Alden Armstrong* was born on this day in 1930 in Wapakoneta, Ohio. His first words after setting foot on the moon were: 'That's one small step for man, one giant leap for mankind.' He wears a US size 13 shoe.

Meaning warrior with a battle axe, strong arm

Ambroise, Ambrose, Emrys, Ambrosio

The French composer *Ambroise Thomas* was born in Metz on this day in 1811. He is best known for his light operas, especially *Mignon* (1866) and *Hamlet* (1868). His treatment of Shakespeare's play differs from the original in ending with Hamlet, now king, alive (and singing).

Meaning immortal

Pierre

Pierre et Jean (1888) is one of the best-known novels by the French writer Guy de Maupassant, who was born in Normandy on this day in 1850. By the time it was published, de Maupassant was already famous and considered the master of the short story. He loved solitude, travelling around the Mediterranean in his yacht *Bel-Ami*, which he named after one of his novels.

Meaning rock, stone

Vern

Country singer *Vern Godsin* was born on this day in 1934. With his brother, Rex, he formed the Godsin Brothers, and they had several hits in the late 1960s. In 1984 his album *There is a Season* was voted best country album of the year by the *Los Angeles Times*.

Meaning growing, flourishing

Selma, Anselma, Zelma, Anselme

Selma Diamond, the Canadian TV actress and comedienne, was born on this day in 1920. She is best known for her role in the long-running TV series *Night Court* (1984–92), for which she received a Golden Globe nomination.

Meaning divinely protected

Loni, Lonie

Loni Kaye Anderson was born on 5 August 1946. The US actress is best known for her role as Jennifer Marlowe on the TV sitcom about a struggling radio station, *WKRP in Cincinnati*, which ran from 1978 to 1982. In 1988 she married Burt Reynolds.

Meaning torch

Afra, Aphra

Today is the feast day of *St Afra*, who lived in Augsburg, Germany. Originally a prostitute, she was converted to Christianity by the bishop of Gerona, but was martyred during the Diocletian persecution by being burned at the stake in about 304. Her mother and three other women who sought to recover her ashes to bury them were also burned to death.

Meaning dark

Kajol, Kajal

The Bollywood star *Kajol Devgan* was born Kajol Mukherjee on this day in 1975. She starred in five films with Shah Rukh Khan, including *Kabhi Khushi Kabhie Gham* (2001), the highest-grossing Indian film overseas, which reached number three in Britain.

Meaning eye-liner

Alfred, Alefred, Ailfrid, Alfredo, Alf, Alfy, Avery

The British poet *Alfred, Lord Tennyson* was born on this day in 1809 in Somersby, Lincolnshire. One of this best-known works, *In Memoriam A.H.H.*, was written in memory of his friend Arthur Henry Hallam, who was engaged to his sister, Emily. Tennyson became poet laureate in 1850, succeeding William Wordsworth.

Meaning wise counsel of the elf

Cherno

The German TV star *Cherno Jobatey* was born in Berlin on this day in 1965. After working as a reporter he joined Germany's Channel 2, turning its morning magazine show into a must-see programme. He then got his own talk show, *Cherno – The Talk Show*.

Meaning black

Andy, Andris, Andrien, Andre, Andie, Anders

The artist and cultural icon *Andy Warhol* was born Andrew Warhola on this day in 1927. His 'factory' was the hub of New York's 1960s Pop Art scene. His paintings and silk-screened images of Campbell's soup cans and Marilyn Monroe were a visual pun on mass-producing mass-production.

From Andrew, meaning warrior

Ballard

The British actor *Ballard Berkeley* was born in Margate, Kent, on 6 August 1904. He had a long career in films and on the stage, but will always be remembered for his role as Major Gowen in John Cleese's classic TV comedy sitcom *Fawlty Towers* (1975, 1979).

Meaning strong, bold

Louella, Luella

Louella Parsons, the US gossip columnist, was born Louella Rose Oettinger on this day in 1881. Her first job was as drama editor on the *Dixon Morning Star*, but her column for the *Los Angeles Examiner* was syndicated to over 600 newspapers around the world.

Meaning shrewd in battle

Geri, Gerianna, Gerrillee, Geralda

It is ex-Spice Girl *Geri Halliwell*'s birthday today. She was born on 6 August 1972 in Watford, in the south of England. Since leaving the Spice Girls band, she has pursued a solo singing and acting career. She has also undertaken work for various charities and is a goodwill ambassador for the United Nations.

From Gerald, meaning ruling spear

Lucille, Lucile

US actress and comedienne *Lucille Desiree Ball* was born on this day in 1911. *I Love Lucy* (1955–61), in which she played Lucy Rocardo, was innovative in many ways. It was the first TV sitcom, the first show to use the three-camera set-up and she was one of the first stars to perform in front of a live audience on TV.

From Lucy, meaning light

Soleil

Soliel Moon Frye, the US actress, was born in Glendora, California, on 6 August 1976. She shot to stardom in the 1980s in the title role of the cult TV sitcom *Punky Brewster*. Later in her career (2000–03) she played the part of Roxy King in *Sabrina The Teenage Witch*.

Meaning sun

Garrison

The US author and radio host *Garrison Keillor* was born on this day in 1942 in Anoka, Minnestoa. He found international fame with his radio monologues *Lake Wobegon Days*, which were published in 1985. He has written for the *New Yorker* and the *Atlantic Monthly*, and had an advice column called Mr Blue on salon.com.

Meaning troops in battle

Caetano

The Brazilian singer and songwriter *Caetano Veloso* was born in Bahia on this day in 1942. One of the most important and best-loved figures in Brazilian contemporary music, he can be seen performing as himself in Pedro Almódóvar's film *Talk to Her* (2001).

Meaning from Gaeta, Italy

Evander, Evandor

US soldier *Evander Law* was born in South Carolina on 7 August 1836. A Confederate general in the Civil War, he led the Fourth Alabama Regiment and fought in many important battles, including the first and second battles of Bull Run in 1861 and 1862.

Meaning bow-carrying warrior

Ulrich, Ulric

The Swedish figure skater *Ulrich Salchow* was born on this day in 1877. He won the world figure skating championships ten times, more than any man before or since. In 1909 he was the first person to land a jump in competition, and the style he used is now known as the Salchow jump. He was president of the International Skating Union from 1925 to 1937.

Meaning powerful, prosperous

Charlize

The actress *Charlize Theron* was born on 7 August 1975 in Benoni, South Africa. She started getting small parts in films after she threw a tantrum in a Los Angeles bank, witnessed by an impressed bystander, talent scout John Crosby. She won an Oscar for her performance in *Monster* (2003).

Meaning manly

Billie, Billy, Billye, Willa

The US actress *Billie Burke* was born Mary William Ethelbert Appleton Burke on 7 August 1885. It was more common at that time for a girl to carry a male ancestor's name. She is best remembered for her role as the Glinda, the Good Witch of the North, in *The Wizard of Oz* (1939).

From William, meaning desiring to defend

Jacqui, Jacque

Jacqui O'Sullivan, a member of the pop group Bananarama, was born in London on this day in 1960. The 1980s group had great success with songs like 'Cruel Summer' (1983), 'Robert de Niro's Waiting' (1984) and the international number one, 'Venus' (1986).

Meaning supplanter

Lydia, Lidia, Lydie, Lidie

The molecular biologist *Lydia Villa-Kimaroff* was born on 7 August 1947. She is a key figure in the field of insulin research and was an important member of Walter Gilbert's team at Harvard University, which proved that bacterial cells could produce insulin.

Meaning cultured one

Dustin, Dustan, Dusty

US actor *Dustin Hoffman* was born Dustin Lee Hoffman on 8 August 1937 in Los Angeles. His first starring role was in *The Graduate* (1967), and he won Oscars for *Kramer versus Kramer* (1979) and *Rain Man* (1988). He has six children: Karin, Jenna, Jacob, Max, Rebecca and Alexandra.

Meaning valiant fighter

Emiliano, Emilio, Emmil, Emile, Emelen, Emlen, Emlyn

The Mexican revolutionary hero *Emiliano Zapata Salazar* was born in Anencuilco, Morelos, on this day in 1879. He was a key player in the Mexican Revolution, and the Zapatistas movement was named after him.

Meaning industrious

Dino

The Italian film producer *Dino de Laurentiis* was born on this day in 1919. He has received 30 Oscar nominations, three Golden Globes, a Palme d'Or and three Golden Lions. His long career spanned such films as *Bitter Rice* (1948), *Flash Gordon* (1980) and *Unforgettable* (1996).

Meaning from the valley

Webb, Webber, Weber, Webster

US country singer *Webb Pierce* was born on this day in 1926 or 1921. He was the king of 1950s honky-tonk and one of the first music stars to live a rock-and-roll lifestyle. He had cars studded with silver dollars and a guitar-shaped swimming pool built in his Nashville home.

Meaning weaver

Esther, Essa, Eister, Etty

The US swimming star *Esther Williams* was born on this day in 1923. She became a Hollywood movie star in the 1940s and 1950s with films featuring special swimming sequences, such as *Million Dollar Mermaid* (1952) and *Jupiter's Darling* (1955).

Meaning bright star

Nita, Bonita

The US actress *Nita Talbot* was born on this day in 1930 in New York. She appeared in many films and TV shows throughout the 1950s and 1960s, but is best known for her performance in the Elvis Presley film *Girl Happy* (1965).

Meaning sweet, good

Kyoko, Kioko

Kyoko Cox, the daughter of Yoko Ono and the US film-maker Tony Cox, was born Kyoko Chan Cox on 8 August 1963. She has a daughter called Emi.

Meaning mirror

Senta, Senthia

The US actress *Senta Moses* was born on 8 August 1973. She was in several TV series in the 1990s, including *Running the Halls* (1993), and she played Delia Fisher in *My So-called Life* (1994).

Meaning assistant

9 AUGUST

Elisha, Eliseo

Elisha Ferry, the US politician, was born on 9 August 1825 in Monroe, Michigan. He served two terms as governor of Washington Territory from 1872 under President Ulysses S. Grant. He was also a successful lawyer.

Meaning God is my salvation

Zino, Zinon, Zine

The French violinist *Zino Francescatti* was born in Marseilles on 9 August 1902. He began playing in orchestras when he was ten years old, making his debut with Beethoven's Violin Concerto. He settled in the USA and joined the New York Philharmonic in 1939.

Meaning beautiful

Rinus

Rinus Gerritsen, of the Dutch heavy rock band Golden Earring, was born on this day in 1946. Golden Earring have been together since the mid-1960s, and in the 1970s they had a UK chart hit with 'Radar Love'. In the late 1990s they were still filling 60,000-seat stadiums.

Meaning not known

Deion, Dion, Dionysus

The US football megastar *Deion Sanders* was born on 9 August 1967 in Fort Myers. He is the only player to have appeared in a Super Bowl and World Series. Although he is a much better footballer than he is a baseball player, he was a regular on offence and defence for the Dallas Cowboys, their first for 34 years.

Meaning god of wine

Whitney

Whitney Houston, the US singer and actress, was born Whitney Elizabeth Houston on this day in 1963. In 1992 she appeared in the film *The Bodyguard* and recorded 'I Will Always Love You' for the soundtrack. It was number one in the US for 14 weeks and in Britain for ten weeks.

Meaning from the white island

Gillian, Gillie, Gilly

US actress *Gillian Anderson* was born in Chicago on 9 August 1968. She was raised in London and then moved back to the US when she was 11. She played FBI agent Dana Scully in *The X-Files* (1994–2002) and is married to *X-Files* assistant art director, Clyde Klotz, with whom she has a daughter, Piper Maru.

Meaning nestling, downy-haired

Melanie, Melonie, Melloney, Melly, Mellie, Melan, Melana

Melanie Griffith, the US actress, was born on this day in 1957. Her mother is the actress Tippi Hedren. Best known for her role as Tess in *Working Girl* (1988), Melanie has three children: Alexander Bauer, Stella del Carmen Banderas Griffith and Dakota Mayi Johnson.

Meaning clad in darkness

Aimee, Aimé

Aimee Mann was born on 9 August 1960. She was the lead singer of the 1980s band Til Tuesday before going solo. In 2000 she had a hit with 'Save Me' from the soundtrack of the film *Magnolia* and was nominated for an Academy Award.

Meaning beloved friend

Jorge, Jorg, Jorgen

The Brazilian novelist *Jorge Amado* was born on 10 August 1912 in Itabuna, Bahia. His best-known novel, *Dona Flor and her Two Husbands* (1966), which is about a widow who remarries and ends up sharing her bed with her dead husband's ghost, was turned into a movie in 1976. Amado wrote more than 20 novels, which have been translated into over 30 languages.

Meaning farmer

Fender

Leo Fender, the guitar-maker, was born Clarence Leonidas Fender on this day in 1909. His first electric guitar was the Telecaster (1950), which was followed by the Precision Bass (1951) and the Stratocaster (1954). He learned the saxophone in school, but never learned to play the guitar.

Meaning enclosing ditch

Antonio, Antone, Antoni

The Spanish actor *Antonio Banderas* was born José Antonio Dominguez Bandera on 10 August 1960. Married to Melanie Griffith and one of the best-known actors in Hollywood, he supplied the voice of Puss in Boots in *Shrek 2* (2004).

Meaning flower

Camilo, Camillo, Camillus, Camillio, Camilio

The first prime minister of the new kingdom of Italy, Count *Camilo Benso di Cavour* was born on this day in 1810. He was a witness of the 1830 revolution in France, and his liberal beliefs enabled him to unite Italy. He became the architect of the Italian constitution.

Meaning free-born

Rosanna, Rosanne, Rose-Anne

US actress *Rosanna Arquette* was born on 10 August 1959 in New York. Her movies include *Pulp Fiction* (1994) and *Crash* (1996). She is from an acting family: her father, Lewis, played J.W. Pickett in *The Waltons*, and her brother, David, and her sisters, Alexis and Patricia, are both actors.

Meaning graceful rose

Norma

Canadian-born US actress *Norma Shearer* was born on this day in 1900. She appeared in silent movies and was one of MGM's major stars in the 1930s. She received Oscar nominations for her performances in *Their Own Desire* (1929), *A Free Soul* (1931), *The Barretts of Wimpole Street* (1934) and *Marie Antoinette* (1938), and received an Academy Award for *The Divorcee* (1930).

Meaning from the north

Neneh, Nenah, Nena

The alternative rap pioneer *Neneh Cherry* was born in Stockholm, Sweden, on this day in 1965 to a Swedish mother and a West African father. Her stepfather was Don Cherry, the famous US trumpet player. She has a brother called, and baptized as, Eagle Eye.

Meaning little girl

Rhonda

The flame-haired movie star *Rhonda Fleming* was born Marilyn Louis on this day in 1923. She appeared in many films of the 1940s and 1950s. Her first lead was opposite Bing Crosby in the Technicolor musical *A Connecticut Yankee in King Arthur's Court* (1949).

Meaning good spear

Erwin, Erwine

The Austrian chemist *Erwin Chargaff* was born on this day in 1905. In his studies of DNA he discovered that in double-stranded DNA, the number of thymine units is the sum of the number of cytosine and adenine units put together.

Meaning army friend

Rice, Rhys, Rhees, Rheese, Reece, Reis, Riess

The US 'president for one day', *David Rice Atchison* was born on 11 August 1807 in Frogtown, Kentucky. Atchison was 'president pro tempore' of the Senate when, on 4 March 1849, Zachary Talyor refused to be inaugurated on the Sabbath.

Meaning passion

Asaph, Asaf

On 11 August 1877 the US astronomer *Asaph Hall* discovered the two moons of Mars. They are named Phobos and Deimos, after the sons of Ares and Aphrodite in Greek mythology. Asaph Hall was awarded the Royal Astronomical Society's gold medal in 1879.

Meaning collector

Gifford, Giffard

America's first environmentalist, *Gifford Pinchot* was born on this day in 1865. Working with Roosevelt, he coined the word conservation and later became governor of Pennsylvania. Gifford Pinchot National Forest in Washington is named after him.

Meaning brave gift

Allegra, Allegria

The US ballerina and ballet teacher *Allegra Kent* was born on this day in 1937. A principal of the New York City Ballet, she was the muse and passion of George Balanchine. She wrote her life story, entitled *Once a Dancer* (1997).

Meaning cheerful

Octavia, Octavie

The writer *Octavia le Vert* was born on 11 August 1811. She was the granddaughter of George Walton, who signed the US Declaration of Independence. Her book *Souvenirs of Travel*, about her travels through Europe, became an international bestseller.

Meaning eighth

May, Mai, Maia

The artist and illustrator *May Preston* was born on this day in 1873. She specialized in the struggle for women's rights and was active in the National Women's Party. She illustrated the book *How It Feels to be the Husband of a Suffragette*.

Meaning born in May

Arlene, Arleen, Arlana, Arlen, Arlena, Arletta, Arlette, Arlina, Arline, Arlynne

Arlene Dahl, the US actress, was born on 11 August 1924. She appeared in many movies throughout the 1950s, including *Journey to the Centre of the Earth* (1959). At the end of the decade she turned to writing and became a beauty columnist and then set up her own lingerie and cosmetics companies.

Meaning pledge

Jacinto

The Nobel Prize-winning Spanish dramatist *Jacinto Benavente y Martinez* was born in Madrid on 12 August 1866. His plays were full of wit and satire, in the style of George Bernard Shaw and Oscar Wilde. One of his best-known plays, *Saturday Night* (1903), ran for an impressive two years in New York.

Meaning hyacinth

Alexei, Alexis, Alexein, Alexey

Alexei I, tsar of Russia, was born on 12 August 1629. Known as Alexei the Quiet, he ruled from 1645 until 1676 and was the father of Peter I, the Great. He had eight children by his first marriage; Peter was the first child of his second marriage.

Meaning protector of mankind

Porter

The country music star *Porter Wagoner* was born on this day in 1927. He had his first hit in 1955 with 'A Satisfied Mind'. His TV show, *The Porter Wagoner Show*, ran for 21 years through the 1960s and 1970s.

Meaning guardian of the door

Norris, Norrie

Norris McWhirter, co-founder with his twin brother, Ross, of the *Guinness Book of Records*, was born on this day in 1925. He presented the TV show of the same name for 23 years. The idea sprang from their fact-finding agency, McWhirter Twins Ltd, which they set up in the 1950s.

Meaning north

Lillie, Lillias

Lillie Devereux Blake, the US novelist, essayist and reformer, was born on this day in 1833. The president of the New York State Women's Suffrage Association, she wrote short stories and novels about women's rights, the best known of which is *A Daring Experiment* (1892).

Meaning lily

Petrovna, Petrova, Petronilla, Petronille

Madame *Helene Petrovna Blavatsky*, the Russian writer and mystic, was born on this day in 1831. She founded the Theosophy Movement, a mixture of scientific thought and Hindu and Buddhist philosophies, which might be described as the first New Age collective.

Meaning rock, stone

Radclyffe, Radcliff, Radclyf, Radclyff

The British author *Radclyffe Hall* was born Marguerite Radclyffe-Hall on 12 August 1880 in Bournemouth, Dorset. She was a controversial figure, and her novel *The Well of Loneliness* (1928) dealt openly with lesbianism. It was banned in Britain for many years.

Meaning red cliff

Leticia

The Italian actress *Leticia Roman* was born on this day in 1939. In 1960 she starred with Elvis Presley in *GI Blues*, but her most memorable performance was in *The Girl Who Knew Too Much* (1964), in which she played a US tourist in Rome.

Meaning joy

Alfred, Alfie, Alf

The British film-maker *Alfred Joseph Hitchcock* was born in Leytonstone, London, on this day in 1899. He made his first film in 1925 and then became world famous with a string of suspenseful, quirky movies, in many of which he himself appeared for only a second or two. Among his many memorable movies are *Spellbound* (1945), *Rear Window* (1955), *Psycho* (1960) and *Frenzy* (1972).

Meaning wise counsel of the elf

Son

The blues singer and guitarist *Son Seals* was born on this day in 1942. He was discovered playing at the Flamingo Club on Chicago's South Side. He released eight albums, the first of which, *Son Seals* (1973), included the well-known 'Hot Sauce'.

Meaning son of

Feargal, Fearghal

Feargal Sharkey, the Northern Irish lead singer of the Undertones, was born in Derry on this day in 1958. Their best-known track is 'Teenage Kicks' (1978), the all-time favourite of British DJ John Peel, and in November 2004 the song was played at Peel's funeral.

Meaning valiant

Sani

The US speed skater *Sani Davis* was born on this day in 1982. He was the first African-American to be in two junior world teams in the same year, and the first African-American ever in this sport to be selected for the US Olympic team.

Meaning illustrious spender

Gretchen

The US actress *Gretchen Corbett* was born on this day in 1947 at Camp Sherman, Oregon. She is best known for her role as Elizabeth 'Beth' Davenport in the long-running 1970s TV series *The Rockford Files* (1975–82) with James Garner.

Meaning pearl

Tiany, Tiana

Tiany Kiriloff, the Belgian model, was born on 13 August 1978 in Zaanst, the Netherlands. She was brought up in Maracaibo, Venezuela, by her Chilean mother and Dutch father. When she was 18 she returned to her homeland and has since settled in Antwerp, Belgium.

Meaning gracious aunt

Midori

The Japanese figure skater *Midori Ito* was born on 13 August 1969. She lit the Olympic flame during the opening ceremonies of the 1998 Winter Olympics. At the 1988 world championships she became the first Asian to win a gold medal in an ice skating event.

Meaning green

Quinn, Quinta, Quintana, Quintelle, Quintella, Quintina

Quinn Cummings, the US TV and film actress, was born on this day in 1967. She was in the TV series *The Family* (1976) and *Starsky and Hutch* (1975), and in the films *Listen to Me* (1989) and *The Goodbye Girl* (1978), among others.

Meaning fifth

Earvin

Earvin 'Magic' Johnson, the US basketball star, was born on this day in 1959. He played with the Lakers through the 1980s, leading them to many victories. He has been called Magic since his high-school days, when his skilled style of playing was already astonishing audiences.

Meaning not known

Wim

Wim Wenders, the German film director, was born on this day in 1945. Among his best-known films are *Paris, Texas* (1985), which starred Natassja Kinski and which won a Palme d'Or at Cannes, and *Wings of Desire* (1987).

Meaning desiring to defend

Rusty, Rusti, Rustin, Rustee

The US racing driver *Rusty Wallace* was born on 14 August 1956. He was the NASCAR Winston Cup champion in 1989 and was runner-up several times. In over 20 years of racing he has won more than $30 million.

Meaning red-haired

Ger

Dutch politician *Ger Koopmans* was born Gerardus Peter Jan Koopmans in Velden, the Netherlands, on this day in 1962. He is a member of the Christian Democratic Party.

Meaning spear

Halle

The beautiful US actress *Halle Berry* was born on this day in 1966 in Cleveland, Ohio. She is named after a shop, Halle's Department Store. In 2002 she became the first African-American woman to win an Oscar; it was for best actress for her performance in *Monster's Ball*.

Meaning rock

Mila

The Ukrainian actress *Mila Kuni* was born on this day in 1983. Her first role was as the young Gia in *Gia* (1998); Angeline Jolie played the older Gia. Mila went on to star in the TV show *That 70s Show*. She starred in *American Psycho 2* (2002) and was in the Aerosmith video *Jaded*.

Meaning favour, glory

Danielle, Daniel, Danelle, Danila, Danita

The bestselling author *Danielle Steel* was born on this day in 1947. She has published more than 55 novels. She also writes for children, and has written two non-fiction books, *Having a Baby* and *His Bright Light*. She has been married five times and has raised nine children.

Meaning God is my judge

Arcangela, Arcangelina, Arcangeline, Arcagolina

Lina Wertmüller, the Swiss-Italian film director, was born *Arcangela Felice Assunta Wertmüller von Elgg Spanol von Braueich* on 14 August 1928. She began her career as Federico Fellini's assistant director, and her film *Seven Beauties* (1976) won four Oscar nominations.

Meaning archangel

Lev, Leon

The Russian inventor *Lev Theremin* was born in St Petersburg on this day in 1896. He invented the musical instrument, the theremin, a strange wailing electronic machine, with a range of five octaves. It has been used for many film scores, but has also been heard in the concert hall: Pashchenko wrote his *Symphonic Mystery* (1924) for theremin and orchestra.

Meaning lion

Napoleon

Napoleon Bonaparte, the emperor of France, was born on this day in 1769 in Ajaccio, Corsica. He ruled France from 1799 until 1814. He was sympathetic to the views of the Enlightenment and even took scholars with him when he invaded Egypt, where they unearthed the Rosetta Stone.

Meaning lion of the woods

Huntz

The US character actor *Huntz Hall* was born on this day in 1920. He was famous throughout the 1930s and 1940s as part of the Bowery Boys, who together made 49 films. He later starred, with Mike Mazurki, in his own TV series, *The Chicago Teddy Bears* (1971).

Meaning not known

Vernon, Vern, Verner, Verne

Vernon Jordan, the Washington insider and close friend of Bill Clinton, was born on this day in 1935. Although he didn't have an official role in Clinton's administration, he was an important player, being known as fixer-without-portfolio.

Meaning growing, flourishing

Eliana

On this day in 2001 *Eliana Sophia Slater* was born, a daughter for Ryan Haddon and Christian Slater and a sister for Jaden Zach Haddon-Slater. In 1995 *Empire* magazine voted Christian Slater as one of the top 100 sexiest film stars ever.

Meaning sun

Julia

The US author and chef *Julia Childs* was born in Pasadena, California, on this day in 1912. After living in France, where her husband was a diplomat, she studied cooking and wrote *Mastering the Art of French Cooking* (1961) with Simone Beck and Louisette Bertholle. In 1966 Mrs Childs won an Emmy for her TV series *The French Chef* (1963–76).

Meaning young in heart and mind

Lori, Loria

The US actress *Lori Nelson* was born on 15 August 1933. She was under contract to Universal Studios in the 1950s and starred in several of their classics, including *Revenge of the Creature* (1955) and *Underwater!* (1955) with Jane Russell.

Meaning laurel

Rita

The British soprano *Rita Hunter* was born in Wallasey on this day in 1933. She made her debut as Inez in Verdi's *Il Trovatore* and became famous for her performances as Brunhilde in Wagner's Ring cycle. Her autobiography was *Wait till the Sun Shines, Nellie* (1986).

From Margarita, meaning pearl

Shimon

Israeli politician *Shimon Peres* was born Shimon Persky in Vishniev, Poland, on this day in 1923. He was prime minister in 1984–6. He won the Nobel Prize for peace in 1994 with Yitzak Rabin and Yasser Arafat. He has three children: a girl, Tzvia (Tziki), and boys, Yoni and Chemi.

Meaning listener

Fess, Festus

Fess Parker, the US actor and real estate developer, was born on this day in 1925. His roles as Davy Crockett and Daniel Boone made him a huge star of the 1960s. He now owns resort hotels, a vineyard and a winery in the Santa Barbara area.

Meaning festive

Massoud, Masud, Massud

Massoud Barzani, the leader of the Kurdistan Democratic Party, was born in Mahabad, Iran, on this day in 1946. The KDP are one of the two most powerful Iraqi Kurdish parties.

Meaning fortunate

Roch, Rock, Roc, Rocco, Rochus

Today is the feast day of *St Roch*, who was a French nobleman, born in 1295 in Montpellier. He nursed villagers during an outbreak of the plague, but then became ill himself. Fortunately, he was rescued by a dog, which fed him and made him well again. He is the patron saint of, among other things, bachelors, dogs, the falsely accused, knee problems and tile-makers.

Meaning rest

Madonna

Singer, actress, author and female icon *Madonna* was born Madonna Louise Veronica Ciccone in Rochester, Michigan, on this day in 1958. She has been a hugely successful, if controversial, singer and entertainer, and she has starred in a number of films, including the lavish biopic of Eva Perón, *Evita* (1996).

Meaning my lady

Lesley, Lesleigh

The actress *Lesley Ann Warren* was born on 16 August 1946 in New York City. Her first important role was in the TV special *Cinderella* (1965). She has since played Dana Lambert in the 1960s series *Mission: Impossible* and appeared in many films, including *Victor/Victoria* (1982).

Meaning small meadow

Georgette, Georgeta, Georgetta, Georgietta

The British author *Georgette Heyer* was born in London on 16 August 1902. She is best known for her historical romances set in the Regency period, but she also wrote detective novels and short stories. She published over 60 books in all.

Meaning farmer

Mateja

Mateja Svet, the most successful alpine skier in Slovenia, was born on this day in 1968 in Ljubljana, Slovenia. Among her wins are the World Cup giant slalom in 1987 and 1988, the Olympic giant slalom silver medal in 1988 and the world championship slalom gold medal in 1989.

Meaning gift of God

17 AUGUST

Vidiadhar

The Trinidadian author *Vidiadhar Surajprasad Naipaul*, better known as V.S. Naipaul, was born on this day in 1932. The novelist and travel writer has won many awards, including the Booker Prize in 1971 and the Nobel Prize for literature in 2001.

Meaning giver of knowledge

Jonathan, Jonathon, Jonathen

The US author *Jonathan Franzen* was born on 17 August 1959. His novel *The Corrections* (2001), about the trials and tribulations of an ordinary American family, was widely praised, won the 2001 US National Book Award for fiction and became an international bestseller.

Meaning God has given

Gilby

Gilby Clark, the guitarist with the band Guns N' Roses, was born on 17 August 1962 in Cleveland, Ohio. Since the mid-1990s he has been a successful solo artist, with albums including *Pawnshop Guitars* (1995), *Hangover* (1997), *Rubber* (1998), *'99 Live* (2000) and *Swag* (2002).

From Gilbert, meaning bright pledge

Bryton

US actor *Bryton McClure* was born in Lakewood, California, on this day in 1986. He is best known for his role in *Family Matters*, the TV sitcom about a middle-class African-American family. He played Richie Crawford from 1990 to 1998.

Meaning from Britain

Mae

US actress *Mae West* was born on 17 August 1893 in Brooklyn, New York City. She wrote several stage plays before going into the movies, including her 1928 hit *Diamond Lil*, which was later turned into the movie *She Done Him Wrong* (1933). The film launched Cary Grant's career and was nominated for a best picture Oscar.

From Mary, meaning bitter

Lene

The Norwegian singer *Lene Marlin* was born Lene Marlin Pedersen on this day in 1980. She achieved success in Norway and Europe with her first album, *Playing My Game* (1999).

Meaning torch

Tarja

Tarja Turunen, who was born on 17 August 1977 in Kitee, Finland, is the lead singer with the Finnish metal band Nightwish. She is one of Finland's most popular rock singers. She also sings classical songs and in opera.

Meaning untamed

Hazel, Hazle

The inventor of the non-smear lipstick, *Hazel Bishop* was born in Hoboken, New Jersey, on this day in 1906. She worked as an organic chemist and perfected the forumla for her lipstick privately. In 1949 she set up her own company and became a successful businesswoman.

Meaning hazel tree

Redford

US actor *Robert Redford* was born on 18 August 1937. As well as being one of the biggest screen stars in the USA, he won an Oscar for directing *Ordinary People* (1980), and owns a restaurant in Utah and a ski resort called Sundance, where he runs an annual film festival.

Meaning of the red crossing

Caspar, Casper

Caspar Weinberger, who was appointed by President Ronald Reagan as the US secretary of defence in 1981 and stayed in the position until 1987, was born on 18 August 1917 in San Francisco, California. After leaving office he became chairman of *Forbes* magazine.

Meaning treasurer

Meriwether

Meriwether Lewis was born in Albemarle County, Virginia, on this day in 1774. As President Thomas Jefferson's private secretary, Lewis, with William Clark, led the exploration of Louisiana and was instrumental in opening up the West. They left St Louis in May 1804 and reached the Pacific coast in November 1805.

Meaning merry weather

Brian, Bryan

British science-fiction writer and novelist *Brian Wilson Aldiss* was born in Dereham, Norfolk, on this day in 1925. Since his first book, *The Brightfoot Diaries* (1955), he has written a score of acclaimed novels as well as non-fiction, including *The Detached Retina* (1994) and *The Twinkling of an Eye: My Life as an Englishman* (1998).

Meaning high-born, noble

Helena, Helen

Today is the feast day of *St Helena*. She was the mother of Constantine the Great, who was born around 274, and when her son became emperor, he raised her from the obscurity, into which her husband (Constantine's father) had plunged her, to the highest honour. Helena is credited with finding the remains of the True Cross.

Meaning bright one

Shelley, Shelli, Shell, Shelly

The actress *Shelley Winters* was born Shirley Schrift in East St Louis, Illinois, on 18 August 1922. She won a best supporting actress Oscar for her role in *The Diary of Anne Frank* (1960).

Meaning meadow on a ledge

Rosalynn, Rosalyn, Rosalynne

Rosalynn Carter, the first lady of the USA from 1977 to 1981, was born on this day in 1927 in Plains, Georgia. As first lady of Georgia, she was on the governor's Commission to Improve Services for the Mentally and Emotionally Handicapped, and has done much work in this area ever since.

Meaning beautiful rose

Marge

Marge Schott, who was born on this day in 1928 in Cincinnati, Ohio, was the primary owner, president and chief executive of Major League team Cincinnati Reds for nearly 15 years. She became the first woman owner of a US baseball team to buy the team outright.

Meaning pearl

19 AUGUST

Magnus

Today is the name day for everyone called *Magnus* living in Sweden. Magnus is traditionally a royal name in Sweden, Norway and Denmark, including Magnus the Good, who ruled Norway in the early 11th century, and Magnus I, who ruled Sweden in the late 13th century. It is also the name of several early Scandinavian saints.

Meaning great one

Orville, Orvil

Orville Wright, one half of the pioneering Wright Brothers, was born on this day in Dayton, Ohio, in 1871. With his brother, Wilbur, Orville opened a bicycle manufacturing and design company in 1892. In 1903 they were the first people to fly a heavier-than-air machine, and by 1909 they had won the first US military aviation contract.

Meaning from the golden town

Quentin

The British painter, sculptor, potter and art historian *Quentin Bell* was born on this day in 1910. He was the son of Clive and Vanessa Bell (sister of Virginia Woolf) and wrote extensively on the Bloomsbury Group. He also wrote about Victorian art.

Meaning fifth

Darius, Dario, Dare, Derry

British singer *Darius Danesh* was born on 19 August 1980. Darius came third in the TV talent contest *Pop Idol* (won by Will Young), and his first single, 'Colourblind', went to number one in Britain in 2002.

Meaning the wealthy man

Gabrielle, Gabriella, Gabriel, Gabrila, Abriella, Avrielle

The great designer and perfumier Coco Chanel was born *Gabrielle Bonheur Chanel* in Samur, France, on this day in 1883. She began her career in fashion in 1909 by selling hats. Two of her most enduring creations are the perfume Chanel No. 5 and the little black dress.

Meaning woman of God

Tammin

The Australian actress *Tammin Sursock* was born on 19 August 1983. Best known for her role as Dani Sutherland in TV's *Home and Away*, Tammin also had a second career as a singer. Her first single, released in 2004, was 'Pointless Relationship'.

Meaning not known

Kyra, Kyrah

The US actress *Kyra Sedgwick* was born on 19 August 1965 in New York City. She married actor Kevin Bacon in 1987 after working with him on the TV film *Lemon Sky*, and in 1989 she played Tom Cruise's girlfriend in the feature film *Born on the Fourth of July* (1989).

Meaning sun

Tipper

Tipper Gore, the wife of former US Vice-president Al Gore, was born Mary Elizabeth Aitcheson in Arlington, Virginia, on this day in 1948. She used to be the drummer in an all-girl band called the Wildcats. They have four children: Karenna, Dristin, Sarah and Albert III.

Meaning star

Quinn, Quin

The US basketball player and coach *Quinn Buckner* was born William Quinn Buckner on this day in 1954 in Phoenix, Illinois. The former Indiana star went on to become an ESPN announcer.

Meaning wise, intelligent

Salvatore, Salvator

The Italian poet *Salvatore Quasimodo* was born on this day in 1901 in Syracuse, Sicily. A classicist who was quite at home with modernity, he was awarded the Nobel Prize for literature in 1959. Among his best-known works are *Life is not a Dream* (1949) and *The Matchless Earth* (1958).

Meaning saviour

Bernard, Bernardo, Bernhard, Bernie

Today is the feast day of *St Bernard of Clairvaux*, born in 1090 near Dijon, France. He entered the strict monastery at Coteaux and was later sent to found an abbey at Clairvaux. No fewer than 68 houses sprang up from his new foundation.

Meaning brave bear

Eero, Ero

The remarkable Finnish architect *Eero Saarinen* was born on this day in 1910. He designed the TWA Terminal Building at Kennedy International Airport, New York (1956–62), the Thomas H. Watson Research Centre, Yorktown (1957–61) and many more, as well as collaborating with Charles Eames on furniture design.

Meaning ever-powerful ruler

Catalina, Catalin

The Romanian gymnast *Catalina Ponor* was born on this day in 1987. In 2004 she was the team, beam and floor event Olympic and European champion. She also won triple silver at the world championships in Anaheim in 2003.

Meaning blessed, pure and holy

Annabella, Annabelle, Anabela, Anabel, Amabel

In Slovakia today is the name day for Annabella. Every girl called Annabelle in the country will receive bunches of flowers and small gifts from their friends and family.

Meaning loveable

Joya

The US jazz vocalist *Joya Sherrill* was born Guilmenot Joya Sherril on this day in 1927 in Bayonne, New Jersey. She sang with Duke Ellington throughout the 1940s and then through the following decade with his protégés Rex Steward and Ray Nance.

Meaning joy

Cherish

US actress and model *Cherish Lee* was born on this day in 1982. She is the daughter of country singer Johnny Lee and of US actress Charlene Tilton. Charlene is best known for her role as Lucy Ewing in the 1970s TV series *Dallas*.

Meaning treasure

21 AUGUST

Booth, Boote, Boot, Both

Booth Garder, the 17th governor of Washington State, was born on 21 August 1936 in Tacoma, USA. He was the US ambassador to the World Trade Organization from 1994 to 1997.

Meaning from a market

Aubrey, Aube, Aulberik

The British illustrator and writer *Aubrey Beardsley* was born in Brighton, Sussex, in 1872. His art nouveau style found its first outlet in the artistic and literary magazine the *Yellow Book* magazine (1894–6). More famously he illustrated Oscar Wilde's *Salome*.

Meaning elf ruler

Liam

Liam Howlett was born Liam Paris Howlett on 21 August 1971. He is the main writer for the UK electronica band Prodigy, working with synthesizers, filters, samplers and computers. The group's hits include 'Firestarter' (1995) and 'Smack My Bitch Up' (1997).

Meaning determined protector

Basie, Base

Count Basie was born on this day in 1904 in Red Bank, New Jersey. His Big Band performed in the New York area from 1936 until 1952, showcasing some legendary performers, including Billie Holliday and Joe Williams.

Meaning short one

Alizée, Alize

Alizée, the French pop star, was born on this day in 1984. After her first hit 'Moi Lolita', made when she was a mere 16-year-old, Alizée took Europe by storm, with world sales totalling over 4 million CDs. In 2003 she released her second album *Mes courants électriques*.

Meaning joyful

Hayden

US actress *Hayden Panettiere* was born on 21 August 1989. She was nominated for the best spoken-word Grammy for her role as Princess Dot in *A Bug's Life* (1995). She has been in many films, including *Raising Helen* (2004).

Meaning from the valley with the hedge

Carrie-Anne, Carieanne, Carieanna, Carianna

The Canadian actress *Carrie-Anne Moss* was born in 1967 in Burnaby, British Columbia. She is best known for her roles in *The Matrix* (1999) and *The Matrix Reloaded* (2003). Other film appearances include *Memento* (2000) and *Chocolat* (2000).

From Caroline, meaning free woman, and Anne, meaning God has favoured me

Alicia, Alichia

The US actress *Alicia Witt* was born on this day in 1975. Her first big role was in the TV comedy *Cybill* (1996). Films she has appeared in include the romantic comedy *Two Weeks' Notice* (2002) and *Vanilla Sky* (2001). She also played the Hollywood executive in *The Sopranos*.

Meaning noble, kind

Mats

The tennis player *Mats Wilander* was born on 22 August 1964 in Vaxjo, Sweden. He won a total of eight grand slam titles, seven of them for singles games. Ranked number one player in 1988, he won the Australian, US and French opens.

Meaning gift of God

Denton

The cardiovascular surgeon Dr *Denton Arthur Cooley* was born in Houston, Texas, on this day in 1920. He was one of the pioneers of open-heart surgery and in 1969 he was the first to implant an artificial human heart. He holds the Medal of Freedom, the highest US civilian award.

Meaning valley town

Elmo

Elmo Langley, the racing driver, was born on this day in 1929 in Cresswell, North Carolina. He had two NASCAR cup wins as a driver. Later he became an owner, with racing drivers including Tommy Gale, Ken Schrader, Curtis Markham and Clark Dwyer.

Meaning protector

Karlheinz

Karlheinz Stockhausen, the German avant-garde composer, was born on 22 August 1928. He has written a wide range of works, from the opera *Licht* (1977) to electronic pieces, such as *Gesang de J.nglinge* (1955) and *Hymnen* (1966).

Meaning man who rules the home

Tori, Toria, Torey, Tory

The singer and songwriter *Tori Amos* was born Myra Ellen Amos on this day in 1963 in North Carolina. A classically trained pianist, her obsession with Led Zeppelin moved her over to pop. Her best-known song is 'Professional Widow', which was number one in the US in 1998.

Meaning victorious conqueror

Leni

Leni Reifenstahl was born in Berlin on August 22 1902. The director of *Triumph of the Will* (1934), a record of the Nuremberg rally, she was also an Olympic cross-country skier, an anthropological photographer and an underwater film-maker. She began diving in her 70s and released *Underwater Impressions* on her 100th birthday.

Meaning torch

Mila

The US country music star *Mila Mason* was born on this day in 1963 in Kentucky. Her first album, *That's Enough of That* (1997), was an immediate success. 'Always find someone who believes in you more than you believe in yourself,' is her advice on getting a start in show business.

Meaning favour, glory

Dorothy, Dorothea, Dorothoe, Dorete, Dorota, Drottya, Dosia, Thea, Dot, Dottie, Dotty, Dora, Dory, Dorothi, Dorothoe, Theodora

On this day in 1893 the US journalist and short story writer *Dorothy Parker* was born in West End, New Jersey. She became drama critic of *Vanity Fair* and joined other great wits of the time at the Round Table luncheon club at the Algonquin Hotel.

Meaning gift of God

23 AUGUST

Constant, Constantine, Constantin, Constantino, Konstantin, Konstantine

The composer and conductor *Constant Lambert* was born on this day in 1905. A child prodigy, he began writing orchestral pieces when he was 13. He wrote the ballet *Romeo and Juliet* (1926) for Diaghilev's Ballet Russe. The character Hugh Moreland in Anthony Powell's 12-novel sequence entitled *A Dance to the Music of Time* was based on Lambert.

Meaning constant and unchanging

Gene

Gene Kelly was born Eugene Curran Kelley in Pittsburgh, Pennsylvania, on this day in 1912. An accomplished actor, director, singer and choreographer, as well as America's best-known dancer, he starred in dozens of classic movies, including *Singin' in the Rain* (1952).

From Eugene, meaning noble, well-born

River

The US actor *River Phoenix* was born on this day in 1970 in Madras, Oregon. His parents were missionaries. His best-known role was in *My Own Private Idaho* (1991), in which he starred with Keanu Reeves. His brother, Joaquin, and sister, Rain, also entered the acting profession.

Meaning river

Tex

The US country musician *Tex William* was born on 23 August 1917. He was an early pioneer of the country music shift from rural and acoustic to dance and pop. He is best known for his talking blues style of singing.

Meaning from Texas

Ethelda, Etheline, Ethelinda, Ethylyn

On this day in 1920 the swimmer *Ethelda Bleibtrey* became the first US woman to win a gold medal at the Olympic Games, which were held in Antwerp, Belgium. She won three medals, all of them in world record times.

Meaning noble serpent

Sophie

The US novelist and short story writer *Sophie Kerr* was born in Maryland on this day in 1880. She established a trust fund, which annually rewards the most promising literary student at Washington College, and at over $50,000 it is one of the biggest literary prizes in the world.

Meaning wisdom

Noor

Queen Noor of Jordan was born in the US on this day in 1951 to an Arab-American family. Before becoming a queen she studied architecture and was the director of planning and design for Royal Jordanian Airways.

Meaning luminous

Rose

Today is the feast day of *St Rose of Lima*, who was born Isabel de Flores y del Olivia. She worked hard to support her parents, growing flowers and doing embroidery, and she cared for the poor and sick in Peru. She is the patron saint of South America.

Meaning rose

Rupert, Ruprecht, Rupes

The British actor *Rupert Grint* was born on this day in 1988 at Watton-at-Stone, Hertfordshire. He is best known for his role as Harry's friend Ron Weasley in the *Harry Potter* films. He also appeared in *Thunderpants* (2002).

From Robert, meaning bright, famous

Isidoro

The Argentine writer Jorge Luis Borges was born *Jorge Francisco Isidoro Luis Borges Acevedo* in Buenos Aires on 24 August 1899. One of the most important writers of the 20th century, Borges's fantastical short stories feature labyrinths, infinity and mirrors.

Meaning god of sky and nature

Durward

Durward Kirby was born on 24 August 1912. He is best remembered for US TV's *Candid Camera*, which he co-hosted for five years. *Candid Camera* was the first reality show, originally airing on the radio as *Candid Microphone* in August 1948.

Meaning door guard

Max

The writer and caricaturist *Max Beerbohm*, known as the Incomparable Max, was born in London on this day in 1872. He succeeded George Bernard Shaw as theatre critic of the *Saturday Review*, and he also contributed to the *Yellow Book*. His best-known work is *Zuleika Dobson* (1912).

Meaning greatest

Joan, Joanie, Joni

Today is the feast day of *St Joan Thouret*, who founded the Sisters of Charity under the protection of St Vincent de Paul in 1799. The movement later spread from France to Switzerland and northern Italy.

Meaning God is gracious

Marlee

Marlee Matlin was born on this day in 1965. She was the youngest person ever to win a best actress Oscar for her performance as the character Sarah Norman in *Children of a Lesser God* (1986). As Josephine in TV's *The West Wing*, she gave birth to an onscreen boy on the same day as her real child, a girl, was born.

Meaning bitter meadow

Letizia, Letitia

Maria Letizia Bonaparte, Napoleon Bonaparte's mother, was born in Corsica, France, on this day in 1749. Napoleon was the fourth of her 12 children. In 1804 she was given the title Madame Mère de l'Empereur but, devoutly religious, she continued to live a simple life.

Meaning joy, gladness

Emily

Today is the feast day of *St Emily de Vialar*. She used a legacy to found a home for children and poor people, and was asked to found a second such home in Algeria. Her movement spread around the world, including to Jerusalem and Australia, and the sisters are now known as the Sisters of St Joseph of the Apparition.

Meaning rival

25 AUGUST

Blair

US actor *Blair Underwood* was born on this day in 1964. In *Sex and the City* he played Miranda's NY Knicks team doctor boyfriend, Robert Leeds. Other appearances include TV's *LAX* (2004) and his one-man show *IM4: From Mountaintop to Hip Hop*, which was written by his brother.

Meaning from the plain

Regis

The US talk-show host *Regis Philbin* was born on 25 August 1931. He was named after his father's high school. As well as hosting his own shows, he hosted the US version of *Who Wants to be a Millionaire?* (1998). He currently holds the Guinness World Record for the most hours on camera: 15,188 hours.

Meaning ruler

Genesius

Today is the feast day of *St Genesius of Arles*. He was a solider and secretary to the magistrat of Arles in the 4th century. He is the patron saint of secretaries and actors, and is also said to protect against chilblains and scurf.

Meaning welcome newcomer

Linus

On this day in 1991 *Linus Torvalds* announced that he was working on a new free computer operating system. It was the beginning of Linux, the free, non-commerical worldwide system. The Finnish computer hero has three daughters: Patricia Miranda, Daniela Yolanda and Celeste Amanda.

Meaning flax-coloured hair

Catarina, Caterina

Catarina Furtado was born on this day in 1972, Catarina is a beautiful and well-known celebrity in Portugal. As well as acting, she writes, produces and hosts her own shows covering a number of different subjects.

Meaning blessed, pure and holy

Althea, Althee, Altheta, Thea, Aletha

The US tennis player *Althea Gibson* was born on this day in 1927. She rose from poverty in Harlem to becoming the first African-American to play at Wimbledon. In 1957 and in 1958 she won both the women's singles and doubles titles at Wimbledon. She also won the French open.

Meaning healer

Claudia, Claude, Claudie, Claudette, Claudell, Claudelle, Claudine

Claudia Schiffer, the German supermodel, was born on this day in 1970. After a long engagement to the magician David Copperfield, she married Matthew de Vere Drummond, the film producer. They have two children, Caspar and Clementine.

Meaning lame one

Ruby

Ruby Keeler, the actress, singer and dancer, was born in Halifax, Nova Scotia, on this day in 1909. She made her name in the Warner Brothers films she made with Dick Powell in the 1930s, including *42nd Street* (1933) and *Footlight Parade* (1933). She came out of retirement in 1971 to appear in a revival of *No, No, Nanette*.

Meaning precious gem

Julio, Julius, Juliun, Juliu

The Argentine-French writer *Julio Cortazar* was born in Brussels on this day in 1914. Sometimes compared with Jorge Luis Borges, Cortazar's writing is surreal and fantastical. Best known for his short stories, his experimental novel *Hopscotch* (1963) is his master work and was filmed in 1966.

Meaning downy-haired

Macaulay, Macauley

The US actor *Macaulay Culkin* was born on this day in 1980. He has six siblings: Quinn, Kieran, Christian, Shane, Rory and Dakota. *Home Alone* (1990) and *Home Alone 2: Lost in New York* (1992) made him the highest-paid child actor ever at the time. Having reached adulthood, he became an accomplished theatre performer.

Meaning righteous

Branford

Saxophonist *Branford Marsalis* was born on this day in 1960. His three brothers are all jazz musicians, as is his father, Ellis. Branford has played with Herbie Hancock, Miles Davis and Sting, among others. He is the musical director of the Jay Leno Show.

Meaning broad crossing

Guillaume, Guillermo

The French poet *Guillaume Apollinaire* was born on 26 August 1880. One of the leaders of the Montmartre set in Paris, he collaborated with Picasso to define the cubist movement, and in his programme notes for the ballet *Parade* (1917) by Jean Cocteau and Erik Satie, he famously coined the word surrealism.

From William, meaning desiring to defend

Thalia, Thalius, Taylee, Taylie

The Mexican actress and singer *Thalia* was born Ariadna Thalia Sodi Miranda on 26 August 1971. After a successful career as a soap actress, Thalia released her first album in 1990. Her first two albums went gold, and her third went platinum. She lives in the USA.

Meaning blooming, plentiful

Elizabeth, Elisabeth, Elisabet, Elisabetta, Lizabeta, Lizbeth, Lizzy, Lizzie, Lize, Liza, Liz, Betty, Bettie, Bet, Eliza, Elisa, Elissa, Elzieta, Elspeth

Today is the feast day of *St Elizabeth Bichier des Ages*. During the French Revolution she helped organize secret meetings for worship among the faithful, and this led her to establishing a community to look after the sick and teach girls. The sisters became known as the Sisters of St Andrew the Apostle.

Meaning consecrated to God

Zona, Zonie

Zona Gale, who was born on this day in 1874 in Portage, Wisconsin, was one of America's best-known writers and the first woman to win a Pulitzer Prize for drama, which was awarded for her 1920 bestseller *Miss Lulu Bett*.

Meaning girdle, belt of Orion

Pilar

Pilar Alma Thomas and her sisters, Barbara Ayala and Gweneth Gonzales, are the triplet daughters of Alma Gonzales and US actor Richard Thomas. Richard Thomas, who was John Boy in the TV series *The Waltons*, starred in the Broadway production *Democracy* (2004).

Meaning pillar

27 AUGUST

Deco, Deck, Decker

Deco, the Brazilian soccer player, was born Anderson Luiz de Sousa on 27 August 1977. He was a key player for Porto, the Portuguese team in 2002–3. After receiving Portuguese citizenship he joined Portugal's national team, and soon after they beat Brazil for the first time since 1966.

Meaning roofer

Lyndon, Lyndan, Lind, Linden

Lyndon Baines Johnson, 36th president of the USA, was born in Stonewell, Texas, on this day in 1908. He had one sister, Rebekah, and three brothers, Josefa, Sam and Lucia. He became president on the assassination of John F. Kennedy, and in his administration the Civil Rights Act (1964) and Voting Rights Act (1965) became law.

Meaning from the lime tree

Ira

The US author, playwright and songwriter *Ira Levin* was born in New York on this day in 1929. His novel *The Boys from Brazil* (1976) was turned into a successful film in 1978. He also wrote the long-running play *Deathtrap*, which was later filmed in 1982, featuring Michael Caine and Christopher Reeve.

Meaning watcher

Emmanuel, Man, Emman, Emanuel, Immanuel, Mano

The surrealist artist Man Ray was born *Emmanuel Rudnitsky* in Philadelphia on this day in 1890. Best known for his pioneering photography, he was also a painter, object maker and film-maker. With Marcel Duchamp he formed the US branch of the dada movement.

Meaning God is with us

Teresa, Terestita, Terese, Teresina, Teressa, Theresa, Therese, Toireasa

On this day in 1910 Agnes Gonxha Bojaxhiu was born in Uskub, in what is now Macedonia, of Albanian parents. She became *Mother Teresa of Calcutta*, the founder of the Missionaries of Charity. In 1979 she won the Nobel Prize for peace. She was beatified by Pope John Paul II in 2003.

Meaning harvest, reap

Jeanette

The British author *Jeanette Winterson* was born on this day in Manchester. Her novel *Oranges Are Not the Only Fruit* (1985) was successfully adapted for BBC TV in 1990. She has won many awards for her writing, including the Whitbread Prize and the Cannes Prix d'Argent.

From Jane, meaning God's gift of grace

Tuesday

US actress *Tuesday Weld* was born Susan Ker Weld in New York on Friday, 27 August 1943. Called Tuesday from early childhood, she was a teenage Hollywood star of the 1950s. She had a love affair with Elvis Presley and married Dudley Moore.

Meaning born on Tuesday

Yolanda, Yolande, Iolanthe

The US gospel and rhythm and blues singer *Yolanda Adams* was born in Houston, Texas, on this day in 1964. She was nominated for a Grammy for her album *More than a Melody* (1995). In 2000 she released a Christmas album with a song called 'Born This Day'.

Meaning violet flower

Sheridan

The Irish author *Sheridan Le Fanu* was born in Dublin on 28 August 1814. He wrote ghost stories and mysteries. 'Carmille', a vampire story, was made into films in 1966, 1990 and 1999, as were many of his other stories, including his best-known novel, *Uncle Silas* (1947).

Meaning wild savage

Robertson

One of Canada's most distinguished novelists, *Robertson Davies*, was born on 28 August 1913 in Thamesville, Ontario. He was also a playwright, critic, journalist, librettist and professor. His novel *What's Bred in the Bone* (1985) was short-listed for the Booker Prize.

Meaning son of Robert

Eliel

The Finnish architect *Eliel Saarinen* was born on 28 August 1873. He moved to the US in the 1920s and became famous for his art nouveau skyscrapers and churches. He formed a partnership with his son, Eero, and also had a daughter, Pipsan.

Meaning my God

Secondo, Secundus, Secondino

The Italian pioneer of the jet engine, *Secondo Campini* was born in Bologna on this day in 1904. He developed the Thermojet and demonstrated it for the first time in 1932 with a jet-powered boat in the waters of Venice.

Meaning second

Gates, Yates

Gates McFadden, the US actress who played Dr Beverly Crusher in *Star Trek: The Next Generation* (1987–94), was born on 28 August 1953. Before joining the crew of the famous *Enterprise* she was a choreographer by profession, working on many Jim Henson productions.

Meaning gates

Shania

The Canadian singer and songwriter *Shania Twain* was born Eileen Regina Edwards in Windsor, Ontario on this day in 1965. She grew up in Timmins, Ontario, where a street and a museum have been named after her. Shania is a Canadian Indian Ojibwa word.

Meaning I'm on my way

Wilhelmina, Wilhelmeni, Wilhelmine, Wilhomena

On this day in 1913 *Queen Wilhelmina*, the queen of the Netherlands, presided over the official opening of the Peace Palace in The Hague. It is the seat of international law and houses the judicial body, the International Court of Justice as well as the Permanent Court of Arbitration.

Meaning desiring protector

Honey

Ann Honey Lantree, who was born on 28 August 1943, was the drummer with the British 1960s group the Honeycombs at a time when it was unheard of for a girl to play in a boy pop group, let alone be the drummer. They had a big hit with 'Have I the Right?' (1964), which reached number one in Britain and number four in the USA.

Meaning honey, sweet girl

Gottlieb, Gotthold

On 29 August 1885 the German inventor and engineer *Gottlieb Daimler* patented the world's first motorcycle. He was a key figure in the development of the gasoline engine, as well as in the invention and development of the motorcar. In 1890 he founded the Daimler-Motoren Gesellschaft in Cannstatt.

Meaning God's love

Elliott, Elliot, Eliott

The US actor *Elliott Gould* was born on 29 August 1938. He was Trapper John in *M*A*S*H* (1970), Philip Marlowe in *The Long Goodbye* (1973), hosted *Saturday Night Live* six times and was a regular guest on the hugely popular TV series *Friends* (1994–2004). He was married to Barbra Streisand, and they have a son, Jason Gould.

Meaning the Lord is God

Preston

The Hollywood film director and screenwriter *Preston Sturges* was born on this day in 1898. He was the first writer to direct his own script, *The Great McGinty* (1940), and it won him the first Oscar for original screenplay writing. His last film was the 1955 *The French, They Are A Funny Race* (*The Diary of Major Thompson* in Britain).

Meaning priest's town

Sterling, Stirling

Sterling Morrison was born on 29 August 1942 in Westbury, New York State. A founding member of the Velvet Underground, he gave it all up in the 1970s and 1980s and became the captain of a Houston tugboat.

Meaning honest, worthy

Eliza, Elisa, Lize, Liza, Liz, Lizzy, Lizzie, Elissa

Eliza Starr, the US religious writer, was born at Deerfield, Massachusetts, on 29 August 1824. She published many books on religion, literature and art, including *Songs of a Lifetime*, *Pilgrims and Shrines* and *The Three Archangels and the Guardian Angels in Art*.

From Elizabeth, meaning consecrated to God

Meshell, Meshelle

The singer and musician *Meshell Ndegocello* was born on 29 August 1969. She recorded her first album, *Plantation Lullabies*, in 1993, and went on to produce further CDs, including *Comfort Woman* in 2003. She sang 'Poison Ivy' on the soundtrack of the movie *Batman & Robin* (1997).

Meaning who is like God

Lurene, Lurena

Lurene Tuttle, the US actress, was born on this day in 1906. She was passionate about radio and was one of the major radio stars of the 1930s and 1940s. She was the first woman president of the Los Angeles division of the American Federation of Radio Artists.

Meaning not known

Wyomia

The US athlete *Wyomia Tyus* was born on this day in 1945. She won the 100 metres Olympic gold medal in 1965 and in 1968, when she also broke the world record. She was the first woman ever to win consecutive gold medals in this event.

Meaning gracious friend

Parker, Park, Parke

The British radio broadcaster *John Robert Parker Ravenscroft* was born on this day in 1939. Better known as John Peel, his widely influential show introducing unusual, innovative new bands on BBC's pop music channel Radio One ran from 1967 until 2004.

Meaning guardian of the park

Claire, Clare, Clarry, Clarice, Clarence, Clavance

Dr *Claire Straith*, the pioneering cosmetic surgeon, was born on 30 August 1891. He founded the Straith Clinic in the 1930s. He spent a great proportion of his time helping people who had been in car accidents and subsequently invented the padded dashboard.

Meaning famous, illustrious one

Elden, Eldon

The US actor *Elden Henson* was born on 30 August 1977 in Maryland, but grew up in California. He was in the films *The Mighty Ducks* (1992), *Cast Away* (2000) and *The Battle of Shaker Heights* (2003), among others.

Meaning elf valley

Rini, Ringan, Ninian

The Dutch singer *Rini Valentine* was born in Roosendaal on 30 August 1955. The name Rini comes from Ringan, which is, in turn, a Scottish dialect form of Ninian, the name of a 5th-century saint who was a missionary in Scotland.

Meaning lively

Stefka, Stepha

On this day in 1987 the Bulgarian athlete *Stefka Kostadinova* set the women's high jump record when she jumped 2.09 metres (6 feet 10 inches). The record, still in place in 2004, is one of the longest-standing in modern athletics. Altogether she set seven world records.

Meaning crowned

Joan

US actress *Joan Blondell* was born on this day in 1909. In the course of a long film career she appeared in dozens of comedies and musicals, from *Sinner's Holiday* (1930) to *The Champ* (1979). She was married to George Barnes, the cinematographer, Dick Powell, the actor, and Mike Todd, the film producer.

Meaning God is gracious

Cameron, Cam, Cameran, Cameren

Cameron Diaz, the US actress, was born on this day in 1972 in San Diego, California. Among her many successes are *My Best Friend's Wedding* (1997), *There's Something About Mary* (1998) and *Being John Malkovich* (1999).

Meaning crooked nose

Shelley, Shelly

The English writer *Mary Wollstonecraft Shelley* was born in London on 30 August 1797. Her father was William Godwin, the philosopher, her mother was the early feminist, Mary Wollstonecraft, and she was married to the poet Percy Bysshe Shelley. She is famous as the author of the Gothic horror novel *Frankenstein, or the Modern Prometheus* (1815).

Meaning meadow on a ledge

Ivan, Van

Van Morrison was born *George Ivan Morrison* on 31 August 1945 in Belfast, Northern Ireland. In the 1960s the singer, songwriter and guitarist was in a band called Them. As a solo artist he has recorded many classics, including the albums *Astral Weeks* (1968) and *Tupelo Honey* (1971).

From John, meaning God has shown me favour

Eldridge, Eldredge, Eldred, Eldrid, Eldwin, Eldwyn

Eldridge Cleaver, the prominent African-American leader and activist and one of the founding members of the Black Panther movement, was born on 31 August 1935 in Wabbaseka, Arkansas. In 1975 he renounced the Panthers and became a born-again Christian.

Meaning wise adviser

DuBose

The US author *DuBose Heyward* was born on 31 August 1885. He is best known as the author of the novel *Porgy* (1924), on which George and Ira Gershwin based their opera *Porgy and Bess* (1935). He also wrote the novels *Angel* (1926) and *Mamba's Daughters* (1929).

Meaning not known

Alan

On 31 August 1918 *Alan Jay Lerner*, the US author and lyricist, was born in New York. He had a long collaboration with Frederick Loewe, with whom he produced a string of musicals. Their first success was *Brigadoon* (1948), and they also worked together on *An American in Paris* (1951) and *My Fair Lady* (1956).

Meaning bright, fair

Rania, Rana, Rani, Ranee, Rayna, Ranique

Queen Rania of Jordan was born in Kuwait on 31 August 1970. Before marrying the future King Abdullah Bin Al-Hussein in 1993 she studied business administration and worked in banking and IT. They have three children: Prince Hussein, Princess Iman and Princess Salma.

Meaning of royal birth

Shekinah, Shekiah, Shekia, Shekeia

Imani Shekinah Alexander, daughter of US comedian and actor Flex Alexander and US singer and actress Shanice Alexander, was born on 31 August 2001. Shanice signed her first record contract when she was 11 years old and released her first album when she was 14.

Meaning hill

Cara, Caralie, Carina, Cariad, Carine, Kara, Karine, Karina

On 31 August 1954 the song 'Cara Mia' was at the top of the British charts. It was by Dave Whitfield with Mantovani and his Orchestra, and it stayed in the charts for 10 weeks, a record at the time, and sold over a million copies.

Meaning friend

Mary

On this day in 1866 the novelist Elizabeth von Arnim was born *Mary Annette Beauchamp* in Sydney, Australia. Her best-known work is *Elizabeth and her German Garden*, which was published anonymously in 1898. Her husband, Count Henning August von Arnim-Schlagenthin, appears in the book as 'the man of wrath'. She was a cousin of Katherine Mansfield.

Meaning bitter

September

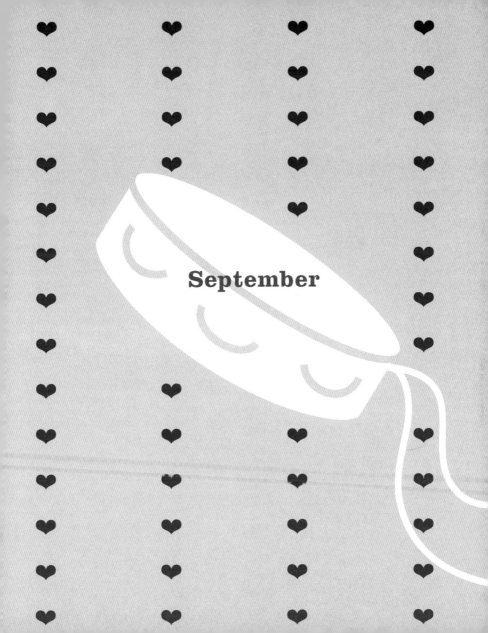

September

Taddeo, Thaddeus, Tad, Tadd

The Italian artist *Taddeo Zuccaro* was born on this day in 1529 in Valdo, near Urbino. His brother, Federico, was also an artist. Taddeo is known for his frescoes, the best known of which are in the Sala Regina in the Vatican, Rome, and in the Villa Farnese, Caprarola.

Meaning father

Engelbert, Engel, Bert

Engelbert Humperdinck, the German composer of the opera *Hansel and Gretel* (1890–93), was born on this day in 1854. He was a friend of Wagner's, whom he helped with *Parsifal*. He taught music to Wagner's son, Siegfried, and was professor of harmony at the Barcelona Conservatoire.

Meaning bright as an angel

Conway

The US singer *Conway Twitty* was born on this day in 1933. He was phenomenally successful throughout the 1950s and 1960s and had no fewer than 55 number one singles and 41 number one albums. 'It's Only Make Believe' and 'Hello Darlin'' are two of his most memorable hits.

Meaning holy water

Ziggy, Zigmund

Ziggy Stardust was born in the USA today. On 1 September 1972 David Bowie released his album *The Rise and Fall of Ziggy Stardust and the Spiders from Mars* in the US. The first single from the album, 'Starman', was already a hit in Britain.

Meaning victorious protector

Marisela, Marise

Marisela Verena, the Cuban singer, was born on this day in 1951 and moved to the USA when she was 11 years old. She received an Emmy for her original score for the documentary *Exile – Trauma to Triumph*. Her album *Somos los que andamos* was released in 2003.

From Mary, meaning bitter

Narcissa, Narcisse, Narcissus

On this day in 1836 *Narcissa Whitman* arrived at Walla Walla in Washington and became one of the first white women ever to settle west of the Rocky Mountains. Her letters and journals, written between 1836 and 1947, vividly describe her pioneering adventures.

Meaning lily

Camile, Camille

The singer *Camile Velasco* was born on this day in 1985. The Filipino-born resident of Hawaii was one of the finalists in the US talent show *American Idol 2004*. Before she entered the competition she was a waitress in a pancake shop.

Meaning noble, righteous

Velma

The US jazz singer *Velma Middleton* was born on 1 September 1917 in St Louis, Missouri. She began as a dancer in the chorus line and an occasional singer. In 1942 she started singing with the great Louis Armstrong and toured the world with his All Stars band.

From Wilhelmina, meaning protectress

Lennox

Lennox Lewis, the British boxer, was born on 2 September 1965 in West Ham, London. When he was 12 he moved to Canada and represented the country in the Los Angeles Olympics. He won a gold medal in the 1988 Seoul Olympics and went on to win many world championship fights.

Meaning grove of elm trees

Romare

Romare Bearden, the African-American painter of the Harlem Renaissance, was born on this day in 1914. His bold, colourful work often represents places he knew well, such as Harlem, St Martin in the Caribbean and Pittsburgh, while his abstracts were inspired by music.

Meaning Roman

Cleveland, Cleve

Cleveland Amory, the writer and founder of New York's Fund for Animals, was born on 2 September 1917. The youngest ever editor of the *Saturday Evening Post*, he wrote many bestsellers and worked tirelessly for animals all his life. His cat books are available as *The Compleat Cat*.

Meaning high cliffs

Keanu

The US actor *Keanu Reeves* was born in Beirut, Lebanon, on this day in 1964. He is best known for his roles in *The Matrix* (1999) and its sequels, and the name Keanu is Hawaiian. His father is Chinese-Hawaiian and his mother is British. He is also a bass player and plays in a band called Becky.

Meaning cool mountain breeze

Lucretia

Lucretia Peabody Hale was born in Boston on this day in 1820. The US author and educator wrote novels, magazine sketches and books of games, but she is best known for her sketches for children, collected together as *The Peterkin Papers* (1880) and *The Last of the Peterkins* (1886).

Meaning riches

Salma

The Mexican actress *Salma Hayek* was born in Coatzacoalcos, Veracruz, on 2 September 1966. She became a star after appearing in the Mexican soap *Teresa* (1989). She produced and played the lead in *Frida* (2002), a film about the life of the Mexican painter Frida Kahlo.

Meaning peace, calm

Lili'uokalani, Lili, Lilika

The last monarch of the kingdom of Hawaii, *Lili'uokalani* was born Lydia Paki Lili'uokalani on this day in 1838. She inherited the throne from her brother Kalakaua in 1891. She was also an author and songwriter, and wrote the Hawaiian anthem 'Aloha 'Oe'.

Meaning lily

Shauna

Shauna Sand Lamas, the US actress and fourth wife of actor Lorenzo Lamas, was born on 2 September 1971. They have three daughters, Alexandra Lynne, Victoria and Isabella Lorenza.

Meaning God is gracious

Ferdinand, Fernand, Ferd, Ferdy, Ferdie, Hernando

The automotive engineer *Ferdinand Porsche* was born on 3 September 1875 in Hafersdorf, Bohemia. His first job was as a mechanic in Vienna, and the only formal education he ever received was through sneaking into university engineering classes.

Meaning bold, daring adventurer

Ryoji, Ryoichi

Ryoji Noyori was born in Kobe, Japan, on 3 September 1938. He won the Nobel Prize for chemistry in 2001 for his pioneering work, together with William S. Knowles, on the study of catalysed hydrogenations.

Meaning first son of Ryo

Starsky, Star

The first episode of *Starsky and Hutch* was shown on 3 September 1975. The long-running TV series, set in Los Angeles, starred David Soul as Ken 'Hutch' Hutchinson and Paul Michael Glaser as Dave Starsky, crime-busting cops, who were helped by their regular informer Huggy Bear (Antonio Fargas).

Meaning star

Kjell, Kjeld, Kjetil

Kjell Magne Bondevik, prime minister of Norway, was born in Molde on this day in 1947. He has served since 1997 and was re-elected in 2001. Ordained as a Lutheran pastor in 1979, he is a theological candidate for the Christian Democratic Party.

Meaning sacrificial cauldron

Angie

On this day in 1973 the Rolling Stones released the single 'Angie' from their album *Goat's Head Soup*. It reached number one in the USA and in Britain. The real Angie is said to be David Bowie's ex-wife, Angie Bowie.

Meaning angel

Dixy, Dixie

US marine biologist, explorer and public official *Dixy Lee Ray* was born on this day in 1914. She starred on TV nature programmes, was chair of the Atomic Energy Commission and, in 1976, became the first woman governor of Washington State. She published many scientific papers and the books *Trashing the Planet* (1990) and *Environmental Overkill* (1993).

Meaning gracious gift of God

Cuthburga

Today is the feast day of *St Cuthburga*, who was the wife of Aldfrid, king of Northumbria. After her husband's death she entered a convent and later founded the nunnery at Wimbourne.

Meaning not known

Pauline

British actress *Pauline Collins* was born on this day in 1940. She became famous for her performance as the parlourmaid Sarah in the popular, long-running TV series *Upstairs, Downstairs* (1971–5). She was nominated for an Oscar for her performance in the film *Shirley Valentine* (1989). She is married to the actor John Alderton.

Meaning small

Jesse, Jess

US outlaw *Jesse Woodson James* was born on this day in 1847 in Clay County, Missouri. After the Civil War he and his brother, Frank, led a gang of outlaws, carrying out numerous train and bank robberies. Betrayed by a member of his gang, Jesse James has been portrayed in numerous books and films about the Wild West.

Meaning gift

Shushilkumar, Shushil, Shush, Kumar

The Indian politician *Shushilkumar Shinde* was born on 4 September 1941 in Sholapur, Maharashtra. He was the chief minister of Maharashtra from January 2003 to November 2004, the first of the Dalit population ever to achieve this office. Shushil and Kumar can be two separate names.

Meaning well-behaved prince

Armin, Armand, Armando, Armond

Armin Kogler, the Austrian world skiing champion, was born on this day in 1959. He won several world championship titles between 1978 and 1982, and in 1980 he set the world ski flying record of 180 metres (590 feet 6 inches). He now works for Austrian TV as a ski-jumping analyst.

Meaning man of the army

Darius, Dario

The French composer *Darius Milhaud* was born in Marseilles on this day in 1892. He wrote all kinds of music, from operas to songs. In 1930 his opera *Christophe Colomb* received its first performance in Berlin, and his popular ballet *Le Boeuf sur le toit* (1919) gave its name to an artists' café.

Meaning benevolent possessor

Mitzi

The US actress and dancer *Mitzi Gaynor* was born in Chicago on this day in 1930. She is best known for her role in the classic film *South Pacific* (1958). In the late 1980s she toured the US with the stage musical *Anything Goes*.

From Mary, meaning bitter

Beyoncé

The African-American singer and actress *Beyoncé* was born Beyoncé Giselle Knowles on 4 September 1981 in Houston, Texas. She is a solo artist and a founding member of the three times Grammy-winning band Destiny's Child. She has also won five solo Grammys.

Meaning beyond others

Daisy

The Dutch singer, actress and TV host *Daisy Dee* was born Daisy Rollocks in Curaçao, Netherlands Antilles, on this day in 1970. Famous in the German-speaking world, her song 'Crazy' reached number one in the US dance charts.

Meaning eye of the day

Khandi

Khandi Alexander was born on 4 September 1957 in New York City. The US dancer, film and TV actress is best known for her role as Jackie Robbins in the TV series *ER*. Previously, she was in the long-running 1990s TV sitcom *NewsRadio*.

Meaning white

John, Jon, Jean, Janons, Jevan, Juan, Eoin, Geno

The US composer *John Cage* was born in Los Angeles on 5 September 1912. In 1952 he composed *4' 33"*, which is silent apart from audience noises. He also wrote poetry, composed for Merce Cunningham's dance company, was an expert on mushrooms and studied Zen Buddhism under Suzuki.

Meaning God has shown me favour

Loudon

US singer and songwriter *Loudon Wainwright III* was born on 5 September 1946 in Chapel Hill, North Carolina. He had a hit in 1972 with 'Dead Skunk (In The Middle of the Road)' and has twice been nominated for a Grammy.

Meaning low valley

Tommaso

The Italian Dominican theologian, philosopher and poet *Tommaso Campanella* was born on this day in 1568. He took the name Tommaso in honour of Thomas Aquinas when he became a monk at the age of 14. He wrote many books, the best known being *The City of the Sun* (1602).

Meaning twin

Dweezil

The US heavy metal guitarist and son of Frank Zappa, *Dweezil Zappa* was born on 5 September 1969. Frank Zappa justified giving his children odd names by saying that it would be their last names that would get them into trouble, not their first names.

Meaning pet name for mother Zappa's little toe

Raquel, Ray, Rahel, Rae

The actress *Raquel Welch* was born on 5 September 1940. She was born Jo Raquel Tejada in Chicago, Illinois. After appearing in films such as *Fantasic Voyage* (1966), her first starring role was in *Myra Breckinridge* (1970). She married three times and had two sons, Andre and Richard.

From Rachel, meaning innocent as a lamb

Benita, Benitia

Benita Ferrero-Waldner, the Austrian diplomat and politician, was born on 5 September 1948. She was Austria's minister for foreign affairs from 2000 to 2004, and she ran for the 2004 presidential election. In November 2004 she became Austria's European Commissioner.

Meaning blessed

Makena, Makalya

Makena Grace Burton, the daughter of Sheree Gustin and Steve Burton, was born on 5 September 2003. The US actor Steve Burton is best known for his role as Jason in the TV soap opera *General Hospital* (1963).

Meaning who is like God

Luella, Lue

The US actress *Luella Gear* was born on this day in 1897. She is best known for appearing in the popular TV sitcom *Joe and Mabel*, which ran from June to September in 1956.

Meaning beautiful light

SEPTEMBER

Yash

The Bollywood film producer *Yash Johar* was born on 6 September 1929. His Hindi films, including *Ka Ho Na Ho* (2003), usually have stories that revolve around Indian traditions and family values, although they are filmed in lavish sets and exotic locations.

Meaning victorious

Moses, Moe, Moise, Moss, Mosie, Mose

The German philosopher *Moses Mendelssohn* was born in Dessau on 6 September 1729. He is known as the father of the Jewish Enlightenment because he was the first Jew to bring secular culture to those living an Orthodox Jewish life.

Meaning saved from the water

Boris

The Russian mathematician *Boris Yakovlovich Bukreev* was born on 6 September 1859. He was a professor of mathematics at the University of Kiev in the Ukraine and worked in the areas of complex functions and different equations.

Meaning small

China, Chyna

The British writer *China Tom Miéville* was born on this day in 1972. He writes fantasy novels in the style known as weird fiction. His third novel, *The Scar*, was nominated for the 2003 Arthur C. Clarke and World Fantasy awards.

Meaning from China

Zadie, Zade

On this day in 2002 British author *Zadie Smith*'s successful novel *White Teeth* was first published in paperback. It was the winner of the Whitbread First Novel Award. The main character in the novel is mixed-race, like Zadie.

Meaning affluent

Bega, Bee

Today is the feast day of *St Bega*, who is believed to have lived in Cumbria, in the north-west of England, in the 7th century. She fled to England from Ireland and is said to have been blessed by St Aidan. She is venerated in Northumbria, and it is possible that the village of St Bees in Cumbria is named after her.

Meaning beautiful Berrigan

Justina

The US actress *Justina Machado* was born in Chicago on this day in 1972. She is best known for her role as Vanessa Diaz in the US TV series *Six Feet Under* (2001). Her films include *She's So Lovely* (1997), *Full Frontal* (2002) and *Torque* (2004), with Ice Cube.

Meaning fair, just

Ce Ce, Cece, Ce-ce

Ce Ce Peniston, the 1980s dance artist, was born in Dayton, Ohio, on 6 September 1969 and raised in Phoenix, Arizona. She is best known for her number one hits 'Finally' (1991) and 'We Got a Love Thang' (1992).

Meaning unseeing

Benmont

Benmont Tench, the keyboard player for Tom Petty and the Heartbreakers and one of the most respected musicians in rock and roll, was born on 7 September 1953 in Gainesville, Florida. He has played sessions with many big stars, including the Rolling Stones, the Ramones and U2.

Meaning not known

Tristan, Tristin, Tristen, Drostan

The French playwright, novelist, journalist and lawyer *Tristan Bernard* was born Paul Bernard on 7 September 1866 in Besançon, Franche-Comté. His amusing and popular works included *L'Anglais tel qu'on le parle* (English as it is Spoken) (1899). A street in Paris is named after him.

Meaning the noisy one

Sonny

The leading jazz saxophonist of the 1950s, *Sonny Rollins* was born in New York on this day in 1930. He recorded with Miles Davis, Thelonious Monk, J.J. Johnson and Bud Powell, among other jazz greats. In 2004 he received a lifetime achievement Grammy award.

Meaning son of

Buddy, Budd

Buddy Holly, the US rock-and-roll pioneer, was born Charles Hardin Holley on 7 September 1936 in Lubbock, Texas. His songs, which included 'That'll be the Day', 'Not Fade Away' and 'Oh Boy', recorded with his band the Crickets, influenced many later singers and writers, including Lennon and McCartney.

Meaning welcome messenger

Anna, Ana, Annika, Anneka, Anula, Anusia, Anuska

The US painter known as Grandma Moses was born *Anna Mary Moses* in Greenwich, New York, on this day in 1880. She took up painting only in her 70s and became famous for her naïve style. At her first exhibition, held in 1938, she was 'discovered' by collector Louis J. Calder. She was received at the White House by President Truman, and in 1960 Nelson Rockefeller proclaimed this day Grandma Moses Day in New York State.

Meaning God has favoured me

Tatia

It is the birthday today of *Tatia Jane Starkey*, Ringo Starr's first grandchild, who was born on 7 September 1985. Her parents are the drummer Zak Starkey, who has played with the Who and Oasis, and his wife, Sarah.

From Tatiana, meaning silver-haired

Edith

British poet Dame *Edith Sitwell* was born in Scarborough, Yorkshire, on this day in 1887. Her innovative poetry was not always well received, and the first performance in 1922 of *Façade*, a setting by William Walton of several of her poems, was controversial.

Meaning fortunate

Grimonia, Germana

Today is the feast day of *St Grimonia of Picardy*. She was the daughter of an Irish pagan chief who lived in the 4th century. Refusing to marry, she ran away and lived in a forest in Laon, Picardy. Miracles occurred at the chapel built over her grave and the region became known as La Chapelle.

Meaning not known

Denys

The British architect *Denys Louis Lasdun* was born on this day in 1914. He designed many buildings in and around London, including the Royal College of Physicians (1960), and also worked on the University of East Anglia, Norwich (1962–8), and the Charles Wilson Building at the University of Leicester (1963).

Meaning lover of wine

Alfred

The French writer *Alfred Jarry* was born in Laval, Mayenne, on this day in 1873. In his first play, *Ubu roi* (1896), a parody of Shakespeare's *Macbeth*, Jarry attacked the bourgeoisie. He later wrote two sequels to this work, *Ubu enchaîné* (1900) and *Ubu cocu* (1944).

Meaning elvish counsel

Antonín, Antonino

The Czech composer *Antonín Leopold Dvořák* was born in Nelahozeves on 8 September 1841. He wrote nine symphonies, of which the best known and most popular is the last, known as 'From the New World'. His operas include *The Devil and Kate* (1899) and *Rusalka* (1900).

Meaning flower

Joaquin, Joachim

The US poet *Joaquin Miller* was born Cincinnatus Hiner Miller on this day in 1841/2. The confusion about his year of birth arose because his parents lost the family bible, and his father said he was born in 1841, but his mother insisted it was 1842. He was named after the bandit Joaquin Murietta.

Meaning judgement of the Lord

Aimee

The US singer and songwriter *Aimee Mann* was born in Richmond, Virginia, on 8 September 1960. In the 1980s she was in the band Til Tuesday before going solo. Her song 'Save Me', from her soundtrack for the film *Magnolia* (1999), was nominated for an Oscar.

Meaning beloved

Virna, Verna

The Italian actress *Virna Lisi* was born on this day in 1937. Her best-known performance was in *How to Murder Your Wife* (1965), in which she starred opposite Jack Lemmon. She was also in *Not with My Wife You Don't* (1966) with Tony Curtis.

Meaning alder tree

Franny, Frannie, Franne

The US actress *Franny Michel* was born on 8 September 1961. She played Patricia Apple in the TV series *Apple's Way* (1974), about a family from the small town of Appleton, Iowa, which moved to the big city.

Meaning of France

Pink

The US rhythm and blues artist *Pink* was born Alicia Moore in Doylestown, Pennsylvania, on this day in 1979. Her rapping hits include 'There You Go' and 'Most Girls'. She got her nickname because she blushed a bright pink whenever she was embarrassed.

Meaning pink

9 SEPTEMBER

Waite, Waitimu

US sportsman *Waite Hoyt* was born in Brooklyn, New York, on 9 September 1899. In the 1920s he was one of the dominant pitchers in baseball. He joined the Giants when he was 15 years old and rose to stardom with the New York Yankees. He was a broadcaster for the Cincinnati Reds for a period of 24 years.

Meaning born of the spear

Chaim, Chaika

The Israeli actor Topol was born *Chaim Topol* in Tel Aviv on 9 September 1935. He rose to stardom after appearing as Tevye the Milkman in *Fiddler on the Roof* (1971), for which he won a Golden Globe and was nominated for an Oscar.

Meaning life

Granville

The US journalist, novelist and critic *Granville Hicks* was born on this day in 1901 in Exeter, New Hampshire. He was one of the foremost Marxist literary critics in the USA at a time when fascism was on the rise. Many of his most memorable pieces appeared in the magazines the *New Leader* and the *Saturday Review*.

Meaning great village

Viking

Viking Eggeling was born on this day in 1880. The Swedish artist and film-maker lived in Switzerland from 1914 and became associated with the dada movement. With his cut-out piece *Symphonie diagonale* (1924), he became a pioneer of animation and film as art.

Meaning Viking

Macy, Maci, Macie

The US singer *Macy Gray* was born Natalie McIntyre on 6 September 1970. In 2001 her song 'I Try', from the album *On How Life Is*, became a big hit. It was nominated for song of the year and record of the year, and she won a Grammy for the best female pop vocal.

Meaning weapon

Inez, Ines

The singer and songwriter *Inez Foxx* was born on this day in 1942 in Greensboro, North Carolina. Inez and her brother, Charlie, wrote and recorded the classic 1960s song 'Mockingbird', their first single, which was arranged by Bert Keyes.

From Agnes, meaning pure, chaste

Lacey, Lacee, Laris

The US actress *Lacey Chabert* was born on 9 September 1982. She was Claudia Salinger in the US TV series *Party of Five*, which ran from 1994 to 2000, and she plays Bianca Montgomery in the TV soap *All My Children*.

From Larissa, meaning cheerful maiden

Osmanna

Today is the feast day of *St Osmanna*, who is also known as St Argariarga. A noblewoman, she was born in Ireland in the 7th century. She moved to Brittany and lived a simple, holy life there. She died at St Brieuc and was enshrined in the Church of St Denys, Paris.

Meaning protective heroine

Lorenzo, Lorenz

The Puerto Rican artist *Lorenzo Homar* was born to Spanish parents on 10 September 1913. The painter, engraver and printmaker moved to New York in 1928. His brightly coloured posters are on exhibition at the Metropolitan Museum of Art, New York.

Meaning laurel

Barriemore

The British drummer with the group Jethro Tull, *Barriemore Barlow* was born in Birmingham on this day in 1949. He began playing with the Blades when he was 14 years old, and the band developed into Jethro Tull, who had a chart-topping hit in 1972 with 'Living in the Past'.

Meaning not known

Colin

The British actor *Colin Firth* was born on this day in 1960. In 1995 he played Mr Darcy in the British TV adaptation of Jane Austen's *Pride and Prejudice*, and since then he has appeared as Mark Darcy in the two *Bridget Jones* movies (2001, 2004).

Meaning victorious, conqueror

Junious, Junius

The US footballer *Junious Buchanan*, known as Buck Buchanan, was born on this day in 1940 in Gainesville, Alabama. He played for the Kansas City Chiefs in 1963–75. Their leading defence player, he only missed one game in 13 years.

Meaning child

Elsa

The French fashion designer *Elsa Schiaparelli* was born in Rome on this day in 1890. She moved to Paris where her innovative and daring designs made her a household name. They often featured bright colours, especially shocking pink, and used traditional fabrics in new ways.

From Elizabeth, meaning consecrated to God

Yma, Ymma

The voice of the Incas, *Yma Sumac* was born in Peru on this day in 1922. She lived in a remote Andean village, but her singing voice was so remarkable that a delegation was sent from Lima, the capital, to hear her. She was taken for training and became world famous.

Meaning how beautiful

Ghada

The Syrian athlete *Ghada Shouaa* was born on this day in 1972. At the 1996 Olympic Games in Atlanta, Georgia, she won the gold medal for the heptathlon, a seven-event track and field marathon. She was the first and, to date, the only Syrian to win an Olympic gold.

Meaning graceful woman

Pulcheria

Today is the feast day of *St Pulcheria*, who was born in Constantinople (now Istanbul). She was the daughter of the Byzantine emperor Arcadius and his wife, Aelia Eudoxia, and she became regent for her young brother, Theodosius II. She commissioned many new churches in Constantinople, dedicated to the Virgin Mary.

Meaning beautiful

11 SEPTEMBER

Arvo

The composer *Arvo Pärt* was born in Paide in the Baltic State of Estonia on 11 September 1935. His music is experimental, and he has used the 12-tone scale pioneered by Schoenberg. Much of his later work consists of settings of scared texts in both Latin and Slavonic.

Meaning valuable

Gherman

Gherman Stepanovich Titov, the Russian cosmonaut and the second person to orbit the earth, was born on 11 September 1935. He made his historic flight in *Vostok* 2 when he was 26, and he remains the youngest person to fly in space.

Meaning not known

David, Dave, Dav, Davey, Davie, Davy, Davon, Davis, Dewi, Dafydd, Dai, Davidson

British writer D.H. Lawrence was born *David Herbert Lawrence* in Eastwood, Nottingham, on this day in 1885. The success of his first novel, *The White Peacock* (1911), enabled him to begin writing full time. *Women in Love* (1921) was filmed in 1969 by Ken Russell with Glenda Jackson, Jennie Linden, Alan Bates and Oliver Reed.

Meaning beloved

William, Bill

The US writer O. Henry was born *William Sydney Porter* on this day in 1862 in Greenboro, North Carolina. He began as a newspaper and magazine editor, but became successful when he moved to New York, where his short stories appeared in many magazines. His first collection, *Cabbages and Kings*, was published in 1904.

Meaning desiring to defend

Rosika

The Hungarian feminist, pacifist and writer *Rosika Schwimmer* was born on this day in 1877. She moved to the USA in 1914 and became a leading figure of the suffragette movement. In 1915 she was a founding member of the Woman's Peace Party, and was later vice-president of the Woman's International League for Peace and Freedom.

Meaning rose

Lola, Loletha, Loleta, Lollie, Lulita

The queen of Las Vegas, *Lola Falana* was born Loletha Elaine Falana on this day in 1942. She was discovered by Sammy Davis Jr, who cast her as the lead in *Golden Boy* on Broadway (1964). She gave up her glamorous life to serve the poor, becoming a poet and Catholic evangelist.

Meaning strong woman

Kristy

US actress *Kristy McNichol*, who played Buddy Lawrence in the TV series *Family* (1976–80), was born on 11 September 1962. She has also appeared in several movies, including *Little Darlings* (1980) and *The Pirate Movie* (1982). She won two Emmys for her role in *Family* (1976) and a Golden Globe for *Only When I Laugh* (1981).

From Christine, meaning follower of Christ

Jessica, Jess

The British writer *Jessica Lucy Mitford* was born in Burford, Oxfordshire, on this day in 1917. She moved to the USA in 1939, where she joined the Communist Party. Her life there provided material for many of her books, including *The American Way of Death* (1963) and *The Trial of Dr Spock* (1970). Her sisters were Unity, Diana and Nancy.

Meaning God's grace

Albizu

The Puerto Rican politician and lawyer Dr *Pedro Albizu Campos* was born on this day in 1891. He was the vice-president of Puerto Rico in 1927, and in the 1930s he was elected president of the Puerto Rican Nationalist Party.

Meaning not known

Stanislaw, Stanislaus, Stanislas, Stanislav

Stanislaw Lem, the science-fiction writer, was born in Lwow, Poland, on this day in 1921. The bestselling author of *Solaris* (1961) and *Imaginary Magnitude* (1973) studied medicine and worked as a car mechanic during the Second World War. His books have sold over 27 million copies.

Meaning stand of glory

Marcel, Marcello, Marcelo, Marsaill

On this day in 1940 the remarkable caves of Lascaux in France were discovered by a dog called Robot. A 17-year-old boy, *Marcel Ravidat*, and his three friends were out treasure hunting when his dog got stuck in a hole, the entrance to the caves.

Meaning war-like

Wilfredo

The Puerto Rican boxer *Wilfredo Benitez* was born on 12 September 1958. In 1976, when he was just 17 years old, he became the youngest boxing champion ever, when he took the world junior welterweight title, beating the Colombian Cervantes in a 15-round fight.

Meaning firm peace-maker

Victoria, Vicky, Tor

Today is the feast day of *St Victoria Fornari-Strata*. After being widowed she decided not to remarry when she had a vision of the Virgin Mary. She and ten friends set up a religious house, and they eventually became known as the Blue Nuns. The order spread from Italy to France.

Meaning victory

Rachel, Rachael, Rachelle, Rachele, Raquel, Rahel, Ray, Rae, Raoghnailt

British-born actress *Rachel Ward* was born on this day in 1957. She moved to the USA, originally as an actress, and has made several films, including *Sharkey's Machine* (1981) and *Wide Sargasso Sea* (1993). She also appeared in the TV films *The Thorn Birds* (1983) and *And the Sea will Tell* (1991). She is married to the actor Bryan Brown.

Meaning innocent as a lamb

Mylené, Malene

Mylené Farmer, the Canadian singer and actress, was born Mylene Gauthier on 12 September 1961. In France she is one of the most successful singers ever. Her song 'Desenchantée' was in the Guinness Book of World Records as the top-selling single of all time.

Meaning tower

Houghton, Hough

On 12 September 1928 *Katharine Houghton Hepburn* appeared on stage for the first time in a play called *The Czarina*. She went on to have a remarkable career in film, with 12 Oscar nominations for best actress; she won four Academy Awards, more than any other actress.

Meaning from the estate on the bluff

13 SEPTEMBER

Roald

The writer *Roald Dahl* was born in Wales on this day in 1916. His popular books for children include *Charlie and the Chocolate Factory* (1964) and *The BFG* (1982). He also wrote the screenplay for *Chitty Chitty Bang Bang* (1968). He was married to Hollywood actress Patricia Neal for 30 years, and they had five children.

Meaning famous ruler

Zac

Zac Starkey, the drummer with the Who, was born on this day in 1965. The son of Ringo Starr, Zac was taught the drums by the Who's original drummer, Keith Moon, who was his idol at the time. He continues to play as a session musician with many famous artists.

From Zachary, meaning Yahweh remembers

Goran

Goran Ivanisevic, the Croatian tennis player, was born in Split on 13 September 1971. After playing in four Wimbledon semi-finals, he won the tournament in 2001. At Barcelona in 1992 he was the first Olympic medal winner for the newly formed Croatia.

Meaning mountain man

Snavely

Milton Snavely Hershey was born in Pennsylvania on this day in 1857. The man whose name would become synonymous with chocolate in the USA started his company when he was in his teens. His early speciality was caramel, and he bought his first chocolate-making machine at the Chicago World's Fair in 1893.

Meaning not known

Claudette

The French actress *Claudette Colbert* was born Lily Claudette Chauchoin in Paris on 13 September 1903. She and her family moved to the USA when she was a teenager, and she soon began to appear on stage. She made 65 films and had many Broadway successes, becoming Hollywood's highest-paid actress in the late 1930s. She won an Oscar for her performance in *It Happened One Night* (1934).

Meaning lame one

Lutie, Lute

Lutie Stearns, the US librarian and reformer, was born on 13 September 1866. As well as campaigning for women's rights, she travelled throughout Wisconsin, establishing over 150 free public libraries and 1,400 travelling libraries.

Meaning instrument

Clara, Clarrie, Klara

Clara Josephine Schumann, the German composer and pianist, was born in Leipzig on this day in 1819. She had a reputation as a brilliant pianist when, against her father's wishes, she married the composer, Robert Schumann. She continued to compose and perform, even travelling to Russia, despite her husband's illness and death.

Meaning famous

Ren, Reena

Ren Farren Martinez, the daughter of US actor Adolfo A. Martinez and Leslie Bryans, was born on this day in 1993. Adolfo plays Cruz in the US TV soap *Santa Barbara*, and he and Leslie have two other children: Dakota Lee and Devon Makens.

Meaning song

Clayton

TV's Lone Ranger, *Clayton Moore* was born on this day in 1914. He will be forever remembered as the masked figure in the white hat, galloping along on his white horse and calling out his catchphrase, 'Hi Yo Silver!', in the popular 1950s western series.

Meaning clay settlement

Ivan

The Russian scientist *Ivan Petrovich Pavlov* was born on this day in 1849. He won the Nobel Prize for physiology or medicine in 1904 for his series of experiments with dogs, in which he measured and analysed their 'conditioned reflexes'.

From John, meaning God has shown me favour

Lehman, Lomman, Loman

US composer and author *Lehman Engel* was born in Jackson, Mississippi, on this day in 1910. The founder of the BMI Musical Theatre Workshop, he was also a conductor and the greatest music teacher on Broadway. His vast library is preserved as the Lehman Engel Collection.

Meaning little bare one.

Winfield, Wynfield

On this day in 1847 US soldier *Winfield Scott* captured Mexico City. The diplomat and presidential candidate, who was nicknamed Old Fuss and Feathers, was ranked as one of the best US generals of his time. As military commander of Mexico City, he was held in high esteem by Mexicans and Americans alike.

Meaning from a friend's field

Mercy

Mercy Otis Warren, the US poet, historian and feminist, was born in 1728 in Barnstable, Massachusetts. Her play *The Adulateur* (1773) was a political satire, and she also wrote poetry, collected as *Poems Dramatic and Miscellaneous* (1790), and non-fiction, including *History of the Rise, Progress and Termination of the American Revolution* (1805).

Meaning mercy

Santa, Sanita

In Latvia today is the name day for *Santa*. Everyone called Santa will receive small gifts and bunches of flowers from their friends and relatives. The name is the female version of the Italian Santo, which comes from the Latin Sanctius, which, in turn, comes from *sanctus*.

Meaning saintly, holy

Ronette, Ronnette

On this day in 1963 the Ronettes released a single called 'Be My Baby'. It came from the album *Presenting the Fabulous Ronnettes* (1963). It was a big hit, reaching number two in the US chart and number four in the UK chart. The group's lead singer, Veronica Bennett, later married Phil Spector, who had produced their record.

Meaning mighty and powerful ruler

Zoe

The Australian actress *Zoe Ada Caldwell* was born in Melbourne on this day in 1934. She has appeared in theatres around the world, making her debut in New York in 1965 in John Whiting's play *The Devils*. She has since moved on to directing plays as well as acting in them.

Meaning life

15 SEPTEMBER

Snooky

US jazz blues harpist *Snooky Pryor* was born in Lambert, Mississippi, on 15 September 1921. He made his first record in 1948, the classic 'Telephone Blues'. He made a comeback in 1987 with the award-winning 'Back to the Country'.

Meaning not known

Gaylord, Gayelord

The US baseball player *Gaylord Perry* was born on this day in 1938 in Williamston, North Carolina. The five-time All Star was, with his brother Jim, the second top-winning brother combination in baseball history.

Meaning cheerful, happy

Harry

Prince Harry, the younger son of Charles, Prince of Wales, and Princess Diana, was born Henry Charles Albert David Mountbatten-Windsor on this day in 1984. Having attended school at Eton, he is destined for a career in the armed services.

Meaning army commander

Adolfo, Adolpho, Adolphe, Adolfus, Ad, Dolph, Dolf

The Argentine writer *Adolfo Bioy Casares* was born in Buenos Aires on this day in 1914. A friend of, and collaborator with, Jorge Luis Borges, Bioy Casares's best-known novel is *La invención de Morel* (1940), a sci-fi terror fantasy, set on an island where all the characters are recordings.

Meaning noble wolf

Jessye, Jessie

Jessye Norman, the great US soprano, was born on 15 September 1945 in Augusta, Georgia. As well as singing in many operas and making concert performances around the world, she made a jazz album, *Jessye Norman Sings Michel Legrand*, in 2004, and sang in the premiere of Judith Weir's *woman.life.song* in 2000.

Meaning God's grace

Wendie

The US actress *Wendie Jo Sperber* was born on this day in 1962 in Hollywood. An early success was her role as Rosie Petrofsky, the Beatles fan, in *I Wanna Hold Your Hand* (1978). She also appeared in the first and third *Back to the Future* movies (1985, 1990).

From Wanda, meaning wanderer

Fay, Fae, Faye, Fayette, Fayina

The actress *Fay Wray* was born Vina Fay Wray in Cardston, Canada, on 15 September 1907 and brought up in the USA. She appeared in more than 100 films, but is best remembered as the girl held at the top of the Empire State Building by an enormous gorilla in *King Kong* (1933).

Meaning raven, fairy-like

Tawny, Tawnie, Tawnee

Tawny Schneider was born Tawny Elaine Godin on this day in 1956. She was Miss America in 1976 and went on to become an actress. She was married to the actor John Schneider.

Meaning light brown

Elgin

The US basketball player *Elgin Baylor* was born on this day in 1934. Famous for his extraordinary grace and acrobatic skills, he played professional basketball for 14 years for the Minneapolis Lakers. He was named rookie of the year in 1959.

Meaning earl of Bruce, Scotland

Morgan, Morgen, Morganica, Morganne

The US actor *Morgan Woodward* was born on 16 September 1925. He got his break with in the 1950s with Disney, and then appeared as Shotgun Gibbs in TV's *The Life and Legend of Wyatt Earp* (1956–62). He was a regular guest star on *Gunsmoke* (1955–75) and *Wagon Train* (1957–65), played the role of Punk Anderson in *Dallas* in the 1973 and starred in many films.

Meaning white sea

Breyten, Breyton

Breyten Breytenbach, the South African writer and painter, was born on this day in 1939. During the 1960s he actively campaigned against apartheid and, after being imprisoned, was exiled to France. He writes in English and Afrikaans, and has had exhibitions of his artwork all over the world.

Meaning Bradan's town

Ninian

Today is the feast day of St Ninian, who is credited with building the first Christian foundation in Britain. This was the White House (Candida Casa) at Whithorn, Galloway, which was dedicated by St Ninian to his friend St Martin of Tours. The saint travelled tirelessly among the southern Picts and was responsible for converting the Welsh.

Meaning not known

Lauren, Lalurena, Laurene, Laurentia

The US actress *Lauren Bacall* was born on 16 September 1924. The first film in which she appeared with Humphrey Bogart was *To Have and Have Not* (1944). She had two children with Bogart, Stephen and Leslie, and one, Sam, with her second husband, Jason Robards.

Meaning laurel wreath

Yolandita

The Puerto Rican singer and actress *Yolandita Monge* was born on this day in 1955. Her single 'Close Your Eyes' (1975) was a hit across South America, and she became an international star in the 1980s with her album *Moonlight*.

Meaning violet

Elisa, Eliza, Lize, Liza, Liz, Lizzy, Lizzie, Elissa

The US artist *Elisa Nadzeija* was born on 16 September 1962. She lets natural forms from nature emerge with as little intellectual interference as possible and then works on the result. She doesn't name her works, leaving the viewer more freedom for interpretation.

From Elizabeth, meaning consecrated to God

Ludmilla, Ludmila

Today is the feast day of St *Ludmilla*. The wife of Borivoy, first Christian duke of Bohemia, Ludmilla lived in the late 9th century. During the regency of her grandson, Wenceslas (of the Christmas carol), Ludmilla was murdered by the pagan queen mother, but when Wenceslas assumed power he promoted Christianity throughout his realm and honoured his grandmother.

Meaning beloved of the people

17 SEPTEMBER

Stirling, Sterling

Stirling Moss, the British Formula One driver, was born in London on 17 September 1929. He came second in the Formula One world championship from 1955 to 1958, and he continues to compete in historic car races.

Meaning good, honest, worthy

Fee

Today is the birthday of *Fee Waybill* of the 1970s US punk band the Tubes. He was born on 17 September 1950. The Tubes were famous for their outrageous costumes with exaggeratedly high platform boots.

Meaning raven

Junius

Sri Lanka politician *Junius Richard Jayawardene* was born in Colombo on this day in 1906. He became his country's first president in 1978 and embarked on a policy of introducing free-market economics. It was during his presidency that disagreements between Tamil separatists and the native Sinhalese began to surface.

Meaning not known

Sil

The US tenor sax player *Sil Austin* was born on 17 September 1929. He had a successful band in the 1950s and recorded over 30 albums, with famous hits such as 'Slow Walk', 'Ping Pong' and, his signature tune, 'Danny Boy'.

From Silas, meaning from the forest

Cassandra, Cassandre, Casondra, Cass, Cassie, Kassandra

The US actress *Cassandra Peterson*, better known as Elvira, Mistress of the Dark, was born on this day in 1949. Elvira, her horror movie host, was nationally syndicated in the 1980s. Her album, *Elvira's Monster Hits* (1995), spawned the singles 'Monster Rap' and 'Haunted House'.

Meaning shining on mankind

Anastacia, Anastasha, Anastasia

The US pop star *Anastacia* was born in Chicago on 17 September 1973. Her first album, entitled *Not That Kind* (2000), was an international success, as was her first single, 'I'm Out of Love'. She made her 2004 hit album *Anastacia* with Dave Stewart of Eurythmics.

Meaning awakening, resurrection

Hildegard, Hildegarde

Today is the feast day of *St Hildegard of Bingen*. She entered a Benedictine convent and soon became abbess. Although her health was always poor, she lived to be 80 years old. She claimed to have visions and sometimes said she could foresee the future. She is largely remembered today for her music.

Meaning war-like

Samantha, Samanta

On this day in 1964 the first episode of *Bewitched* was shown on ABC TV in the USA. The much-loved series starred Elizabeth Montgomery as the suburban witch Samantha, married to mortal Darrin, who was always feuding with her witch mother, Endora.

Meaning guarded by God, listener

Lance, Lancelot, Lancey, Launcelot, Launce

Lance Armstrong was born on this day in 1971. The inspirational US cyclist recovered from cancer and went on to win the Tour de France a record six consecutive times between 1999 and 2004. His girlfriend is the singer Sheryl Crow.

Meaning attendant of the spear

Rossano

The Italian actor and director *Rossano Brazzi* was born on this day in 1916. Before his international success in the film classics *Three Coins in the Fountain* (1954) and *South Pacific* (1958), he was already a well-known star of stage and screen back home in Italy.

Meaning from the peninsula, horse

Dee Dee, Didi

Dee Dee Ramone was born Douglas Colvin on this day in 1952. The Ramones, formed in 1974, are known as the first punk band. A residency in New York's CBGB earned them a cult following, and they became the inspiration for the punk rock revolution that was to follow two years later.

Meaning people's warrior

Samuel, Sam, Sammy

The English writer and lexicographer Dr *Samuel Johnson* was born in Lichfield, Staffordshire, on this day in 1709. His life's work was his *Dictionary of the English Language*, which was published in 1755. He founded the Literary Club in London in 1764 with fellow writers Edmund Burke and Oliver Goldsmith. His biography was written by his friend James Boswell.

Meaning asked of God

Greta, Grete, Gretta, Griet

The Swedish actress and icon *Greta Garbo* was born Greta Lovisa Gustafsson on this day in 1905. Her first roles were in silent movies in the 1920s, and she was one of the few actresses to make a successful transition to the talkies. One of her best performances was in *Camille* (1937).

From Margaret, meaning pearl

Shabana, Shabina, Shaba

The Indian actress *Shabana Azmi* was born on 18 September 1950 in New Delhi, India. The daughter of the Urdu poet Kaify Azmi, she has starred in the films *Amar Akbar Anthony* (1977), *Makdee* (2002) and *Tehzeeb* (2003).

Meaning rose

Grayson

The US actress *Grayson Hall* was born in Philadelphia, Pennsylvania, on 18 September 1923. She is best known for her role as Dr Julia Hoffman in the long-running TV series *Dark Shadows*; she played the role from 1967 to 1971.

Meaning son of bailiff

Jada

The US actress and model *Jada Pinkett Smith* was born in Baltimore, Maryland, on this day in 1971. Her film performances include *Collateral* (2004), *The Matrix Revolutions* (2003) and *The Matrix Reloaded* (2003).

Meaning daughter

19

Lol, Lolonyo

British singer *Lol Crème* was born in Manchester on 19 September 1947. As a member of 10cc he had hits including 'I'm Not in Love' and 'Life is a Minestrone' (both 1975). He and Kevin Godley subsequently left the band and formed their own group, Godley and Crème.

Meaning love is beautiful

Basil, Basile, Basileus, Base

A TV classic was born on this day in 1975 when the first episode of *Fawlty Towers* was shown in Britain. Written by and starring John Cleese as *Basil Fawlty* and his then wife Connie Booth as the maid, the whole series is regarded as the best of comedic genius.

Meaning king

Mika, Mikal, Mikali

The Finnish novelist *Mika Tiomi Waltari* was born on this day in 1908. He is famous for his historical novels, especially *The Egyptian* (1945), which was made into a Hollywood film in 1954. The novels he has penned, totalling some 29, have been translated into more than 30 languages.

From Michael, meaning like the Lord

Januarius, Jenaro, Genaro, Jennaro, Gennaro, Janus

Today is the feast day of *St Januarius of Benevento*, who lived in the 4th century. A special miracle associated with him concerns a small phial of his blood, which, legend recounts, stopped the eruptions of Mount Vesuvius. When it is put in front of a statue of Januarius it bubbles.

Meaning of Janus

Twiggy

The model, actress and singer *Twiggy* was born Lesley Hornby in Neasden, London, on this day in 1949. After her successful modelling career, her first big acting role was the lead in Ken Russell's film *The Boyfriend* (1971), since when she has had many other successes.

Meaning skinny

Soledad

The US TV news anchor *Soledad O'Brien* was born on this day in 1966. She studied at Harvard and began her career at Boston's KISS-FM. She was the only journalist allowed to travel to Moscow with Laura Bush on her 2003 trip.

Meaning solitude

Lurleen, Lurline, Lurlina

Lurleen Wallace, the first woman governor of Alabama, was born in Tuscaloosa on this day in 1926. She was elected in November 1966, running as her husband's surrogate. Her husband, the popular George Wallace, was not allowed to succeed himself at the time.

Meaning temptress

Cass, Cassia

Mama Cass Elliot, vocalist with the US band the Mamas and the Papas, was born on 19 September 1943 in Baltimore, Maryland. The group's hits, which helped define the era of the 1960s, include 'California Dreamin'' and 'Monday, Monday'. Mama Cass also had a huge solo hit with 'Dream a Little Dream'.

From Cassandra, meaning prophetess ignored by men

Upton

The US socialist author and journalist *Upton Beall Sinclair* was born on this day in 1878. His novel *The Jungle* (1906), about the meat-packing industry, caused such a public outcry that it led to the Meat Inspection Act of 1906. He ran for governor of California twice.

Meaning upper town

Leland, Leyland

The US child actor of the silent screen, *Leland Benham* was born on this day in 1905. He was the son of debonair actor Harry Benham and actress Ethyle Cooke. With his parents and his sister, Dorothy, Leland appeared in the pioneering Thanhouser Company movies.

Meaning residence

Eustace, Eustis, Eustazio

Today is the feast day of *St Eustace*. He was a powerful Roman general who, while out hunting, had a vision of a stag with a crucifix between its antlers and was converted to Christianity. He is the patron saint of huntsmen, and his symbol is the stag with the cross.

Meaning fruitful

Zeke

Zeke Bonura was born Zeke Henry John Bonura on 20 September 1908. The US baseball player played for the Chicago Cubs, the New York Giants, the Washington Nationals as well as the Chicago White Sox.

Meaning strength of God

Gogi

The 1950s US singing star *Gogi Grant* was born Myrtle Audrey Arinsberg on this day in 1924. *Billboard* magazine voted her the most popular female vocalist of 1956. Her hits included 'Strange are the Ways of Love' (1958) and 'The Wayward Wind' (1956).

Meaning meat

Sugar

On this day in 1969 *Sugar Sugar* by the Archies hit the number one slot in the US charts. The Archies was a bubblegum band based on the Archies comic-book cartoon show. The lead singer of the famous track, which became Record of the Year in the US, was Ron Dante.

Meaning sugar, sweet

Asia, Asija

The Italian actress *Asia Argento* was born in Rome on this day in 1975. Her full name is Asia Aria Anna Maria Vittoria Rossa Argento. In 1989 she won the Ciah, the Italian equivalent of a Golden Globe, for her leading role in the film *Zoo*. She has a daughter, Anna Lou.

Meaning east

Thursday

On this day in 1999 the song *Thursday's Child* was released as a single. It was the first single to be taken from David Bowie's album *Hours* and was supposedly based on the old nursery rhyme 'Thursday's child has far to go, Friday's child...'. Bowie himself was born on a Wednesday.

Meaning born on Thursday

21 SEPTEMBER

Aristotle, Ari

The Greek shipping magnate *Aristotle Onassis* was born on this day in 1906 in Smyrna (now Izmir, Turkey). Besides his involvement in shipping, he started Olympic Airways in 1957. He had a well-publicized affair with the opera singer Maria Callas and married Jacqueline Kennedy.

Meaning the best

Matthew, Matt

Today is the feast day of *St Matthew*. Originally a tax collector, he was called by Christ to be one of the apostles. From the earliest times the authorship of the first Gospel was ascribed to him, and it is believed that he was martyred in Ethiopia or Persia.

Meaning gift of God

Fazlur

Fazlur Rahman Malik, who was born on 21 September 1919, was a well-known and highly respected Muslim scholar and author of several publications on Islam. He was born in Hazara, in what is now Pakistan. He developed the Near Eastern Studies programme at Chicago University.

Meaning not known

Luke, Loukas

The US actor *Luke Wilson* was born on 21 September 1971. His films have included *Charlie's Angels* (2000), *Old School* (2003) and *Anchorman* (2004). The younger brother of Owen Wilson, he has been romantically linked with Drew Barrymore and Gwyneth Paltrow.

Meaning from Luciana

Suzanne, Susanna, Sousanna

The poet, singer, songwriter, author and Buddhist monk Leonard Cohen was born on 21 September 1934 in Montreal, Canada. One of his best-known songs, 'Suzanne', comes from his first album *The Songs of Leonard Cohen* (1967). It was also a hit for Judy Collins.

Meaning lily, rose

Fannie

US comedienne *Fannie Flagg* was borne on 21 September 1944. She wrote the Oscar-nominated *Fried Green Tomatoes at the Whistle Stop Café*. She was a TV anchor and actress before she became a writer, appearing in the film *Grease* (1978) as well as many others.

Meaning free

Ricki, Riki, Rikki, Richelle, Ricielle, Ricca, Rika

Ricki Lake, the talk-show host and actress, was born on this day in 1968. She hosted her own talk show from 1993 until 2004, working with ordinary members of the public rather than celebrities. She has appeared in a number of films, including *Hairspray* (1988) and *Cecil B. Demented* (2000).

Meaning hard ruler

Sigrid, Sigrath, Sigurd, Sigwald

US actress *Sigrid Valdis* was born on 21 September 1935. She is best remembered for the TV series *Hogan's Heroes* (1965–71), in which she played Colonel Klink's secretary Fraulein Hilda. In real life she married the star of the show, Bob Crane.

Meaning winning adviser

Ronaldo, Ronaldinho

The Brazilian soccer player *Ronaldo Luiz Nazario de Lima* was born on this day in 1976. Known the world over as Ronaldo, he is considered one of the best strikers in the game's history. He was named the world's best player in 1996 and 1997.

Meaning rules with counsel

Dannie

Dannie Abse, the Welsh poet and doctor, was born on this day in Cardiff in 1923. His work as a doctor and his Jewish and Welsh heritages are themes for his work. He has published numerous works and won the Cholmondeley Award in 1985.

Meaning God is my judge

Sunday, Sunny, Sun

The Nigerian music star *King Sunny Ade* was born Sunday Adeniyi on this day in 1946. The Grammy-nominated performer is known as the African Bob Marley. He is one of the most powerful people in his home country, where he is known as the minister of enjoyment.

Meaning born on Sunday

Lute, Lantos

The basketball coach *Lute Olsen* was born on 22 September 1934. A top coach for four decades, Lute is one of just 38 head coaches who has won over 600 games, and he holds the best winning percentage in the USA over 15 seasons.

Meaning lutenist

Christabel, Christa

The suffragette activist Dame *Christabel Harriette Pankhurst* was born on this day in 1880. Arrested for calling for votes for women at a Liberal Party meeting, she went to jail rather than pay the fine, gaining huge publicity. She later moved to the USA and became an evangelist.

Meaning beautiful follower of Christ

Rosamunde, Rosamunda

The British novelist *Rosamunde Pilcher* was born on this day in 1924. Her novels, which include worldwide bestsellers *The Shell Seekers* (1987) and *Coming Home* (1996), contain vivid descriptions of some of the most beautiful landscapes of the British Isles.

Meaning famous defender

Emeline, Emelina, Emeleen, Emeleena

Emeline Horton Cleveland, the distinguished US physician and college professor, was born on this day in 1829. The first woman recorded to perform major surgery, she was the most respected female physician of her time, gaining entry to several all-male medical societies.

Meaning industrious

Freia, Freya

On 22 September 1869 the first performance of Richard Wagner's opera *Das Rheingold* (The Rhine Gold) was given in Munich; it is the prologue to his Ring cycle. In one element of the plot, Wotan has promised to give *Freia*, the goddess of love and eternal youth, to the giants who have built Valhalla for him. If he does so, the gods will age and die.

Meaning lady, mistress

23 SEPTEMBER

Constantius, Constantinus, Constantios, Conus, Constantinianus, Constantino

Today is the feast day of *St Constantius*, a layman who cleaned and lit the lamps of St Stephen's Church, Anona, in Italy. Known for his humility and holiness, when he was once ridiculed he hugged his accuser and thanked him for pointing out his faults.

Meaning firm, unwavering

Walter, Walters, Walther, Wally, Wal, Walt, Walterpierce

The US journalist and political commentator *Walter Lippmann* was born on this day in 1889. One of the most influential thinkers of his time, he was the adviser to President Woodrow Wilson during the First World War. He coined the phrase the Cold War in his 1947 book of the same title.

Meaning mighty warrior

Octavius

Gaius Octavius Augustus Caesar, the first Roman emperor, was born on this day in 63BC. Heir to his great-uncle Julius Caesar, when Julius was murdered, he changed his name to Gaius Julius Caesar Octavianus. He was a brilliant politician and took a firm hold on Rome.

Meaning eighth

Kahori, Kaori

The Japanese actor *Kahori Fujii* was born in Oita, Japan, on 23 September 1965. His best-known role is as Yoshimi Kitada in the Japanese movies *Ju-on* and *Ju-on II* (2000).

Meaning add a man's strength

Chiyoko

Pat Chiyoko Suzuki, the US actress and singer, was born on 23 September 1931. Discovered by Bing Crosby, in 1957 she recorded her first album, *The Many Faces of Pat Suzuki*. She starred in the Broadway musical *The Flower Drum Song*, popularizing the song 'I Enjoy Being a Girl'.

Meaning child of a thousand generations

Lita

Lita Ford, the heavy metal guitarist known as the queen of noise, was born in London in 1958. After playing in the Runaways, she went solo, has recorded six solo albums and has been nominated for a Grammy.

Meaning luminous, white

Emmuska

Baroness *Emmuska Orczy* was born Emma Magdalena Rosalia Maria Josefa Barbara Orczy in Hungary on this day in 1865. She was an accomplished novelist, artist and playwright, and is best known for her adventure romance *The Scarlet Pimpernel* (1905), which she followed with *The Elusive Pimpernel* in 1908.

Meaning not known

Cherie

Cherie Booth Blair was born on this day in 1954. The wife of British prime minister Tony Blair is also a lawyer. She studied at the London School of Economics, where she was, and still is, the only student to gain a law degree with a first in every subject. She also succeeded in coming top of her year in the Bar exams.

Meaning beloved

Gordon, Gorden, Gordan, Gordy, Gordie

The US actor *Gordon Clapp*, who plays Detective Greg Medavoy in US TV's *NYPD Blue*, was born on this day in 1948. He is married to Deborah Taylor, who plays Marie Medavoy in the same show. They have a son called William.

Meaning from the cornered hill

Kermit

On this day in 1936 the great puppeteer Jim Henson was born in Greenville, Mississippi. *Kermit the Frog* of the Muppets was his signature character. The TV shows and films appealed to adults as well as children and spawned the children's TV classic *Sesame Street*.

Meaning freeman

Francis

US author *Francis Scott Key Fitzgerald* was born on this day in 1896. He became known as the chronicler of the Jazz Age in his novels *This Side of Paradise* (1920), *The Beautiful and the Damned* (1922) and *The Great Gatsby* (1925). He was also a Hollywood screenwriter.

Meaning free man

Girolamo, Girolimo

Girolamo Cardano was born on this day in 1501 in Pavia, Italy. A respected doctor, a successful gambler, a pioneering mathematician and a sought-after astrologer, he wrote prolifically, publishing two encyclopaedias of natural science and many mathematical papers.

Meaning holy name

Linda, Lind, Lindie, Lynda, Lynd, Lyndy

Linda McCartney was born Linda Eastman in Scarsdale, New York, on this day in 1941. An established photographer when she met Paul McCartney in 1967, she ran a vegetarian food business, played keyboards in Wings and had four children: Heather, Stella, Mary and James.

Meaning pretty one

Nia

The Canadian actress *Nia Vardalos* was born on 24 September 1962 in Winnipeg, Manitoba. She is also a screenwriter and producer, her best-known screenwriting success being *My Big Fat Greek Wedding* (2002).

Meaning purpose

Mikeli, Mikesha, Mikela

Today, 24 September, is the second day of *Mikeli*, an ancient Latvian festival held for three days during the *dzelzs denela* (week of iron). On this day there were feasts and parties, and the third day was the only day of the year on which men could propose to their girlfriends.

Meaning who is like God

Fern

US actress *Fern Barry* was born on 24 September 1900. She was a film and TV actress through the 1930s to the 1960s, appearing in many episodes of *Perry Mason* and *Wagon Train*.

Meaning fern

Aldo, Aldis

The US actor *Aldo Ray* was born on this day in 1926. After his debut in *Saturday's Hero* (1951), he appeared in many features, including *Battle Cry* (1955), *Let's Do it Again* (1953), *We're No Angels* (1955) and *The Naked and the Dead* (1958).

Meaning old and wise

Hammer

The founding president of Nauru, an island in the south-west Pacific, *Hammer DeRoburt* was born on 25 September 1922. Elected head chief in 1955, he negotiated with the Australian government and led the country to independence in 1968. He stayed in power almost continually until 1989.

Meaning hammer

Onnie

Onnie McIntyre, the Scottish rhythm guitarist with the jazz funk group the Average White Band, was born on 25 September 1945 in Lennoxtown. The Average White Band had a big hit in the 1970s with their instrumental 'Picking up the Pieces'.

From Lonnie, meaning noble and ready

Sergius, Sergiu

Today is the feast day of *St Sergius of Radonezh*, who lived in Russia in the early 14th century. He became a hermit, and soon other hermits joined him, developing a monastery, whose reputation spread throughout Russia.

Meaning servant

Vinnie

Vinnie Ream, the first woman to be commissioned by the US government to make a statue, was born on this day in 1847. The sculpture is of Abraham Lincoln at the Capitol Rotunda. She was just 18 years old. The town Vinita, Oklahoma, is named after her.

Meaning conqueror

Felicity, Felicita, Flick

The British actress *Felicity Kendall* was born on this day in 1946. The accomplished stage and film actress became famous in the 1970s for her role as Barbara Good in the hit UK TV sitcom *The Good Life*. Decades later, the show is still periodically repeated on primetime TV.

Meaning good fortune

Aida, Ada

US actress *Aida Turturro* was born on 25 September 1962. She plays Janice in the TV series *The Sopranos*, and she and her co-star James Gandolfini have also appeared together in the films *Angie* (1994) and *Fallen* (1998). They also performed together on Broadway in *A Streetcar Named Desire* (1947).

Meaning noble

Kayley and Ashlyn

The actresses *Kayley Yvonne Messick* and *Ashlyn Lexandra Messick* were born on 25 September 1993. The twins have already had a successful career, appearing together and individually. They appeared as babies in the TV movie *A Time to Heal* (1994).

Meaning battle maid and vision, dream

Cosmas

Today is the feast day of *St Cosmas* and St Damian. They were said to be twins who practised as physicians for no payment. They were martyred and buried in Cyus, Syria, after which miracles connected to their relics began to occur. They are the patron saints of chemists, midwives, the blind, surgeons and hairdressers.

Meaning order

Stearns

The poet T.S. Eliot was born *Thomas Stearns Eliot* on 26 September 1888 in St Louis, Missouri. He lived in London and worked in a bank while writing some of the most widely read poetry in the English language. His master works are *The Waste Land* (1922) and *The Four Quartets* (1943), and for the stage include *Murder in the Cathedral* (1935).

Meaning not known

Clip

Clip Payne, who was born on 26 September 1956, was the vocalist with Funkadelik. Together with the band the Parliaments, Funkadelik were responsible for the genre of music known as P-Funk, which put black rock music on the map. P-Funk stands for Pure Funk and Plainfield Funk.

Meaning attached

Manmohan, Manmathan, Manmath, Manmatha

The 13th prime minister of India *Manmohan Singh* was born on this day in 1932. A Sikh, he is India's first non-Hindu prime minister. He studied economics at Oxford and Cambridge, and his widely popular economic reforms rescued the country from potential bankruptcy.

Meaning handsome, loved

Serena

US tennis player *Serena Williams* was born on 26 September 1981 in Saginaw, Michigan. With her sister Venus she dominated women's world tennis for a period in the early 2000s and was ranked number one on many occasions.

Meaning serene

Carlene

The country singer *Carlene Carter* was born on this day in Madison County, Tennessee, in 1955. She is famously quoted as saying that she hoped she would be the woman who took the 'o' out of country music.

From Caroline, meaning free woman

Abbey, Abbie, Abby, Abbe, Abbas, Aby

The Beatles LP *Abbey Road* was released in the UK on this day in 1969. The last of their albums was recorded at EMI Studios, 3 Abbey Road, London. The cover features the four walking across a zebra crossing in the street, now a haunt of tourists.

Meaning joyous one

Lysette, Lizette, Lysetta, Lizetta

The British actress and producer *Lysette Anthony* was born Lysette Chodzko on 26 September 1963. Before she became an actress she was a model. Her first major role was in the TV serial *Oliver Twist* (1982), and since then she has been in many films, including Woody Allen's *Husbands and Wives* (1992).

From Elizabeth, meaning consecrated to God

Vincent, Vince

Today is the feast day of *St Vincent de Paul*, who became chaplain to Margaret of Valois. His move to Paris brought him into contact with Philip de Gondi, whose children he taught, and he used his society contacts to raise money to found hospitals for the poor. He lived to be 85 years old.

Meaning conquering

Wilford

The US character actor *Wilford Brimley* was born on this day in 1934 in Salt Lake City. He didn't become an actor until quite late in life, beginning as a rodeo rider. He has appeared in many films, including the lead in *Coccoon* (1985). He was Gus Witherspoon in TV's *Our House* (1986).

Meaning ford by the willows

Gaston

The French mathematician *Gaston Tarry* was born in Villefranche de Panat, Aveyron, on this day in 1843. His main achievement was confirming Leonard Euler's conjecture that two orthogonal Latin squares of order 6 did not exist.

Meaning from Gascony

Sture

The Swedish saxophonist and bass clarinettist *Sture Ericson* was born on this day in 1912. He was in the group Position Alpha from 1979 until 1995 and then formed the free improvisational band the Electrics with Axel Dorner.

Meaning contrary

Grazia

The Nobel Prize-winning author *Grazia Deledda* was born in Nouro, Sardinia, on 27 September 1871. She won the prize in 1926 for her many novels, including *Cenere* (Ashes) (1904) and *La madre* (The Mother) (1920), depicting life on the island of Sardinia with remarkable depth, sympathy and clarity.

Meaning grace

Avril

Avril Lavigne, the Canadian singer songwriter, was born on 27 September 1984. Her first album, *Let Go* (2002), took just six months to become quadruple platinum. It sold over 14 million worldwide and spawned five hit singles, including 'I'm with You' and 'Complicated'.

Meaning April

Sada, Saida

The US actress *Sada Thompson* was born in Des Moines on this day in 1929. A star of the Broadway stage, she also won a best actress Emmy for her role as the mother in the 1970s TV series *Family* and was nominated for her role as Carla's mother in *Cheers*.

Meaning pure

Minnie, Minta, Minda, Mindy

Minnie Vautrin was born on this day in 1886. The missionary and educator went to China when she was 26 years old and spent 30 years helping the poor. She helped thousands during the Japanese occupation, turning her school into a sanctuary for 10,000 women and children.

Meaning remembered with love

Avery

Avery Brundage, the US athlete, businessman, art collector and philanthropist, was born in Detroit on this day in 1909. He competed in the 1912 Olympic Games in the pentathlon and decathlon events, and he became president of the International Olympic Committee in 1952, a position he held until 1972.

Meaning elf ruler

Seymour

The supercomputer architect and founder of Cray Research, *Seymour R. Cray*, was born in Chippewa Falls, Wisconsin, on 28 September 1925. He worked on the ERA 1103, the first commercially successful scientific computer.

Meaning marsh near the sea

Prosper, Prospero, Prosperus

The French dramatist, historian and archaeologist *Prosper Mérimée* was born on this day in 1803. He was also a writer of short stories, and Bizet's opera *Carmen* is based on his 1846 book. He also became a senator and the inspector-general of historical monuments.

Meaning successful, fortunate

Merisi, Meris

One of the greatest painters of all time, *Michelangelo Merisi da Caravaggio* was born on 28 September 1573 in the town of Caravaggio, near Bergamo, Italy. Much of his work was controversial with his contemporaries, as he used models from the streets for biblical characters.

Meaning of the sea

Lata

Lata Mangeshkar, the most revered female singer in India, was born on this day in 1929. She and her sister, Asha Bhosle, are world famous as the queens of Bollywood. At a function in 1963 her singing moved the prime minister, Jawaharlal Nehru, to tears.

Meaning creeper plant

Brigitte

The French actress *Brigitte Bardot* was born on 28 September 1934 in Paris. She made her first film, *Le Trou normand* (Crazy for Love), in 1952 and became a sex symbol in 1956 with Roger Vadim's *Et Dieu créa la femme* (And God Created Woman). She became famous in later years for her passionate stand on animal rights. She has one son, Nicolas-Jacques Charrier.

From Bridget, meaning strong

Moon Unit

Moon Unit Zappa was born in New York City on this day in 1967. She sang on the song 'Valley Girl' by her father Frank Zappa, which was a Top 40 hit in the USA. She appeared in the TV sit-com *Normal Life* (1990) and in 2001 published a novel, *America, The Beautiful*.

Meaning one that orbits the moon

Lioba, Liobgotha

Today is the feast day of St Lioba, who was a Benedictine abbess and related to St Boniface. After training in Wimbourne, Dorset, she founded several monasteries in Germany. She became Abbess of Bischofheim Monastery in Mainz.

Meaning beloved

Nelson

Horatio Nelson, the British admiral and naval hero, was born in Burnham Thorpe, Norfolk, on 29 September 1758. For his heroism in the Napoleonic Wars, Nelson's Column was built in Trafalgar Square, where it is one of London's best-known landmarks.

Meaning son of a champion

Mackensie, Mackenna, Makenzie

Mackensie Crook, the British actor famous for his role as Gareth in the UK TV comedy *The Office* (2001), was born in this day in 1971. He started out as a stand-up comedian, but has since appeared in many feature films, including *The Merchant of Venice* (2004) and *Brothers Grimm* (2005).

Meaning son of wise leader

Jacopo

The great Italian Renaissance painter *Jacopo Robusti Tintoretto* was born, probably in Venice, on this day in 1518. He got the name Tintoretto because his father was a dyer. Tintoretto was assisted in his studio by his sons, Domenico and Marco, and his daughter Marietta.

Meaning supplanter

Lech

The Polish trade union leader, *Lech Walesea*, was born in Popowo on this day in 1943. The founder of Solidarity, the first independent trade union in the Soviet bloc, was the son of a carpenter, but he became president of Poland from 1990 to 1995. He married Danuta Walesowa and they have seven children.

Meaning forest spirit

Greer

The actress *Greer Garson* was born on this day in 1904. She was discovered in London by Louis B. Mayer who was on a talent-spotting trip, and she received an Oscar nomination for her first US film, *Goodbye Mr Chips* (1939). She won a best actress Oscar for *Mrs Miniver* (1942).

Meaning alert and watchful

Lila

Lila Grace, the daughter of UK supermodel Kate Moss, was born on 29 September 2002. Kate Moss, the face of Calvin Klein, began modelling when she was just 14 years old. Lila's father is the magazine publisher Jefferson Hack.

Meaning lily

Alouette, Alouetta, Aleta, Alitah, Aletah, Aleyta, Aleata

On this day in 1962 Canada launched her first satellite, which was named *Alouette*. Canada thus entered the space age and became the first nation outside the USA and Russia to design and build its own artificial earth satellite.

Meaning lark, winged wanderer

Jolie

Jolie Gabor, who was born in Hungary on this day in 1899, was the mother of Zsa-Zsa Gabor and her two actress sisters, Eva and Magda. She lived in California and became a celebrity in her own right. Jolie is a French name.

Meaning pretty

Bolan, Boylan

British singer *Marc Bolan* was born in London on this day in 1947. His first album with his band Tyrannosaurus Rex was called *My People Were Fair and Had Sky in Their Hair But Now They're Content to Wear Stars on Their Brows* (1968). In the 1970s he shortened the group's name to T. Rex and had a string of hits, including 'Ride a White Swan', 'Get it On' and 'Hot Love'.

Meaning from Mahon

Truman

The US novelist and man about town *Truman Capote* was born on this day in 1924 in New Orleans. His books include *Breakfast at Tiffany's* (1958) and *In Cold Blood* (1966), which was turned into a classic film of the same name in 1967.

Meaning trusty man, loyal man

Elie, Eliezer

Elie Wiesel was born on this day in 1928 in Sighet, Transylvania (now Romania). The professor, journalist and humanitarian, who survived both Auschwitz and Buchenwald, was awarded the Nobel Prize for peace in 1986. In addition, he has received over 100 honorary degrees. His memoir, *Night* (1958), was universally acclaimed.

From Eleanor, meaning light

Decimus

The British architect and garden designer *Decimus Burton* was born on this day in 1800. Famous for his designs of Hyde Park, the Palm and Temperate Houses at Kew Gardens and London Zoo, he also designed the grand façades of Tunbridge Wells and St Leonards on Sea.

Meaning tenth child

Cissy, Sissy

The US soul singer *Cissy Houston* was born on this day in 1933. She recorded the original version of 'Midnight Train to Georgia', which was later a hit for Gladys Knight. Cissy will always be best known as the mother of Whitney.

From Cicely, meaning patron saint of music

Rula

The actress *Rula Lenska* was born on this day in 1947 in St Neots, Cambridgeshire, to Polish parents. She rose to fame in Britain after her appearance in the 1970s TV serial *Rock Follies*. Her father was head of Radio Free Europe in Poland.

Meaning one who rules by right

Deborah, Debbie

The actress *Deborah Kerr* was born in Helensburgh, Strathclyde, on this day in 1921. She played typically 'English' roles until 1953, when she took the role of a nymphomaniac in *From Here to Eternity*. She starred in *The King and I* (1956) and *Separate Tables* (1958). In 1994 she received a special Oscar for her career achievements.

Meaning bee

Shanesia, Shane

The US actress *Shane Williams*, formerly known as Shanesia Davis-Williams, was born in Detroit on this day in 1966. She now lives in Chicago. The stage, film and TV actress was Marissa Clark in the TV series *Early Edition* (2004).

Meaning spirit

October

October

1 OCTOBER

Slapsie

The film actor and boxer *Slapsie Maxie Rosenbloom* was born in Harlem, New York City, on this day in 1903. He was light heavyweight world champion from 1932 to 1934 and appeared in many Hollywood movies in the 1930s.

Meaning not known

Youssou, Youssouf, Youssuf

The African music star *Youssou N'Dour* was born on this day in 1959. His music, which blends African traditional music with jazz, rock and reggae, has made him an international star. He works tirelessly for the well-being of Africa and is a UN food aid ambassador.

Meaning God will increase

Fletcher

US novelist and journalist *Fletcher Knebel* was born on 1 October in Dayton, Ohio. He wrote a number of novels to popular acclaim, including *Seven Days in May* (1988), but is best remembered for the following remark: 'smoking is one of the leading causes of statistics.'

Meaning maker of arrows

Dizzee, Dizzy, Dizzie

The British rap artist *Dizzee Rascal* was born in London on this day in 1985. His album *Boy in Da Corner* (2003) won the 2003 Mercury Music Prize for best album. At the age of 19 he was the youngest, and the first rapper, to receive the coveted award.

Meaning dizzy

Faith

The US writer *Faith Baldwin* was born on this day in 1893 in New Rochelle, New York. The successful novelist published over 85 romances over a period of 56 years. The story lines were usually of the boy-meets-girl kind, and the hero and heroine always got together in the end.

Meaning loyalty

Brie

The US actress *Brie Larson* was born on 1 October 1989. She became a star at the early age of 12 when she landed the role of Emily in the US TV series *Raising Dad* (2001).

Meaning region in France

Mariska

Mariska Veres, the lead vocalist with the Dutch 1960s band Shocking Blue, was born in The Hague, the Netherlands, on 1 October 1948. Her father was Hungarian and her mother was German. She is now a solo artist.

Meaning of the sea

Jurnee

The US child actress *Jurnee Smollett* was born on this day in 1986. Her first big film role was in *Eve's Bayou* (1997). She has also made regular appearances on TV, including *Selma, Lord, Selma* (1999) and *Wanda at Large* (2004).

Meaning not known

Sting

The British pop star and actor *Sting* was born Gordon Matthew Sumner on this day in 1951. He was the lead singer of the 1970s band the Police, who had many international hits, including 'Roxanne' and 'Every Breath She Takes'. He then became a successful solo artist. With his wife, Trude, he is an ecology activist.

Meaning spike of grain

Cordell

The US politician *Cordell Hull*, who was secretary of state under Franklin Delano Roosevelt, was born in Pickett County, Tennessee, on 2 October 1871. One of the founders and most robust supporters of the United Nations, he was awarded the Nobel Prize for peace in 1945.

Meaning rope maker

Groucho

The Marx brother with the moustache and the cigar, *Groucho* was born Julius Henry Marx on this day in 1890. Woody Allen called him a genius in the mould of Picasso and Stravinsky. With his brothers he made some of the finest comic films, including *Horse Feathers* (1933), *A Night at the Opera* (1935) and *A Day at the Races* (1937).

Meaning one with a grouch

Mohandas

Mohandas Gandhi, known as Mahatma, was born on this day in 1869. This remarkable man led India to independence from British rule without holding a political office or using physical force of any kind. Richard Attenborough's film *Ghandi* (1982), about his life, won nine Academy Awards.

Meaning not known

Lani, Lanny, Laina, Lane, Laney

The US actress *Lani O'Grady* was born on 2 October 1954 in Walnut Creek, California. She appeared on many TV shows in the 1970s and 1980s, including *Baby Blue Marine* (1976), *A Family Reunion* (1987) and *Eight is Enough* (1989).

Meaning noble woman

Tiffany, Tiphany, Tifanee, Tiffy, Tiffie, Tifany

The US singer *Tiffany* was born on this day in Norwalk, southern California, in 1971. She began her first album when she was just 13 years old. The result was two number one singles, 'I Think We're Alone Now' and 'Could've Been', and millions of records sold worldwide.

Meaning appearing to God

Ayumi, Ayu

Ayumi Hamasaki, known affectionately in Japan as Ayu, was born on this day in 1978. She is one of Japan's most successful pop stars and also one of the most prolific, having released 24 albums and 34 singles. She won the Japan Recording Award for three years running, the only artist to have ever done so.

Meaning walk on

Romina, Romola, Romona

The actress *Romina Power* was born on this day in 1951, the daughter of the actor Tyrone Power and Linda Christian. She starred in the film *Justine* (2002). Romina is married to Al Bano Carrisi, and they have four children: Ylena, Yari, Cristel and Romina Jolanda.

Meaning from Rome

Gore

The US writer *Gore Vidal* was born Eugene Luther Gore Vidal on this day in 1925. Gore is the surname of his maternal grandfather. He writes on political, historical and literary themes. His novel *Myra Breckinridge* (1968) was made into a film starring Raquel Welch in 1970.

Meaning triangular

Chubby

US singer *Chubby Checker* was born on this day in 1941. He is forever linked to his 1960s hit 'The Twist', which popularized the dance now synonymous with the era. He followed up with 'Let's Twist Again' and 'Slow Twistin''. He married Miss World 1962, Catharina Lodders.

Meaning chubby

Lindsey, Lindsay, Lindsie

Fleetwood Mac's guitarist and singer *Lindsey Buckingham* was born on this day in 1949. After he joined the band they released their classic album *Fleetwood Mac* (1975), also known as *The White Album*. It spawned three hits, 'Over My Head', 'Rhiannon' and 'Say You Love Me'.

Meaning Lincoln's marsh

Fulke, Fulk

Fulke Greville was born on 3 October 1554 in Warwickshire, in the Midlands of England. A politician and a writer, he was knighted by Queen Elizabeth I in 1597. His writing includes the sonnet cycle *Caelica* (1633) and *The Life of the Renowned Sir Philip Sidney* (1652).

Meaning people

Neve

Neve Campbell, the Canadian actress, was born on 3 October 1973 in Guelph, Ontario. Her first important acting role was as Julia Salinger in the TV drama *Party of Five* (1994–2000). She appeared in the three *Scream* movies (1996, 1997, 2000), and she produced, co-wrote and starred in *The Company* (2004).

Meaning radiant

Sonnet

Sonnet Noel Whitaker, the daughter of Forest Whitaker, was born on 3 October 1996. The US actor and movie director Forest and his wife, model Keisha Nash, also have a daughter called True Summer. Forest has a son from a previous relationship called Ocean.

Meaning poem

Elonora, Elona, Elon

Italian actress *Elonora Duse* was born on this day in 1858. She was the leading actress of her day in Italy and appeared in both London and New York. One of her great triumphs was in the Italian version of *La Dame aux camélias*, in which she took the part made famous by Sarah Bernhardt.

Meaning God loves me

Madlyn

Madlyn Rhue, the popular US character actress, was born on this day in 1934. She appeared on many TV shows in the 1950s, 1960s and 1970s, including *Days of Our Lives*, *Executive Suite* and *Bracken's World*.

Meaning tower of beauty

Alvin, Alwyn, Alvan, Alva, Aloin, Aluin, Aluino

Alvin Toffler, the US futurist author, was born on this day in 1928. His books take on the digital and corporate revolutions in contemporary society. Juan Atkins, one of the founders of techno music, got the name of his musical style from Toffler's phrase 'techno rebels'.

Meaning noble friend

Charlton, Carlton, Carleton

US actor *Charlton Heston* was born on 4 October 1924. He shot to international stardom after appearing as Moses in *The Ten Commandments* (1956), and he won a best actor Oscar for playing the title role in *Ben Hur* (1959).

Meaning Carl's town

Rutherford

Rutherford Birchard Hayes, the 19th US president, was born on this day in 1822. His election was the closest run in history: 4,036,000 for Rutherford and 4,300,000 for his Democratic opponent, Samuel J. Tilden. To win he got all the disputed electoral votes; if one had gone the other way he would have lost. He retired after a single term.

Meaning from the cattle ford

Buster

Buster Keaton, the US star of silent movies, was born on 4 October 1895. He was born in Piqua, Kansas, while his parents were with a travelling medicine show. His godfather, Harry Houdini, gave him his nickname. After he became famous Buster became a legitimate name.

Meaning breaker of things

Felicia, Feliciah, Feliciana, Felice, Felica

The US actress *Felicia Farr* was born on this day in 1932. She was discovered while waitressing in a Hollywood restaurant, and she went on to appear in many films, including *The Venetian Affair* (1967) and *Charley Varrick* (1973). In 1962 she married Jack Lemmon, and they had a daughter, Courtney Noel.

Meaning good fortune

Spring

On this day in 1954 the US comedienne *Spring Byington* made her TV debut in the series *December Bride*. She was already a big star of the movies, and in 1935 she appeared in eight films, including *Mutiny on the Bounty* (1935).

Meaning spring

Dahlia

On this day in 1926 the *dahlia* was designated the official flower of the city of San Francisco. All US cities have their special symbols and flags. San Francisco's flag is a phoenix rising from the ashes, its patron saint is St Francis and its musical instrument is the accordion.

Meaning flower

Seija, Saija, Saila, Saige

In Finland today is the name day today for *Seija*. It is a modern name, invented by Yrjo Karalis, the head of the national board of education, for his first daughter, born in 1917. He combined Seia, the name of a Roman god, with the word *seijas*, which means calm and serene.

Meaning beam of light

Monty, Monte

On this day in 1969 TV history was made when the first British broadcast of *Monty Python's Flying Circus* took place. The show, starring John Cleese, Michael Palin, Eric Idle, Terry Jones, Graham Chapman and the cartoons of Terry Gilliam, became an international phenomenon.

Meaning mountain hunter

Vaclav

The president of Czechoslovakia, later the Czech Republic, playwright and democratic hero, *Vaclav Havel*, was born on this day in 1936. He was one of the founders of the human rights group Charter 77 and in 1979 he was imprisoned for five years. He studied drama at evening classes and through a correspondence course.

Meaning more glory

Flann, Flannan

The Irish writer *Flann O'Brien* was born Brian O'Nolan on this day in 1911. The Joyce-inspired author's best-known novel is *At Swim Two Birds* (1939), in which the characters, all recycled as there are too many fictional characters already, are in hilarious conflict with the author.

Meaning red

Chester, Cheston

Chester Allen Arthur, the 21st US president from 1881 until 1885, was born on 5 October 1829 in Fairfield, Vermont. The Republican was very popular with the people and known for his smart appearance, which earned him the nickname the Gentleman Boss.

Meaning fortress, camp

Galla, Gallia

Today is the feast day of *St Galla of Rome*. She was the daughter of Symmachus the Younger, the Roman patrician consul, and lived in the 5th century. She founded a convent and a hospital, and it is said that she blessed some water and administered it to a deaf and mute girl who was consequently cured.

Meaning gutsy

Shell, Shella

Shell Kepler, the US soap actress, known to all as Amy Vining from the TV series *General Hospital* (1972), was born on this day in 1961. Shell decided to be an actress after she saw *The Wizard of Oz* when she was two years old.

Meaning shell, who is like God

Parminder, Parminda, Parmida

The actress *Parminder Nagra* was born on this day in 1975. She shot to fame as the soccer-playing British teenager in the film *Bend it Like Beckham* (2002) – she had never kicked a ball before taking on the starring role. She also plays Neela Rasgotra in TV's *ER*.

Meaning princess

Alberta, Albertha, Albertine, Albertina

Alberta Mary Bizeau-Weiss, the daughter of Roberta Bizeau-Weiss and soap opera star Roscoe Born, was born on 5 October 1997. Roberta Weiss played Caroline Morse in the film *Audition* (2004).

Meaning noble, bright

Thor, Thorin, Tor, Tyrus

The Norwegian explorer *Thor Heyerdahl* was born on this day in 1914. He sailed 6,920 kilometres (4,300 miles) from South America to the Taumomtu Islands in the wooden raft *Kon-Tiki*, proving that South Americans could have migrated in that direction. As a teenager he was scared of water.

Meaning God of thunder

Formosus, Formosius

On this day in 891 *Formosus* began his reign as the pope in Rome. He wasn't ambitious and clung to the altar of his church in Porto when it was time for him to go to Rome. He was a pope of the political persuasion, holding councils in Rome and encouraging them elsewhere.

Meaning good looking

Karol

The Polish composer and pianist *Karol Maciej Szymanowski* was born in Tymoszowka, in what is now the Ukraine, on this day in 1882. He wrote the ballet *Harnaise* (1923–31) and the operas *Hagith* (1912–13) and *King Roger* (1920–24). He also wrote piano music and songs, some based on texts by James Joyce.

Meaning man

Jacopo, Jacoup, Jacomus

On 6 October 1600 the earliest surviving opera received its premiere in Florence. *Euridice* was written by the Italian composer *Jacopo Peri*, often described as the inventor of opera. He wrote it in collaboration with another Jacopo, Florence's leading patron of music, Jacopo Corsi.

Meaning supplanter

Shana, Shanana, Shanara

The US news commentator and journalist *Shana Alexander* was born on this day in 1925. She presented the CBS show *60 Minutes* (1968) and wrote the book *Nutcracker, Money, Madness and Murder*, made into a film in 1987.

Meaning wise river

Britt, Britta

Britt Ekland, the Swedish actress, was born on this day in 1942. She was in the cult movie *The Wicker Man* (1973) and the Bond film *The Man with the Golden Gun* (1974). She was married to Peter Sellers, with whom she had her daughter, Victoria.

Meaning high goddess

Jenny, Jen

On this day in 1820 the Swedish soprano *Jenny Lind* was born in Stockholm. She became known as the Swedish nightingale, and appeared all over the world, including the USA and Cuba under the auspices of Phineas T. Barnum. The great composer Chopin heard her sing.

From Jennifer, meaning kinswoman

Marita, Maritza, Marith

On this day in 1985 the German athlete *Marita Koch* set the 400 metres women's record, running it in 47.6 seconds. She won 16 team and individual world records in outdoor events and 14 world records in indoor events.

Meaning bitter

Desmond, Desmund

Desmond Mpilo Tutu, the South African archbishop, was born in Klerksdorp on 7 October 1931. The man who played such a big part in bringing apartheid to an end has four children: Trevor Thamsanqua, Theresa Thandeka, Naomi Nontombi and Mpho Andrea.

Meaning sophisticated

Yo-Yo, Yo

The Chinese-American cellist *Yo-Yo Ma* was born in Paris on this day in 1955. One of the best-known and most widely respected contemporary cellists, he was a child prodigy, appearing on TV aged eight in a concert conducted by Leonard Bernstein. He has two children, Nicholas and Emily.

Meaning honest

Niels

The Danish mathematician *Niels Bohr* was born on 7 October 1885. A contemporary of Einstein, his work on quantum mechanics and atomic structures paved the way for quantum theory. He received the Nobel Prize for physics in 1922.

Meaning victorious people

Sherman

The poet and novelist *Sherman Alexie* was born on this day in 1966. He is a Spokane-Coeur d'Alene Indian and grew up on a reservation in Wellpinit, Washington. He was one of *Granta*'s best of young American novelists and has won many awards for his writing.

Meaning cutter of cloth

Charleszetta, Charleszita

Charleszetta Waddles, known as Mother Waddles, was born on 7 October 1912. She was a religious leader and writer who sold donated used cars to fund her Perpetual Mission, which fed the poor of the community. She was known as Detroit's Mother Teresa.

From Charles, meaning free man

Ludmilla, Ludmila

The Russian gymnast *Ludmilla Tourischeva* was born on this day in 1972. She dominated gymnastics from 1971 to 1974, winning nine Olympic medals and being crowned world champion four times. She is remembered for her particularly elegant style.

Meaning favour, grace

Melinda, Mel

The US actress *Melinda O Fee* was born on this day. She became famous in the 1960s playing Dr Kate Westin in the TV series *Days of Our Lives*. Throughout the 1980s she appeared in many TV dramas and the movie *A Nightmare on Elm Street Part 2: Freddy's Revenge* (1985).

Meaning dark beauty

Portia, Porcia, Porchia

On this day in 1940 the US radio soap opera *Portia Faces Life* was aired for the first time. The series, created by Mona Kent, was a popular and long-running show. It transferred to TV in 1954 and was shown every weekday for 15 minutes.

Meaning offering to God

Toru

The composer *Toru Takemitsu* was born in Tokyo, Japan, on 8 October 1930. He explored both Western and Japanese principles of composition, and his main influences were Debussy and Messiaen. He incorporated Japanese instruments into his orchestral works.

Meaning sea

Ejnar, Einar, Einer

Ejnar Hertzsprung was born on this day in 1873. The Danish astronomer was the first to publish colour-magnitude diagrams and discovered that some stars, named giants, are of much lower density than others, named dwarfs.

Meaning leader, fighter

Spark

The Japanese-American Hawaiian senator *Spark Matsunga* was born Masayuki Matsunaga on 8 October 1916. Spark was a childhood nickname he legally adopted. The Matsunaga Institute for Peace at the University of Hawaii was founded in his honour.

Meaning spark

Chevy, Chevi, Chevalier

Chevy Chase, the US actor and comedian, was born on this day in 1943. He was in the original *Saturday Night Live* line-up in 1975. He has appeared in many movies, the most memorable of which is *Three Amigos!* (1986), starring Chevy, Steve Martin and Martin Short.

Meaning knight, hunter

Pelagia, Pelageya, Pelagie

Today is the feast day of *St Pelagia the Penitent*. She was a beautiful dancing girl from Antioch, but she heard the bishop of Edessa preach and was converted to Christianity. She gave away all her belongings and disguised herself as a man, living as a hermit on the Mount of Olives, Jerusalem.

Meaning open sea

Meighan

The New Zealand actress *Meighan Desmond* was born on this day in 1977. She plays the role of the Goddess Discord in TV's *Xenia: Warrior Princess* (1998). and is in the *Hercules* series (1994). She is well known in New Zealand for her appearances in TV's *Shortland Street*.

Meaning the strong one

Sigourney

Famed for her role as Ellen Ripley in the *Alien* series of films, the US actress *Sigourney Weaver* was born Susan Weaver on this day in 1949. She changed her name to Sigourney after reading F. Scott Fitzgerald's *The Great Gatsby* when she was a teenager. She has won many awards and been Oscar-nominated several times.

Meaning victorious

Rona

The US gossip columnist *Rona Barrett* was born on this day in 1936. She began her career in the 1950s, first in print and then on TV. As well as continuing *The Rona Report,* she has a business selling lavender products and runs a charitable foundation for the elderly.

Meaning mighty power

Lennon, Len, Lenn

John Lennon was born on this day in 1940 in Liverpool, England. After the Beatles split, he married Yoko Ono and continued to write classic songs, including 'Beautiful Boy' for their son, Sean, who was also born on 9 October.

Meaning little cloak

Dinis

Dinis, the sixth king of Portugal, was born on 9 October 1261 and became king in 1279. He smoothed relationships between his country and the Catholic Church, granted asylum to the Templar Knights and created the Order of Christ. This day is also the feast day of St Denis of Paris.

From Dennis, meaning wine lover

Shep, Shepherd

The soccer goalkeeper *Shep Messing* was born on 9 October 1949. He was the US team goalkeeper in the 1972 Olympic Games in Munich. In the 1970s he played with the Boston Minutemen with Pelé and Beckenbauer. He later joined the New York Cosmos.

Meaning sheep-herder

Linwood

Linwood Boomer was born in Canada on this day in 1955. He played Adam Kendall in TV's *Little House on the Prairie* (1974) before going behind the scenes. He was the co-executive producer of *The Boys are Back* (1995) and executive producer of *Third Rock from the Sun* (1996).

Meaning beautiful wood

Shona, Shonaugh

The New Zealand singer *Shona Laing* was born on 9 October 1955. She was a finalist on the TV talent show *New Faces* in 1972 when she was just 17 years old. She went on to join the 1970s supergroup Manfred Mann's Earthband.

Meaning God is gracious

Autumn

Autumn Isabella Chiklis, the daughter of US actor Michael Chiklis and his wife Michelle, was born on 9 October 1993. For five years Michael Chiklis was in the TV series *The Commish* (1991) and its three TV movie specials.

Meaning autumn

Carling

Carling Bassett-Seguso, the Canadian tennis player and actress, was born on 9 October 1967. She reached the quarterfinals of the Australian open in 1983, the French open in 1984 and 1986 and in 1984 was in the semi-final of the US open. She was in the movie *Spring Fever* (1983).

Meaning hill where old women gather

Publia, Publias

Today is the feast day of *St Publia*, the mother of John, bishop of Antioch. She lived in Syria in the 4th century and organized a group of Christian women who sang psalms and prayed together.

Meaning not known

Giuseppe

The Italian composer *Giuseppe Verdi* was born Giuseppe Fortuno Francesco Verdi on this day in 1813. His first success was the opera *Nabucco*, which opened at La Scala, Milan, in 1842. Giuseppina Strepponi, who played Abigaille, later became his wife.

From Joseph, meaning he will add

Daido

The Japanese photographer *Daido Moriyama* was born on this day in 1938. His photographs, gathered in the collection entitled *Nippon gekijo shashincho*, record the breakdown of traditional values in post-war Japan, often by portraying everyday objects.

Meaning large

Midge

Midge Ure, the Scottish guitarist, singer and songwriter, was born on 10 October 1953 in Cambuslang, Lanarkshire. Formerly of Ultravox, he co-wrote the Band Aid song 'Do They Know it's Christmas'. His real name, Jim, was reversed to Mij and then became Midge.

Meaning supplanter

Benjamin, Ben, Benny, Benjie

On this day in 1738 the painter *Benjamin West* was born in Springfield, Pennsylvania. He worked in Italy and in 1763 established a studio in London, where he stayed for the rest of his life. He is best known for his portraits and historical pictures, which included *The Death of General Wolfe* (1771) and *Saul and the Witch of Endor* (1777).

Meaning son of the south

Katherine

US journalist *Katherine Mayo* was born in Ridgeway, Pennsylvania, on this day in 1868. Her books, such as *Isles of Fear* (1925) and *Mother India* (1927), exposed social evils. She condemned the administration of the Philippines and was opposed to child marriage.

Meaning pure maiden

Mya

The singer *Mya* was born on 10 October 1979. She was the background singer on the 1998 hit song 'Ghetto Supastar' by Ol' Dirty Bastard. Her voice, a combination of hip hop and soul, can also be heard on the track 'Dirty Dancing Havana Nights' (2004).

Meaning not known

Florida, Floreeda, Florrie, Floreida

TV actress *Florida Friebus* was born on this day in 1909. She played Dobie Gillis's mother in *The Many Loves of Dobie Gillis* (1959), in which she starred alongside Dwayne Hickman, Bob Denver, Sheila James and Frank Faylen. She also appeared in *Jennifer* (1978).

Meaning flowering

Kirsty

The British singer *Kirsty MacColl* was born on this day in 1959, the daughter of folk singer Ewan MacColl. She had two big hits in Britain in the 1980s, 'Fairytale of New York' with the Pogues and 'There's a Guy Works Down the Chip Shop Swears He's Elvis'.

Meaning anointed one

Elmore

Elmore Leonard, the US novelist, was born on 11 October 1925 in New Orleans, Louisiana. He began by writing westerns but then moved into mystery, crime and screenwriting, where his convoluted plots are widely admired. His novel *Get Shorty* was made into a film in 1995; *Rum Punch* became *Jackie Brown* (1997).

Meaning dweller by the elm tree

Octavio, Octavius, Octavion

On this day in 1990 the Mexican novelist and diplomat *Octavio Paz* won the Nobel Prize for literature. He worked in the diplomatic service with Pablo Neruda, who encouraged his writing. He fought in the Spanish Civil War. His best-known work is *The Labyrinth of Solitude* (1959).

Meaning eighth

François, Franco

The French writer *François Mauriac*, one of the greatest Roman Catholic writers of the 20th century, was born on this day in 1885. He published his first work, a book of poems called *Clasped Hands*, in 1909. He wrote over 30 novels and won the Nobel Prize for literature in 1952.

Meaning of France

Harlan, Harlon, Harland

Harlan Fiske Stone, the US jurist, was borne in Chesterfield, New Hampshire, on this day in 1872. He started out as a lawyer in New York City in 1898 and became US attorney general in 1924 and the chief justice of the Supreme Court in 1941.

Meaning from the battle land

Dottie, Dotty, Dot

The US country singer *Dottie West* was born in McMinnville, Tennessee, on this day in 1932. She wrote and sang 'Here Comes My Baby' and became the first female country artist to win a Grammy. She achieved great success in Nashville at a time when female singers were rare, paving the way for other stars to follow.

From Dorothy, meaning gift of God

Lindy

Lindy Boone was born on October 11 1955, the daughter of the singer Pat Boone. With her three sisters, Cherry, Debby and Laurie, Lindy was in the musical group the Boone Family. Their idealized family image was no fabrication.

From Linda, meaning pretty one

Maryrose, Mary Rose

On this day in 1982 the old English ship *Mary Rose* was raised from the bottom of the sea near Portsmouth, in the south of England. She was Henry VIII's warship, and her last battle was against France in 1545. A special museum has been built in Portsmouth to house her.

Meaning bitter flower

Loleatta, Loliatta, Loliata

On 11 October 1991 'Good Vibrations' by Marky Mark and the Funky Bunch with *Loleatta Holloway* reached the top of the US charts. Loleatta, whose contribution was a sample from her 1980 recording, became known as the diva of salsoul. It reached number 14 in the British charts.

Meaning sorrowful

Columbus, Columban, Columbo, Colum

The second Monday in October is Columbus Day in the USA, and the first time it was celebrated was 12 October 1792. *Christopher Columbus* was born in Italy in 1451 to a wool weaver called Domenico Columbo. He discovered America in 1492.

Meaning dove

Luciano, Lucian, Lucianus

The great tenor *Luciano Pavarotti* was born in Modena on this day in 1935. He received the longest applause ever recorded after he sang in Donizetti's *L'elisir d'amore* in Berlin in 1988. The clapping went on for one hour and seven minutes.

Meaning light

Vaughan, Vaughn

Ralph Vaughan Williams (who pronounced his first name 'Rafe') was born on October 12 1872 in Down Ampney, Gloucestershire. The British composer collected old English folksongs and used some in his music. He wrote nine symphonies, chamber music, opera and film scores. His great uncle was Charles Darwin.

Meaning small

Paluvayi, Paluvai

The Indian film producer, director and editor of Telugu and Tamil films Sri P.S. Ramakrishna Rao was born *Paluvayi Shiva Ramakrishna Rao* on this day in 1918. He married the film star Padmaşri Dr Bhanumathi Ramakrishna and they had one son.

Meaning not known

Martie

Martie Seidel of the Dixie Chicks was born Martha Elenor Erwin Maguire on this day in 1969. The contemporary country music group, formed in 1989, hit the big time in 1998 with their quadruple platinum album *Wide Open Spaces*. It won a Grammy for best country album.

Meaning war-like

Perle

Perle Mesta, the US socialite and diplomat, was born on this day in 1889 in Sturgis, Michigan. After helping Harry S. Truman to get elected she was appointed the American ambassador to Luxembourg. Irving Berlin's musical comedy *Call Me Madam* (1950), featuring the songs 'It's a Lovely Day Today' and 'Washington Square Dance', was based on her story.

Meaning pearl

Helena, Helene

The Polish actress *Helena Modrzejewska* was born on 12 October 1840 in Krakow, Poland. She emigrated to the USA and became one of the leading Shakespearean actresses of the time. She took the role of Nora in the US premiere of Henrik Ibsen's *A Doll's House* (1973).

Meaning light

Ethelburga

Today is the feast day of *St Ethelburga of Barking*, who was abbess of Barking in Essex. She died in about 676 having lived, according to the Venerable Bede, 'an upright life, as the sister of a bishop ought to do'.

Meaning noble fortress

Ashok

One of the greatest Indian film stars of the 20th century, *Ashok Kumar* was born on this day in 1911. He had a natural style and a social conscience that hadn't been seen before in Indian cinema. His breakthrough film was *Acchut Kanya*, and his later films include *The Return of the Jewel Thief* (1997).

Meaning one without sorrow

Cornel, Cornell

The US actor *Cornel Wilde* was born on 13 October 1915. An Olympic fencer, he was discovered after he became Laurence Olivier's fencing instructor on Broadway for *Romeo and Juliet* and was given a small part in the film. He received an Oscar nomination for his role of Frederic Chopin in *A Song to Remember* (1945).

Meaning battle horn

Nipsey

The African-American comedian *Nipsey Russell* was born on 13 October 1924. He was a regular guest on 1970s TV quiz and game shows, including *Match Game* and *To Tell the Truth*. One of his earliest TV appearances was on *Car 54 Where Are You?* (1960).

Meaning not known

Arna

The Harlem Renaissance writer *Arna Wendell Bontemps* was born on this day in 1902 in Alexandria, Louisiana, and brought up in Watts, Los Angeles. He wrote poetry and books for children. His *Story of the Negro* (1948) won several awards.

Meaning cedar

Cherelle

Cherelle Jardine, the Canadian singer songwriter and producer, was born on this day. She played for a short while with the band AZ IZ in 1992 before going solo. She has produced several solo CDs, the first, *Born Naked* (1994), the fourth, *Head Traffic* (2005).

Meaning dear one

Lillie

The British actress *Lillie Langtry*, nicknamed the Jersey Lily, was born on this day in 1853. Her nickname arose because of the title of the portrait of her painted by John Millais. He became the mistress of the Prince of Wales (later Edward VII) and managed the Imperial Theatre in London.

Meaning flower

Henrietta

British writer and traveller *Mary Henrietta Kingsley* was born in Islington, London, on this day in 1862. She travelled to West Africa, living there among native people, and wrote about her experiences in *Travels in West Africa* (1899). She served as a nurse during the South African War.

Meaning powerful ruler

Cady, Kady

The US actress *Cady McClain* was born on this day in 1969. Her early TV appearances include *Cheers*, *St Elsewhere* and *Lou Grant*. She played Peter O'Toole's daughter Tess in the feature *My Favourite Year* (1982) and in Dennis Potter's TV classic *Pennies From Heaven* (1981).

From Katherine, meaning pure maiden

Eamon, Eamonn

Eamon de Valera was born on this day in 1882. The US-born president of Ireland began his political career fighting for independence from Britain as a member of the Republican opposition. He was the prime minister of Ireland three times before becoming president.

Meaning blessed guardian

Cliff, Clifford

The British singer Sir *Cliff Richard* was born on 14 October 1940. The international star has been consistently at the top of the charts since the 1950s. He is a big fan of tennis and takes particular care of his looks, earning him the nickname the Peter Pan of pop.

Meaning cliff by a ford

Dwight

Dwight David Eisenhower, the 34th president of the USA, was born in Denison, Texas, on this day in 1890. He married Mamie Geneva Doud, and they had two children, Doud Dwight and John Sheldon David Doud. John's son, David Eisenhower, married Richard Nixon's daughter, Julie, and Camp David was named after him.

Meaning light-haired

Elwood

The US automobile pioneer *Elwood Haynes* was born on this day in 1857. He built his first prototype car in Kokomo in 1894 and took it out for a test. They towed it to the countryside with a horse and buggy so as not to frighten the horses in the busy town.

Meaning from the ancient forest

Arleen, Arlene, Arlana, Arlina, Arlen, Arletta, Arlyne

The actress *Arleen Sorkin* was born on 14 October 1967. She was the voice of Harley Quinn in *Batman* (1997). She is also a screenwriter and producer, producing the movie *Fired Up* (1997). She wrote *Picture Perfect* (1997) and several *Tiny Toon* adventures.

Meaning pledge

Hannah

Hannah Arendt, the German political theorist, was born in Hanover on this day in 1906. Raised in Konigsberg and Berlin, in the Second World War she fled to the USA to escape from the Nazis. She wrote *The Origins of Totalitarianism* (1951), which explored the roots of communism and fascism and their link to anti-Semitism.

Meaning full of grace

Miles

The Australian writer *Miles Franklin* was born Stella Maria Sarah Miles Franklin on this day in 1879. She sometimes wrote under the pseudonym of Brent of Bin Bin. She is best known for her generosity, and her estate funds the annual Miles Franklin award, which is worth $43,000, making it the richest literary prize in Australia.

Meaning soldier

Lourdes

It is the birthday today of *Lourdes Maria Ciccone Leon*, the daughter of Madonna and Carlo, who was born on 14 October 1996 in Los Angeles, California. Lourdes, a small town in the south of France, has been a site of pilgrimage since the Virgin Mary appeared to a young girl in 1858.

Meaning Lourdes, France

Virgil, Vergil, Virge, Virgy

On this day 70BC *Virgil*, the Latin poet Publius Vergilius Maro, was born near Mantua in the region named Cisalpine Gaul by the Romans, the area south of the Alps. The Latin poet is the author of the *Ecologues* and the *Georgics*. He also wrote the *Aeneid*, which became the Roman Empire's creation epic.

Meaning staff bearer

Pelham

P.G. Wodehouse, the British comic novelist, was born *Pelham Grenville Wodehouse* on 15 October 1881 in Guildford, Surrey. He wrote the Jeeves and Wooster stories, starting with *Right Ho, Jeeves* (1934), and Blandings Castle novels. As a lyricist he worked with Cole Porter on the musical *Anything Goes.*

Meaning town of furskin

Ginuwine

The US rhythm and blues singer *Ginuwine* was born Elgin Baylor Lumpkin on this day in 1975. He is one of the most successful rhythm and blues artists of the late 1990s, with many of his albums and singles going platinum. He has worked with Missy Elliott, Aaliyah and R. Kelly.

Meaning not known

Mario

Mario Puzo, the author of *The Godfather* (1969), was born on 15 October 1920 in Hell's Kitchen, New York. He published his first book, *Dark Arena*, in 1955. He co-wrote the screenplays for the film trilogy *The Godfather* (1972, 1974, 1990) with the director Francis Ford Coppola.

Meaning male

Lucy

On this day in 1951 the first *I Love Lucy* show was broadcast on CBS TV. Starring Lucille Ball, it was an instant hit and ran for six years, staying in the top three of the ratings all that time. In 1953 a pregnant Lucy gave birth to 'Little Ricky' in an episode watched by 44 million viewers.

Meaning light

Debby

On this day in 1977 *Debby Boone*'s single 'You Light up My Life' got to number one in the US charts. It stayed at number one for ten weeks. Debby Boone is the daughter of singer Pat Boone, and she is married to Gabriel Ferrer, the son of Rosemary Clooney and José Ferrer.

Meaning the bee

Teresa

Today is the feast day of *St Teresa of Avila*, who entered a Carmelite convent when she was about 20. She founded a monastery at Durelo (Spain), the first of 17 new convents, where the emphasis was on prayer. She had a series of visions and ecstasies and is best known from the statue of her by Bernini in Rome.

Meaning not known

Madge

Jan Miner was born on this day. She is better known as *Madge*, the Palmolive Dishwashing Detergent manicurist. She played the role for 27 years, and has made the international versions in French, German, Danish and Italian. Jan was married to the actor Richard Merrell.

From Margaret, meaning pearl

Gunter, Gunther, Gunner, Gunar, Gunthar

The German author *Gunter Grass* was born in Danzig (Gdansk, now Poland) on 16 October 1927. His best-known novel is *The Tin Drum* (1959). In 1979 it was made into a film, which won an Oscar and the Palme d'Or at Cannes. In 1999 he won the Nobel Prize for literature.

Meaning bold warrior

Flea

Flea, the bassist with the Red Hot Chili Peppers, was born Michael Peter Balzary on this day in 1962 in Melbourne, Australia. His family emigrated to the USA when he was ten years old, and he was brought up in Los Angeles. He is widely considered to be one of the best bass guitarists in recent history.

Meaning flea

Zahir

Zahir Shah, king of Afghanistan, was born Mohammed Zahir Shah on 16 October 1914. After the coup of 1973, he left the country to live in exile in Italy. The symbol of unity in his homeland, he is known as the father of the nation.

Meaning splendid

Manute

The Sudanese-American basketball player *Manute Bol* was born on this day in 1962. At 2.31 metres (7 feet 7 inches) he was one of the two tallest men ever to play in the national game. Since retiring he has established his own charitable foundation and works hard for famine relief.

Meaning man

Nico, Nicoe

Nico, a friend of US pop artist Andy Warhol, was the vocalist with the Velvet Underground and a central part of the New York 1960s scene. She was born Christa Paffgen on 16 October 1938 in Cologne, Germany. She got the name Nico from one of her photographers.

From Nicole, meaning people's victory

Merrilee, Merilie

Merrilee Rush was born on 16 October 1948. She was a singer in the 1960s band the Turnabouts, known as Merrilee and the Turnabouts. The group, which came from Seattle, Washington, were together from 1965 to 1974 and had a hit in 1968 with 'Angel of the Morning'.

Meaning Saint Mary's field

Fania, Fani

On this day in 1916 the 'women rebels' *Fania Mindell*, Margaret Sanger and Ethel Burns opened the first birth control clinic in Brooklyn, New York, for the poor and needy. Far ahead of their time, all three women were arrested for disseminating birth control information.

Meaning free

Hema, Hima, Himalaya

Hema Malini, the Bollywood film star, was born in Madras, India, on 16 October 1948. She was a trained classical Bharat Natyam dancer before becoming one of the biggest stars in the industry, with films like *Seeta aur Geeta* (1972) and *Amir Garib* (1974).

Meaning snow, Himalayas

Nathanael, Nataniel

The US author *Nathanael West* was born Nathan Wallenstein Weinstein on this day in 1903. He is best known for his surreal novels *Miss Lonelyhearts* (1933) and *The Day of the Locust* (1939), one of the best books ever written about the dark underside of Hollywood.

Meaning gift of God

Eminem

The white rapper *Eminem* was born Marshall Bruce Mathers II in St Joseph, Missouri, on 17 October 1972. He started his career when he was 14 years old in a group called Soul Intent. He has a daughter, Haile Jade, who was born on Christmas Day 1995.

Meaning Marshall & Mathers, M&M

Montgomery

The US actor *Montgomery Clift* was born on this day in 1920 in Omaha, Nebraska. After a decade on Broadway, his movie career began in 1948. He went on to be nominated for an Oscar as best actor in four films, including *The Search* (1948) and *From Here to Eternity* (1953).

Meaning mountain hunter

Arthur

The US playwright and screenwriter Arthur Miller was born on this day in 1915. His first play, *All My Sons* (1947), is set in the Second World War and is about a factory worker who sells faulty aircraft parts. *The Crucible* (1953), based on the Salem witch trials, is really about the McCarthy anticommunist trials.

Meaning strong as a rock

Elinor, Elinora, Eleanor

The author *Elinor Glyn* was born Nellie Sutherland on the island of Jersey on 17 October 1864. Her racy novels, including *Beyond the Rocks* (1906), *Three Weeks* (1907) and *Did She?* (1934), were the forerunners of mass-market women's fiction. Her sister, Lady Lucy Duff Gordon, was a survivor of the *Titanic*.

Meaning light

Rita

On this day in 1918 US actress *Rita Hayworth* was born in New York City. Her real name was Margarita Carmen Sansino. Known as the 'love goddess', she starred in many films in the 1940s, including *Gilda* (1946) and *The Lady from Shanghai* (1948). She was married five times.

From Margaret meaning pearl

Marsha, Marsa, Marsella

The US actress *Marsha Hunt* was born Marcia Virginia Hunt on 17 October 1917. She appeared in 62 Hollywood films and went on to work tirelessly for a variety of charities and foundations, including the Screen Actors Guild, Equity and the United Nations.

Meaning male

LaWanda

LaWanda Page was born on this day in 1920. She was an African-American comic actress and comedienne, best remembered for her role as Aunt Esther in the 1970s TV show *Sanford and Son*, the US version of the British classic comedy serial *Steptoe and Son*.

Meaning of the Wend

Baldassare, Balthazar

The Venetian composer *Baldassare Galuppi* was born on this day in 1706. He lived and worked in Venice for most of his life and was the musical director of St Mark's Cathedral, the top musical job in the city at the time. He wrote operas, oratorios and pieces for the harpsichord.

Meaning not known

Wynton, Winton

Wynton Marsalis was born on 18 October 1961 in New Orleans. The classically Juilliard-trained trumpet player is the artistic director of the Jazz at Lincoln Centre programme in New York and was the first jazz musician to win the Pulitzer Prize.

Meaning from a friend's farm

Chuck, Chick, Chic

Chuck Berry was born on this day in 1926. One of the fathers of rock and roll, Chuck Berry had more than 30 top ten hits, including 'Johnny B. Goode', 'Sweet Little Sixteen' and 'Roll Over Beethoven'. His influences on bands like the Rolling Stones cannot be overestimated.

From Charles, meaning free man

Logan

Logan Pearsall Smith was born in Millville, New Jersey, on this day in 1865. Educated at Harvard and Oxford universities, he wrote fiction, biographies and criticisms. Among his many acclaimed works are *Afterthoughts* (1931), *On Reading Shakespeare* (1933) and *Unforgotten Years* (1938), his autobiography.

Meaning little hollow

Lotte

The Austrian singer *Lotte Lenya* was born on this day in 1898. Her distinctive style of singing was encouraged by her husband, Kurt Weill, who also composed many musicals for her.

From Charlotte, meaning free woman

Erin, Erina

The US actress *Erin Moran* was born on this day in 1961 in Los Angeles. A child actress on the TV shows *Daktari* (1968–9) and *The Don Rickles Show* (1972), she is best known for her role as Joanie Cunningham in the long-running TV hit series *Happy Days*.

Meaning from Ireland

Dusa, Duscha

The British mathematician *Dusa McDuff* was born on 18 October 1945. The Cambridge graduate's career took off when she solved a well-known mathematical problem relating to von Neumann algebras. Since then she has written standard textbooks and received many honours.

Meaning soul

Amber, Ambur, Amberley

On this day in 1944 the historical romance *Forever Amber* by the US writer Kathleen Windsor was published. Scandalously steamy for its time, it was an immediate success, film rights were snapped up and the movie appeared in 1947, starring Cornel Wilde and Jessica Tandy.

Meaning jewel, sky

19 OCTOBER

Jaap

The Dutch athlete *Jaap Eden* was born in Groningen, the Netherlands, on 19 October 1873. Holland's first-ever sporting hero, he was the world champion speed skater and the world champion cyclist, the only person ever to have held these two records.

From Jacob, meaning supplanter

Geirr, Geir

The Norwegian composer *Geirr Tveitt* was born in Oslo on 19 October 1908. Most of his music wasn't composed in classical major and minor keys but in modes, which are series of musical intervals that, with the key, define the pitches of the sounds.

Meaning spear

Evander

The US boxer *Evander Holyfield* was born on this day in 1962. In the first pay-per-view boxing telecast he knocked out James 'Buster' Douglas and became the undisputed heavyweight champion of the world. Among many honours he has had a Sega computer game named after him.

Meaning benevolent ruler

Ferdinand, Ferdie, Ferdy

The French diplomat and entrepreneur *Ferdinand de Lesseps* was born on this day in 1805. While he was stationed in Cairo he conceived the idea for the Suez Canal, and in 1856 he obtained a concession from the ruler of Egypt. Building began in 1860 and was completed in 1869. He wrote *Histoire du canal de Suez* (1875–9).

Meaning courageous traveller

Frideswide

Today is the feast day of *St Frideswide*. It is said that she was the daughter of Didian, a prince of Mercia in the 8th century, and that she fled from home to escape from marriage. She established a nunnery at Oxford, which flourished, becoming its first abbess and living there until her death.

Meaning peaceful

Amanda, Manda

The US poet and inventor *Amanda Jones* was born Amanda Theodosia Jones on this day in 1835. She wrote poetry and war songs during the Civil War. She invented a way of canning food called the Jones process and then developed a type of oil heating furnace.

Meaning worthy of love

Johnnetta

The US anthropologist Dr *Johnnetta Betsch Cole* was born on this day in 1936. The first African-American woman to become president of Spelman College, she has received many awards and is the holder of 50 honorary degrees.

From John, meaning God has shown me favour

Buff

The actress *Buff Cobb* was born in Florence, Italy, on this day in 1928. With her husband, Mike Wallace, she hosted the US TV show *All Around the Town* in the early 1950s. She was in many films, including *Anna and the King of Siam* (1946).

Meaning buffalo, from the plains

Chauncey

Senator *Chauncey Goodrich* was born in Durham, Connecticut, on 20 October 1759. He was elected to Congress in 1794 and served until 1813. Elected mayor of Connecticut in 1812, he served as mayor and lieutenant governor for the rest of his life.

Meaning chancellor

Viggo, Viggio, Vigoleis

The Danish-US actor *Viggo Mortensen* was born on 20 October 1958 in New York City. He is best known for his role as Aragorn in *The Lord of the Rings* film trilogy (2001, 2002, 2003). He is also a photographer, a published poet and a painter. He has a son called Henry Blake.

Meaning war

Snoop

Rapper *Snoop Dogg* was born Calvin Cordozar Braodus on this day in 1971. His album *Doggystyle* (1993) was the first debut album ever to enter the charts at number one. It spawned the hit singles 'What's My Name' and 'Gin and Juice'.

Meaning snoop

Fayard, Fayad

Fayard Nicholas was born on this day in 1914. He and his brother Harold were the Nicholas Brothers, the tap-dancing sensations of the 1920s. They were auditioned by Duke Ellington for the Cotton Club and bowled him away, regularly appearing in the club thereafter.

Meaning generous

Elfriede, Elfrieda, Elfrid

The Austrian feminist playwright and novelist *Elfriede Jelinek* was born on 20 October 1946. The novels to her credit include *Wonderful Wonderful Times* (1980), *The Piano Teacher* (1983) and *Lust* (1989), and she was awarded the Nobel Prize for literature in 2004.

From Alfreda, meaning wise counsellor

Anna, Ana, Annika, Anneka, Anula, Anusia, Anuska

The British actress Dame *Anna Neagle* was born Marjorie Robertson in London on this day in 1904. She started her career in the theatre as a chorus girl and was a West End star before becoming a film star, portraying British heroines such as Florence Nightingale, Amy Johnson and Odette.

From Anne, meaning God has favoured me

Mirage

Today is the birthday of *Mirage Burdon*, the daughter of Rose and Eric Burdon. Eric Burdon was the lead singer with the 1960s group the Animals, who recorded the classic 'The House of the Rising Sun' (1964).

Meaning mirage

Chase

Chase Rolison was born in Los Angeles on this day in 2000. She is the daughter of Dedrick Rolison, the hip hop singer Mack 10, and Tionne T-Boz Watkins of the superstar hip hop band TLC. Chase can be a boy's or a girl's name.

Meaning hunter

Dizzy, Dizzie

The jazz trumpeter *Dizzy Gillespie* has a birthday today. He was born John Birks Gillespie on 21 October 1917 in Cheraw, South Carolina. He was a key player in the development of bebop and modern jazz, and his endearing personality did much to bring it to a wider audience.

Meaning dizzy

Alphonse, Alphonsus

The French poet *Alphonse de Lamartine* was born on 21 October 1790 at Macon, Saone-et-Loire. He wrote his first major work, *Les Méditations poètiques*, in 1820. He wrote *Histoire des Girondins* (1847) in veiled praise of the French Revolution and became a minister of foreign affairs in the provisional government of 1848.

Meaning noble and ready

Lux

Lux Interior, the singer with the 1970s New York punk band the Cramps, was born Erick Purkhiser on this day in 1946. Lux got his name from a car advertisement. His girlfriend, guitarist Kirsty, called herself Poison Ivy Rorschach.

Meaning luxury

Manfred, Manfried

Manfred Mann was born on this day in 1940. The singer and keyboard player with the group Manfred Mann was born Manfred Lubowitz in South Africa. The band had many hits in the 1960s, including two number ones in Britain: 'Do Wah Diddy Diddy' and 'Pretty Flamingo'.

Meaning peaceful hero

Jade, Jada

Jade Jagger was born in Paris on 21 October 1971. The daughter of Mick and Bianca Jagger, she is a successful jewellery designer. Her collections are popular among celebrities, including Madonna. She has two children, Assisi and Amba.

Meaning daughter

Marga

Marga Richter was born on this day in 1926. The works of this successful US composer have been performed around the world by more than 45 orchestras and many top stars, including the celebrated soprano Jessye Norman. One of her more than 75 compositions is *Quantum Quirks of a Quick Quaint Quark No. 2*.

From Margaret, meaning pearl

Piper

Piper de Palma is the daughter of the film producer and director Brian de Palma and his then wife Darnelle. She was born on 21 October 1996. Among de Palma's most successful films is *The Untouchables* (1987), which starred Kevin Costner and Sean Connery.

Meaning pipe player

Breeze

On this day in 1972 a group called Seals and Croft released 'Summer Breeze'. The song by Jim Seals and Dash Crofts was later covered by the Isley Brothers and became a big hit. It was also covered by Nicki Richards, Jason Mraz and Shinehead.

Meaning light wind

Drazen, Drazan, Draze

The Croatian basketball player *Drazen Petrovic* was born on this day in 1964 in Sibenik. He played for the Yugoslav national team and won a bronze medal in the 1984 Olympic Games. He has also played for Real Madrid, the Portland Trail Blazers and the New Jersey Nets.

Meaning not known

Stiv

The US punk rock singer *Stiv Bators* was born in Cleveland, Ohio, on 22 October 1949. He played in Rocket from the Tombs, the Wanderers and the Lords of the New Church, and co-starred in the John Waters film, *Polyester* (1981).

From Stephen, meaning garland, crown

Curly

Curly Howard of the Three Stooges comedy act was born Jerome Lester Horwitz in New York on 22 October 1903. The slapstick trio, often just called Larry, Moe and Curly, appeared in many features. Curly's catchphrases were 'N'yuk N'yuk N'yuk' and 'Woooo Woooo Woooo'.

Meaning curly

Dámaso, Damase, Damasse

The Spanish poet *Dámaso Alonso* was born on this day in 1898. His works include *Poemillas of the City* (1921), *Children of Wrath* (1944) and *Hombre and God* (1955).

Meaning not known

Alodia

Today is the feast day of *St Alodia* and St Nunilo, sisters born of a Christian mother and a Muslim father. They lived in the 9th century in the Huesca region of Spain. Raised as Christians, they were both committed to Christ, much to their mother's second husband's disapproval.

Meaning great force, great courage

Valeria, Valora

The Italian actress and model *Valeria Golino* was born on 22 October 1966 in Naples, Italy. In 1988 she appeared in *Rain Man* and in *Big Top Pee Wee*. In one famous scene she and Pee Wee Herman kiss for 3 minutes 16 seconds, although it is cut down in the final version.

Meaning strong

Sarah

French actress *Sarah Bernhardt* was born Henriette Rosine Bernard in Paris on this day in 1844. She trained at the Paris Conservatoire and made frequent appearances in London and the USA as well as in Europe. She founded the Théâtre Sarah Bernhardt in 1899.

Meaning princess

Dory

US singer and songwriter *Dory Previn* was born on 22 October 1925 in New Jersey. Her solo albums include *On My Way to Where* and *Mythical Kings and Iguanas*, and she has received three Academy Award nominations for her work in films.

From Dora, meaning golden girl

Pelé

The soccer legend *Pelé* was born Edson Arantes de Nascimento on 23 October 1940 in Tres Coracoes, Brazil. One of the greatest players of all time, he was totally two-footed, a precision scorer, a brilliant dribbler and passer, and not a bad defender either.

Meaning not known

Banz

Banz Alexander Baldwin, the son of Billy Baldwin and the singer Chynna Phillips, was born on 23 October 2001. The US actor Billy Baldwin has been in many films and is also a celebrity backgammon player.

Meaning town in Germany

Chi-Chi

The great golfing showman *Chi-Chi Rodriquez* was born in Rio Piedras, Puerto Rico, on this day in 1935. The highly successful player is also the founder of the Chi-Chi Rodriquez Youth Foundation for troubled and abused youths in Clearwater, Florida.

Meaning God

Gummo

The Marx Brother *Gummo Marx* was born Milton Marx on 23 October 1892. He didn't appear in any of the movies; instead, he went into the dressmaking business and later set up a theatrical agency with his brother Zeppo, who represented Groucho Marx.

Meaning not known

Blanche, Bellanca, Blanch, Blanka, Blunise, Branca

On this day in 1910 the pioneer aviatrix *Blanche Stuart Scott* became the first woman ever to make a solo flight. Before this she had driven a car from coast to coast in 1910. She went on to fly for exhibition teams doing daredevil stunts.

Meaning fair, white

Oda, Odalis

Today is the feast day of *St Oda*. The daughter of King Childebert, she lived in Belgium in the 8th century. She was married to the duke of Aquitaine, but devoted her life to caring for the sick, poor and suffering. There is a shrine to her at Amay, near Liège, Belgium.

Meaning wealthy

Dimitra

The US actress *Dimitra Arliss* was born on this day in 1932. She played the clerk with the big secret in *The Sting* (1973) and has the distinction of playing roles in bed with both Paul Newman and Robert Redford. When asked who was sexier, she always replies Robert Shaw.

Meaning earth goddess

Allegra, Alegria

Today is the birthday of *Allegra Sky Leguizamo*, the daughter of actor and comedian John Leguizamo and Justine Maurer. Allegra was born on 23 October 1999 in New York, a sister to Ryder Lee. John Leguizamo was Benny Blanco in the film *Carlito's Way* (1993).

Meaning cheerful

Moss

The theatre playwright and director *Moss Hart* was born in New York on this day in 1904. He directed the original 1956 production of *My Fair Lady* at the Mark Hellinger Theatre on Broadway, casting Julie Andrews and Rex Harrison in their celebrated roles. It ran for 2,717 performances.

From Moses, meaning saved from the water

Preston

The US actor *Preston Foster* was born in Ocean City, New Jersey, on 24 October 1900. In 1937 one of his many roles was as a coast guard in *The Sea Devils*, and he took on the job for real in the Second World War, becoming a captain in the Reserves and later an honorary commodore with the Coast Guard Auxiliary.

Meaning from the priest's farm

Santo

The guitarist *Santo Farina* was born on 24 October 1937 in New York. In the 1950s he played in the duo Santo and Johnny, and in 1959 they had a big hit with the instrumental 'Sleepwalk'. Other hits include 'Tear Drop' and 'Twistin' Bells'.

Meaning saintly

Kweisi

Kweisi Mfume, the politician and president of the National Association of the Advancement for Colored People, was born on this day in 1948. A congressman for ten years, he holds hundreds of awards. Kweisi is pronounced Kwah-E-see.

Meaning born on Sunday

Belva

The US feminist and reformer *Belva Ann Lockwood* was born on this day in 1830. A teacher and member of the American Woman Suffrage Association, she was a key figure in the fight for equal wages for women, culminating in Congress passing the 1872 equal pay for equal work bill.

Meaning beautiful view

Caprice, Capriccia

The US model and actress *Caprice Bourret*, known by her first name Caprice, was born on 24 October 1974 in California. She moved to Britain and achieved success as a model, TV hostess and actress, and has appeared in the one-woman stage show *The Vagina Monologues* (2002).

Meaning fanciful

Basia

The Polish pop star *Basia* was born on 24 October 1956. Her jazz style of pop has produced several successful albums, including *Time and Tide* (1987), which went platinum, and *Basia on Broadway* (1995). She writes and produces with Danny White.

Meaning daughter of God

Marghanita

On this day in 1915 *Marganhita Laski*, the British journalist and novelist, was born in Manchester. The niece of the political scientist Harold Laski, she wrote extensively for various newspapers. Among her novels are *Love on the Supertax* (1944), *Tory Heaven* (1948) and *The Victorian Chaise-longue* (1953).

From Margaret, meaning pearl

25

Chad, Chadda, Cadda, Chaddie

Chad Smith, drummer with the Red Hot Chili Peppers, was born on this day in 1962. The multi-platinum US band performed at Woodstock in 1999 with Chad wearing a big lightbulb on his head. He has also appeared in *The Simpsons*, one of the few rock drummers ever to have the honour.

Meaning warlike

Pablo

Pablo Picasso was born in Malaga, Spain, on 25 October 1881. He was baptized Pablo Diego José Santiago Francisco de Paula Juan Nepomuceno Crispin Crispiniano de los Remedios Cipriano de la Santisima Trinidad Ruiz Blasco y Picasso Lopez.

From Paul, meaning little

Evariste, Evaristo

The French mathematician *Evariste Galois* was born in Bourg-la-Reine on this day in 1811. A child prodigy, his contribution to mathematics was to lay the foundations for Galois theory, a major branch of abstract algebra, which he did while still a teenager.

Meaning pleasing

Zoot

The tenor saxophonist *Zoot Sims* was born on 25 October 1925. He played with a variety of bands, including Benny Goodman's Big Band, on and off for 30 years. Other notable artists with whom he played include Woody Herman, Buddy Rich, Artie Shaw, Gerry Mulligan and Al Cohn.

Meaning flashy dresser

Midori

The violinist *Midori* was born on this day in 1971 in Osaka, Japan. A child prodigy, she hummed a Bach theme when she was just two years old. The international star has started several foundations to help the less fortunate, including Midori and Friends and Partners in Performance.

Meaning green

Chely, Chelly, Chellie, Chellia

The country music star *Chely Wright* was born Richelle Renee Wright on 25 October 1970 in Kansas City, Missouri. She had her first success with *Single White Female* (1999), a hit album as well as a number one single. Her name is pronounced Shelly.

Meaning meadow on a ledge

Taffy

Taffy Danoff was born on 25 October 1944. With her husband, Bill, she was in the 1970s group the Starland Vocal Band, which had a US number one with 'Afternoon Delight' (1976) and their own TV show in 1977. Fledgling comic David Letterman made a guest appearance.

Meaning beloved

Maudie

The US actress *Maudie Prickett* was born on 25 October 1915. Among the films in which she appeared were *The Phantom Stagecoach* (1957), *North by Northwest* (1959), *The Maltese Bippy* (1969) and *Sweet Charity* (1969).

Meaning strong in battle

Bootsy, Boote, Boot, Boothe, Both, Booth

The US funk bassist *Bootsy Collins* was born on 26 October 1951 in Cincinnati, Ohio. His first band, the Pacesetters, formed in 1968, played with James Brown as the JBs. Later in his career he appeared on two Fatboy Slim records.

Meaning from a market

Desiderius, Desidario, Desidarius, Desi

The Dutch writer and the leader of German humanism *Desiderius Erasmus* was born on this day in 1466. He is known as the great saviour of theology. His writings, including *Colloquia familiaria* (1518) and his annotated *New Testament* (1516), paved the way for Martin Luther.

Meaning longing, desire

Eros

The Italian pop idol *Eros Ramazzotti* was born on 26 October 1964. Ramazzotti is a superstar in Europe and South America. In 1997 his ninth album, *Eros*, which included a duet with Tina Turner, was launched worldwide.

Meaning love

Cedd

Today is the feast day of *St Cedd*, who lived on the island of Lindisfarne, Northumbria, in the 7th century. In 654 he became bishop of the East Saxons. Monasteries he founded include Bradwell on Sea, Tilbury and Lastingham. His brother was St Chadd of Lichfield.

Meaning bishop's name

Hillary, Hillery, Hilary, Hilaria, Hilaire

Today is the birthday of *Hillary Rodham Clinton*, who was born on 26 October 1947 in Park Ridge, Illinois. She was the first lady of the USA from 1993 to 2001 and became a politician in her own right, serving as a senator for New York.

Meaning cheerful

Mahalia, Mahelia, Mahala, Mahela, Mahalah, Mahalar

One of the best gospel singers who ever lived, *Mahalia Jackson* was born on this day in 1911 in New Orleans, Louisiana. Her first hit was 'Move on up a Little Higher' (1948), and she had her own radio show and sang at the funeral of Martin Luther King Jr.

Meaning tenderness, marrow

Tennessee

The colourfully unorthodox feminist *Tennessee Celeste Claflin* was born on this day in 1845. She ran séances with her sister, Victoria, and started a newspaper advocating free love, which caused much scandal. The sisters left the USA to settle in Britain, where Tennessee married well, becoming the marchioness of Montserrat.

Meaning child of Dennis

Jaclyn, Jacklyn

One of the original 1970s *Charlie's Angels*, *Jaclyn Smith*, was born on October 26 1947. Jaclyn played Kelly Garrett in the TV series, which ran from 1976 to 1981. She was nominated for a Golden Globe for her role as Jacqueline Onassis in the TV film of her life.

Meaning supplanter

Conlon, Conlin, Conlan, Conan, Connal, Conal

Conlon Nancarrow was born in Texarkana, Arizona, on this day in 1912. He composed pieces for the player piano that couldn't possibly be played by human hands, creating extraordinary pieces of music. He is recognized as one of the most original composers of the 20th century.

Meaning beloved

Theodore, Teodore, Theod, Teddy

The 26th president of the USA, *Theodore Roosevelt*, was born in New York City on this day in 1858. He was president from 1901 to 1909 and was awarded the Nobel Prize for peace in 1906. He pressed for US intervention in the First World War and promoted social reform. He had six children: Alice Lee, Theodore Jr, Kermit, Ethel, Archibald and Quentin.

Meaning gift of God

Kenyon

The US academic and artist *Kenyon Cox* was born on 27 October 1856 in Warren, Ohio. He spent five years in Paris studying with Carolus Duran and Gerome. Best known for his decorative work and murals, his work includes *Lady in Black* (1880) and *Thistledown* (1883).

Meaning fair-haired

Lula

Lula da Silva, the president of Brazil, was born on this day in 1945 to a very poor family in the northeast of Brazil. On 1 January 2003 the popular former trade-union worker became the 37th president of his country, and he appointed music star Gilberto Gil his minister for culture.

Meaning all encompassing

Sabina, Sabine

In Hungary, Lithuania, Poland, Slovakia and Sweden it is the name day for everyone called Sabina. The Sabines lived in central Italy, around Rome. When the Sabine women were kidnapped by the Romans, their men came to rescue them and the women were able to mediate between the two factions.

Meaning Sabine woman

Kelly, Kell, Kel, Kellie

Kelly Osbourne, the daughter of Sharon and Ozzy Osbourne, was born in London on this day in 1984. Famous for her forthright appearances on TV celebrity reality show *The Osbournes*, she and her father had a British number one hit in 2004 with the duet 'Changes'.

Meaning battle maid

Maxine, Maxina, Maxie

The Chinese-American novelist *Maxine Hong Kingston* was born on this day in 1940. Her books on the Chinese perspective of life in the USA have been a success since she produced her first book, *The Woman Warrior: Memoirs of a Girlhood Among Ghosts* (1976).

Meaning the greatest

Enid

The British writer *Enid Bagnold* was born in Jamaica on 27 October 1889. She was educated in Europe and was a contemporary and friend of Katherine Mansfield and John Middleton Murry. She wrote plays and novels, the best known of which is *National Velvet* (1935), filmed in 1944 with Elizabeth Taylor.

Meaning pure of soul

Eliphalet

The US manufacturer *Eliphalet Remington* was born on 28 October 1793 in Suffield, Connecticut. A blacksmith, he learned his trade with his father, making farming tools. The Mexican and Civil War produced a demand for guns, and he designed and made the famous Remington rifle.

Meaning the God of deliverance

Leaf

The US actor *Leaf Phoenix* was born Joaquin Rafael Phoenix on this day in 1974 in San Juan, Puerto Rico. He was a child star, appearing in the movies *Space Camp* (1986), *Russkies* (1987) and *Parenthood* (1989). He has now changed his name back to Joaquin.

Meaning leaf

Bill

The wealthiest person in the world was born on this day. William Henry Gates III, known universally as *Bill Gates*, was born in 1955 in Seattle, Washington. The founder of Microsoft is married to Melinda French, and they have three children: Jennifer Katharine, Rory John and Phoebe Adele.

From William, meaning desiring to defend

Jonas

Jonas Salk, the man who discovered the polio vaccine, was born in New York City on this day in 1914. Salk did not attempt to profit from his discovery, stating that it was owned by the people and asking: 'Could you patent the sun?' The Salk Institute in California is named after him.

Meaning dove

Liberty, Libby

The *Statue of Liberty* was officially unveiled in New York on this day in 1886. A gift from the French, the statue's official title is Liberty Enlightening the World. The sculptor was Frederic-Auguste Bartholdi. Gustave Eiffel, who designed the Eiffel Tower, sculpted the armature.

Meaning freedom

Telma

The US singer and actress *Telma Hopkins* was born on this day in 1948 in Louisville, Kentucky. After playing Rachel Crawford, the restaurant owner, in the US TV sitcom *Family Matters* from 1989 to 1997, she went on to appear in another sitcom, *Half and Half*.

Meaning ambitious

Dody, Dodie

The US actress *Dody Goodman* was born on this day in 1929 in Columbus, Ohio. A regular on Jack Paar's TV talk show in the 1950s, she was in the movie *Grease* (1978) and was a voiceover artist in the cartoon *The Chipmunk's Adventure* (1987).

Meaning gift of God

Cleo

The British jazz singer *Cleo Laine* was born in London on this day in 1927. In 1983 she became the first British person ever to win a Grammy. Her arranger is her husband, John Dankworth. Together since the late 1950s, they have achieved lasting success.

Meaning father's glory

John

On this day in 1998 *John Herschel Glenn* took off from the earth on the space shuttle *Discovery*. He was 77 years old at the time, making him the oldest person ever to go into space. In February 1960 he also became the first American to make an orbit of the earth.

Meaning God has shown me favour

Akim

The Russian actor *Akim Tamiroff* was born on 29 October 1899. He appeared in many Hollywood films in the 1930s and was nominated for a best supporting actor Oscar for *The General Died at Dawn* (1935). He starred in Jean Luc-Godard's *Alphaville* (1965).

From Joachim, meaning judgement of the Lord

Isao, Isa

Isao Takahata was born on this day in 1935 in Ise, Japan. He is one of Japan's best-known *anime* (animated film) directors. His masterpiece, *Graves of the Fireflies* (1988), is considered by many pundits to be one of the best animated films ever made.

Meaning not known

Amit

The Swedish pop star and member of the A Teens, *Amit Paul* was born Amit Sebastian Paul on 29 October 1983 in Boden, Sweden. The A Teens rose to fame by covering Abba songs, and they later recorded 'School's Out' with Alice Cooper (2002).

Meaning endless

Winona

The US actress *Winona Ryder* was born Winona Laura Horowitz on this day in 1971. She gets her name from her birthplace, Winona, Minnesota. When she was seven her family lived on a commune called Elk in California. Her godparents were Timothy Leary and Allen Ginsberg.

Meaning first born

Fanny

The US singer and comedienne *Fanny Brice* was born in New York City in 1891. She appeared in the *Ziegfeld Follies* of 1910 and in 1913 was in *Honeymoon Express*. She became famed for singing 'Second-hand Rose' and 'Rose of Washington Square'. Barbra Streisand played her in the film *Funny Girl* (1964).

From Frances, meaning French woman

Melba

The US singer and actress *Melba Moore* was born on this day in 1945. She was a Broadway star, replacing Diane Keaton in *Hair* and winning a Tony award for her role in *Purlie* (1963). She had a British and Australian hit with 'This is It' (1976) and won a Grammy for 'Lean on Me' (1976).

Meaning soft, slender

Finola

The British Emmy-winning actress *Finola Hughes* was born on 29 October 1960. Famous for her role as Anna Devane, Alex's presumed dead twin in the US TV soap *General Hospital* (1963), she also appeared in TV's *All My Children* (1999).

Meaning white-haired

Ezra, Ez, Esra

The US poet *Ezra Pound* was born Ezra Weston Loomis Pound on 30 October 1885 in Hailey, Idaho. He lived in Europe and, with T.S. Eliot, was a key player in the founding of modernism in 20th century poetry. He was the friend and secretary of W.B. Yeats, his favourite living poet.

Meaning the one who helps

Hamilton

Hamilton Camp was born in London on this day in 1934. As an actor he has appeared in many films and TV shows, including *Star Trek*. As a singer and songwriter he has recorded six albums, and his songs have been covered by Gordon Lightfoot and Quicksilver, among others.

Meaning beautiful mountain

Herschel, Hirschel, Herschell, Hersch, Herzi

The actor *Herschel Bernardi* was born on this day in 1923. Best known for his starring role in the TV sitcom *Arnie* (1969), in the 1950s he was in the TV series *Peter Gunn*. On Broadway he played the title role in *Zorba the Greek* and starred in *Fiddler on the Roof*.

Meaning deer

Alonso, Alonzo

Today is the feast day of St Alonso. A healer through the power of fervent prayer, he was the doorkeeper of the Jesuit college of Motesion, Palma, for 46 years. *The Spiritual Works of Blessed Alonso Rodriguez* was published in 1885. His relics are enshrined on Majorca.

Meaning noble and ready

Kassidy

The country singer *Kassidy Osborn* has a birthday today, born on 30 October 1976. With her two sisters, Kristyn and Kelsi, she sings in SheDaisy, native American for 'my sisters'. They released their first album, *The Whole SheBang* (1999), to much acclaim.

Meaning clever

Irma, Irme, Irmina, Irmine, Erma, Erme

The author of America's favourite cookbook, *The Joy of Cooking*, was born on this day in 1877. *Irma Rombauer* self-published her collection of recipes in 1931, and her daughter Marion contributed the illustrations. Her extraordinary story can be read in her biography, *Stand Facing The Stove*.

Meaning noble

Nia

The US actress *Nia Long* was born in Brooklyn, New York, on this day in 1970. Her name is taken from one of the seven days of Kwanza, a modern celebration of African heritage. Nia was in the film *Boyz N The Hood* (1991) and TV's *The Fresh Prince of Bel Air* (1990).

Meaning life purpose

Angelica

Angelica Kauffman was born on this day in 1741. A close friend of Sir Joshua Reynolds, she painted classical mythology and portraits. She was one of only two female founders of London's Royal Academy of Arts. It accepted no more women until the 1920s.

Meaning God's messenger

31 OCTOBER

Romulus

On this day in 475 *Romulus Augustus* was proclaimed emperor of Rome. His abdication a year later would mark the end of the Roman Empire in the West. The Eastern, Byzantine, Empire carried on until 1453. He is the main character in Friedrich Dürrenmatt's play *Romulus der Grosse* (1949).

Meaning citizen of Rome

Helmut

The German photographer *Helmut Newton* was born on 31 October 1920. His fashion work appeared extensively in the top glossy magazines in the 1960s. In the 1980s he produced a classic collection, *Big Nudes*, which sealed his position among the greats of photography.

Meaning courageous

Blue

The US basketball player *Blue Edwards* was born on this day in 1965. His real name was Theodore Edwards, but he acquired the name Blue when he was a baby. He played in the league for a period of ten years, with Utah Jazz, Milwaukee Bucks, Boston and Vancouver Grizzlies and the Greek team, Olympiakos.

Meaning blue

Dermot

The US actor *Dermot Mulroney* was born on 31 October 1963 in Alexandria, Virginia. His many films include *My Best Friend's Wedding* (1997), *The Safety of Objects* (2003) and *The Wedding Date* (2005). He is married to Catherine Keener, and they have one son, Clyde.

Meaning free of envy

Willow

Willow Camille Reign Smith, the daughter of actress Jada Koren Pinkett-Smith and her husband, Will Smith, was born on 31 October 2000, a sister to Jadan Christopher Syre Smith.

Meaning symbol of healing

Nevada

On this day in 1864 *Nevada* became the 36th US state, and it is now the fastest-growing state in the USA. The name Nevada comes from the Spanish, but it is not pronounced Ne-vah-da locally, but with an abbreviated 'a', like cat or mat. The state colours are silver and blue.

Meaning snowy

Myant

Annabella Lwin, the lead singer with Bow Wow Wow, was born in Burma on this day in 1965. Bow Wow Wow was a much-acclaimed 1980s jungle funk band. Malcolm McClaren discovered Annabella working in a dry cleaners and changed her name from *Myant Myant Aye*, which means cool cool high.

Meaning cool

Deidre

The US actress *Deidre Hall* was born on this day in 1948. For 18 years she played Dr Marlena Evans in the TV soap *Days of Our Lives*, which turned her into a household name. She and her husband have a son conceived through artificial insemination with a surrogate mother.

Meaning beloved of Ireland

November

November

Lyle, Lisle, Liall, Lyall, Lyell

The singer, musician and actor *Lyle Lovett* was born on this day in 1957 in Klein, Texas. He has won three Grammys for his individual style of country and western and rock music. He was married to film star Julia Roberts for two years.

Meaning from the island

Penn

The US actor *Penn Badgley* was born in 1986 in Baltimore, but grew up in Seattle. His TV roles have included an appearance on *Will and Grace* (1998) and a starring role in the comedy series *Do Over* (2002).

Meaning enclosure

Grantland

Sports writer *Grantland Rice* was born on this day in 1880 in Tennessee. His unique style of writing contributed to the 1920s sometimes being known as the golden age of sports in the USA. He coined the phrase: 'It isn't whether you win or lose, but how you played the game.'

Meaning from the great lands

Crane

The writer *Stephen Crane* was born in New Jersey on this day in 1871. He began his career as a journalist in New York City. His first novel, *Maggie, A Girl of the Streets* (1893), was not a commercial success, but his next book, *The Red Badge of Courage* (1895), a powerful tale of the American Civil War, received international acclaim.

Meaning cry

Victoria, Vittoria, Victoire, Victorine, Vicky

The great Spanish soprano *Victoria de los Angeles* was born in Barcelona on 1 November 1923. She made her debut in her home town as the Countess in *The Marriage of Figaro*. Her celebrated appearances at the Metropolitan Opera House in New York included singing 'Mimi, Manon and Marguerite' (in *Faust*). She was also a great interpreter of Spanish folksongs.

Meaning victory

Lydia

The US author *Lydia Howard Sigourney* was born in Norwich, Connecticut, on this day in 1791. She wrote more than 60 volumes, including *Moral Pieces in Prose and Verse* (1815), *How to be Happy* (1833) and *The Faded Hope* (1853).

Meaning cultured

Katja, Katia

The German actress *Katja Riemann* was born Katja Hannchen Leni Riemann in Bremen on this day in 1963. She is a film, TV and stage actress. Her films have included *Balzac: A Life of Passion* (1999) and *Rosenstrasse* (2004).

From Catherine, meaning pure

Cosima, Cosina

Australian singer *Cosima de Vito* was born on this day in 1976 into a musical family of Italian descent. She first sang in public at the age of nine. Her debut single was 'When the War is Over', and she has released one album.

Meaning the perfect order of the universe

Burt

The US actor *Burt Lancaster* was born Burton Stephen Lancaster on this day in 1913. An athletic figure, he was good at gymnastics and for a time worked as a circus acrobat. He won an Oscar, a Golden Globe and the New York Film Critics award for *Elmer Gantry* (1960).

Meaning of bright and glorious fame, one who lives at the fortified town

Luchino, Lucius

The Italian film and theatre director *Luchino Visconti* was born on 2 November 1906 in Milan. He was the son of the duke of Modrone, and he started his career in Paris as Jean Renoir's assistant before moving back to Italy. Among his best-known films are *The Leopard* (1963), with Burt Lancaster, and *Death in Venice* (1971).

Meaning light

Gamaliel

Warren Gamaliel Harding, the 29th president of the USA, was born in Ohio on this day in 1865. He came from a publishing family: his father owned a local newspaper in Caledonia, and he himself owned the *Marion Daily Star*, which he won in a card game.

Meaning the recompense of the Lord

Boone

The great pioneer and frontiersman *Daniel Boone* was born in Birdsboro, Pennsylvania, on 2 November 1734. He explored most of Kentucky and Tennessee as regions of the American colonies, and fought the Indians and British during the American War of Independence. He founded Boonesborough, Kentucky, in 1775.

Meaning good one

Dawn

The singer k d lang was born *Kathryn Dawn Lang* on this day in 1961 in Alberta, Canada. She has lent her voice to a wide range of musical styles and often performs the works of Canadian songwriters, such as Neil Young, Joni Mitchell and Leonard Cohen.

Meaning break of the day

Helga

The Swedish writer Moa Martinson was born *Helga Maria Swartz* in Vardnas, Sweden, on 2 November 1890. She wrote about the plight of agricultural labourers and became actively involved in the socialist movement, campaigning for better living conditions and wages for farm and factory workers.

Meaning pious, religious and holy

Shere

Today is the birthday of the US feminist writer *Shere Hite*, who was born Shirley Diana Gregory on 2 November 1941 in St Joseph, Missouri. She is famous for the findings of her five-year research, published in 1976 as *The Hite Report: A Nationwide Study of Female Sexuality*. In 1989 she published *Good Guys, Bad Guys*.

From Shirley, meaning bright clearing

Alfre

Alfre Woodard was born on this day in 1953. The multi-Emmy-winning US actress has starred in many films, including *Cross Creek* (1983), for which she was nominated for an Oscar, and *Passionfish* (1998), for which she was nominated for a Golden Globe. She has also been in TV's *St Elsewhere* and *People's Century*, among others.

Meaning elf power

3 NOVEMBER

Bronson

The actor *Charles Bronson* was born Charles Buchinski on 3 November 1920. He was born in Pennsylvania to Lithuanian immigrant parents. His unusual looks suited his tough-guy screen image. He films include *The Magnificent Seven* (1960), *The Great Escape* (1963) and *Death Wish* (1974), among many others.

Meaning the brown-haired one's son

Montagu, Montague

John Montagu, 4th earl of Sandwich, was born on this day in 1718. The 'inventor' of the original fast food, it is said that the sandwich was created to sustain Montagu and his friends, who were gambling, so that they did not have to leave the card table to take refreshment.

Meaning from the jagged mountain

Terrence, Terence, Terry

The US playwright *Terrence McNally* was born in Florida on 3 November 1939. He is best known for his plays *Frankie and Johnny at the Claire de Lune*, an unlikely romance between a middle-aged waitress and a short-order cook, and *Kiss of the Spider Woman* (1991).

Meaning smooth, polished

Shadoe, Shadrach

Shadoe Stevens, who was born on this day in 1947 in North Dakota, was the host of the national countdown show *American Top 40* from 1988 to 1995. Previously, he had gained a cult following in the 1970s when he appeared as Fred Rated in a series of TV commercials.

Meaning survivor of the fiery furnace

Roseanne, Rosanne, Rosanna

The actress and comedienne *Roseanne Barr* was born today in 1952 in Salt Lake City. Sometimes known by her first name, she started as a stand-up comic and became world famous in the hugely popular TV show *Roseanne*, which ran from 1988 until 1997.

Meaning graceful rose

Lulu

The Scottish singer *Lulu* celebrates her birthday today. Born Marie Lawrie in Glasgow in 1948, she shot to fame with her hit single 'Shout' when she was 15. Small in stature but with a powerful voice, she has had a successful career as a singer, TV and film actress.

Meaning pearl

Elmira, Almira, Almeira, Almeria

Elmira Gulch is a character in the film *The Wizard of Oz*. It was shown on TV for the first time on 3 November 1956. The viewing audience was estimated at 45 million, and through this and subsequent TV broadcasts the film has achieved iconic status.

Meaning truth without question

Maty, Matty, Matya, Matti, Mattie, Matui

Maty Monforth, the US TV hostess, was born on this day in 1965. She rose to fame in the 1990s US TV programme *The Mike and Maty Show*. In 1999 she hosted *Smart Solutions*, a show of tips, hints and how-to information.

Meaning strength in battle

Adair

Will Rogers, humorist, actor and American folk hero, was born *William Penn Adair* on this day in 1879 in Oolagah, Oklahoma, then Indian Territory. Part Cherokee Indian, he was a real-life cowboy before he became an actor in Vaudeville and Broadway musicals.

Meaning from the oak tree near the ford

Eden

The British novelist, poet and dramatist *Eden Phillpotts* was born on 4 November 1862 in Mount Aboo, India, and educated in Plymouth, Devon. He was the author of many novels, plays and poems about Dartmoor. His play *The Farmer's Wife* (1917) became a silent movie directed by Alfred Hitchcock in 1928.

Meaning place of delight and pleasure

Skeeter, Skeat, Skeet, Skeets

The major league baseball player *Skeeter Webb* was born on this day in 1909 in Meridian, Mississippi. He played for five different teams, including the St Louis Cardinals and the Detroit Tigers, for 12 seasons before ending his big league playing career in 1948.

Meaning swift

Harlen

Harlen Curruher, the US actor, was born on this day in 1960. He is best known for his role as Jonathan Muir in the hit TV series *The Ghost and Mrs Muir* (1970), which ran for 50 episodes.

Meaning from the battle land

Nellie, Nelie, Nela, Nelly

On 4 November 1924 *Nellie Taylor Ross* became the first female governor in the USA when she was elected Democratic governor of the state of Wyoming. In May 1933 she became the first woman director of the US Mint, a position she held until 1953. She lived to be 101 years old.

Meaning womanly virtue

Mildred, Mildrid

The actress Doris Roberts, who played *Mildred Krebs* in the 1980s TV series *Remington Steele*, was born on this day in St Louis, Missouri, in 1929. She went on to star in *Everybody Loves Raymond* (1996), receiving three Emmys for outstanding supporting actress in a comedy series.

Meaning gentle counsellor

Lane

Laura Lane Bush, wife of George Walker Bush, 43rd president of the USA, was born in Midland, Texas, in 1946. She was an elementary schoolteacher and a librarian until 1977, when she married George W. They have twin daughters, Jenna and Barbara, who were born in 1981.

Meaning from the narrow road

Pauline, Paulina, Paulette, Pauletta

The French fashion designer *Pauline Trigere* was born in Paris on this day in 1909. She started her own fashion house in the USA in 1942. In 2000 she introduced a range accessories for the elderly, including a red ostrich box for pills and stylish purses for hearing aids.

From Paul, meaning small

Sinclair

On 5 November 1930 the writer *Sinclair Lewis* became the first American to win the Nobel Prize for literature. Born in Minnesota in 1885, he won the prize for his books *Main Street* (1920), *Babbitt* (1922) and *Arrowsmith* (1925).

Meaning shining light

Haldane, Halden, Haldan, Halfdan

The geneticist *John Burdon Sanderson Haldane*, known as J.B.S. Haldane, was born in Scotland on this day in 1892. He was one of the founders of population genetics and an early 'popular' scientist. His famous book *The Causes of Evolution*, published in 1932, was the first major work on what came to be known as the 'modern evolutionary synthesis'.

Meaning half-Danish

Shepard

Playwright, writer and actor *Sam Shepard* was born Samuel Shepard Rogers in Illinois in 1943. He often writes about the modern American west, and he received a Pulitzer Prize in 1979 for *Buried Child*. His partner is the actress Jessica Lange.

Meaning sheep tender, shepherd

Art

Art Garfunkel was born Arthur Ira Garfunkel on 5 November 1941 in Forest Hills, New York. With Paul Simon, he recorded some of the most memorable songs of the 1960s and 1970s, including 'Bridge Over Troubled Water' (1970).

From Arthur, meaning strong as a rock

Tatum, Tate

Actress *Tatum O'Neal* was born on this day in 1963 in Los Angeles, the daughter of the actor Ryan O'Neal. In 1974 she became the youngest person ever to win an Academy Award as best supporting actress in the film *Paper Moon*. She has three children by her former husband, tennis player John McEnroe.

Meaning to be cheerful

Elke, Elkie

The German actress *Elke Sommer* was born in Berlin in 1940, and moved to Hollywood in the 1960s. Her films included *The Prize* (1963) and *A Shot in the Dark* (1964). Since the 1990s she has concentrated on painting.

Meaning noble, kind

Tilda, Mathilda, Matilda, Tilly

The British actress *Tilda Swinton* was born on this day in 1961. A graduate of Cambridge University, she has acted with the Royal Shakespeare Company and had a long association with the director Derek Jarman, appearing in many of his films, including *War Requiem* (1988).

Meaning strong in battle

Ella, Ela

The US author and poet *Ella Wheeler Wilcox* was born on this day in 1850. A popular writer of plainly written, rhyming verse, her poem 'Solitude' opens with her most memorable lines: 'Laugh and the world laughs with you, weep and you weep alone.'

Meaning beautiful fairy maiden

Alois

The Bavarian playwright *Alois Senefelder*, who was born on 6 November 1771, was trying to find a cheap way of publishing his plays. He experimented with a slab of Bavarian limestone and invented lithography, a method of printing on a smooth surface.

From Aloysius, meaning famous warrior

Colley

Colley Gibber, the English actor, playwright and poet laureate, was born on this day in 1671. The French artist John Baptist Vanloo travelled to Britain and painted a portrait of Gibber in the 1730s, which helped make his reputation.

Meaning swarthy, victorious people's army

Harold, Hal, Harry

Harold Ross, journalist and co-founder of the *New Yorker*, was born today in 1892 in Aspen, Colorado. He was able to attract the best writers to the new magazine, among them James Thurber, Robert Benchley and Dorothy Parker. He edited every issue from 1925 until his death in 1951.

Meaning army commander

Antoine, Anthony, Antony, Anton, Ant, Tony

Musician and inventor *Antoine-Joseph Sax*, who is now better known as Adolphe Sax, was born on this day in Dinant, France, in 1814. With his father he invented a valved brass wind instrument, which he named the sax-horn or saxophone. He moved to Paris to promote his invention and subsequently became an instructor at the Paris Conservatoire in 1858.

From Anthony, meaning not known

Thandie, Thandiwe

Actress *Thandie Newton* was born in 1972 in Zambia, the daughter of a British father and Zimbabwean mother, and grew up in England. She appeared in the film *Mission: Impossible 2* (2000) and has made several appearances in the TV series *ER*.

Meaning beloved

Susie, Suzy

Writer and psychotherapist *Susie Orbach* was born on this day in 1946. She became well known after the publication of her book *Fat is a Feminist Issue* (1998) and is a frequent contributor to newspapers and magazines, TV and radio.

Meaning graceful lily

Vashti

Vashti Cromwell McCollum was born on this day in 1912 in Lyons, New York. She served as president of the American Humanist Association and has been inducted into the National Women's Hall of Fame. She was named after a biblical character who was the first exponent of women's rights

Meaning the most beautiful

Travers, Travis

Mary Travers of the US folk group Peter, Paul and Mary was born on this day in 1937. They had many hits in the 1960s and early 1970s, including 'Leaving on a Jet Plane', 'If I Had a Hammer' and 'Where Have All the Flowers Gone?' They continue to perform in concert.

Meaning from the crossroads

Dickson, Dixon

The US diplomat, author and teacher *Andrew Dickson White* was born on this day in 1832 in Homer, New York. With Western Union tycoon, Ezra Cornell, he was the co-founder of Cornell University, which is one of the world's leading educational institutions.

Meaning son of Richard

Raman

The Indian physicist Sir *Chandrasekhara Venkata Raman* was born on this day in 1888 in Tamil Nadu. He is famous for his work on optics. In 1930 he won the Nobel Prize for physics for his work on the scattering of light. The discovery of the effect was named after him, the Raman effect.

Meaning one who brings joy

Albert

The French existentialist writer *Albert Camus* was born on 7 November 1913 in Algeria. He was active in the Resistance during the Second World War. He wrote the nihilistic *L'Etranger* (The Outsider) in 1942. This was followed by *La Peste* (1947) and *La Chute* (1956).

Meaning bright, well-born

Wolf

The British writer *Wolf Mankowitz* was born in London on this day in 1924. He has written the screenplays for *The Millionairess* (1960), *The Long and the Short and the Tall* (1961) and *Casino Royale* (1967). He has also written novels, including *A Kid for Two Farthings* (1953).

Meaning wolf

Sigrun, Sigrud, Sigrid

Sigrun Wodars, the former German middle distance athlete, was born on this day in 1965. She started as a 400 metre runner but switched to 800 metres. She won her first national title in 1986, and won at the world championships in 1987 and the Seoul Olympics in 1988.

Meaning victorious counsellor

Marie, Marya, Maria

Marie Curie was born Marya Sklodowska in Warsaw, Poland, on this day in 1867. A pioneer in the study of radiology, she was the first woman to win a Nobel Prize. She won the physics prize in 1903 with her husband, Pierre, and Antoine Henri Becquerel, and the chemistry prize in 1911.

Meaning bitter

Joni, Joan, Joanna

The Canadian musician and painter *Joni Mitchell* was born Roberta Joan Anderson on this day in 1943. She is one of the most influential singers and songwriters of the late 20th century, and among her best-known compositions are 'Both Sides Now', 'Big Yellow Taxi' and 'Woodstock'.

Meaning God's gift of grace

Lotta, Lotte

The US comedienne and stage actress *Lotta Crabtree* was born Lotta Mignon Crabtree on 7 November 1847. She began performing as a child and became the darling of Broadway in the 1880s. She was a master of the *double entendre* decades before Mae West.

From Charlotta, meaning little woman born to command

Frederick, Frederic, Fred, Freddie, Fritz

The British painter *Frederick Gore* was born in Richmond, Surrey, on this day in 1913. He studied at the Ruskin School of Drawing in Oxford and was elected to the Royal Academy in 1972. He was the son of the painter Frederick Spencer Gore.

Meaning peaceful ruler

Bram, Bramwell

Bram Stoker, who was born in Dublin on this day in 1847, was the author of the vampire tale *Dracula* (1897). Count Dracula has become one of the most recognizable characters of film and fiction, appearing in countless plays and films. Bram Stoker wrote many other novels and short stories, but none of them is much remembered today.

Meaning from the bramble bush, spring

Leif

US singer and teen idol *Leif Garrett* was born today in 1961 in Hollywood. He was a child actor, appearing in the film *Bob & Carol & Ted & Alice* (1969) when he was five years old.

Meaning beloved

Halley

The astronomer and mathematician *Edmond Halley* was born in London on 8 November 1656. He calculated that the comet sightings of 1531, 1607 and 1682 were the same comet, and he correctly predicted its return in 1758. It then became known as Halley's Comet.

Meaning from the manor house meadow, holy

Nerys

The British actress *Nerys Hughes* was born in Wales on this day in 1941. She is best known for her role as Sandra in the successful BBC TV series *The Liver Birds*, which ran from 1969–1996.

Meaning lordly one

Posey, Posy

The US actress *Parker Posey* was born in Mississippi on this day in 1968. In the early 1990s she appeared in the TV soap *As the World Turns* and is now best known for her roles in independently produced films, such as *Basquiat* (1996). She was named after the 1950s supermodel Suzy Parker.

Meaning small bunch of flowers

Lizzie, Lizzy, Liza, Lisa, Lize, Liz

The US philanthropist *Lizzie Merrill Palmer* was born on 8 November in 1838. In her will she left the sum of $3 million for the foundation of the Merrill Palmer Institute, a school for motherhood and home training.

From Elizabeth, meaning consecrated to God

Alfre, Alfreda, Elfrida, Elfride

The film and TV actress and film producer *Alfre Woodard* was born on this day in 1952 in Tulsa, Oklahoma. She played Dr Roxanne Turner in *St Elsewhere* (1983–9), and her film work includes *Passion Fish* (1992), *How to Make an American Quilt* (1995) and *Star Trek: First Contact* (1996).

Meaning wise counsellor

Imre

The Hungarian author and concentration camp survivor *Imre Kertész* was born today in 1929. His best-known work, *Fateless*, is partially based on his own experiences. He won the Nobel Prize for literature in 2002, and the citation noted that it was 'for writing that upholds the fragile experience of the individual against the barbaric arbitrariness of history'.

Meaning an industrious ruler

Spiro

US politician *Spiro Theodore Agnew* was born on 9 November 1918 in Baltimore, Maryland. He was governor of Maryland before he became vice-president of the USA in 1969, serving under President Richard Nixon until 1973.

Meaning breath of the gods

Giles, Gyles

The British architect Sir *Giles Gilbert Scott* was born on this day in 1880. His father and grandfather were also both noted architects. He is probably best known for his prize-winning design of the new Anglican cathedral in Liverpool, which was begun in 1904, consecrated in 1924 but not completed until the 1980s.

Meaning shield bearer

Ingvar, Ingar

The Swedish politician *Ingvar Carlsson* was born on this day in 1934. He was leader of the Social Democrat Party and prime minister of Sweden from 1986 to 1991, succeeding Olof Palme, and again in 1994–6.

Meaning a son's army

Cornelia, Cornela, Cornelie, Cornelle, Cornie

The US painter *Cornelia Strong Fassatt* was born on 9 November 1831. Her painting *The Florida Case Before the Electoral Commission*, which hangs in the Capitol, Washington D.C., contains the likenesses of 260 prominent people of the day.

Meaning womanly virtue

Hedy, Heddy

The glamorous Austrian actress *Hedy Lamarr* was born Hedwig Kiesler on this day in 1914 in Vienna. Interestingly, she was also an inventor: she co-patented the 'secret communication system' in 1942, which would lead to the development of cellular telephone technology.

From Hedwig, meaning safe place in time of trouble

Tula, Tulia

Tula Pajeau Goodman, the daughter of US actress Carrington Garland and Carlos Goodman, was born on 9 November 1999. Carrington Garland is best known for her role as Kelly Capwell in the US TV soap *Santa Barbara* (1984).

Meaning destined for glory

Kezia, Kesia

Physician and reformer *Harriot Kezia Hunt* was born in Boston, Massachusetts, on this day in 1805. Although she was refused entrance to Harvard medical lectures because she was a woman, she was eventually awarded her MD. She was also active in the women's rights movement.

Meaning favourite

Vachel

The US poet *Vachel Lindsay* was born on 10 November 1879 in Springfield, Illinois. He dropped out of medical school and travelled around the US, trying to make a living as a poet. He published several collections of poems including *The Tree of the Laughing Bells* (1905) and *Every Soul is a Circus* (1929).

Meaning little cow

Jared

The US naturalist Dr *Jared Potter Kirtland* was born on this day in 1793 in Wallingford, Connecticut. He was a horticulturist and politician as well as a physician, and co-founded the Western Reserve University's medical school.

Meaning descendant

Ennio, Enio

The Italian composer *Ennio Morricone* was born on 10 November 1928. He is mainly a composer of film music and is especially known for his scores for Sergio Leone's spaghetti westerns, such as *A Fistful of Dollars* (1964) and *The Good, the Bad and the Ugly* (1967). He received four Academy Award nominations for his music.

Meaning not known

Pawel, Pavel

Pawel Jusienlcu was the penname of Leon Lech Beynar, who was born on this day in 1909 in Simbirsk, Russia, the son of Russian Poles. At first a soldier in the Polish army, after the fall of Poland he joined the underground movement and was known for his bravery. After the war he was a journalist, writer and amateur historian.

Meaning little

Mackenzie

The US actress *Mackenzie Phillips* was born today in 1959, the daughter of John Phillips, lead singer of the Mamas and the Papas. Her first major acting role was in the film *American Graffiti* (1973), but she is best known for her role as Julie Cooper in the TV series *One Day at a Time* (1975).

Meaning handsome

Alaina, Alana, Alanah, Lana

Alaina Reed-Hall celebrates her birthday today. The US stage, screen and TV actress was born in Springfield, Ohio, in 1946. She is best known for her appearances on the 1980s TV shows *Sesame Street* and *227*, and she has also appeared in *Friends*, *Ally McBeal* and *NYPD Blue*.

Meaning bright, fair

Natalene, Natalena

Today is the feast day of *St Natalene*. She is an obscure French saint, and few details are known about her life. The name Natalene is still quite common in France, especially for girls born on the days leading up to Christmas. It is a variant of the name Natalie.

Meaning born at Christmastide

Roxette, Roxetta

On this day in 1989 the group *Roxette* hit the top of the charts in the US and Britain with their song 'Listen to Your Heart'. The highly successful Swedish group are a duo: guitarist, Per Gessle, and vocalist, Marie Fredriksson.

Meaning dawn

Mose, Moise, Moses, Moss

The US jazz pianist, singer and songwriter *Mose Allison* was born on this day in 1927 in Tippo, Mississippi. In New York he played with Stan Getz and Gerry Mulligan before forming his own trio. His songs have been recorded by, among others, Van Morrison and Bonnie Raitt.

Meaning saved from the water

Fyodor, Feodore, Theodore, Tudor

The writer *Fyodor Dostoevsky* was born on this day in 1821 in Moscow. He was arrested by the Russian government in 1849 for distributing socialist pamphlets and was imprisoned for four years. His best-known works are *Crime and Punishment* (1866) and *The Brothers Karamazov* (1879–80).

Meaning gift of God

Kurt, Curtis

The US writer *Kurt Vonnegut* was born on this day in 1922 in Indianapolis, Indiana, into a German immigrant family. His best-known book, *Slaughterhouse Five* (1969), is based on his experiences in the US army during the Second World War when he was imprisoned in a slaughterhouse in Dresden.

Meaning courteous one

Jesse

The US folksinger *Jesse Colin Young* was born on 11 November 1944. He started his career in Greenwich Village in the 1960s and released two solo albums before forming the Youngbloods. Their self-titled debut album was released in 1967 and included the hit song 'Get Together'.

Meaning God's gift

Calista, Callista, Kallista

US actress *Calista Flockhart* celebrates her birthday today. She was born in Illinois in 1964. She has appeared in films and theatre, but is best known for her role as Ally McBeal in the TV series of the same name, about a young single lawyer working for a Boston law firm.

Meaning fair, good

Gemini

On this day in 1966 the spacecraft *Gemini* 12 took off from earth with astronauts Jim Lovell and Buzz Aldrin on board. This was the last flight of the *Gemini* programme, which had 12 launches, two unmanned, and ten manned. After this the *Apollo* missions took over.

Meaning twins

Demi, Demetria, Demeter

The actress *Demi Moore* was born on this day in 1962. She became the highest-paid Hollywood actress when she received $12 million for her role in *Striptease* (1996). She was married to the actor Bruce Willis, by whom she had three daughters.

Meaning fertility

Bibi, Biba

Swedish theatre and film actress *Bibi Andersson* was born in Stockholm on this day in 1935. She appeared in several of Ingmar Bergman's films, including *Smiles of a Summer Night* (1955), *The Seventh Seal* (1956) and *Wild Strawberries* (1957), and gave her best performance in *Persona* (1966).

Meaning lady

Ross

The character *Ross Geller* in the successful TV series *Friends* was played by David Schwimmer, who was born in Astoria, New York, on this day in 1966. He grew up in Los Angeles and studied speech and theatre at Northwestern University.

Meaning from the peninsula

Auguste, Augustus, Augustine, Gus

The great French sculptor *Auguste Rodin* was born on this day in Paris in 1840. Among his best-known sculptures are *The Burghers of Calais* (1884–6), *The Kiss* (1901–4) and *The Thinker* (1904). His fascination with dance and movement is often evident in his work.

Meaning exalted one

DeWitt

DeWitt Wallace, founder of the *Reader's Digest*, was born on this day in 1889 in St Paul, Minnesota. His first sample issue of the magazine was rejected by several publishers, but it eventually became one of the most profitable and widely read publications in the world.

Meaning blond

Salim

India's foremost ornithologist Dr Salim Moizuddin Abdul Ali, known as Dr *Salim Ali*, was born on this day in 1896. He was the author of several authoritative volumes about the birds of India and Pakistan.

Meaning safe, healthy

Letitia, Laetitia, Leda, Lettice

Letitia Tyler was born on this day in Virginia in 1790. Married when she was 23 years old, she had no formal education, but was a skilled manager of the family plantation and a homemaker. Her husband, John Tyler, became the tenth president of the USA in 1841.

Meaning joyous gladness

Rhonda

The TV host and actress *Rhonda Shear* was born on this day in 1954 in New Orleans. She hosted the USA Network's weekend movie show, *USA Up All Night* (1986). Before working in TV she was a beauty queen, winning Miss Louisiana in the Miss America and Miss USA pageants.

Meaning grand

Valerie, Valeria, Velorey, Valora, Valorie, Valory, Vallie, Valery

The actress *Valerie Leon* was born today in London in 1945. She was a theatre and TV actress before the first of her appearances in seven of the much-loved *Carry On...* comedy films. She also appeared in *The Revenge of the Pink Panther* (1978) and *The Spy Who Loved Me* (1977).

Meaning strong

Brielle, Briella, Brie

Brielle Nicole Underwood, the daughter of Desiree DeCosta and US actor Blair Underwood, was born on 12 November 1998. Blair appeared in *LAX* (2004) and played Miranda's neighbour in *Sex and the City*. She has two siblings, Paris and Blake.

Meaning region in France

13

Brice, Bryce, Bryse, Britius, Bricius

Today is the feast day of *St Brice*. He was bishop of Tours in 397, but had to leave his see and was in exile for seven years. When he returned to France he formed several new communities.

Meaning speckled

Fielding

Joseph Fielding Smith, who was born today in 1838, was the sixth president of the Church of Jesus Christ of Latter-day Saints, or the Mormons. He was the nephew of Joseph Smith, the founder of the Mormon faith, and a son of Hiram Smith. He is remembered for the construction and dedication of the Seagull Monument at Temple Square in Salt Lake City, Utah.

Meaning one who lives near the field

Takuya, Takuyou

The singer and actor *Takuya Kimura* was born on this day in 1972. He is one of the most popular artists of all time in Japan and has starred in many TV dramas. He won the Best Jeanist award, given annually to one male and one female celebrity who look good in jeans.

Meaning not known

George

The US composer *George Whitfield Chadwick* was born in Lowell, Massachusetts, on this day in 1854. He studied music at the New England Conservatory, where he later taught, and also in Germany. He is known for incorporating folk music into his symphonic works.

Meaning farmer

Caryn, Karyn, Carin, Karin

The actress Whoopi Goldberg was born *Caryn Johnson* in New York on this day in 1955. Originally a stand-up comic, she was nominated for an Oscar for her performance in the 1985 film *The Color Purple*, adapted from Alice Walker's novel, and she won a best supporting actress Oscar for *Ghost* (1990).

Meaning pure

Adrienne, Adriane, Adrianna, Adrianne, Adria, Hadria

The theatre and film actress *Adrienne Corri* was born on this day in 1933. Born in Scotland to Italian parents, she attended the Royal Academy of Dramatic Arts in London. Her most memorable film role was in *A Clockwork Orange* (1971).

From Adrian, meaning from the coast

Frances

Today is the feast day of *St Frances Cabrini*, who was the first American to be canonized. She was born in Lodigiano, Lombardy, Italy, in 1850 and became a nun, travelling to the USA with a missionary order. She travelled throughout the USA for 28 years, founding hospitals, orphanages and schools. She is the patroness of immigrants.

Meaning free woman

Columba

Today is the feast day of *St Columba of Cornwall*. She is one of the earliest saints and not much is known about her other than she was a virgin martyr. She lives on, however, as the patron saint of two Cornish parishes.

Meaning dove

Ellis, Elias, Elijah, Eliot, Elliot

The US jazz pianist and composer *Ellis Marsalis* was born in New Orleans on this day in 1934. In recent years he has also come to be known as a leading jazz teacher. His four sons, Branford, Wynton, Delfeayo and Jason, are jazz musicians.

Meaning the Lord is God

Claude, Claud

The French painter *Claude Monet* was born in Paris on this day in 1840. He was the co-founder, with Pierre-Auguste Renoir, of the impressionist movement. The beautiful garden at his house in Giverny, Normandy, is much visited for its famous bridge and pond with water lilies.

Meaning the lame one

Sherwood

The US TV producer *Sherwood Schwartz* was born today in 1916. During a long career he has been involved in many TV projects, but is best known as the producer of two popular 1960s programmes, *Gilligan's Island* and *The Brady Bunch*.

Meaning bright forest

Fulton

The US engineer and inventor *Robert Fulton* was born in Pennsylvania on this day in 1765. He is widely credited with developing the first steam-powered ship. An engine built to his plans by Boulton and Watt powered the first commercially successful paddle steamer.

Meaning from the field

Condoleezza, Condie, Condy

Condoleezza Rice was born on this day in 1954 in Birmingham, Alabama. She trained as a classical musician before turning to politics. She was US national security adviser from January 2001, and after his re-election in November 2004, President George W. Bush appointed her to replace Colin Powell as secretary of state.

Meaning with sweetness

Astrid

The Swedish writer *Astrid Lindgren* was born on this day in 1907. She is best known for *Pippi Longstocking* (1945), and the stories that followed, about a nine-year-old orphan with red pigtails, one black and one brown stocking and enormous black shoes. More than 80 million copies have been sold worldwide.

Meaning divine strength

Claribel

Claribel Cone was born on 14 November 1864 in Baltimore, Maryland. Together with her sister, Etta, she assembled one of the most important art collections in the world, with many paintings by Matisse and Picasso. The sisters left their collection to the Baltimore Museum of Art.

Meaning fair, bright

Sandahl, Sandrell

The US actress *Sandahl Bergman* was born on 14 November 1951. Her first film role was in *All That Jazz* (1979). In 1981 she starred as Valeria in *Conan the Barbarian* and won a Golden Globe for new female star of the year.

Meaning protector of mankind

Whitman

The TV actor *Whitman Mayo* was born on 15 November 1930 in New York City. He played the role of Grady Wilson in the popular series *Sanford and Son* (1972), and had his own spin-off show, *Grady* (1975). He also appeared in *Hill Street Blues* and *ER*.

Meaning white-haired

William, Will, Bill

The author of the *Olney Hymns*, the English poet *William Cowper* (pronounced cooper) was born on this day in 1731 in Great Berkhamstead, Hertfordshire. He was one of the most popular poets of his time, and he wrote about everyday life and scenes from the English countryside.

Meaning desiring to defend

Averell, Averill

The US politician and businessman *William Averell Harriman* was born on 15 November 1891 in New York City. He was the US ambassador to the Soviet Union and to Britain. He was a governor of New York in the 1950s and a candidate for the Democratic presidential nomination in 1952 and again in 1956.

Meaning boar-like

Clyde

The influential US rhythm and blues singer *Clyde McPhatter* was born on this day in 1932. In 1950 he joined Billy Ward and the Dominoes, and their hit, 'Sixty Minute Man', was one of the earliest rock-and-roll records. After several more hits he formed his own group, the Drifters.

Meaning heard from the distance

Richmal

The British writer *Richmal Crompton* was born on this day in 1890. She wrote for both adults and children, but is best known for her series of children's stories about an 11-year-old boy called William, the first of which, *Just William*, was published in 1922.

Meaning brave one

Beverly, Beverley

The US actress *Beverly D'Angelo* was born on 15 November 1951 in Columbus, Ohio. She gave an impressive performance as the country singer Patsy Cline in *Coal Miner's Daughter* (1980), singing all her own songs. She has two children by her former partner, Al Pacino.

Meaning ambitious

Nova, Novia

The British actress *Nova Pilbeam* was born on this day in 1919. She was already a stage performer when she appeared in Alfred Hitchcock's *The Man Who Knew Too Much* (1934) at the age of 14. She was also in the same director's film *Young and Innocent* (1937).

Meaning newcomer

Janita

In Finland 15 November is the name day for *Janita*. The name Janita comes from Janet, which itself is derived from Jane, which originally came from the old French name Jehane. This popular group of names is the female form of the equally popular and enduring John.

From Jane, meaning God's gift of grace

Fleming

On 16 November 1904 the British electrical engineer and physicist Professor Sir *John Ambrose Fleming* patented his invention, the two-electrode radio rectifier, which he called the oscillation valve and which is also known as a Fleming valve. The invention is widely considered to have been the beginning of electronics.

Meaning Dutchman

Burgess

The US actor *Burgess Meredith* was born on this day in 1909. He played both dramatic and comedy roles, and was the Penguin in the TV series *Batman* (1966–8). In the first three *Rocky* films (19176, 1979, 1982) he played the part of Rocky's trainer, Mickey.

Meaning one who lives in a fortified town

Chinua

The Nigerian writer *Chinua Achebe* was born Albert Chinualumogu Achebe on 16 November 1930. He is considered one of Africa's greatest writers. His novels, which deal with the impact Western customs have had on traditional African society, include *Things Fall Apart* (1958) and *Anthills of the Savannah* (1987).

Meaning God's blessings

Paul

The German composer *Paul Hindemith* was born in Hanau, near Frankfurt, on 16 November 1924. Initially regarded as being at the forefront of the avant-garde, he was later viewed as a conservative composer. Among his best-known works are the operas *Neues vom Tage* (1929) and *Mathis der Maler* (1933–5), which was banned by the Nazis.

Meaning small

Zina, Zena

The US tennis player *Zina Garrison-Jackson* was born in Houston, Texas, on this day in 1963. She was the runner-up in the women's singles final at Wimbledon in 1990, when she was beaten by Martina Navratilova.

Meaning hospitable

Hedwig, Hedvig, Jadwiga, Jadvyga, Hedwigis

On this day in 1384 *Hedwig* became perhaps the only woman to be made a king when she was crowned king of Poland. This was so that she would be seen as a monarch in her own right and not as a consort. She was a tall, blue-eyed blonde, famed for being kind as well as beautiful.

Meaning safe place in time of trouble

Margaret

Today is the feast day of *St Margaret of Scotland*, who was married, at the age of 12, to the English king, Edward the Confessor, but who lived in exile in Scotland after the Norman Conquest. She married King Malcolm III, and under her influence Christianity spread through the Scottish court.

Meaning pearl

Lisa, Liza, Lize, Lizzie, Lizzy, Liz

The US actress *Lisa Bonet* was born on 16 November 1967. She made her name in TV's *The Cosby Show* (1984), in which she played Denise. She has also appeared in several films, including *Enemy of the State* (1999) and *High Fidelity* (2000).

From Elizabeth, meaning consecrated to God

Danny, Daniel, Dan

The US actor, producer and director *Danny DeVito* was born on this day in 1944. He starred in the NBC TV series *Taxi* (1978) and has appeared in many films, including *One Flew Over the Cuckoo's Nest* (1975), *LA Confidential* (1997) and *Matilda* (1996), which he also directed.

Meaning the Lord is my judge

Shelby

The US writer and historian *Shelby Foote* was born on this day in 1916 in Greenville, Mississippi. He wrote historical fiction and non-fiction about the American Civil War. He also wrote several novels and a three-volume history of the Civil War.

Meaning from the estate at the cliff edge

Ralegh, Raleigh, Rawley

On 17 November 1603 the English explorer, writer and poet Sir *Walter Ralegh* was put on trial for treason. Sir Walter, who had been a favourite of Queen Elizabeth I, was imprisoned in the Tower of London until 1616 and passed the time by writing *A History of the World*.

Meaning one who lives in the meadow of the roe deer

Auberon, Oberon

The British author and journalist *Auberon Waugh* was born on this day in 1939, the son of the writer Evelyn Waugh. During his prolific career he wrote for the *Spectator*, the *New Statesman* and various newspapers, but achieved his greatest fame for his diary in the satirical magazine *Private Eye*.

Meaning noble

Winifred

The US welfare worker *Winifred Holt* was born on this day in 1870, the daughter of the publisher Henry Holt. She saw a group of blind students at a concert, and their obvious enjoyment made a lasting impression on her. She devoted her life to helping the blind, establishing the New York Association for the Blind in 1905.

Meaning peaceful friend

Fenella, Finella, Fionnula

The husky-voiced British theatre and film actress *Fenella Fielding* was born in London on this day in 1934. She appeared in *Carry on Screaming* (1966) and many other British comedies, and she was the voice of the Village announcements in the 1960s cult TV series *The Prisoner*.

Meaning white-shouldered

Salomea

Today is the feast day of *St Salomea*. She lived in Poland in the 13th century and was married to the Hungarian duke, Boleslas the Chaste. She founded a convent in the Ojcow valley, and she features in a beautiful stained glass window in the Franciscan Church in Cracow.

Meaning peace

Lesley, Leslie

The US actress *Leslie Bibb* was born in 1973. In 1990 she won Oprah Winfrey's nationwide search for a model, which was judged by John Casablanca, Iman, Naomi Campbell and Linda Evangelista. She was Brooke McQueen in the US TV series *Popular* (1999).

Meaning keeper of the fort

Wyndham, Windham

The British painter and author *Percy Wyndham Lewis* was born on this day in 1882. During the First World War he served as an official war artist. One of his best-known paintings, *A Battery Shelled*, comes from this time. He founded and edited the vorticist review, *Blast*, in 1914.

Meaning from the village with the winding path

Klaus, Claus

The German author *Klaus Mann* was born in Munich on this day in 1906. He was the son of the writer Thomas Mann. He is best known for his book *Mephisto* (1936), which blends the mythological world of Mephistopheles with the Third Reich.

From Nicholas, meaning victorious, conqueror

Caxton

On 18 November 1477 *Dictes and Sayengis of the Phylosophers* was printed by *William Caxton* at his press in Westminster. It was the first book known to have been printed there. The most important books printed by Caxton were *Le Morte d'Arthur* and Geoffrey Chaucer's *The Canterbury Tales*.

Meaning from a small town in England

Joris, Jorin, Jurgen

The Dutch film-maker *Joris Ivens* was born on this day in 1898. He moved to the USA in 1936 and made anti-fascist films. *The Spanish Earth* (1937), a film made for the Spanish loyalists, was narrated by Ernest Hemingway. He was knighted by the Dutch government in 1989.

Meaning farmer

Amelita, Ameline

The Italian opera singer *Amelita Galli-Curci* was born in Milan on this day in 1882. She is considered to be one of the best coloratura sopranos of the early 20th century. She made her debut as Gilda in Verdi's *Rigoletto* in 1906.

Meaning hard-working

Chloe

The US actress *Chloe Sevigny* was born in Springfield, Massachusetts, on 18 November 1974. She was nominated for an Oscar for best supporting actress for her role in the film *Boys Don't Cry* (1999), and then appeared in *American Psycho* (2000).

Meaning young blossom

Peta

The Australian actress and model *Peta Wilson* was born on this day in 1970. She played the title role in the Canadian TV series *Nikita* (from 1997), which ran for five seasons and totalled 96 episodes. Her film appearances include *Vanishing Point* (1971) and *The League of Extraordinary Gentlemen* (2003).

Meaning rock, stone

Sojourner

Sojourner Truth was born Isabella Baumfree on this day in 1797, one of 13 children of slave parents. After slavery ended in New York State in 1828, she changed her name and later worked with abolitionists, helping the freed slaves of the Southern states after the end of the Civil War.

Meaning visitor

19

Calvin

The US fashion designer *Calvin Klein* was born Calvin Richard Klein in New York on this day in 1942. A marketing, as well as a design, genius, his name is as internationally recognizable as Coca-Cola or Nike. He is particularly popular for his underwear range and perfumes such as CK One and Obsession.

Meaning little bald one

Ted, Teddy, Teddie

The US media mogul and philanthropist *Ted Turner* was born on 19 November 1938. America's largest landowner started his career by taking over his father's billboard business when he was just 24 years old. As well as founding numerous TV channels, he won the America's Cup in 1977 and has pledged £1 billion to the United Nations.

Meaning prosperous guardian

Garrick, Garek, Garrek

The US journalist *Garrick Utley*, correspondent for CNN's New York bureau since 1997, was born on this day in 1939. As chief foreign correspondent for ABC News, and before that for NBC News, he has covered foreign affairs from over 70 countries.

Meaning spear ruler

Lemar, Lemarr, Lamar, Lamarr

The US politician *Lemar S. Smith* was born on 19 November 1947 in San Antonio, Texas. He was elected to the Texas House of Representatives as a Republican in 1980, and to the House of Representatives in 1986.

Meaning famous throughout the land

Jodie, Jody, Judith, Juditha, Judy

The US actress and director *Jodie Foster* was born Alicia Christian Foster in Los Angeles on 19 November 1962. When she was just 14 years old she was nominated for an Oscar as best supporting actress for her performance in *Taxi Driver* (1976). She has won two best actress Oscars, for *The Accused* (1988) and *The Silence of the Lambs* (1991).

Meaning admired

Kathleen, Cathleen, Caitlin

The US actress *Kathleen Quinlan* was born on this day in 1954. She has appeared in many films, including *Airport '77* (1977) and *Trial by Jury* (1994). She was nominated for an Oscar for her performance in *Apollo 13* (1995).

Meaning pure

Mechtildis, Mechthild, Mechthilde, Mechtild, Mechtilde

Today is the feast day of *St Mechtildis*. She was born in Saxony in 1240, and her sister, Gertrude (later St Gertrude of Helfta), was the abbess of Hackeborn. Mechtildis was a mystic and healer who had a beautiful singing voice. Gertrude wrote *The Book of Special Grace*, an account of her sister's teachings.

Meaning not known

Kerri, Kerry

The gymnast *Kerri Strug* was born in Tucson, Arizona, on this day in 1977. She was a member of the US gold medal-winning team at the 1995 world championships and 1996 Olympic Games, and won a bronze medal at the 1992 Olympics.

Meaning dark one

Powell

The astronomer *Edwin Powell Hubble* was born on this day in 1889 in Marshfield, Missouri. He is credited with discovering that the universe is expanding, a concept known as Hubble's law. The orbiting Hubble Space Telescope was also named after him.

Meaning alert

Kenesaw

The first commissioner of professional baseball, *Kenesaw Mountain Landis* was born on 20 November 1866 in Milville, Ohio. The former judge took firm control of the game, giving hundreds of minor leaguers free agency and restoring the public's faith after the Black Sox scandal of 1919.

Meaning town in Nebraska

Chester

The cartoonist *Chester Gould*, creator of the *Dick Tracy* comic strip, was born in Pawnee, Oklahoma, on 20 November 1900. He joined the *Chicago Tribune* as cartoonist in 1931, and he wrote and drew the comic strip for 46 years.

Meaning fortified camp

Peregrine, Perry

The first child to be born to the Pilgrim Fathers in the New World was *Peregrine White*. He was born on 20 November 1620, the son of Susannah and William White, on board the ship *Mayflower*, which was in Cape Cod harbour. He was, therefore, the first child of English parents to be born in New England.

Meaning wanderer

Nadine, Nadia

The South African writer *Nadine Gordimer* was born on this day in 1923 near Johannesburg. She writes novels, short stories and non-fiction, and was awarded the Nobel Prize for literature in 1991. She has lived all her life in South Africa.

Meaning hope

Corita

The US artist *Corita Kent*, known as Sister Corita, was born Frances Kent on 20 November 1918. She became a nun in 1936 and taught art before leaving her order to devote all her time to her art. Her boldly coloured silkscreen prints were often used to express her anti-war feelings.

From Cora, meaning maiden

Susannah, Suzanna, Suzanne

Susannah Annesley was born in England on this day in 1669, the youngest of 25 children. She married Samuel Wesley, who, like her father, was a minister, and they had 19 children. Ten of these survived to adulthood, of whom John and Charles Wesley were the founders of Methodism.

Meaning lily, rose

Dulcie

The softly spoken British actress *Dulcie Gray* was born on this day in 1919. Among the films she appeared in were *A Place of One's Own* (1944) and *Angels One Five* (1953). She was married to the actor Michael Denison.

Meaning charming

Livingston

The US singer and songwriter *Livingston Taylor* was born today in 1950. His bestselling single, 'I Will be in Love with You' (1970), was from his album *Three Way Mirror*. His siblings, James, Alex, Hugh and Kate, are also musicians, James being the best known.

Meaning from Leif's town

Coleman, Col, Cole

The tenor saxophonist *Coleman Hawkins* was born on this day in 1904 in St Joseph, Missouri. Sometimes called the father of jazz saxophonists, he influenced many bebop players and recorded and performed with dozens of well-known jazz artists of the time.

Meaning keeper of the doves

Telly, Terry, Tel

The US actor *Telly Savalas* was born on this day in 1924. He became best known for his role in the TV series *Kojak* (1974–8) and for his catchphrase 'Who loves ya, baby?' He also made many films, including *The Dirty Dozen* (1967) and *Kelly's Heroes* (1970).

From Terence, meaning instigator

Foster, Forster, Forrie, Foss

The Canadian radio pioneer *Foster Hewitt* was born in Toronto on 21 November 1902. In March 1923 he made the second ever ice hockey broadcast, using a telephone, and for the next 60 years he was Canada's number one hockey broadcaster. His famous phrase was 'He shoots – he scores!'

Meaning guardian of the forest

Beryl, Beril

Dame *Beryl Bainbridge*, who was born in Liverpool on 21 November 1934, is one of Britain's finest novelists. Her books include *Harriet Said...* (1972) and *According to Queenie* (2001). *An Awfully Big Adventure* (1989) was made into a film in 1995 starring Hugh Grant and Alan Rickman.

Meaning precious jewel

Lorna, Lorne

The US actress *Lorna Luft* was born on this day in 1952 in Santa Monica, California. She is the daughter of Judy Garland and Sidney Luft, and half-sister to Liza Minnelli. She started acting when she was very young and has appeared on stage, TV and film.

From Laura, meaning laurel wreath

Jena, Jenna

The US actress *Jena Malone* was born at Lake Tahoe, Nevada, on this day in 1984. She won a Golden Globe as best supporting actress in the TV movie *Hope* in 1998, and was in the film *Stepmom* (1998) with Julia Roberts and Susan Sarandon.

Meaning small bird

Vivian, Viv

The US actress and singer *Vivian Blaine* was born Vivienne Stapleton on this day in 1921. She made several films in the 1940s, including *State Fair* (1945) and *Three Little Girls in Blue* (1946), but enjoyed her greatest successes on Broadway.

Meaning lively

Hoagy, Hogan, Hoagland

Hoagy Carmichael was born Hoagland Howard Carmichael on this day in 1899. He is one of the USA's greatest popular composers, and his songs include 'Star Dust', 'Georgia on My Mind' and 'Lazy Bones'. He won an Oscar for 'In the Cool, Cool, Cool of the Evening', which was performed by Bing Crosby in *Here Comes the Groom* (1951).

Meaning youth

Rodney, Rod, Roddy

The comedian *Rodney Dangerfield* was born on this day in 1921 in Long Island, New York. Born Jacob Cohen, he began writing jokes when he was 15 and was performing in public by the age of 20. His big break came with appearances on TV's *Saturday Night Live* (1975).

Meaning famous, renowned

Wade

US baseball player *Wade Blasingame* was born today in 1943 in New Mexico. He was signed by the Milwaukee Braves in 1961 and has also played for the Atlanta Braves, Houston Astros and New York Yankees.

Meaning wanderer

Huxley

The physiologist and biophysicist Sir *Andrew Fielding Huxley* was born in London on this day in 1917. In 1963 he won the Nobel Prize for physiology or medicine with Alan Lloyd Hodgkin for their work on nerve 'action potentials'. Aldous Huxley was his half-brother.

Meaning Hugh's meadow

Jamie, Jaime

The actress *Jamie Lee Curtis* was born on this day in Los Angeles in 1958, the daughter of Janet Leigh and Tony Curtis. Her performance in *Halloween* (1978) earned her the nickname the Scream Queen. She was also in *A Fish Called Wanda* (1988), proving that she had a talent for comedy as well as horror.

Meaning I love

Mariel

The US actress *Mariel Hemingway* was born on this day in 1961 in Mill Valley, California. She is the granddaughter of the writer Ernest Hemingway, and her sister, Margaux, who died in 1996, was also an actress. Mariel has appeared in *Superman IV: The Quest for Peace* (1987), *Personal Best* (1982) and Woody Allen's *Manhattan* (1979).

From Mary, meaning bitter

Ludmilla, Ludmila

The Russian ice skater *Ludmilla Protopopov* was born on this day in 1935. She and her husband, Oleg, were Olympic figure skating pairs champions in 1964 and 1968. The pair were still showcase skating at the ages of 72 and 68, respectively, training for up to seven hours a day.

Meaning beloved of the people

Rosamond, Rosamonde, Rosemond, Rosemonde, Rosemund

Rosamond Vincy is a character in *Middlemarch*, regarded by many as the greatest novel by the British writer George Eliot, who was born Mary Ann Evans on this day in 1819. She wrote under a male name because she wanted her work to be taken seriously.

Meaning rose of the world

Manuel, Manolo, Manny, Mano

The Spanish composer *Manuel de Falla* was born in Cadiz on 23 November 1876. His early interest in native Spanish music, particularly Andalusian flamenco, is apparent in much of his music. His first important piece was the opera *La vida breve* (Life is Short) (1904–5), and later works included the ballet *El sombrero de tres picos* (The Three-cornered Hat) (1916–19).

From Emmanuel, *meaning* God is with us

Prospero, Prosper

The Italian physicist and botanist *Prospero Alpini* was born on this day in 1553 in Venice. He studied medicine at Padua and practised as a physician, but his real interest was in botany. In 1593 he was appointed professor of botany at Padua; his son Alpino Alpini succeeded him.

Meaning fortunate

Harpo, Harper

Arthur Marx, better known as *Harpo Marx*, was born on this day in 1888, the second eldest of the Marx Brothers. Harpo was always known by his nickname, as were his brothers. He was always silent in the films that made them famous, including *Monkey Business* (1931) and *Duck Soup* (1933), but he could, in fact, speak.

Meaning harp player

Valdemar, Waldemar

The Danish engineer *Valdemar Poulsen* was born on 23 November 1869. In 1898 he demonstrated magnetic recording in his Telegraphone, for which he received a patent. This led to his development of a magnetic tape recorder in 1899.

Meaning famous ruler

Dominique, Dominica, Domenica, Domini, Dominga

The US actress *Dominique Dunne* was born today in 1959, the daughter of journalist Dominick Dunne and sister of the actor Griffin Dunne. She is best known for her role as Dana in the 1982 horror film *Poltergeist*.

Meaning born on Sunday

Elmarie, Elmaria

Elmarie Wendel, who was born on 23 November 1939, is best known for her role as Mrs Dubeck in the popular TV series *Third Rock from the Sun* (1996–2001).

Meaning not known

Maria, Marya

On this day in 1860 the Russian painter and diarist *Maria Bashkirtseff* was born Marya Konstantinovna Baskirtseva. She studied painting in Paris, where she exhibited at the 1880 Salon. Her *Journal* was a candid account of her life.

Meaning bitter

Felicity

Today is the feast day of *St Felicity*. Little is known about her beyond the fact that she lived in Rome and is buried on the Salarian Way in the cemetery of Maximus. She is believed to have had four sons: Felix, Philip, Martial and Vitalis.

Meaning happiness

Zachary, Zacharias, Zack

The 12th president of the United States, *Zachary Taylor* was born in Orange County, Virginia, on this day in 1784. He was the first president not previously elected to any other public office, having come to the presidency after a long military career, during which he was nicknamed Old Rough and Ready.

Meaning the Lord has remembered

Garson

The film and stage writer and director *Garson Kanin* was born on this day in 1912. He wrote the classic Tracy-Hepburn film comedies *Adam's Rib* (1949) and *Pat and Mike* (1952), in collaboration with his wife, actress Ruth Gordon. He wrote the play *Born Yesterday*, which he adapted for the screen in 1950.

Meaning garrison, young man

Dale, Dael, Dal

Dale Carnegie was born on this day in Maryville, Missouri, in 1888. A pioneer of the self-help industry, his book *How to Win Friends and Influence People* has sold more than 15 million copies since its publication in 1936.

Meaning one who lives in the valley

Laurence, Lawrence, Larry, Lars

The writer *Laurence Sterne* was born in Ireland on this day in 1713. The publication between 1760 and 1765 of his great comic novel *The Life and Opinions of Tristram Shandy, Gentleman* made him famous. His second book was *A Sentimental Journey Through France and Italy* (1768).

Meaning crowned with laurels

Yoshiko

The writer *Yoshiko Uchida* was born on this day in 1922 in California to Japanese-American parents. During the Second World War she and her family were sent to an internment camp with other Japanese-Americans. She wrote more than 25 books for children.

Meaning good

Arundhati, Arunda

The Indian writer *Arundhati Roy* was born on this day in 1961 in Meghalaya in northeastern India. She grew up in Kerala. She won the Booker Prize in 1997 for her semi-autobiographical novel, *The God of Small Things*, but has since focused her talents on non-fiction and environmental and humanist causes.

Meaning sunrise

Flora

Today is the feast day of *St Flora* and St Mary, who were martyred in Spain during the persecution of Christians under the Moorish rulers. They were threatened with being forced to become prostitutes if they did not renounce their faith, but were beheaded together.

Meaning flower

Frances, Francesca, Francine, Fran, Fanny

The British author *Frances Hodgson Burnett* was born on this day in 1854 in Manchester, but in 1865 her family emigrated to Tennessee in the USA. She wrote for both adults and children, but is best known today for her children's books, *Little Lord Fauntleroy* (1886), *The Secret Garden* (1911) and *A Little Princess* (1905).

Meaning free woman

Donovan, Donn

Donovan McNabb, the football player for the Philadelphia Eagles, was born on this day in 1976. Before turning professional, he attended Syracuse University, where he was a star basketball player.

Meaning dark brown

Virgil, Virgy, Virge, Virgie

The US composer *Virgil Thomson* was born on this day in 1896 in Kansas City, Missouri. He studied with Nadia Boulanger, and in New York City was a contemporary of Aaron Copland. He was also music critic for the *New York Herald Tribune* from 1940 to 1954. He won a Pulitzer Prize for music in 1949 for his film score for *Louisiana Story*.

Meaning staff bearer, strong and flourishing

Imran

Charismatic former cricketer *Imran Khan* celebrates his birthday today. Born in 1952, he was considered Pakistan's finest all-rounder, captaining the national team several times between 1982 and 1992. He retired from cricket in 1992 and is now a politician. He was married to British heiress Jemima Goldsmith.

Meaning strong

Dougray, Douggie, Douggy, Dugal, Dugald, Duggy

The actor *Dougray Scott* was born on this day in 1965 in Fife, Scotland. His first major role was in the popular British TV series *Soldier, Soldier* (1990). He has also appeared in the feature films *Enigma* (1982), *Twin Town* (1997) and *Mission: Impossible 2* (2000).

From Douglas, meaning from the dark stream

Liana, Lianne, Leanna

The Puerto Rican swimmer *Liana Vicens* was born on 25 November 1956. She was the 100 metres breaststroke champion at the 1968 Olympic Games. Liana can either mean a climbing vine, or it can be derived from Eliane, which comes from *helios*, the Greek word for sun.

Meaning climbing vine, sun

Trisha, Trish

The US dancer and choreographer *Trisha Brown* was born on this day in 1936. She studied modern dance in California and was a founding member of the innovative Judson Dance Theatre in New York. In 1970 she formed the Trisha Brown Dance Company, which was all-woman until 1979.

Meaning well-born

Catherine, Catharine, Katherine, Katharine, Kathryn, Cathryn, Cathy, Kathy, Catharina, Cathelle, Cathie, Cathleen, Catriona

Today is the feast day of *St Catherine of Alexandria*, after whom the firework is named. In 305 the Roman emperor Maxentius carried away the wives and daughters of Alexandria and employed 50 philosophers to persuade them to abandon Christianity. Catherine managed to convert them, and the enraged emperor had her put to death.

Meaning pure maiden

Yvonne

The Australian soprano *Yvonne Kenny* was born in Sydney, New South Wales, on this day in 1950. She made her London debut in 1975 in Donizetti's opera *Rosamunde d'Inghilterra* and has since appeared in operas around the world.

Meaning yew

Emlyn, Emlin, Emlen

The Welsh playwright and actor *Emlyn Williams* was born on this day in 1905. His first major success was the thriller *Night Must Fall* (1935), which was later made into a film. He toured the world in a one-man show in which he played Charles Dickens, reading from the much-loved author's novels.

Meaning one who lives on the border

Harvard, Harv

John Harvard was born on this day in 1607 in Southwark, London. In 1637 he emigrated to New England, and he bequeathed half of his estate, together with his library of some 400 volumes, to New College, which was renamed Harvard College and later became Harvard University.

Meaning not known

Willis, Willet, Will

The inventor of air conditioning, *Willis Haviland Carrier* was born on this day in 1876. His Carrier Engineering Company, formed in 1915, pioneered the design and manufacture of refrigeration machines to cool large spaces, and it revolutionized American life.

From William, meaning desiring to defend

Norbert, Norbie

The US mathematician *Norbert Wiener* was born on this day in 1894 in Columbia, Missouri. He received his first degree in mathematics at the age of 14 and his PhD (from Harvard) at the age of 18. He is credited with establishing the science of cybernetics in his book *Cybernetics* (1948).

Meaning brilliant sea hero

Maia, Maya

The actress *Maia Campbell* was born today in 1976 in Takoma Park, Maryland. She is mainly known for her role as Tiffany Warren in the NBC TV comedy series *In the House* (1995). She is the daughter of the author Bebe Moore Campbell.

From Mary, meaning bitter

Tina

On this day in Brownsville, Tennessee, in 1939 *Tina Turner* was born Annie Mae Bullock. She and Ike, later her husband, had their first hit in 1960 with 'A Fool in Love'. In the 1980s Tina launched a successful solo career, and her life story was told in the 1993 movie, *What's Love Got to Do with It*.

From Christina, meaning follower of Christ

Garcelle

The actress *Garcelle Beauvais* was born in Haiti in 1966 and moved to the mainland of the USA when she was seven. Formerly a model, she is best known for her roles in the TV series *Models Inc.* (1994) and the *Jamie Foxx Show* (1996). She has also appeared in *NYPD Blue*.

Meaning not known

Moore, Mor

The US abolitionist and feminist *Sarah Moore Grimke* was born on 26 November 1792. Her father was a plantation owner who believed in slavery and the subordinate status of women. Sarah, who was self-taught, fought strongly against both. During the Civil War she lectured in support of Abraham Lincoln.

Meaning great

Anders

The Swedish astronomer *Anders Celsius* was born on this day in 1701. The astronomer was one of the founders of the first modern observatory in Sweden, but he is best known as the inventor of the Celsius, or centigrade, temperature scale.

Meaning strong, manly

Sprague

The science-fiction and fantasy writer *L. Sprague de Camp* was born in New York City on 27 November 1907. He wrote numerous novels, short stories and non-fiction books in his long career. His best-known works were his short novels *Lest Darkness Fall*, *The Wheels of If* and *The Glory That Was*.

Meaning lively

Benigno

The brave Filipino politician *Benigno S. Aquino* was born on this day in 1932. Known throughout the country by his nickname Ninoy, he offered peace to the corrupt President Marcos and paid for it with his life. His wife, Cory, continued the fight and succeeded in winning, eventually replacing Marcos as president.

Meaning kind, friendly

Ernest, Ernie

On this day in 1925 Ernie Wise was born *Ernest Wiseman*. He was one half of the much-loved British comedy duo Morecambe and Wise, who were the undisputed kings of comedy on British TV throughout the 1970s and early 1980s.

Meaning purposeful, serious

Verity

Verity Lambert, one of Britain's leading TV and film producers, was born on this day in 1935. She was behind many of Britain's best-known TV programmes, including *Dr Who*, *Rumpole of the Bailey* and *Edward and Mrs Simpson*. She produced the film *A Cry in the Dark* (1988).

Meaning truth

Anne, Ann, Annie

On 27 November 1582 William Shakespeare married *Anne Hathaway*. She was born at Shottery, near Stratford-upon-Avon, and although little of her early life is known, her cottage can still be seen near Stratford. She and Shakespeare had three children, Susanna (born in 1583) and twins, Hamnet and Judith (born in 1585).

Meaning God has favoured me

Molly, Moya

On this day in 1966 Mitch Ryder and the Detroit Wheels hit the top of the US charts with 'Good Golly, Miss Milly'. The song, written by Robert Blackwell and John Marascalco, had been a hit for Little Richard in 1958, but was first released by the Valiants in 1957.

From Mary, meaning bitter

Elsie, Elsa, Else, Elyse, Elysa

The US anthropologist and folklorist *Elsie Clews Parsons* was born into a wealthy New York family on this day in 1874. The accomplished pacifist, socialist and feminist is best known for her work among the Native Americans of the southwestern United States.

From Elizabeth, meaning consecrated to God

Berry

Berry Gordy, the US record producer and founder of Tamla Motown, was born in Detroit on 28 November 1929. He discovered Smokey Robinson and the Miracles in 1957, and among the many other artists he signed were the Supremes, Marvin Gaye and the Four Tops.

Meaning berry

Randy, Randall, Randal, Randolph, Randolf

The US songwriter *Randy Newman* was born on 28 November 1943 in Los Angeles. Also known as a singer, arranger and pianist, he wrote the songs 'Sail Away' and 'Baltimore', and his film scores include *Ragtime* (1981), *Toy Story* (1995) and *A Bug's Life* (1998).

Meaning shield wolf

Ferdinand

The German pianist and composer *Ferdinand Ries* was born in Bonn on this day in 1784. His father, Franz Anton, had been one of Beethoven's teachers, and when young Ferdinand travelled to Vienna he became one of Beethoven's pupils. The great composer is said to have remarked: 'He imitates me too much.'

Meaning peace

Manolo, Manno, Manny, Mani

Manolo Blahnik, one of the world's leading designers of women's shoes, was born on this day in 1942 in the Canary Islands. His shoes were mentioned so often in the TV series *Sex and the City* that he was said to be the fifth star of the show.

Meaning God is with us

Hope

The US actress *Hope Lange* was born on this day 1931. She appeared in the film *Bus Stop* (1956) with Marilyn Monroe and was nominated for an Oscar for best supporting actress for her performance in *Peyton Place* (1957). She received two Emmys for her role as Carolyn Muir in the TV series *The Ghost and Mrs Muir* (1968–70).

Meaning optimism

Dervla, Dervia

The travel writer *Dervla Murphy* was born on 28 November 1931 in County Waterford, Ireland. She is famous for her autobiographical novels about her adventures abroad on a bicycle. Her first book, *Full Tilt*, tells of her self-supported solo bicycle ride from Ireland to India in 1963.

Meaning daughter of the poet

Marina, Marnie

The Dutch actress *Marina Duvekot* was born on this day in 1967. She starred in the Dutch TV series *Volgems Hem, Volgens Haar* (According to Him, According to Her) (2002).

Meaning lady from the sea

Lilia

The Austrian actress *Lilia Skala* was born in Vienna on 28 November 1896. She received an Oscar nomination for best supporting actress for her role in *Lilies of the Field* (1963), in which she starred with Sidney Poitier.

Meaning lilac

Clive, Clyve, Cleve, Cleeve

The Irish writer C.S. Lewis was born *Clive Staples Lewis* on this day in 1898 in Belfast. He is best remembered for *The Chronicles of Narnia*, a series of seven books beginning with *The Lion, the Witch and the Wardrobe*, published in 1950.

Meaning cliff

Wendell, Wendall

The abolitionist *Wendell Phillips* was born on 29 November 1811 in Boston, Massachusetts. He gave up his law practice to devote all his time to the abolitionist cause. After the 15th amendment to the US Constitution was passed, he focused on other issues, including women's rights.

Meaning wanderer

Ryan

The Manchester United soccer player *Ryan Giggs* was born on this day in 1973. He was born in Wales, but was brought up in England after the age of seven. He also plays for the Welsh national team.

Meaning small king

Lucas, Lukas

The US actor *Lucas Black* was born today in Alabama in 1982. He made his film debut when he was 11 years old in a small role in the Kevin Costner film *The War* (1996). He appeared as Caleb Temple in the TV series *American Gothic* (1996), and was in the films *Ghosts of Mississippi* (1996) and *Cold Mountain* (2003).

Meaning light

Dagmar

The US actress *Dagmar* was born Virginia Egnor in Huntingdon, West Virginia, on this day in 1921. She started her working life as a fashion model before moving into TV work. She created a successful 'dumb blonde' act and appeared in several shows, including Milton Berle's *Texaco Star Theatre* (1948) and *Hollywood Squares* (1966).

Meaning glory of the Danes

Norina, Norine

Norina is a character in the opera *Don Pasquale* (1880). It was composed by Gaetano Donizetti, who was born in Italy on this day in 1797, and tells how Norina, who is in love with Ernesto, pretends to be a termagant so that Don Pasquale will allow her to marry his nephew, Ernesto.

From Honora, meaning honour

Gena

The US actress and model *Gena Lee Nolin* was born on this day in 1971 in Duluth, Minnesota. After appearing in the TV soap *The Young and the Restless* (1973), she replaced Pamela Anderson in the cast of the US TV series *Baywatch* (1989).

From Georgina, meaning farmer

May

The US writer *Louis May Alcott* was born on this day in 1832. She is known today as the author of children's books, especially *Little Women* (1868), which was followed by *Little Men* (1871) and *Jo's Boys* (1886).

Meaning spring

Ridley

The film director *Ridley Scott* was born on this day in 1937. After working at the BBC he left to produce high-quality commercials. He moved to Hollywood and embarked on a successful career as a film director. His films include *Alien* (1979), *Blade Runner* (1982), *Thelma and Louise* (1991) and *Gladiator* (2000).

Meaning from the reed clearing

Mark

The US writer *Mark Twain* was born Samuel Langhorne Clemens on this day in 1835 in Missouri. His best-known books are *The Adventures of Tom Sawyer* (1872) and its sequel, *The Adventures of Huckleberry Finn* (1884). He also wrote *The Prince and the Pauper* (1881), which was filmed in 1937 (with Errol Flynn) and 1977 (with Oliver Reed).

Meaning war-like

Colin, Colan, Collin

The actor and comedian *Colin Mochrie* celebrates his birthday today. He was born in Scotland in 1957 and grew up in Canada. He appeared regularly on the British TV improvisation series *Whose Line is it Anyway?* (1988) and on the US version of the show on ABC, hosted by Drew Carey.

From Nicholas, meaning victorious, conqueror

Lemuel, Lemmie, Lem

The Anglo-Irish novelist and satirist Jonathan Swift was born on this day in 1667 in Dublin, Ireland. His masterpiece, *Gulliver's Travels* (1726), the story of Dr *Lemuel Gulliver*'s journeys through a series of exotic places, is considered one of the most forceful moral satires ever written.

Meaning devoted to God

Marilla, Amaryllis, Amarillis

The Canadian author Lucy Maud Montgomery was born on this day in 1874. The character *Marilla* appears in her best-known work, *Anne of Green Gables* (1908), the first in a series of popular novels featuring Anne Shirley, a red-haired, freckled orphan.

Meaning fresh, sparkling

Verna, Verena, Verneta, Verda, Vernis, Vernice, Vernita, Virina, Virna

The US actress Virginia Mayo was born on this day in St Louis, Missouri, in 1920. She was one of the most beautiful and successful actresses of the 1940s and 1950s, and one of her best performances was as *Verna Jarrett* in the 1949 film *White Heat*, which also starred James Cagney.

Meaning spring-like

Des'ree, Desiree, Desirée

The British pop singer *Des'ree* was born on this day in 1968 in London. Her music is a mixture of reggae, calypso, rap and pop. Her 1994 album, *I Ain't Movin'*, spawned the single 'You Gotta Be', the most played video on the VH1 channel. The album sold over 16 million copies.

Meaning desired

Christel

The US actress *Christel Khalil* was born in Los Angeles on 30 November 1987. She plays Lily Winters in the TV soap *The Young and the Restless* (1973). She has been in several films, including *Matilda* (1996) and *White Like the Moon* (2003).

Meaning crystal

December

December

1

Pip, Pippin

Pip is the protagonist and narrator of *Great Expectations* by Charles Dickens. The first instalment was published on 1 December 1860 in the magazine *All the Year Round*. Each edition sold more than 100,000 copies, and today it is one of the most popular of Dickens's novels.

From Philip, meaning lover of horses

Turner

Stansfield Turner was born in Highland Park, Illinois, on this day in 1923. In 1975 he was made admiral and became commander in chief of NATO's southern flank. He was president of the Naval War College and director of the CIA from 1977 until 1981.

Meaning lathe-worker

Kirby

The British contractor and multimillionaire Sir *Kirby Laing* was born today in 1918. He is the benefactor of numerous awards and donations through the charitable trust he has established, the Kirby Laing Foundation.

Meaning from the church village

Treat

The US actor *Treat Williams* was born on 1 December 1951. He gets his name from his l8th-century ancestor, Robert Treat Paine, who was one of the people who signed the US Declaration of Independence. Treat works on TV, in films and in the theatre.

Meaning reward

Jasmine, Jasmina, Yasmin, Jessamy

The Dutch TV and film actress *Jasmine Sendar* was born in Curaçao, largest island of the Netherlands Antilles, on this day in 1977. She has appeared in the films *Mindhunters* (2004) and *Volle Maan*, also known as *Full Moon Party* (2002).

Meaning fragrant flower

Golden

Golden Brooks, the US actress, was born on 1 December 1970. She was in the TV show *Girlfriends* (2000) and the film *Imposter* (2000). She is also a singer and dancer, and holds a masters degree in creative writing.

Meaning golden

Destry

Destry Allyn Spielberg was born on 1 December 1996. She is the daughter of the film producer and director Stephen Spielberg and his wife, the actress Kate Capshaw. The couple have five children together, two of them adopted, and one child each from previous relationships.

Meaning warhorse

Violette

The French ballerina and dance director *Violette Verdy* was born in Point-l'Abbé-Lambour on this day in 1933. She was a principal dancer with the New York City Ballet from 1958 to 1977 and subsequently the director of the Paris Opera Ballet from 1977 to 1980.

Meaning shy flower

Agostino, Agosto, August, Augustus

The Italian composer and music theorist *Agostino Agazzari* was born on this day in 1578 into an aristocratic family in Siena, where he became organist and choirmaster at the cathedral. He wrote both sacred and secular music.

Meaning exalted one

Botho, Boto, Botolfe, Botolf, Botulf

On this day in 1944 the German playwright *Botho Strauss* was born. His best-known play is *Die Besucher* (The Visitors). He has also written a novel, *The Night with Alice When Julia Prowled Around the House.*

Meaning wolf

Gianni

The Italian designer *Gianni Versace* was born in Reggio di Calabria on this day in 1946. He opened his first boutique in 1978 and rose to become one of the most important and influential designers of the late 20th century. In 1993 he won the American fashion 'Oscar'.

From John, meaning God has shown me favour

Dagfinn

The Norwegian politician *Dagfinn Høybråten* was born on 2 December 1957. He is the leader of the Christian Democratic Party and was minister for health from 1997 to 2004.

Meaning day finn

Elna, Elnora, Elnore

The South African tennis player *Elna Reinach* was born in Pretoria on this day in 1968. Of her 31 Federation Cup games for her country, she lost only eight. She reached the fourth round of the Wimbledon singles before being beaten by Martina Navratalova.

From Helen, meaning light

Maria

On this day in 1923 the Greek-US soprano *Maria Callas* was born in New York. Although raised in the USA, she trained at the Athens Conservatory, making her debut in Athens. She became known after appearing in *La Gioconda* in 1947 and made her last stage appearance in *Tosca* in 1965.

Meaning bitter

Nelly, Nell, Nela, Nellis, Nelle, Nella, Nellia, Nelina, Nelita, Nellwyn

The popular Canadian singer and songwriter *Nelly Furtado* was born on 2 December 1978 in Victoria, British Columbia. She studied trombone, ukulele and piano as a child. Her first recording, 'I'm Like a Bird' (2002), was a big hit and won a Grammy. She has a daughter, Nevis.

Meaning bright one

Britney, Brittnee, Britne, Britni

Pop icon *Britney Spears* was born in McComb, Mississippi, on 2 December 1981 and then grew up in Kentwood, Louisiana. She embarked on the road to stardom in TV's *New Mickey Mouse Club* (1993), along with cast-mates Justin Timberlake and Christina Aguilera.

Meaning from Bretagne, France

Godard, Goddard

The French film-maker *Jean-Luc Godard* was born in Paris on this day in 1930. One of the most influential members of the French *nouvelle vague*, his first feature film was *A bout de souffle* (Breathless) (1960). His other films include *Alphaville* (1965), *Pierrot le fou* (1966) and *Sauve qui peut* (1980).

Meaning divinely firm

Conrad, Konrad

Józef Teodor Naleçz Konrad Korzeniowksi was born in Berdichev (now Ukraine) on 3 December 1857. He is better known as the novelist *Joseph Conrad*, the author of the short story 'Heart of Darkness' (1902). It was written in English, which was, remarkably, Conrad's third language.

Meaning brave counsel

Ikeda

Ikeda Hayato, who was prime minister of Japan in the early 1960s, was born on 3 December 1899. He resolved a long-running mining strike at the beginning of his term and became one of the key figures in masterminding Japan's extraordinary economic growth.

Meaning pond, rice field

Ferlin, Ferlon

The US country singer *Ferlin Husky* was born in Flat River, Missouri, on this day in 1927. He had several big hits in the 1950s and 1960s, including 'I Feel Better All Over (More Than Anywhere Else)' (1955). He had several pseudonyms, including Simon Crum and Terry Preston.

Meaning not known

Katarina, Katrina, Katrin

The German figure skater *Katarina Witt* was born on this day in 1965 in the city of Staaken. She won two gold medals at the Winter Olympics in Sarajevo in 1984 and again in 1988 in Calgary. She also won the world championship title four times.

Meaning pure maiden

Julianne, Julieanne, Julianna

The actress *Julianne Moore* celebrates her birthday today. She was born in 1961 in Fayetteville, North Carolina. After appearances in TV movies, mini-series and theatre, she has become an established film actress. Her films include *The End of the Affair* (1999), *The Hours* (2002) and *Far From Heaven* (2002).

Meaning young in heart and mind

Daryl, Darel, Darelle

The American actress *Daryl Hannah* was born in Chicago on this day in 1960. Her film debut was in the horror movie *The Fury* in 1978. Other memorable roles have been in *Blade Runner* (1982), *Splash!* (1984), *Roxanne* (1987) and *Northfork* (2002).

Meaning dear little one

Freda, Halfrida, Wilfreda

On this day in 1910 *Freda du Faur* became the first woman to climb Mount Cook, New Zealand, in a record-breaking six hours. She was born in Australia in 1882. On all her climbs she wore a skirt, which came to just below the knee, underneath which she wore knickerbockers and long puttees.

Meaning peace

Rainer

The lyric poet *Rainer Maria Rilke* was born in Prague (then in the Austrian Empire) on 4 December 1875. He was educated in Germany, and after travelling in Europe he settled in Paris. Considered one of the greatest lyric poets to have written in German, his best-known works are *The Tale of the Love and Death of Cornet Christopher Rilke* (1905), and *Duino Elegies* and *Sonnets to Orpheus* (both 1923).

Meaning ruler

Wassily, Vassily

The painter *Wassily Kandinsky* was born in Moscow on this day in 1866. He is considered one of the most important 20th-century artists, and with Picasso and Matisse he is credited with painting the first abstract works of modern art.

Meaning unwavering protector

Cornell, Cornelius, Neil

The US crime writer *Cornell Woolrich* was born on this day in 1903. His story, *It Had to be Murder*, which he wrote under the pseudonym William Irish, was retitled *Rear Window* and made into a film by Alfred Hitchcock in 1954. Another story, *The Bride Wore Black* (1940), was made into a film by French director François Truffaut in 1968.

Meaning battle horn

Shawn

Shawn Carter was born in Brooklyn, New York, on 4 December 1970. Better known as the rapper star Jay-Z, and variously as the Jigga, HOV and Hova, he got his name from his local nickname Jazzy. After many hits, he became the president and CEO of Def Jam Recordings.

Meaning God's gracious gift

Deanna, Dee, Diandra

The Canadian actress and singer *Deanna Durbin* was born Edna Mae Durbin on this day in 1921 in Winnipeg. Known for her wholesome, sweet image, one of her first films was *Three Smart Girls* (1936), and she received a special Academy Award in 1939 for 'bringing to the screen the spirit and personification of youth'.

Meaning moon goddess

Tyra

The supermodel *Tyra Banks* was born in Los Angeles in 1973. As well as modelling, she has appeared in the TV series *The Fresh Prince of Bel Air* (1990) and *Felicity* (1998). Her film work includes *Halloween Resurrection* (2002).

Meaning battler

Anke, Anika, Anneke, Annika

The tennis player *Anke Huber* was born in Bruchsal, Germany, on this day in 1974. She was introduced to tennis at the tender age of seven and won several junior championships in Europe before competing in major tournaments all over the world.

From Anne, meaning God has favoured me

Celeste

On 4 December 1872 the US brigantine *Mary Celeste* was found drifting in the Atlantic Ocean, between the Azores and Portugal. The ship was deserted, but there was only slight damage to its rigging. There have been many theories about what happened, but the mystery of the ship has never been solved.

Meaning heavenly

Disney, Dis, Disnai

Walt Disney was born Walter Elias Disney in Chicago on 5 December 1901. He had been interested in films since an early age and started making short animated films based on well-known fairytales in the early 1920s. The rest, as they say, is history.

Meaning De Isigney (from Isigney, a French village)

Nunnally

Screenwriter and producer *Nunnally Johnson* was born on this day in 1897 in Columbus, Georgia. He wrote the screenplays for many Hollywood films, including *The Grapes of Wrath* (1940) and *How to Marry a Millionaire* (1953).

Meaning one who is by the monk or nun

Sheldon

US physicist *Sheldon Lee Glashow* was born on 5 December 1932. He worked on the development of theories of electromagnetic and nuclear particle interaction and in 1979 shared the Nobel Prize for physics with Abdus Salaam and Steven Weinberg.

Meaning from the hill ledge

José

The Spanish opera singer *José Carreras* was born in Barcelona on this day in 1946. He was especially known for his performance of the works of Verdi and Puccini, but he became internationally famous as one of the Three Tenors with Placido Domingo and Luciano Pavarotti.

Meaning he will add

Christina

The poet *Christina Georgina Rossetti* was born on this day in London in 1830. She was the sister of the painter and poet Gabriel Dante Rossetti, and their father was a political asylum-seeker from Naples, Italy. Her most popular poem was 'Remember', and many of her other poems were written for children.

Meaning follower of Christ

Kree, Kreeli

Kree Louise Crisman, the daughter of US actress Mariel Hemingway and Stephen Crisman, was born on 5 December 1987. Mariel Hemingway, who has two daughters, starred in the TV film *First Daughter* (1999).

Meaning charming

Crispina

Today is the feast day of *St Crispina*, who lived in Numidia in the early 4th century. During the Diocletian persecutions she was brought before the proconsul because she refused to offer sacrifices to the gods. She was condemned to death by the sword.

Meaning curly-haired

Shalom

The Canadian model and actress *Shalom Harlow* was born in Ontario on 5 December 1973. In 1995 she was the winner of the VH-1 model of the year award. Since then her acting career has blossomed, and she has appeared in many films, including *Vanilla Sky* (2001).

Meaning peace

Nicholas, Nicolas, Niccolo, Nichol, Nicol, Nicolai, Nick, Nik, Nikki, Nickie, Nikos

Today is the feast day *St Nicholas*, who is believed to have lived in the 4th century and who is the patron saint of children, known today as Santa Claus. He was born in Patara, Asia Minor, and was bishop of Myra. A number of miracles are ascribed to him, but not a lot is known about him.

Meaning victorious, conqueror

Osbert, Osborn, Osborne, Osmond, Osmar, Osted, Osman, Ossie

British writer *Osbert Sitwell* was born Sir Francis Osbert Sacheverell Sitwell, 5th baronet Sitwell, on 6 December 1892. His first poem, on his experiences in the trenches in the First World War, was published in 1916. His autobiography ran to five volumes.

Meaning divine

Wulstan, Wulfstan

The British stop-animation film-maker Nick Park was born *Nicolas Wulstan Park* on 6 December 1958. The Oscar winner is the creator of Wallace and Gromit, the stars of several films, including the Oscar-winning *The Wrong Trousers* (1992) and *A Close Shave* (1995).

Meaning wolf stone

Xander

The US actor *Xander Berkeley* was born on this day in 1958. He has appeared in many films, including *Terminator 2: Judgement Day* (1991) and *Apollo 13* (1995). He played George Mason in the hit TV series *24* (2004).

From Alexander, meaning protector of mankind

JoBeth, Jobeth

The US actress *JoBeth Williams* was born in Houston, Texas, on 6 December 1948. She has appeared in many films, most notably *Kramer versus Kramer* (1979), *Poltergeist* (1982) and *Poltergeist II* (1986). She directed *On Hope* (1994), which won her an Oscar nomination for best short film, live action.

From Josephine, meaning God is good, and Elizabeth, meaning consecrated to God

Libbie, Libby

The zoologist *Libbie Hyman* was born on this day in 1888 in Iowa. Her first interest was botany, but she switched to zoology, which she studied at the University of Chicago. She wrote a six-volume study of invertebrates and took art lessons so that she could illustrate her work professionally.

From Elizabeth, meaning consecrated to God

Janine, Janina

Janine Turner, the US actress, was born in Lincoln, Nebraska, on this day in 1962. She is best known for her role in the hit TV show *Northern Exposure*, which ran from 1990 to 1995. She was also in *General Hospital* (1982–3).

From Jane, meaning God's gift of grace

Lina, Lena, Lonette

The German actress *Lina Carstens* was born on this day in 1892. The stage star began working in silent films in the 1920s. In the 1930s she starred in *April April* (1935) and *Das Mädchen vom Moorhof* (1935), and appeared in films until the late 1970s.

Meaning enchanting one

Heywood, Hayward, Haywood

The newspaper columnist and critic *Heywood C. Broun* was born on this day in 1888. He began writing his column 'It Seems to Me' in 1921 for the *New York World*, and it was later syndicated to other newspapers. Always a champion of the underdog, he said: 'The tragedy of life is not that man loses, but that he almost wins.'

Meaning keeper of the hedged field

Noam

The US linguist and political activist *Noam Chomsky* was born on this day in 1928 in Philadelphia. As well as being professor of linguistics at Massachusetts Institute of Technology, he is internationally known as a writer and lecturer on current affairs, philosophy and US foreign policy.

Meaning friendship

Eli, Ely

The US film and stage actor *Eli Wallach* was born on this day in 1917 in Brooklyn, New York. He has had a prolific film career, making his debut in Elia Kazan's *Baby Doll* (1956). His other films include *The Misfits* (1961) and *The Good, the Bad and the Ugly* (1967).

Meaning highest

Gianlorenzo, Gian Lorenzo

The Italian sculptor, architect and painter *Gianlorenzo Bernini* was born on 7 December 1598 in Naples. A child prodigy, he dominated the art scene in Rome for 50 years. He is best known for his sculptures, which transformed Rome into the city of fountains.

Meaning God's gracious gift crowned with laurels

Willa

The US writer *Willa Sibert Cather* was born on this day in Winchester, Virginia, in 1873. When she was 12 years old the family moved to Red Cloud, Nebraska, which became the setting and inspiration for many of her works. She won the Pulitzer Prize for her novel *One of Ours* (1922).

Meaning desiring

Shiri, Shirin, Shirina, Shira, Shirah

The US actress *Shiri Appleby* was born Shiri Freda Appleby on 7 December 1978. Best known for her role as Liz Parker in the US TV soap *Roswell* (2004), she was born in Los Angeles and raised in the San Fernando Valley.

Meaning song

Benedetta

Today is the feast day of *Benedetta Rosello*, also known as St Mary Joseph Rosello. She was born in 1811 at Liguaria, Savona, Italy, and she devoted her life to teaching young girls and was the founder of the Institute of the Daughters of Mercy.

Meaning blessed

Marcella, Marcela, Marcelle

The Italian actress and author *Marcella Albani* was born on this day in 1923. She was a big star of the silent movies in the 1920s, making an impressive 20 films between 1927 and 1929. Her novel *La citta dell'amore* was turned into a film in which she herself starred.

Meaning belonging to Mars

Llewellyn

The author *Richard Llewellyn* was born in St David's, Wales, on this day in 1906. He is best known for his novel *How Green Was My Valley* (1939), a sometimes sentimental depiction of the life of the mining communities of South Wales. The book was a big hit and was made into a Hollywood film in 1941.

Meaning lion-like

Chandler

The journalist and writer *Joel Chandler Harris* was born on this day in 1848 in Eatonton, Georgia. He is best known for his stories about Br'er Rabbit and Uncle Remus, beginning with *Uncle Remus: His Songs and His Sayings* (1880). The Walt Disney film *Song of the South* (1946) was adapted from his work.

Meaning candle-maker

Galway, Galloway

The flautist *James Galway*, who was born in Belfast in 1939, is sometimes called 'the man with the golden flute'. One of the first flautists to have a career as a soloist, his expressive playing features in the soundtracks of *The Lord of the Rings* trilogy (2001, 2002, 2003).

Meaning man from the stranger land

Clerow

The US comedian Flip Wilson was born *Clerow Wilson* on 8 December 1933. He was given the nickname Flip when he was serving in the US air force because of his flippant sense of humour. He hosted *The Flip Wilson Show* (1970–74) and made many other TV appearances.

Meaning not known

Camarin

Today is the feast day of *Our Lady of Camarin* and a public holiday on the Pacific island of Guam. In the apse of Agana Cathedral a small wooden statue of the Lady of Camarin stands guard and protects the people. Camarin is a very popular name on this island.

Meaning shelterer, protector

Teri

The US actress *Teri Hatcher* was born on this day in 1964. She has starred in many films and TV series, including roles as Lois Lane in *Lois and Clark* (1994–7) and Susan Mayer in *Desperate Housewives* (2004–5).

Meaning harvester

Carina, Karina, Caryn, Carynn

The Hong Kong Chinese actress *Carina Lau* was born in the province of Xuzhou on 8 December 1965. She is a big star who has appeared in many films, including *Days of Being Wild* (1990) and *No More Love, No More Death* (1993).

Meaning dear little one

LeAnna, Leanna

LeAnna Croom, the US actress, was born on this day in 1974. She has appeared in film and on TV, and her work has included *Someone Like You* (2001) and *The Door In the Floor* (2004).

Meaning climbing vine

9 DECEMBER

Sebastian, Seb

The Canadian actor *Sebastian Spence* was born in St John's, Newfoundland, on this day in 1969. He has appeared in the TV series *Dawson's Creek* (1998) and *The X-Files* (1998), but is best known for his role as Cade Foster in the Sci-Fi Channel's *First Wave* (1998).

Meaning reverenced one

Sanford

US comedian Redd Foxx was born *John Elroy Sanford* on 9 December 1922. He became a star in the 1970s appearing in the long-running TV series *Sanford and Son*. Later, in 1986, he starred in *The Redd Foxx Show*.

Meaning from the sandy ford

Dalton

US screenwriter and novelist *Dalton Trumbo* was born in Colorado today in 1905. A successful Hollywood scriptwriter in the 1940s, he won an Oscar for *The Brave One* (1956) and another for *Roman Holiday* (1953), awarded in 1993, 40 years after the film's release.

Meaning from the farm in the valley

Beau, Beal, Beale

The actor *Beau Bridges* was born Lloyd Vernet Bridges III on this day in 1941. The son of Lloyd Bridges and the older brother of Jeff Bridges, he was nicknamed Beau after a character in *Gone with the Wind*, the book that both his parents were reading at the time.

Meaning handsome

Judi, Judie, Judy

One of Britain's most distinguished actresses, Dame *Judi Dench*, was born in York on this day in 1934. She made her stage debut as Ophelia in Shakespeare's *Hamlet* in 1957 and has since had a prolific and varied career on stage, film and TV.

Meaning admired

Hermione, Hermina

The actress and comedienne *Hermione Gingold* was born on this day in 1897. She began her career in British musical revues before moving to the USA in 1951. She appeared in the film *Gigi* (1958) and in the Broadway production and film of *A Little Night Music*.

Meaning of the earth

Masako

Crown Princess Masako of Japan was born on 9 December 1963. She became a princess in 1993 on her marriage to Crown Prince Naruhito. She is a graduate of Harvard, Oxford and the University of Tokyo, and before her marriage worked in Japan's ministry of foreign affairs.

Meaning child of Masa

Elisabeth, Elizabeth, Elisabet, Elisabetta, Lizabeta, Lizbeth, Lizzy, Lizzie, Lize, Liza, Liz, Betty, Bettie, Bet, Eliza, Elisa, Elissa, Elzieta, Elspeth

Elisabeth Schwarzkopf, the German lieder and opera singer, was born in Jarotschin, Posen province, on this day in 1915. She was one of the leading sopranos of the 1940s–1960s, and she has recorded all the major roles. She created the part of Anne Trulove in the premiere of Igor Stravinsky's *The Rake's Progress* in Venice in 1951.

Meaning consecrated to God

César, Césare

The composer and organist *César Franck* was born on this day in 1822 in Liège, Belgium. He moved to Paris when he was 22. He was a fine pianist, but made his living as an organist and teacher. His fame as a composer comes from a small number of compositions from his later years.

Meaning emperor

Adrien, Adrian

On this day in 1825 the opera *La Dame blanche* (The White Lady) by the French composer *François Adrien Boieldieu* received its first performance in Paris. Boieldieu was ranked with Auber as the uncrowned king of comic opera in the 1820s.

Meaning from the coast

Hildemar, Hildimar, Hildegard, Hildemara

Today is the feast day of *St Hildemar*, a French Benedictine monk who lived in the 9th century in Corbie, Picardy. In 821 he was made bishop of Beauvais. He attended the councils of Paris in 829 and Beauvais in 844.

Meaning battle renowned

Nobel, Noble, Nolan, Noland

On this day in 1901 the first Nobel Prizes were awarded in Stockholm. They were instituted in the will of *Alfred Nobel*, the Swedish chemist and engineer, who had made a vast fortune from his discovery of dynamite. The prizes are awarded annually on 10 December, the date on which Nobel died in 1896.

Meaning famous, well-born

Rumer

The British author *Rumer Godden* was born in Eastbourne, Sussex, on this day in 1907, but grew up in India. She wrote for children and adults. Her best-known novels are *Black Narcissus* (1939), *The River* (1946) and *The Greengage Summer* (1956), all of which were made into films.

Meaning gypsy

Yelena, Jelena

On this day in 1975 *Yelena Bonner* accepted the Nobel Prize for peace on behalf of her husband, Andrei Sakharov, the nuclear physicist and writer. He was unable to leave the Soviet Union, where the couple were leading dissidents at the helm of the human rights and civil liberties campaigns.

Meaning shining light

Leta, Lita

Mary Leta Dorothy Slaton was born on this day in 1914. Better known as the Hollywood screen goddess Dorothy Lamour, she began her career as Miss New Orleans. Her first big role was as Ulah in *The Jungle Princess* (1936).

Meaning joy

Ada, Adar, Adara

Ada Lovelace, the world's first computer programmer, was born on 10 December 1815, the daughter of the poet Lord Byron. She worked in collaboration with Charles Babbage and devised a method for calculating Bernoulli numbers for his analytical engine.

Meaning happy, prosperous

Fiorello

Fiorello Henry LaGuardia, who was mayor of New York from 1934 to 1945, was born on this day in 1882. He was elected during the Great Depression on an anti-corruption ticket. During a newspaper strike he read comics on the radio. LaGuardia Airport is named after him.

Meaning little flower

Hector, Hec, Heck, Eachan, Eachunn, Eachann

The French composer *Hector Berlioz* was born on 11 December 1803 near Lyons. He is best known for his *Symphonie fantastique* and *Requiem*. He was drawn to the French Romantic movement and became friends with writers such as Alexandre Dumas, Victor Hugo and Honoré de Balzac.

Meaning steadfast

Rider, Ryder

The US actor *Rider Strong* was born on this day in 1979 in San Francisco. He played Shawn Hunter in TV's *Boy Meets World* (1993) and has appeared in the films *Cabin Fever* (2002), *The Secret Pact* (1999) and *My Giant* (1998). His brother, Shiloh, is also an actor.

Meaning horse rider

McCoy

The US jazz pianist *McCoy Tyner* was born on 11 December 1938 in Philadelphia. He played with the famous John Coltrane Quartet and has had many successful recordings on his own for the Blue Note label, including *The Real McCoy* and *Tender Moments*.

Meaning son of Aodh, son of fire

Severine

The Belgian model *Severine van de Voorde* was born on this day in 1980. She was a finalist in the Miss Belgium competition in 2004. The name Severine is French and comes from the Latin Severinus. There was a pope called Severinus and many saints have this name.

Meaning stem

Teri, Terentia, Terencia

The film actress *Teri Garr* was born on this day in 1949 in Lakewood, Ohio. Among the films she has appeared in are *Young Frankenstein* (1974), *Close Encounters of The Third Kind* (1977) and *Tootsie* (1982), for which she was nominated for an Oscar as best supporting actress.

Meaning guardian

Clemence, Clemency, Clementine

Dr *Clemence Harned Lozier* was born on this day in 1813 in New Jersey, the youngest of 13 children. She studied medicine in Syracuse, and in 1863 founded the New York Medical College and Hospital for Women, the first institution to be founded in New York City where women could study medicine.

Meaning merciful, kind

Rosita

The Puerto Rican singer, dancer and actress Rita Moreno was born *Rosita Dolores Alverio* on this day in 1931. She won a best supporting actress Oscar for her role in the film *West Side Story* (1961) and was the second person in history to have won an Emmy, a Grammy, a Tony and an Oscar.

From Rose, meaning rose

Osborne, Osborn

The playwright *John James Osborne* was born in London on this day in 1929. The main character, Jimmy Porter, in his best-known play, *Look Back in Anger* (1956), was the prototype of the 'angry young man', a phrase that came to be used to describe a generation of artists who rebelled against the establishment.

Meaning divine warrior

Emerson

The racing driver *Emerson Fittipaldi* was born today in 1946 in São Paulo, Brazil. He started his successful career in Europe in 1969 and was a Formula One championship winner. His nephew, Christian, is also a racing driver.

Meaning industrious ruler

Frank, Franklin, Francklin, Frankie, Franklyn

US singer and actor *Frank Sinatra* was born Francis Albert Sinatra on 12 December 1915. He was one of the finest vocalists that has ever lived, and his rise to fame and riches from a poor childhood in Hoboken, New York, epitomized the American Dream.

Meaning free man

Manès

Manès Sperber was born on 12 December 1905 in Zablotow, Galizien (now in Ukraine). He was an Austrian-French writer, psychologist and philosopher most famed for his trilogy *Wie eine Träne im Ozean* (1961).

Meaning god of the underworld

Concetta

One of the bestselling female singers of all time, Connie Francis was born *Concetta Franconero* on this day in 1938 in Newark, New Jersey. Her first hit, 'Who's Sorry Now' (1958), launched her into super-stardom status. She had many other hit records, including 'Don't Break the Heart that Loves You' (1962).

Meaning ingenious thought

Dionne, Dione, Dionia

US singer *Dionne Warwick* was born on 12 December in 1940 and is best known for her work with songwriters, Hal David and Burt Bacharach. Among her most successful songs were 'Anyone Who Had a Heart' (1964), 'Walk on by' (1964) and 'Do You Know the Way to San José?' (1967).

Meaning daughter of heaven and earth

Honor, Honora

British actress *Honor Blackman* was born on this day in 1927. She became famous for her roles as Cathy Gale in the cult British 1960s TV series *The Avengers* and as Bond-girl Pussy Galore in the film *Goldfinger* (1964).

Meaning honour

Sheila, Sheilah, Shelagh

The singer and percussionist *Sheila E* was born today in 1959. Her father is Pete Escovedo, Latin-jazz artist and band leader. Sheila dropped her surname after meeting Prince in 1983; he helped her to record her first solo album, *The Glamorous Life*, in 1984.

Meaning musical

Yevgeny

The writer *Yevgeny Petrov* was born in Odessa on 13 December 1903. Together with fellow journalist and novelist Ilya Ilf, he wrote two successful satirical novels in the 1930s, *The Twelve Chairs* and *The Little Golden Calf*, the first of which was made into a film in the USA by Mel Brooks.

Meaning noble

Ferguson, Fergus, Feargus

The baseball player *Ferguson Jenkins* was born on this day in 1943 in Ontario, Canada. He played with the Philadelphia Phillies, the Chicago Cubs and the Texas Rangers. He was the first Canadian ever to be elected to the US National Baseball Hall of Fame.

Meaning best choice

Laurens, Loren, Lorin

Sir *Laurens van der Post* was born on 13 December 1906 in Philipolos, Orange River, a British colony in South Africa, to a Dutch father and German mother. The explorer, writer, philosopher, farmer, educator, humanitarian and conservationist is best known for his book *The Lost World of the Kalahari* (1958).

Meaning laurel crown

Haven, Havyn

Haven Jude Cain, the son of Schae Harrison and Mick Cain, was born on 13 December 2003. His parents are both stars of the popular daytime US TV drama *The Bold and the Beautiful* (1987).

Meaning safe place

Tonja

Tonja Yevette Buford-Bailey, the US athlete, was born on 13 December 1970. The 400 meter hurdler won the bronze medal at the 1996 Olympic Games at Atlanta, Georgia.

Meaning worthy of praise

Anouska, Anuska

Anouska Hempel, Lady Weinberg, was born in New Zealand on this day in 1941. The actress, designer and hotelier moved to Britain in the 1960s. Married to Sir Mark Weinberg, her achievements include the fashionably minimalist Hempel Hotel in London.

From Anne, meaning God has favoured me

Lucy

Today is the feast day of *St Lucy*, who lived in Syracuse, Sicily, in the early 4th century. During the Diocletian persecution of Christians she was denounced as a Christian by a rejected suitor. She is renowned for healing diseases of the eyes.

Meaning light

Paula

The British actress *Paula Wilcox* was born in Manchester on this day in 1949. She has appeared in many British TV series, including *Coronation Street* and the long-running *On the House* and *Man About the House* in the 1970s.

Meaning small

Tycho, Tyge

The Danish astronomer *Tycho Brahe* was born on this day in 1546 at his family's ancestral seat, Knudstrup Castle, Sweden. He coined the term 'nova' for a 'new' star in his book *De stella nova* (1573), when he was recording the appearance of a very bright star, now known as Tycho's star, in the constellation Cassiopeia.

Meaning he who hits the mark

Roger, Rodger

The British artist and art critic and member of the Bloomsbury Group *Roger Fry* was born on this day in 1866 in London. In 1913 he founded the Omega Workshops, whose members included Vanessa Bell, the sister of writer Virginia Woolf.

Meaning renowned warrior

Morey, Morrie, Morse, Moritz, Moriz, Morets, Meuriz

Morey Amsterdam, the US actor and comedian, was born in Chicago on 14 December 1908. He began his show business career as his brother's straight man and also worked in Al Capone's speakeasy. Commonly known as the Human Joke Machine, he played Buddy Sorrel in *The Dick Van Dyke Show* (1962–6).

From Maurice, meaning dark, swarthy

Binion, Binyamin

Binion Louis Haggard, the son of Theresa and Merle Haggard, was born on 14 December 1992. The country music star Merle Haggard has had a massive 95 country music hits, with a total of 38 number ones.

Meaning son of my right hand

Aphra

The British writer *Aphra Behn*, who was born in Wyte, Kent, was baptized on this day in 1640. The first British woman to earn a living as a writer, she wrote poetry, several novels and 15 plays. Virginia Woolf was a great admirer, crediting her as the one who allowed all women to speak their minds.

Meaning female deer

Cynthia, Cindy

The actress *Cynthia Gibb* was born on this day in 1963 in Bennington, Vermont. She trained as a dancer and played a minor part in the Woody Allen film *Stardust Memories* (1980). Her TV work includes three years appearing in *Fame* (1982), and she played Karen Carpenter in *The Karen Carpenter Story* (1989).

Meaning moon goddess

Lee

The US actress *Lee Remick* was born on this day in 1935. She had a long career in films, from her debut in *A Face in the Crowd* (1957). She was in *The Omen* (1976) and was nominated for an Oscar for her performance in *Days of Wine and Roses* (1963).

Meaning wood, clearing

Noelle, Noel

The US actress *Noelle Beck* was born on 14 December 1968 in Baltimore, Maryland. She has appeared in many TV soaps, including playing the roles of Trishia Alden McKenzie in *Loving* (1983), and Jordan Tate in *Central Park West* (1995).

Meaning Christmas

15 DECEMBER

Baichung

The Indian soccer player *Baichung Bhutia* was born in Tinkitam on this day in 1976. India's top player, he attracted big sponsorship deals and in 1994 was voted Indian player of the year. In the 1999 season he played for the English team, Bury Football Club.

Meaning not known

Nero

The fifth and last Roman emperor of the Julio-Claudian dynasty, *Nero* was born Lucius Domitius Ahenobarbus on 15 December AD37. He was emperor during the years 54 to 68 and is probably best remembered for his interest in singing, acting and chariot racing rather than his administrative successes. He allegedly continued playing his lyre while Rome burned to the ground in the year 64.

Meaning powerful

János

The Hungarian mathematician *János Bolyai* was born in Kolozsvár, Transylvania, on this day in 1802. He mastered calculus by the time he was 13 years old and went on to do important work relating to complex numbers and real numbers.

Meaning God's gracious gift

Freeman, Freedman

The British physicist and mathematician *Freeman John Dyson* was born in Berkshire on this day in 1923. He worked on quantum electrodynamics at Princeton University and on the subsequently abandoned Orion space project. He published speculations about space and the future, and is renowned for his work on quantum theory.

Meaning born a free man

Atlanta, Atalanta, Atlantia, Atlan

On 15 December 1939 the world premiere of the film *Gone with the Wind* was held in Atlanta, Georgia. The British actress Vivien Leigh played Scarlett O'Hara, but many actresses were tested for the role, including Katharine Hepburn, Barbara Stanwyck and Tallulah Bankhead. It was one of the highest-grossing films of all time.

Meaning mighty bearer

Vida

The writer, teacher and reformer *Vida Scudder* was born on this day in 1861 in Madura, India. She and her mother returned to the USA in 1862 after the death of her father, who was a Congregationalist missionary. She became active in social welfare and went on to help organize the Women's Trade Union League.

Meaning beloved

Surya

The French ice skater *Surya Bonaly* celebrates her birthday today. She was born in Nice in 1973 and began skating at the age of 18 months. She was once a world champion gymnast and is famous for her unique back flip when she lands.

Meaning sun

Una, Oona, Oonagh, Ona

The British writer, physician and feminist *Una Kroll* was born today in 1925. After studying medicine she was a nun for five years. She became a doctor, married, had four children and campaigned against sex discrimination. She was ordained in 1997.

Meaning the one and only girl

Ludwig, Ludvig, Ludovik

One of the greatest composers of all time, *Ludwig van Beethoven* was born on this day in 1770 in Bonn, Germany. His talent was noticed at a very early age. Many of his greatest works were written after the onset of deafness, which began when he was about 28.

From Lewis, meaning famous warrior

Zoltán, Zoltan, Zoltin

The composer *Zoltán Kodály* was born on this day in 1882 in Hungary. He spent most of his childhood in what is now Slovakia and studied music at the Franz Liszt Academy in Budapest. His fervent interest in folk music influenced many of his compositions.

Meaning ruler, sultan

Boston

On 16 December 1773 the *Boston Tea Party* took place. It was a political protest by the residents of Boston, who were infuriated by the British government's decision to levy a tax on tea in America, even though the same tax had been repealed in Britain.

Meaning town near a thicket

Jaromir

On this day 1997 the opera *Shwanda the Bagpiper* by the Czech US composer *Jaromir Weinberger* received its first performance in Wroclaw, Poland. Weinberger was unable to match the success of his popular opera, which was subsequently translated into 17 languages.

Meaning not known

Jane

On this day in 1775 the writer *Jane Austen* was born in Steventon, Hampshire, where her father was rector. Of her six great novels, four were published anonymously during her lifetime. *Persuasion* and *Northanger Abbey* were published under her name after her death in 1818.

Meaning God is gracious

Elayne

The US comedienne *Elayne Boosler* was born in Brooklyn on this day in 1952. As well as performing in live stand-up shows, she hosts the US TV game show *Balderdash*, based on the board game of the same name, in which (as in *Call My Bluff*) contestants have to work out which definition of a word is true and which is balderdash.

From Helen, meaning light

Lenita, Leni, Lenitia

The US actress *Lenita Lane* was born in Pennsylvania on 16 December 1901. She was a big star from the 1930s to the 1950s and appeared in many films, including *The Bat* (1959). She was married to the screenwriter Crane Wilbur.

Meaning gentle

Adelaide

Today is the feast day of *St Adelaide*. After the death of her first husband, Lothair, king of Italy, she married Otto I (Otto the Great), king of the Germans from 936 to 973 and holy Roman emperor from 962 onwards. As queen mother during the reign of Otto II and joint-regent (with Empress Theophano) for Otto III, she influenced state affairs, but also conducted herself with modesty and piety.

Meaning well-born, kind

Madox, Maddox, Maddock

The British novelist, poet and literary critic *Ford Madox Ford* was born Ford Hermann Hueffer in Merton, Surrey, on this day in 1873. In 1919 he changed his name in honour of his grandfather, the Pre-Raphaelite painter Ford Madox Brown. His best-known novel is *The Good Soldier* (1915).

Meaning beneficent

Erskine

The US writer *Erskine Caldwell* was born on 17 December 1903 in White Oak, Georgia. As a young man he had a variety of jobs, and these gave him a deep insight into the lives of poor sharecroppers, which was later reflected in his novels *Tobacco Road* (1932) and *Gold's Little Acre* (1933).

Meaning from the cliff's height

Armin

Armin Mueller-Stahl, the leading German film actor, was born on 17 December 1930. He began his career in East Germany and emigrated to the West in 1980. He was nominated for an Oscar for best supporting actor for his performance in the film *Shine* (1996).

Meaning army man

Takeo

Takeo Spikes was born on this day in 1976 in Sandersville, Georgia. The US football player began his career with the Cincinnati Bengals, who drafted him out of Auburn University. He then moved to the Buffalo Bills.

Meaning strong, like bamboo

Oxana, Ozana

The first Miss Russia to win the Miss Universe contest, *Oxana Fedorova*, was born on 17 December 1977. After her win in 2002 she received many awards and honours. She gave up her crown for personal reasons, and became an advocate of Russian youth causes.

Meaning treasure

Begga

Today is the feast day of *St Begga*, who was the sister of St Gertrude of Nivelles. Begga married Ansegis, a son of St Arnulf of Metz, and their son was Pepin of Heristal. After her husband's death, Begga founded seven churches, and nuns from her sister's convent joined her in the abbey she founded at Andenne in France.

Meaning small

Milla, Militza

Milla Jovovich was born Militza Natasha Jovovich in Kiev, Ukraine, on 17 December 1975. Raised in the USA, she became a child model and then starred in *Return to the Blue Lagoon* (1980). She is also a singer, and her first album, *The Divine Comedy*, was released in 1994.

Meaning not known

Napiera

Napiera Danielle Groves, the US actress best known for her role as Bonnie in the TV soap *As the World Turns* (1956), was born on 17 December 1975. In 1997 she was crowned Miss Washington D.C. and Miss Congeniality.

Meaning valley

Keith

Keith Richards, songwriter and guitarist with the Rolling Stones, was born in Dartford, Kent, on this day in 1943. He co-founded the group in 1962 with Mick Jagger and Brian Jones.

Meaning from the forest

Robson, Robinson

The British actor *Robson Green* was born in Northumberland on this day in 1964. He has starred in many TV dramas, and a one-off performance of 'Unchained Melody' in an episode of the drama series *Soldier, Soldier* (1990) led to a surprise British number one hit for Robson and his co-star, Jerome Flynn.

Meaning son of Robert

Brad, Bradley

The US film star *Brad Pitt* was born on this day in 1963 in Shawnee, Oklahoma. One of Hollywood's most successful actors, he was nominated for an Oscar as best supporting actor for his role in Terry Gilliam's film *Twelve Monkeys* (1995). Later films include *Ocean's Eleven* (2001) and *Troy* (2004).

Meaning from the broad meadow

Henderson

The African-American jazz musician *Fletcher Henderson* was born on this day in 1897 in Cuthbert, Georgia. A pianist, bandleader, arranger and composer, he was influential in the development of big band jazz and swing music, and his pieces include 'Hot Mustard' (1926) and 'Grand Terrace Rhythm' (1936).

Meaning son of Henry

Arantxa

The Spanish tennis player *Arantxa Sanchez-Vicario* was born on 18 December 1971 in Barcelona. In 1989 she became the first Spanish player to win a grand slam event when she beat Steffi Graf in the French open singles final.

Meaning thornbush

Eugenia, Eugenie, Gina

The Russian gymnast *Eugenia Kuznetsova* was born on this day in 1980 in St Petersburg. Her best events are the beam and bars, and she was European champion on the beam in 1998. She moved to Bulgaria in 2001, the nation she has since represented at international events.

Meaning noble, well-born

Gladys, Gladine, Gleda

The British actress Dame *Gladys Cooper* was born on this day in 1888 in Lewisham, London. She had a long and distinguished career in Hollywood from 1940, appearing in classic movies such as *Rebecca* (1940), *The Bishop's Wife* (1947) and *My Fair Lady* (1964).

Meaning frail, delicate flower

Annette, Annetta

The ballet dancer *Annette Page* was born on this day in 1932. She was a dancer with the Royal Ballet, and in 1962 she toured Australia with Margot Fonteyn, Michael Soames, Rowena Jackson and Bryan Ashbridge. This celebrated group was known as the Fonteyn Follies.

From Anne, meaning God has favoured me

19 DECEMBER

Carter

The US historian and teacher *Carter G. Woodson* was born on this day in 1875 in New Canton, Virginia. In 1912 he became only the second African-American to earn a Harvard doctorate; his subject was history. He was an active promoter of black education.

Meaning cart driver

Eamonn, Eamon

The Irish TV personality *Eamonn Andrews* was born on this day in 1922 in Dublin. He was a popular presenter of BBC programmes in the 1960s, including *What's My Line*, *This is Your Life* and the children's show, *Crackerjack*.

Meaning rich guardian

Italo

The Italian writer Ettore Schmitz, who wrote under the penname *Italo Svevo*, was born in Trieste on this day in 1861. His classic psychological novel *Confessions of Zeno* was self-published in 1923, but was not a success until it was championed by James Joyce.

Meaning to hold fast

Jake

US actor *Jake Gyllenhall* was born in Los Angeles on 19 December 1980. His first big role was the lead in the cult classic *Donnie Darko* (2001). Other film appearances include *Bubble Boy* (2001) and *The Good Girl* (2002).

Meaning supplanter

Alyssa

The US actress *Alyssa Jayne Milano* was born on this day in 1972. She is best known for her appearances on the US TV show *Who's the Boss?* (1984–92), in which she starred with Tony Danza. Her image was used as a template for Ariel in the Disney cartoon *The Little Mermaid* (1989).

From Alice, meaning noble, well-born

Zanzibar, Zanzi

On this day in 1963 *Zanzibar* gained its independence from Britain. The country consists of two islands, Zanzibar and Pemba, and, together with nearby Mafia Island and the Maluku Islands, they are sometimes called the Spice Islands.

Meaning land of the blacks

Samthana, Sam

Today is the feast day of *St Samthana of Meath*. An Irish abbess, she lived in the 6th century and founded the Benedictine monastery of Cluain-Bronach in Meath, Ireland's 'royal' county.

Meaning not known

Janie

The country music singer *Janie Fricke* was born on 19 December 1952. She sang on albums with Elvis Presley before becoming a star in her own right. She has won many awards, including the Country Music Association's female vocalist of the year in 1982 and 1983.

Meaning God's gift of grace

Nalo

The Canadian author *Nalo Hopkinson* was born on 20 December 1960. His novels, which combine traditional Caribbean storytelling with science fiction, include *Brown Girl in the Ring* (1998) and *Midnight Robber* (2000).

Meaning loveable

Suleiman, Suleyman

On this day in 1522 the sultan of the Ottoman Empire, *Sulieman the Magnificent*, accepted the surrender of the Knights of Rhodes. They then moved to Malta and became known as the Knights of Malta.

From Solomon, meaning peaceful, wise

Uri, Yuri, Uriah, Urias, Uriel

The TV personality and alleged psychic *Uri Geller* was born in Tel Aviv, Israel, on this day in 1946. He started out as a magician in Israeli night-clubs, and in the 1970s he became internationally famous for his telekinetic and telepathic abilities, bending spoons and distorting watches.

Meaning the Lord is my light

Branch

The US baseball executive *Branch Rickey* was born on 20 December 1881. He was the executive who helped get rid of baseball's colour barrier. His many innovative achievements, including the invention of the minor league system, earned him the nickname the Mahatma.

Meaning extension

Mitsuko

The pianist *Mitsuko Uchida* was born at Atami near Tokyo on 20 December 1948. She is known particularly for her interpretation of the works of Mozart, Beethoven and Schubert. She has recorded all Mozart's piano sonatas and is artistic director of Marlboro Music School and Festival.

Meaning child of Mitsu

Louisiana

Today commemorates the day in 1803 on which the *Louisiana Purchase* was completed. For $15 million the USA bought the French territory of Louisiana, an area of some 2,144,500 square kilometres (828,000 square miles), extending from Canada to the Gulf of Mexico and from the Mississippi River to the Rocky Mountains, thereby doubling the size of the United States.

From Louis, meaning famous warrior

JoJo

The US pop singer *JoJo* was born Joanna Noelle Levesque in Foxborough, Massachusetts, on this day in 1990. She had a hit with 'Leave (Get Out)' when she was just 13 years old. She is the youngest female solo artist ever to have had a number one hit in the US.

From Johanna, meaning God's gift of grace

Irene

On this day in 1898 the US actress *Irene Dunne* was born. She starred in many films in the 1930s and 1940s, often playing well-bred, rather sensible women. She was nominated for Oscars for her performances in *Theodora Goes Wild* (1936), *The Awful Truth* (1937), *Love Affair* (1939) and *I Remember Mama* (1948).

Meaning peace

Keifer

The TV and film actor *Keifer Sutherland* was born in London on this day in 1966. His father is the Canadian actor Donald Sutherland and his mother is the actress Shirley Douglas. Keifer is best known for his role as Jack Bauer in the cult TV show *24* (from 2003).

Meaning barrel-maker

Marco

The Dutch pop singer *Marco Borsato* was born on this day in 1966. His self-titled first album was a big hit, and he has since released several more successful albums. A patron of the charity War Child, he has given benefit concerts and heads an awareness campaign in the Netherlands.

Meaning follower of Mars, the warrior

Wynn, Wynne

On this day in 1913 the very first crossword puzzle appeared in a newspaper. It was the invention of *Arthur Wynne*, a journalist with the *New York World*. He called it a word-cross, but a mistake was made by the typesetter who called it a cross-word.

Meaning fair one

Sewall

The US geneticist *Sewall Green Wright*, who was born on 21 December 1889, was one of the primary founders of population genetics. He emphasized the importance of the interaction of genetic drift and natural selection in determining the outcome of evolution.

Meaning sea powerful

Karmen, Karmina, Karmia, Karmine, Karma, Karmacita, Karmelita, Karmita

The Slovenian musician and pop singer *Karmen Stavec* was born on 21 December 1973 in Berlin in what was then West Germany. She represented Slovenia in the 2003 Eurovision Song Contest with the song 'Nanana'.

Meaning singer with beautiful voice

Delorez

The US athlete *Delorez Florence Griffith Joyner* was born on this day in 1959. Known as Flo Jo, she first came to the world's attention as a 200 metres silver medallist in the 1984 Olympic Games. Known as a 200 metres runner, she startled everyone when she set a new world record of 10.49 seconds for the 100 metres.

Meaning lady of sorrow

Karrie

The Australian golfer *Karrie Webb* was born on 21 December 1974 in Ayr, Queensland. She is one of the most successful players in the world, winning, among other tournaments, the British women's open in 1995, 1997 and 2002, and the US open in 2000 and 2001.

Meaning gracious melody

Chala, Chalae

Chala King, the daughter of the US TV talk-show host Larry King, was born on 21 December 1967. *The Larry King Show* is CNN's most popular and highest-rated show.

Meaning neither one thing nor another

Mathias, Mattias

The Belgian-born actor *Mathias Sercu* was born today in 1970. He is best known for his role as Ubi Stevens in the TV series *Buiten de Zone* (1995). He has also appeared in Flemish-speaking films and is a theatre writer and director.

Meaning gift of God

Srinivasa, Srinivas, Srini

The Indian mathematician *Srinivasa Aiyanger Ramanujan* was born on 22 December 1887. A child prodigy who never went to university, he had mastered trigonometry by the age of 12. He is famous for many summation formulas, including *pi*, prime numbers and the partition function.

Meaning not known

Obadiah, Obie, Obed, Obe

British entomologist *John Obadiah Westwood* was born in Sheffield, Yorkshire, on this day in 1893. He was the president of the Entomological Society of London and the curator of the Hope Entomological Collection at Oxford.

Meaning servant of God

Hawkshaw, Hawk

The country music singer *Hawkshaw Hawkins* was born on this day in 1921. A big star in the 1940s, he played honky-tonk blues and traditional country, and his shows were unique western entertainments, featuring rope tricks, stand-up comedy and horses.

Meaning detective

Manon

Manon Lescaut was the third opera by Giacomo Puccini, who was born on this day in 1858 in Lucca, Italy. His operas are extremely popular, their beautiful arias making them attractive to a wide audience. *Manon Lescaut* was the first of his works with librettists Giuseppe Giacosa, Luigi Illica, Giulio Ricordi and Domenico Oliva.

From Mary, meaning bitter

Alma

The British singer *Alma Cogan* began her career on 22 December 1948 in the chorus of the first London performance of *High Button Shoes*, the musical by Jule Styne and Sammy Cahn, which was based on the novel by Stephen Longstreet. The songs included 'I Still Get Jealous' and 'Can't You Just See Yourself'.

Meaning kind, nourishing

BernNadette

The US actress *BernNadette Stanis* was born on 22 December 1953. She is best known for her role as Thelma in the US TV comedy *Good Times* (1974). She was also in the hip hop video *Camp Lo* (1998) and produces off-Broadway shows with her husband.

Meaning brave as a bear

Estella

The Canadian actress and model *Estella Warren* was born in Peterborough, Ontario, on this day in 1978. She starred in *Driven* (2001) with Sylvester Stallone and played Daenna in *The Planet of the Apes* (2001). She has been placed top of *Maxim* magazine's hot 100 babe list.

Meaning bright star

23 DECEMBER

Akihito

Akihito, the emperor of Japan, was born on 23 December 1933. He is the 125th emperor of his country, and he and Empress Michiko have three children: Crown Prince Naruhito, Prince Akishino and Princess Sayako.

Meaning bright

Corey, Correy, Corry, Cory, Corrie

The Canadian actor *Corey Haim* was born in Toronto on 23 December 1971. He made many films in Hollywood in the 1980s, including *The Lost Boys* (1987) and *Dream a Little Dream* (1989).

Meaning raven, from the hollow

Jorma

Jorma Kaukonen, one of the founding members of the US 1960s band Jefferson Airplane, was born on this day in 1940 in Washington D.C. He has since run a music and guitar camp in Ohio called the Fur Peace Ranch.

Meaning farmer

Severo

Severo Bonini, the Italian composer, organist and writer on music, was born in Florence on 23 December 1582. He was a Benedictine monk, who was the organist at Santa Trinità, Florence. He wrote an important book about the rise of opera.

Meaning victory guard

Carla, Carly

The model and singer *Carla Bruni* was born in Turin, Italy, on this day in 1968, but grew up in France. After retiring from modelling, she established a new career as a singer, releasing her debut album, *Quel qu'un m'a dit*, in 2002.

Meaning woman born to command

Micheline, Michaela, Michelle

The French athlete and pianist *Micheline Ostermeyer* was born on this day in 1922 in France, but grew up in Tunisia. She managed to mix her music career with athletics, and at the 1948 Olympic Games she won gold medals in the shot put and discus events as well as a bronze medal in the high jump.

Meaning likeness to God

Catriona

The speed skater *Catriona LeMay Doan* was born in 1970 in Saskatchewan, Canada, of Scottish descent. She won the 500 metres speed skating title at both the 1998 and 2002 Winter Olympics, becoming the fastest woman on ice.

Meaning pure maiden

Beth

It is the birthday today of the popular Spanish singer known as *Beth*, who was born on this day in 1981 in Suria, near Barcelona. Her song 'Dime' (2003), Spain's entry for the Eurovision Song Contest, was a big hit in Spain.

From Elizabeth, meaning consecrated to God

Hadley, Hadleigh

The British author of mystery books *James Hadley Chase* was born René Brabazon Raymond in London on this day in 1906. His best-known book, *No Orchids for Mrs Blandish* (1939), was filmed in 1948, and another story, *Eve*, was made into a film (1962) starring Jeanne Moreau and Stanley Baker.

Meaning from the hot meadow

Anil

The Indian actor *Anil Kapoor* celebrates his birthday today. He was born in 1969 and is a star of many Bollywood films, including *Shakti* (1993). A member of a film-making dynasty, his father is a cousin of Raj Kapoor. One of his brothers is a film producer and another is an actor.

Meaning god of the wind

Prescott

The British physicist *James Prescott Joule* was born in Manchester on this day in 1818. He studied the nature of heat, and his discovery of its relationship to mechanical work led to the first law of thermodynamics. The SI unit of work, the joule, is named after him.

Meaning from the priest's house

Diedrich

The US actor *Diedrich Bader* was born on 24 December 1968 in Washington D.C. He spent part of his childhood in France. He played both twins, Jethro and Jethrine, in *The Beverly Hillbillies* (1993) and Oswald in the US TV comedy hit *The Drew Carey Show* (1995).

Meaning ruler of people

Myrtle

Lulu Belle, named the queen of all radio in 1936, was born *Myrtle Cooper* on this day in 1913. She and her husband Scott Wiseman were the country music act Lulu Belle and Scotty. In the 1970s she went into politics and represented North Carolina for the Democrats.

Meaning evergreen shrub, myrtle

Zola

Zola Murphy, the daughter of Nicole and Eddie Murphy, was born on 24 December 1999. Eddie Murphy is one of the most popular actors and comedians in the US. Zola has two sisters, Brya and Shayne, and a brother, Myles.

Meaning quiet, tranquil

Irmina, Irmine, Erme, Erma

Today is the feast day of *St Irmina of Oehren* and her sister St Adela of Pfalzel. They lived in Germany in the 8th century and were the daughters of the king of the Franks, Dagobert II, who was himself later canonized, and the Anglo-Saxon princess, Matilda.

From Irma, meaning strong

Ava, Avis

The actress *Ava Gardner* was born on this day in 1922 in North Carolina. A leading film actress of the 1940s and 1950s, she was once voted the world's most beautiful woman. She had three husbands, including Mickey Rooney and Frank Sinatra, and many lovers, including Howard Hughes and the matador Luis Miguel Dominguin.

Meaning bird

Maurice, Morris, Morrell

The French painter *Maurice Utrillo* was born on this day in 1883. He was born and raised in the Montmartre quarter of Paris and is best known for his paintings of the area in which he grew up. He had no real training in art, other than what his mother, Suzanne Valadon, a painter and artist's model, taught him.

Meaning dark, swarthy

Cabell, Cab

The jazz singer and bandleader *Cabell 'Cab' Calloway III* was born in Rochester, New York, on 25 December 1907. He was a master of 'scat' singing and led one of America's most popular big bands from the early 1930s to the 1950s. He recorded his best-known song, 'Minnie the Moocher', in 1931.

Meaning crooked mouth

Bogart

The legendary US film actor *Humphrey Bogart* was born in New York City on this day in 1899. He won the best actor Oscar for *The African Queen* (1951) and was voted the greatest male star of all time by the American Film Institute in 1999.

Meaning strong bow

Ismail, Ishmael

The film producer *Ismail Merchant* was born on this day in 1936. He and director James Ivory founded Merchant-Ivory productions in 1961, and they often worked with the screenwriter Ruth Prawer Jhabvala. Their films include *Heat and Dust* (1983), *A Room with a View* (1985) and *The Remains of the Day* (1993).

Meaning the wanderer

Cecily, Cecilia, Cicely, Celia

The writer Dame Rebecca West was born *Cecily Isabel Fairfield* in Ireland on this day in 1892. She trained as an actress and took the name Rebecca West from a play by Ibsen. She wrote non-fiction and fiction, and her best-known novel is *The Return of the Soldier* (1918).

Meaning patron saint of music

Sissy, Sissie, Sisley

The US actress *Sissy Spacek* was born Mary Elizabeth Spacek on this day in 1949 in Quitman, Texas. Her first notable role was in *Badlands* (1973) with Martin Sheen. She has been an Oscar nominee five times, and won the best actress award for her performance in *Coal Miner's Daughter* (1980), in which she played Loretta Lynn and sang.

Meaning musical

Dido

The pop singer *Dido* was born Dido Florian Cloud de Bouneville Armstrong in London on this day in 1971. Her hit singles 'Thank You' and 'Here with Me' were from her debut album *No Angel*, which was Britain's top-selling album in 2001.

Meaning teacher

Clarissa, Clarice

The founder of the American Red Cross, *Clarissa Harlowe Barton*, known as Clara Barton, was born on this day in 1821 in Oxford, Massachusetts. At the start of the Civil War she began work as a volunteer, organizing deliveries of bandages and other supplies to wounded soldiers.

Meaning little shining one

Lars

Lars Ulrich, drummer with the heavy metal band Metallica, was born today in 1963 in Denmark. He moved with his family to Los Angeles when he was ten. His early interest in jazz changed after he became a big fan of the rock group Deep Purple.

From Lawrence, meaning laurel crown

Josias

Prince *Frederick Josias of Saxe-Coburg-Sallfeld* was born on this day in 1737. He was an accomplished general in the Holy Roman Empire and the winner of many battles, including several in the Turkish War of 1788.

From Josiah, meaning fire of the Lord

Laurent

Laurent Clerc was born on this day in 1785 near Lyons, France. He became deaf when he was one year old following an accident. In 1916 he went to the USA with Thomas Hopkins Gallaudet, and together they founded America's first school for the deaf in Connecticut.

Meaning crowned with laurels

Carlton, Carleton, Carl, Charlton

Former major league baseball catcher *Carlton Fisk* was born on 26 December 1947 in Bellows Falls, Vermont. He played for 24 years with the Boston Red Sox and Chicago White Sox. He caught 2,226 games, more than any other catcher in history.

Meaning farmers' meeting place

Tahnee, Tahn, Tann, Tan

The US actress *Tahnee Welch* was born Le Tahn Rennee Welch in San Diego on 26 December 1961. The beautiful daughter of Raquel has starred in many films, including *Cocoon* (1985) and *Cocoon: The Return* (1988).

Meaning fire

Dominique, Dominiqua, Dommie, Dominca, Dom

On this day in 1963 the single 'Dominique' by the Singing Nun hit the top of the US charts. The Singing Nun, known as Sister Smile, was born Jeanine Deckers in Belgium. In 1967 she released an album called *I am Not a Star*.

Meaning belonging to the Lord

Vincentia

Today is the feast day of *St Vincentia Maria Lopez y Vicuna*. She was born in Cascante, Spain, in 1847 and founded the institute of the Daughters of Mary Immaculate for Domestic Service, which helped oppressed servant girls. She was canonized in 1975.

Meaning triumphant, conqueror

Tapania

In Finland 26 December is the name day for *Tapania* and Tapani, which is the male form of this name. Tapani is the Finnish version of the name Stephen, and Tapania is the Finnish form of the name Stephanie.

Meaning garland, crown

27 DECEMBER

Gérard, Gerard, Garrard, Garrett

The actor *Gérard Depardieu* was born in Chateauroux, France, on this day in 1948. He is France's leading actor, and his films include *The Last Metro* (1980), *Le Retour de Martin Guerre* (1982), *Jean de Florette* (1986) and *Cyrano de Bergerac* (1990).

Meaning mighty spear warrior

Hinton

The writer *Hinton Rowan Helper* was born on this day in 1829. His book *The Impending Crisis in the South and How to Meet It* (1957) was a strident anti-slavery treatise. An earlier work, *The Land of Gold*, was an account of his three unsuccessful years searching for gold in California during the Gold Rush.

Meaning old town

Barrie, Barry

On 27 December 1904 the first performance of Sir *James Barrie*'s stage play *Peter Pan, or The Boy Who Wouldn't Grow Up*, took place in London. *Peter Pan* has been adapted many times, including a Disney animated version in 1953. Another notable play by the Scottish dramatist was *The Admirable Crichton* (1902).

Meaning spear-like

Crawford

On this day in 1845 ether anaesthetic for childbirth was used for the very first time. It happened in Jefferson, Georgia, and was applied by *Crawford Williamson Long*, the US physician and pharmacist. Crawford Long Hospital in Atlanta, Georgia, is named after him.

Meaning river crossing

Marlene, Marlena

The German actress and singer *Marlene Dietrich* was born on this day in 1901 in Berlin. Her first notable role was in Josef von Sternberg's film *The Blue Angel* (1930), playing one of the several femme-fatale roles with which she became associated and in which she memorably sang 'Falling in Love Again'.

Meaning tower of strength

Verona

The Dutch gymnast *Verona Van de Leur* was born in Waddinxveen on 27 December 1985. She started training when she was five years old and competes in both team and individual competitions. In 2002 she won the all-around gymnastic event in the Vize European Championships.

Meaning lady of Verona

Fabiola, Fabienne, Fabiana, Fabia

Today is the feast day of *St Fabiola*, who used her wealth to do good works in Rome. In 395 she travelled to Bethlehem to be with St Jerome, but returned to Rome, where she established a hospice for indigent travellers.

From Fabian, meaning bean

Cokie

Cokie Roberts, the TV news and congressional analyst, was born Mary Martha Corrine Morrison Claiborne Boggs on 27 December 1943. She has received many coveted awards for her work, including an Emmy for her ABC news special *Who is Ross Perot?* (1991).

Meaning not known

Woodrow

The 28th president of the USA, *Thomas Woodrow Wilson* was born on 28 December 1856 in Staunton, Virginia, of Scottish-Irish ancestry. He served as president from 1913 to 1921 and was the second Democrat to serve two consecutive terms.

Meaning from the hedge in the wood

Mortimer

The US philosopher and author *Mortimer Adler* was born on this day in 1902 in New York City. He started teaching philosophy at the University of Chicago in 1930. He was said to have brought philosophy to the masses, as some of his books, such as *How to Read a Book*, became bestsellers.

Meaning from the quiet water

Denzel, Denzil

The US actor *Denzel Washington* was born on this day in 1954 in Mount Vernon, New York. Two of his critically acclaimed film roles were as Steve Biko in *Cry Freedom* (1987) and Malcolm X in the 1992 film of the same name. He has won two Oscars: best supporting actor in *Glory* (1989) and best actor in *Training Day* (2002).

Meaning high stronghold

Ludolf

The painter *Ludolf Bockhuysen* was born on this day in 1631 in Emden in the Netherlands. He painted mostly maritime subjects; one of his best-known pictures is *Ships Running Aground in a Storm*, and it is said to have influenced Turner.

Meaning famous wolf

Sienna

The actress *Sienna Miller* was born in New York City on this day in 1981, but grew up in Britain. She studied drama at New York's Lee Strasberg Institute. She has appeared in the TV series *Bedtime* (2001) *and Keen Eddie* (2003), as well as in the film *Alfie* (2004).

Meaning from the city of Siena

Hildegard, Hildegarde

The German actress and singer *Hildegard Knef* was born on 28 December 1925 in the city of Ulm. She has made more than 50 films, mostly in Europe. In the USA her work included Cole Porter's Broadway musical *Silk Stockings* and the film *The Snows of Kilimanjaro* (1952).

Meaning battle stronghold

Jordan, Jordane, Jordana

Elizabeth Jordan Carr, the first US test-tube baby, was born in Norfolk, Virginia, on 28 December 1981. Louise Brown, the world's first test-tube baby, had been born in Britain three years earlier. Since then over a million babies have been conceived in this way.

Meaning flow, descend

Atherton

Atherton Grace Johnson was born on 28 December 1999, the daughter of Kelley Phleger and US actor Don Johnson. Don Johnson rose to fame as the star of the 1980s TV series *Miami Vice*. He has two other children, a son, named Jesse, and a daughter, Dakota.

Meaning one who lives at the spring farm

Archibald, Archie, Archer, Archimbald, Arkady

The English historian Sir *Archibald Alison* was born on this day in Shropshire in 1792. He is best known for *The History of Europe During the French Revolution* (1833–42, 1852–9), which was once popular and translated into many languages.

Meaning noble, truly bold

Jude, Judd, Judah

The actor *Jude Law* was born in Lewisham, London, on this day in 1972. His films have included *The Talented Mr Ripley* (1999), *Cold Mountain* (2003) and *Alfie* (2004). He was formerly married to the actress Sadie Frost, by whom he has three children.

Meaning extolled

Ewart, Everard, Everett

The British liberal politician and four-time prime minister *William Ewart Gladstone* was born in Liverpool on this day in 1809. He was a political reformer and a fine orator, and it was no secret that he was often at odds with Queen Victoria, who displayed her preference for his main political rival, Benjamin Disraeli.

Meaning strong as a boar

Aled

The Welsh singer *Aled Jones* was born on 29 December 1970 in Bangor, where he was a chorister in the cathedral choir. When he was 12 he had a hit single with his recording of 'Walking in the Air', the song from the animated film *The Snowman*. He has since become a successful classical singer and radio and TV presenter.

Meaning name of a Welsh river

Merrill, Merrila, Merila, Merilla, Merrilla

The US actress *Dina Merrill* was born Nedinia Hutton Rumbough on 29 December 1925. Her first film was *The Desk Set* (1957). The second of her three husbands was the actor Cliff Robertson.

Meaning fragrant

Viveca

The actress *Viveca Lindfors* was born on this day in 1920 in Uppsala, Sweden. She had a long stage and screen career in Sweden and Hollywood, where her first film was Don Siegel's *Night unto Night* (1949), which also starred Ronald Reagan.

Meaning living voice

Gelsey, Gelasia, Gelasie

The US ballet dancer *Gelsey Kirkland* was born on 29 December 1952 in Pennsylvania. She joined the New York City Ballet when she was 15 and became a soloist after two years. She joined the American Ballet Theatre in 1974 as principal dancer opposite Mikhail Baryshnikov.

Meaning laughing water

Tamara, Tamar

In Hungary 29 December is the name day for *Tamara*. The best-known Tamara in history was the early-13th-century Queen Tamara of Georgia. From the age of 25 she reigned successfully for a quarter of a century, and in Russian history, this era is known as the Tamar period.

Meaning palm tree

Ellas, Ellis, Elias

Ellas Bates was the real name of Bo Diddley, the influential blues singer, songwriter and guitarist, who was born on this day in 1928. He was inspired to become a blues artist after seeing John Lee Hooker. He was known for the Bo Diddley beat, a rhumba-based rhythm on the 'hambone' style used by street performers.

Meaning the Lord is God

Rudyard, Rud

The British author and poet *Rudyard Kipling* was born in India on this day in 1865. He is best known for *The Jungle Book* (1894), *Kim* (1901) and his poems 'Gunga Din' and 'If'. In 1907 he became the first British writer to be awarded the Nobel Prize for literature.

Meaning from the red enclosure

Eldrick, Eldrich, Eldric, Aldrich, Aldric, Alric

Golfer *Eldrick 'Tiger' Woods* was born in Cypress, California, on this day in 1975. One of only five players to have won all four major professional championships, he is credited with prompting an increased interest in golf, particularly among minorities and young people.

Meaning wise old ruler

Darnell

The rhythm and blues artist, actor and model *Tyrese Darnell Gibson*, often known simply as Tyrese, was born today in 1978. His debut album went platinum and his second album, *2000 Watts*, is also the name of an organization he founded to help inner-city children.

Meaning from the hidden nook

Tracey, Tracy

The British-born comedian, actress and singer *Tracey Ullmann* was born in London on 30 December 1959. *The Simpsons* was first shown on her US TV show, *The Tracey Ullmann Show*, appearing as a cartoon short (1987). The show has won four Emmys.

Meaning battler

Patti, Patrice

The singer, songwriter and guitarist *Patti Smith* was born in Chicago on this day in 1946. She was a rock star by the mid-1970s and formed the Patti Smith Group. The band's debut album was *Horses*, a fusion of rock and roll, punk rock and spoken poetry.

Meaning well-born

Noley, Nolly, Nolley, Nollie

The US actress *Noley Thornton* was born on this day in 1983. She made her TV debut in *The Little Riders* (1996) and subsequently went on to become a child star, taking the title role in the 1993 TV adaptation of *Heidi*.

Meaning magnolia

Anysia, Anya

Today is the feast day of St Anysia of Salonika. She was born in Thessalonika, Greece, in the 4th century. She was from a wealthy family, but lived a life of contemplation, chastity and poverty.

Meaning complete

Barton, Bart

The musician *Barton Cummings* was born on this day in 1947 and lives in Los Angeles. He is an author, composer, conductor and performer, as well as a teacher of music. He has also played a role in redefining the importance of the tuba as a solo instrument.

Meaning barley farmer

Dieter, Dietrich

The German writer *Dieter Noll* was born on 31 December 1928. His novel *The Adventures of Werner Holt* was about two 17-year-old friends conscripted into Hitler's army, one of whom questions the cause he is fighting for. The book was made into a film in 1965.

Meaning from strong people

Fermin

Fermin Goytisolo, the conga player with the 1970s group KC and the Sunshine Band, was born in Havana, Cuba, on this day in 1953. Their biggest hit, 'That's the Way (I Like It)' (1974), was covered by the Backstreet Boys in 1999.

Meaning strong

Broderick, Broderic

The tennis player *Broderick Dyke* was born on this day in 1960 in Gumerocha, Australia. A left-hander, he turned professional in 1982 and won both singles and doubles titles.

Meaning from the broad ridge

Arden, Ardene

Elizabeth Arden was born Florence Nightingale Graham in Ontario, Canada, on 31 December 1884. She opened her beauty salon on Fifth Avenue, New York, in 1910 and is one of the great names in the beauty business.

Meaning eagle valley

Lilith

The US actress Bebe Neuwirth celebrates her birthday today. She was born in New Jersey in 1958 and started her career as a dancer. She is known for her role as Dr *Lilith Sternin Crane* in two popular TV series: *Cheers*, which ran from 1982 to 1993, and *Frasier*, which ended in 2004.

Meaning woman of the night

Chandra, Chandre, Candra, Candre

The actress *Chandra West* was born today in Edmonton, Canada, in 1970. She was a dancer before she became an actress. On TV she has appeared in *NYPD Blue* (1993) and *Crime Scene Investigation* (2000), and her film appearances include *The Perfect Son* (2000) and *The First $20 Million* (2002).

Meaning the moon that outshines the stars

Odetta

The Grammy-winning US folk and blues singer *Odetta* was born in Birmingham, Alabama, on this day in 1930. Her album *Odetta Sings Ballads and Blues* (1956) was a great influence on Bob Dylan and inspired him to play acoustic guitar.

Meaning melody

A

Aaron 131
Abbey 301
Abby 88
Abel 30
Abigail 88, 211
Abraham 55
Abriella 146, 260
Absalom 49
Ace 136
Ada 383
Adair 345
Adam 242
Adan 242
Adar 383
Adara 383
Adela 67, 212
Adelaide 212, 389
Adeline 212
Adlai 48
Adolfo 290
Adrian 18, 33, 383
Adrianna 354
Adrien 18, 383
Adrienne 354
Aeron 122
Aesta 202
Aestas 202
Afra 246
Agape 112
Agatha 48
Agnes 29, 129
Agnetha 114
Agostino 375
Agosto 136, 375
Agueda 48
Ahmet 238
Aida 300
Aidan 83
Aiden 83
Aigail 88
Ailee 203
Aileen 203
Aimée 62, 146, 250, 283
Aisha 116
Akarija 105
Akarova 105
Akbar 123
Aki 113
Akihito 396
Akim 233, 336
Akira 98
Al 121
Alaina 351
Alan 60, 272
Alana 51, 351
Alanis 176
Alanson 178
Alaska 186
Alban 197
Albanus 197
Alben 197
Albéric 184
Albert 89, 104, 348
Alberta 76, 312
Albertina 312

Albertine 76
Albin 33, 197
Albizu 287
Albrecht 162
Aldis 233, 300
Aldo 233, 300
Aldous 233
Aldric 403
Aldrich 403
Aled 402
Alegria 330
Alejandro 196
Aleksander 196
Alex 128, 196
Alexander 196
Alexei 253
Alexis 128
Alf 130
Alfie 129
Alfonso 95, 189
Alfre 343, 349
Alfred 247, 254, 283
Alfreda 349
Algar 177
Alger 177
Ali 110, 228
Alice 52
Alichia 262
Alicia 262
Alina 51, 168
Alison 154
Alitha 114
Aliyah 228
Aliza 114
Alizée 262
Allan 60
Allegra 252, 330
Allen 178
Alleye 110
Allie 110, 178
Allyn 178
Allyson 154
Alma 191, 395
Almira 344
Alodia 329
Alois 347
Alonso 189, 231, 336
Alonzo 189
Alouette 304
Alphonse 231, 328
Alphonso 95, 189
Alric 403
Althea 266
Aluino 311
Alva 25
Alvan 217
Alvar 46
Alverta 76
Alvin 311
Alwin 121
Alwyn 121
Alyce 52
Alyssa 392
Amabel 261
Amadeo 156
Amadeus 156
Amala 186
Amalya 186

Amanda 326
Amandine 208
Amantee 208
Amaryllis 371
Amber 325
Amberley 325
Ambroise 199, 246
Ambrose 199, 246
Amelia 20
Ameline 359
Amelita 359
Amerigo 84
Ami 17
Amia 186
Amie 17
Amit 336
Amos 145
Amrita 192
Amritha 192
Amy 62, 146
An 50
Ana 13, 20, 40, 64, 149, 197, 282, 327
Anaïs 64
Anastacia 292
Anastasia 13
Anatoli 164
Anatolio 164
Ancel 35
Anders 106, 144, 247, 368
Anderson 106
Andie 130
Andonis 144
André 115
Andreas 115
Andrej 61
Andrés 61
Andrew 106
Andrey 134
Andy 247
Aneka 163
Aneurin 212
Angela 36
Angelica 336
Angelina 36, 179
Angelique 179
Angelita 179, 291
Angie 278
Anika 163, 377
Anil 397
Anise 86
Anissa 86
Anita 199
Anjelica 215
Anke 377
Ann 49, 72, 197, 368
Anna 20, 40, 149, 197, 282, 327
Annabella 261
Annabeth 88
Anne 49, 72, 197, 368
Anneka 149, 163, 197, 327
Anneke 377
Annetta 391
Annette 391
Annie 49, 72, 197, 368

Annika 20, 40, 149, 163, 197, 377
Anouska 386
Ansard 52
Ansbert 52
Ansel 63
Ansell 63
Anselm 63, 83
Anselme 198, 246
Ansgar 154
Anshelm 83
Anthaniel 201
Anthelm 201
Anthony 21, 68, 347
Antoine 68, 347
Antoinette 157
Anton 38, 68, 137, 347
Antonetta 157
Antonia 25
Antonín 283
Antonina 157
Antonino 283
Antonio 21, 38, 68, 251
Antony 21, 68, 347
Anula 20, 40, 149, 197, 282, 327
Anusia 20, 149, 197, 327
Anuska 20, 40, 149, 197, 327
Anya 403
Anysia 403
Aphra 387
Apple 155
Aprile 123
Arabella 164
Aram 181
Arantxa 391
Arbel 164
Arcadius 21
Arcangela 255
Arcangelo 60
Archer 402
Archibald 148, 226, 402
Archie 148, 226, 402
Archimbald 226, 402
Arden 404
Ardene 404
Ardito 127
Ardley 126
Aretha 12
Ari 206
Ariel 151
Ariella 151
Aristide 103
Aristotle 206
Arkady 402
Arleen 320
Arlene 252
Arletty 156
Arlina 252
Arline 156
Arlo 217
Arlyne 156
Armand 162, 279
Armando 162, 279
Armin 162, 279, 390

Armond 279
Armstrong 246
Arna 320
Arnetia 218
Arnetta 238
Arnette 238
Arnold 237
Arron 122
Art 91, 346
Artel 169
Artemis 135
Artemisia 215
Arthur 91, 324
Artis 97
Artley 169
Arto 169
Arton 169
Arturo 91
Arunda 365
Arundhati 365
Arvo 286
Asa 40
Asaph 252
Ase 40
Asgerd 154
Asha 210
Ashbok 320
Ashia 116
Ashley 128, 188
Ashlyn 300
Asia 235, 295
Asija 295
Astrid 355
Atalanta 388
Atherton 401
Atlanta 388
Auberon 184, 358
Aubert 89
Auberta 76
Aubrey 262
Audie 145
Audrey 145, 198
August 136, 375
Augusta 149, 229, 242
Auguste 149, 353
Augustine 242, 353
Augustus 353, 375
Aung San 194
Aura 184
Aure 184
Aurelia 10
Aurelio 134
Auria 184
Aurora 10
Austen 230, 242
Austin 230
Autumn 316
Ava 397
Aveline 191
Averell 356
Averill 356
Avery 303
Avis 191, 397
Avital 216
Avitus 216
Avrielle 260
Avril 302
Axi 49

Ayrton 96
Ayumi 309

B

Babe 201
Babette 139, 201
Babita 139, 201
Baichung 388
Balbina 106
Baldassare 325
Ballard 247
Ballington 235
Banz 330
Barbara 19
Barbie 56
Barbra 133
Barnabas 186
Barnaby 186
Barrie 400
Barriemore 285
Barrington 139
Barry 400
Bart 10, 23, 404
Bartholomew 10
Bartolomé 10
Barton 404
Base 262
Basia 331
Basie 262
Basil 294
Bea 154
Beah 219
Beale 382
Beata 154
Beatrice 31
Beatrix 40
Beau 182, 382
Beauregard 182
Beck 199
Becka 185
Beckham 143
Becky 128, 185
Bee 281
Bega 281
Bekka 128
Bekky 128
Bel 164
Bela 100
Bella 193, 231
Bellanca 330
Belle 47
Bellona 178
Beltrando 78
Belva 331
Belvia 231
Ben 26, 317
Benazir 196
Benedetta 380
Benedict 21
Benet 171
Bengt 171
Benigno 368
Benita 280
Benitia 280
Benjamin 25, 317
Benmont 282
Benny 171
Benoit 171